AN INTRODUCTION TO ANCIENT GREEK

A Literary Approach

C. A. E. LUSCHNIG

University of Idaho

CHARLES SCRIBNER'S SONS

New York

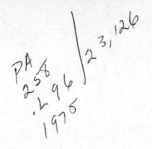

PREFACE

The Book's Approach

In this book it has been assumed that the student who studies Greek at the University really wants to learn Greek, and not something else; and that he wants to learn Greek so that he will be able to read Greek or some particular thing in Greek. It is not so that he will be able to recite paradigm after paradigm in endless and meaningless succession. But still he must learn the paradigms. The other beginning Greek textbooks currently in use tend to give the student little more than the bare bones of Greek, and these not in a very interesting way. The choice of Xenophon's *Anabasis* (and that Xenophon adapted so that it is barely recognizable and even less comprehensible) strikes me as a most unfortunate choice. Readings from Greek authors, chosen to introduce students to Greek literature, should be intellectually stimulating: they should make him want to read Greek. Many of the readings in this book were chosen because they illustrated grammatical points; but many were selected in the hope that they would be interesting to the student, to encourage him to learn the new paradigms, to expand his consciousness of Greek, so that he can read more. The readings were taken from a variety of sources of different ages and different philosophies, some of which the student will not have heard of before reading them.

Languages, Living and Dead

To call Greek a dead language is to take a narrow-minded, exclusively pragmatic view of time and of life and death (at least of the life and death of languages). A language is only dead when it has passed from the memory of men, leaving no literature and no

living descendants. Perhaps we could say that Hittite and Tochar-
ian are 'dead' languages, because their literatures are so scanty
and because so little is know about them. And yet they live for
some ardent Indo-European philologists . . . after their fashion.
The life of a language is a relative thing. To call Greek a dead
language is to admit that one knows no Greek, and to imagine that
it cannot be known, and indeed is not worth knowing. The literature of the ancient Greeks is alive and always exciting; it is
set down for all time, not for the past only. All literature is,
of necessity, conscious: conscious of itself and conscious of
time: for it sees itself as a way of by-passing human mortality,
by being a thing that *is*, *was*, and *shall be*. Greek, I insist, is
a living language, not only because it never died (but has continued to develop and change, and can still be heard in its heir,
Modern Greek), but also because it has left to us a literature
which is our common heritage and which continues to influence the
way we think and write.

Traditional Method

On the other hand, the language spoken in fifth century
Athens is no longer spoken in the same way. There is nowhere we
can hear it and no one with whom we can speak it. For this reason, I have taken the traditional, rational approach to teaching
Greek, rather than the 'natural method'. The study of Greek has
traditionally been a bookish pursuit, and rightly so. For we
have only the books of the ancients to study. We have only part
of a language: the sophisticated literary language of a literate
people. We have only the part of the language that can be written down. (The few 'conversations' included in this book are
based on literary texts.) It is for this reason that the system
of learning ancient Greek through recordings and responses seems
more 'unnatural' than simply learning the forms in a reasonable
order from a book, through constant use, repetition and review.
In any case, the forms must be memorized, and the rational approach seems to be the most efficient way of doing so. The student should be treated as an intelligent, rational human being, a

potential equal of the teacher; he should always know what he is
doing.

The study of grammar and grammatical forms can seem tedious,
but this is only an attitude (albeit a prevalent one) toward it:
students can also become fascinated by means of expression different from their own. I have, therefore, introduced immediately,
in the first lesson, a concept that will be new to most beginning
students, the middle voice. The usual approach is to start off
with things that will seem familiar, and gradually let in the
more unfamiliar aspects of the Greek language. It seemed to me
both formally and psychologically more profitable to introduce
the middle voice at once. The student will know that he is dealing with an altogether different language than he has studied before. He will not be encouraged to make comparisons between
Greek and Latin, which in the early stages tend to be detrimental
to his understanding of Greek. (In this book, it has not been
assumed that the student knows any Latin; but it is assumed that
the student is aware of, or at least interested in learning, how
language works.)

From the first principal part of -ω verbs, the book progres-
ses inevitably and in an orderly fashion through the tenses of
the indicative to the sixth principal part, and from there to the
contract and -μι verbs, and then to the other moods. There is no
sudden spate of verb forms in the middle of the book to inundate
the unsuspecting student. There is, it is true, a great deal of
material in each lesson. It will be impossible to say 'prepare
Lesson I for tomorrow.' Each lesson contains paradigms and ex-
planations to be introduced on the first day. For these, purely
formal exercises in conjugating or declining and parsing are included. This will make up the first day's lesson and assignment.
The second day, the student will indicate whether he has understood the formal part. Once he has learned the forms, he will do
the translation exercises (concoctions made up to illustrate the
vocabulary and the new forms: it is to be stressed that these
are grammatical exercises and not real Greek) and translations

into Greek of simple sentences. Lastly he will work on the selections from ancient authors, for some of which he will certainly need help from his instructor. Each section will take from three to five days (perhaps longer at first). Most lessons are divided into sections, one on nouns, adjectives, or pronouns, and the other on verbs. Not all the material in the exercises needs to be covered in class time; some can be left for the students' own use, for practice and review. The reading sections become more and more copious; but reading is, after all, the objective. Furthermore, the pause gives the students time to learn the forms and vocabulary thoroughly before new material is introduced. It is hoped that the fourteen lessons can be finished (in a four or five hour course) in two quarters of study, and that the rest of the year can be spent on the reading section (now in progress) which will include material for review, composition, and new vocabulary with each set of readings. It will also be possible to use this text in an intensive Greek course or as a teach-yourself-manual-for-adults.

Material is included which the students need not learn, but is added to increase their interest in the Greek language. I refer particularly to the lexical and linguistic notes (under the heading 'vocabulary notes') to be found in many lessons, and other notes in single space. These are instead of pictures. The assumption I have made is that the students who will use this book are adults (if growing ones) and are interested in the Greek *language* (more than the Greek landscape): that a note on ἀρετή will be of more interest to them than a picture of an ἀγορά.

SUGGESTIONS FOR CLASS USE

This text was used with success by the author and two teaching assistants at the University of Washington. It was found that some of the readings might be profitably omitted to save time: these have been marked with brackets in the text. The author suggests going over these optional readings with the students in class, but not requiring the students to prepare them as home work.

The following suggestions are offered for using the text in the classroom: introduce the new material and then turn to the formal exercises which accompany each section and go over several of each type (to make sure that the students understand the process of forming and the meaning and use of the new forms) at sight. For homework, have the students work on the formal exercises until they are familiar with the new forms, and then do the translation exercises (if there seem to be too many, have them do alternate numbers, and go over the others at sight in class, or save them for review work), and then the English to Greek sentences (these are the only exercises to be written; it may be found useful to have the students turn these in from time to time). The next day review the forms by going over a few more of the formal exercises, especially the parsing (it is neither necessary nor desirable to go over all of these exercises unless the students are having trouble with them; again, some may be used for review work), and then go over the translation exercises. The following day or two days, go over the reading selections carefully (the emphasis in this text has been placed on the readings from the ancient authors), and then introduce the new material. The author has found it useful to give a quiz at the end of every lesson (or every two lessons during the summer session): these quizzes usually include forms (and use of the forms), vocabulary, translation (simple sentences similar to those in the translation exercises), a little (but very little) translation from English to Greek, and some brief selections from the readings. At the end of the second quarter the students read Plato's *Euthyphro* (a running vocabulary was supplied), and at the end of the third quarter they read the *Alcestis* of Euripides (in the St. Martin's Elementary Classics edition): these were found to be excellent texts for the students' first connected material.

ACKNOWLEDGMENTS

The author takes this opportunity to thank Professor H. A. Hultgren of Ohio University, friend and former colleague, for invaluable help at the initial stages of the book.

To the Classics Department of the University of Cincinnati for generous financial support during the last year of work on the book (1972-1973), and for support in the production of the first experimental edition, the author expresses gratitude.

To the following individuals for encouragement, helpful suggestions, and corrections of the original typescript, the author wishes to express appreciation: to the late Professor D. W. Bradeen; to Professors J. A. Cameron, A. J. Christopherson, J. E. Keefe, C. R. Trahman, and J. M. Vail; and to Mr. Jack Davis, Mr. Charles Lowry, Dr. Sherrilyn Martin, and Ms. Elaine Willey of the University of Cincinnati; to Professors Cynthia and William King and Eva Stehle of Wright State University; and to Miss Sabina Magliocco of Walnut Hills High School. Much appreciation is owed also to Mr. Bruce Taylor of Cincycopy in Cincinnati, Ohio, for printing the first three experimental editions.

The author wishes to thank the two Teaching Assistants, Rochelle Snee and Bruce Perry, who helped teach the beginning Greek course at the University of Washington in 1973-1974, and who made many suggestions and corrections. Thanks are due also to the students in Greek 101-102-103, who bravely put up with the first experimental edition.

The teachers who used the book in their classes, in its awkward experimental form, rendered an immeasurable service to the author. To the following teachers of elementary Greek, for enthusiastic encouragement, for comments and corrections, and for kind words at critical times, the author expresses heartfelt thanks: Dr. Catherine Roth, Dr. Laurence Bliquez, and Mr. Michael Riley of the University of Washington; Dr. Anne Bergren of Princeton University; Dr. Cynthia King of Wright State University; Dr. Catherine Pearson of the University of Cincinnati; Dr. Rachel Kitzinger of Amherst University; Dr. Gisela Berns of Saint John's College; Dr. Sherrilyn Martin of Rockford, Illinois. To Dr. Helene Foley of Stanford University, who not only used the book, but spread the word about it to teachers at other fine universities, the author offers special thanks.

To Mr. John Peter Givler, director of the College Department at Charles Scribner's Sons, and to Mr. Charles Scribner, for their interest in the book, the author expresses grateful appreciation.

Finally, to the typist, Mr. Harry Fulton of the University of Washington, for undertaking so enormous a task and for doing such a professional job, many thanks.

Many mistakes were corrected through the good services of colleagues, but for those that remain, the author takes full responsibility.

Moscow, Idaho
March, 1976

CONTENTS

INTRODUCTION

The Greek Alphabet

The Greek alphabet has twenty-four letters (γράμματα: *grammata*), given below with their names, usual transliterations into our alphabet, and the recommended pronunciation for classroom use.

Character	Name		Transliteration	Pronunciation
Α α	ἄλφα	alpha	*a*	short: c*u*p; long: f*a*ther
Β β	βῆτα	beta	*b*	b
Γ γ	γάμμα	gamma	*g* (*ng*)	g, hard, *g*oing (ng, below p. 6)
Δ δ	δέλτα	delta	*d*	d
Ε ε	᾿ἒ ψιλόν	epsilon	*e*	short e, b*e*t
Ζ ζ	ζῆτα	zeta	*z*	sd, wi*sd*om (or dz, a*dz*e, p. 7)
Η η	ἦτα	eta	*e*	long e, French t*ê*te
Θ ϑ	ϑῆτα	theta	*th*	*th*ing (but see below, p. 6)
Ι ι	ἰῶτα	iota	*i*	short: b*i*n; long: b*ea*n
Κ κ	κάππα	kappa	*k, c*	k
Λ λ	λάμβδα	lambda	*l*	l
Μ μ	μῦ	mu	*m*	m
Ν ν	νῦ	nu	*n*	n
Ξ ξ	ξῖ	xi	*x*	ks/x: ta*cks*, ta*x*
Ο ο	᾿ὂ μικρόν	omicron	*o*	short o: p*o*t (German G*o*tt)
Π π	πῖ	pi	*p*	p
Ρ ρ	ῥῶ	rho	*r, rh*	trilled as in Italian
Σ σ, ς	σίγμα	sigma	*s*	as in *s*ay
Τ τ	ταῦ	tau	*t*	t
Υ υ	᾿ὒ ψιλόν	upsilon	*y*	French *u*; German *ü*
Φ φ	φῖ	phi	*ph*	*f*oot (but see below, p. 6)
Χ χ	χῖ	chi	*ch*	lo*ch* (but see below, p. 6)
Ψ ψ	ψῖ	psi	*ps*	hi*ps*
Ω ω	᾿ὦ μέγα	omega	*o*	g*o* (or s*aw*)

The capitals are the forms originally used, but the small letters are now used for the most part; the capitals are used for proper nouns and for the beginnings of paragraphs in modern printed texts.

Greek Punctuation

The punctuation marks now used in Greek printed texts are as follows: the period (.) and comma (,) have the same use in Greek

1

as in our system of punctuation. A raised period (·) is equivalent to both our semicolon [;] and colon [:]. A semicolon in
Greek (;) is equivalent to our question mark [?].

Assignments and Exercises

1. Learn the names, sounds, and shapes of the Greek letters
(concentrating on the small letters).

2. Pronounce the following words. Try to write English e-
quivalents for them. Do you recognize any words that are similar
to English words? (For the time being, stress the syllable that
has the accent mark (´`˜).

1.	δρᾶμα	8.	σκηνή
2.	θεός	9.	βάρβαρος
3.	φίλος	10.	ψυχή
4.	ξένος	11.	ποταμός
5.	λόγος	12.	ζῷον
6.	ἀρχή	13.	μικρός
7.	δένδρον	14.	ἀγορά

3. Pronounce the following and write English equivalents.

1.	ἀλφάβητος	8.	Κύκλωψ
2.	βαρβαρισμός	9.	μητρόπολις
3.	ζωδιακός	10.	τεχνολογία
4.	ὀρθογραφία	11.	ἐπιτομή
5.	συμβίωσις	12.	ἀποθέωσις
6.	ῥινόκερως	13.	ἄνθρωπος
7.	ἐτυμολογία	14.	ἀδελφός

4. Pronounce and memorize:

Ἐν ἀρχῇ ἦν ὁ λόγος.   (John)

In (the) beginning was the word.

*Notes on the Alphabet and the Sounds of Greek Vowels and Vowel
  Combinations*

1. Vowels. The vowels (φωνήεντα) are α, ε, η, ι, ο, υ, ω.
Of these, α, ι, and υ are of variable quantity, that is to say,
they can be either long or short. Of the others, ε (ἐ φιλόν,
'plain e') and ο (ὃ μικρόν, 'little o') are always short; and η
and ω (ὦ μέγα, 'big o') are always long. Long vowels were origi-

nally pronounced for about twice as long as the short ones.
Length of vowel affects pronunciation and accent (and the meter
of poetry as well).

2.   Diphthongs (δίφθογγοι) and Vowel Combinations. "A diphthong is a continuous glide from one vowel quality to another
within the bounds of a syllable" (Allen, *Vox Graeca*). The following words contain the various vowel combinations of Greek.
(Listen as the teacher pronounces them):

εἰμί εἶμι καί οὐ οὖ ὗς υἱός
οἴκοι εὖ αὐτός ναῦς τοῖς φίλοις
αὐτοῦ ταῖς ψυχαῖς ᾧ τῷ φίλῳ
ᾗ τῇ ψυχῇ τῇ πείρᾳ Ζεύς ὦ ᾦ

The diphthongs in Greek are:

	Transliteration	Pronunciation
αι	ae, e	(ai) *aisle*, h*i*gh [i]
αυ	au	(au) *sauerkraut* [ou] (*house*)
ει	ei, e, i	(ei) sl*ei*gh [ā]
ευ (also ηυ)	eu	(ε + υ)
οι	oe, e, i	(oi) *coin*, t*oy*
ου	u	(ou) *soup* [oo]
υι	ui	(uy) (cf. *New York*)

(The combination υι in Attic Greek always occurs before another vowel and is pronounced as υ followed by the semi-vowel *y;*
there is no exact English equivalent.)

The Long Diphthongs

When a long vowel (ā, η, or ω) combines with ι to form a
diphthong, the ι is (in modern texts) written under the line:
this is called ι-*subscript,* ᾳ, ῃ, ῳ. This is not an ancient custom, but dates from the Byzantine Age when scholars were attempting to standardize the spelling of ancient Greek although the
pronunciation had changed over the years.

Note on ι-subscript:

In the Classical period, and in fact until the ninth century A.D., the
capital letters were used for all formal writing. The small letters are sim-

plified forms of these for faster writing, and began in the ninth century A.D. to be used as a formal (or book) hand. Before this time the long diphthongs were written with *iota* on the line with the other letters: ΑΙ, ΗΙ, ΩΙ, as in ΤΗΙ ΚΩΜΩΙΔΙΑΙ: ΤΗΙ ΤΡΑΓΩΙΔΙΑΙ (τῇ κωμῳδίᾳ, τῇ τραγῳδίᾳ, 'to the comedy', 'to the tragedy'), and was (doubtless) pronounced: spelling originally represents pronunciation (i.e. language), but often becomes standardized (as it were, fossilized) as pronunciation changes. By the second century B.C. this *iota* had been lost from the pronunciation in Attica, and it gradually ceased to be written. The Byzantines put it back as a necessary part of the spelling, but put it under the line to show that it no longer affected the pronunciation. When this little *iota* occurs, it must be learned as a part of the spelling of the word: e.g. it is necessary to distinguish -ῃ (a dative ending) from -η (a nominative ending). After a capital letter, this ι is still written on the line in modern texts, Αι, Ηι, Ωι (= ᾳ, ῃ, ῳ).

The Rough and Smooth Breathings

1. In Greek, the symbol ', though not a letter, represents one of the sounds of the language, the *h* sound (or aspiration).

2. Every word beginning with a vowel or diphthong must be marked with either the ' (rough breathing for the *h*) or the ' (smooth breathing for the absence of an *h*): εἰς (*eis*) 'into'; εἷς (*heis*) 'one'; ὀδός (*odos*) 'threshold'; ὁδός (*hodos*) 'road'. Note that the breathing mark goes over the second member of a diphthong: οὐ 'not'; οὗ 'of whom'.

3. Words beginning with ρ and υ always have the rough breathing: ῥόδον 'rose'; ὑπέρ 'over' (cf. hyper).

Note on the Breathings:

The alphabet given above (on page 1) is the *Ionic* alphabet, which was the one used by the Ionian Greeks and adopted by the Athenians (officially in 403 B.C.) and gradually by all the Greeks. Before this universal acceptance of the Ionic alphabet, each city-state not only had its own dialect, but might even have its own version of the alphabet. Now the Ionic alphabet is the one used both for modern Greek and for classical Greek texts. The old Attic alphabet (and some of the others as well) used the H symbol for the *h* sound (the aspiration), but the Ionians used the same symbol to represent the long *e* sound: in their dialect, speakers tended to drop their *h*'s. In some places, a new symbol was developed to represent the *h* sound, at first used only to differentiate words that were otherwise the same (as ὄρος *horos* 'boundary' from ὄρος *oros* 'mountain') but later adopted universally. This symbol was developed from the H, by splitting it in half: Ⱶ (used in inscriptions from the Greek colonies in Southern Italy, Ⱶορος). It was later adopted in the form ⌐

by the Alexandrian scholars from which it developed into our ', the rough breathing (πνεῦμα δασύ, 'hairy breath'). The Alexandrian grammarians also introduced the complementary ⊣ (which became ⌐ and then ') to indicate the absence of aspiration (calling it by the name πνεῦμα ψιλόν 'plain breath', 'bald breath') again to indicate the correct reading of words otherwise spelled the same. It is now conventional to mark a rough (') or smooth (') breathing *over* every initial vowel (and it *must* be learned as part of the spelling of the word); it is written beside (to the left of) a capital letter, Ἡ, Ἡ, Ἀ, Ἀ.

   The rough breathing is pronounced and transliterated as the letter *h*; the smooth breathing is sort of like the emperor's new clothes; it is not heard and is not transliterated.

Ὀρέστης 'Orestes' Ὅμηρος 'Homer(-us)'

   The rough breathing is also used over an initial ρ, to indicate that it too is aspirated (we usually represent this by trilling the ρ). ῥήτωρ *rhetor* 'orator'.

The Consonants

   The consonants (σύμφωνα) are divided into *mutes* (or stops) and *continuants* (including liquids, nasals, a spirant and double consonants).

   Mutes (ἄφωνα) are nine in number and are divided according to (1) where they are produced, into labials, dentals, and palatals, and (2) the effort in breathing, into unvoiced, voiced, and aspirated (or rough).

   The following chart shows the two classifications:

	un-voiced	voiced	aspi-rated	
LABIALS	π	β	φ	produced with the LIPS
DENTALS	τ	δ	ϑ	produced with the TEETH
PALATALS	κ	γ	χ	produced with the soft PALATE

Unvoiced or voiceless (ψιλά) consonants are produced without vibration of the vocal chords.

Voiced consonants (called μέσα in Greek) are produced with vibration of the vocal chords: the difference between (for example) τ and δ or κ and γ or π and β (*t* and *d* or *k* and *g* or *p* and *b)* can be felt if you place your fingers on your Adam's apple;

you will feel δ, γ, and β, but not τ, κ, π.

Aspirated (δασέα) consonants are followed by a blast of air, or the *h* sound (ʽ), the rough breathing in Greek.

Note on the Aspirated Consonants:

The three aspirates, φ, θ, χ, are equivalent to the three unvoiced mutes π, τ, κ plus the *h* sound. This means that they are pronounced more or less as follows: φ like *ph* in flo*p*-*h*ouse; θ like *th* in po*t*-*h*ead; and χ like *kh* in bloc*k*-*h*ead; except that in Greek the two sounds would be in the same syllable. Actually in English our initial *p* is aspirated (and so probably very much like Greek φ): if you hold your hand in front of your mouth when saying *p*ut or *p*ot, you will feel a blast of air (which is the aspiration). Then try s*p*ot or sto*p*, and you will find that *p* in these positions is much less heavily aspirated. The same is true of our *t* and *k* sounds, as in *t*op, s*t*op; *c*at, s*c*at. English does not make the distinction in spelling between these two variants of *p, t, k,* but Greek does. An English speaker would have difficulty in hearing the difference between π and φ, τ and θ, κ and χ in their ancient pronunciations: that is why we give them their modern Greek pronunciations for classroom use. Knowing that φ = π'; θ = τ'; and χ = κ' will be helpful later on.

The Nasals. There are three nasals in Greek: μ (a labial nasal), ν (a dental nasal), and nasal γ (a palatal nasal).

Nasal γ: when γ occurs before another palatal, that is γ, κ, χ, or ξ, it is pronounced as *ng* (as in si*ng*):

ἄγγελος	'messenger' (cf. angel) the sound of the γγ would	
	resemble that of *ng* in a*ng*er.	
ἀνάγκη	'necessity' γκ as in i*nk*, a*nk*le	
σύγχορος	'partner in the chorus' γκ as in si*nk*-hole,	
	Ba*nkh*ead	
Σφίγξ	'Sphinx' γξ as in i*nks*, Sphi*nx*	

The Liquids are ρ and λ. The only *Spirant* in Greek is σ. (Note that sigma at the end of a word is written ς, anywhere else σ.

The Double Consonants (διπλᾶ): the double consonants, ζ, ξ, ψ, are two consonant sounds represented by one letter.

Any labial mute combines with σ to become ψ.

π, β, or φ + σ → ψ

Any palatal mute combines with σ to become ξ.

κ, γ, or χ + σ → ξ

The symbol ζ represents the sound combination σδ. There is, however, some dispute over the pronunciation of this letter: it may originally have indicated the sound *dz* and is pronounced in this way by most English-speaking Greek scholars. It is derived from several Indo-European sound combinations: *sd, dy, gy.* The continual change in language often makes it difficult to find exactly how a given letter was pronounced at a given time: either combination (*sd* or *dz*) is acceptable for classroom use.

Exercises: diphthongs, ι-subscript, breathings, nasal γ.

1. Pronounce the words on page 3.

2. Pronounce the following words aloud. (Try to guess at their meanings or find English words derived from them.)

1. δαίμων	6. αἰθήρ	11. εἰρήνη	16. οἰκονομικός
2. φαινόμενον	7. ψευδής	12. ἄγγελος	17. εἰρωνεία
3. ἔκλειψις	8. αὐστηρός	13. σφίγξ	18. ηὕρηκα
4. χαρακτήρ	9. ῥαφῳδός	14. ἐγκώμιον	19. ἵππος
5. οὐρανός	10. οἶκος	15. αὐτόματος	20. ὑποκριτής

(For the transliteration of diphthongs, see p. 3)

3. Read the following aloud. Write English equivalents. All are proper names: do you know who they are?

1. Αἴσωπος	9. Ἀγαμέμνων	17. Εὐκλείδης	25. Ἰφιγένεια
2. Ἀλκιβιάδης	10. Ἕκτωρ	18. Βάκχος	26. Θουκυδίδης
3. Ἀριστοφάνης	11. Κάδμος	19. Ὄλυμπος	27. Ἀθῆναι
4. Ἀριστοτέλης	12. Σοφοκλῆς	20. Ῥόδος	28. Ἀθηνᾶ
5. Ἡσίοδος	13. Σωκράτης	21. Μήδεια	29. Ἡρακλῆς
6. Αἰσχύλος	14. Δελφοί	22. Εὐριπίδης	30. Ἀπόλλων
7. Αἴγυπτος	15. Οἰδίπους	23. Ἥρα	31. Κλυταιμνήστρα
8. Ἄρτεμις	16. Ἐπίκουρος	24. Ζεύς	32. Διογένης Λαέρτιος

4. Read and memorize the following quotation (from Aristotle's *Politics*):

Ἄνθρωπος φύσει πολιτικὸν ζῷον.

Man (is) by nature (a) political/social animal.

Obsolete Letters:

In the earliest Greek alphabets, there were three other letters which, though not found in manuscripts, are found in some inscriptions. They are (1) Ϝ (also written ⨍) called *digamma* because of its shape (i.e. it looks like

two capital gammas Γ on top of each other) or *vau* because of its pronunciation
(it was pronounced like our *w* sound, or the Latin *v*). (It is also called
stigma because in later times, the symbol ϛ was used for the στ combination;
but digamma is the most common name). (2) ϙ, called *koppa* (corresponding to
q) and used in place of κ before ο and υ; and (3) ϡ, *san* or *sampi*, whose original sound is a little more obscure: it was probably another spirant (perhaps the *sh* sound). A form of it (Ϡ) seems to have been used in certain
places for the σσ (Attic ττ) which at that time may have been pronounced as
our *tch* or *ts*. In the alphabet, ϝ is the sixth letter (between ε and ζ); ϙ is
between π and ρ; and ϡ comes at the end, after ω. These were used for numerical notation along with the other letters of the alphabet (see below for numerals and numerical notation). The sounds these three obsolete letters represent were lost very early in the history of the Greek language, though traces
of the digamma sound are found in Homer, the earliest poetry. (See p. 12 on
numerals.)

Accents (τόνοι)

The predominant accent of classical Greek was one of pitch
rather than of stress (until about the fourth century A.D., by
which time it had probably become a stress accent like that of
Modern Greek). We know that it was a musical pitch accent from
the descriptions of it by Greek grammarians beginning in the Hellenistic Age, and from the very terminology used to describe it.
In spite of this knowledge, we moderns usually treat it as a
stress accent, stressing the syllable that has the mark over it.
There are many practical difficulties in using the Greek pitch
accents as such, among them being that (in spite of enthusiastic
and scholarly research) we do not know exactly what they sounded
like. It is therefore recommended in this book to use the accent
marks as guides for stress, though no one should be discouraged
from attempting the musical accent.

There are three accent marks in Greek:
    ´   acute: ὀξύς *(sharp)*
    `   grave: βαρύς *(heavy, deep)*
    ~   circumflex: περισπώμενος (originally written ^)
which represent respectively a rising pitch (´); a falling pitch
(`); and a rising-falling pitch (^). Most Greek words have one
accent mark to indicate the dominant accent (κύριος τόνος) of the

word. There are many rules on the placing of the accent, some
few of which will be given in this book, as they are needed, beginning now.

Practical Point. Where to put the accent mark: the accent
is written over a vowel or diphthong (over the second member of
the diphthong): θάνατος 'death'; νῆσος 'island'; πλοῦτος 'wealth'.
Should accent and breathing mark fall on the same letter, the
acute or grave is written beside the breathing mark, to the right
of it; the circumflex over it: ὅς or ῾ὸς 'who'; ᾦ 'to whom'; οἷς
'to whom' (pl.). With capital letters, both accent and breathing
are put to the left of the letter: Ὅμηρος 'Homer'; Ὦ 'Oh!'. If
the word begins with an accented diphthong, the breathing and accent are put over its second member as usual: Αἴγυπτος 'Egypt'.

Accent Rules

1. *The accent mark can fall on only one of the last three
syllables[1] of a word.* These are usually called by Latin names:
the last syllable is called the *ultima* (i.e. 'last' in Latin); the
next to last is called the *penult(ima)* (i.e. 'almost the last');
and the third from the last is called the *antepenult* (i.e. 'before
the next to last'). These terms are used to save time and effort,
instead of the awkward English phrases, and will be easy once they
become familiar. (We need not bother with the anteante- or any
others further back than the antepenult, since they are out of the
running for the accent mark.)

2. The *acute* accent (ὁ τόνος ὀξύς) can fall on any of the last
three syllables; the *circumflex* (ὁ τόνος περισπώμενος) only on one of
the last two; and the *grave* (ὁ τόνος βαρύς) only on the ultima.

3. The *circumflex* (which required a rising and falling pitch
within the same syllable) can fall only on a long vowel or diph-

---

[1]See p. 16 for definition of a syllable.

thong. The acute and grave can fall on either long or short vowels or diphthongs.

4. How far back (i.e. away from the end of the word) the
accent *can* go is determined by the *length-of-the-ultima*. For purposes of accent a syllable is long if it contains a long vowel
(η, ω, ᾱ, ῑ, ῡ) or a diphthong, short if it contains a short vowel (ε, ο, ᾰ, ῐ, ῠ). The diphthongs οι and αι as *endings* are considered *short* in determining accent (usually: except in the optative mood of verbs). (Note, however, that -οις, -αις are *long*,
and that -οι-, -αι- in other positions are long, as in Ἀθηναῖος.)

5. If the ultima is *short*, the *acute* can fall as far back
as the *antepenult;* and the *circumflex* as far back as the *penult*
(and no farther).

Examples (short ultima):

ἄνθρωπος, ἄνθρωποι	'man', 'men'
παιδίον, παιδία	'child', 'children'
θεός, θεοί	'god', 'gods'
δῶρον, δῶρα	'gift', 'gifts'
Ἀθηναῖος, Ἀθηναῖοι	'Athenian', 'Athenians'

6. If the ultima is *long*, the acute can fall only as far
back as the penult and the circumflex only on the ultima (i.e.
the circumflex cannot fall on the penult if the ultima is long).

Examples (long ultima):

ἀνθρώπου	'man's'
παιδίου	'child's'
δώρου	'of a gift'
ἀρετή	'goodness'
θεοῦ	'god's'

These rules will be treated again when we deal with the declension and accent of nouns.

7. The *grave* accent falls only on the ultima and is used
only when a word, normally having the acute on the ultima, is
followed by another word without intervening punctuation (to lead

into the next word, the pitch is slightly lower than the normal acute).

ἀγαθός	'good'
ὁ ἀγαθὸς ἄνθρωπος	'the good man'

Note: the accent of nouns and adjectives is inherent: that is, it belongs to the word and is *not* imposed on it by the rules for accent. The accent of nouns or adjectives may fall on any one of the last three syllables, and it is persistent, that is, it remains in the same place unless forced, by the rules of accent, to move forward. (See pp. 41f.)

Notes on the Accents:

In classical times, of course, the accent marks were unnecessary, and they are not found in inscriptions. A native speaker of Greek did not need to be told where to raise and lower his pitch any more than we normally need to have the stress marked in order to pronounce English words correctly. According to tradition, the marking of accents was started about 200 B.C. in Alexandria by the great Homeric scholar Aristophanes of Byzantium. There are two theories about why accent marks had become necessary at this time: either Aristophanes instituted them in connection with his work on Homer, to guide even native speakers in the proper pronunciation of the ancient epic forms that had by then become unfamiliar; or, because Greek had become the international language in the Hellenistic world, accent marks may first have been developed for teaching foreigners the correct accentuation. Whichever the reason, accent marks are a great help to us all, since (unfortunately) we must all learn classical Greek as a foreign language. The system used now in all texts was developed by Byzantine scholars from the Alexandrian systems and is a very practical and economical way of indicating an important aspect of the Greek language: its tonal accent.

Accent Exercises

According to the rules of accent given above, only one in each group is correctly accented: choose it. Be prepared to say why the other two are wrong. Be rational.

	a)	b)	c)
1.	ἄνθρωπου	ἄνθρωποι	ἀνθρῶπου
2.	πλοῦτου	πλουτὸς	πλοῦτος
3.	περίσπωμενος	περισπῶμενος	περισπώμενος
4.	λδγος	λόγος	λόγος
5.	τό δῶρον	τὸ δῶρον	τοῦ δώρου
6.	ἀρετή	ἄρετη	ἄρέτη
7.	δἷς	οἷς	ʽδις
8.	Θουκυδίδης	Θοῦκυδιδῆς	Θουκυδίδης
9.	δαῖμων	δαῖμων	δαίμων
10.	τόν θεόν	τὸν θεόν	τὸν θεόν
11.	μᾶχη	τὴν καλήν ψυχήν	κῶμαι

12. a) ἄθανατος   b) ἀθάνατοι   c) ἀθάνατους
13. a) ῥοδον   b) ῥοδον   c) ῥόδον
14. a) ἀθάνατους   b) ἀθάνατῳ   c) ἀθάνατον
15. a) καλός καὶ ἀγαθός b) καλὸς καὶ ἀγαθός   c) καλὸς καὶ ἀγαθὸς

Read aloud and learn the following saying (of Menander):

διπλοῦν ὁρῶσιν οἱ μαθόντες γράμματα.

(double they see, those having learned the letters)
People who have learned to read see twice as much.

Vocabulary: Numerals and Numerical Notation

The earliest system of Greek numerical notation was alphabetic, that is, they used the letters of the alphabet (including the three that have since become obsolete, Ϝ, Ϙ, ϡ) as numbers, with the sign (´) to mark them as numbers. The following list gives the names of the numbers one to twelve, and the letter used to represent each one. This system of numerical notation lacked a sign for zero and was therefore far inferior to the Arabic system in use today. The Greek system was an additive system rather than a place system (they used a separate figure for 10: ι´; 11 is then 10 + 1: ια´ , etc.).

Learn the names for the numbers 1-12 and 20.

α´	1	εἷς, μία, ἕν	ζ´	7	ἑπτά
β´	2	δύο	η´	8	ὀκτώ
γ´	3	τρεῖς, τρία	θ´	9	ἐννέα
δ´	4	τέτταρες, τέτταρα	ι´	10	δέκα
ε´	5	πέντε	ια´	11	ἕνδεκα
ϛ´	6	ἕξ	ιβ´	12	δώδεκα
		κ´	20	εἴκοσι	

The first four, εἷς, δύο, τρεῖς, τέτταρες, and their compounds are declinable (i.e. they change endings according to gender and case). This will be treated later (Lesson X).

The Readings

Dionysius Thrax (Διονύσιος Θρᾷξ)(born ca. 166 B.C., d. ca. 90 B.C.) was the author of the earliest Greek grammar textbook, late in the second or early in the first century B.C. His treatise (τέχνη γραμματική) became a standard

textbook and continued to be used until the eighteenth century. The work is
an admirable example of brevity and orderliness, beginning with a definition
of Grammar (γραμματική), listing its parts, and discussing the letters and
syllables (γράμματα καὶ συλλαβαί); from this part the reading passages that
follow have been excerpted. The most interesting thing about this, the earliest grammar book in our tradition, is not that it has many faults and omis-
sions (notable among them is the absence of any treatment of syntax), but that
so much of it is still useful: e.g. the way of presenting vowels and consonants is almost the same as in a modern grammar (this one, for example).
Later in the book, Dionysius lists and defines the parts of speech; his list
is a little different from our usual list and in some ways superior. (It will
be discussed in the next section of the introduction.)

   About the readings: It is not expected that the student will 'get'
everything in these early readings on his own. Many hints have to be provi-
ded and references made to pages of the English text where the point has been
treated. But the readings from the ancient authors should be read not once
only, but again and again, as more information comes under the student's con-
trol. These selections from Dionysius were chosen to impress on the student's
mind certain grammatical points, and to give them the respectability of age.
They were chosen too because they were felt by the author to be interesting
and amusing: the student may soon come to believe that a grammarian's sense
of fun is somehow distorted.

Read aloud and try to understand and translate the following
short sentences from Dionysius Thrax, on the letters of the alphabet. The numbers in parentheses tell you on what page the
point has been treated above. The grammar and vocabulary are
briefly explained to the left of the passage.

ἐστιν: (he, she, it) 'is'; (they, neuter) 'are', 'there are'; ἀπό 'from'; μέχρι 'to', 'up to'; τοῦ 'the', gen.; τέσσαρα = τέτταρα

1. Γράμματά ἐστιν εἰκοσιτέσσαρα ἀπὸ τοῦ ᾱ μέχρι τοῦ ῶ.

(p. 1)

τούτων 'of these' (refers to γράμμα-τα); μέν . . . δέ (in 3) point to the two parts of a contrast

2. τούτων φωνήεντα μέν ἐστιν ἑπτά ᾱ ε̄ η̄ ῑ ō ῡ ῶ.

(p. 2)

λέγεται 'is/are called'; ὅτι 'be-cause'; φωνήν (acc.) 'voice', 'sound'; ἀφ' ἑαυτῶν 'from them-selves'; ἀποτελεῖ 'it/they produce(s)

3. φωνήεντα δὲ λέγεται, ὅτι φωνὴν ἀφ' ἑαυτῶν ἀποτελεῖ.

(optional)

τῶν φωνηέντων 'of the . . .' (geni-tive plural); μακρά 'long'; βραχέα 'short'; δίχρονα 'of variable quan-tity'; καί 'and'

4. τῶν δὲ φωνηέντων μακρὰ μέν ἐστι δύο, η̄ καὶ ῶ, βραχέα δύο, ε̄ καὶ ō, δί-χρονα τρία, ᾱ, ῑ, ῡ.

(p. 2)

εἰσιν 'they are'

5. δίφθογγοι δέ εἰσιν ἕξ· αι αυ ει ευ οι ου. (p. 3)

τὰ λοιπά 'the remaining' (καὶ τὰ λοιπά, κ.τ.λ. = 'etc.')

6. σύμφωνα δὲ τὰ λοιπὰ ἑπτακαίδεκα· β γ δ ζ θ κ λ μ ν ξ π ρ σ τ φ χ ψ. (p. 5)

"They are called consonants (σύμφωνα) because they do not have a sound (φωνή) by themselves, but arranged with the vowels they produce a sound."

7. σύμφωνα δὲ λέγεται, ὅτι αὐτὰ μὲν καθ' ἑαυτὰ φωνὴν οὐκ ἔχει, συντασσόμενα δὲ μετὰ τῶν φωνηέντων φωνὴν ἀποτελεῖ. (optional)

ἄφωνα: α-privative, 'without', 'non-', 'un-', 'a-' + φων- (φωνή 'voice', 'sound', cf. *phon*etics

8. ἄφωνα δέ ἐστιν ἐννέα· β γ δ κ π τ θ φ χ. (p. 5)

μέσα 'in between' (cf. the Latin name for these sounds, *mediae;* we call them "voiced.")

9. τούτων ψιλὰ μέν ἐστι τρία, κ π τ, δασέα τρία, θ φ χ, μέσα δὲ τούτων τρία β γ δ. (p. 5-6)

ἔτι 'furthermore'; -ων endings imply 'of', the genitive case, plural

10. ἔτι δὲ τῶν συμφώνων διπλᾶ μέν ἐστι τρία· ζ ξ ψ. (p. 6)

εἴρηται 'is/are called/; ἓν ἕκαστον 'each one'; αὐτῶν 'of them'; ὅτι 'because'; σύγκειται 'consists'; ἐκ 'from' (here 'of')

11. διπλᾶ δὲ εἴρηται ὅτι ἓν ἕκαστον αὐτῶν ἐκ δύο συμφώνων σύγκειται, τὸ μὲν ζ ἐκ τοῦ σ καὶ δ, τὸ δὲ ξ ἐκ τοῦ κ καὶ σ, τὸ δὲ ψ ἐκ τοῦ π καὶ σ.

οὖν 'then'; χρόνοι 'times', 'quantities'

12. τόνοι μὲν οὖν εἰσι τρεῖς· ὀξύς ´, βαρύς `, περισπώμενος ῀. χρόνα δύο: μακρὸς ¯ καὶ βραχύς ˘. (p. 8)

Read aloud and learn the following statement from Aristotle's *Politics* (slightly altered):

ἡ γραμματικὴ καὶ ἡ γραφικὴ χρήσιμοι πρὸς τὸν βίον.

The arts of reading and writing are useful for life.

Notes on the Alphabet:

How important the art of writing was to the Greeks can be seen in the fact that it was the subject of myth, its invention being attributed to one of the gods or to a folk-hero. One of the most popular stories of the origin of writing was that Cadmus (the founder of Thebes), after living in Poenicia for a long time, brought back the alphabet (or some of it) with him on his return to Greece. This story is told as history by Herodotus (Book V, 58-9), where he explains why the letters of the alphabet are called Φοινικήια γράμματα

(Phoenician letters): i.e. because the Phoenicians taught the letters to the Greeks, who used them with a few changes in form (ῥυθμός) and in pronunciation (φωνή). Herodotus goes on to say that he had seen some of the early letters in inscriptions in a temple, and that they were for the most part like his own Ionian alphabet.

Like most Greek legends, this one has a great deal of truth in it. Scholars now believe that the Greek alphabet is derived from a Semitic form of writing (the North Semitic Alphabet) which originated in ancient Palestine or Syria and was spread by the Phoenicians, a Semitic people with trading stations throughout the Mediterranean world. The borrowing of this alphabet seems to have taken place independently in different parts of the Greek world, because there are many different versions of it in the various cities until the Ionic alphabet becomes the standard.

The date at which the Greeks became literate is still a matter of dispute: the earliest inscriptions (in the alphabet) are from the eighth century B.C.; some scholars therefore think that it must have been adopted by the Greeks in the ninth century. Others, however, using the shapes of the Semitic letters at different periods of their development, favor a much earlier date (even as early as the eleventh century B.C.).

As evidence for the North Semitic origin of the Greek alphabet, and through it directly or indirectly of all the alphabets in use, we have, first, the shapes of the early Greek letters which are similar to their Semitic counterparts. And, then, the names of the Greek letters and their order correspond to Semitic. Most of the names of the signs in the Greek alphabet are meaningless in the Greek language, but can be explained in Semitic (e.g. ἄλφα *aleph* 'ox'; βῆτα *beth* 'house'; γάμμα *gimel/gamel* 'camel'; δέλτα *daleth* 'door'; etc.). Naturally the names have been changed a little to fit the Greek language, which prefers words to end in vowels: the only consonants used to end words in Greek are ν, ρ, and ς.

The letters expressing sounds which Greek and Semitic had in common were adopted by the Greeks without change, others were adapted to express different Greek sounds (as Herodotus implies). The Greeks furthermore added the signs Υ, Φ, Χ, Ψ, and Ω at the end of the alphabet to represent sounds not existing in Semitic. But the most striking contribution of the Greeks to alphabetic writing was the full development of a vowel system, used only irregularly in the Semitic writing. Instead of using each sign to represent a consonant plus a variable vowel, the Greeks adapted certain of the signs as specifically vowel signs: this (the use of distinct consonant and vowel signs, each representing a single sound) is the main characteristic of *alphabetic* writing as opposed to any of the earlier syllabic or pictographic systems.

Some interesting books on the subjects treated in this lesson:

1. On the alphabet

David Diringer, *The Alphabet: A Key to the History of Mankind*. New York, 1948 (reprinted 1953)

--------------, *Writing*. London, 1962

I. J. Gelb, *A Study of Writing*. Chicago, 1963.

2. On the sounds of Greek

W. Stanley Allen, *Vox Graeca*. Cambridge, 1968.

W. B. Stanford, *The Sound of Greek*. Berkeley, 1967.

Note on Syllables:

1. For each separate vowel or diphthong in a Greek word there is a syllable (i.e. there are no silent vowels in Greek).

2. A syllable consists of a vowel or diphthong alone or with one or more consonants.

3. Some rules for syllabification:

a. A single consonant between two vowels in one word goes with the second vowel (e.g. ἄ-φω-να, φαι-νό-με-νον).

b. Any group of consonants that can begin a word in Greek goes with the following vowel as does a mute with μ or ν (e.g. πρᾶ-γμα, μη-τρός, τύ-πτω).

c. If the group of consonants cannot begin a word, it is divided, as are double consonants (e.g. ἄν-θος, ἐλ-πίς, ἄγ-γε-λος, ἵπ-πος).

Part II - Grammatical Outline of the Greek Language (or a preview of what you are in for if you stay in the course)

Γραμματική ἐστιν ἐμπειρία τῶν παρὰ ποιηταῖς τε καὶ συγγραφεῦσιν
ὡς ἐπὶ τὸ πολὺ λεγομένων.

Grammar is a practical knowledge of the usage of poets and writers
of prose

--Dionysius Thrax

The Greek language is very different from the English (language): this is one thing that makes it endlessly exciting (and exacting) to learn. In studying Greek, one must study grammar. Grammar, though no longer stylish, is a good thing. A knowledge of grammar enables us to speak and write correctly, clearly, elegantly; and to recognize the same qualities in others. Studying a foreign grammar forces us to see and to ponder the different ways in which things can be and have been said; it gives us a chance to look at other modes of expression than our own and to glimpse other modes of thought behind them. It makes us more a-ware (and more wary) of what we are reading and writing, hearing and saying. In short, grammar is a safe and legal way of expand-ing one's consciousness.

To begin with, Greek is a highly inflected language. Eng-lish is not. English has 'lost' most of its inflections. In English often only the context (environment of words) can tell us even what kind of word (noun, adjective, adverb, verb, etc.) we are dealing with. Take, for example, the word *right* in the fol-lowing phrases:

(1) the *right* of way

(2) to *right* a wrong

(3) go West and turn *right*

(4) the *right* way to do something

(5) do it *right* away/*right* now

In (1) *right* is a noun; in (2) it is a verb form; in (3) and (5) it is an adverb; and in (4) an adjective. We cannot take the word *right* out of its environment and say that it is a particular part of speech. In Greek, on the other hand, it is usually pos-sible to recognize what part of speech a word is by how it looks: its *form* goes a long way in telling what part of speech it is, and what it is doing in the sentence.

Again, English syntax is one of position. If we were to say such a thing as, 'the warden gave Socrates a cup of hemlock,' we would know who gave what to whom by the order of the words: the subject is first, then the verb, followed by the indirect object (to whom) and the direct object. Change that order and you change the meaning. In Greek, however, it is not the order of the words, but their form which indicates their relationships to each other (i.e. their syntax). 'Socrates' will have a different *case-ending* from the 'warden.' The warden will be *nominative* be-cause he is the subject, Socrates as indirect object (the recipient of the cup) will be *dative*; the cup (the direct object) will be in the *accusative* case in Greek. The order of the words will make very little difference because the endings (or inflexions) tell the whole story.

Of course English does have some inflexions left: the personal and relative pronouns change their forms from subject to object. We must say "*I* like you," but " you like *me*." Even so, we cannot reverse or meddle with the word order ("me like you," "you me like," or "you like I," because the syntax of *word order* in English has taken precedence over that of case inflection to such an extent that these series of words are not only ungrammatical, but nonsensical.

English still has some (though simple) verb inflexion: add -s to form the third person singular of the present (work, work*s)* add -d or -ed to form the regular simple past (work*ed)* and so forth. Greek has a very elaborate verb system, expressing by inflexional variations all the subtleties for which English uses its rich system of auxiliary verbs and compound verb formations (shall, will, may, might, should, would, used to, going to, etc., besides the forms of *be* and *have)*.

Both English and Greek are rich and subtle languages: but their richness lies in different directions. For the varieties of tense, mood, and voice, Greek has an abundance of verb endings, and English of compound and periphrastic expressions. It is a tendency of language to simplify, to regularize, to analogize (to get rid of the differences). Greek and English are languages at different stages of development. There is no sense in making value judgments about whether an inflected language is 'better' or 'worse' than a non-inflected one. In the last century, linguists and comparative grammarians considered our modern spoken languages as the decadent progeny of the pure Aryan mother tongue. And they considered English among the worst of a bad lot. Now in our own less romantic age, it is recognized that all languages tend to move in the same direction, from complexity of form to simplicity.

It is sobering for Greek scholars and beginning Greek scholars to bear in mind the opinion of the great Danish scholar of the English language, Otto Jespersen: "The so-called full and rich forms of the ancient languages are not a beauty but a deformity." This is perhaps going too far in the other direction, but let us not rhapsodize excessively about the wealth of Greek from its numbers of forms ("tell me not in mournful numbers..."). But considered and judged in the only way a language can be judged, as a means of expressing thought, Greek will not be found wanting.

Note: The material treated below will be considered in more detail throughout the book. It is given now in the hope that the student will feel safer and happier after getting a rational overview of the parts of speech of the Greek language and their equivalents in English.

The Parts of Speech (τὰ τοῦ λόγου μέρη)

In English the parts of speech are usually listed as these eight: *noun, pronoun, adjective, verb, adverb, preposition, conjunction,* and *interjection.* In Greek there are also eight parts of speech (by some ancient counts at least), but the Greeks listed them differently: noun (ὄνομα), pronoun (ἀντωνυμία), verb (ῥῆμα), adverb (ἐπίρρημα), *article* (ἄρθρον), *participle* (μετοχή), preposition (πρόθεσις), and conjunction (σύνδεσμος). In English we define our parts of speech according to what role(s) each can play in a sentence. In Greek it is possible to define them according to their form (the shapes they can take).

Noun (ὄνομα): a noun is the *name* of a thing, anything that has been given a name. The Greek word ὄνομα means "name." In Greek a noun is described as a word that has case, number, and gender.

Case-declension (πτῶσις: literally, a "falling") tells what part a noun is playing in a sentence. In English we use prepositional phrases and word order to show the relationship between a noun and other words in a sentence. Greek uses cases. Greek too has prepositions used with the cases to further define the relationships: it would be impossible to have a separate case for every possible relationship a noun can have with the other members of its sentence.

The cases in Greek are:

Nominative (ὀρθή) for the subject of the sentence.

Genitive (γενική) for relationships for which we use the preposition "of" (such as possession, origin); and for separation ("from").

Dative (δοτική) for the 'indirect object' and other relations for which we use "to" and "for"; for the locative relationship (the place "at" which a thing is located: "by," "at," "in," "on," etc.); for the instrumental relationship (the means "by" which, the manner "in" which).

Accusative (αἰτιατική) for the 'direct object' of the verb; for the end of motion ("to," "into").

These are the important cases to learn; there is a fifth case in Greek, the *vocative* (κλητική), the case of direct address (for calling people or addressing them).

We are fortunate that Greek reached such an advanced state of development as to have dropped some few of its original cases by the time it became a literary language. The parent of Greek *and* of English (and of the other Germanic languages) and of Latin (and of the Romance languages) and of the Indo-Iranian, Slavic, Armenian, Albanian, and Celtic languages had more than these simple five. This parent, called Indo-European (or Aryan) by the Comparative Grammarians had at least eight cases:

Nominative

Genitive

Dative

Accusative

Ablative (for separation)

Instrumental (for means by which)

Locative (for place where)

Vocative

In Greek, the genitive and ablative became melded into one form, and the dative, instrumental, and locative uses all drifted into one form (the dative). Old English had an elaborate case system too, but modern English has lost the case endings for all its adjectives, and nouns as well, except for the genitive or possessive endings of nouns, 's, s' (of course we do have a plural of nouns, but this is not a case).

Gender: There are three genders (γένη) in Greek:

Masculine (ἀρσενικόν)

Feminine (θηλικόν)

Neuter (οὐδέτερον neither)

In English we do not have grammatical gender: if we know or believe (or wish to say) that a person or animal or thing (such as a ship, machine or hurricane) is male or female, we use "he" or "she" (respectively); all other things are "it." Greek and many other languages have grammatical gender: a noun is either masculine, feminine, or neuter (and must have its article and adjective in agreement with that gender), sometimes quite regardless of its sex or lack thereof. Usually for persons, grammatical gender follows natural gender: but things (things which we do not think of as having gender) are often either masculine or feminine grammatically, and sometimes people are neuter, grammatically (as παιδίον 'a small child', and other diminutives).

Number: There are three numbers (ἀριθμοί) in Greek (yes, *three):*

Singular (ἐνικός) for *one*.
Dual (δυϊκός) for *two*.
Plural (πληθυντικός) for *more* (than two).

We need not worry about the dual in Greek because it had grown obsolete by classical times and was used only for such natural pairs as hands and feet, a yoke of oxen. Even English has some remnants of the dual (cf. the word "both," the words "twin" and "between" used only of two, and both related to the word "two"). Usually in Greek, the plural is used for more than one. (Dual forms will be given in the appendix for reference.)

Since adjectives have the same properties as nouns in Greek (i.e. undergo changes in form to indicate case, gender, and number), they are considered to belong to the same part of speech as the noun (ὄνομα). Furthermore, any adjective in Greek can be used as a noun when the article is put before it. In English we say that an adjective *modifies* a noun (or better that it gives an attribute of a noun). The adjective does not really change the meaning of the noun, but rather offers a subclass: *good men* are none the less *men* for their goodness, but they are a *part* of the whole class of *men*. In Greek if we want to say "the good men," we can actually leave out the word for "men" because the gender of the article and adjective tells us that we mean *men* as opposed to women or neuter things: οἱ ἀγαθοὶ ἄνθρωποι 'the good men', or simply οἱ ἀγαθοί 'the good', with "men" understood from the gender.

A *pronoun* (ἀντωνυμία) is a word used instead of a noun: it has no meaning of its own, but is used when we choose not to name, or not to repeat the name of whatever we are speaking/writing about. The reader is expected to know what the noun is to which the pronoun refers. Pronouns in Greek undergo declension with respect to case, number and gender.

The *article* (τὸ ἄρθρον) we recognize (in English grammar) as belonging to the same class as adjectives. In Greek (ὁ, ἡ, τό) and in English ("the"), it is really a demonstrative (cf. "this,"

"that"): in both languages etymologically related to the demonstratives.   The definite article is used when we want to refer
to a particular (definite) member/members of a class. (The differences between English and Greek usage of the article will be
treated in Lesson I.) Greek has no indefinite article (a, an),
which we use in English to indicate that we do not mean a particular member of a class: in Greek the noun by itself suffices.

A *verb* (ῥῆμα) in Greek is a word showing the following properties: tense, voice, mood, person, and number. The Greek verb
has many forms to express these properties. In English too we
can express them all, not through changes in the form of the
verb, but rather through auxiliary verbs and compound tenses.

Tense: the tense in Greek tells us two things: time and
aspect. *Time* tells us whether the action or state expressed by
the verb is past, present, or future. *Aspect* tells us the relationship of the action or state to the passage of time: is it
going on, momentary, or completed?

Greek has seven tenses of the indicative mood: present, imperfect, future, aorist, perfect, pluperfect, and future perfect,
which we can chart according to their *time* and *aspect*:

(aspect)	*Present*	*Past*	*Future*	(time)
Durative	Present	Imperfect	Future	
Momentary		Aorist		
Completed	Perfect	Pluperfect	Future Perfect	

Voice tells us the relationship of the subject to the action, whether the subject acts or is acted upon. The Greek verb
has three voices: *active*, *middle*, and *passive* (it will probably
occur to the student that the Greek verb has more than its share
of everything). The active and passive are simple enough, since
they are common in English.

Active voice: the subject performs the action ('I stop
the car.').

Passive voice: the subject receives (suffers) the

action ('I am stopped.').

   Middle voice: the subject is both the doer and receiver of the action ('I stop myself,' 'I cease'). It can be reflexive, the subject does something directly to himself, but usually it is more subtle; the subject does something for herself/himself or for something belonging to her/him (thus the middle voice can have an object). The middle voice implies that the subject is more directly (or more deliberately) involved in the activity. (Examples in Lesson I)

   Mood (mode): the moods (ἐγκλίσεις) tell us the manner of the action. Greek has four moods: Indicative, Imperative, Subjunctive, and Optative, besides the Infinitive and Participle, which are properly a verbal noun and a verbal adjective (respectively).

   The Indicative is, generally speaking, used to state a fact; the Imperative to give an order. The other two moods are less distinct. The Subjunctive was originally used for futurity, and many of its relationships have to do with the future: for exhortations, prohibitions, purpose, after verbs of fearing, in conditions (both future and general). The Optative is even less distinct than the Subjunctive: its independent uses are the optative of wish and the potential optative ('maybe,' 'might').

   Person and *Number:* the Greek verb changes its form to express the subject of the action: first, second, or third person, singular or plural ('I, you, he/she/it; we, you, they' are expressed by the ending, and the pronoun can be omitted unless special emphasis is needed). Greek also has a dual form for the second ("you two") and third ("they two") persons.

   Infinitive: the infinitives are formed from the various verb stems, but are not inflected. They are verbal nouns and share the characteristics of both nouns and verbs: as nouns they can be used with the article (τό) in different cases; they can be subjects or objects; as verbs they have tense and voice and can take objects. Infinitives are fairly common in English, with or without "to."

The *participle* (μετοχή) shares the characteristics of verb and adjective: it was considered a separate part of speech by the Greek grammarians. The Greek language is φιλομέτοχος ('fond of participles'). Their uses are numerous, though not very difficult, once the concept is grasped that the same word can be two parts of speech. The participles are formed from the different tense stems of the verb and they are declined (according to case, gender, and number) because they are adjectives.

The possible forms of a (full) verb:

Present	*Imperfect*	*Future*	*Aorist*	*Perfect*	*Pluperfect*	*Fut. Perfect*
Indic.	Indic.	Indic.	Indic.	Indic.	Indic.	Indic.
Subj.			Subj.	Subj.		
Opt.		Opt.	Opt.	Opt.		(Opt.)
Imper.			Imper.	Imper.		
Infin.		Infin.	Infin.	Infin.		(Infin.)
Partic.		Partic.	Partic.	Partic.		(Partic.)

All tenses and moods have the active voice, although the future perfect is very rare. The middle and passive voices are combined into one form for the present, imperfect, and the perfect tenses. Aorist and future have separate forms for the passive and middle. (See Appendix II for a complete verb.)

The other parts of speech present no difficulties: an adverb (ἐπίρρημα) indicates an attribute of a verb; a conjunction (σύνδεσμος) is used to join; a preposition (πρόθεσις) is used with a noun case to further define the use of the case. (Interjections are outside the grammatical structure of the sentence.) None of these elements is inflected even in Greek.

The Readings

The following sentences are taken from the grammar of Dionysius Thrax, from the sections defining the parts of speech.

μέρη plural of μέρος (neuter) subject of the sentence, 'parts' (for vocab., see p. 19); τοῦ λόγου 'of (the) speech' (genitive)

1. τοῦ δὲ λόγου μέρη ἐστὶν ὀκτώ· ὄνομα, ῥῆμα, μετοχή, ἄρθρον, ἀντωνυμία, πρόθεσις, ἐπίρρημα, σύνδεσμος.

Zeno, the Stoic, gives a shorter list (D.L.VII,57); προσηγορία 'common noun'; ὄνομα 'name' (i.e. 'proper noun')

2. τοῦ δὲ λόγου ἐστὶ μέρη πέντε· ὄνομα, προσηγορία, ῥῆμα, σύνδεσμος, ἄρθρον.

"A noun is a part of speech, having case declension (πτωτικόν), signifying an object (σῶμα 'body') or an abstraction (πρᾶγμα 'action, deed'), an object such as "stone" (λίθος), an abstraction such as "education" (παιδεία), called common and proper, common such as "man" (ἄνθρωπος), "horse" (ἵππος), proper as "Socrates."

3. ὄνομά ἐστι μέρος λόγου πτωτικόν, σῶμα ἢ πρᾶγμα σημαῖνον, σῶμα μὲν οἷον λίθος, πρᾶγμα δὲ οἷον παιδεία, κοινῶς τε καὶ ἰδίως λεγόμενον, κοινῶς μὲν οἷον ἄνθρωπος ἵππος, ἰδίως δὲ οἷον Σωκράτης.

(See p. 21); οὖν 'then, therefore, accordingly'

4. γένη μὲν οὖν εἰσι τρία· ἀρσενικόν, θηλυκόν, οὐδέτερον.

(See pp. 21-2); ὁ 'the', nominative masculine sing.; τῶ 'the', nom. masc. dual; οἱ 'the', nom. masc. plural; Ὅμηρος 'Homer'

5. ἀριθμοὶ τρεῖς· ἑνικός, δυϊκός, πληθυντικός· ἑνικὸς μὲν ὁ Ὅμηρος, δυϊκὸς δὲ τῶ Ὁμήρω, πληθυντικὸς δὲ οἱ Ὅμηροι.

(See p. 20); πτώσεις 'cases'; ὀνομάτων 'of nouns'

6. πτώσεις ὀνομάτων εἰσὶ πέντε· ὀρθή, γενική, δοτική, αἰτιατική, κλητική.

πρόσωπα 'persons'; ἀφ' οὗ 'from whom'; πρὸς ὅν 'to whom'; περὶ οὗ 'about whom'; πρῶτον, δεύτερον, τρίτον 'first, second, third'; ὁ λόγος 'the word, the speech'

7. πρόσωπα τρία, πρῶτον, δεύτερον, τρίτον· πρῶτον μὲν ἀφ' οὗ ὁ λόγος, δεύτερον πρὸς 'ὃν ὁ λόγος, τρίτον δὲ περὶ οὗ ὁ λόγος.

λέξις 'word'; μετέχουσα 'sharing' (+ gen.); τῆς . . . ἰδιότητος (gen.) 'the peculiarity' (See p. 25)

8. μετοχή ἐστι λέξις μετέχουσα τῆς τῶν ῥημάτων καὶ τῆς τῶν ὀνομάτων ἰδιότητος.

Read aloud and memorize the following expression:

χρόνος τὰ κρυπτὰ πάντα πρὸς τὸ φῶς ἄγει.

(time the hidden things all to the light leads)

Time brings all hidden things to the light.   --Menander

Some interesting books on the subjects considered in this section:

Jack E. Conner, *A Grammar of Standard English*. Boston, 1968.

Otto Jespersen, *The Philosophy of Grammar*. London, 1924.

R. H. Robins, *Ancient and Medieval Grammatical Theory in Europe*. London, 1951.

John Edwin Sandys, *A History of Classical Scholarship*, vol. I. Second edition, Cambridge, 1906.

LESSON I

A. Present Indicative Active and Middle-Passive of -ω verbs

Definitions

In Greek there are two types (or conjugations) of verbs:
(1) -ω verbs (or *thematic* verbs) and (2) -μι verbs (*non-thematic*
or *athematic*). The -ω verbs are characterized by the *thematic*
vowel o/ε (that is, o or ε) which connects the endings to the
stem; the -μι verbs on the other hand lack the thematic vowel
(in certain tenses, as will be explained later).

There are three voices in Greek: *active*, *middle*, and *passive*. *Voice* indicates the relation of the subject to the action:
in the active voice, the subject performs the action; in the passive voice, the subject suffers or experiences the action (is
acted upon); in the middle voice, the subject acts upon himself
(the reflexive use of the middle), or he acts for himself or in
his interest, or on something or someone belonging to himself:
the subject is intimately involved in the action of the verb.

Uses of the Voices: Examples

1. The Greek verb form παύω (active voice, first person singular, present indicative) means "I stop," in the sense of "I
bring to a stop" (i.e. *I bring* someone or something *to a stop*).
In the passive sense παύομαι (a form which is middle *or* passive
voice, first person singular present indicative), means "I am
stopped"; in the middle sense, παύομαι means "I stop myself" or
"I come to a stop." The difference between the middle and passive is that the *middle* implies that I stop of my own free will,
and the passive that I am forced to stop by someone or something
outside myself. The active form is transitive (that is, it takes
an object: I stop someone or something other than myself). The
middle in the example given is intransitive (since it is used re-
flexively).

2.   πείθω 'I stop' (in the active voice); πείθομαι in the middle voice means 'I persuade myself', and in the passive 'I am persuaded'. From this, the middle and passive have the meanings of 'I trust in, believe, or obey'.

3.   Often the middle voice means to have something done *for* oneself. For example, παιδεύω means 'I educate'; παιδεύομαι (as middle), 'I have (someone) educated or trained': as 'the parents *have* their children *educated* in the best institutions'. In this example the middle voice is transitive, that is, it takes an object; and there is no implication that the parents are actually doing the teaching, but rather that they are *having* it done.

Λύω means 'I release'; λύομαι (the middle form), 'I have (someone) released (by ransom)'; it can also mean 'I release' something of my own. These uses of the middle are not reflexive and may take objects.

4.   Other examples:

γράφω 'I write'; γράφομαι 'I write for myself', i.e. I write something down for my own use (e.g. of taking notes).

πέμπω 'I send'; πέμπομαι 'I send for'.

φέρω 'I bear or carry'; φέρομαι 'I carry or bring (with me for my own use)'.

ἄρχω 'I make a beginning'; the middle voice, ἄρχομαι, is used where personal action is emphasized.

βουλεύω 'I plan'; βουλεύομαι 'I take counsel with myself, make plans for myself'.

Although in some of these examples, the meaning of the verb appears to change significantly from the active to the middle or passive, a close look will show that these changes are only logical progressions caused by the differences in the uses of the voices. It is always possible to translate the word literally when unsure of the exact meaning, and then as the context becomes clearer, to substitute a more suitable word in the translation. On the other hand, in some of the examples given above, the translations of the active and middle will be identical. The differences in meaning will be clear in the Greek, but will be lost in the translation into English. This is but one of the many subtleties of the Greek language which make it difficult to translate adequately, but worth the effort of reading and understanding.

The same forms are used for middle and passive in the present system (which includes present and imperfect) and in the perfect system (perfect and pluperfect), but the meaning will usually be clear from the context. Just as in English, if you take the word "sets" by itself, you cannot even tell whether it is a noun or a verb, but in a sentence its meaning will usually be clear: in the same way, παύομαι in isolation may mean either 'I stop (myself)' or 'I am stopped', but in a sentence the surrounding words will tell you which is meant.

The Greek verb has seven tenses (see Introduction, p. 23), divided into primary and secondary tenses: the primary tenses being present, future, perfect, and future perfect; the secondary tenses aorist, imperfect, and pluperfect.

The present tense is used for action going on in the present time. The Greek present tense can be translated by any of the three English present tenses: λύω may mean 'I am freeing', 'I do free', or 'I free'; λύεις; 'are you freeing?', 'do you free?'

Formation of Present Indicative and Infinitive:
     present stem + thematic vowel + primary endings

	Active Endings		Middle-Passive Endings	
Thematic Vowel	Endings		Thematic Vowel	Endings
		Singular		
	-ω	1st	-ο-	-μαι
	-εις	2nd	[-ε-σαι] →	-ει / -ῃ
	-ει	3rd	-ε-	-ται
		Plural		
-ο-	-μεν	1st	-ο-	-μεθα
-ε-	-τε	2nd	-ε-	-σθε
	-ουσι(ν)	3rd	-ο-	-νται
	-ειν	Infinitive	-ε-	-σθαι

Notes:

    1. Note that the thematic vowel has been absorbed in the long endings, -ω, -εις, -ει, -ουσι. Otherwise it can be seen quite clearly as an element used to join the endings to the stem.

    2. It is a characteristic of the Greek language that -s- between two vowels tends to drop out. In the second person singular of the middle-passive the ending was originally -σαι, but the -σ- comes between the -αι of the ending and the thematic vowel, and so it drops out; the resulting -ε-αι contracts to -ει, for which the alternative form -η is also found.

    3. -ουσι(ν): the movable ν: certain forms ending in vowels add ν if the word following begins with a vowel, or if the form ends a sentence. This is true of words ending in -σι (whether nouns or verbs) and third person singular forms ending in -ε (see Lesson II). Compare the ν-movable to our indefinite article: *a* confrontation, *an* ultimatum.

Example: λύω in the Present Indicative and Infinitive: Present Stem, λυ-

		Active		*Middle-Passive*
		Singular		
	λύω	1st		λύομαι
	λύεις	2nd		λύει (*or* λύη)
	λύει	3rd		λύεται
		Plural		
	λύομεν	1st		λυόμεθα
	λύετε	2nd		λύεσθε
	λύουσι(ν)	3rd		λύονται
	λύειν	Infinitive		λύεσθαι

    Accent: The accent of verbs is *recessive*. This means that the accent goes back as far as the length of the ultima permits. If the ultima is long the accent will be an acute on the penult; if the ultima is short, the accent will go back to the antepenult if there is one. There are some exceptions to this rule and they will be given later.

Deponent Verbs

    Many verbs in Greek lack active forms for some or all of their tenses. If a verb has no active forms, it is called "deponent"; if it lacks the active in only some of its tenses, it is called "semi-deponent." Such verbs are easily recognized because they will show principal parts in the middle-passive ending (-ομαι) rather than in the active ending (-ω). Although deponent verbs are middle or passive in form, they are active in meaning.

Vocabulary

In the following vocabulary list, the first principal part is given for each verb: the first person singular present active indicative, or the first person singular present indicative middle-passive (if the verb is deponent).

The present stem of the verb is to be found by removing the first person ending, -ω or -ομαι. Examples: λύω: stem, λυ-; λείπω: stem, λειπ-; ἔρχομαι: stem, ἐρχ-; γίγνομαι: stem, γιγν-.

In the list that follows, find the present stem of each verb. Which of these verbs are deponent?

ἄγω	*lead, drive, bring* (paedagogue, παιδαγωγός)
ἄρχω	*begin, rule* (+ genitive)(archaeology, anarchy) ἄρχων - ruler
βουλεύω	*plan* (+ infinitive, *resolve* to do)(bouleuterion, βουλευτή-
βουλή →	ριον, *council chamber*) Deliberate
βούλομαι	*wish, want* (+ infinitive)(Cf. Lat. *volo*, Ger. *wollen*, Eng. *will*)
γίγνομαι	*become, be born, be* (the root of this word is γεν-, γν-, hence, genesis, γένεσις)
γράφω	*write* (epigraphy, palaeography)
ἐθέλω	*wish, be willing* (+ infinitive)
ἔρχομαι	*come, go*
ἔχω	*have*
κρίνω	*judge* (critic)
λέγω	*say* (Cf. Lat. *lego*; Greek, λόγος, *word*), *speak, mean*
λείπω	*leave* (eclipse, ellipse)
λύω	*free, loosen, release, destroy, break* (catalyst, analysis)
μένω	*remain, wait*
νομίζω	*think, believe* (from νόμος) usage, custom, law → use customarily
παιδεύω	*educate, train* (from παῖς, παιδός *child*)
παύω	*stop*, mid. *cease* (pause)
πείθω	*persuade*, in mid-pass. *obey, trust* (+ dative)(Πειθώ, Peitho, *Persuasion*, patron goddess of politicians)
πέμπω	*send* (pomp)
πράττω	*do, make* (practical, pragmatic)
φέρω	*bring, carry* (Cf. Lat. *fero*, Eng. *bear*)
πιστεύω	√. *trust* (+ dative) πίστις (trust, faith) n.
καί	*and, even, also*
καί . . . καί	*both . . . and*
ἤ	*or*
ἤ . . . ἤ	*either . . . or*

Vocabulary Notes:

1. ἄρχω means 'be first', whether of time ('begin', 'make a beginning') or of place or station ('govern', 'rule'). The word ἄρχων, the present parti-

ciple of ἄρχω, used in the masculine as a noun, means 'ruler', 'commander', or
'archon', and is the title of the three top administrative magistrates in ancient Athens.

2. βούλομαι and βουλεύω are related words. From βούλομαι 'wish' comes
the noun βουλή which means (1) 'will', 'determination', and (2) the 'Council'
or 'Senate' at Athens, referring to the Council of Five Hundred, established
by Cleisthenes in 507 B.C. From the noun βουλή is derived the verb βουλεύω,
'take counsel', 'deliberate', 'be a member of the βουλή'.

3. βούλομαι and ἐθέλω both mean 'wish', but βούλομαι implies choice or
preference (εἰ βούλει . . . 'if you please', 'if you like'), and ἐθέλω is
used of consent rather than desire: εἰ βούλει, ἐγὼ ἐθέλω: 'if you want to, I
am willing to go along'. (εἰ 'if', ἐγώ 'I')

4. νομίζω is derived from the noun νόμος meaning 'usage', 'custom',
'law'. The original meaning of νομίζω is 'use customarily', as in the expression νομίζειν γλῶσσαν, 'to have a language in common use'; but has the secondary meaning of 'own', 'acknowledge', 'believe', as in νομίζειν θεοὺς εἶναι,
'to believe that the gods exist'.

5. Verbs in -ιζω and -ευω are called denominatives, that is, they are
derived from nouns: νομίζω from νόμος; βουλεύω from βουλή; παιδεύω derived
from παῖς ('child'), means 'bring up, rear a child'; πιστεύω from πίστις
('trust', 'faith') means 'put faith in'.

Learning by Rote

Sit down with your textbook and go over the new forms a few
times; write them down from memory. This is a good start, but
only a start. Later in the day, say them over to yourself, sing
them in the shower (paying attention to the pitch accents), mut-
ter them at breakfast, mumble them in rhythm as you walk along,
count them over as you fall asleep (you may even begin to dream
in Greek, a good sign): make them a part of your memory, and in
that way you will never forget them, not even when the crunch (of
the examination) comes. Learning a new language necessitates
taxing your memory to the utmost . . . because you cannot know
the language in the abstract, you must know its forms and structure (i.e. grammar) and its vocabulary.

Exercises

1. Fill in the correct accents (p. 32):

1. ἀγομαι	3. βουλευεις	5. βουλεται
2. ἀρχεσθαι	4. ἀγομεθα	6. γιγνονται

7. γραφει	12. λεγεται	17. παιδευειν
8. ἐθελομεν	13. λειπουσι	18. παυει
9. ἐρχεσθαι	14. λυονται	19. πειθεσθαι
10. ἐχομεν	15. μενειν	20. πεμπομεθα
11. κρινετε	16. νομιζω	21. πιστευομεν

2. Conjugate (i.e. write out all the forms you have learned so far, in the order given; include infinitives) in the present active (where it exists) and middle-passive:

1. ἄγω	2. βούλομαι	3. γίγνομαι
4. γράφω	5. λείπω	6. ἔρχομαι
7. ἔχω	8. φέρω	9. παύω
10. πέμπω		

3. Parse the following (i.e. identify them grammatically) and then translate them. E.g. πέμπεσθαι: present middle-passive infinitive of πέμπω; meaning 'to send for, to be sent'; ἄγετε: present active indicative, second person plural of ἄγω; meaning 'you lead, are leading'.

1. φέρεσθαι	8. γίγνεται	15. λέγεσθαι
2. ἀρχόμεθα	9. βουλεύεσθε;	16. πιστεύεις
3. βούλει	10. ἔρχονται	17. παυόμεθα
4. ἐθέλεις;	11. ἔρχει;	18. μένει
5. πέμπομεν	12. νομίζουσιν	19. λείπεται
6. ἄγομεν;	13. γράφεσθε	20. ἔχειν
7. ἔχετε	14. λύειν	21. φέρεις καὶ ἄγεις.

22. βουλευόμεθα καὶ κρίνομεν.
23. βούλομαι ἄρχειν. ἐθέλεις ἄρχεσθαι;
24. βουλεύουσι γράφειν.
25. λύετε 'ἢ λύεσθε;
26. βούλεται ἔρχεσθαι 'ἢ μένειν;
27. τί πράττεις;   (τί 'what?')
28. τίνι πείθεσθε;   (τίνι 'to whom?', dat.)
29. βούλει λύεσθαι;
30. τί βούλονται γράφεσθαι;

3(a). Change 1-10 to the opposite voice, if it exists (act. to m-p; m-p to active).

3(b). Change 11-20 to the opposite number (sing. to plur.; plur. to sing.). (Note that an infinitive has no person and number.)

4. Translate the following into Greek verb forms:

1. we are being taught   2. I cease (stop myself)
3. she trusts (persuades herself)   4. they are being carried

5. we are led
6. you (pl.) persuade
7. you (sg.) begin
8. you (sg.) obey (are persuaded)
9. we are ruled
10. they plan
11. do you wish?
12. they make plans for themselves
13. you (sg.) become
14. he is writing
15. are you (sg.) going?
16. I am willing (consent)
17. he has
18. are you (pl.) writing?
19. they are being sent
20. he judges
21. you (pl.) say
22. it is said
23. she is being released
24. to remain
25. I think
26. to become
27. do you (pl.) believe?
28. to plan
29. to wish
30. to be left

31. He wants to write.
32. We wish to be educated.
33. They are willing to remain.
34. Do you (pl.) wish to be led?
35. Are you (sg.) willing to stop (yourself)?
36. He is willing both to rule and to be ruled.
37. Do you (pl.) wish to plan (make plans for your-selves) or to judge?
38. Is he writing or speaking?
39. I both wish and consent to obey.
40. They are either coming or remaining.

Read aloud and memorize the following Greek proverb:

ἀκρὸν λάβε, καὶ μέσον ἕξεις.

Seize the top, and you will have the middle.

B. Nouns of the -η (first) and -o- (second) Declensions

Characteristics of Nouns

Number tells how many: one (*singular*) or more than one (*plural*). There is one set of endings for singular and another for plural. Besides the singular and plural, Greek has a third number, the *dual*, for two persons or things. The student will not be burdened with learning the dual at this time, since it was archaic in classical times and is not very common even in the earliest Greek literature. By the classical age, the dual was used for certain obvious pairs, as feet, hands, a team of oxen.

Gender: there are three genders in Greek: *masculine, feminine,* and *neuter*. All nouns have gender, which may be natural gender, or purely grammatical gender: usually nouns for males are masculine, those for females feminine; as ὁ ἀνήρ 'the man', ἡ γυνή 'the woman'. But names of things are very often masculine or feminine and nouns for people are sometimes neuter: e.g. all diminutive nouns in -ιον are neuter, as τὸ παιδίον 'little child'. The gender of every noun must be learned. Each noun in the vocabulary is accompanied by a form of the article which will tell you what gender it is: ὁ (masc.), ἡ (fem.), τό (neuter).

Case: the cases tell the relationship of a noun or pronoun to the other words in the sentence. There are five cases in Greek: nominative, genitive, dative, accusative, and vocative. The *nominative* is the case of the subject and of the predicate nominative (used with copulative verbs such as 'be', 'become'). The *genitive* is the case of possession, denoting the relationship expressed by the preposition 'of', or by the ''s, s' in English. The *dative* is the case of the indirect object, expressed in English by 'to' or 'for'. The *accusative* is the case of the direct object. The *vocative* is the case of direct address.

There are other meanings for the genitive, dative, and accusative cases, besides the basic ones given above. As was mentioned in the introduction, there were three other cases in the Indo-European language from which Greek was developed: the ablative, the instrumental and the locative. (In Latin, the ablative assumed the meanings of the instrumental and locative.) In Greek, the genitive has taken over the meaning of *separation* ('from'), or the old ablative case; and the dative has the meanings of the *instrumental* ('by', 'with') and of the *locative* ('in', 'on', 'at'). The accusative has the meaning of the end of motion (called the *terminal* accusative: the place, thing, or person toward which motion is directed). These relationships in English are, for the most part, expressed by the use of prepositions.

It is impossible to have a separate case for every possible relationship a noun can play in a sentence. The Finnish language

has sixteen cases and even that is not enough. There are in
Greek a number of prepositions which further define the case
uses. Some of these prepositions are used with one case only,
as ἐν 'in', which is used only with the dative case (the locative
dative, the case for *place at which)*; or εἰς 'into', 'to', used
only with the accusative case (cf. the terminal accusative, the
case for *place to which)*. Other prepositions are used with more
than one case; and the word we use to translate them depends on
which case follows. One such preposition is παρά 'alongside of'
('at the side of', 'near'): with the genitive, παρά means 'from
beside', 'from the side of' (or simply 'from'): the genitive of
separation; with the dative, παρά means 'at the side of' ('with',
'beside', 'near'): the locative dative; with the accusative,
παρά may be translated as 'to the side of' ('to'): the terminal
accusative. It is important to remember that the meaning of the
case is generally retained when a preposition is used with it.
The uses of the cases will be discussed in more detail and various special uses will be given in the future.

It is of great importance to be familiar with the case endings and uses, for the cases alone tell you what part a noun
plays in a sentence: Greek, as an inflected language, is not
bound by the place system of syntax as English is. The use of a
word is not dependent on the order in which it appears in the
sentence, but rather on its form.

The Definite Article

Corresponding to the English "the" is ὁ, ἡ, τό in Greek.
Like any other adjective, it is declined: it has singular and
plural, all three genders, and all the cases (except the vocative). Its endings are similar to those of the -η and -ο- declensions (which follow the treatment of the article), though not
identical with them. It should be learned thoroughly, the soon-
er, the better.

Article

	Singular			Plural		
	M.	F.	N.	M.	F.	N.
NOM.	ὁ	ἡ	τό	οἱ	αἱ	τά
GEN.	τοῦ	τῆς	τοῦ	τῶν	τῶν	τῶν
DAT.	τῷ	τῇ	τῷ	τοῖς	ταῖς	τοῖς
ACC.	τόν	τήν	τό	τούς	τάς	τά

Remarks on the Article:

Notice that the forms of the nominative masculine and feminine both singular and plural (ὁ, ἡ, οἱ, αἱ), the forms without τ, have no accent. They are *proclitics*, that is, they lean on the word following them for their accent. Only the forms ὁ and τό differ in endings from the regular -o- (second) declension endings; the endings of the feminine are the same as the -η type of the first declension.

Uses of the article: in general, the definite article corresponds to English "the," but it is used in some instances where English would omit it.

1. Often proper names are accompanied by the article, e.g. ὁ Πλάτων (Plato).

2. Abstract nouns may be used with or without the article: ἡ ἀρετή or ἀρετή ('excellence').

3. Demonstrative adjectives are always used with the article: οὗτος ὁ ἀνήρ ('this man'). (Lesson III)

4. The definite article is used with a noun in the generic sense, designating a person or thing as representing a class, ὁ ἄνθρωπος ('man', in general), οἱ ἄνθρωποι ('mankind').

The article can also be used as a possessive, to indicate that a thing belongs to someone mentioned in the sentence: that is, it may sometimes be translated as 'my, your, his/her/its, their', etc.

Greek has no indefinite article equivalent to our 'a/an'.

Nouns of the -η and -o- Declensions

There are three declensions of nouns in Greek: first declension (or η/α nouns, so called because -η or -α is characteristic of their declension; the -η type will be discussed in this lesson, the -α type in Lesson III); second declension (or -o- type, -o- being their characteristic vowel; they are divided into two types, -ος and -ον); third declension (sometimes called the consonant declension, although it includes other types, to be treated in Lesson V).

1. -η type nouns of the first declension: all nouns of this type are feminine.

Formation: to the base of the noun, add:

-η type, Endings:

	Singular	Plural
NOM.	-η	-αι
GEN.	-ης	-ῶν
DAT.	-ῃ	-αις
ACC.	-ην	-ας (long -α-)

(The vocative will only be given separately when it differs from the nominative.)

The general rule for finding the *base* of a noun is: remove the genitive ending; for this reason, the genitive is always given with a new noun in the vocabulary.

Examples (with the article), ἡ δίκη 'justice'; ἡ ἀρετή 'excellence':

	Singular	Plural	Singular	Plural
NOM.	ἡ δίκη	αἱ δίκαι	ἡ ἀρετή	αἱ ἀρεταί
GEN.	τῆς δίκης	τῶν δικῶν	τῆς ἀρετῆς	τῶν ἀρετῶν
DAT.	τῇ δίκῃ	ταῖς δίκαις	τῇ ἀρετῇ	ταῖς ἀρεταῖς
ACC.	τὴν δίκην	τὰς δίκας	τὴν ἀρετήν	τὰς ἀρετάς

2. -ο- type: second declension

To the base of the noun, add the following endings:

-ος type: mostly masc., some fem.   -ον type, all neuter

	Singular	Plural	Singular	Plural
NOM.	-ος	-οι	-ον	-α
GEN.	-ου	-ων	-ου	-ων
DAT.	-ῳ	-οις	-ῳ	-οις
ACC.	-ον	-ους	-ον	-α
VOC.	-ε			

Examples (with article), ὁ λόγος 'word'; ἡ ὁδός 'road'; ὁ πλοῦτος 'wealth'; ὁ ἄνθρωπος 'man':

                    Singular

NOM.	ὁ λόγος	ἡ ὁδός	ὁ πλοῦτος	ὁ ἄνθρωπος
GEN.	τοῦ λόγου	τῆς ὁδοῦ	τοῦ πλούτου	τοῦ ἀνθρώπου
DAT.	τῷ λόγῳ	τῇ ὁδῷ	τῷ πλούτῳ	τῷ ἀνθρώπῳ
ACC.	τὸν λόγον	τὴν ὁδόν	τὸν πλοῦτον	τὸν ἄνθρωπον
VOC.	λόγε	ὁδέ	πλοῦτε	ἄνθρωπε

                    Plural

NOM.	οἱ λόγοι	αἱ ὁδοί	οἱ πλοῦτοι	οἱ ἄνθρωποι
GEN.	τῶν λόγων	τῶν ὁδῶν.	τῶν πλούτων	τῶν ἀνθρώπων
DAT.	τοῖς λόγοις	ταῖς ὁδοῖς	τοῖς πλούτοις	τοῖς ἀνθρώποις
ACC.	τοὺς λόγους	τὰς ὁδούς	τοὺς πλούτους	τοὺς ἀνθρώπους

-ον type: τὸ ἔργον 'deed';   τὸ δῶρον 'gift':

NOM.	τὸ ἔργον	τὰ ἔργα	τὸ δῶρον	τὰ δῶρα
GEN.	τοῦ ἔργου	τῶν ἔργων	τοῦ δώρου	τῶν δώρων
DAT.	τῷ ἔργῳ	τοῖς ἔργοις	τῷ δώρῳ	τοῖς δώροις
ACC.	τὸ ἔργον	τὰ ἔργα	τὸ δῶρον	τὰ δῶρα

Remarks on the endings:

Be sure to learn the ι-subscript of the dative singular endings, -ῃ and -ῳ: the forms are not correct without it. -ι- is characteristic of the dative case: -ῃ, -ῳ, -οις, -αις.

Note that the endings for the -ος type and the -ον type are the same except for the nominative singular and the nominative and accusative plural.

Neuters always have the same ending in the nominative and accusative.

The numerous examples given above have been chosen to illustrate the accentuation of nouns; the endings are the same within each type, and should be the student's first concern at this point.

Remarks on Accent (Consult the paradigms given above)

The accent of nouns is *persistent*, that is, it regularly stays on the syllable on which it starts, unless forced to move. Where it starts must be learned by observation and by saying the new words over and over to yourself.

An exception to this rule is that nouns of the *first* declension have the circumflex on the ultima in the genitive plural (regardless of where the accent falls in the other forms). Historically the -ῶν ending is the result of a contraction from -άων or -έων to -ῶν.

It is necessary to know where the accent starts in order to be able to accent the nouns correctly. This can most easily be learned by saying the word aloud several times, stressing the accented syllable, until it is familiar to you.

Using the nouns declined above as examples, study the following rules:

1. The accent is persistent, and so, will stay where it starts: thus the word δίκη: the accent is on the penult, which in this word is short: it remains on this syllable except in the genitive plural, as noted above. Study δίκη and λόγος and ἔργον.

2. In the word ἀρετή, the accent is on the ultima and remains there throughout the declension. Note that in certain cases, the accent changes from the acute to the circumflex: in the first and second declensions, if the accent falls on the ultima, the circumflex is used in the *genitive* and *dative, singular* and *plural*. Study the examples, ἀρετή and ὁδός.

3. In the words πλοῦτος and δῶρον, again the accent is on the penult. In these two words, the penult is long.

If the penult is *long* and *accented*, and the ultima is short, then the accent on the penult must be the *circumflex*. Remember that the endings -αι and -οι are short for the purposes of accentuation.

The circumflex can fall on the penult only if the ultima is *short*. If the ending is long (as -ου, -ῳ, -αις, -οις, -ους, -ων) then the accent must change from the circumflex to the acute. Study the declensions of πλοῦτος and δῶρον. What is the length of the -α in the neuter plural, long or short?

4. In the declension of ἄνθρωπος, you will notice that the accent shifts from the antepenult to the penult. The accent is forced to move by the length of the ultima.

An accent can go as far back as the antepenult only if the ultima is *short*. If the ultima is *long*, the furthest

back an accent can go is the penult: thus ἄνθρωπος, ἄνθρωποι, but
ἀνθρώπῳ, ἀνθρώπου.

5. The grave accent is used when a word, accented with
the acute on the ultima, is followed immediately by another word
(without any intervening punctuation mark), e.g. τὸν ἄνθρωπον; ὁ λόγος καὶ τὸ ἔργον.

Vocabulary: Nouns

Nouns can always be recognized in the vocabulary or dictionary because they are given in the following way: nominative singular, genitive singular, article (in the nominative singular):
e.g. ἄνθρωπος, ἀνθρώπου, ὁ, *man*. The article given with each noun
tells what gender it is. It is not always possible to determine
the gender from the nominative form (cf. ὁδός, which is feminine).
It is not correct to think of declensions as having gender. As
you will learn in Lesson III, there is a class of nouns of the
first declension that is masculine; and as you already know, certain (only a few) nouns of the second declension are feminine.
Therefore it is a good idea to get in the habit of learning the
article with each new noun. The genitive should be learned as
well because the base of a noun is usually found from the genitive singular. As will become clear later (Lesson V), the base
is not always clear from the nominative. The nominative and genitive together show you what paradigm (pattern) the noun will
follow. Always learn the accent of a noun (by saying it aloud)
when you study the vocabulary word, and notice what changes (if
any) in accent take place from the nominative to the genitive.

ἀνάγκη, ἀνάγκης, ἡ	*necessity*
ἄνθρωπος, ἀνθρώπου, ὁ	*man* (anthropomorphic)
ἀρετή, ἀρετῆς, ἡ	*goodness, excellence, virtue*
ἀρχή, ἀρχῆς, ἡ	*beginning, origin; power, empire, office, first prin-* *ciple* (cf. the meanings of ἄρχω)
βίος, βίου, ὁ	*life, livelihood* (macrobiotic)
βουλή, βουλῆς, ἡ	*will, determination; Council, Senate*
γνώμη, γνώμης, ἡ	*thought, opinion* (gnome, gnomic)
δίκη, δίκης, ἡ (ῐ)	*justice, order, right; lawsuit, trial*
δῶρον, δώρου, τό	*gift* (Pandora)

εἰρήνη, εἰρήνης, ἡ   *peace* (Irene)
ἔργον, ἔργου, τό   *deed, work* (erg, energy)
ἥλιος, ἡλίου, ὁ   *sun* (helium; Helius, the sun god)
θάνατός, θανάτου, ὁ   *death* (euthanasia, thanatopsis)
θεός, θεοῦ, ὁ/ἡ   *god, goddess* (πρὸς θεῶν 'good heavens!')(θεός is com-
                             mon gender, masc. or fem. The voc. θεός is irreg.)
λίθος, λίθου, ὁ   *stone* (lithograph)
λόγος, λόγου, ὁ   *reason, word; speech; account; principle*
μέτρον, μέτρου, τό   *measure, moderation* (meter)
νῆσος, νήσου, ἡ   *island* (Peloponnesian)
νόμος, νόμου, ὁ   *usage, custom, law* (cf. νομίζω)(κατὰ νόμον *according
                             to law,* παρὰ νόμον *contrary to law,* νόμῳ *by custom,
                             conventionally*)
ξένος, ξένου, ὁ   *guest-friend, stranger, foreigner* (xenophobic)
ὁδός, ὁδοῦ, ἡ   *road, street, way*
οὐρανός, οὐρανοῦ, ὁ   *heaven, sky* (uranium, Uranus)
παιδίον, παιδίου, τό   *little child, young slave* (pediatrician)
πλοῦτος, πλούτου, ὁ   *wealth, riches* (Πλοῦτος, Plutus, god of wealth)
πόλεμος, πολέμου, ὁ   *war*
πόνος, πόνου, ὁ   *toil, labor*
φίλος, φίλου, ὁ   *friend, loved one* (includes family)
χρόνος, χρόνου, ὁ   *time* (can refer both to time in the abstract and to a
                             definite period of time)
ψυχή, ψυχῆς, ἡ   *life, soul* (Psycho)

γάρ   *for,* conjunction, postpositive (i.e. cannot come first
                             in a sentence or clause, and is usually put second,
                             often between the article and noun). Note that γάρ
                             is not a preposition (the English preposition 'for'
                             is usually expressed in Greek by the dative case
                             without a preposition), but a causal conjunction, a
                             milder way of saying 'because'. In translation it
                             may often seem to begin a sentence, but in Greek it
                             is used to connect a sentence or thought to the one
                             before it.
δέ   *but,* postpositive conjunction
μέν . . . δέ   *on the one hand . . . on the other hand* (both μέν and
                             δέ are postpositives and are used to point out that
                             the words with which they are associated are being
                             contrasted)

Prepositions

εἰς   *into, to,* a preposition with the accusative case: cf.
                             the terminal accusative, the place to which, with
                             verbs of motion
ἐν   *in,* preposition with the dative case: cf. the loca-
                             tive dative, the place where
παρά   *alongside, by, near* (usually used of persons and per-
                             sonified things), preposition with genitive, dative,
                             and accusative
        with genitive: *from the side of, from beside, from* (παρὰ τῶν θεῶν
                             from the gods)

with dative: *by the side of, beside, with, near* (παρὰ τοῖς φίλοις
                    with/beside the friends)

with accusative: *to the side of, to, along; in addition to, contrary to*
                    (παρὰ νόμον *contrary to the law*)

σύν   *with* (older Attic spelling ξύν), preposition with the
                    dative case (it is used both of accompaniment: *a-
                    long with, in company with;* and of instrument:
                    with, by means of)

Vocabulary Notes:

1. ἀρετή ('excellence') is a very important word and concept in the
Greek language and in the Greek mind. It is the word that comes to mind when
we think of the Greek ideal--striving for perfection of the mind and body, and
for the fullest development of human capabilities. Naturally the understanding of the word changed over the years. In Homer's heroic world, ἀρετή was
martial valor, the quality of the hero, the ideal for which men lived and
died. Later it came to have a more political connotation: under the influence of the Sophists, man's highest goal came to be political ἀρετή. Socrates' mission was spiritual perfection (ἀρετή), which he believed could be at-
tained through knowledge of the truth. The word ἀρετή is related to ἄρσην,
the Greek word for 'male' (cf. Latin *virtus* and *vir*, 'virtue' and 'man'), and
originally referred to manly qualities. Other kindred words are Ἄρης (Ares)
the god of war and destruction, a very masculine deity indeed; and ἄριστος
'best' (there is also an emphatic prefix ἀρι- 'very').

2. γνώμη (cf. γιγνώσκω, root γνω- 'know'), although often defined as
meaning 'opinion', has as its first meaning, 'a means of knowing' and so 'an
organ by which one knows or perceives' and thence 'intelligence', 'thought',
'judgment', 'opinion'. The phrase γνώμην ἔχειν means 'to understand' ('to
have intelligence' rather than 'to have an opinion'). The philosopher Hera-
clitus wrote, "Knowledge is one thing (ἓν τὸ σοφόν): to know true judgment
(ἐπίστασθαι γνώμην, fragment 41)." Here the meaning of γνώμη is obviously
quite different from our use of the word 'opinion'. γνῶμαι are 'maxims', the
'opinions' of wise men: cf. English 'gnome', a short saying which expresses a
general truth. To express a general truth (or a habitual action) in a vivid
way, the aorist tense is often used in Greek, hence the designation *gnomic aorist*.

3. δίκη is another word for which the usual translation (in this instance 'justice') is somewhat misleading. The first meaning of δίκή is 'custom' or 'usage', that is, 'the normal rule of behavior'. δίκη is from the
same root as δείκνυμι (Lesson XII) 'point out', 'show'. From this come the
meanings 'order', 'right', as opposed to βία 'might'. In a technical sense,
δίκη refers to a 'lawsuit' or 'trial' (that is, the proceedings instituted to
determine legal rights). In the writings of the Greek tragedians, especially
Sophocles, the word δίκη seems to represent a balance: if this balance is up-
set, all nature rebels until it is set right. A great crime against nature or
society (such as Oedipus' marriage to his mother, or Creon's refusal to bury
the dead and burying of the living Antigone) destroys the balance of δίκη,
bringing disaster, sometimes upon the whole city, until the balance is re-
stored.

4. λόγος (derived from λέγω): in the large dictionary, one finds six long columns under the λόγος entry; these have been condensed into the following ten items, to give an idea of the ways this word is used.

1. computation, reckoning, account
2. relation, correspondence, ratio, proportion
3. explanation, plea, case; statement of a theory, argument, thesis, reason, formula, law, rule of conduct
4. debate (internal): reason, abstract reasoning
5. continuous statement, narrative, story, speech
6. verbal expression, opposite to ἔργον; common talk, repute
7. a particular utterance: saying, oracle, proverb
8. the thing spoken of: subject matter (in art, the subject of a painting)
9. expression, speech: intelligent utterance: language
10. the Word, or Wisdom of God: in the New Testament, λόγος is identified with the person of Christ: ἐν ἀρχῇ ἦν ὁ λόγος.

George Kennedy in *The Art of Persuasion in Greece* writes, "The Greek word for speech is *logos,* an ambiguous and sometimes mystical concept which may refer concretely to a word, words, or an entire oration, or may be used abstractly to indicate the meaning behind a word or expression or the power of thought and organization or the rational principle of the universe or the will of God. On the human level it involves man's thought and his function in society, and it includes artistic creativity and the power of personality."

5. ξένος, *guest-friend*: the word ξένος applies to persons or states bound by treaty or ties of hospitality. When applied to a person, it may mean 'guest' or 'host' (though most commonly 'guest'), i.e. a person giving or receiving hospitality: the people you stay with when you go to another town and who stay with you when they come to yours are your ξένοι. The relationship between guest and host was a very sacred one and very important to survival in a land that was divided into many separate political entities. To harm or betray one's guest or host was considered a serious and unholy crime: many tales from Greek legend and folklore are concerned with the guest-host relationship (cf. the cause of the Trojan War in Paris' theft of his generous host's beautiful wife, etc.). The stranger, wanderer, or refugee is also a ξένος and was under the special protection of Ζεὺς ξένιος. Any stranger or foreigner, as opposed to a native or citizen, is called ξένος, and one addresses any stranger ὦ ξένε. The word is also used as opposite to φίλος, that is, the ξένος is *not* a member of the family. Thus we have and hopefully have explained the anomaly of the same word meaning both 'friend' and 'stranger'. One last meaning of ξένος is 'hireling', especially in the sense of 'mercenary soldier'. In present day Greece, in the villages and small towns, foreigners are often greeted excitedly with the words ξένοι, ξένοι; in a friendly way, for the Greeks have remained through the ages a most hospitable people.

6. ψυχή, 'life' or the 'force of life' which escapes from the person at death: from this it carries the idea of the departed spirit, the shadow or ghost of the man which goes to Hades after death. In Homer, this shadowy

realm is described: the spirits flit around in a vague and bleak eternity, clinging to the life they have lost. For Homer the real life of man was spent on earth under the sun. But this is not so for many later writers: the ψυχή becomes the more important part, the immaterial and immortal soul, one of the eternal verities. It still survives the man but at death it escapes from the pollution of the body and returns to its essence: here we see the division into body and soul (σῶμα καὶ ψυχή). To Plato, the ψυχή is the immaterial principle of life and movement. To him we owe the tripartite division of the soul into λογισμός ('reason'), θυμός ('spirit'), and ἐπιθυμία ('appetite'), in which arrangement reason must rule. ψυχή can also mean the conscious self or personality, whence our use of the term "psyche."

7. Diminutives (cf. παιδίον from παῖς, 'child', stem: παιδ-) formed from noun stems by adding -ιον are all neuter, even when they denote a person. They may be used to express endearment or contempt: πατρίδιον (from πατήρ, 'father'), 'Daddy' is a term of affection; but the names Σωκρατίδιον and Εὐριπίδιον ('little Euripides' and 'little Socrates') are used by Aristophanes as two of his favorite butts. Many diminutive forms are not diminutive in meaning (e.g. βιβλίον, 'book'; πεδίον, 'plain'; this is especially true in Modern Greek, where diminutives abound).

Exercises

1. Decline (i.e. give all the cases, in the order given in the paradigms):

1. ἡ νῆσος		6. ἡ βουλή	
2. ὁ ἥλιος		7. τὸ μέτρον	
3. ὁ βίος		8. ἡ γνώμη	
4. ὁ οὐρανός		9. ὁ θάνατος	
5. τὸ παιδίον		10. ὁ φίλος	

What happens to the accent in the nominative plural of γνώμη? What is the length of ι in φίλος? How can you tell?

2a. Parse the following (example: ὁδῷ, dative singular of ὁδός, ἡ, 'road'):

1. ἀνθρώπους	2. νόμῳ	3. χρόνου
4. φίλου	5. βουλῇ	6. ξένε
7. πλούτῳ	8. γνωμῶν	9. ἀρχῇ
10. ἀρετῆς	11. δῶρα	12. ὁδῶν
13. παιδίον	14. νήσων	15. θανάτου
16. οὐρανός	17. λόγος	18. ἀνάγκη
19. ἀρχῶν	20. λίθῳ	21. πολέμους
22. βίους	23. θανάτους	24. εἰρήναις
25. ὁδόν	26. θεόν	27. μέτρα
28. ξένους	29. ψυχαί	30. πόνους

2b. Change to the opposite number (example: ὁδῷ, dat. sg., ὁδοῖς, dat. pl.).

2c.   What form of the article should be used with each of the above?

Syntax

Study the following points before proceeding to the translation exercises and readings.

1.   Instrumental Dative

Besides being used for the indirect object and with many prepositions (e.g. ἐν, 'in'; παρά, 'by the side of') denoting place where (locative), and with the preposition σύν ('with') denoting accompaniment, the dative is commonly used for *means* or *manner*: the instrumental dative.

   A.   *Dative of Means* (Instrument)

   The means by which anything is or is done is in the dative case.   (It answers the question "with what?")
Examples:

   τοὺς θεοὺς πείθομεν δώροις. We persuade the gods *by means of gifts*.

   ὁρῶμεν τοῖς ὀφθαλμοῖς. We see *with our (the) eyes*.

   B.   *Dative of Manner*

   The manner in which anything is or is done is in the dative case.   (It answers the question "how, in what way?")
Examples:

τῇ ἐμῇ γνώμῃ	'in my opinion'
δρόμῳ	'on the run'
σιγῇ	'in silence'

2.   Verbs of ruling such as ἄρχω take the genitive case.

3.   The verb πιστεύω and the verb πείθω in the middle (πείθομαι) take the dative case.

4. A neuter plural subject takes a singular verb: the neuter plural is thought of collectively.

Exercises

3a. Translate the following:

1. ἡ μὲν εἰρήνη φέρει τὸν βίον, ὁ δὲ πόλεμος θάνατον.
2. ὁ ἥλιος τοῖς ἀνθρώποις τὴν ἀρχὴν τοῦ βίου φέρει.
3. ὁ πλοῦτος τὴν τοῦ ἀνθρώπου ψυχὴν λύει.
4. ἀνάγκη μέτρον ἔχειν. (ἀνάγκη [ἐστί] + infinitive: 'it is necessary')
5. τὸ παιδίον ἐθέλει παιδεύεσθαι.
6. ὁ δὲ χρόνος παιδεύει τὸ παιδίον.
7. ὁ ἄνθρωπος παιδεύεται τὸ παιδίον.
8. τὰ παιδία εἰς τὴν νῆσον πέμπεται.
9. τοῖς γὰρ θεοῖς ἀνάγκη τὰ δῶρα ἄγειν.
10. οἱ μὲν ἄνθρωποι τῷ νόμῳ πείθονται· τὰ δὲ παιδία τοῖς φίλοις πείθεται.
11. ὁ λόγος ἐστὶ παρὰ τῶν θεῶν. (ἐστί 'is')
12. τὰ γὰρ δῶρα ἄγομεν παρὰ τοὺς θεούς.
13. σὺν τοῖς φίλοις ἔρχονται.
14. εἰς ἀνθρώπους λέγει ὁ θεός. (εἰς here 'before')
15. σὺν θεῷ εἰρήνην πράττετε. (πράττω 'bring about')
16. ὁ μὲν ἄνθρωπος λέγει, ὁ δὲ θεὸς πράττει.
17. τὸν πόνον λείπομεν.
18. οἱ ἐν ταῖς νήσοις ἄνθρωποι ἡμῶν ἄρχουσιν. (ἡμῶν 'us' gen.)
19. παρὰ τοῖς φίλοις βουλόμεθα μένειν.
20. παρὰ τῇ ὁδῷ τὸν φίλον λείπετε;

3b. Translate. Change to the opposite number where appropriate. (1-10 into the plural; 11-24 into the singular)

1. ἡ μὲν ὁδὸς ἄγει εἰς τὸν θάνατον, ἡ δὲ εἰς τὸν βίον. (ἡ μέν . . . ἡ δέ 'the one . . . the other')
2. ὁ ἄνθρωπος τὸ παιδίον λύεται τῷ δώρῳ. (p. 30: λύω in the middle voice)
3. ὁ μὲν θεὸς ἄρχει τοῦ ἀνθρώπου, ὁ δὲ ἄνθρωπος ἄρχεται ὑπὸ τοῦ θεοῦ. (ὑπό + genitive 'by')
4. ὁ ἄνθρωπος ἄγει τὸν φίλον εἰς δίκην παρὰ νόμον.
5. εἰς λόγους ἔρχομαι τῷ ξένῳ. (εἰς λόγους ἔρχεσθαι + dat. 'enter into speech with')

6. ὁ ἄνθρωπος ἐθέλει φίλος γίγνεσθαι.

7. ἡ ψυχὴ κρίνεται ἐν οὐρανῷ.

8. ἡ γὰρ ἀρετὴ γίγνεται ἡ τοῦ βίου ἀρχὴ τῷ ἀνθρώπῳ.

9. βούλει Ἑλλάδα λείπειν; βούλει μένειν; (Ἑλλάδα 'Greece' acc.)

10. πιστεύεις τῷ θεῷ;

11. οἱ ἄνθρωποι ἄγουσι τὰ δῶρα καὶ τοῖς θεοῖς καὶ ταῖς θεοῦς.

12. δώροις γὰρ πείθομεν τοὺς θεούς.

13. οἱ θεοὶ τῶν ἀνθρώπων ἄρχουσιν.

14. βουλεύονται καὶ κρίνουσιν.

15. βούλονται οἱ ἄνθρωποι φίλους ἔχειν.

16. νομίζουσι τοὺς ἀνθρώπους εἶναι ξένους. (εἶναι 'to be')

17. εἰς λίθους γράφομεν τοὺς λόγους καὶ τὰς γνώμας.

18. οἱ γὰρ ἄνθρωποι γράφουσι τοῖς παιδίοις.

19. αἱ τῶν ἀνθρώπων ψυχαὶ εἰς τὸν οὐρανὸν ἔρχονται.

20. τοῖς μὲν τῶν θεῶν λόγοις πιστεύομεν· τοῖς δὲ τῶν ἀνθρώπων νόμοις πειθό-
μεθα.

21. τοῖς μὲν λόγοις φίλοι εἰσίν· τοῖς δὲ ἔργοις οὔ. (εἰσί(ν) 'they are'; οὐ/
οὔ ('not')

22. οἱ θεοὶ παύουσι τὸν πόλεμον· ὁ μὲν πόλεμος παύεται, ἡ δὲ εἰρήνη γίγνεται.

23. καὶ οἱ θεοὶ καὶ οἱ ἄνθρωποι βούλονται εἰρήνην ἄγειν.

24. σὺν θεοῖς εὖ πράττομεν. (εὖ 'well')

    4a. Write in Greek:

1. The man brings gifts to his guests.
2. The gods bring both life and death to men.
3. Does man rule over the god?
4. Do you trust the opinions of men?
5. Do we judge our friends by the gifts?
6. Both men and gods wish to stop the war and to have peace.
7. Does the road lead to the island?
8. I am willing to wait, but I wish to leave.
9. Is justice destroyed by gifts?
10. Do the gifts of men persuade the god?

    4b. Make up some Greek sentences using the following words.
Change the forms of the nouns and verbs. Think out the sentences
in Greek. Be creative.

1. τὸ δῶρον, ἐν, θεός, οὐρανός, φέρω

2. ἡ γνώμη, γράφω, ὁ φίλος

3. ὁ ἄνθρωπος, κρίνω, καί, τὸ ἔργον, ὁ λόγος, φίλος

4. βούλομαι, βίος, εἰρήνη, ἔχω, καί

5. μέν, δέ, ἐθέλω, βούλομαι, ἔρχομαι, μένειν, εἰς ἡ νῆσος

Readings

ἦν 'was' (3rd sg. imperfect tense);
πρός prep. with acc. 'to', 'with',
'in the presence of'; οὗτος 'this'
(refers to λόγος)

1. Ἐν ἀρχῇ ἦν ὁ λόγος, καὶ ὁ λόγος ἦν
    πρὸς τὸν θεόν, καὶ θεὸς ἦν ὁ λόγος.
    οὗτος ἦν ἐν ἀρχῇ πρὸς τὸν θεόν.

     John

ἐποίησεν 'made' (3rd sg. aorist
tense); γῆν (acc. sg. of γῆ) 'earth'

2. Ἐν ἀρχῇ ἐποίησεν ὁ θεὸς τὸν οὐρανὸν
    καὶ τὴν γῆν.

     Genesis

εἰσί 'are' (3rd pl.); ζωή 'life';
πολλή 'much' (with διαφορά); διαφορά
'difference'; μεταξύ 'between' (+
gen.); μία see p. 12

3. ὁδοὶ δύο εἰσί, μία τῆς ζωῆς καὶ μία
    τοῦ θανάτου, διαφορὰ δὲ πολλὴ μεταξὺ
    τῶν δύο ὁδῶν.

     Teaching of the Twelve Apostles

οὐδέ 'and not', 'not even'; μάχομαι
'fight' (+ dative: i.e. 'fight
against')

4. ἀνάγκῃ οὐδὲ θεοὶ μάχονται.

     Greek Proverb

ὄνομα 'name' (acc.); οὐ, οὐκ, οὐχ
'not'; ὡς 'as'

5. ὁ θεὸς ὄνομα οὐκ ἔχει ὡς ἄνθρωπος.

     Eusebius, *Ecclesiastical History*

πᾷ Doric for πῇ 'where'; οὐκ ἔβαν
ἐγώ; 'have I not gone?'

6. πόνος πόνῳ πόνον φέρει.
    πᾷ πᾷ
    πᾷ γὰρ οὐκ ἔβαν ἐγώ;

     Sophocles, *Aias*
    The chorus is searching for Aias,
    fearing the worst.

δεόμενος 'lacking', 'in need of (+
gen.); ἔστιν 'is'; both meanings of
βίος are used

7. βίος βίου δεόμενος οὐκ ἔστιν βίος.

     Menander

οἷον 'such as', 'as if', 'as it
were'; ζῴων 'of living things'
(ζῷον, -ου, τό 'living being', 'animal')

8. ἔστι γὰρ [ἡ ψυχή] οἷον ἀρχὴ τῶν
    ζῴων.

     Aristotle
    (ἡ ψυχή is bracketed because it is
    supplied from the previous sen-
    tences.)

γεωργός, -οῦ, ὁ 'farmer' (γῆ + ἔρ-γον); κἄν = καὶ ἐν; πέτραις (dat. pl.) 'rocks', 'rocky terrain' (πέτρα, -ας, ἡ 'rock'); τρέφω 'nourish'; καλῶς 'well'; κακῶς 'badly'; πεδίον, -ου, τό 'plain' (the best land)

9. εἰρήνη γεωργὸν κἄν πέτραις τρέφει καλῶς, πόλεμος δὲ κἄν πεδίῳ κακῶς.

    Menander

μί' = μία; τὸν ἄτοπον 'the wicked' (person); φεύγω 'flee', 'avoid'; ἀεί 'always'

10. μί' ἐστιν ἀρετὴ τὸν ἄτοπον φεύγειν ἀεί.

    Menander

11. δῶρα θεοὺς πείθει.

    Greek Proverb

12. θάνατον 'ἢ βίον φέρει.

    Sophocles, *Aias*

δικαιοσύνη 'justice'; (ὦ) Σώκρατες voc. of 'Socrates'

13. ἡ γὰρ δικαιοσύνη, ὦ Σώκρατες, ἀρετή ἐστιν.

    Plato, *Meno*

Elision

In both prose and verse, a final short vowel often drops out before a word beginning with a vowel: this is called elision; it is marked by the apostrophe (').

μί' ἐστιν   for   μία . . .
δ' ἔργοις   for   δέ . . .

Read aloud and learn the following quotation:

νόμῳ ψυχρόν, νόμῳ θερμόν, ἐτεῇ δὲ ἄτομα καὶ κενόν.

"By convention cold, by convention hot, but in reality atoms and void." (From Diogenes Laertius, *Lives of the Philosophers*, quoting Democritus the Atomist.)

Conversation

χαῖρε (χαῖρε, ὦ φίλε).	Hello. (Hello, my friend.)
καὶ σύ, χαῖρε.	Hello to *you* too.
τί πράττεις; (πῶς ἔχεις)	How are you?
καλῶς πράττω (καλῶς ἔχω).	I'm well, and how are you?
καὶ σύ, τί πράττεις;	

κακῶς πράττω.   Not well.

From Menander, *The Misogynist:*

    A.   χαῖρ' ὦ Γλυκέριον   Hello, Glycerium.

    Γλ.   καὶ σύ.   Same to you.

    A.   πολλοστῷ χρόνῳ   Long time, no see.
            ὁρῶ σε.

LESSON II

A. Imperfect Active and Middle-Passive

The *imperfect* tense is formed from the present stem (found by removing the personal ending from the first principal part) and is therefore said to belong to the present tense system.

The imperfect is a secondary (or historical) tense. It is used for a continuous, habitual, or repeated act in past time (that is, for action *going on* in the past) as opposed to the *aorist* tense which is used for a single act in past time (or action simply taking place in the past).

Like all secondary tenses (in the indicative), the imperfect receives the *augment* (or increase, at the beginning of the form). The augment was originally an adverbial particle used to indicate past time, but became attached to the verb, to mark a past tense. The augment is ε- and it occurs in two ways: the *syllabic* augment and the *temporal* augment. The syllabic augment is so called because it adds a syllable to the word; the temporal augment is merely the lengthening of an initial vowel, and adds no syllable; it is therefore only temporal. It is to be understood that the augment is always temporal (i.e. it refers to time) and that these terms are used for convenience only.

1. Syllabic Augment: verbs beginning with a consonant simply prefix the syllable ε- to the tense stem:

E.g. λύω   stem λυ-:   ἐλυ-,   imperfect ἔλυον

λείπω   stem λειπ-:   ἐλειπ-, imperfect ἔλειπον

βούλομαι   stem βουλ-:   ἐβουλ-, imperfect ἐβουλόμην

Note: verbs beginning with ῥ, double the ρ after the augment:

ῥίπτω ('throw'), stem ῥιπτ-: ἐρριπτ-, imperfect ἔρριπτον

2. 'Temporal' Augment: verbs beginning with a vowel or diphthong are usually augmented by lengthening the initial vowel, according to the following pattern:

*α → η	αι → η	ᾳ → ῃ	αυ → ηυ	ἄγω	: ἦγον
*ε → η	ει → η		ευ → ηυ	ἔρχομαι:	ἠρχόμην
ο → ω	οι → ῳ				
ι → ῑ					
υ → ῡ					

*These are the most common and should be learned at once.

Note: there are several instances in which verbs beginning with a vowel take the syllabic (ε-) augment. These will be treated as irregular forms. They occur when an initial consonant, Ϝ (w-sound) or σ has been lost; and the most common is ε augmenting to ει (contraction of ε + ε): ἔχω, imperfect, εἶχον.

Formation of the Imperfect Active and Middle-Passive

Augment + present stem + thematic vowel + secondary endings: Endings (with thematic vowel):

Singular

Active			Middle-Passive
ο-ν	1st		ο-μην
ε-ς	2nd	[ε-σο] →	ου
ε(ν)	3rd		ε-το

Plural

ο-μεν	1st	ο-μεθα
ε-τε	2nd	ε-σθε
ο-ν	3rd	ο-ντο

There is no imperfect infinitive.

Example: λύω in the imperfect active and middle-passive:

Singular

ἔλυον	1st	ἐλυόμην
ἔλυες	2nd	ἐλύου
ἔλυε(ν)	3rd	ἐλύετο

Plural

ἐλύομεν	1st	ἐλυόμεθα
ἐλύετε	2nd	ἐλύεσθε
ἔλυον	3rd	ἐλύοντο

Translation of the imperfect: ἔλυον may be translated in the following ways: 'I was freeing', 'I used to free', 'I kept on freeing'. (It also sometimes has the meaning of 'I tried to free': this is known as the *conative* imperfect.)

Irregular Imperfect: as noted above, certain verbs augment irregularly. Among these is ἔχω, which has εἶχον as the imperfect. When a verb deviates from the norm in the imperfect, the form will be given in the vocabulary.

Accent: remember that the accent of verbs is recessive, i.e. it goes back as far as the length of the ultima will permit. Explain the accent of εἶχον and ἦγον.

B. Irregular Verb: εἰμί, present and imperfect indicative.

1. Forms. The Greek verb εἰμί, like the English verb 'be', is very irregular. Learn by rote the present and imperfect indicative and the present infinitive of εἰμί.

Present			Imperfect	
εἰμι	'I am'	1st	ἦν/ἦ	'I was'
εἶ	'you are'	2nd	ἦσθα	'you were'
ἐστί(ν)	'he, she, it is' 'there is'	3rd	ἦν	'he, she, it was' 'there was'
ἐσμέν	'we are'	1st	ἦμεν	'we were'
ἐστέ	'you are'	2nd	ἦτε	'you were'
εἰσί(ν)	'they are'	3rd	ἦσαν	'they were'

Present Infinitive: εἶναι 'to be'

2. Accent. The forms of the present indicative of εἰμί, except for εἶ, the second person singular, are enclitics; that is, they lean on the preceding word for their accent. Often enclitics are not accented at all, but are pronounced with the preceding word. Under certain circumstances, an enclitic will cause changes in the accent of the preceding word.

Study these rules explaining the accent of enclitics, along with the examples. Remember that the enclitic affects the accent of the word before it. The accent of a word, as you know, can fall no further back than the third syllable from the end of the word: the enclitic, as it were, adds one or more syllables to the end of the word.

      a. Two accents will be marked on the word preceding the enclitic, if it (the preceding word) has either an acute on the antepenult or a circumflex on the penult. In either case an acute is added to the ultima.

ἄνθρωπός εἰμι (ἄνθρωπος: acute on the antepenult)

δῶρόν ἐστι   (δῶρον: circumflex on the penult)

      b. If an enclitic of two syllables follows a word with the acute on the penult, then the enclitic has an accent on the ultima. (But the preceding word remains unchanged.) Under these circumstances, an enclitic of one syllable will not have an accent.

ξένοι εἰσίν   but   ξένος τις

(τις is the indefinite pronoun-adjective 'some', 'any'; and is enclitic.)

      c. An accent on the ultima of the preceding word remains unchanged. That is, an acute does not change to a grave. The enclitic itself does not take an accent in this instance.

θεός ἐστιν   θεοί εἰσίν

θεῶν τινων   θεοῦ τινος

      d. In a series of enclitics, the first ones are accented and the last remains unaccented. (In the example, the enclitics are underlined.)

εἴ ποῦ τίς τινα ἴδοι ἐχθρόν (Thucydides)

Since enclitics lean for their accent upon the word that comes before them, they usually do not come first in the sentence. If, however, existence or possibility is stressed, ἐστί can come first in the sentence, and is accented, ἔστι (i.e. it is not enclitic under these conditions). Other enclitics too when emphasized keep their accents.

Exercises

   1.   Accent the following words or phrases:

1. ἐβουλου	6. εἰχε
2. ἐγιγνεσθε	7. ἐμενετε
3. ἐγραφον	8. ἐφεροντο
4. ἠθελες	9. ἐπιστευομεν
5. ἠρχομεθα	10. ἐβουλευετο

   Enclitics other than εἰμί are underlined:

11. λογοι <u>τινες</u>	16. ἐστιν ἀνθρωπος
12. ἀνθρωπος ἐστιν	17. βουλη <u>τις</u>
13. ξενοι ἐσμεν	18. βουλης <u>τινος</u>
14. θεοι ἐστε	19. ἀνθρωπου τινος
15. δωρον <u>τι</u>	20. θεων τις

   2a. Form and conjugate (orally or in writing) the imperfects of:

   1. ἄρχω   2. ἐθέλω   3. κρίνω   4. λέγω
   5. νομίζω   6. πράττω   7. ἔρχομαι   8. γίγνομαι

   2b. Conjugate in full (present and imperfect) including infinitives:

   1. ἄγω   2. ἔχω   3. παυω   4. ἔρχομαι   5. βούλομαι

   3a.   Parse and translate.

   3b.   Change to the opposite number.

   3c.   Give the corresponding forms of the present or imperfect.

1. ἐκρινου	6. εἶ	11. ἐφέρετε	16. πιστευουσιν
2. γίγνεσθε	7. ἦγεν	12. φέρεσθαι	17. ἐπείθετο
3. ἐβουλευόμεθα	8. ἔλειπον	13. ἐπαύοντο	18. ἦ
4. βούλονται	9. ἔμενες	14. ἐσμέν	19. ἠρχετε
5. ἦσαν	10. ἐθέλεις	15. ἦσθα	20. ἤρχοντο

   4.   Translation exercises:

1. ἤγομεν τὰ δῶρα εἰς τὴν νῆσον.

2. οἱ ἄνθρωποι ἐνόμιζον τὸν ἥλιον εἶναι θεόν.

3. τοὺς γὰρ φίλους παρὰ τῇ ὁδῷ ἐλείπομεν.

4. σὺν τοῖς φίλοις εἰς τὴν νῆσον ἔρχεσθαι ἐβούλοντο.

5. οἱ μὲν ἄνθρωποι ἤθελον εἰρήνην ἄγειν, οἱ δὲ ἐβουλεύοντο πόλεμον ποιεῖν.
   (οἱ μέν . . . οἱ δέ 'some . . . others'; ποιεῖν 'to make' (infinitive))

6. ἡ ὁδὸς πλούτου ἔφερε θάνατον τῇ ψυχῇ.

7. ἔλεγε τοὺς τῶν θεῶν λόγους ἐν ἀνθρώποις.   (ἐν 'among')

8. οἱ ἐν οὐρανῷ θεοὶ ἔφερον τὴν δίκην τοῖς ἀνθρώποις.

9. ὁ ἄνθρωπος πόνους εἶχεν.

10. τοὺς θεοὺς δώροις ἔπειθον.

11. οἱ ξένοι φίλοι ἦσαν καὶ τοῖς θεοῖς καὶ τοῖς ἀνθρώποις.

12. θεὸς μὲν ἦν ὁ πλοῦτος, φίλος δ' οὔ. (δ' see p. 52; οὐ, οὔ 'not')

   (note: usually the subject has the article, and the predicate nominative usually does not)

13. ἐβούλεσθε ἄρχειν μέν, ἄρχεσθαι δ' οὔ;

14. ὁδοὶ ἦσαν δύο· ἡ μὲν ἦγεν εἰς τὴν ἀρετήν, ἡ δὲ εἰς τὸν πλοῦτον.

15. τὰ δῶρα ἦν παρὰ τῶν φίλων.

16. οἱ γὰρ ἄνθρωποι τὸν πλοῦτον εἶχον ἐν ταῖς ψυχαῖς.

17. παρὰ τῇ ὁδῷ ἐμένομεν.

18. παρὰ τοὺς ξένους ἠρχόμεθα σὺν τῷ παιδίῳ.

19. τὰ παιδία δώροις ἐλύοντο. τὰ παιδία δώροις ἐλύετο.

20. καὶ λόγοις καὶ ἔργοις φίλοι ἦτε.

   5. Write in Greek:

1. Justice was a gift of the gods.

2. We took counsel for ourselves and we judged.

3. Were you a friend to men and gods?

4. The children were writing to their friends.

5. Were the men bringing gifts to their guests?

6. The friends of the gods used to go into the heavens.

7. Men used to want to live in peace.

8. Were we left on (ἐν) the island?

9. There were two roads, the one led to war, the other to peace.

10. They were persuading the gods with gifts.

   Read aloud and memorize the following quotation:

      ἔστι ἡ ψυχὴ τοῦ ζῶντος σώματος αἰτία καὶ ἀρχή.
                  of the living body cause

   The soul is the cause and the first principle of the living body.

            Aristotle, Περὶ Ψυχῆς (De anima, or On the Soul)

C. Adjectives of the -ος, -η, -ον type.

1. Adjectives are words used to 'modify' nouns (or, better, to name attributes of nouns). In Greek they must agree grammatically (i.e. in gender, number, and case) with the noun they modify. This does not mean that the endings of the noun and adjective are necessarily identical, since the noun and adjective may belong to different declensions. (Remember that a declension in itself does not have gender.)

'The good man' in Greek is ὁ ἀγαθὸς ἄνθρωπος, but 'the good road' is ἡ ἀγαθὴ ὁδός, because ὁδός is *feminine* of the second declension.

2. Although there are several types of adjectives, the most common is the -ος, -η, -ον (of second-first declension type: that is, the masculine and neuter forms are declined in the second declension like λόγος and ἔργον, and the feminine is declined in the first declension like δίκη). The accent of adjectives is persistent like that of nouns. The endings are the same as those you have already learned, and will give you an opportunity to review the declensions.

3. Endings for the -ος, -η, -ον adjectives: to the base of the adjective, add:

	Singular			Plural		
	M	F	N	M	F	N
NOM	-ος	-η	-ον	-οι	-αι	-α
GEN	-ου	-ης	-ου	-ων	-ων	-ων
DAT	-ῳ	-ῃ	-ῳ	-οις	-αις	-οις
ACC	-ον	-ην	-ον	-ους	-ας	-α
VOC	-ε					

Example: καλός, καλή, καλόν 'good', 'fine', 'fair'

	M	F	N	M	F	N
NOM	καλός	καλή	καλόν	καλοί	καλαί	καλά
GEN	καλοῦ	καλῆς	καλοῦ	καλῶν	καλῶν	καλῶν
DAT	καλῷ	καλῇ	καλῷ	καλοῖς	καλαῖς	καλοῖς
ACC	καλόν	καλήν	καλόν	καλούς	καλάς	καλά
VOC	καλέ					

The adjectives will be given in the vocabulary in the three genders: as καλός, καλή, καλόν, and thus will be easily recognizable. Some adjectives, mostly compounds, have only two sets of endings, the -ος and -ον, with the -ος serving for both masculine and feminine, e.g. ἀθάνατος, ἀθάνατον 'immortal', 'deathless'. They are declined in the same way as καλός, omitting the feminine (-η) endings:

| | Singular | | Plural | |
	M & F	N	M & F	N
NOM	ἀθάνατος	ἀθάνατον	ἀθάνατοι	ἀθάνατα
GEN	ἀθανάτου	ἀθανάτου	ἀθανάτων	ἀθανάτων
DAT	ἀθανάτῳ	ἀθανάτῳ	ἀθανάτοις	ἀθανάτοις
ACC	ἀθάνατον	ἀθάνατον	ἀθανάτους	ἀθάνατα
VOC	ἀθάνατε			

Of this same type are ἄλογος, ἄλογον and ἄδικος, ἄδικον.

4. The position of adjectives:

There are two possible positions (with certain variations) which the adjective may occupy. These are--simply stated--(1) directly after the article or (2) *not* directly after the article.

a. The first of these positions is called the *attributive* position and is used when the adjective is simply qualifying the noun. The most common order is *article-adjective-noun* (the same as the usual English order):

ὁ σοφὸς ἄνθρωπος	'the wise man'
ἡ ἀθάνατος ψυχή	'the immortal soul'
τὸ καλὸν παιδίον	'the good child'

But this position can be varied in the following ways: the article and the noun may be followed by a second article, as:

ὁ ἄνθρωπος ὁ καλός 'the good man'

or the first article may be omitted:

ἄνθρωπος ὁ καλός   'the good man'
(cf. κατὰ γνώμην τὴν ἐμήν 'in my opinion')

without changing the meaning: only the emphasis is slightly
changed. The first arrangement is by far the most common, the
most direct and natural; the second is formal, putting the emphasis on the noun, with the attributive being used as a further explanation, almost as an afterthought: 'the man (that is), the
good one'. The important thing to remember is that the adjective
must come directly after the article for it to be in the attributive position.

Other words and phrases which are used in the same way as
adjectives are put in the attributive position (any one of the
three arrangements). That is, any expression which tells an attribute of a noun, or qualifies its meaning in the same way as an
adjective does, goes into the attributive position. Genitives
and prepositional phrases are commonly used in this way.

Examples:

i.   ἡ ψυχή 'the soul'
       ἡ ἀθάνατος ψυχή 'the immortal soul'
    ἡ τοῦ ἀνθρώπου ψυχή 'the soul of man'

Note that the article τοῦ is used with 'man' (generic article, ὁ ἄνθρωπος 'man in general'). The dependent genitive usually
has the article, if the noun on which it depends has it. It is
not uncommon to have a series of articles, each agreeing with its
own noun:

τὰ γὰρ τῆς τῶν πολλῶν ψυχῆς ὄμματα
'the eyes of the soul of the many' (Plato)

Another example:

       τὰ καλὰ παιδία 'the good children'
    τὰ τοῦ ἀνθρώπου παιδία 'the man's children'

ii.   οἱ καλοὶ ἄνθρωποι 'the good men'
       οἱ τότε ἄνθρωποι 'the men of that time' (the then men)
       οἱ νῦν ἄνθρωποι 'men of the present day' (now people)

τότε and νῦν are adverbs and are not declined. In these expressions they are used in the same way as adjectives, i.e. they tell *which* men.

>   iii.   ὁ ἐξ ὁδοῦ ἄνθρωπος 'the man from the street'
>   οἱ ἐν ἄστει ἄνθρωποι ⎫
>   οἱ ἄνθρωποι οἱ ἐν ἄστει ⎭ 'the men in the city'

Which men?--the men in the city: considered in the Greek mind as the same type of expression as 'the good man'.

Other examples:

τὸ παρὰ τὸν Ἀλφειὸν ποταμὸν πεδίον 'the plain by the river Alpheius'
        ὁ ἐν τῇ ἐμῇ ψυχῇ πλοῦτος 'the wealth in my soul' (Xenophon)

>   b.   The second position the adjective may occupy (i.e. not directly following the article) is the *predicate* position. A predicate adjective may precede the article or follow the noun and its article. A whole sentence may be formed, with the verb 'to be' understood:

>   σοφὸς ὁ ἄνθρωπος
>   ὁ ἄνθρωπος σοφός 'the man is wise'

The forms ἐστί and εἰσί are often omitted, especially in short sentences and proverbial sayings. But it is not common to leave out other forms of εἰμί.

>   5.   Adjectives used as nouns: Attributive adjectives with the article are often used as nouns ('the noun-making power of the article'):

οἱ ἀγαθοί means 'the good (men)': the masculine gender of article and adjective makes it clear that *men* is understood. (Cf. also οἱ τότε 'men of former times' and οἱ νῦν 'men of the present day', 'now people')

>   ἡ κακή means 'the wicked woman'
>   τὰ καλά 'good things'

The neuter singular of an adjective (and sometimes the neuter plural) is very commonly used as an abstract noun:

τὸ καλόν 'the beautiful', 'beauty'

τὸ ἄδικον 'injustice'

In the sentence χαλεπὰ τὰ καλά, the verb ἐστί is omitted (cf. p. 49: neuter plurals take a singular verb), in the short proverbial statement. The article and adjective (τὰ καλά) are used as a noun. Note that although the word order does not tell which of the two adjectives is the subject and which the predicate nominative adjective, we can tell that the sentence means 'good things are hard', rather than 'hard things are good', because the subject is usually accompanied by the article, the predicate rarely so.

An extension of this use of the article with an adjective (omitting the noun) may be seen in the expression ὁ μέν . . . ὁ δέ 'the one . . . the other' and οἱ μέν . . . οἱ δέ 'some . . . others'. This expression can, of course, be used in any gender and any case; so, do not be surprised to see τὰ μέν . . . τὰ δέ 'some things . . . other things'; or τοῦ μέν . . . τοῦ δέ 'of the one . . . of the other', etc.

In this instance, the article retains an original demonstrative force (see Lesson III on demonstratives) which has largely been lost in Attic Greek (but is generally still retained in Homer, the earliest Greek literature). Thus the original force of ὁ μέν . . . ὁ δέ would have been 'this (man), on the one hand . . . this (man), on the other hand' (or simply 'this one . . . that one').

D. The Relative Pronoun

The Greek relative pronoun (corresponding to the English 'who', 'whose', 'whom'; 'which', 'that') is ὅς, ἥ, ὅ. The inflection is similar to that of the first and second declensions: discover where the differences are.

	Singular			Plural			English
	M	F	N	M	F	N	
NOM	ὅς	ἥ	ὅ	οἵ	αἵ	ἅ	who, which, that
GEN	οὗ	ἧς	οὗ	ὧν	ὧν	ὧν	whose, of whom/which
DAT	ᾧ	ᾗ	ᾧ	οἷς	αἷς	οἷς	to whom/which
ACC	ὅν	ἥν	ὅ	οὕς	ἅς	ἅ	whom, which, that

The relative pronoun introduces a relative clause, and refers to a noun or pronoun (called the antecedent) in the main clause. In the sentence

'The man to whom you are writing is coming.'

ὁ ἄνθρωπος ᾧ γράφεις ἔρχεται.

"the man" is the antecedent . . . "(to) whom" is the relative pronoun.

The relative pronoun agrees with its antecedent in number and gender, but its case depends on the part it plays in its own clause. In our example, 'the man' is masculine singular, and is nominative, since it is subject of the main clause: ὁ ἄνθρωπος. '(To) whom' will therefore be masculine and singular, but in its own clause, it is indirect object, and so is dative, ᾧ.

Be careful not to confuse the forms of the relative with the definite article. Set the relative and the article side by side, and list the differences between them, including differences in accent.

A note on the relative pronoun: The antecedent is often omitted, especially when it is indefinite and can be supplied from the context. E.g. ἔχει ἃ βούλεται 'he has (those things) which he wants', or 'he has what he wants'. Often the relative pronoun can best be translated by 'the one who', 'that which', or some such phrase. Cf. the phrase from Hippocrates, χρόνος ἐστὶν ἐν ᾧ καιρός, καὶ καιρὸς ἐν ᾧ χρόνος οὐ πολύς, "Time is that in which there is a critical time [καιρός], and a critical time is that in which there is not much time."

Vocabulary: Adjectives

Adjectives are easily recognized in the vocabulary because their three (or two) genders are given.

ἀγαθός, ἀγαθή, ἀγαθόν	*good*
ἄδικος, ἄδικον	*unjust*
ἀθάνατος, ἀθάνατον	*immortal, deathless* (cf. θάνατος)
ἄλογος, ἄλογον	*irrational* (cf. λόγος)
ἄριστος, ἀρίστη, ἄριστον	*best* (superlative of ἀγαθός)(aristocrat)
δεινός, δεινή, δεινόν	*fearful, terrible; clever (dinosaur)*
Ἑλληνικός, -ή, -όν	*Greek* (Journal of *Hellenic* Studies)

ἐσθλός, ἐσθλή, ἐσθλόν   *noble, good, brave*
κακός, κακή, κακόν   *bad, evil (cacophony)*
καλός, καλή, καλόν   *good, fine, fair, beautiful (calligraphy)*
κοινός, κοινή, κοινόν   *common, public* (koinē)
μόνος, μόνη, μόνον   *alone, only (monotheistic)*
ὅλος, ὅλη, ὅλον   *whole, entire, complete (holograph)*
πρῶτος, πρώτη, πρῶτον   *first, foremost (protein)*
σοφός, σοφή, σοφόν   *wise, clever, skilled (sophisticated)*
χαλεπός, χαλεπή,   *hard, difficult*
   χαλεπόν
χρηστός, χρηστή,   *good*
   χρηστόν

Nouns

βιβλίον, βιβλίου, τό   *book* (bibliography; βιβλιοθήκη 'library')
γάμος, γάμου, ὁ   *marriage* (monogamous)
ἡδονή, ἡδονῆς, ἡ   *pleasure* (hedonist)
ἰατρός, ἰατροῦ, ὁ   *physician* (pediatrician, psychiatrist)
κόσμος, κόσμου, ὁ   *order, ornament, credit, world-order, universe* (cosmo-
    logical) (κατὰ κόσμον, κόσμῳ 'in order', 'duly')
οἶνος, οἴνου, ὁ   *wine*
τύχη, τύχης, ἡ   *fortune, luck*
ὕπνος, ὕπνου, ὁ   *sleep* (hypnosis)

Adverbs, Pronouns, Prepositions

διά   preposition *through*
    with genitive   *through*
    with accusative   *because of, on account of*
εἰ   *if*
νῦν   *now, as it is* (also enclitic νυν, νυ)(καὶ νῦν 'even
    so'; οἱ νῦν 'men of the present day')
ὅς, ἥ, ὅ   *who, which, that* (relative pronoun)
ὅσπερ, ἥπερ, ὅπερ   *the very one who* (accented like ὅς, ἥ, ὅ)
οὐ (οὐκ, οὐχ, οὐχί,   *not* (οὐκ before smooth breathing; οὐχ before rough
   οὔ)   breathing; οὐχί emphatic; οὔ with accent, as last
    word or as answer, "No!")
οὐδέ   *but not, not even, nor*
περί   preposition *about, around*
    with genitive   *about, concerning* (περὶ ψυχῆς, the title of a work of
    Aristotle)
    with dative   *about* (mostly poetic)
    with accusative   *about, around, near* (of place or time)(ᾤκουν περὶ πᾶ-
    σαν τὴν Σικελίαν 'they settled all around Sicily')
πρός   preposition expressing direction *on the side of, in
    the direction of*
    with genitive   *from*
    with dative   *at, near, besides, in addition to*
    with accusative   *to, towards*
τότε   *at that time*

Vocabulary Notes:

1.   Greek words for 'good': ἀγαθός, ἐσθλός, καλός, and χρηστός. Ἀγαθός 'good' is used as widely as the English word "good." It generally means
'good', in the sense of 'capable', 'well-fitted' to something. In Homer ἀγαθός usually refers to physical excellence, hence the meanings 'valiant',
'brave (in battle)'; but is extended to moral goodness as well. Frequently
ἀγαθός is used with the accusative of respect to show what specific thing it
refers to. οἱ ἀγαθοί in the political sense are the aristocrats (i.e. the
'well-born'), especially in the phrase καλοὶ κἀγαθοί (καλοὶ καὶ ἀγαθοί)

Ἐσθλός is equivalent to ἀγαθός, in all its senses, but is mainly poetic.

Καλός properly means 'beautiful' and may be used either of persons or
things. In the moral sense (extending its meaning from beautiful to 'good',
'virtuous', 'honorable'), it refers to noble deeds, differing from ἀγαθός,
which would mean 'advantageous', 'useful'. In Attic Greek, the word καλός is
added to the name of a person (usually a boy) as a token of love: this is
commonly seen on painted vases (as Λέαγρος καλός), appearing again and again
for the favorite of the day.

Χρηστός also means 'good', but more definitely in the sense of 'useful',
'serviceable', 'good of its kind'; it is in fact derived from χράομαι 'use'.

2.   Κοινός: the Κοινή (Koinē) Dialect). The ancients cite five major
dialects of Greek: διάλεκτοί εἰσι πέντε, Ἀτθὶς Δωρὶς Αἰολὶς Ἰὰς καὶ κοινή,
that is, Attic (spoken in Athens and environs), Doric (used in the Peloponnese
and Northwest Greece), Aeolic (used in Lesbos, and with variations in Boeotia
and Thessaly), Ionic (spoken on the coast of Asia Minor and on some of the islands) and Koinē, the common dialect as opposed to the four local dialects.
It is not a combination of the other dialects, but is the common, or universal,
Greek language that was used in the Alexandrian Age and after, when Greek culture and the Greek language had spread over the world as a result of the con-
quests of Alexander. The κοινή is based largely on the Attic dialect (both
the written and vulgar, or spoken, forms) with some Ionian influence. From
the fourth century B.C. there was a gradual disappearance of the local dialects as the κοινή came into general use. Koinē is the language of the New
Testament and of the Septuagint (the Greek translation of the Old Testament)
and of the Jewish historian Josephus, but was used by many secular writers as
well: for example, Polybius, Diodorus, Plutarch, Dio. From the Koinē is de-
scended Modern Greek, which in the puristic form (Καθαρεύουσα, used for scholarly, formal, and official writing and speaking) is remarkably close to ancient Greek.

Exercises

1.   Decline in full (orally or in writing), paying some attention to accents, the following adjectives, in all genders:

1. ἀγαθός   2. ἄδικος   3. χαλεπός   4. ἄριστος   5. πρῶτος

2.   Noun-adjective combinations: translate into Greek and

decline (orally or in writing):

   1. the wise man   2. the only opinion   3. the difficult child

   4. the immortal soul   5. the beautiful island   6. the irrational

   3.   Parse the following: example, adjective: ἀγαθῷ, dative singular masculine or neuter of ἀγαθός 'good'; pronoun: ᾗ, dative singular feminine of ὅς, relative pronoun, 'to whom'.

1. ὅλη	2. μόνῳ	3. ὄν	4. δεινοῖς	5. αἱ	6. ἤ
7. τοῖς	8. κακούς	9. κοινά	10. ἄδικος	11. ὅς	12. Ἑλληνικοῦ
13. τά	14. ἐσθλόν	15. ἅ	16. σοφῆς	17. ὁδόν	18. αἷς
19. τῷ	20. νήσου	21. ἄλογα	22. τόν	23. οὗ	24. οὕ

   4.   Relative-pronoun-antecedent fill-ins: translate the underlined words:

   1. The gods to whom we gave offerings were unjust.

   2. I saw the man who did it.

   3. He does not give presents to the children who are naughty.

   4. Is that the man whose book you are reading?

   5. The island which we see is very beautiful.

   6. The evils that men do live after them.

   7. Where is the book which I was reading?

   8. The man whom we saw was Socrates.

   9. Did you see the goddess whose temple you were in?

  10. The gods who made heaven and earth are just.

Syntax: Accusative and Dative of Respect

   1. Accusative of Respect

The accusative is used to tell in what specific respect an expression is true.

If we say ἀγαθός ἐστι ('he is good'), it is a general statement; but if we want to say that someone is good in or at something, we use the accusative for the quality or part.

Examples:

$$\text{ἀγαθὸς γνώμην}\quad\text{good in intellect}$$

$$\text{ἀγαθός ἐστι πᾶσαν ἀρετήν}\quad\text{he is good in every (πᾶσαν) virtue}$$

$$\text{βουλὴν κακός ἐστιν}\quad\text{he is bad in council}$$

This accusative is very common with adjectives, but can be used with nouns or verbs as well:

ἀλγῶ τὴν κεφαλήν   I have a pain in my head (I hurt as to my head)

2. Dative of Respect

The dative of respect, used similarly to the accusative of respect, is a form of the dative of manner (see Lesson I).

Examples:

λόγῳ μὲν φίλοι εἰσίν, ἔργῳ δ' οὔ   They are friends in word, but not in deed.

ἀγαθός ἐστι πολέμῳ   He is good at war.

Exercises continued:

5. Translate:

1. οἱ μὲν ἦσαν ἀγαθοί, οἱ δὲ κακοί.

2. ἀγαθοὶ ἦτε γνώμην;

3. πλοῦτος ἄδικος ἔφερε τύχην κακήν.

4. ἀθάνατος ἡ ἀρετή.

5. ὁ ἄνθρωπος ὁ σοφὸς οὐκ ἐπείθετο τῷ ἀδίκῳ λόγῳ.

6. ἔργον ἐστὶ τοῦ χρηστοῦ ἀνθρώπου παύειν τὸν πόλεμον. (ἔργον ἐστί + gen. 'it is the business of')

7. οὐκ εἶχον 'ἃ ἐβούλοντο. (see p. 66, n.)

8. καλὴ γὰρ ἦν ἡ νῆσος εἰς 'ἣν ἤγομεν τὰ δῶρα.

9. καλὸς καὶ ἀγαθὸς ὁ σοφὸς ἄνθρωπος.

10. ἔλεγεν ὁ σοφὸς κακά;

11. ὁ ἀγαθὸς ἐβούλετο τοὺς κακοὺς φίλους ἄγειν πρὸς τὴν δίκην.

12. ἄδικον ἦν πλοῦτον ἔχειν παρὰ νόμον.

13. ὁ ὕπνος φέρει ἡδονήν.

14. κακόν ἐστι 'ὃ λέγεις. κακὸν ἦν 'ὃ ἔλεγες.

15. ἐλέγομεν ὅτι ὁ σοφὸς ἦν ἀγαθὸς καὶ γνώμαις καὶ βουλαῖς. (ὅτι 'that')

16. τοὺς μὲν ἀγαθοὺς ἔλυον, τοὺς δὲ κακοὺς ἦγον πρὸς τὴν δίκην.

17. οἱ θεοὶ ἔφερον τὰ καλὰ δῶρα τοῖς ἀνθρώποις.

18. οἱ τότε ἤρχοντο εἰς τὴν νῆσον.

19. οἱ ἀγαθοὶ ἄνθρωποι τὰ παιδία ἐπαιδεύοντο τοῖς τῶν σοφῶν λόγοις καὶ ταῖς γνώμαις.

20. οἱ τότε Ἑλληνικοὶ ἔγραφον εἰς λίθους.

21. οἱ μὲν τότε τῷ νόμῳ ἐπείθοντο, οἱ δὲ νῦν πείθονται τοῖς φίλοις.

22. ὁ ἄδικος ἦν δεινὸς λέγειν. (δεινὸς λέγειν 'clever at speaking')

23. οἱ ἄριστοι ἦρχον τῶν ἀνθρώπων.

24. οἱ ἄνθρωποι οἷς ἐπιστεύομεν ἦσαν φίλοι.

25. ὁ ἥλιος ὃς ἔφερε τὸν βίον τοῖς ἀνθρώποις θεὸς ἐνομίζετο.

26. εἶχε ἡ θεὸς μόνον παιδίον.

27. ἐν τοῖς πρώτοις λόγοις ἔλεγε πολλὰ καὶ καλὰ καὶ ἀγαθά. (πολλά 'many things')

28. χαλεπόν ἐστι τὰς γνώμας τὰς τῶν σοφῶν λύειν.

29. καλαὶ μὲν αἱ τῶν σοφῶν γνῶμαι, χαλεποὶ δὲ οἱ λόγοι.

30. ὁ σοφὸς ἔλεγε ὅτι ὁ βίος ἐστὶ χαλεπόν. (ὅτι 'that')(Note: χαλεπόν is neuter: 'a difficult thing')

31. οἱ ἰατροὶ σὺν τοῖς φίλοις ἤρχοντο παρὰ τὴν ὁδόν.

32. ὁ ἀγαθὸς ὃς τῷ νόμῳ ἐπείθετο εἶχε τοὺς θεοὺς ὡς φίλους. (ὡς 'as')

33. ὁ σοφὸς ἐγράφετο πέντε βιβλία περὶ ψυχῆς.

34. ἀγαθοὶ οἱ νόμοι οἱ περὶ τοὺς γάμους.

35. πρὸς δὲ πλούτῳ φίλους ἔχειν ἐβουλόμεθα.

Write in Greek:

1. We did not have what we wanted.

2. The soul of the wise man is immortal.

3. Some were good in deed, others in word.

4. It is the business of the wise man to have good opinion.
   (Ex. 5, 6)

5. Did you wish to live in peace?

6. The war was being stopped.

7. We used to trust the gods, who used to bring good (things)
   to men of former times.

8. The men who were saying wicked things were led to court.

9.   The man to whom we were bringing gifts was our (= the) guest.

10.   On account of wealth, they did not wish to have peace.

Readings

τά + gen. of possession 'the pos-
sesions of'

    1.   κοινὰ τὰ τῶν φίλων.

        Plato

ὅττι (an Epic form of ὅ τι) 'whatever'; φίλος, -η, -ον (as adj.)
'dear'

    2.   ὅττι καλόν, φίλον ἐστί, τὸ δ'οὐ
      καλὸν οὐ φίλον ἐστίν.

        Theognis

ἀεί 'always'

    3.   ὅ τι καλὸν φίλον ἀεί.

        Euripides

    4.   ἀθάνατος ὁ θάνατός ἐστιν.

        Amphis (a comic writer)

πατρίς 'homeland', 'country'; ξύμπας
'whole'

    5.   ψυχῆς ἀγαθῆς πατρὶς ὁ ξύμπας κόσμος.

        Democritus

πάντα accusative of respect 'in
everything, all things' (neut. pl.
nom./acc.)

    6.   πάντα γὰρ οὐ κακός εἰμι.

        Homer, *Odyssey*

ἐπὶ Κρόνου 'in the age of Cronus'

    7.   ὁ ἐπὶ Κρόνου βίος

      (a Greek proverb, not a full sen-
      tence)

μέγα 'big' (neut. sg. nom./acc.)

    8.   μέγα βιβλίον, μέγα κακόν.

        Callimachus

ὁ γραμματικός 'the grammarian'; ἴσον
'equal' (to, + dative); μεγάλῳ 'big'
(dative, m./n. sg.)

    9.   Καλλίμαχος ὁ γραμματικὸς τὸ μέγα
      βιβλίον ἴσον ἔλεγεν εἶναι τῷ μεγάλῳ
      κακῷ.

        Athenaeus

ἴδιος 'private', 'personal'

   10.   νόμος δ'ἐστὶν ὁ μὲν ἴδιος ὁ δὲ κοι-
      νός.

        Aristotle, *Rhetoric*

   11.   ὕπνος δεινὸν ἀνθρώποις κακόν.

        Menander

λύπη, -ης, ἡ 'pain', 'grief'

   12.   λύπης ἰατρός ἐστιν ὁ χρηστὸς φίλος.

        Menander

ἐν νυκτί 'in the night'; σοφοῖσι =
σοφοῖς; γίνεται = γίγνεται

   13.   ἐν νυκτὶ βουλὴ τοῖς σοφοῖσι γίνεται.

        Menander

τὸ θεῖον 'the divine', 'divinity'

14. ἄγει τὸ θεῖον τοὺς κακοὺς πρὸς τὴν δίκην.

   Menander

τὸ λυπεῖν (infinitive used as a noun) 'to hurt'; ἑκουσίως 'willingly, on purpose'

15. ἄδικον τὸ λυπεῖν τοὺς φίλους ἑκουσίως.

   Menander

ἕνεκα τοῦ λαβεῖν 'for the sake of gain'

16. λέγεις, 'ἃ δὲ λέγεις ἕνεκα τοῦ λαβεῖν λέγεις.

   Menander

λύπη, -ης, ἡ (see #12); οὗτος 'this' (masc. nom. sg.); θελητήριον, -ου, τό 'charm'

17. λύπης ἰατρός ἐστιν ἀνθρώποις λόγος· ψυχῆς γὰρ οὗτος μόνος ἔχει θελητήρια.

   Menander

πάνθ' (= πάντα) 'all things'; φαύλως 'badly'; ὅτε 'when'; σοι 'to you' (dat.); ἐγώ 'I' (nom.)

[18. τότ' ἦν ἐγώ σοι πάνθ' ὅτε φαύλως ἔπραττες

   Menander]

19. ʽεν γὰρ καὶ δύο καὶ τρία καὶ τέσσαρα δέκα γίγνεται.

   Sextus Empiricus (On the Pythagoreans' "proof" that ten is the perfect number.)

ἐδυνάστευσε 'had power over' (+ genitive) 3rd pers. sg.; παντός gen. masc. sg. of πᾶς 'whole', 'entire'

20. Οὐρανὸς πρῶτος τοῦ παντὸς ἐδυνάστευσε κόσμου.

   Apollodorus

τις 'anyone' (masc. nom. sg.); Μέγαρα, -ων, τά Megara (a city); Ἀθῆναι, -ῶν, αἱ 'Athens'; ἄρα 'therefore'

21. εἴ τίς ἐστιν ἐν Μεγάροις, οὐκ ἔστιν ἐν Ἀθήναις· ἄνθρωπος δ'ἐστὶν ἐν Μεγάροις· οὐκ ἄρ' ἐστὶν ἄνθρωπος ἐν Ἀθήναις.

   Diogenes Laertius (quoting a paradox of Chrysippus)

οὐδέν 'nothing' (n. sg. nom./acc.); ἄπορος, -ον 'impossible'; ξένος, -η, -ον (used as adj.) 'strange', 'foreign'

22. τῷ σοφῷ ξένον οὐδὲν οὐδ' ἄπορον.

   Diogenes Laertius (a saying of Antisthenes)

μὴ δύνασθαι 'not to be able'; μέγα 'big', 'great' (n. sg. nom./acc.)

23. μέγα κακὸν τὸ μὴ δύνασθαι φέρειν κακόν.

   Diogenes Laertius (a saying of Bion)

οὗδε 'these', 'the following' (masc. nom. pl.)

[24. The Seven Sages: σοφοὶ δὲ ἐνομίζοντο οὗδε· Θαλῆς, Σόλων, Περίανδρος, Κλεόβουλος, Χείλων, Βίας, Πιττακός.

   Diogenes Laertius]

εἴδωλον, -ου, τό 'image', 'phantom' 25. "Ελεγε δὲ τὸν μὲν λόγον εἴδωλον εἶναι τῶν ἔργων.

Diogenes Laertius (a saying of Solon)

τῶν ὄντων 'of the things that exist' 26. τῶν ὄντων τὰ μέν ἐστι κακά, τὰ δὲ
οὐδέτερος 'neither', 'neuter' ἀγαθά, τὰ δὲ οὐδέτερα.

Diogenes Laertius (quoting Plato)

σώματι dat. of σῶμα 'body'; ἐκτός 27. τῶν ἀγαθῶν ἐστι τὰ μὲν ἐν ψυχῇ, τὰ
'outside' (an adverb) δὲ ἐν σώματι, τὰ δὲ ἐκτός.

Diogenes Laertius (quoting Plato)

μέγιστος, -η, -ον 'greatest'; μανία, 28. τὰ μέγιστα τῶν ἀγαθῶν ἡμῖν γίγνεται
μανίας, ἡ 'madness'; ἡμῖν 'to us' διὰ μανίας.
(dat. pl.)

Plato, Φαῖδρος

δεχόμεσθα = δεχόμεθα from δέχομαι 29. τῶν ἀγαθῶν οὐ δεχόμεσθα κόρον.
'receive'; κόρος, -ου, ὁ 'a sur-
feit' (i.e. 'too much') Greek Anthology

καρτερός 'strong', 'staunch'; τόδε [30. καρτερὸς ἐν πολέμοις Τιμόκριτος, οὗ
σᾶμα (σῆμα) 'this tomb'; φείδομαι τόδε σᾶμα·
'spare' (+ gen.); "Αρης, -εως, ὁ "Αρης δ'οὐκ ἀγαθῶν φείδεται, ἀλλὰ
'Ares' (the god of war) κακῶν.

Anacreon]

31. χαλεπὰ τὰ καλά.

Greek Proverb (quoted by Plato, in *Republic*)

32. χαλεπὸν ὁ βίος.

Xenophon

δίκαιος 'just' 33. Σωκράτης γὰρ σοφὸς ἦν καὶ δίκαιος.

'Aristotle', Rhetoric to Alexander

Syntax

The Articular Infinitive:

Under the 'Noun-Making Power of the Article' we may include the *articular infinitive*: that is, the infinitive used as a noun with the article. It can be used in any case, as subject, object, with prepositions, etc. Several examples occur in the readings of this lesson:

$$\text{τὸ λυπεῖν} \quad \text{'to hurt'} \quad (\#15)$$

$$\text{ἔνεκα τοῦ λαβεῖν} \quad \text{'for the sake of gain'} \quad (\#16)$$

$$\text{τὸ μὴ δύνασθαι} \quad \text{'not to be able'} \quad (\#23)$$

(The negative used with the articular infinitive is μή.)

Conversation

A	τί ἐστι καινόν;	What's new?
B	οὐδὲν καινότερον.	Nothing (newer).
A	πῶς ἔχεις;	How are you?
B	ἔχω κακῶς.	I'm ill.
A	τί πάσχεις, ὦ φίλε;	What's wrong, my friend?
B	ἀλγῶ τὴν κεφάλην· χθὲς γὰρ ἐμεθύσθην	I have a headache. For I got drunk yesterday.

Some Sayings on the Art of Drinking

1. χειμερίας μεθύων μηδαμὰ νυκτὸς ἴῃς.

Never go out drunk on a winter's night.   --Greek Anthology

2. τί μικρόλογος εἶ; πλεῖαί τοι οἴνου κλισίαι.

Why are you so stingy? Your tents are full of wine.   Athenaeus

3. τὸ δὲ ζῆν, εἰπέ μοι, τί ἐστι; πίνειν φημ' ἐγώ.

Living, tell me what it is? I say, to drink.   --Antiphanes

4. οἴνῳ τὸν οἶνον ἐξελαύνειν.

'A hair of the dog that bit you.'   (Lit. to drive out wine with
   wine. --Antiphanes

5. οἶνος, ὦ φίλε παῖ, καὶ ἀλάθεα (= ἀλήθεια).

Wine, dear boy, and truth. (*In vino veritas*)   --Alcaeus

6. οἱ μὲν οἶνον ἔμισγον ἐνὶ κρητῆρσι καὶ ὕδωρ.

Some were mixing wine and water in craters (mixing bowls).
   --Homer, *Odyssey* (I.110)

7. οὐδεὶς φιλοπότης ἐστὶν ἄνθρωπος κακός.

No one who is fond of drinking is a wicked man.   --Athenaeus
   (quoting Alexis)

8. νῦν χρῆ μεθύσθην . . .

Now is the time for drinking. (*Nunc est bibendum*) --Alcaeus

9. ἄριστον μὲν ὕδωρ . . .

Water is best. --Pindar

Read aloud and learn the following quotation:

τυφλὸς τά τ'ὦτα τόν τε νοῦν τά τ'ὄμματ' εἶ.

(τὰ ὦτα, τὸν νοῦν, τὰ ὄμματα accusatives of respect)

"You are blind in your ears, your mind and your eyes."

Sophocles, *Oedipus*

LESSON III

A. The Future Active and Middle: Second Principal Part of Verbs
      (ω-type)

The second principal part of (most) verbs is the first person singular future active indicative; of deponent verbs, the future middle indicative. The future belongs to a different tense system than the present and has a different stem. Henceforth, when a new verb is introduced, the future will be given along with the present. The future middle and passive are different in form (the future passive is formed from the sixth principal part and will be treated later). (Lesson X)

The future is regularly formed from the present stem by adding -σ- before the endings. For irregular verbs, however, special forms must be learned. For verbs with stems ending in a consonant, certain changes in spelling take place when -σ- is added, as described below.

Formation of the Future: Regular

Present stem + σ + primary endings (with thematic vowel), same as present

Active		Middle
λύ-σ-ω	1st	λύ-σ-ο-μαι
λύ-σ-εις	2nd	λύ-σ-ει (or λύσῃ)
λύ-σ-ει	3rd	λύ-σ-ε-ται
λύ-σ-ο-μεν	1st	λυ-σ-ό-μεθα
λύ-σ-ε-τε	2nd	λύ-σ-ε-σθε
λύ-σ-ουσι(ν)	3rd	λύ-σ-ο-νται
λύ-σ-ειν	Infinitive	λύ-σ-ε-σθαι

No problem arises in the regular formation of the future of verbs with stems ending in a vowel, as λύω, λύσω; παύω, παύσω; κτλ. When the verb stem ends in a consonant, certain changes take place, depending on the type of consonant involved.

Orthographic Changes for Verbs with Mute Stems:

> A LABIAL   (π, β, φ) + σ → ψ
>
> A PALATAL   (κ, γ, χ) + σ → ξ
>
> A DENTAL   (τ, δ, θ) drops out before σ

Examples:

> Labial, πέμπω, stem: πεμπ-; future, πέμψω
>
> Palatal, ἄγω, stem: ἀγ-; future, ἄξω
>
> Dental, πείθω, stem: πειθ-; future, πείσω

Form the futures of the following:

1.	ἄρχω	2.	παιδεύω
3.	βουλεύω	4.	παύω
5.	γράφω	6.	πιστεύω
7.	λέγω	8.	δέχομαι ('receive', deponent)
9.	λείπω	10.	θύω ('sacrifice')

The following verbs which have already been given in the vocabulary have irregular futures (and must be learned). These are formed irregularly, but are conjugated regularly.

βούλομαι	future	βουλήσομαι
γίγνομαι	future	γενήσομαι
ἐθέλω	future	ἐθελήσω
ἔρχομαι	future	ἐλεύσομαι
ἔχω	future	σχήσω ('I shal get')
		ἕξω ('I shall have')
πράττω	future	πράξω (stem: πραγ-)
φέρω	future	οἴσω

Deponent Futures

There are a number of verbs which have their futures in the middle (though they have other forms in the active). These are usually verbs of perception or of physical activity, as:

ἀκούω, ἀκούσομαι	'hear'
μανθάνω, μαθήσομαι	'learn'
ὁράω, ὄψομαι	'see' (present to be explained later)(XI)
ἀποθνῃσκω, ἀποθανοῦμαι	'die' (a contract future)(Lesson XI)
λαμβάνω, λήψομαι	'take'

These futures are to be translated as if they were active.

Among verbs with deponent future is εἰμί 'be', future ἔσομαι
'I shall be':

$$\begin{aligned}
&\text{ἔσομαι}\\
&\text{ἔσῃ or ἔσει}\\
&\text{ἔσται}\\[4pt]
&\text{ἐσόμεθα}\\
&\text{ἔσεσθε}\\
&\text{ἔσονται}
\end{aligned}$$

Infinitive: ἔσεσθαι

The forms are conjugated regularly, except for ἔσται, which lacks
the thematic vowel. This completes the principal parts of εἰμί.

Vocabulary

Along with the new verbs, the student should study the futures of all
verbs given so far. The future is not given for a few of the verbs: verbs
with liquid or nasal stems (μ, ν, λ, ρ) have a special kind of future which
will be treated in Lesson XI (this affects κρίνω, μένω, and νομίζω of the
verbs given previously).

ἀγγέλλω	*announce* (angel, evangelist)
ἀκούω, ἀκούσομαι	*hear* (+ gen. of person)(acoustics)
ἀποθνήσκω	*die* (cf. θάνατος), *be killed* (contr. fut.)
ἀποκτείνω	*kill*
βάλλω	*throw, hit* (ballistics)
δέχομαι, δέξομαι	*receive* (cf. Mod. Gr. ξενοδοχεῖον 'hotel')
θύω, θύσω	*sacrifice*
λαμβάνω, λήψομαι	*take, seize* (epilepsy, syllable)
μανθάνω, μαθήσομαι	*learn, understand* (stem μαθ-, mathematics)
πάσχω, πείσομαι	*suffer, be affected* (stem παθ-, pathos)
φαίνω	*bring to light;* passive, *appear* (phantom, epiphany)

Note: the imperfects of ἀποθνήσκω ('die') and ἀποκτείνω ('kill') are
respectively ἀπέθνησκον and ἀπέκτεινον: the *verb* being augmented rather than
the prefix (ἀπο- in these two examples); before another vowel, the final vowel
of the prefix is elided. (See Lesson IV)

ἀεί (αἰεί)	*always*
οὔτε . . . οὔτε	*neither . . . neither*
οὔ ποτε or οὔποτε	*never, not ever*

Exercises

1. Form and conjugate the futures of:

1. ἄρχω	2. βούλομαι	3. πάσχω	4. δέχομαι
5. πείθω	6. λείπω	7. ἐθέλω	5. ἀκούω

2.   Conjugate in full (all voices, all tenses that you have had), orally, or in writing:

   1. παύω   2. πέμπω   3. φέρω   4. ἔχω   5. γίγνομαι

3.   Parse the following.   3b.   Change to opposite number (except infin.).

1. ἔσται	2. οἴσουσι	3. ἄξομαι	4. ἦρχον
5. ἐβουλεύετο	6. βουλήσεσθαι	7. ἦν	8. ἐγίγνεσθε
9. γράφονται	10. ἐθελήσεις	11. ἤθελες	12. ἐλευσόμεθα
13. σχήσομεν	14. ἔκρινεν	15. κρίνειν	16. ἐλείπετε
17. λέξονται	18. ἐμένομεν	19. νομίζειν	20. ἐπαύοντο
21. ἕξει	22. πείθεται	23. πιστεύεις	24. πράξω
25. οἴσειν	26. εἶ	27. φαίνομαι	28. φέρεσθαι
29. ἔπασχον	30. μαθήσεται	31. ληψόμεθα	32. δέχεσθαι
33. γράφεται	34. ἔθυε	35. ἔσομαι	36. δέξεται
37. ἐλάμβανον	38. ἤκουον	39. ἀποθνῄσκειν	40. ἦσθα

4.   Translate:

1. ὁ χρόνος ἄξει τοὺς κακοὺς καὶ ἀδίκους πρὸς τὴν δίκην.

2. ἡ δίκη τοὺς τῶν ἀνθρώπων βίους κρίνει.

3. ὁ μὲν ἄδικος ἄνθρωπος σχήσει πλοῦτον, ὁ δὲ ἀγαθὸς ἕξει ἀρετὴν καὶ φίλους.

4. ὁ γὰρ ἄνθρωπος ὁ ἀγαθὸς οὐ βουλήσεται ἔχειν ἄδικον πλοῦτον.

5. τὸ γὰρ ἄδικον ἔσται ἄδικον ἀεί.

6. ἐν ὕπνῳ φαίνεται ὁ θεός.

7. ἀγγέλλεις πόλεμον;

8. ἀκουσόμεθα τοὺς λόγους τῶν σοφῶν.

9. οἱ καλοὶ καὶ ἀγαθοὶ ἀπέθνῃσκον ὑπὸ τῶν κακῶν καὶ ἀδίκων.   (ὑπό + gen. 'by')

10. ἐβάλλετε τοὺς ξένους τοῖς λίθοις;

11. ὁ ἀγαθὸς ἄνθρωπος οὐ θύσει τὸ παιδίον τοῖς θεοῖς.

12. οἱ ἄδικοι λήψονται τὰ τῶν φίλων παρὰ νόμον.   (See p. 72 #1)

13. τὰ γὰρ δῶρα δεξόμεθα.

14. ἔστι καὶ ἦν καὶ ἔσται ἀεὶ ὁ θεός.

15. τὸ παιδίον γράψει τῷ φίλῳ.

16. ἀεὶ οἱ θεοὶ τῶν ἀνθρώπων ἄρξουσιν· οὐ γὰρ ἀποθνῄσκουσιν οἱ θεοί.

17. βουλεύσομαι καὶ κρινῶ.   (κρινῶ = future of κρίνω, 1st sg.)

18. ἐθελήσεις θύειν τὰ δῶρα τῷ ἡλίῳ;

19. ἐλεύσεται ὁ ἄριστος εἰς τὴν νῆσον καὶ λύσεται τὰ παιδία, ἃ ὁ κακὸς ξένος τοῖς θεοῖς βούλεται θύειν.

20. ταῖς καλαῖς θεοῖς τὰ χρηστὰ δῶρα οἴσουσιν, ἁὶ πέμψουσιν ἀγαθὰς βουλὰς πρὸς τοὺς ἀνθρώπους.

21. ἐν τῷ πρώτῳ βιβλίῳ γράφομαι τὰς γνώμας.

22. τὰ δῶρα φέρει ἡδονὴν τοῖς παιδίοις.

23. τὰ δῶρα ἄγεται παρὰ τοὺς θεοὺς ὑπὸ τῶν ἀνθρώπων.   (ὑπό: see p. 80 #9)

24. οὔποτε ἀποθνήσκει ὁ θεός.

25. οἱ θεοὶ ἀπέκτεινον τοὺς ἀδίκους οἳ οὐκ ἔθυον.

26. τὰ παιδία τοὺς σοφοὺς ἔβαλλε λίθοις· οὐ γὰρ ἐπείθετο τοῖς τῶν σοφῶν λόγοις.

27. δέξεται τὰ δῶρα ἐκ τοῦ φίλου.   (ἐκ 'from')

28. τῶν κακῶν ἀνθρώπων μαθησόμεθα ἔργα κακά.

29. μανθάνεις ἃ λέγω;

30. ἐλευσόμεθα εἰς τὴν νῆσον ἧς ἄρχουσιν οἱ φίλοι.

    5.   Translate into Greek.

1.   Shall we sacrifice to the gods in heaven?

2.   Will you hear the wise men?

3.   We shall trust the opinions of the good, but not of the wicked.

4.   The island over which we shall rule is beautiful.

5.   Were you hitting the unjust men with stones?

6.   The island of the sun is ruled by the best men.   ('by': ὑπό + gen.)

7.   Good men will have their children educated.

8.   The possessions of wise and good men will be in common. (See p. 72 #1 and p. 80 #12)

9.   Unjust wealth will bring war and unjust deeds.

10. What you are saying is unjust.

     Read and learn the following quotation:

          ἀεὶ κολοιὸς παρὰ κολοιῷ ἱζάνει.   --Greek proverb

     Birds of a feather flock together. (lit. A jackdaw always perches beside a jackdaw.)

First Declension Nouns (Consult the chart given below)

The first declension has several variations. One type (cf. Lesson I) has -η as characteristic of the singular, as in δίκη, ἀρετή, etc.[1] If the base of a first declension noun ends in ε, ι, or ρ, however, -α is found rather than -η in the singular[2]. This -α is long in some words and short in others, which is not terribly important except that it does affect the accent in certain places. It is always long in the genitive and dative singular, but the length of the -αν in the accusative singular will be the same as that of the -α in the nominative. There are also a few nouns with bases ending in letters other than ε, ι, or ρ which have -α (short) in the nominative and accusative singular, but -η in the genitive and dative singular[3]. Nouns of these first three types are all *feminine*.

In addition there are a number of masculine nouns of the first declension which end in -ης in the nominative singular[4], or in -ας (long α) if the base ends in ε, ι, or ρ[5], with the genitive in -ου for both types (cf. the second declension genitive singular).

All nouns of the first declension have the same endings for the plural.

The pattern that each noun is to follow can be easily recognized from the nominative and genitive.

Summary of endings:

Singular

	[1] -η type	[2] α type after ε, ι, ρ	[3] ᾰ/η type	[4] masc. -ης type	[5] masc. in -ας after ε, ι, ρ
NOM.	-η	-α	-α	-ης	-ας
GEN.	-ης	-ας	-ης	-ου	-ου
DAT.	-ῃ	-ᾳ	-ῃ	-ῃ	-ᾳ
ACC.	-ην	-αν	-αν	-ην	-αν
VOC.				-α	-α

Plural

NOM. -αι   GEN. -ῶν   DAT. -αις   ACC. -ᾱς

Examples:

	¹δίκη 'justice'	²μοῖρα 'fate' (short α)	²χώρα 'land' (long α)
N	ἡ δίκη	ἡ μοῖρα	ἡ χώρα
G	τῆς δίκης	τῆς μοίρας	τῆς χώρας
D	τῇ δίκῃ	τῇ μοίρᾳ	τῇ χώρᾳ
A	τὴν δίκην	τὴν μοῖραν	τὴν χώραν
N	αἱ δίκαι	αἱ μοῖραι	αἱ χῶραι
G	τῶν δικῶν	τῶν μοιρῶν	τῶν χωρῶν
D	ταῖς δίκαις	ταῖς μοίραις	ταῖς χώραις
A	τὰς δίκας	τὰς μοίρας	τὰς χώρας

	³θάλαττα 'sea'	⁴πολίτης 'citizen' (long ι)	⁵νεανίας 'young man' (short ι)
N	ἡ θάλαττα	ὁ πολίτης	ὁ νεανίας
G	τῆς θαλάττης	τοῦ πολίτου	τοῦ νεανίου
D	τῇ θαλάττῃ	τῷ πολίτῃ	τῷ νεανίᾳ
A	τὴν θάλατταν	τὸν πολίτην	τὸν νεανίαν
V		πολῖτα	νεανία
N	αἱ θάλατται	οἱ πολῖται	οἱ νεανίαι
G	τῶν θαλαττῶν	τῶν πολιτῶν	τῶν νεανιῶν
D	ταῖς θαλάτταις	τοῖς πολίταις	τοῖς νεανίαις
A	τὰς θαλάττας	τοὺς πολίτας	τοὺς νεανίας

Besides these nouns, the adjectives with bases in ε, ι, or ρ have -α (long) in the feminine.

δίκαιος, δικαία, δίκαιον   'just'

	Singular			Plural		
	M	F	N	M	F	N
N	δίκαιος	δικαία	δίκαιον	δίκαιοι	δίκαιαι	δίκαια
G	δικαίου	δικαίας	δικαίου	δικαίων	δικαίων	δικαίων
D	δικαίῳ	δικαίᾳ	δικαίῳ	δικαίοις	δικαίαις	δικαίοις
A	δίκαιον	δικαίαν	δίκαιον	δικαίους	δικαίας	δίκαια
V	δίκαιε					

Note of the Accent of Adjectives:

The accent of adjectives like that of nouns is persistent. In the genitive plural, the feminine form, if the same as the masculine and neuter, is accented like them.

Demonstrative Adjective-Pronouns

The three most important demonstratives are οὗτος ('this', 'that'), ὅδε ('this (here)'), ἐκεῖνος ('that (there)'). They are declined as follows:

	Singular			Plural		
	M	F	N	M	F	N
N	οὗτος	αὕτη	τοῦτο	οὗτοι	αὗται	ταῦτα
G	τούτου	ταύτης	τούτου	τούτων	τούτων	τούτων
D	τούτῳ	ταύτῃ	τούτῳ	τούτοις	ταύταις	τούτοις
A	τοῦτον	ταύτην	τοῦτο	τούτους	ταύτας	ταῦτα

Observations:

1. Notice that οὗτος has τ where the article has it, but not where the article does not have it.

2. The endings are like those of the relative pronoun (i.e. the same as the -ος, -η, -ον adjectives except for neuter singular nominative and accusative.

3. The spelling is -ου- in some forms and -αυ- in others. Can you find any pattern in this?

4. οὗτος refers to what is near in place, time, or thought, and so can mean 'the latter' (i.e. 'the one more recently mentioned'). It can also mean 'the aforesaid'.

	Singular			Plural		
	M	F	N	M	F	N
N	ὅδε	ἥδε	τόδε	οἵδε	αἵδε	τάδε
G	τοῦδε	τῆσδε	τοῦδε	τῶνδε	τῶνδε	τῶνδε
D	τῷδε	τῇδε	τῷδε	τοῖσδε	ταῖσδε	τοῖσδε
A	τόνδε	τήνδε	τόδε	τούσδε	τάσδε	τάδε

Observations:

1. ὅδε is formed by the article plus the enclitic particle -δε. It is, therefore, declined like the article, except that all forms are accented.

2. The fact that -δε is enclitic explains the accent of ἥδε, τήνδε, τοῦσδε, etc., which according to the rule should be circumflexed.

3. Meanings: ὅδε is a weaker demonstrative. It also generally refers to what is near. It is sometimes used to mean 'the following'. ὅδε may be used to call attention to the presence or approach of a person and in this sense should be translated 'here' or 'there': Πλάτων δ' ὅδε . . . 'but Plato here' (and the speaker, Socrates in this case, would point at Plato).

	Singular			Plural		
	M	F	N	M	F	N
N	ἐκεῖνος	ἐκείνη	ἐκεῖνο	ἐκεῖνοι	ἐκεῖναι	ἐκεῖνα
G	ἐκείνου	ἐκείνης	ἐκείνου	ἐκείνων	ἐκείνων	ἐκείνων
D	ἐκείνῳ	ἐκείνῃ	ἐκείνῳ	ἐκείνοις	ἐκείναις	ἐκείνοις
A	ἐκεῖνον	ἐκείνην	ἐκεῖνο	ἐκείνους	ἐκείνας	ἐκεῖνα

Observations:

    1. ἐκεῖνος has the same endings and accents as οὗτος.

    2. ἐκεῖνος sometimes appears as κεῖνος (especially in Herodotus and in poetry).

    3. Meanings: 'that', ἐκεῖνος generally refers to what is remote in place, time, or thought. Thus it can mean 'the former', and sometimes refers to what is to follow, as being unfamiliar and therefore remote.

Position

The demonstratives may be used as pronouns or as adjectives.

When used as adjectives, they must be used with the article, but put in the predicate position:

        οὗτος ὁ πολίτης or
        ὁ πολίτης οὗτος 'this citizen'

The use of the demonstratives is flexible and varies from writer to writer. The student will learn more about them gradually by observation, but for the present should be content with knowing their forms and basic meanings.

Vocabulary

ἀλήθεια, ἀληθείας, ἡ	truth, reality
γλῶττα, γλώττης, ἡ	tongue, language (polyglot, glottology)(also γλῶσσα)
δέσποινα, δεσποίνης, ἡ	mistress, lady (fem. form of δεσπότης)
δεσπότης, δεσπότου, ὁ	master (despot)
δημοκρατία, δημοκρατί-ας, ἡ	democracy
δικαστής, δικαστοῦ, ὁ	judge, juryman (cf. δίκη, δίκαιος, ἄδικος)
Εὐριπίδης, Εὐριπίδου, ὁ	Euripides
ἡμέρα, ἡμέρας, ἡ	day (ephemeral, cf. Mod. Grk. καλημέρα)
ἡσυχία, ἡσυχίας, ἡ	rest, quiet, stillness
θάλαττα, θαλάττης, ἡ	sea (also spelled θάλασσα, θαλάσσης)
θεά, θεᾶς, ἡ	goddess
μοῖρα, μοίρας, ἡ	fate, part, portion, lot
Μοῦσα, Μούσης, ἡ	Muse
ναύτης, ναύτου, ὁ	sailor (cf. Latin nauta, -ae, m.)
νεανίας, νεανίου, ὁ	youth, young man (cf. νέος)
οἰκία, οἰκίας, ἡ	house, dwelling (economic)
πεῖρα, πείρας, ἡ	test, trial, attempt (empiric)
ποιητής, ποιητοῦ, ὁ	poet (maker)
πολίτης, πολίτου, ὁ	citizen (long ι)(politics, from πόλις, 'city state')

σκηνή, σκηνῆς, ἡ	tent, stage (scene)
στρατιώτης, στρατιώ-του, ὁ	soldier (strategy, from στρατηγός, general)
συμφορά, συμφορᾶς, ἡ	misfortune (cf. φέρω)
ταμίας, ταμίου, ὁ	steward, dispenser, treasurer
τιμή, τιμῆς, ἡ	honor, esteem, office (timocracy: Plato, Rep. 545b)
ὑγίεια, ὑγιείας, ἡ	health (hygiene)
φιλία, φιλίας, ἡ	friendship (cf. φίλος)
χώρα, χώρας, ἡ	land, country; place, position, (one's) post, station
ὥρα, ὥρας, ἡ	time (any fixed period of time), season, hour (ὥρα [ἐστί] + infinitive: 'it is time to . . .')

Adjectives

αἰσχρός, αἰσχρά, αἰσχρόν	shameful, ugly
ἄξιος, ἀξία, ἄξιον	worthy (axiom) (ἄξιός εἰμι 'I deserve to')
δίκαιος, δικαία, δίκαιον	just (cf. δίκη) (δίκαιός εἰμι 'I have the right to')
μικρός, μικρά, μικρόν	small (microwave)
νέος, νέα, νέον	new, young (Neoplatonic)
παλαιός, παλαιά, παλαιόν	ancient, old (palaeography)
πονηρός, πονηρά, πονηρόν	wicked (cf. πόνος)
φίλιος, φιλία, φίλιον	friendly (to + dative)
ἐκεῖνος, ἐκείνη, ἐκεῖνο	that
ὅδε, ἥδε, τόδε	this
οὗτος, αὕτη, τοῦτο	this, that
ἀπό	preposition with genitive, away from, from
ἐκ	preposition with genitive, out of, from

Vocabulary Notes:

1. On the first declension. It is the -α which is originally the characteristic ending for the first declension. In the Attic and Ionic dialects, it changes to -η; in Ionic even after ε, ι, and ρ: so in an Ionic writer such as Herodotus one finds χώρη, οἰκίη, ἡμέρη where Attic has χώρα, οἰκία, ἡμέρα. In other dialects (Doric, Aeolic, etc.) -α is retained (ἀλάθεια, ἀμέρα, σκανά for ἀλήθεια, ἡμέρα and σκηνή).

Another characteristic of Attic is the spelling ττ for σσ, as in θάλαττα for θάλασσα; γλῶττα for γλῶσσα of the other dialects. Early writers of Attic prose (such as Thucydides) did not use the ττ, although it is known to have been in use at that time from inscriptions. Probably ττ seemed too provincial in the early period, when Ionic culture and literature were still the most important. Atticisms became respectable, however, when Attic became top dialect.

2. A δικαστής is a member of the jury, usually of five hundred men, chosen by lot, fifty from each tribe (there were ten tribes). All (male) citizens over thirty were eligible for jury duty. Six thousand (six hundred from

each tribe) were chosen annually as panels from which the jury of five hundred would be chosen for each case, by an elaborate system of selection designed to prevent bribery (which nevertheless remained a problem). The great Athenian statesman Pericles introduced pay to the jury. The δικασταί not only heard the case and made the verdict, but set the penalty as well. The defense and the prosecution would each propose a sentence and the δικασταί would make a choice between the two possible penalties.

3. The original meaning of μοῖρα is 'part': a 'portion' of land, a 'division' of a people, a political 'party', a geographical or astronomical 'degree'; and then the 'lot' or 'share' which falls to each person, especially in the distribution of booty. The word means the 'lot' or rightful portion of an individual; but from this it came to mean the doom of death, man's ines- capable lot. Thus μοῖρα came to have a fatalistic connotation and was person- ified first as the goddess of fate and then as the three fates: Lachesis, who assigns the lot; Clotho, who spins the thread of life; and Atropos, who cuts it. In Greek folklore, the Μοῖραι come to the room where a child is born and at the time of his birth determine his destiny, the whole course of his life between his birth and his death.

4. The Muses were daughters of Zeus and Mnemosyne (Memory), and acted as patron deities of music, poetry, literature, and dance; in heaven they pro- vided the gods with entertainment at the Olympian feasts (feasting being the Olympians' chief activity, the Muses kept very busy). They inspired poets and gave them true knowledge. Homer calls on the Muse to tell him the story, to refresh his memory: Memory personified was their mother. Poets (both Greek and Latin) from Homer to the end of the Roman Empire celebrated the Muses as the inspiration of their art. Hesiod in the *Theogony* (lines 75 ff.) gives the following list of them:

> ταῦτ' ἄρα Μοῦσαι ἄειδον Ὀλύμπια δώματ' ἔχουσαι
> ἐννέα θυγατέρες μεγάλου Διὸς ἐκγεγαυῖαι,
> Κλείω τ' Εὐτέρπη τε Θάλειά τε Μελπομένη τε
> Τερψιχόρη τ' Ἐράτω τε Πολύμνιά τ' Οὐρανίη τε
> Καλλιόπη θ' ἢ δὲ προφερεστάτη ἐστὶν ἁπασέων.

These things then the Muses sang, who have their homes on Olympus,
Nine daughters of great Zeus born,
Clio and Euterpe and Thalia and Melpomene and
Terpsichore and Erato and Polymnia and Urania and
Calliope; but she is the greatest of them all.

A museum (μουσεῖον) is a place connected with the Muses and their arts, but, even in antiquity, the word had a literary and educational significance rather than a religious one. Plato and Aristotle both organized their schools as associations of the Muses and their cult. The Museum at Alexandria was the most famous in antiquity. Scholars from all parts of the civilized world (i.e. the Mediterranean area) congregated there, and were generously supported by the government.

5. The word σκηνή originally meant 'tent' or 'booth' (a booth in the marketplace). Perhaps the Greek plays--before permanent theatres with stage buildings were erected--were first performed in front of a tent or hut from and to which the actors made their entrances and exits and in which they changed masks. Later the word continued to refer to the stage building or

'scene', as the background for the plays. οἱ ἀπὸ σκηνῆς are 'actors' (as opposed to the chorus who do not enter or exit from the stage building).

6. Demonstratives and the article: the article was originally a demonstrative and is generally so used in Homeric Greek. In Attic this original meaning can still be seen in such expressions as ὁ μέν . . . ὁ δέ 'the one . . . . . the other'. (Also in the expressions τὸ καὶ τό 'this and that' and τὸν καὶ τόν 'this man and that one'.) This relationship between article and demonstrative can be seen in the fact that ὅδε, ἥδε, τόδε is formed from the article, by the addition of the particle -δε. οὗτος is also from the article, perhaps with the article doubled as τούτου.

Exercises

1. Determine to which of the five types of first declension nouns each of the nouns in the vocabulary belongs.

2. Decline (orally or in writing):

1. ὁ ποιητής   2. ἡ θεά   3. ἡ γλῶττα   4. ὁ ταμίας
5. ἡ ἡμέρα   6. ἡ εἰρήνη   7. Εὐριπίδης   8. ἄξιος, ἀξία,
                                          (sing. only)   ἄξιον

3. Choose the correct adjective/article/demonstrative form to agree with the following noun forms:

1. πολῖται   a. καλός   b. καλαί   c. καλοῦ
2. θάλατταν   a. κακήν   b. κακάν   c. κακάς
3. ταμίᾳ   a. ἀξία   b. ἀξίᾳ   c. ἀξίῳ
4. θεᾶς   a. τῆς   b. τᾶς   c. τοῦ   d. τάς
5. σκηνήν   a. νεόν   b. νέην   c. νέαν
6. δεσπότου   a. ταύτης   b. οὔτου   c. τούτου
7. ποιητής   a. πονηρός   b. πονηρῆς   c. πονηρά   d. πονηρᾶς
8. πεῖρα   a. ταύτη   b. αὕτη   c. ταῦτα   d. αὕτα
9. νεανίας   a. ταύτης   b. τούτου   c. τούτους   d. ταύτας
10. ναύταις   a. αἰσχραῖς   b. αἰσχρῷ   c. αἰσχροῖς
11. συμφοράν   a. ἄδικαν   b. ἄδικον   c. ἀδίκην
12. δικασταί   a. ταί   b. αἱ   c. οἱ
13. ὁδός   a. παλαιός   b. παλαιόν   c. παλαιά
14. γλώττης   a. φιλίας   b. φιλίης   c. φιλίου
15. Εὐριπίδη   a. αἰσχρᾷ   b. καλῷ κἀγαθῷ c. ἀδίκη
16. Μουσῶν   a. τούτων   b. ταυτῶν   c. αὕτων

4. Translate and decline in Greek (orally or in writing):

1. this citizen   2. that misfortune

3. the small tent   4. the immortal goddess

5. the shameful   6. the dishonest (unjust)
     tongue   treasurer

Syntax

1. Genitive of separation

The genitive case is used to denote separation ('from'). It
can be used with verbs meaning remove, deprive, release, cease,
etc., and with adjectives (as a rule with those that imply depri-
vation, or some such thing). With verbs of motion, a preposition
is used: two of the most common prepositions used with a genitive of separation are:

> ἀπό   'away from', 'from'
>
> ἐκ   'out of', 'from' (from within)

Cf. also παρά and πρός with the genitive.

2. The genitive of agent with ὑπό

A subdivision of the genitive of source is the genitive of
agent. The person *by whom* the action of a passive verb is performed is put into the genitive case, in prose, usually with the
preposition ὑπό 'by'.

> πέμπονται ὑπὸ τῶν θεῶν 'they are sent by the gods'

3. Other uses of ὑπό ('under')

With genitive of place: 'under', 'from under'
> ὑπὸ γῆς 'under the earth'
>
> τὰ ὑπὸ γῆς 'the things under the earth'

With dative: 'beneath', 'under', 'at the foot of' (of
rest under)

With accusative: 'under' (to a place under: terminal
acc.); also of time: 'toward'

> ὑπὸ νύκτα 'at nightfall'
>
> ὑπὸ τὴν εἰρήνην 'at the time of peace'

Exercises

5.   Translate:

1.   ὁ σοφὸς βούλεται τὴν ἀλήθειαν λέγειν ἀεί.

2.   οὗτος ὁ ἄνθρωπος οὐ μὲν σοφός ἐστι, γλώσσῃ δὲ δεινός.

3.   ἐκεῖνος ὁ θεὸς ἦν ὁ δεσπότης ὁ τῆς θαλάττης.

4.   ὁ δεσπότης καὶ ὁ δοῦλος οὐκ ἔσονταί ποτε φίλοι.

5.   ὁ ἀγαθος δικαστὴς ὅδε οὐκ ἐλάμβανεν ἄδικα δῶρα.

6.   Εὐριπίδης ἦν ὁ τῆς σκηνῆς σοφός.

7.   οἱ ἐκ τῆς θαλάσσης εἰσὶν αἰσχροὶ καὶ ἄδικοι.

8.   τὰ δὲ τῶν τῆς θαλάσσης θεῶν ἔργα ἐστὶ καλά.

9.   Εὐριπίδης ὁ ποιητὴς ἔλεγε τάδε· ὅ τι καλὸν φίλον ἀεί.

10. τῇδε τῇ ἡμέρᾳ ἐλευσόμεθα εἰς ἐκείνην τὴν μικρὰν νῆσον.   (τῇδε τῇ ἡμέρᾳ
     dative of time when 'on this day')

11. ὁ ἥλιος φέρει τὴν ἡμέραν.

12. καλὰ ἡ ἡσυχία καὶ ἡ εἰρήνη.

13. κακῶν θάλατταν ὁ κακὸς ἄνθρωπος φέρει.

14. οἱ θεοὶ καὶ αἱ θεαὶ πέμπουσι καὶ καλὰ καὶ κακά.

15. ἀγαθῇ γαρ μοίρᾳ ἄξεσθε ἡσυχίαν.

16. ὁ δίκαιος δικαστὴς κρίνει δίκῃ.

17. μοῖρα γάρ ἐστι ἀποθνήσκειν τοὺς ἀνθρώπους καὶ δικαίους καὶ ἀδίκους.
     (acc. subject of inf.)

18. ὁ ναύτης ἔχει τὸν βίον ἐκ τῆς θαλάττης.

19. οὗτος ὁ νεανίας ἦν ποιητής.

20. οἱ ποιηταὶ ἐπαίδευον τοὺς πολίτας καλὰ καὶ ἀγαθά.

21. ἐν δημοκρατίᾳ οἱ πολῖται βουλεύονται.

22. ὁ γὰρ νόμος καὶ ἡ βουλὴ ἄρχουσι τῶν πολιτῶν ἐν δημοκρατίᾳ.

23. ἡ ἡμέρα ἥδε ἀγαθὸν 'ἢ κακον οἴσει;

24. οἱ ποιηταὶ ἐλέγοντο οἱ τῶν Μουσῶν ταμίαι.   (ἐλέγοντο 'were said to be',
     'were called')

25. ὁ σοφος ἄνθρωπός ἐστι ὁ ταμίας ὁ τῆς γνώμης καὶ τῆς γλώσσης.

26. οἱ θεοὶ καὶ αἱ θεαὶ ἦσαν οἱ ταμίαι οἱ τῶν ἐν τοῖς οὐρανοῖς.

27. συμφορά ἐστι κακὰ πράττειν.

28. ὁ Ζεὺς ἦν ταμίας τῶν ψυχῶν καὶ τῶν ἀγαθῶν καὶ τῶν κακῶν.

29. τοῖς φίλοις τιμὰς ἐφέρομεν.

30. ὁ σοφὸς λόγος ἔξει τιμὴν ἀεί.

31. οἱ ἐν τιμαῖς ἄρχουσι τούτων τῶν πολιτῶν.

32. ὁ ἄδικος δικαστὴς ἐξεβάλλετο ἐκ τῆς τιμῆς. (ἐκ-βάλλω 'cast out')

33. ἡ ὑγίεια νομίζεται ἀγαθὸν τῷ βίῳ.

34. ἄριστον ἀνθρώποις ἡ ὑγίεια ἡ τῆς ψυχῆς.

35. ὁ κακὸς στρατιώτης λείψει τὴν χώραν.

36. ὥρα ἐστὶ βουλεύεσθαι καὶ κρίνειν.

37. τῶν ἐν τιμαῖς ἔργον ἐστὶν ἄρχειν τῶν πολιτῶν δίκῃ καὶ ἀγαθῇ βουλῇ. (ἔργον ἐστί + gen.: see p. 70 #6)

38. τὸ δίκαιον διορίζει τὰ καλὰ καὶ τὰ αἰσχρά. (διορίζω 'distinguish')

39. τὰ ἔργα τὰ τοῦ ἀγαθοῦ ποιητοῦ ἄξιά ἐστιν τιμῆς.

40. ὁ τοῦ σοφοῦ λόγος ἄξιος τιμῆς τοῖς ἀνθρώποις.

41. ὁ ἄνθρωπος ὃς ἄδικα ἔπραττεν ἄξιος ἦν θανάτου.

42. οἱ δίκαιοι ἄξιοι ἔσονται τιμὴν καὶ δῶρα λαμβάνειν.

43. δίκαιοι οἱ πολῖται κολάζειν τοὺς ἀδίκους. (κολάζειν 'to punish')

44. δίκαιός εἰμι λέγειν τάδε.

45. οἱ πολῖται οὓς ἀπεκτείνετε οὐκ ἦσαν ἄξιοι θανάτου.

46. ἡ γὰρ θεὰ ᾗ θύετε ἀξία ἐστὶν τῶν δώρων.

47. οὐκ ἔστιν αἰσχρὸν τὴν ἀλήθειαν λέγειν.

48. οὐ δίκαιος εἶ ἀποκτείνειν τούσδε τοὺς ἀνθρώπους.

49. οὗτος ὁ ἄνθρωπος ξένος παλαιός ἐστιν.

50. τὸ μικρὸν παιδίον τοὺς μικροὺς λίθους οἴσεται.

51. ἡ μὲν τῶν νέων ἀρετή ἐστι ἀνδρεία, ἡ δὲ τῶν παλαιῶν ἐστι ἀγαθὴ βουλή. (ἀνδρεία 'courage')

52. ὁ πονηρὸς ἄξιος μικροῦ.

53. οἱ γὰρ ποιηταὶ νέοι ἀεί.

54. αἱ γνῶμαι αἱ τῶν παλαιῶν ἄξιαί εἰσι πιστεύεσθαι.

55. ἄξιόν ἐστι πείθεσθαι τοῖς ἀνθρώποις οἳ λέγουσι τὰς ἀληθείας.

56. ἥδε ἡ χώρα φιλία ξένοις.

57. ἐκεῖνος ὁ στρατιώτης ὃς εἰρήνην ἄγειν ἐβούλετο φίλιος ἦν τοῖς πολίταις.

58. ἄξια λόγου τὰ ἔργα τὰ τῶν θεῶν καὶ τὰ μικρά.

59. οὗτοι μὲν ἐκείνοις ταῦτα ἔλεγον· ἐκεῖνοι δὲ τούτοις ἔλεγον τάδε.

60. οὐ δίκαια ἃ λέγεις· ἄδικον γὰρ πλοῦτον ἐθέλεις ἔχειν.

6. Translate into Greek

1. It is time to go to that small island. (cf. #36 above)

2. This man will not be a friend to his master.

3. The work of the good poet will be immortal forever.

4. On that day we were bringing gifts to the gods. (cf. #10, p. 90)

5. Will you sacrifice to the goddess who is killing the young men?

6. The good citizen will never have unjust wealth.

7. The wise men said this (the aforesaid), but the poet said the following.

8. The opinion of the wise man will have honor.

9. The good soldier will never leave his place. (cf. #35, p. 91)

10. Do you wish to have the friendship of these men, but not of the gods?

7. Make up sentences in Greek using the following words:

1. ἀγαθός   ἡμέρα   ὅδε   φέρω

2. θεά   θύω   ὅς/ἥ/ὅ   ἄδικος   ὅδε/ἥδε/τόδε

3. ἀλήθεια   ἀγαθός   λέγω

4. ἄνθρωπος   δῶρον   ἐκεῖνος   οὗτος   φέρω

5. ἄνθρωπος   βουλεύω   ὥρα

Readings: Translate

τις 'one', 'anyone' (nom. m. sg.); ἐποίησεν 'made' (3rd sg. aorist); πῦρ 'fire' (nom./acc. neut. sg.)

1. κόσμον τόνδε οὔτε τις θεῶν οὔτε ἀνθρώπων ἐποίησεν, ἀλλ' ἦν ἀεὶ καὶ ἔστιν καὶ ἔσται πῦρ.

    Heraclitus

φῶς 'light' (acc.)

2. ἄγει δὲ πρὸς φῶς τὴν ἀλήθειαν χρόνος.

    Menander

τὰ πάντα 'all things' (acc.); καλῶς adverb (-ως = -ly)

3. ὥρα τὰ πάντα τοῦ βίου κρίνει καλῶς.

    Menander

ξένιζε 'entertain!' (2nd sg. imperative); σύ 'you' (nom.); γ' = γέ 'at least'

4. ξένους ξένιζε, καὶ σὺ γὰρ ξένος γ' ἔσῃ.

    Menander

ἀνήρ 'man' (nom. m. sg.)

5. ἀνὴρ δίκαιος πλοῦτον οὐκ ἔχει ποτέ.

   Menander

κλύζει 'washes' (3rd sg. pres.);
πάντα 'all' (neut. pl. nom./acc.);
τἀνθρώπων = τὰ ἀνθρώπων

6. θάλασσα κλύζει πάντα τἀνθρώπων
   κακά.

   Euripides

οὐχί emphatic form of οὐ

7. οὐχὶ δώδεκά εἰσιν ὧραι τῆς ἡμέρας;

   John

φησίν 'he says'; μόνιμος, -ον 'sta-
ble', 'steady'; ἔοικε 'it seems';
μήν 'indeed'; ῥᾴδιος, -α, -ον 'easy';
οὕτως (adv. of οὗτος) 'thus' (note
-ως is adverbial ending)

8. καὶ περὶ ἀληθείας δ᾽ἐν τοῖς Νόμοις
   φησὶν οὕτως· καλὸν μὲν ἡ ἀλήθεια,
   ὦ ξένε, καὶ μόνιμον· ἔοικε μὴν οὐ
   ῥᾴδιον πείθειν.

   Diogenes Laertius (quoting Plato)

οὐδέν 'nothing' (n. sg. nom./acc.)

9. οὐδὲν κακὸν μικρόν ἐστιν.

   Demetrius (*On Style*)

10. ὁ νέος ἔσται νέος.

    Greek Proverb

11. οὐ πόλεμον ἀγγέλλεις.

    Greek Proverb (meaning 'that is
    good news')

πολλῶν 'of many' (gen. pl.); αἰτία,
-ας, ἡ 'cause'

12. ἡ γλῶσσα πολλῶν ἐστιν αἰτία κακῶν.

    Menander

με 'me' (acc. sg. m./f.); μέλλω 'be
about to', 'intend to' (+ infinitive); κελεύω 'order', 'bid'; βῆ
ba-a-a

13. θύειν με μέλλει καὶ κελεύει βῆ λέ-
    γειν.

    Aristophanes

δοκεῖν 'to seem' (infinitive); θέλει
= ἐθέλει

14. οὐ γὰρ δοκεῖν ἄριστος, ἀλλ᾽ εἶναι
    θέλει.

    Aeschylus

φιλοῦσιν '(they) love' (3rd pl.)

15. ὃν οἱ θεοὶ φιλοῦσιν ἀποθνῄσκει
    νέος.

    Menander

χαῖρε (see p. 52)

16. χαῖρε, θάλασσα φίλη.

    Greek Anthology

υἱός, -οῦ, ὁ 'son'; ὀργή, -ῆς, ἡ
'anger'; πατήρ 'father' (nom. m.
sg.)

17. πρὸς υἱὸν ὀργὴν οὐκ ἔχει χρηστὸς
    πατήρ.

    Menander

ἐμὸς πόσις 'my husband' (nom. sg.);
νεκρός 'corpse' (nom. sg.); δεξιός,
-ά, -όν 'right'; χερός (= χειρός)
'hand' (gen.); τέκτονος 'worker'
(gen. m./f.); τάδ' ὧδ' ἔχει 'this is
how it is'

ὤνθρωποι = οἱ ἄνθρωποι; οὐκι = οὐχί

σώματι 'body' (dat. sg.); ἐκτός
'outside' (adv.); οἷον 'such as';
δικαιοσύνη 'justice'; φρόνησις 'intellect'; ἀνδρεία 'manliness',
'courage'; τὰ τοιαῦτα 'such things';
κάλλος 'beauty' (cf. καλός); εὐεξία
'bodily vigor'; ἰσχύς 'strength';
ἡ τῆς πατρίδος εὐδαιμονία 'the pros-
perity of one's country'

δοῦλος 'slave' (nom. sg. m.)

τε 'and' (enclitic); ποιοῦσι 'make'
(3rd pl.); μακρολόγος = μακρός +
λόγος

ἀπονέμω 'assign'; τὸ πλῆθος 'multitude', 'the masses'; ἐστέρηται (pf.
mid.) 'is deprived (from στερέω);
χειροτονία and ψηφηφορία are two
kinds of voting: by the show of
hands and by ballot. Both are gen.
of separation after στερέω; μήτε . .
. . μήτε 'neither . . . nor'

ζῶμεν (from ζάω) 'we live'; αἰσθάνομαι 'perceive'; διανοούμεθα (διανοέομαι) 'we think'; πρώτως adv. of
πρῶτος

ὅτι 'because'; κινεῖ (κινέω) 'it
moves'; σίδηρος, -ου, ὁ 'iron'

---

18. οὗτός ἐστιν Ἀγαμέμνων, ἐμὸς πόσις,
νεκρὸς δὲ τῆσδε δεξιᾶς χερὸς ἔργον
δικαίας τέκτονος. τάδ' ὧδ' ἔχει.

Aeschylus (Clytemnestra over Agamemnon's dead body)

19. αἱ συμφοραὶ τῶν ἀνθρώπων ἄρχουσι,
καὶ οὐκὶ ὤνθρωποι τῶν συμφορῶν.

Herodotus

[20. τῶν ἀγαθῶν ἐστι τὰ μὲν ἐν ψυχῇ τὰ
δὲ ἐν σώματι, τὰ δὲ ἐκτός· οἷον ἡ
μὲν δικαιοσύνη καὶ ἡ φρόνησις καὶ ἡ
ἀνδρεία καὶ ἡ σωφροσύνη καὶ τὰ τοιαῦτα ἐν ψυχῇ· τὸ δὲ κάλλος καὶ ἡ
εὐεξία καὶ ἡ ὑγίεια καὶ ἡ ἰσχὺς ἐν
σώματι· οἱ δὲ φίλοι καὶ ἡ τῆς πατρίδος εὐδαιμονία καὶ ὁ πλοῦτος ἐν
τοῖς ἐκτός.]

Diogenes Laertius (in his summary
of Plato's thought)

21. εἷς ἐστι δοῦλος οἰκίας ὁ δεσπότης.

Menander

22. αἵ τε γὰρ συμφοραὶ ποιοῦσι μακρο-
λόγους.

Appian

[23. δημοκρατία μὲν ἀρίστη ἐν ᾗ οἱ νόμοι
τοῖς ἀρίστοις τὰς τιμας ἀπονέμουσι,
τὸ δὲ πλῆθος μήτε χειροτονίας μήτε
ψηφηφορίας ἐστέρηται.]

'Aristotle' (Rhetoric to Alexander)

[24. ἡ ψυχὴ δὲ τοῦτο ᾧ ζῶμεν καὶ αἰσθανόμεθα καὶ διανοούμεθα πρώτως . . .]

Aristotle, περὶ ψυχῆς

25. Θαλῆς . . . τὸν λίθον ἔφη ψυχὴν
ἔχειν, ὅτι τὸν σίδηρον κινεῖ.

Aristotle, περὶ ψυχῆς (quoting
Thales' remark about the magnet)

26. τῷ δικαίῳ παρὰ θεῶν δῶρα γίγνεται.

Plato, *Republic*

πάντα see pp. 92-93 #3, 6   27. πάντα μὲν τὰ νέα καὶ καλά ἐστιν.

                                      Democritus (on style)

θησαυρός, -οῦ, ὁ 'treasury'; προφέρω   28. ὁ ἀγαθὸς ἄνθρωπος ἐκ τοῦ ἀγαθοῦ θη-
'bring forth'; καρδία, -ας, ἡ   σαυροῦ τῆς καρδίας προφέρει τὸ ἀγα-
'heart'   θόν, καὶ ὁ πονηρὸς ἐκ τοῦ πονηροῦ
                                           προφέρει τὸ πονηρόν.

                                      Luke

ἐκβάλλω 'cast out', 'produce'   29. ὁ ἀγαθὸς ἄνθρωπος ἐκ τοῦ ἀγαθοῦ θη-
                                           σαυροῦ ἐκβάλλει ἀγαθά, καὶ ὁ πονη-
                                           ρὸς ἄνθρωπος ἐκ τοῦ πονηροῦ θησαυ-
                                           ροῦ ἐκβάλλει πονηρά.

                                      Matthew

σῴζω 'save', 'preserve'; ἐς = εἰς   30. καὶ τόνδ' ἔσῳζον οἶκον ἐς τόδ'
('to this day'); οἶκον = οἰκία   ἡμέρας.

                                      Euripides, *Alcestis*

Crasis

   In both prose and verse, a vowel or diphthong at the end of
one word may contract with a vowel or diphthong at the beginning
of another word. This is called *crasis* ('a mixing'); an apostrophe (called the coronis)(') is used to mark it.

Examples: ταγαθά for τὰ ἀγαθά

           καλὸς κἀγαθός for καλὸς καὶ ἀγαθός

                ὦριστε for ὦ ἄριστε

           τἀνθρώπων for τὰ ἀνθρώπων

           ὤνθρωποι for οἱ ἄνθρωποι

   An invitation to dinner (from a papyrus of the third century
A.D.):

       καλεῖ σε Εὐδαίμων δειπνῆσαι ἐν τῷ γυμνασίῳ ἐπὶ
   τῷ στέψει τοῦ υἱοῦ αὐτοῦ Νείλου τῇ α ἀπὸ ὥρας η.

       Eudaimon invites you to dine in the gymnasium at the crown-
   ing of his son Neilos on the first, from the eighth hour (about
   2:00 p.m.)

Read and learn the following saying of Democritus:

       ἐτεῇ δὲ οὐδὲν ἴδμεν· ἐν βυθῷ γὰρ ἡ ἀλήθεια

   In reality we know nothing: for the truth is in an abyss.

LESSON IV

A. Aorist Active and Middle: Third Principal Part

The *Aorist* is a secondary (or past) tense. It is used for a single act in past time, as opposed to the imperfect, which is used for a continuous or habitual act in past time.

Imperfect ἔλυον 'I was releasing', 'used to release', 'kept on releasing', 'tried to release'

Aorist ἔλυσα 'I released'

The aorist, like the future, has separate forms for the middle and passive.

There are two forms of the aorist called, for convenience, first and second aorist. These differ only in formation and conjugation, but not in meaning and use. If a verb has a first aorist, it will not have a second aorist (there are some few exceptions to this rule, but they will be dealt with as needed). The first aorist is formed regularly from the present stem. To form the second aorist, certain changes usually take place in the verb stem. The two types correspond to our regular and irregular (weak and strong) verbs as:

Regular	look	looked	(looked)
Irregular	sing	sang	(sung)
	see	saw	(seen)
	drink	drank	(drunk)

Note that in the three irregular verbs there is a variation in the stem vowel in the different forms; this is also a common occurrence in the Greek verbs with second aorists (it is known as vowel gradation or ablaut).

Like the imperfect (and the other secondary tense, the pluperfect), the aorist (both first and second) is augmented, but only in the indicative. The infinitive and all other moods than the indicative are *not* augmented.

The aorist active indicative, first person singular, is the third principal part of verbs. Fully deponent verbs, of course, have no aorist active; the deponent verbs are divided into two classes, those which have their aorists in the middle and those with passive aorists, called respectively middle or passive deponents.

Formation and Conjugation of the First Aorist

   1. Vowel and Mute Stems (Sigmatic Aorist)

      a. Vowel Stems

      Augment (ε) + stem + σ - α (tense sign) + secondary endings (the secondary endings show slight modifications in the active of the first aorist):

Active		Middle
	Singular	
-σ-α	1st	-σ-αμην
-σ-ας	2nd	[-σ-ασο] → -σω
-σ-ε(ν)	3rd	-σ-ατο
	Plural	
-σ-αμεν	1st	-σ-αμεθα
-σ-ατε	2nd	-σ-ασθε
-σ-αν	3rd	-σ-αντο
-σ-αι	Infinitive	-σ-ασθαι (not augmented)

   Note: These endings differ from the other secondary endings mainly in that they do not have the thematic vowel ο or ε; rather -α- is the characteristic vowel of the first aorist endings.

Example: λύω, aorist ἔλυσα:

	Singular	
ἔλυσα	1st	ἐλυσάμην
ἔλυσας	2nd	ἐλύσω
ἔλυσε(ν)	3rd	ἐλύσατο
	Plural	
ἐλύσαμεν	1st	ἐλυσάμεθα
ἐλύσατε	2nd	ἐλύσασθε
ἔλυσαν	3rd	ἐλύσαντο
λῦσαι	Infinitive	λύσασθαι

Accent of the first aorist infinitive active: the first aorist infinitive *active* is accented on the penult: λῦσαι, βουλεῦσαι, γρά-ψαι.

b. Mute (Consonant) Stems

Before the -σ- of the first aorist, the mute stems undergo orthographic changes (as in the future):

a labial (π, β, or φ) + σ becomes ψ

πέμπω: ἔπεμψα   (cf. future πέμψω)
γράφω: ἔγραψα   (future γράψω)

a palatal (κ, γ, or χ) + σ becomes ξ

ἄρχω: ἦρξα   (future ἄρξω)
πράττω (πραγ-): ἔπραξα (future πράξω)

a dental (τ, δ, or θ) drops out before σ (ζ also drops out)

πείθω: ἔπεισα   (cf. future πείσω)
νομίζω: ἐνόμισα

These forms are conjugated in the same way as the vowel stems; the -σ- is present in the double consonants ψ and ξ.

2. The Liquid First Aorist

Verbs with stems ending in μ, ν, λ, or ρ (the nasals and liquids) do not add -σ- to form the first aorist. (The combinations μσ, νσ, λσ and ρσ were generally avoided in Greek.) The Liquid First Aorist is formed as follows:

Augment + stem + -α- with the secondary endings as given above.

Note on the stem of the liquid first aorist: *Compensatory Lengthening:* In the formation of the liquid first aorist, the sigma is lost and, to make up for this loss, the stem vowel of the verb is often lengthened, according to the following pattern: ε becomes ει; α becomes η.

Examples:

μένω   stem μεν-   aorist ἔμεινα

ἀγγέλλω   stem ἀγγελ-   aorist ἤγγειλα
φαίνω   stem φαν-   aorist ἔφηνα
κρίνω   stem κριν-   aorist ἔκρινα

These are conjugated in the same way as ἔλυσα.

Active		Middle
Singular		
ἤγγειλα	1st	ἠγγειλάμην
ἤγγειλας	2nd	ἠγγείλω
ἤγγειλε(ν)	3rd	ἠγγείλατο
Plural		
ἠγγείλαμεν	1st	ἠγγειλάμεθα
ἠγγείλατε	2nd	ἠγγείλασθε
ἤγγειλαν	3rd	ἠγγείλαντο
ἀγγεῖλαι	Infinitive	ἀγγείλασθαι

Exercises: For the First Aorist

1. a. Fill in the accent; b. Parse and translate each form; c. Give each in the opposite number:

1. ἠγγειλας	2. ἠκουσαμεν	3. ἀπεκτειναν
4. ἠρξαντο	5. ἐπραξατε	6. ἐγραφατο
7. ἐβουλευσαμεθα	8. ἐδεξαμην	9. ἐπεμφασθε
10. ἐπαυσε	11. ἐπεισω	12. ἐμεινα
13. ἠθελησατε	14. ἐθυσαμεθα	15. ἐνομισαντο
16. ἐκρινασθε	17. ἐλεξαν	18. ἐλυσω
19. ἐφηνα	20. ἐπαιδευσαμην	21. ἐτειναμεν*
22. ἐστειλατο*	23. ἠκουσας	24. ἐλεξεν
25. ἐπεμψω	26. ἐπαυσαν	27. ἐτειναν*
28. ἠρξας	29. ἐκριναν	30. ἠθελησε

*τεινω 'stretch'; στελλω 'send'

2. a. Fill in the accent; b. Parse and translate the form; c. Give each in the corresponding form of the middle:

1. ἀκουσαι   2. ἀγγειλαι   3. φηναι   4. λεξαι   5. κριναι (ῑ)
6. παυσαι   7. πεμφαι   8. πεισαι   9. ἀρξαι   10. βουλευσαι

3. For each of the following present forms, give the corresponding form in the imperfect, future and aorist:

(Example: λύεις - impf. ἔλυες, fut. λύσεις, aor. ἔλυσας)

1. λύετε   2. παύομαι   3. ἄρχονται
4. παιδευόμεθα   5. ἀποκτείνω*   6. νομίζειν*

*omit future

7.	γράφουσι	8.	δέχεσθαι	9.	ἀγγέλλει
10.	πείθεται	11.	δέχει	12.	φαίνομεν
13.	πέμπεσθε	14.	βουλεύεσθε	15.	μένεις

The Second Aorist

The second aorist is formed as follows:
Augment + second aorist stem + secondary endings (the same endings as for the imperfect):

Active		Middle
	Singular	
-ον	1st	-ο-μην
-ες	2nd	-ου
-ε(ν)	3rd	-ε-το
	Plural	
-ο-μεν	1st	-ο-μεθα
-ε-τε	2nd	-ε-σθε
-ο-ν	3rd	-ο-ντο
-εῖν	Infinitive	-έσθαι	note the accent

The second aorist is a thematic tense, i.e. it has a vowel, ο or ε added to the stem before the endings.

The Second Aorist Stem

There is no one way in which second aorists are formed, but a general characteristic is a variation in the stem vowel of the given verb. The second aorist is to be learned from the principal parts: the stem is found by removing the augment and personal ending. Very often the second aorist stem shows the root (the most basic part) of the verb.

Examples:

λείπω	aorist stem:	λιπ-	second aorist:	ἔλιπον
λαμβάνω	aorist stem:	λαβ-	second aorist:	ἔλαβον
βάλλω	aorist stem:	βαλ-	second aorist:	ἔβαλον
γίγνομαι	aorist stem:	γεν-	second aorist:	ἐγενόμην
μανθάνω	aorist stem:	μαθ-	second aorist:	ἔμαθον

There are some other kinds of changes which certain verbs undergo in the formation of the second aorist. Examples:

ἄγω   aorist stem αγαγ-   second aorist ἤγαγον, which is a re-duplication (or doubling) of the present stem ἀγ- to ἀγαγ-.

ἔχω   aorist stem σχ-   second aorist ἔσχον. (This stem is related to that of the future σχήσω; its relation to the other forms will be discussed below in the vocabulary notes.)

φέρω   aorist stem ἐνεγκ-   second aorist ἤνεγκον. (This is also a reduplication, but unrelated to the present; a comparison could be made between this verb and the English verb 'go, went' in which the parts are taken from different verb stems.)

ἔρχομαι   aorist stem ἐλθ-   second aorist ἦλθον. (Note that the second aorist of this verb is active in form as well as in meaning.)

Example of Second Aorist, of λείπω: aorist stem, λιπ-:

Active		Middle
	Singular	
ἔλιπον	1st	ἐλιπόμην
ἔλιπες	2nd	ἐλίπου
ἔλιπε(ν)	3rd	ἐλίπετο
	Plural	
ἐλίπομεν	1st	ἐλιπόμεθα
ἐλίπετε	2nd	ἐλίπεσθε
ἔλιπον	3rd	ἐλίποντο
λιπεῖν	Infinitive	λιπέσθαι

The endings are the same as those of the imperfect, but even so, it is, generally speaking, easy to distinguish the two tenses because the imperfect is always formed from the present stem, and the second aorist from a different, usually simplified, stem.

Vocabulary

Review of Principal Parts (both regular and irregular of verbs given in the previous lessons). * indicates irregular verbs: pay special attention to the verbs so marked. Be sure that you know the meanings of all the verbs. Many of these verbs, though irregular, do follow a pattern.

   *ἀγγέλλω --- ἤγγειλα

   *ἄγω ἄξω ἤγαγον (ἀγαγ-)

   *ἀκούω ἀκούσομαι ἤκουσα

   *ἀποθνῄσκω --- ἀπέθανον

   *ἀποκτείνω --- ἀπέκτεινα

   ἄρχω ἄρξω ἦρξα

   *βάλλω --- ἔβαλον

   βουλεύω βουλεύσω ἐβούλευσα

   *βούλομαι βουλήσομαι (the aorist of this verb is passive, Lesson X)

   *γίγνομαι γενήσομαι ἐγενόμην

   γράφω γράψω ἔγραψα

   δέχομαι δέξομαι ἐδεξάμην

   *ἐθέλω ἐθελήσω ἠθέλησα

   *ἔρχομαι ἐλεύσομαι ἦλθον (ἐλθ-)

   *ἔχω ἕξω/σχήσω ἔσχον (σχ-)

   θύω θύσω ἔθυσα

   *κρίνω --- ἔκρινα

   *λαμβάνω λήψομαι ἔλαβον

   λέγω λέξω ἔλεξα (εἶπον)

   *λείπω λείψω ἔλιπον

   λύω λύσω ἔλυσα

   *μανθάνω μαθήσομαι ἔμαθον

   *μένω --- ἔμεινα

   *νομίζω --- ἐνόμισα

   παιδεύω παιδεύσω ἐπαίδευσα

   *πάσχω πείσομαι ἔπαθον

   παύω παύσω ἔπαυσα

   πείθω πείσω ἔπεισα

   πέμπω πέμψω ἔπεμψα

   πιστεύω πιστεύσω ἐπίστευσα

   πράττω (πραγ-) πράξω ἔπραξα

   *φαίνω --- ἔφηνα

   *φέρω οἴσω ἤνεγκον

Note on finding the aorist stem: the aorist stem is found by removing the augment and the personal ending. It is necessary to know what the form looks like without its augment, for forming and recognizing infinitives and the other dependent moods, and for recognizing at a glance what verb a particular aorist is from. The only difficulty that may present itself is among augmented forms beginning with η, which may represent a lengthened ε or α. In most cases it can be determined whether an η deaugments to ε or α, from the relationship of the aorist to the present. For example: ἦρξα, first aorist of ἄρχω, will have ἀρξ- as its aorist stem because the η simply represents a lengthened α.   Similarly ἤγγειλα (ἀγγειλ-) from ἀγγέλλω; ἤκουσα (ἀκουσ-) from ἀκούω; ἤγαγον (ἀγαγ-) from ἄγω; ἠθέλησα (ἐθελησ-) from ἐθέλω. The only real difficulty arises in aorists that bear little or no resemblance to the other principal parts, as ἤνεγκον (ἐνεγκ-), aorist of φέρω; or ἦλθον (ἐλθ-) from ἔρχομαι. In such cases, the aorist stem is given in the vocabulary along with the aorist indicative.

Vocabulary Notes - Notes on Stems and on the Aorist Tense:

     The second aorist stem often represents the simplest form of the verb. It is often the present that has something added to it: λείπω, ἀγγέλλω, etc. are lengthened forms. μανθάνω and λαμβάνω and several other verbs of their class have the whole syllable -αν- as well as an additional nasal added to form the present stem; their roots are μαθ- and λαβ-, respectively. We may say that this simplest form of the verb (the root) contains the basic meaning of the verb--but why is it found in the aorist rather than the present? The aorist is in fact the simplest tense. The meaning of the term "aorist" (from the Greek ἀόριστος) is "unlimited," and it is so called because it has none of the limitations of repetition, continuance, or completion which the other tenses have: it refers to a simple act (in the indicative, in past time). The present refers to action going on, in progress; the imperfect to continued or repeated action, again, action in progress; the perfect to completed action. This is what we mean by the *aspect* of Greek tenses: the tenses refer not only to time (as present, past, or future) but also to the character of the action: whether it is in progress, simply taking place, or finished.

     As has been mentioned above, the augment was originally a floating temporal particle and only later became attached to the verb: in Homer, secondary tenses of the indicative often appear without the augment. Only the indicative has the augment and it is only in the indicative that the aorist is strictly a past tense. That is, the infinitive, optative, subjunctive, and imperative (all unaugmented forms) usually express the aspect rather than the time. An aorist infinitive (except in indirect statement, which will be treated below) differs in meaning from a present infinitive only in that the present refers to the action as going on, the aorist to a single act. (The present and aorist infinitives are by far the most commonly used of the infinitives.) The infinitive is a verbal noun and therefore does not express time any more than a noun does.

Examples:

λύειν	'to be releasing'
λῦσαι	'to release'
γίγνεσθαι	'to go through the process of becoming'
γενέσθαι	'to become'

A linguistic note: the original stem of the verb ἔχω is σεχ-. Initial
σ often changes to the rough breathing, leaving us with ἔχω. The difficulty
in pronouncing two successive aspirations (the rough breathing and the aspirated consonant χ) caused the change to ἔχω. In the future, however, when the
second aspiration is lost in the combination of χ + σ = ξ, the first aspiration is free to return, giving ἕξω. The aorist ἔσχον, with the stem σχ is
from the original stem σεχ- with the stem vowel's total disappearance (by vowel gradation). The irregular imperfect εἶχον has also been affected by the
original initial σ that dropped out. The augment ει is really a syllabic (or
ε) augment resulting from ε-ε (ε-σ-εχον): ει is the regular contraction for
ε-ε.

Compound Verbs

Compound verbs are most commonly formed by prefixing a preposition to the verb. In these compounds, the meaning of the
verb is the fundamental part, with the preposition-prefix modifying it more or less. The most important thing to remember at
this point is that the augment is added after the preposition:
that is, the verb is augmented and not the preposition, as ἀποκτείνω, aorist ἀπ-έκτεινα. Prepositions ending in a vowel drop the
final vowel before another vowel, by elision (περί and πρό are exceptions to this rule). There are some other changes that take
place when prepositions are added to verbs.

1. ἀπό, κατά, ἐπί, μετά, ὑπό before a rough breathing change
their final consonant to the aspirated form (having dropped the
vowel by elision):

ἀφαιρέω	'take from', 'take away':	ἀπό + αἱρέω
καθίστημι	'set down':	κατά + ἵστημι
ἐφίημι	'send to':	ἐπί + ἵημι
μεθίστημι	'change':	μετά + ἵστημι
ὑφαρπάζω	'filch', 'snatch away from under':	ὑπό + ἁρπάζω

2. ἐξ before a vowel, ἐκ before a consonant:

ἐκβάλλω	'throw, put out'; aorist ἐξέβαλον
ἐκφέρω	'bring forth'; future ἐξοίσω

3. ἐν, σύν before a labial (π, β, φ) become ἐμ and συμ:

ἐμβάλλω	'throw, put in'; aorist ἐνέβαλον

συμβαίνω   'come to pass', 'happen'; aorist συνέβην

συμβάλλω   'throw together'; aorist συνέβαλον

ἐν, σύν before a palatal (γ, κ, χ) become ἐγ-, συγ-:

ἐγγράφω   'inscribe'; aorist ἐνέγραψα

συγχρονέω   'be contemporary with' (cf. χρόνος)

συγγίγνομαι   'keep company with'; aorist συνεγενόμην

συγκομίζω   'bring together'; aorist συνεκόμισα

συν before λ becomes συλ- (ἐλ- is not very common, but ἐλλείπω, ἐνέλιπον):

συλλέγω   'collect'; aorist συνέλεξα

συλλύω   'help in loosing'; aorist συνέλυσα

συλλαμβάνω   'take with one'; aorist συνέλαβον

συν before σ, ζ becomes συ (this does not happen to ἐν):

συζῶ   'live with' (σύν + ζάω, 'live')

συστέλλω   'draw together' (σύν + στέλλω)

Exercises on Second Aorist and Compound Verbs

1. a) put in correct accent; b) parse and translate;
c) give the opposite number for each form:

1. ἤγαγε	11. ἐλαβόμεθα	21. ἔλιπες
2. ἐγενόμην	12. ἐλίποντο	22. ἔλυσω
3. ἤλθετε	13. ἔσχετε	23. ἔπαθον
4. ἐλίπομεν	14. ἔλιπεν	24. ἐγένοντο
5. ἠνέγκεσθε	15. ἠνέγκου	25. ἔπεισας
6. ἔμαθες	16. ἐμάθετο	26. ἠνέγκου
7. ἔλαβον	17. ἠγαγόμεθα	27. ἔφηνα
8. ἐβάλου	18. ἐλαβόμην	28. ἔσχομεν
9. ἀπέθανον	19. ἀπεθνῃσκον	29. οἴσουσιν
10. ἐγένετο	20. ἐμάθομεν	30. ἠγάγετε

2. Parse:

1. λαβεῖν	6. ἀποθανεῖν	11. λιπέσθαι
2. σχεῖν	7. βαλεῖν	12. βαλέσθαι
3. ἀγαγεῖν	8. ἐλθεῖν	13. μαθέσθαι
4. μαθεῖν	9. παθεῖν	14. λαβέσθαι
5. γενέσθαι	10. ἐνεγκεῖν	15. ἐνεγκέσθαι

3. For each of the following imperfect forms, give the corresponding form in the aorist:

1. ἐλάμβανον
2. ἔφερες
3. ἤγετε
4. ἐγίγνοντο
5. ἐμανθάνομεν

6. ἐβάλλετο
7. ἐγίγνου
8. ἐλειπόμην
9. ἠρχόμεθα
10. εἶχε

4. Compounds: for each of the following present forms, give the corresponding imperfect, future, and aorist:

1. ἀπέχω   'be away', 'be distant from'

2. ἐκφέρεσθε   'carry out/away'

3. εἰσβάλλει   'throw into'

4. ἀποφαίνομεν   'show forth'

5. περιγίγνομαι   'get the better of'

6. προφέρετε   'bring forth'

7. ἐμβάλλεται   'throw into'

8. ὑποτείνουσι   'subtend'   ὑπο + τείνω --- ἔτεινα

9. ἀποθυόμεθα   'pay off a vow'

10. εἰσπράττεις   'get in', 'exact a debt'

11. συλλαμβάνονται   'collect', 'gather together'

12. ἐγγράφει /-ῃ   'inscribe'

Irregular Verb, φημί 'say'

Principal Parts: φημί, φήσω, ἔφησα

Only the present system is irregular; the future and first aorist are conjugated like λύσω, ἔλυσα. φημί, like εἰμί, belongs to the class of verbs known as -μι verbs, and like εἰμί is enclitic in the present indicative (except for the second person singular).

	Present	Singular	Imperfect
	φημί	1st	ἔφην
	φῄς	2nd	ἔφησθα or ἔφης
	φησί	3rd	ἔφη
Infinitive		Plural	
φάναι	φαμέν	1st	ἔφαμεν
	φατέ	2nd	ἔφατε
	φασί	3rd	ἔφασαν

Indirect Statement (Constructions after verbs of *saying* and
  thinking)

There are in Greek, several ways of quoting a statement indirectly. The construction to be used depends on the introduc-
tory verb of saying or thinking.

The three ways of expressing indirect quotations are: (1)
with ὅτι or ὡς, 'that' and a finite verb (similar to English usage; (2) with the infinitive and subject accusative (similar to
Latin usage); and (3) with the participle (see Lesson VII).

Of the verbs of *saying*, φημί regularly takes the infinitive
construction; εἶπον (infinitive εἰπεῖν) 'I said' takes ὅτι or ὡς,
with the indicative (or optative); and λέγω in the active usually
takes the ὅτι/ὡς construction; in the passive, the infinitive.
Verbs of *thinking* or *believing* such as νομίζω usually take the infinitive construction. Verbs of *seeing*, *hearing*, and *learning*
take the participle construction (Lesson VII).

1.   In indirect statement after ὅτι or ὡς, each verb
retains both the mood and tense of the direct quotation. (After
past tenses an alternate construction is possible, using the optative; see Lesson XIII).

Examples:

Direct	Indirect
μανθάνω 'I understand'	λέγω ὅτι μανθάνω 'I say that I understand'
	λέγει ὅτι μανθάνει 'he says that he under-stands'

Sometimes ὅτι introduces a direct quotation (quotation marks
had not yet been invented): εἶπον ὅτι ἱκανοί ἐσμεν 'they said "we
are able"' (Xenophon, *Anabasis*).

2.   The verbs φημί and νομίζω (among others) take a construction in which the verb of the original statement is changed
to the infinitive of the corresponding tense. The following examples will illustrate:

Direct	Indirect

γράφω 'I am writing'

νομίζω γράφειν 'I think that I am writing'

νομίζει γράφειν 'he thinks that he is writing'

ἐνόμισα γράφειν 'I thought that I was writing'

ἐνόμισε γράφειν 'he thought that he was writing'

Note that in the last two examples, the tense of the English translation changes to comply with the rules of English tense sequence. In Greek, the tense of the infinitive remains the same because the infinitive still represents the same form of the indicative, the present: that is, it still stands for the same implied direct statement, γράφω, 'I am writing'. The present infinitive can also be used to stand for the imperfect indicative.

γράφω 'I shall write'

νομίζω γράφειν 'I think that I will write'

νομίζει γράφειν 'he thinks that he will write'

ἐνόμισα γράφειν 'I thought that I would write'

ἔγραφα 'I wrote'

νομίζω γράψαι 'I think that I wrote'

νομίζει γράψαι 'he thinks that he wrote'

ἐνόμισα γράψαι 'I thought that I had written'

The Subject of the Infinitive in Indirect Statement:

1. In the examples given above, the subject of the indirect statement has been omitted. If the subject of the infinitive is the same as the subject of the main verb (i.e. the verb of saying or thinking) then it is usually omitted, unless it is to be emphasized, in which case it will be in the nominative (because it agrees with the subject of the main clause), and anything which agrees with it will be nominative.

The infinitive can stand for any person and number: ἔφην γράφειν 'I said that I was writing', the infinitive stands for the first person singular. ἔφασαν γράφειν 'they said that they were writing', the infinitive stands for the third person plural.

2. If the subject of the infinitive is different from that of the main verb, then it goes into the accusative case and it

may not be omitted:

ὁ ἄνθρωπος γράφει 'the man is writing'

νομίζω τὸν ἄνθρωπον γράφειν 'I think that the man is writing'

ὁ πολίτης ἐστὶ καλός 'the citizen is good'

νομίζω τὸν πολίτην εἶναι καλόν 'I think that the citizen is good'

But, ὁ πολίτης νομίζει εἶναι καλός 'the citizen thinks that he (himself) is good'

In the last example, καλός is nominative because it refers to the same subject as that of the main verb

Exercises

1. Go over the list of principal parts (p. 103) and classify the various verbs: which have first aorist, liquid first aorist, second aorist? Which are deponent, which semi-deponent? Which have futures in the middle?

2. Conjugate the following in the aorist (active and middle); include infinitives: (1) παύω (2) μανθάνω (3) κρίνω (4) δέχομαι mid. only (5) ἀποθνήσκω act. only (6) ἀποκτείνω act. only.

2b. Conjugate orally in full, giving all forms you know (review):   (1) λύω (2) ἔρχομαι (3) φαίνω (4) λαμβάνω (5) ἀκούω

3. **Parse and translate:**

1. δέξασθαι	19. σχήσειν	37. ἀπέθνησκον
2. γίγνεσθαι	20. σχεῖν	38. νομίσαι
3. γενέσθαι	21. ἀκοῦσαι	39. ἐλεύσει
4. γενήσεσθαι	22. λιπεῖν	40. παύσω
5. ἔφερεν	23. ἐδέξαντο	41. ἐπαύσω
6. ἤνεγκον	24. ἦρχον	42. ἀπέκτειναν
7. ἔξουσιν	25. ἤρχετο	43. ἀπέκτεινον
8. ἐβουλευσάμεθα	26. ἄρχονται	44. κρίνομεν
9. βουλήσονται	27. ἔρχεσθε	45. ἐκρίνομεν
10. φέρεις	28. λήψει	46. ἐκρίναμεν
11. ἔφηναν	29. νομίζειν	47. ἐλύσαντο
12. λύεις	30. γράφει	48. βάλλειν
13. ἐλύσω	31. γράψαι	49. βαλεῖν
14. μεῖναι	32. πείσειν	50. ἐξέφερεν
15. ἐπράξατε	33. πεῖσαι	51. φάναι
16. πέμψουσι	34. πάσχομεν	52. φῆναι
17. λείπειν	35. ἐλεύσεται	53. ἔσεσθαι
18. οἰσόμεθα	36. ἔθυσαν	54. ἔφη

55. εἶναι   57. οἴσειν   59. εἶ
56. φησί   58. φαίνεται   60. ἔφασαν

4.   Translate the following: Direct and Indirect Statement:

1. ξένος εἰμί. ἔφη ξένος εἶναι.

2. οὗτος ὁ πολίτης ἐστὶ ἀγαθός. νομίζω τοῦτον τὸν πολίτην εἶναι ἀγαθόν.

3. ἐκεῖνος ὁ νεανίας ἐστὶ ποιητής. ἐκεῖνος ὁ νεανίας νομίζει εἶναι ποιητής.
   νομίζεις ἐκεῖνον τὸν νεανίαν εἶναι ποιητήν.

4. ἐλευσόμεθα εἰς τὴν νῆσον. ἐνομίζομεν ἐλεύσεσθαι εἰς τὴν νῆσον.

5. ὁ λίθος ἔχει ψυχήν. ὁ σοφὸς νομίζει τὸν λίθον ἔχειν ψυχήν. ἔφη τὸν λίθον
   ἔχειν ψυχήν. (see Lesson III, Readings, sentence #25)

6. οἱ ποιηταὶ ἐπαίδευον τοὺς πολίτας. ἐνόμισαν τοὺς ποιητὰς παιδεύειν τοὺς
   πολίτας.

7. οὗτος ὁ ἄνθρωπος ἤνεγκε καλὰ δῶρα τοῖς θεοῖς. νομίζετε τοῦτον τὸν ἄνθρωπον ἐνεγκεῖν καλὰ δῶρα τοῖς θεοῖς; οὗτος ὁ ἄνθρωπος ἔφη ἐνεγκεῖν καλὰ
   δῶρα τοῖς θεοῖς.

8. ὁ πονηρὸς ἀπέκτεινε τοὺς φίλους. τὸν πονηρόν φαμεν ἀποκτεῖναι τοὺς φίλους.

9. ἄγει δὲ πρὸς φῶς τὴν ἀλήθειαν χρόνος. ὁ ποιητὴς ἔφη τὸν χρόνον ἄγειν πρὸς
   φῶς τὴν ἀλήθειαν.

10. ἐλύσατο ὁ ἄνθρωπος τὸ παιδίον. ἔφασαν τὸν ἄνθρωπον λύσασθαι τὸ παιδίον.

5.   Translate into Greek: Indirect Statement:

1. The children will bring stones.

   We think that the children will bring stones.

   The children said that they would bring stones.

2. We went to that island.

   We think that we went to that island.

   They said that they had gone to that island.

3. The soul of man is immortal.

   The poets say that the soul of man is immortal.

4. That wise man was put to death (ἀποθνῄσκω, active voice) by the
   unjust citizens.

   I thought that the wise man had been put to death by the
   unjust citizens.

5. This man whom they wish to kill speaks the truth.

   They denied that this man whom they wished to kill was
   speaking the truth. ('deny' = 'say not' = οὐ φημί)

6. Write the following as indirect statements, using forms
of φημί or νομίζω:

    1. ὁ σοφὸς ἄνθρωπος λέγει τὴν ἀλήθειαν ἀεί.

    2. ὁ ἀγαθός δικαστὴς οὐκ ἔλαβε τὰ ἄδικα δῶρα.

    3. οἱ χρηστοὶ ἤνεγκον τιμὰς τοῖς φίλοις.

    4. ὁ ἀγαθὸς στρατιώτης οὐ λείψει τὴν χώραν.

7. Translate:

1. ἤγγειλεν ὁ ἄγγελος πόλεμον; (ὁ ἄγγελος 'the messenger')

2. ἠγάγομεν τὰ δῶρα τοῖς θεοῖς, ὃ ἔχουσι τὰς οἰκίας ἐν οὐρανῷ.

3. ἤκουσα τοῦ σοφοῦ, ὃς τὴν ἀλήθειαν ἔλεγεν.

4. ἀπέθανον οἱ ἀγαθοὶ στρατιῶται ὑπὸ τῶν ἀδίκων πολιτῶν.

5. οὗτοι γὰρ ἐκείνους ἀπέκτειναν λίθοις παρὰ νόμον.

6. οἱ θεοὶ ἦρχον τοῦ κόσμου.

7. οἱ ξένοι ἔβαλον τοὺς πολίτας λίθοις.

8. ὁ μὲν ποιητὴς ἔφη τὴν ἀλήθειαν λέγειν· οἱ δὲ πολῖται οὐκ ἐπείσαντο αὐτῷ.
    (αὐτῷ = 'him', dat.)

9. ἐκείνη τῇ ἡμέρᾳ ἐβουλεύσασθε. (see p. 90, #10)

10. ἔγραψας τῷ φίλῳ;

11. ἐδεξάμην τοὺς ξένους ὃι ἔφερον τὰ καλὰ δῶρα.

12. λιπεῖν μὲν Ἑλλάδα ἠθελήσαμεν· μεῖναι δὲ ἐβούλου. (Ἑλλάδα 'Greece',
    acc.)

13. εἰς λόγους τοῖς πολίταις ἦλθον οἱ ξένοι.

14. ἐνόμισα μὲν τοῦτον τὸν ποιητὴν πλοῦτον σχεῖν· ἔσχε δὲ οὔ.

15. ἔφασαν τοὺς πολίτας παθεῖν ὑπὸ τῶν ἀδίκων λόγων.

16. οὐκ ἔκριναν· οὐ γὰρ κρίνεσθαι ἐβούλοντο.

17. τῇδε τῇ ὥρᾳ ἔλαβε τὴν χώραν. (see #9 above)

18. τὰ παιδία ἔμαθεν ἐσθλὰ ἀπ’ ἐσθλῶν.

19. οἱ χρηστοὶ ἐπαιδεύσαντο τὰ παιδία ὑπὸ τῶν ποιητῶν.

20. οἱ μὲν ἄνθρωποι ἔθυσαν καλὰ δῶρα τοῖς θεοῖς· οὗτοι δ’ οὐκ ἤκουσαν ἐκεί-
    νων.

21. ὁ νόμος ἔπαυσε τὸν δικαστὴν τῶν κακῶν ἔργων.

22. ἐνόμισαν γὰρ τὸν δικαστήν, ὃς δῶρα ἔλαβεν, ἄξιον εἶναι θανάτου.

23. οἱ ἀγαθοὶ ἐπίστευσαν τῇ ἀρετῇ.

24. ὁ ἥλιος ἤνεγκε τὸν βίον.

25. ἡ αἰσχρὰ ἔπεμψε κακὰ δῶρα πρὸς τὴν βασίλειαν ἣν ἀποκτεῖναι ἐβούλετο.

26. ὁ ταμίας ἔπραξεν ἀγαθά.

27. ἀεὶ ἔφηνε τὴν ἀρετὴν ὁ σοφός.

Vocabulary (for readings)

Learn the following:

ἀλλά (ἀλλ')	*but*
ἄλλος, ἄλλη, ἄλλο	*other, another* (declined like ἐκεῖνος)(τί ἄλλο 'what else')
γέ	*at least* (postpositive, enclitic particle, used to emphasize a word; sometimes attached to the word, ἔμοιγε 'to me at least'. In conversation it is often to be translated as 'yes'.)
γιγνώσκω, γνώσομαι, (aor. Lesson XII)	*know* (cf. γνώμη)
δή	*of course, indeed, quite* (postpositive emphatic particle)
δήπου	*probably, doubtless, I presume* (often with a touch of irony)(οὐ δήπου 'certainly not', 'is it not so')
δικαιοσύνη, δικαιοσύνης, ἡ	*righteousness, justice*
δικαίως	*justly* (adv. of δίκαιος)
ἀδίκως	*unjustly* (adv. of ἄδικος)
δοκεῖ	*it seems, he/she seems* (from δοκέω Lesson XI)(δοκοῦσι(ν) 'they seem'; δοκεῖν 'to seem')
εἶπον	*said* (aorist, defective vb. for present λέγω)
μάλιστα	*especially;* an emphatic *yes, of course*
μή	*not* (to be further explained)
οἴομαι	*think*
οἷος, οἵα, οἷον	*such, what a* (οἷός τε εἰμί 'be able'; οἷον 'as', 'such as')
οὖν	*therefore, then, in fact, at all events* (postpositive particle)
σωφροσύνη, -ης, ἡ	*soundness of mind, discretion, moderation, self-control*
τε	*and* (postpositive enclitic, follows the word it is connecting)(. . . τε . . . καί 'both . . . and'; . . . τε . . . τε 'both . . . and')
χαίρω	*rejoice* (+ dat., 'rejoice in'; χαῖρε 'hello')
τοιοῦτος, τοιαύτη, τοιοῦτον	*such, of such a kind, such as this*

Learn the following words only for recognition in the context of the readings:

ἄρα	*then* (postpositive particle, denoting interest of surprise)
ἆρα	*an interrogative particle which leaves the question open* (need not be translated)

ἀργύριον, ἀργυρίου, τό   *silver, coin*

ἐγώ / ἐμοί, μοι   *I / to me* (dat.)

εἴπερ   *even if, if indeed* (emphatic form of εἰ 'if')

ἐπιθυμέω   *set one's heart upon (a thing), long for, desire* (+ genitive)(contract verb, Lesson XI)

ἐπιθυμητής, ἐπιθυμη-   *one who longs for; lover, follower*
   τοῦ, ὁ

ἕτερος, -α, -ον   *one or the other of two*

ἦ   *in truth* (affirmative particle); *is it that?* (interrogative particle)

καίπερ   *even, although* (usually with participles)

καλέω   *call* (contract verb, XI)

κινδυνεύω   *run the risk, be likely to*

ναί   *yes*

ὁμοίως   *in like manner*

ὅμως   *still, nevertheless, all the same*

ὁσίως   *piously*

οὐκοῦν   *(not) . . . then?; therefore* (interrogative)

πορίζω   *bring about, provide;* mid. *furnish oneself with, procure*

πόρος, πόρου, ὁ   *means of passing; way, means of achieving, acquiring*

πότερον   *introduces a double question, whether* (πότερον . . . ἦ *'whether . . . or')*

σύ / σοι   *you / to you* (dat.)

τοίνυν   *well then, well now, then* (a colloquial particle used mostly in dialogue)

χρυσίον, χρυσίου, τό   *gold, piece of gold* (diminutive of χρυσός)

Exercises (for readings)

1. οἱ ἄνθρωποι οὐκ ἐπιθυμοῦσι τῶν κακῶν. (-οῦσι 3rd pl. ending of contract verb)

2. οὐκ οἴομαι τὰ κακὰ ἀγαθὰ εἶναι.

3. οἱ μὲν ἐπιθυμοῦσιν τῶν ἀγαθῶν, οἱ δὲ τῶν κακῶν.

4. εἶπεν ὁ Μένων ὅτι ἡ ἀρετή ἐστι βούλεσθαι τὰ ἀγαθά.

5. ἐνόμισε τὰ ἀγαθὰ εἶναι ὑγίειάν τε καὶ πλοῦτον.

6. οἱ ἄνθρωποι βούλονται τὰ ἀγαθὰ γενέσθαι αὐτοῖς. (γενέσθαι + dat. 'to belong'; αὐτοῖς 'to them' (dat.))

7. οὐ γιγνώσκουσι τὰ κακὰ ὅτι κακά ἐστιν.

8. ὁ ἄδικος οὐχ οἷός τε ἐστὶ πορίζεσθαι τὰ ἀγαθά.

9. οὐδεὶς βούλεται κακὸς εἶναι. (οὐδείς 'no one')

10. ὁ ποιητὴς ἔφη τὴν ἀρετὴν εἶναι καλοῖς χαίρειν.

Reading: selections from Plato's *Meno*

Socrates (Σωκράτης) and Meno (Μένων), a young Thessalian gentleman, are discussing the problem of whether virtue (ἀρετή) can be taught. Socrates, disclaiming any knowledge of his own, first wants to discover what virtue is. This being the first reading of connected prose, it is not expected that the student will grasp everything the first time through it. He should, however, go over it a few times both before and after it has been more fully explained in class. Since this is a conversation, aiming at some degree of verisimilitude, there are a number of elliptical sentences. Pay special attention to the use of the particles.

καθάπερ 'as'; καλοῦσι = καλοῖς; δύνασθαι 'to be capable (of it)'; ἐπιθυμοῦντα 'the one who desires' (+ gen.)(participial form, masc., sg., acc.); δυνατὸν εἶναι 'to be able (to)'

ὡς ὄντων τινῶν '(assuming) that there are some . . .'; πάντες 'all (men)' (masc., nom., pl.); ὤριστε = ὦ ἄριστε (voc.) 'my good man' (see p. 95)

τινες (encl.) 'some (men)' (masc. nom. pl.)

οἰόμενοι (ptcpl., n. pl. m.); γιγνώσκοντες (ptcpl., n. pl. m.); αὐτῶν 'of them'

ἀμφότερα 'both (things)'

τις 'anyone' (n. sg. m.); γιγνώσκων ptcpl. (n. sg. m.)

γενέσθαι αὐτῷ 'to be/belong to him' (dat. of possession)

Meno: Δοκεῖ τοίνυν μοι, ὦ Σώκρατες, ἀρετὴ εἶναι, καθάπερ ὁ ποιητὴς λέγει, 'χαίρειν τε καλοῖσι καὶ δύνασθαι·' καὶ ἐγὼ τοῦτο λέγω ἀρετήν, ἐπιθυμοῦντα τῶν καλῶν δυνατὸν εἶναι πορίζεσθαι.

Socrates: ᾽Αρα λέγεις τὸν τῶν καλῶν ἐπιθυμοῦντα ἀγαθῶν ἐπιθυμητὴν εἶναι;

Meno: Μάλιστά γε.

Socrates: ᾽Αρα ὡς ὄντων τινῶν οἳ τῶν κακῶν ἐπιθυμοῦσιν, ἑτέρων δὲ οἳ τῶν ἀγαθῶν; οὐ πάντες, ὤριστε, δοκοῦσί σοι τῶν ἀγαθῶν ἐπιθυμεῖν;

Meno: Οὐκ ἔμοιγε.

Socrates: ᾽Αλλά τινες τῶν κακῶν;

Meno: Ναί.

Socrates: Οἰόμενοι τὰ κακὰ ἀγαθὰ εἶναι, λέγεις, 'ἢ καὶ γιγνώσκοντες, ὅτι κακά ἐστιν, ὅμως ἐπιθυμοῦσιν αὐτῶν;

Meno: ᾽Αμφότερα ἔμοιγε δοκεῖ.

Socrates: ᾽Η γὰρ δοκεῖ τίς σοι, ὦ Μένων, γιγνώσκων τὰ κακὰ ὅτι κακά ἐστιν ὅμως ἐπιθυμεῖν αὐτῶν;

Meno: Μάλιστα.

Socrates: τί ἐπιθυμεῖν λέγεις; ἢ γενέσθαι αὐτῷ;

Meno: Γενέσθαι· τί γὰρ ἄλλο;

. . . . .

ὅστις 'anyone who' (masc. nom.
sg.); ἄθλιος, -α, -ον 'unhappy';
κακοδαίμων 'unlucky' (m/f nom. sg.)

Socrates: Ἔστιν οὖν ὅστις βούλεται ἄθλιος καὶ κακοδαίμων εἶναι;

Meno: οὔ μοι δοκεῖ, ὦ Σώκρατες.

οὐδείς 'no one' (masc. nom. sg.);
κτᾶσθαι 'to possess' (pres. inf.)

Socrates: Οὐκ ἄρα βούλεται, ὦ Μένων, τὰ
κακὰ οὐδείς, εἴπερ μὴ βούλεται τοιοῦτος
εἶναι. τί γὰρ ἄλλο ἐστὶν ἄθλιον εἶναι,
ἢ ἐπιθυμεῖν τε τῶν κακῶν καὶ κτᾶσθαι.

ἀληθῆ 'the truth' ('true things')
(neut. nom./acc. pl.)

Meno: κινδυνεύεις ἀληθῆ λέγειν, ὦ Σώκρα-
τες· καὶ οὐδεὶς βούλεσθαι τὰ κακά.

Socrates: Οὐκοῦν νῦν δὴ ἔλεγες, ὅτι ἔστιν
ἡ ἀρετὴ βούλεσθαί τε τἀγαθὰ καὶ δύνασθαι;

γάρ in conversation is often
equivalent to 'yes'

Meno: Εἶπον γάρ.

. . . . .

τἀγαθά (crasis, see p. 95)

Socrates: Τἀγαθὰ φὴς οἷόν τ᾽ εἶναι πορίζεσθαι ἀρετὴν εἶναι;

Meno: Ἔγωγε.

Socrates: Ἀγαθὰ δὲ καλεῖς οὐχὶ οἷον ὑγίειάν τε καὶ πλοῦτον;

ἐν πόλει 'in the city'

Meno: καὶ χρυσίον λέγω καὶ ἀργύριον κτᾶσθαι καὶ τιμὰς ἐν πόλει καὶ ἀρχάς.

εἶεν 'O.K.'; τοῦ μεγάλου βασιλέως
'of the great king' (the King of
Persia)(gen. sg.); πατρικός 'hereditary', 'ancestral'; προστιθεῖς
'you add'; οὐδέν 'nothing' (neut.
nom./acc. sg.); οὐδὲν διαφέρει 'it
makes no difference'; κἄν . . .
'even if one should acquire them
unjustly . . .'

Socrates: Εἶεν· χρυσίον δὲ δὴ καὶ ἀργύριον πορίζεσθαι ἀρετή ἐστιν, ὥς φησι Μένων
ὁ τοῦ μεγάλου βασιλέως πατρικὸς ξένος.
πότερον προστιθεῖς τούτῳ τῷ πόρῳ, ὦ Μένων, τὸ δικαίως καὶ ὁσίως, ἢ οὐδέν σοι
διαφέρει, ἀλλὰ κἂν ἀδίκως τις αὐτὰ πορί-
ζηται, ὁμοίως σὺ αὐτὰ ἀρετὴν καλεῖς.

Meno: Οὐ δήπου, ὦ Σώκρατες.

κακία, -ας, ἡ (opp. of ἀρετή)

Socrates: Ἀλλὰ κακίαν.

πάντως 'absolutely', 'altogether'

Meno: Πάντως δήπου.

δεῖ 'it is necessary'; ὡς ἔοικε
'as it seems'; ὁσιότητα 'piety'
(acc. sg.); ἄλλο τι μόριον 'some
other part'; ἐκπορίζουσα 'acquiring' (n. sg. f.); προσεῖναι inf.
of πρόσειμι 'be added to', 'belong
to'

Socrates: Δεῖ ἄρα, ὡς ἔοικε, τούτῳ τῷ πόρῳ δικαιοσύνην ἢ σωφροσύνην ἢ ὁσιότητα
προσεῖναι, ἢ ἄλλο τι μόριον ἀρετῆς· εἰ
δὲ μή, οὐκ ἔσται ἀρετή, καίπερ ἐκπορίζουσα τἀγαθά.

Read and learn the following quote from Palladas in the Palatine Anthology:

Σύνταξις γὰρ ἐμοὶ καὶ θάνατον παρέχει.
Syntax is the death of me.

LESSON V

Third Declension Nouns

The third declension presents some difficulties because of the variety of base endings, which bring about some variations in the declension. The difficulties will be resolved with familiarity.

The endings given below are added to the base of the noun, which is usually found by removing the -ος ending from the genitive singular (which will always be given in the vocabulary). If the student is thoroughly familiar with these endings he/she will have less trouble later on in sticking them on to nouns properly. It is now very important to learn both nominative and genitive, as the pattern which a word is to follow is only clear if both forms are known. Also the base is often not complete in the nominative.

Endings:

Singular

M and F		N
variable, often -ς	NOM	base
-ος	GEN	-ος
-ι	DAT	-ι
(short) -α or -ν	ACC	same as nom
(like nom. or base)	(VOC)	same as nom

Plural

-ες	NOM	-ᾰ
-ων	GEN	-ων
-σι(ν)	DAT	-σι
-ᾰς	ACC	-ᾰ

Consonant Bases

For convenience in teaching and learning, we divide the third declension nouns into consonant bases and vowel bases. The following examples show some of the more common types of consonant bases. Look at each example and then consult the notes about it.

The accent of these nouns is usually persistent, but monosyllabic bases accent the ultima in the genitive and dative singular and plural (e.g. κλώψ, base κλωπ-, gen. sg. κλωπός, dat. sg.
κλωπί, gen. pl. κλωπῶν, dat. pl. κλωψί.)

Third Declension Consonant Bases

Masculine and Feminine

		Labial	Palatal	Dental (1)	Dental (2)
	Base:	ὁ κλώψ κλωπ-	ἡ κύλιξ κυλικ-	ἡ ἐλπίς ἐλπιδ-	ὁ/ἡ ὄρνις ὀρνιθ-
		'thief'	'drinking cup'	'hope'	'bird'
	NOM.	κλώψ	κύλιξ	ἐλπίς	ὄρνις
	GEN.	κλωπός	κύλικος	ἐλπίδος	ὄρνιθος
S	DAT.	κλωπί	κύλικι	ἐλπίδι	ὄρνιθι
	ACC.	κλῶπα	κύλικα	ἐλπίδα	ὄρνιν
	VOC.	(κλώψ)	(κύλιξ)	(ἐλπί)	(ὄρνις)
	NOM.	κλῶπες	κύλικες	ἐλπίδες	ὄρνιθες
P	GEN.	κλωπῶν	κυλίκων	ἐλπίδων	ὀρνίθων
	DAT.	κλωψί	κύλιξι	ἐλπίσι	ὄρνισι
	ACC.	κλῶπας	κύλικας	ἐλπίδας	ὄρνιθας
	Rules:	1, 2	1, 2	1, 2, 4	1, 2, 4

		ν- base	-οντ-	Neuter Dental
	Base:	ὁ δαίμων δαιμον-	ὁ ἄρχων ἀρχοντ-	τὸ ὄνομα ὀνοματ-
		'divinity'	'ruler'	'name'
	NOM.	δαίμων	ἄρχων	ὄνομα
	GEN.	δαίμονος	ἄρχοντος	ὀνόματος
S	DAT.	δαίμονι	ἄρχοντι	ὀνόματι
	ACC.	δαίμονα	ἄρχοντα	ὄνομα
	VOC.	(δαῖμον)	(ἄρχων)	
	NOM.	δαίμονες	ἄρχοντες	ὀνόματα
S	GEN.	δαιμόνων	ἀρχόντων	ὀνομάτων
	DAT.	δαίμοσι	ἄρχουσι	ὀνόμασι
	ACC.	δαίμονας	ἄρχοντας	ὀνόματα
	Rules:	2, 3	2, 3	2, 3

Notes on the Consonant Bases:

    1. -ς is the nominative singular ending of masculine and feminine nouns of the third declension except those with base ending in ν, ρ, or -οντ-.

    2. -ς of the nominative and -σι of the dative plural cause the same orthographic changes as in the futures ond first aorists of verbs, that is:

>   a. A labial (π, β, φ) + σ → ψ (e.g. κλώψ, base κλωπ-, dat. pl. κλωψί).
>
>   b. A palatal (κ, γ, χ) + σ → ξ (e.g. κύλιξ, base κύλικ-, dat. pl. κύλιξι).
>
>   c. A dental (τ, δ, θ) is dropped before σ (e.g. ἐλπίς, base ἐλπιδ-, dat. pl. ἐλπίσι; ὄρνις, base ὀρνιθ-, dat. pl. ὄρνισι). Cf. also the neuter plural nouns of the ὄνομα type: base ὀνοματ-, dat. pl. ὀνόμασι. -ν is also dropped before σ (e.g. δαίμων, base δαιμον-, dat. pl. δαίμοσι). -οντ- bases have -ουσι in the dative plural, for -οντσι: both ν and τ are dropped before -σ-, and the base vowel is lengthened to compensate for the loss of two consonants: ο is lengthened to ου.

    3. For the nominative of bases in ν, ρ, σ and -οντ-, no σ is added, but the last vowel is lengthened to form the nominative.

    Examples:

>   Nom. δαίμων base δαιμον-
>   Nom. ἄρχων   base ἀρχοντ-
>   Nom. ῥήτωρ   base ῥητορ-

Note that ν, ρ, and σ are the only consonants which can end a word in Greek. So, τ is dropped from the -οντ- type for the nominative singular, e.g. ἄρχων, base ἀρχοντ-; and from the -ατος (genitive) type of neuter nouns, as ὄνομα, ὀνόματος: base ὀνοματ-.

    4. The accusative singular ending is usually -α for consonant bases, masculine and feminine, but -ν is used for dental bases if the dental is preceded by an *unaccented* ι or υ (in which case, the dental is dropped from the accusative singular).

    Examples:

>   ἐλπίς, base ἐλπιδ-, acc. sg. ἐλπίδα accented ι.
> BUT: ὄρνις, base ὀρνιθ-, acc. sg. ὄρνιν no accent on -ι-.
>   χάρις, base χαριτ-, acc. sg. χάριν no accent on -ι-.

    (This will be easier to remember if you are in the habit of pronouncing the words aloud.)

    There are a number of other types of third declension consonant base nouns, but the ones given are the most common and will be sufficient for now.

Exercises

1. Parse:

1. κλῶπα	6. ἐλπίδα	11. ὄνομα
2. ὀνόματι	7. ἄρχοντι	12. δαίμοσι
3. ἄρχοντας	8. κύλικος	13. ἄρχουσι
4. δαίμονες	9. ἐλπίσι	14. ῥήτορες
5. ὄρνιν	10. ὄρνιθος	15. κλωπῶν

2. Decline (orally):

1. θεράπων, θεράποντος, ὁ 'attendant'
2. ἀσπίς, ἀσπίδος, ἡ   'shield'
3. θαῦμα, θαύματος, τό 'marvel'
4. χάρις, χάριτος, ἡ   'grace'
5. νύξ, νύκτός, ἡ   'night'
6. ὕδωρ, ὕδατος, τό 'water'
7. Ἕλλην, Ἕλληνος, ὁ   'Greek'

Vowel Bases

		-ευς nouns	ι or υ bases		neuters in -ος: -εσ- base
		ὁ βασιλεύς	ἡ πολις	τὸ ἄστυ	τὸ γένος
		'king'	'city'	'town'	'race'
S	NOM.	βασιλεύς	πόλις	ἄστυ	γένος
	GEN.	βασιλέως	πόλεως	ἄστεως	γένους
	DAT.	βασιλεῖ	πόλει	ἄστει	γένει
	ACC.	βασιλέα	πόλιν	ἄστυ	γένος
	VOC.	(βασιλεῦ)	(πόλι)		
P	NOM.	βασιλεῖς /-ῆς	πόλεις	ἄστη	γένη
	GEN.	βασιλέων	πόλεων	ἄστεων	γενῶν
	DAT.	βασιλεῦσι	πόλεσι	ἄστεσι	γένεσι
	ACC.	βασιλέας	πόλεις	ἄστη	γένη

Syncopated Nouns

		ὁ πατήρ	ὁ ἀνήρ
		'father'	'man'
S	NOM.	πατήρ	ἀνήρ
	GEN.	πατρός	ἀνδρός
	DAT.	πατρί	ἀνδρί
	ACC.	πατέρα	ἄνδρα
	VOC.	(πάτερ)	(ἄνερ)

	NOM.	πατέρες	ἄνδρες
P	GEN.	πατέρων	ἀνδρῶν
	DAT.	πατράσι	ἀνδράσι
	ACC.	πατέρας	ἄνδρας

Declined like πατήρ are: ἡ μήτηρ, μητρός 'mother'; ἡ θυγάτηρ, θυγατρός 'daughter'; and ἡ γαστήρ, γαστρός 'belly'.

Notes for Vowel Bases and Syncopated Nouns:

1. -ευς nouns

    a. all nouns of this type are masculine.

    b. -υ- (of -ευς) drops out before a vowel (i.e. in all cases except nominative and vocative singular and dative plural).

    c. -ως in the genitive singular instead of -ος.

    d. ε + ε contracts to -ει (in nom. pl., thus -εις; the -ης form was, however, more common until 350 B.C.).

2. -ι and -υ bases

    a. bases in ι and υ have ε in place of ι or υ in all cases except nominative, accusative and vocative singular.

    b. -ως in genitive singular (for -ος).

    c. masculines and feminines have -εις in nominative and accusative plural (the accusative ending is borrowed from the nominative). Neuters have -η for -εα in nominative and accusative plural.

    d. accent of genitive in -εως is explained by transfer of quantity from -ηος.

3. Neuters in -ος originally had base in -εσ-: γένος, original base γενεσ-

    a. -σ- between two vowels drops out

    b. contraction occurs: ε + ο becomes ου; ε + α becomes η.

	N.		γένος
S.	G.	[γένεσος → γένεος] →	γένους
	D.	[γένεσι → γένε-ι] →	γένει
	A.		γένος
	N.	[γένεσα → γένε-α] →	γένη
P.	G.	[γενέσων → γενέων] →	γενῶν
	D.	[γένεσ-σι] →	γένεσι
	A.	[γένεσα → γένε-α] →	γένη

4. Syncopated nouns

    a. drop ε of base in genitive and dative singular and dative plural. (μήτηρ, base μητερ-, gen. sg. μητρός, dat. sg. μητρί, dat. pl. μητράσι).

    b. dative plural in -ασι (πατράσι, μητράσι, θυγατράσι, γαστράσι, ἀνδράσι).

    c. ἀνήρ drops -ε and inserts δ in all cases but nom. and voc. singular (i.e. decline as if the base were ἀνδρ-).

It is not expected that the student will memorize these notes; rather they are intended to help by pointing out the similarities and differences among these many patterns. Time will be better spent studying the patterns themselves.

Exercise

Decline:

1. ἱππεύς, ἱππέως, ὁ   'horseman'
2. τέλος, τέλους, τό   'end'
3. θυγάτηρ, θυγατρός, ἡ   'daughter'
4. ὄψις, ὄψεως, ἡ   'vision'
5. ἱερεύς, ἱερέως, ὁ   'priest'
6. ἔτος, ἔτους, τό   'year'

Vocabulary

Words marked with an asterisk (*) should be learned thoroughly, others should be studied as recognition vocabulary. Any irregularities in the declension or accent will be noted.

*ἀνήρ, ἀνδρός, ὁ   *man, husband* (polyandry)

*ἄρχων, ἄρχοντος, ὁ   *archon, ruler*

ἀσπίς, ἀσπίδος, ἡ   *shield* (aspidistra)

*ἄστυ, ἄστεως, τό   *city, town*

*βασιλεύς, βασιλέως, ὁ   *king* (Basil)

*γένος, γένους, τό   *race, birth* (geneology, genesis)

*γέρων, γέροντος, ὁ   *old man* (geriatrics) (γέρον, voc. sg.)

*γυνή, γυναικός, ἡ   *woman, wife* (misogynist) (declined: γυνή, γυναικός, γυναικί, γυναῖκα, (γύναι)· γυναῖκες, γυναικῶν, γυναιξί, γυναῖκας)

*δαίμων, δαίμονος, ὁ   *divinity*

δράκων, δράκοντος, ὁ   *snake, serpent*

ἔθνος, ἔθνους, τό   *nation, tribe* (ethnic)

ἔθος, ἔθους, τό   *custom* (ethics) (also ἦθος . . .)

εἴκων, εἰκόνος, ἡ   *image* (icon)

*Ἑλλάς, Ἑλλάδος, ἡ   *Greece* (Hellas)

Ἕλλην, Ἕλληνος, ὁ   *(a) Greek (man)* (Hellenic, Hellene)

Ἑλληνίς, Ἑλληνίδος, ἡ   *(a) Greek (woman)*

*ἐλπίς, ἐλπίδος, ἡ   *hope*

ἔπος, ἔπους, τό   *word* (epic)

*ἔτος, ἔτους, τό   *year* (Etesian)

θαῦμα, θαύματος, τό   *marvel* (thaumaturgy, thaumatology) (τὰ θαύματα 'magic tricks')

θαυμάζω, θαυμάσομαι, ἐθαύμασα   *wonder at*

*θεράπων, θεράποντος, ὁ   *attendant, servant* (therapeutic)

θεραπεύω	wait on, attend, serve, treat, tend
*θυγατήρ, θυγατρός, ἡ	daughter
ἱερεύς, ἱερέως, ὁ	priest (hieratic, hierarchy)
ἱππεύς, ἱππέως, ὁ	horseman, knight
ἵππος, ἵππου, ὁ	horse (hippopotamus, hippodrome)
*κάλλος, κάλλους, τό	beauty (from καλός; calligraphy)
κέρδος, κέρδους, τό	gain, profit
*κῆρυξ, κήρυκος, ὁ	herald
*κλέος, το	fame, glory (only nom. & acc.)
κλώψ, κλωπός, ὁ	thief
κλέπτω	steal (kleptomania, biblioklept)
κτῆμα, κτήματος, τό	possession
κύλιξ, κύλικος, ἡ	drinking cup (cylix)
λέων, λέοντος, ὁ	lion (Leo) (λέον, voc. sg.)
μάθημα, μαθήματος, τό	lesson, learning, knowledge (mathematics, polymath)
*μαθητής, μαθητοῦ, ὁ	learner, pupil, disciple (cf. ἔμαθον, aorist of μανθάνω)
μάντις, μάντεως, ὁ/ἡ	seer (Praying mantis, mantic)
*μέρος, μέρους, τό	part (isomer)
*μήτηρ, μητρός, ἡ	mother
νύξ, νυκτός, ἡ	night (Mod. Grk. καληνύχτα) (nyctophobe)
ὀδούς, ὀδόντος, ὁ	tooth (orthodontist)
ὄμμα, ὄμματος, τό	eye
*ὄνομα, ὀνόματος, τό	name, noun (onomatopoeia)
ὀνομάζω	name, call by name
ὄρνις, ὄρνιθος, ὁ/ἡ	bird (ornithology)
ὄρος, ὄρους, τό	mountain (orogeny, orology)
*πάθος, πάθους, τό	experience, suffering (pathos, pathology) (cf. ἔπαθον, aorist of πάσχω)
*παῖς, παιδός, ὁ/ἡ	child, slave (orthopedics, pediatrics) (gen. pl. παίδων, voc. sg. παῖ)
*πατήρ, πατρός, ὁ	father (patronymic)
*πατρίς, πατρίδος, ἡ	native land, country
πνεῦμα, πνεύματος, τό	breath, breeze (pneumonia) (τὸ ἅγιον πνεῦμα 'the Holy Ghost')
*πόλις, πόλεως, ἡ	city-state (politics)
*πούς, ποδός, ὁ	foot (tripod, Oedipus)
*πρᾶγμα, πράγματος, τό	deed, affair, thing (pragmatism) (cf. πράττω, stem πραγ-)
πῦρ, πυρός, τό	fire (pyromaniac) (pl. τὰ πυρά, dat. πυροῖς: declined in 2nd decl. 'watchfires')
ῥήτωρ, ῥήτορος, ὁ	orator (rhetoric)
στόμα, στόματος, τό	mouth (stomatopod)
*σῶμα, σώματος, τό	body (psychosomatic)
τεῖχος, τείχους, τό	wall (teichoscopy)
*τέλος, τέλους, τό	end (teleology) (acc. as adverb, τέλος 'finally')
τυραννίς, τυραννίδος, ἡ	tyranny
τύραννος, τυράννου, ὁ	tyrant
*ὕδωρ, ὕδατος, τό	water (dehydrated)
υἱός, υἱοῦ, ὁ	son

φύλαξ, φύλακος, ὁ	*watchman* (phylacteries)
*χάρις, χάριτος, ἡ	*grace, favor* (charity)(acc. sg. χάριν)
*χείρ, χειρός, ἡ	*hand* (chiropractor)(dat. pl. χερσί)
*χρῆμα, χρήματος, τό	*thing*, pl. *money* (chrematheism)
ἔτι	*still, yet, besides* (adverb)
ὅτι	*that* (conjunction); *because* (causal particle)
οὕτως	*in this way, thus, so* (οὕτω)
ὡς	*as* (rel. adv.)
ὥσπερ	*just as, even as* (adverb)

Vocabulary Notes:

1. ἀνήρ, 'man', corresponds to the Latin *vir* (as ἄνθρωπος is the equivalent of *homo*). Ἄνθρωπος means 'man' in the sense of 'human being', or 'man'
as opposed to the animals, but ἀνήρ is primarily used as 'man' as opposed to
'woman', or 'man' as opposed to the gods (cf. Homer's epithet for Zeus, πατὴρ
ἀνδρῶν τε θεῶν τε). Usually ἀνήρ is a man in the prime of life rather than a
youth (Xenophon gives the ages of man as παῖς, μειράκιον, ἀνήρ, πρεσβύτης:
i.e. child, youth, <u>man</u>, elder). Frequently ἀνήρ is used to mean 'a real man'
(cf. Mensch), as in the expression (from Herodotus) πολλοὶ μὲν ἄνθρωποι, ὀλίγοι δὲ ἄνδρες.

2. Ἄρχων is the participle of ἄρχω (see Lesson VII on participles),
used as a noun, 'one who rules', 'ruler', 'chief', 'commander', etc. As an
official title, it meant one of the chief magistrates at Athens, οἱ ἐννέα ἄρχοντες ('the nine archons'). Archons were also found in most states of cen-
tral Greece, and the term generally refers to the highest office of the state.
In Athens at first there were three ἄρχοντες: ὁ (ἄρχων) βασιλεύς, ὁ Ἄρχων
(or ὁ ἄρχων ἐπώνυμος) and ὁ πολέμαρχος who were elected yearly; and later
their number was increased to nine (the other six being called θεσμοθέται,
'lawgivers'). In 487 B.C. they began to be chosen by lot, and at this time
seem to have lost any real political power, but to have become administrators
merely; at this time, the elected στρατηγοί ('generals') became the most important officials. The ἄρχων ἐπώνυμος (eponymous) gave his name to the year:
i.e. from 683 B.C. a continuous list of the archons was kept, by which the
year was referred to (e.g. ἄρχοντος Ἀθήνησι Δαμασίου 'when Damasias was archon at Athens', that is, in the year 582 B.C.). The Archon remained the nom-
inal head of the state even after 487. The ἄρχων βασιλεύς seems to have had
primarily religious duties, and the πολέμαρχος, though originally head of mil-
itary affairs, later had only judicial and sacrificial duties.

3. Δαίμων: it is hard to give an exact definition of the word δαίμων,
perhaps because even to the ancients it was a vague term, used in different
ways by different writers. It can be applied to one of the great gods, but
more usually corresponds to "Divine Power," not exactly as an abstract idea,
but rather in its specific manifestations to men; the word θεός on the other
hand refers to a 'god' in person. Sometimes the word δαίμων comes near to
meaning 'fate' (as in κατὰ δαίμονα 'by chance'). And more particularly it
may refer to the 'destiny' of an individual, his 'fortune' or 'lot' (as in
δαίμονα δώσω 'I will give (you your) fate', that is 'I will kill you', from
the *Iliad*). The poet Hesiod (whose works along with those of Homer are sometimes considered the 'Bible' for the ancient Greeks, because Hesiod organized
the myths about the origin of the gods and the ages of man) tells us that δαι-

μονες are the souls of men of the golden age acting as protective deities.

To Plato and other philosophers, the δαίμονες had a more exact position in the universe. Being intermediate in nature, between gods and men, they had an intermediate dwelling place, in the air between heaven and earth. To the philosophers, though not to the poets, to be sure, a god had to be morally perfect: this is the major bone of contention between the two, that the poets depicted the gods as being even more wicked than men (and enjoying it more); and this was one reason Plato considered the poets as corrupting influences and would ban them from his ideal state. But though a god must be perfect, a δαίμων need not be so, and thus many later philosophers used δαίμονες to explain certain difficulties in the moral order and to help them to a solution of the problem of evil. Ancient stories about amorous, cruel and vindictive behavior on the part of the divinities could be transferred to δαίμονες and not genuine gods. Late Greek philosophy, particularly Neoplatonism, contained a large admixture of magic: again, real gods could not be influenced by sorcerers, but maybe δαίμονες could be: anyway it would not hurt to try. To the pagans, these spirits were both good and evil--but to the Christians, since they were rivals to the one God, they became all bad, hence our *demons* are devils.

4. Word Formation: We have had by now a number of words derived from παῖς, παιδός, 'child'. It will be noted that all have as their root the base of παῖς, παιδ-: παιδίον, παιδίου, τό, 'little child' is the diminutive of παῖς, the ending -ιον being the most common diminutive ending. Παιδεύω, ('teach', 'educate') 'bring up a child' is a denominative verb, i.e. derived from a noun, as the -ευω ending indicates. Other examples are βουλεύω from βουλή; βασιλεύω 'be king' from βασιλεύς; πιστεύω from πίστις. Παίδευμα, παιδεύματος 'that which is taught' (can mean either a 'pupil' or a 'lesson') is derived from παιδεύω, with the suffix -μα (-ματ-) added, denoting the result of an action. E.g. πρᾶγμα 'act', from πράττω, stem πραγ-, 'do'; μάθημα from μαθ-, root and aorist stem of μανθάνω, 'learn'.

5. Πόλις and ἄστυ: The territory of a πόλις included both the town and the country: what we call the 'city-state'. The center of the government is in the town, and the surrounding country is politically, economically, and militarily dependent upon it, and is called after it. Ἄστυ is the actual 'city' or 'town' as opposed to the ἀγρός (the 'country'), both of which make up the πόλις. The Athenians used the word ἄστυ as *the* city, that is *Athens,* just as the Romans used *urbs* to mean *Rome.* Sometimes πόλις is used more specifically to mean πόλις ἄκρη (or ἀκρόπολις), that is, the fortified part of the city or 'citadel'; while the lower town is called ἄστυ. But usually when ἄστυ and πόλις are used together, the former is the town in the material sense, buildings and so forth, while πόλις is the citizen body (who were actually *citizens* depended of course on the constitution of the particular state).

6. τυραννίς: "tyranny" is a form of government in which the sovereignty is obtained by force or fraud, rather than by legitimate succession. Aeschylus in the *Prometheus Bound* speaks of the tyranny of Zeus, ἡ Διὸς τυραννίς, because Zeus had seized the throne by violence, and his rule is furthermore given all the characteristics of a tyranny in the worst sense: might makes right, and justice is only for the strong. But the original tyrants (τύραννοι), who usurped the power in many oligarchic city-states (πόλεις) throughout

Greece in the seventh and sixth centuries B.C. (during what is called "the age of tyrants"), generally brought improvement to their states. Sometimes tyranny was a step toward democracy, because the early tyrants had come to power through political and economic leadership of the lower classes, opposing the feudal rule of the nobles. The first tyrants did not change the constitutions but, as a rule, used the laws and institutions they had received as instruments of their own policy: their major contributions being in economic modernization. They also contributed to culture, attracting the great musicians, painters, poets and philosophers to their courts. Of course there is a danger inherent in tyranny, because the absolute ruler is potentially unlimited by law or constitution, and so there is no appeal beyond the man in power: everything depends upon the character of the tyrant. It is noteworthy that most tyrannies did not last beyond the second generation. (There is a story, no doubt apocryphal, but amusing nevertheless, that Thales the philosopher, when asked what was the strangest thing he had ever seen, replied "γέροντα τύραννον", 'an old tyrant'.) The bad sense of the word tyranny was attached to it by the fifth century Athenian philosophers, and especially Plato, who considered it the worst form of government, and finally by the later tyrants (especially the Syracusan dynasty) who proved that Plato was right. Thus, like the word δαίμων, which for religious reasons has given us "demon," τυραννίς for philosophical and political reasons has deteriorated from a technical word for "monarchy (whether good or bad) obtained through extra-legal means" to "tyranny," a wicked and despotic rule.

Exercises

1. Go over the vocabulary and determine to which paradigm (if any) each noun conforms.

2. Parse the following:

1. τυραννίδα	21. ἔθνη	41. κήρυξιν
2. ἀσπίσι	22. Ἑλλάδι	42. γένεσι
3. ἱερέως	23. θαύματα	43. πόλεων
4. γύναι	24. ἔτει	44. μαθητοῦ
5. ἄνδρας	25. θεράποντος	45. ἄνδρας
6. ἄστυ	26. ἄστει	46. δαιμόνων
7. πατέρες	27. ἐλπίδα	47. μάντιν
8. γένους	28. θυγατήρ	48. ἔθους
9. χερσί	29. ἀνδρῶν	49. θυγατράσι
10. τέλους	30. ἱερεῦσι	50. μητρός
11. βασιλέα	31. κάλλος	51. νυκτί
12. γυναιξί	32. κλῶπα	52. ὀνόμασιν
13. δαίμονι	33. γένη	53. πυρά
14. γέρουσιν	34. κύλικι	54. μαθηταί
15. ἀνδρί	35. ἀνδράσι	55. πατρί
16. ἄρχοντες	36. μέρους	56. παισί
17. βασιλέας	37. κέρδους	57. πάθει
18. πατράσι	38. γυναῖκα	58. πόλιν
19. ἀσπίδα	39. ἐλπίδι	59. τυραννίδες
20. γένει	40. βασιλεῦ	60. ὄρνιθος

61. πρᾶγμα	66. πυρός	71. χειρός
62. ῥήτορες	67. πνεύματά	72. χρήματα
63. πάθη	68. τεῖχος	73. πῦρ
64. χάριν	69. χάριτος	74. ὕδατι
65. πατρίδα	70. ὄρνιν	75. παίδων

3. Translate:

1. οὐκ ἔστιν ὑγίεια ἐν τυραννίδι.

2. κήρυκες ἦσαν οἱ ἄγγελοι οἱ τῶν θεῶν καὶ τῶν ἀνδρῶν.

3. ὁ στρατιώτης ἀπέβαλε τὴν ἀσπίδα, οὐ γὰρ χρηστὸς ἦν.

4. ἔφη ὁ ποιητὴς τὸν νόμον εἶναι τὸν πάντων βασιλέα. (πάντων 'of all')

5. ὁ δὲ σοφὸς ἔφη πόλεμον εἶναι πάντων βασιλέα.

6. ὁ πονηρὸς λέγεται ἄρχων τοῦ κόσμου τούτου.

7. οἱ στρατηγοὶ ἦσαν ἄνθρωποι, οὐ δὲ ἄνδρες.

8. Ζεύς ἐστι πατὴρ ἀνδρῶν τε θεῶν τε.

9. ἤλθομεν τότε ἐξ ἄστεως εἰς θάλατταν.

10. ὁ παῖς ἐστι Ἕλλην γένος. (γένος 'by birth')

11. ἀθάνατον τὸ τῶν θεῶν γένος.

12. τῶν γερόντων ἔργον ἐστὶ συμβουλεύειν. (συμβουλεύειν 'to advise')

13. τί τῶν βασιλέων ἔργον ἐστίν; (τί 'what?')

14. οὐ θεοὶ μέν, οὐκ ἄνθρωποι δὲ οἱ δαίμονες.

15. σὺν δαίμονι ἕξομεν εἰρήνην.

16. τοὺς λόγους τοὺς ἐκείνων τῶν ἀνδρῶν εἰς ὕδωρ γράφω.

17. λέγεται ὁ Ζεὺς εἶναι βασιλεὺς τῶν θεῶν τε καὶ τῶν δαιμόνων.

18. περὶ τῆς ψυχῆς οὐκ ἐλπίδας εἶχεν ὁ κακὸς ἀνήρ.

19. ἐλπίς ἐστί μοι σχήσειν τὰ χρήματα. (μοι 'to me')

20. ἔτος εἰς ἔτος οἱ ἄνδρες ἀποκτείνουσιν ἄνδρας.

21. τοὺς ποιητὰς φασι θεράποντας εἶναι Μουσῶν.

22. θεράποντες τῶν θεῶν οἱ ἱερεῖς, οἳ θύουσι καὶ χάριν φέρουσι τοῖς θεοῖς καὶ
    ταῖς θεαῖς.

23. ὁ ἀγαθὸς ἀνὴρ οὔποτε βούλεται ἐκ πονηροῦ πράγματος κέρδος λαβεῖν.

24. κέρδος ἐστί μοι μανθάνειν τοὺς τῶν σοφῶν λόγους.

25. ἡ ἀρετὴ λέγεται κάλλος τῆς ψυχῆς.

26. τὸ τούτου τοῦ ἀνδρος κλέος εἰς οὐρανὸν ἔρχεται.

27. ἐκ μικρῶν ἔργων ἔρχεται μικρὸν κλέος.

28. ὁ χρόνος κλώψ ἐστι τῶν ἐν βίῳ ἀγαθῶν.

29. τούτῳ τῷ ἀνθρώπῳ ὄνομά ἐστιν Οὖτις. (οὖτις 'no one')

30. ὁ ἀγαθὸς οὐκ ἐβούλετο μαθεῖν τὰ τῶν πονηρῶν ἤθη.

31. βιβλίον ἀγαθόν ἐστι κτῆμα εἰς ἀεί.

32. ἡ ἡμέρα ἐστὶ ἡ τῆς νυκτὸς θυγάτηρ.

33. λέγει ἡ μάντις τὴν τῶν θεῶν καὶ δαιμόνων βουλήν.

34. οἱ γὰρ δαίμονες λέγουσι διὰ τοῦ στόματος τοῦ τῆς μάντεως, 'ἡ μόνη ἀκούει
    τοὺς τῶν δαιμόνων λόγους, καὶ μανθάνει.

35. ὁ παῖς τῆς νυκτός ἐστι ὕπνος.

36. ἡ πόλις ἐστὶ οἱ ἄνδρες καὶ αἱ γυναῖκες καὶ οἱ παῖδες.

37. τέλος δὲ εἰς τὴν κοινὴν πατρίδα πάντες ἐλευσόμεθα.

38. πρᾶγμά ἐστί μοι ἀρετὴν μανθάνειν.

39. ἔφη ὁ ποιητὴς τὸ ὕδωρ εἶναι ποταμοῦ σῶμα, καὶ τὸν ἥλιον εἶναι πῦρ ἀθάνα-
    τον.

40. ὅδε ὁ ἀνὴρ βουλεύει τυραννίδα, φύλακας γὰρ ἔχειν τοῦ σώματος βούλεται.

4. Translate into Greek:

1. The poets say that heralds are the servants of men and gods.

2. The divinities are children of the gods.

3. They bring both good and evil to men and women.

4. The birds wished to become divinities; for they wished to
    receive gifts.

5. In a tyranny the city is not ruled by an archon.

6. The good father wants his child to learn virtue.

7. On account of money, evils come into being.

8. The whole world is the native land of the wise and good man.

9. An old man wants to hear an old man and a child (wants to
    hear) a child.

10. Was it profitable (i.e. a gain, cf. p. 129, #24) for that
    man to kill his father?

Readings

σύν + γράφω

1. Θουκυδίδης Ἀθηναῖος συνέγραφε τὸν
    πόλεμον τῶν Πελοποννησίων καὶ Ἀθη-
    ναίων.

    Thucydides, the opening sentence
    of his *History of the Pelopon-
    nesian War.*

Lacedaemonian is another name for
Spartan; μηδὲν ἄγαν 'nothing in excess'; καιρός, -οῦ, ὁ 'proper time';

2. ἦν Λακεδαιμόνιος, Χίλων σοφός, 'ὃς
    τάδ' ἔλεξε· μηδὲν ἄγαν· καιρῷ πάντα
    πρόσεστι καλά.

πρόσεστι 'belongs to' (πρός +
ἐστι); πάντα (neut. pl. nom./
acc.) 'all things'

ὀργή, -ῆς, ἡ 'anger'

3. πρὸς υἱὸν ὀργὴν οὐκ ἔχει χρηστὸς πατήρ.

    Menander

κτῆσις, -εως, ἡ 'possession';
πάντες 'all' (N. pl. m.); ἡμῖν
'to us' (dat. pl.)

4. διὰ τὴν τῶν χρημάτων κτῆσιν πάντες οἱ
πόλεμοι ἡμῖν γίγνονται.

    Plato

5. τοῦ πατρὸς τὸ παιδίον.

    Greek Proverb--"A chip off the old
        block."

νῆες (N. pl. f. of ναῦς)
'ships'; κενός, -ή, -όν 'empty'
(+ gen.)

6. ἄνδρες γὰρ πόλις, καὶ οὐ τείχη, οὐδὲ
νῆες ἀνδρῶν κεναί.

    Thucydides

ἔνιοι 'some' (N. pl. m.); αὐτόν
'him' (acc.)

7. ἔνιοι δὲ καὶ αὐτὸν πρῶτον εἰπεῖν φασιν
ἀθανάτους τὰς ψυχάς.

    Diogenes Laertius (refers to Thales)

8. (ἔλεγε) εἶναί τε πατρίδα τὸν κόσμον.

    Diogenes Laertius (refers to Theodor-
        us)

ἥδιστος, -η, -ον 'sweetest'

9. γέρων γέροντι γλῶσσαν ἡδίστην ἔχει.

    Greek Comic Fragment

δίς 'twice'

10. δὶς παῖδες οἱ γέροντες.

    Menander

σῴζω 'save'

11. ἀνὴρ γὰρ ἄνδρα καὶ πόλις σῴζει πόλιν.

    Menander

γίνεται = γίγνεται

12. βίου δικαίου γίνεται τέλος καλόν.

    Menander

πάσαις 'all' (D. pl. f.); σιγή
'silence'

13. γυναιξὶ πάσαις κόσμον ἡ σιγὴ φέρει.

    Menander

πῆμα, -ατος, τό 'calamity',
'misery'; σωτηρία, -ας, ἡ
'salvation'; οἶκος, -ου, ὁ =
οἰκία

14. γυνὴ γὰρ οἴκῳ πῆμα καὶ σωτηρία.

    Menander

εὑρίσκω 'find'; τέχνη, -ης, ἡ
'skill', 'way', 'art'

15. δειναὶ γὰρ αἱ γυναῖκες εὑρίσκειν τέχνας.

    Menander

16. διὰ τὰς γυναῖκας πάντα τὰ κακὰ γίνεται.

    Menander

ἀφικνεῖται 'arrives at', 'reaches' (3rd sg., contract verb)

17. κοὔτε τις ἄγγελος οὔτε τις ἱππεύς ἄστυ
τὸ Περσῶν ἀφικνεῖται.

Aeschylus, *The Persians*

διά + ἔρχομαι; ἅμαξα, -ης, ἡ 'wagon'; τι 'anything'; λαλεῖς 'you talk of' (+ acc.); σου 'of you', 'your'; ἄρα 'therefore'

18. εἴ τι λαλεῖς, τοῦτο διὰ τοῦ στόματός σου
διέρχεται· ἅμαξαν δὲ λαλεῖς· ἅμαξα ἄρα
διὰ τοῦ στόματός σου διέρχεται.

Diogenes Laertius (quoting a paradox of Chrysippus)

ἕλκω 'draw', 'drag'; βοῦς 'ox', 'cow'

19. ἡ ἅμαξα τὸν βοῦν ἕλκει.

Greek Proverb

δόμος, -ου, ὁ 'house' (often in the plural); παρουσία 'presence'

20. ὄμμα γὰρ δόμων νομίζω δεσπότου παρουσίαν.

Aeschylus, *The Persians*

εἰσιδεῖν aor. inf. 'to see'; νυκτός 'during the night'

21. καὶ ταῦτα μὲν δὴ νυκτὸς εἰσιδεῖν λέγω.

Aeschylus, *The Persians*

χαρακτήρ --; γνωρίζω 'make known'

22. ἀνδρὸς χαρακτὴρ ἐκ λόγου γνωρίζεται.

Menander

τί 'what?', 'why?'; δηλαδή 'clearly'; μάν = μήν 'indeed', 'truly'; τρί-πους, τετρά-πους; τέτορας = τέτταρας; τοίνυν 'therefore', 'well then'; αἴνιγμα --; νοέω 'think', 'devise'; τοι particle, 'let me tell you', 'look here'

[23. Α. τί δὲ τόδ' ἐστί; Β. δηλαδὴ τρίπους.
Α. τί μὰν ἔχει πόδας
τέτορας; οὐκ ἔστιν τρίπους, ἀλλ' ἐστὶν
οἶμαι τετράπους.
Β. ἐστὶ δ' ὄνομ' αὐτῷ τρίπους, τέτοράς
γε μὰν ἔχει πόδας.
Α. Οἰδίπους τοίνυν ποτ' ἦν, αἴνιγμά τοι
νοεῖς.]

Fragment of Epicharmus, quoted in Athenaeus

ἡμᾶς 'us' (acc., subj. of infin.); ἱερός 'holy'; τὰ ἱερά 'offerings', 'rites'; δῆμος 'the popular assembly'; κατασκευή 'construction', 'condition'; συμμαχία, ἡ 'alliance'; συμβόλαιον 'mark', 'contract'; πόρος 'way', 'means'

24. ἀνάγκη γάρ ἐστι καὶ βουλεύεσθαι καὶ λέγειν ἡμᾶς ἐν βουλῇ καὶ δήμῳ 'ἢ περὶ ἱερῶν 'ἢ περὶ νόμων 'ἢ περὶ τῆς πολιτικῆς
κατασκευῆς, 'ἢ περὶ τῶν πρὸς ἄλλας πόλεις συμμαχιῶν καὶ συμβολαίων 'ἢ περὶ
πολέμων 'ἢ περὶ εἰρήνης 'ἢ περὶ πόρου
χρημάτων.

'Aristotle', *Rhetoric to Alexander*

25. κρίνει φίλους ὁ καιρός, ὡς χρυσὸν τὸ
πῦρ.

Menander

πάντων 'of all' (gen. pl. m./n.)

26. πάντων χρημάτων μέτρον ἐστὶν ἄνθρωπος.

Protagoras

σκιά 'shadow' (-ᾶς, ἡ)

27. ἄνθρωπός ἐστι πνεῦμα καὶ σκιὰ μόνον.

    Sophocles

ὅρκος, -ου, ὁ 'oath'

28. ὅρκους γυναικὸς εἰς ὕδωρ γράφω.

    Sophocles

ἑλληνίζω 'speak Greek'

29. Ἕλλην μέν ἐστι καὶ ἑλληνίζει.

    Plato, *Meno*

σύ 'you' (N. sg.); ἀττικίζω cf. ἑλληνίζω

30. σὺ μὲν ἀττικίζεις, οἱ δὲ Ἕλληνες ἑλληνίζομεν.

    Posidippus (comic poet)

αὐτοῖς 'them' (dat.)

31. ἔτι ἐν αὐτοῖς εἰσιν ἐλπίδες, νέοι γάρ.

    Plato, *Protagoras*

32. ἄριστον μὲν ὕδωρ.

    Pindar

γῆ, γῆς, ἡ 'earth'; περίμετρον --; σφαῖρα 'sphere', 'globe'; κατασκευάζω 'equip', 'construct'

[33. καὶ γῆς καὶ θαλάσσης περίμετρον πρῶτος ἔγραψεν, ἀλλὰ καὶ σφαῖραν κατεσκεύασε.]

    Diogenes Laertius, on Anaximander

34. καὶ ἐγὼ λέγω οὐ μόνον δικαιοσύνην ἀλλὰ καὶ ἄλλας εἶναι ἀρετάς.

    Plato, *Meno*

στρατηγός, -οῦ, ὁ 'general'; σωτήρ, σωτῆρος, ὁ 'savior'; στρατόπεδον, -ου, τό 'camp'; παιδεία, -ας, ἡ 'education'; ἡγεμών, -όνος, ὁ 'leader'; μετά (+ gen.) 'with'

35. ἔτι δὲ ὥσπερ ὁ στρατηγός ἐστι σωτὴρ στρατοπέδου, οὕτω λόγος μετὰ παιδείας ἡγεμών ἐστι βίου.

    'Aristotle' *Rhetoric to Alexander*

ἀναφαίρετος, -ον 'not to be taken away'; βροτός, -οῦ, ὁ 'a mortal man' (as adj. 'mortal')

36. ἀναφαίρετον κτῆμ' ἐστὶ παιδεία βροτοῖς.

    Proverb

ἀχώριστος 'inseparable' ('from' + gen.); φυσικός, -ή, -όν 'natural', 'physical'; ὕλη, -ης, ἡ 'material', 'stuff'; ζῷον, -ου, τό 'living being'

37. ἐλέγομεν δ' ὅτι τὰ πάθη τῆς ψυχῆς ἀχώριστα τῆς φυσικῆς ὕλης τῶν ζῴων.

    Aristotle

ἀσφαλέστατος 'most secure'; ἡγοῦ (imperative) 'consider!'; εὔνοια 'goodwill', 'favor'; σαυτοῦ 'of yourself'; φρόνησις, -εως, ἡ 'good sense', 'wisdom'; φυλακή, -ῆς, ἡ 'a watching/guarding', 'guard'

38. φυλακὴν ἀσφαλεστάτην ἡγοῦ τοῦ σώματος εἶναι τήν τε τῶν φίλων ἀρετὴν καὶ τὴν τῶν πολιτῶν εὔνοιαν καὶ τὴν σαυτοῦ φρόνησιν.

    Isocrates

ἀκούσας (participle) 'having   39. 'Ὦ Σόλων, Σόλων, Ἕλληνες ἀεὶ παῖδές
heard'; πῶς τί 'how and what'   ἐστε, γέρων δὲ Ἕλλην οὐκ ἔστιν.'
                                              'Ἀκούσας οὖν, 'Πῶς τί τοῦτο λέγεις;'
                                         φάναι.
                                              'Νέοι ἐστέ,' εἰπεῖν, 'τὰς ψυχὰς πάν-
                                         τες. . .'

                                         Plato, *Timaeus*

Conversation

τί γὰρ ὁ Ζεὺς ποιεῖ;   How's the weather?   (What is Zeus doing?)

ὕει ὁ θεὸς καὶ βροντᾷ.   It's raining and thundering.   (The god is . . .)

λάμπει ὁ ἥλιος.   The sun is shining.

πηνίκα ἐστὶν τῆς ἡμέρας;   What time of day is it?

μικρόν τι μετὰ μεσημβρίαν.   A little after noon.

Quotation: Read and learn:

                    ὕβρις φυτεύει τύραννον.
          Hubris produces the tyrant.
                              --Sophocles

LESSON VI

A. Third Declension Adjectives

There are two important types of adjectives declined in the third declension only: the -ης, -ες type and the -ων, -ον type. Both are of two terminations (cf. ἀθάνατος, -ον), the same form being used for masculine and feminine (many of these adjectives are compounds).

1. -ης, -ες type. Review γένος (stem γενεσ-) for the declension: these adjectives also have bases in -εσ-, but -σ- drops out as in γένος and the -ε- contracts with the vowel of the endings.

Example: (review the third declension endings)

ἀληθής, ἀληθές (base ἀληθεσ-), 'true'

	Singular		Plural	
	M, F	N	M, F	N
NOM	ἀληθής	ἀληθές	ἀληθεῖς [έ-ες]	ἀληθῆ [έ-α]
GEN	ἀληθοῦς [έ-ος]	ἀληθοῦς	ἀληθῶν	ἀληθῶν
DAT	ἀληθεῖ	ἀληθεῖ	ἀληθέσι	ἀληθέσι
ACC	ἀληθῆ [έ-α]	ἀληθές	ἀληθεῖς	ἀληθῆ
VOC	(ἀληθές)			

The masculine-feminine accusative plural (ἀληθεῖς) takes the form of the nominative (as also happens with πόλις and some other types of third declension nouns).

2. -ων, -ον type. Review δαίμων.

Example:

εὐδαίμων, -ον 'happy'

	Singular		Plural	
	M, F	N	M, F	N
NOM	εὐδαίμων	εὔδαιμον	εὐδαίμονες	εὐδαίμονα
GEN	εὐδαίμονος	εὐδαίμονος	εὐδαιμόνων	εὐδαιμόνων
DAT	εὐδαίμονι	εὐδαίμονι	εὐδαίμοσι	εὐδαίμοσι
ACC	εὐδαίμονα	εὔδαιμον	εὐδαίμονας	εὐδαίμονα
VOC	(εὔδαιμον)			

(Besides compound adjectives like εὐδαίμων (base εὐδαιμον-), there are also certain comparatives declined similarly, which will be treated in Lesson X.)

Throughout this lesson, the student should refer to the rules and examples of third declension nouns in the previous lesson.

There are several types of adjectives which are declined in the third and first declensions: that is, masculine and neuter forms follow the third declensions while the feminine ones follow the first.

1. Bases in -υ-, with the nominative in -υς (m.), -εια (f.), -υ (n.). Example: εὐρύς, εὐρεῖα, εὐρύ 'wide'. Review πόλις, ἄστυ and the notes on -ι- and -υ- bases, to which the masculine and neuter are similar except that they have -εος in the genitive singular (not -εως) and the neuter plural -εα is not contracted. The feminine is declined in the first declension, α-type (see Lesson III), but with short -α- in the nominative and accusative singular.

Singular

	M	F	N
NOM	εὐρύς	εὐρεῖα	εὐρύ
GEN	εὐρέος	εὐρείας	εὐρέος
DAT	εὐρεῖ	εὐρείᾳ	εὐρεῖ
ACC	εὐρύν	εὐρεῖαν	εὐρύ
VOC	(εὐρύ)		

Plural

	M	F	N
NOM	εὐρεῖς	εὐρεῖαι	εὐρέα
GEN	εὐρέων	εὐρειῶν	εὐρέων
DAT	εὐρέσι	εὐρείαις	εὐρέσι
ACC	εὐρεῖς	εὐρείας	εὐρέα

2. Bases in -ντ-: a few adjectives and many participles have bases in -ντ-.

A very common adjective of this sort is πᾶς, πᾶσα, πᾶν 'all', with the base παντ- (ν and τ dropping out before σ). The feminine is of the α/η type (like θάλαττα, θαλάττης, Lesson III).

Singular

	M	F	N
NOM	πᾶς	πᾶσα	πᾶν
GEN	παντός	πάσης	παντός
DAT	παντί	πάσῃ	παντί
ACC	πάντα	πᾶσαν	πᾶν

Plural

	M	F	N
NOM	πάντες	πᾶσαι	πάντα
GEN	πάντων	πασῶν	πάντων
DAT	πᾶσι	πάσαις	πᾶσι
ACC	πάντας	πάσας	πάντα

πᾶς (and σύμπας) usually is found in the predicate position, as in οἱ ἄνδρες πάντες 'all the men'. In the attributive position it is used to mean the entire number or amount or the sum total, as ἡ πᾶσα Σικελία 'the whole of Sicily', οἱ πάντες ἄνθρωποι 'all mankind'. These distinctions are not very great. πᾶς can also be used without the article to mean 'all', 'every'.

Vocabulary

Adjectives:

ἀληθής, ἀληθές	*true* (alethorama)
ἅπας, ἅπᾱσα, ἅπαν	*quite all, everyone* (cf. πᾶς)
ἀσθενής, ἀσθενές	*weak, feeble, poor* (cf. σθένος, 'strength')
ἀσφαλής, ἀσφαλές	*safe, steadfast, sure* (asphalt)
βαρύς, βαρεῖα, βαρύ	*heavy, tiresome, oppressive* (baritone)
βραχύς, βραχεῖα, βραχύ	*short, brief* (brachycephalic)
γλυκύς, γλυκεῖα, γλυκύ	*sweet, pleasant* (glucose)
δυστυχής, δυστυχές	*unfortunate, unlucky* (cf. τύχη)
εὐτυχής, εὐτυχές	*lucky, fortunate, successful*
εὐγενής, εὐγενές	*well-born, generous* (cf. γένος, γίγνομαι)
εὐδαίμων, εὔδαιμον	*lucky, happy, wealthy* (cf. δαίμων)
δυσδαίμων, δύσδαιμον	*ill-fated*
εὐκλεής, εὐκλεές	*glorious, of good fame, famous* (cf. κλέος)
εὐρύς, εὐρεῖα, εὐρύ	*wide, spacious, far-reaching* (eurypterid)
ἡδύς, ἡδεῖα, ἡδύ	*sweet, pleasant* (cf. English "sweet," Latin *suavis*)
ἥμισυς, ἡμίσεια, ἥμισυ	*half* (hemisphere, cf. Latin *semis*)
θῆλυς, θήλεια, θῆλυ	*female, feminine, soft, effeminate*
ὁμοῖος (or ὅμοιος), ὁμοία, ὁμοῖον	*like, resembling; equal*
ὀξύς, ὀξεῖα, ὀξύ	*sharp, keen* (oxytone, oxygen)

πᾶς, πᾶσα, πᾶν   *every* (sg.), *all,* with art. *all, whole* (pandaemonium)
σαφής, σαφές   *clear, plain, distinct*
ταχύς, ταχεῖα, ταχύ   *swift, fleet* (tachygraphy)
ὑγιής, ὑγιές   *healthy, sound* (cf. ὑγίεια)
ψευδής, ψευδές   *false, lying, untrue* (pseudo-)
μέγας, μεγάλη, μέγα*   *big, large, great* (megaton, omega)
πολύς, πολλή, πολύ*   *much,* pl. *many* (Monopoly)

        *These irregular adjectives are declined below.

καιρός, καιροῦ, ὁ   *proportion, critical time, opportunity*
παιδεία, παιδείας, ἡ   *rearing of a child, training and teaching, education*
κατά   *down,* preposition with genitive and accusative
        + genitive: *down from, down upon, beneath, against*
      + accusative: *down along, over, against, through, during, according*
                             to, opposite
οὐκέτι   *no more, no longer, not now*

Irregular Adjectives

1. μέγας, μεγάλη, μέγα **'big'**, base μεγαλ-:

| | Singular | | | Plural | | |
	M	F	N	M	F	N
NOM	<u>μέγας</u>	μεγάλη	<u>μέγα</u>	μεγάλοι	μεγάλαι	μεγάλα
GEN	μεγάλου	μεγάλης	μεγάλου	μεγάλων	μεγάλων	μεγάλων
DAT	μεγάλῳ	μεγάλη	μεγάλῳ	μεγάλοις	μεγάλαις	μεγάλοις
ACC	<u>μέγαν</u>	μεγάλην	<u>μέγα</u>	μεγάλους	μεγάλας	μεγάλα
VOC	(μεγάλε)					

The irregular forms are underlined.

2. πολύς, πολλή, πολύ **'much'**, **'many'**, base πολλ-:

| | Singular | | | Plural | | |
	M	F	N	M	F	N
NOM	<u>πολύς</u>	πολλή	<u>πολύ</u>	πολλοί	πολλαί	πολλά
GEN	πολλοῦ	πολλῆς	πολλοῦ	πολλῶν	πολλῶν	πολλῶν
DAT	πολλῷ	πολλῇ	πολλῷ	πολλοῖς	πολλαῖς	πολλοῖς
ACC	<u>πολύν</u>	πολλήν	<u>πολύ</u>	πολλούς	πολλάς	πολλά

        (no vocative)

Exercises

    1. Decline in all genders and numbers (orally or in writing):

    1. ἄπας   2. θῆλυς   3. ψευδής   4. γλυκύς   5. δυσδαίμων

2.   Which is the proper adjective form to agree with the
following article-noun groups?

		a.	b.	c.
1.	τῷ _____ ἀνδρί	εὐγένῳ	εὐγενῆς	εὐγενεῖ
2.	τὴν _____ ψυχήν	θήλειαν	θῆλυν	θηλείην
3.	τοῖς _____ μαθηταῖς	ὀξαῖς	ὀξέσι	ὀξείαις
4.	τὸ _____ δῶρον	ἡδύ	ἡδόν	ἡδὺν
5.	τῇ _____ ὁδῷ	παντί	πάσῃ	πάσα
6.	τοῦ _____ γένους	ἀληθοῦς	ἀληθές	ἀληθοῦ
7.	ἡ _____ πόλις	εὐδαίμων	εὐδαιμόνη	εὐδαίμονα
8.	τοῦ _____ βασιλέως	μέγους	μεγαλέως	μεγάλου
9.	τὸν _____ δαίμονα	ἡμίσονα	ἡμίσεον	ἥμισυν
10.	τὰς _____ χάριτας	ἀληθείας	ἀληθεῖς	ἀληθῆ
11.	τοὺς _____ πολέμους	μεγάλους	μεγάλου	μέγας
12.	τὰ _____ ἤθη	πολλά	πολλαί	πολύ
13.	οἱ _____ ξένοι	ἄπαντοι	ἄπαντες	ἄπασοι
14.	ταῖς _____ συμφοραῖς	βάρεσι	βαρύσι	βαρείαις
15.	ὁ _____ πολίτης	ἀσθενοῦς	ἀσθενῆς	ἀσθενές

(Which of the above are not proper forms at all of the words
in question?)

3.   Decline the following groups (for review):

1.	ὁ ἀγαθὸς βασιλεύς	2.	ἡ ψευδὴς μάντις
3.	τὸ εὔδαιμον γένος	4.	ὁ πᾶς Ἕλλην
5.	ἡ ἀληθὴς ὁδός	6.	τὸ βραχὺ μέτρον
7.	ὁ ἡδὺς ποιητής	8.	ὁ εὐκλεὴς ἀνήρ
9.	τὸ ἀσθενὲς σῶμα	10.	ἡ μεγάλη θάλασσα

4.   Compose Greek sentences using the following word groups
(add appropriate verbs, articles, pronouns, etc. to make sentences):

1.	ἄπας παῖς	2.	βαρεῖα χείρ
3.	ἡ ὁδὸς ἡ ἀσφαλής	4.	ὕπνος γλυκύς
5.	ἀληθὴς λόγος	6.	βασιλεὺς ὁ μέγας
7.	ὁ βίος ὁ δυστυχής	8.	λόγοι ψευδεῖς
9.	πόλις ὑγιής	10.	οὐρανὸς εὐρύς

5.   Translate:

1.   οὐκ αἰσχρὸν τὸ ἀληθὲς εἰπεῖν ἀεί.

2.   ἐκεῖνος ὁ ποιητὴς οὐκ ἦν βαρὺς τὸ σῶμα.

3.   ἥδε ἡ ὁδὸς ἀσφαλὴς ἦν γυναιξὶ καὶ παισίν.

4.   ἐν βραχεῖ εἶπον μακρὸν λόγον.

5.   κατὰ βραχὺ μανθάνομεν τὸ ἀληθές.   (κατὰ βραχύ 'little by little')

6.   ἄπας γὰρ βούλεται εὐδαίμων εἶναι καὶ εὖ πράττειν.

7.   γλυκύ ἐστι πολλὰ μανθάνειν.

8. δυστυχὴς ὁ τοῦ χρήμασι ἀσθενοῦς βίος.

9. ἐνομίζομεν τὰς Ἀθήνας εἶναι πόλιν μεγάλην καὶ εὐδαίμονα.

10. αἱ γλαῦκες ὄρνιθες εὐγενεῖς εἰσίν. (γλαῦξ, -κός, ἡ 'owl')

11. τὸ τούτου τοῦ ἀνδρος κλέος εἰς εὐρὺν οὐρανὸν ἔρχεται.

12. οἱ δικασταὶ κατὰ τοὺς νόμους κρίνουσιν.

13. ὁ ὕπνος ἡδύς ἐστι πᾶσι ἀνθρώποις.

14. ὁ νέος ἔσχεν εὐρείας ἐλπίδας.

15. ἡ γῆ ἐστι μεγάλη μήτηρ τῶν θεῶν τε καὶ τῶν ἀνθρώπων.

16. οὐ ψευδῆ λέγει ὁ πολίτης ὁ καλὸς κἀγαθός.

17. βασιλευς ὁ μέγας ἦρχε πάντων τῶν βαρβάρων.

18. ταχὺν ἄγγελον ἔπεμψας;

19. ψευδεῖς λόγοι οὔκ εἰσι τῆς ὑγιοῦς ψυχῆς.

20. νέος μὲν καὶ ὀξὺς εἶ· γέρων δὲ καὶ βραδύς εἰμί.

21. κατὰ θάλατταν ἠρχόμεθα εἰς τὴν νῆσον.

22. ὁ κῆρυξ τὸ ἥμισυ τοῦ λόγου ἤγγειλε καὶ ἀπέθανεν.

23. λίθους ἔβαλλον κατὰ τοῦ τεύχους.

24. ὁ ῥήτωρ ὁ ἄδικος πολλὰ καὶ ψευδῆ ἔλεγεν κατὰ τῶν δικαίων πολιτῶν.

25. ὁ νεανίας ἐθέλει ἀρετὴν κατὰ πάντα ἔχειν.

B. Syntax

1. *Result Clauses*

The conjunction ὥστε (or sometimes ὡς), 'so that', 'so as to' is used to express result, either (1) the *actual* result, or (2) a result which the action of the main verb *tends* or *intends* to produce or is *capable* of producing.

1. ὥστε with the *indicative* expresses the actual result, that is, it implies that the second action *actually* happened or is happening as a *result* of the first. The negative with this type of result clause is οὐ.

2. ὥστε with the *infinitive* implies a possible or intended result or a tendency, rather than an actual fact. The negative after ὥστε with the infinitive is μή.

Examples:

    1.   τὸ ἀληθὲς λέγει ὥστε πιστεύεται.

He tells the truth with the (actual) result (so that) he is trusted.

    2.   τὸ ἀληθὲς λέγει ὥστε πιστεύεσθαι.

He tells the truth so as to be trusted (so that it is natural for him to be trusted).

    3.   οὕτως αἰσχρός ἐστιν ὥστε τὸν ξένον ἀπέκτεινεν.

He is so shameless that he killed his guest.

    4.   οὕτως αἰσχρός ἐστιν ὥστε τὸν ξένον ἀποκτεῖναι.

He is so shameless that he would kill his guest. (He is shameless enough to do it; but there is no implication that he actually did it. The indicative, on the other hand, emphasizes the actual occurrence of the result.)

Some Examples from Greek Authors:

    πᾶν ποιοῦσιν ὥστε δίκην μὴ διδόναι.

They do everything so as not to be punished. (Infinitive)
            --Plato, *Gorgias*

    οὕτως ἀγνωμόνος ἔχετε, ὥστε ἐλπίζετε αὐτὰ χρηστὰ γενήσεσθαι;

Are you so witless that you (actually) expect them to become good?

        --Demosthenes

2. *Temporal Clauses*

A temporal clause is introduced by a conjunction of time such as:

          ὅτε   'when'
          ἕως   'as long as', 'until'
          ἐπεί   'after', 'since'
        ἐπειδή   'after', 'since'
          πρίν   'before', 'until'

When they refer to a definite time in the present or past, they are used with the indicative mood (except for πρίν, see below). For temporal clauses referring to indefinite time, see section on the uses of the subjunctive and optative. The negative is οὐ (unless the clause is conditional).

Examples of temporal clauses:

1. γράφω, ἐπειδὴ (ἐπεὶ) γράφειν οὐκ ἐθέλεις.

I am writing since you do not wish to write.

2. ὅτε τὸ ἀληθὲς ἐμάθομεν, τοὺς ἀδίκους ἐκρίναμεν.

When we had learned the truth, we judged the guilty.

3. ἐμείναμεν ἕως Ἑλλάδα ἐλίπετε.

We waited until you left Greece.

πρίν 'before', 'until':

1. After a negative clause, πρίν means 'until' and takes the indicative (of a definite time), in the aorist or imperfect.

2. After an affirmative clause, πρίν means 'before' and takes the *infinitive*.

Examples:

1. οὐκ ἤλθομεν πρὶν Ἑλλάδα ἐλίπετε.

We did not come until you left Greece.

2. Ἑλλάδα ἐλίπομεν πρὶν τῶν σοφῶν ἀκούειν.

We left Greece before hearing the philosophers.

Conditions

A condition consists of two clauses, the *protasis* (or 'if' clause) and the *apodosis* (or conclusion-clause). The negative used in the protasis is usually μή; in the apodosis, οὐ.

1. A *simple condition* has εἰ ('if') with the indicative in the protasis, and the indicative (or whatever mood the sense requires) in the apodosis. A simple condition implies nothing as to actual fulfillment.

Examples:

      1. εἰ βούλει, ἐγὼ ἐθέλω.

If you wish, I am willing.

      2. εἰ μὴ τῷδε πιστεύεις, σοφὸς οὐκ εἶ

If you do not trust this man, you are not wise.

      2. A *condition contrary-to-fact* has εἰ with a past
tense of the indicative (imperfect or aorist) in the protasis,
and ἄν with a past tense of the indicative in the apodosis. A
condition contrary-to-fact (or unreal condition) implies that the
supposition cannot be or could not be fulfilled. The imperfect
refers to present time (or to continued action in the past) and
the aorist to simple action in the past.

Examples:

      1. εἰ ταῦτα ἔλεγες, οὐκ 'ἂν τὴν ἀλήθειαν ἔλεγες.

If you were saying these things, you would not be speaking
the truth.

      2. εἰ μὴ ἤλθετε, ἐλίπομεν 'ἂν τὴν χώραν ἐκείνην.

If you had not come, we would have left that place.

      3. εἰ οἱ δικασταὶ δίκαιοι ἦσαν, οὐκ 'ἂν τὰ ἄδικα δῶρα ἔλαβον.

If the jurors were just, they would not have received the
unjust gifts.

Exercises

1. οὗτος ὁ ἀνὴρ οὕτως κακὸς ἦν ὥστε μὴ ἔχειν φίλους.

2. πολλοὺς δὲ φίλους ἔχει ὥστε εὐτυχής ἐστιν.

3. οὕτως σοφὸς εἶ ὥστε πάντα ἐπίστασθαι. (ἐπίστασθαι 'to know' (present in-
    finitive))

4. ἐκεῖνος ὁ βασιλεὺς ἦν οὕτως αἰσχρὸς ὥστε τὴν καλὴν θυγατέρα τοῖς θεοῖς
    τοῖς τοῦ πολέμου ἔθυσεν.

5. ἐκεῖνος ὁ πολίτης οὕτως ἐστὶ δεινὸς λέγειν ὥστε πάντας πεῖσαι.

6. οἱ δικασταὶ οὐδε οὕτως ἦσαν ἄδικοι ὥστε παρὰ νόμον πολλὰ καὶ ἄδικα δῶρα
    ἔλαβον.

7. ἐπειδὴ οὐκ ἤθελες, οὐκ ἤλθομεν εἰς τὴν μικρὰν σκηνήν.

8. εὐτυχεῖς ἐστε ἕως ἔτι νέοι ἐστέ.

9. ἐπειδὴ ταύτην τὴν χώραν ἔλιπον, κατὰ θάλατταν πρὸς τὰς νήσους ἦλθον.

10. ὅτε τὴν ἀλήθειαν ἔλεγε, ἤκουον τὸν πάντα λόγον.

11. οἱ γὰρ δικασταὶ οὐκ ἔκριναν πρὶν τὴν ἀλήθειαν ἔμαθον.

12. οἱ πολῖται ἐβουλεύσαντο πρὶν κρίνειν.

13. ἀπεθάνομεν ἂν, εἰ μὴ οἵδε οἱ ἄνδρες ἦλθον.

14. εἰ ἦτε ἄνδρες δίκαιοι, οὐκ ἂν ἐλέγετε ταῦτα.

15. εἰ τοῖς θεοῖς ἐθύσαμεν, οὐκ ἂν ταῦτα τὰ κακὰ ἐπάσχομεν.

16. τῷδε τῷ στρατιώτῃ ἂν ἐπίστευον, εἰ ἐνόμιζον αὐτὸν δίκαιον εἶναι. (αὐτόν 'him')

17. εἰ εὐδαίμονές ἐστε, εὐδαίμων εἰμί.

18. εἰ μέγα ἐστὶ τὸ βιβλίον, κακόν ἐστιν.

19. οὐκ ἂν ἔχειν πολὺν πλοῦτον ἐβούλου, εἰ σοφὸς ἦσθα.

20. εἰ ἀγαθοὶ δικασταί εἰσιν, κατὰ τοὺς νόμους κρίνουσιν.

Translate into Greek:

1. If you had left that place, we would not have remained.

2. He would have died, if his friends had not come.

3. He is so wicked that he would take away (ἀπάγω) his host's wife.

4. If we had money, we would go by sea to the islands.

5. He did not come until his father died.

6. He wished to judge before he knew the truth.

7. If they had freed that man, he would have fled.

8. If he were unjust, he would not do these things.

Readings

ἵκανε 'reached' (3rd sg. impf.)

ἀγών, ἀγῶνος, ὁ 'contest', 'struggle'

σφαλερός, -ά, -όν 'perilous'

1. κλέος οὐρανὸν εὐρὺν ἵκανε.

    Homer, *Odyssey*

2. μικροῦ δ' ἀγῶνος οὐ μέγ' ἔρχεται κλέος.

    Sophocles, fragment

3. ὁ βίος βραχύς, ἡ δὲ τέχνη μακρά
    ὁ δὲ καιρὸς ὀξύς, ἡ δὲ πεῖρα σφαλερά.

    Demetrius, quoting aphorisms of Hippocrates (cf. *Ars longa, vita brevis.*)

πλεῖστος, -η, -ον 'most'; καλοῦσι '(they) call'; πάσαις understand πόλεσι; ἀκήρυκτον 'unher-
alded', 'undeclared'; κατὰ φύσιν
'according to nature'

τίκτω 'bring forth'; πάλιν 'a-
gain'; κομίζω 'conduct'; mid.
'take back for oneself';

δόξα, -ης, ἡ 'reputation'

περὶ πλείονος ποιοῦ 'make more
of' (imperative); ἤ 'than';
κατά + λείπω; θνητός, -ή, -όν
'mortal'

ἀήρ, ἀέρος, ἡ 'the lower air',
'mist'; περί + ἔχω 'hold a-
round', 'surround', 'encompass'

οὐσία 'substance', 'wealth';
πλούσιος adj., cf. πλοῦτος, καλοῦμαι 'I am called'; μακάριος,
-α, -ον 'happy'; οὐδενός 'no
one'

γηρῶν 'growing old' (Nom.,
masc., sg.); οἰκτρός 'pitiable';
ἀμφότερος 'both'; χρῆσθαι 'to
use'; ὁπότε 'when'; δύναμαι 'I
am able/can'; (ἐ)δυνάμην 'I was
able/could'

ἐπίστασθαι 'know' (pres. inf.)

εὐκταῖος, -α, -ον 'desirable',
'prayed for'

ὡς 'how', as preposition 'to'

4. ῾ὴν γὰρ καλοῦσιν οἱ πλεῖστοι τῶν ἀνθρώπων εἰρήνην, τοῦτ' εἶναι μόνον ὄνομα, τῷ
δ' ἔργῳ πάσαις πρὸς πάσας τὰς πόλεις ἀεὶ
πόλεμον ἀκήρυκτον κατὰ φύσιν εἶναι.

   Plato, *Laws*

5. γῆ πάντα τίκτει καὶ πάλιν κομίζεται.

   Menander

6. γίνεται γὰρ δόξα καὶ ἀληθὴς καὶ ψευδής.

   Aristotle, περὶ ψυχῆς (*de anima*)

7. περὶ πλείονος ποιοῦ δόξαν καλὴν 'ἢ πλοῦτον μέγαν τοῖς παισὶ καταλιπεῖν ὁ μὲν
γὰρ θνητός, ἡ δ' ἀθάνατος.

   Isocrates, *Nicocles*

8. ὅλον τὸν κόσμον πνεῦμα καὶ ἀὴρ περιέχει.

   Anaximenes

9. ἔχω δὲ πολλὴν οὐσίαν καὶ πλούσιος κα-
λοῦμ' ὑπὸ πάντων, μακάριος δ' ὑπ' οὐδενός.

   Menander

[10. ῍Ην νέος, ἀλλὰ πένης· νῦν γηρῶν πλούσιός
εἰμι
   ὦ μόνος ἐκ πάντων οἰκτρὸς ἐν ἀμφοτέ-
ροις·
῍ὃς τότε μὲν χρῆσθαι δυνάμην, ὁπότ' οὐδὲ
῍ἓν εἶχον,
   νῦν δ' ὁπότε χρῆσθαι μὴ δύναμαι, τότ'
ἔχω.]

   Greek Anthology (Anon.)

11. ἄριστόν ἐστι πάντ' ἐπίστασθαι καλά.

   Menander

12. γάμος γὰρ ἀνθρώποισιν εὐκταῖον κακόν.

   Menander

13. ὡς αἰεὶ τὸν ὁμοῖον ἄγει θεὸς ὡς τὸν ὁ-
μοῖον.

   Homer, *Odyssey*

14. ὅμοιον ὁμοίῳ φίλον.

   Greek Proverb

ἔσοπτρον, -ου, τό 'mirror'; βλέπω 'see', 'look' ('at' + acc.);
αὐτό 'it' (neut. nom./acc. sg.);
ὅλως (adv.) 'wholly', 'altogether'; οὐχ ὅλως 'not at all'

[15. ψευδες ἔσοπτρον ἔχει Δημοσθενίς· εἰ γαρ
ἀληθὲς
ἔβλεπεν, οὐκ ᾽αν ὅλως ἤθελεν αὐτο βλέ-
πειν.]

Greek Anthology

γέλως, -ωτος, ὁ 'laughter'; ἄ-
καιρος, -ον 'unseasonable'; βροτός, -οῦ, ὁ 'mortal'

16. γέλως ἄκαιρος ἐν βροτοῖς δεινὸν κακόν.

Menander

πρεσβύτερος, -α, -ον 'elder';
παραμυθία, -ας, ἡ 'consolation';
πένης, πένητος, ὁ 'poor man';
'pauper'

17. τὴν παιδείαν εἶπε τοῖς μὲν νέοις σωφροσύνην, τοῖς δὲ πρεσβυτέροις παραμυθίαν,
τοῖς δὲ πένησι πλοῦτον, τοῖς δὲ πλουσί-
οις κόσμον εἶναι.

Diogenes Laertius (the subject is Diogenes)

ῥίζα, -ης, ἡ 'root'; πικρός, -ά,
-όν 'bitter'; καρπός, -οῦ, ὁ
'fruit'

18. τῆς παιδείας ἔφη τὰς μὲν ῥίζας εἶναι πι-
κράς, τὸν δὲ καρπὸν γλυκύν.

Diogenes Laertius (the sayings of
Aristotle)

κενός, -ή, -όν 'void' ('empty')

19. ἀλλὰ μὴν καὶ τὸ πᾶν ἐστι σώματα καὶ κενόν.

Diogenes Laertius (quoting Epicurus)

ἐρωτηθείς 'asked', 'having been
asked' (aor. pass. ptcpl.); τί
γηράσκει 'what grows old?'; ταχύ
(as adv.) 'quickly'

20. ἐρωτηθεὶς τί γηράσκει ταχύ, 'χάρις' ἔφη.

Diogenes Laertius (a saying of Aristotle)

προσεπιμετρεῖ 'assigns over and
above' (3rd sg. pres.)

[21. τὸ πολὺ τῆς ἡμέρας προσεπιμετρεῖ τῷ ὕπνῳ.]

Athenaeus

ἐλεύθερος, -α, -ον 'free' (as
noun, 'free man')

22. ἐλευθέρου γάρ ἐστι τἀληθῆ λέγειν.

Menander

διδάσκαλος, -ου, ὁ 'teacher'

23. πολλῶν ὁ καιρὸς γίνεται διδάσκαλος.

Menander

νόσος, -ου, ἡ 'illness'

24. ὕπνος δὲ πάσης ἐστὶν ὑγίεια νόσου.

Menander

γαῖα, -ας, ἡ 'earth'; τροφός,
-οῦ, ὁ 'nurse'

25. μήτηρ ἁπάντων γαῖα καὶ κοινὴ τροφός.

Menander

πάντως adv. of πᾶς; νιν 'him';
εὐπιθής, -ές 'compliant', 'ready
to obey'

[26. πάντως γὰρ οὐ πείσεις νιν· οὐ γὰρ εὐπιθής.]

Aeschylus, *Prometheus* (Prometheus
speaks to Oceanus, referring to
Zeus)

φοβερός, -ά, -όν 'fearful'; πρόσωπον, -ου, τό 'face', 'mask'; ὁρῶ 'I see'

27. ἐκ τῶν φοβερῶν τῶνδε προσώπων μέγα κέρδος ὁρῶ τοῖσδε πολίταις.

Aeschylus, *Eumenides*

συνήθεια, -ας, ἡ 'association'; Φανία voc. of Φανίας

28. ἔργον ἐστί, Φανία, μακρὰν συνήθειαν βραχεῖ λῦσαι χρόνῳ.

Menander

ὧδε 'here' (adv.); κεῖται 'lies' (3rd sg. present); Διός, Διά gen. & acc. of Ζεύς; τάφος, -ου, ὁ 'tomb'; κικλήσκουσιν 'they call'

29. ῟Ωδε μέγας κεῖται Ζᾶν ὃν Δία κικλήσκουσιν. (εἰς τάφον τοῦ Διὸς ἐν Κρήτῃ)

Pythagoras (in Greek Anth.)

κύκνος 'swan'; ταῦρος 'bull'; σάτυρος 'satyr'; χρυσός 'gold'; ἔρως, ἔρωτος, ὁ 'love'

30. Ζεὺς κύκνος, ταῦρος, σάτυρος, χρυσὸς δι' ἔρωτα
Λήδης, Εὐρώπης, Ἀντιόπης, Δανάης.

Greek Anthology (the many faces of Zeus and his many indiscretions with the ladies)

ἀπόλωλεν 'has passed away', 'is dead' (3rd sg. perfect tense)

31. ἀπόλωλεν ὁ Ζεύς.

Aristophanes

ὀφθαλμός, -οῦ, ὁ 'eye'; ἐκεῖ 'there' (adv.)

32. ὀξὺς θεῶν ὀφθαλμὸς εἰς τὰ πάντ' ἐκεῖ κακά.

Menander

33. σκηνὴ πᾶς ὁ βίος.

Euripides

τίς 'who?' (nom. sg. m./f.); σε 'you' (acc. sg.)

34. τίς οὕτως ἐστὶ δεινὸς λέγειν ὥστε σε πείσει;

Xenophon, *Anabasis*

ἐρημία, -ας, ἡ 'desert'

35. μεγάλη πόλις μεγάλη ἐρημία.

Greek Proverb

στοά, -ᾶς, ἡ 'stoa', 'Stoic school' (of philosophy)

36. εἰ μὴ γὰρ ἦν Χρύσιππος, οὐκ 'ἀν ἦν στοά.

Diogenes Laertius

ἐξ + ἔρχομαι; ἐξ + ἀγγέλλω; κρίσις noun (cf. κρίνω); Ὀρόντα gen. of Ὀρόντας

[37. ἐπεὶ δ' ἐξῆλθον, ἐξήγγειλε τοῖς φίλοις τὴν κρίσιν τοῦ Ὀρόντα ὡς ἐγένετο.]

Xenophon, *Anabasis*

παρθένος, -ου, ἡ 'maiden', 'virgin'; φρέσιν dat. pl. of φρήν, φρενός, ἡ 'mind', 'heart'; τάχα (adv. cf. ταχύς) 'quickly', 'soon'

38. εἰ δ' ἡ Διὸς παῖς παρθένος Δίκη παρῆν ἔργοις ἐκείνου καὶ φρέσιν, ταχ' 'ἀν τόδ' ἦν.

Aeschylus, *Seven against Thebes* (Eteocles is referring to the claim of his brother, Polynices, that he will return home with justice: but justice is only pictured on his shield; she is not in his heart.)

σχεδόν 'near', 'almost' (adv.); μέσος 'middle', 'in the middle of' (-η, -ον)

39. ὅτε ταῦτα ἦν, σχεδὸν μέσαι ἦσαν νύκτες.

    Xenophon

δεῖ 'it is necessary'

40. εἰ ἡσυχίαν Φίλιππος ἄγει, οὐκέτι δεῖ λέγειν.

    Demosthenes

41. εἰ ἦσαν ἄνδρες ἀγαθοί, ὡς σὺ φῇς, οὐκ ἂν ποτε ταῦτα ἔπασχον.

    Plato, *Gorgias*

συμφέρον 'advantageous' (neut. sg. nom./acc.); ῥώμη, -ης, ἡ 'strength'; σοφία (noun, cf. σοφός); τὰ ἐπίκτητα 'acquired things'

42. σώματι μὲν οὖν ἐστὶ συμφέρον ῥώμη κάλλος ὑγίεια, ψυχῇ δὲ ἀνδρεία σοφία δικαιοσύνη, τὰ δ' ἐπίκτητα φίλοι χρήματα κτήματα.

    'Aristotle' (Rhetoric to Alexander)

ἱκόμην (aor. of ἱκνέομαι) 'come' (1st sg.); ἐκάλεις impf. of 'call' (2nd sg.)

43. οὐδ' ἱκόμην ἔγωγ' ἄν, εἰ σὺ μὴ 'κάλεις.

    Sophocles *O.T.* (Teiresias speaking to Oedipus)

ὁρᾷς 'you see' (pres. of ὁράω, 2nd sg.); ὡς ἔχει 'how it is/ they are'; σοι 'to you' (dat. sg.)

44. Ἄδμηθ', ὁρᾷς γὰρ τἀμὰ πράμαθ' ὡς ἔχει, λέξαι θέλω σοι πρὶν θανεῖν ἃ βούλομαι.

    Euripides, *Alcestis* (Alcestis about to make her last request)

ἀφίκοντο (aor. of ἀφικνέομαι) 'arrive' (3rd pl.); στρατηγός, -οῦ, ὁ 'general'

45. ἔμειναν ἕως ἀφίκοντο οἱ στρατηγοί.

    Xenophon

διδάσκω 'teach'; μ' = με 'me' (acc. sg.); βίοτος = βίος

46. πολλὰ διδάσκει μ' ὁ πολὺς βίοτος.

    Euripides

47. πόλεμος πάντων μὲν πατήρ ἐστι, πάντων δὲ βασιλεύς.

    Heraclitus

48. οὐκ εἶπον μὲν ταῦτα, οὐκ ἔγραψα δέ.

    Demosthenes

Read and learn:

    ἐὰν ᾖς φιλομαθής, ἔσει πολυμαθής.

If you are a lover of learning, you will be learned.

    --Isocrates *To Demonicus*

LESSON VII

Participles: Present, Future, Aorist Active and Middle/Middle-
  Passive

Definition

Participles are *verbal adjectives:* that is, they have the
qualities of both verbs and adjectives. Dionysius Thrax defines
the participle as follows: Μετοχή ἐστι λέξις μετέχουσα τῆς τῶν ῥημάτων
καὶ τῆς τῶν ὀνομάτων ἰδιότητος: "A participle is a part of speech
which shares (lit. sharing) the peculiarities both of verbs and
nouns/adjectives" (remember that adjectives are classed under ὀνόματα in Greek grammatical theory). As adjectives they are declined in gender, number, and case, and agree with a noun (whether expressed or implied). As verbs they have tense and voice.
Participles are very common in English, but even more so in
Greek.

Some examples of the uses of participles in English:

1. As adjective (Attributive Use)
    The *established* Church
    The *ruling* class
    The *missing* link

2. As a descriptive clause (Circumstantial or Adjective Clause)
    The soup is on the stove, *boiling* away.
    The Greek troops, *led* by Agamemnon, defeated Troy
in ten years' time.
    Does she really learn while *sleeping?*

3. Objective and Supplementary
    He stopped *talking.*

(4. Treatment of the use of participles in forming compound tenses, as 'I wasn't *talking*'; 'I have never *done* that--
since this use is so well known--will be omitted.)

The most important thing to keep in mind is that *particles are adjectives derived from verbs*. A participle can have *tense:* this can be seen in the first two examples: "established" is in form a *past* participle; "ruling" is *present*. In Greek there are present, future, aorist, and perfect participles. Furthermore, the participle has *voice:* again in the two examples, "established" is passive; "ruling," active. Greek has separate forms for active, middle/middle-passive, and in certain tenses passive participles.

Formation and Declension of Participles

Review ὁ ἄρχων (Lesson V) and πᾶς πᾶσα πᾶν (Lesson VI) for the declension.

All tenses of participles are formed from the corresponding tense stem. (Participles are not augmented.) Thus, the present participle of λύω is formed by adding the proper participial endings to the present stem λυ-. Likewise the future participle is formed from the future stem λυσ- (from λύσω); the aorist from the stem λυσ(α) (from ἔλυσα), etc. (The student should review the principal parts of the various verbs.)

Active Participles

All the active participles (except the perfect, see Lesson VIII) have bases in -ντ-. The thematic tenses (present, future, and second aorist) form active participles in -οντ- (cf. ἄρχων). The first aorist, with its characteristic α, has -αντ- (as in πᾶς, base παντ-). The masculine and neuter are declined in the third declension, the feminine in the first.

a. Participles of λύω: present, future, first aorist:

		Active			
		M.	F.	N.	
Present:	stem λυ-:	λύων	λύουσα	λῦον	base λυοντ-
Future:	stem λυσ-:	λύσων	λύσουσα	λῦσον	base λυσοντ-
First Aorist:	stem λυσ-α:	λύσας	λύσασα	λῦσαν	base λυσαντ-

b. of λείπω: second aorist:

Second Aorist: ἔλιπον stem: λιπ-   λιπών λιποῦσα λιπόν   base: λιποντ-

Paradigms

Present Active Participle of λύω, λύων 'releasing'

Singular

	M	F	N
NOM	λύων	λύουσα	λῦον
GEN	λύοντος	λυούσης	λύοντος
DAT	λύοντι	λυούσῃ	λύοντι
ACC	λύοντα	λύουσαν	λῦον

Plural

	M	F	N
NOM	λύοντες	λύουσαι	λύοντα
GEN	λυόντων	λυουσῶν	λυόντων
DAT	λύουσι(ν)	λυούσαις	λύουσι(ν)
ACC	λύοντας	λυούσας	λύοντα

Future Active Participle of λύω, λύσων 'being about to release'

Singular

	M	F	N
NOM	λύσων	λύσουσα	λῦσον
GEN	λύσοντος	λυσούσης	λύσοντας
DAT	λύσοντι	λύσούσῃ	λύσοντι
ACC	λύσοντα	λύσουσαν	λῦσον

Plural

	M	F	N
NOM	λύσοντες	λύσουσαι	λύσοντα
GEN	λύσόντων	λυσουσῶν	λυσόντων
DAT	λύσουσι(ν)	λυσούσαις	λύσουσι(ν)
ACC	λύσοντας	λυσούσας	λύσοντα

First Aorist Active Participle of λύω, λύσας 'having released'

Singular

	M	F	N
NOM	λύσας	λύσασα	λῦσαν
GEN	λύσαντος	λυσάσης	λύσαντος
DAT	λύσαντι	λυσάσῃ	λύσαντι
ACC	λύσαντα	λύσασαν	λῦσαν

Plural

	M	F	N
NOM	λύσαντες	λύσασαι	λύσαντα
GEN	λυσάντων	λυσασῶν	λυσάντων
DAT	λύσασι(ν)	λυσάσαις	λύσασι(ν)
ACC	λύσαντας	λυσάσας	λύσαντα

Second Aorist Active Participle of λείπω, λιπών 'having left'

Singular

	M	F	N
NOM	λιπών	λιποῦσα	λιπόν
GEN	λιπόντος	λιπούσης	λιπόντος
DAT	λιπόντι	λιπούσῃ	λιπόντι
ACC	λιπόντα	λιποῦσαν	λιπόν

Plural

	M	F	N
NOM	λιπόντες	λιποῦσαι	λιπόντα
GEN	λιπόντων	λιπουσῶν	λιπόντων
DAT	λιποῦσι(ν)	λιπούσαις	λιποῦσι
ACC	λιπόντας	λιπούσας	λιπόντα

Present Active Participle of εἰμί, ὤν 'being'

	Singular			Plural		
	M	F	N	M	F	N
NOM	ὤν	οὖσα	ὄν	ὄντες	οὖσαι	ὄντα
GEN	ὄντος	οὔσης	ὄντος	ὄντων	οὐσῶν	ὄντων
DAT	ὄντι	οὔσῃ	ὄντι	οὖσι(ν)	οὔσαις	οὖσι(ν)
ACC	ὄντα	οὖσαν	ὄν	ὄντας	οὔσας	ὄντα

Learn this as a review of the endings of the participles in -οντ-. Note that the accent of the second aorist participle is like that of εἰμί.

Middle and Middle-Passive Participles

The middle and middle-passive participles are formed quite simply by adding -μενος, -́η, -ον to the appropriate stem: -ομενος to thematic tense stems; -αμενος to the first aorist.

Middle/Middle-Passive Participles of λύω

Present (M-P): stem λύ-: λυόμενος, λυομένη, λυόμενον 'ransoming', or 'being freed'

Future (M): stem λύσ-: λυσόμενος, λυσομένη, λυσόμενον 'about to ransom'

First Aorist (M): stem λυσ-α-: λυσάμενος, -́η, -ον 'having ransomed'

of λείπω: second aorist (ἔλιπον)

Second Aorist (M): stem λιπ-: λιπόμενος, λιπομένη, λιπόμενον

These are declined in the same way as -ος, -η, -ον adjectives (cf. ἄριστος).

Example: Present Middle-Passive Participle of λύω: λυόμενος.

Singular

	M	F	N
NOM	λυόμενος	λυομένη	λυόμενον
GEN	λυομένου	λυομένης	λυομένου
DAT	λυομένῳ	λυομένῃ	λυομένῳ
ACC	λυόμενον	λυομένην	λυόμενον

Plural

	M	F	N
NOM	λυόμενοι	λυόμεναι	λυόμενα
GEN	λυομένων	λυομένων	λυομένων
DAT	λυομένοις	λυομέναις	λυομένοις
ACC	λυομένους	λυομένας	λυόμενα

Participles are not so very difficult once one recognizes the logic of them and understands what they are: adjectives derived from verbs. The word "participle" comes from the Latin word *participium* (a 'sharing' or 'partaking'), which is a direct translation of the Greek word μετοχή. The Greeks thought of the participle as a separate part of speech, but as the name implies they recognized clearly enough that it shared the characteristics of two other parts of speech. We do not usually think of the participle as a separate part of speech, but we should realize that the parts of speech are not necessarily mutually exclusive.

Uses of the Participle in Greek

There are in general three ways of using participles:

General Usage:

1. *Attributive:* The participle is used as an adjective, modifying the noun in the same way as the adjective does, often with the article (e.g. a *moving* vehicle, a *dangling* participle).

2. *Circumstantial:* The participle, used without the article, in agreement with a noun or pronoun (expressed or implied) and introducing a clause which defines the circumstances of an action (i.e. an action as expressed by the main verb). "He went home, *disgusted* at the behavior of his colleagues." Under this heading also comes the genitive absolute.

3. *Supplementary:* The participle is used to complete the idea expressed by the verb; there are a number of Greek uses that differ from our usage. Also under this heading we may place the use of the participle after verbs of perception and in indirect statement. ("Stop *doing* that!" or "Keep on *going*!" or "He finished *eating*" which correspond to Greek usage.)

Examples of the Uses of Participles in Greek

   1. *Attributive (as adjective)*

      a. Used with a noun and often with an article:

         ὁ παρὼν χρόνος 'the present time' (παρών,
         present participle of πάρειμι 'being present')

Many English participles do not lend themselves to this use, and for this reason, many of the Greek participles must be paraphrased in the English translation either by a relative clause or by an adjective or noun: this is especially true of the attributive participle used as a noun (b).

      b. Like any adjective, the participle may be used as a noun with the article (the *man*, *woman*, or *thing* being omitted; cf. οἱ ἀγαθοί 'the good': the masculine gender makes it clear that 'the good men' is implied). In the same way, a participle may be used as a noun with the article:

   Examples:

οἱ φεύγοντες	'those who flee'; 'the fugitives', 'the exiles'
ὁ διώκων and ὁ φεύγων	'the one who pursues' and 'the one who flees': in a courtroom context, 'the prosecutor' and 'the defendant'.
ὁ ἄρχων	'the one who rules', originally a participle from ἄρχω ('the ruling man'), hence 'the ruler', so common that it is considered a noun.
τὸ ἄρχον	in the neuter, 'that which rules' ('the ruling thing') can best be translated as 'the ruling party'.

   Interesting too are the uses of the neuter participles of εἰμί: τὸ ὄν and τὰ ὄντα 'that which is/exists'; 'those things which are/exist' (lit. 'existing' things) respectively; but both may be translated as 'the universe'. Cf. also τὰ πάροντα 'the present circumstances'.

οἱ ἔχοντες and οἱ οὐκ ἔχοντες 'those who have' and 'those who do not have', i.e. 'the rich' and 'the poor' or 'the haves' and 'the have-nots'.

c. Remember that the participle is a verbal form, and so can take an object: ὁ ταῦτα εἰπών (lit. 'the one having said these things') 'the one who said these things'.

2. *Circumstantial*

The circumstantial participle defines the circumstances surrounding the action of the main verb, and may express *time, manner/means, cause, condition, concession,* that is, *when, in/by, since/because, if, although* respectively. It can also be merely *descriptive.* The context (or sense) of the sentence will usually tell you which is intended, though sometimes more than one of these relations may be implied. These different types of the circumstantial participle do not differ from one another *except in context;* therefore it is not necessary or desirable to make a sharp distinction among them. When translating them, first translate them literally, even though it may be awkward in English (having done, doing, having been done, etc.), and then as the whole sentence becomes clearer, an appropriate word such as "if," "when," "although" may be added. There are, to be sure, some clues which will sometimes make the meaning clearer (e.g. whether οὐ or μή is used, and a number of particles).

1. *Time ("when," "after"): Temporal*

In narration, the participle is very common (see the sections from Apollodorus in the readings: Apollodorus in fact tends to over-use them, making his style predictable and rather dull; the stories, however, should be interesting, and the syntax, at this point, challenging) for a series of events. The use of the participle can extend the sentence indefinitely as you will see when you read long passages from Thucydides and Isocrates.

In English, when narrating a series of events, we tend to use a series of finite verbs in separate clauses (whether coordinate or subordinate). We may say (for example) "After killing the man, he got away," or "He killed the man and got away," or "After he killed the man, he got away," etc. The first uses a participle; the second two coordinate clauses, and the third a subordinate clause. In Greek the verb of the first clause would be expressed by a participle in the *aorist*, that of the second by a finite verb:

> τὸν ἄνθρωπον ἀποκτείνας, ἔφυγεν.

There are other ways of expressing this in Greek, but this would be the most common and the easiest. (Note that when you have the word "after," it is best to use the *aorist* participle.)

Another example:

> φεύγοντες ἀπέθανον '*fleeing* (while they were fleeing) they
>   were killed'

Participles used with temporal particles:

ἅμα   'at once', 'at the same time'

   ἅμα εἰπὼν ἔβαλε τὸν λίθον 'at the same time as speaking he threw the
     stone.'

αὐτίκα   'forthwith', 'at once'

   αὐτίκα γενόμενος 'as soon as born'

μεταξύ   'in the midst of', 'meanwhile', 'while'

   μεταξὺ θύων 'while sacrificing'

   λέγοντα μεταξύ 'in the midst of the discourse'

2. *Causal ("because," "since")*

Examples:

> πολλα εἶπε, βουλόμενος τον βασιλέα πεῖσαι.

He said many things, *because he wished* to persuade the king.

The causal particles that can be used with participles are:

ἅτε   'inasmuch as', 'seeing that'

ἅτε τὰ χρήματα ἔχων 'seeing that he has the money'

ὡς, ὥσπερ   as causal particles give an alleged cause for which
                            the speaker/writer does not wish to take credit.
                            They may be translated as 'as if', 'as though', 'as
                            thinking', 'on the ground that'.

θαυμάζονται ὡς σοφοὶ ὄντες 'They are admired as if (on the ground that)
    they are wise.'

δεδίασι τὸν θάνατον ὡς εὖ εἰδότες ὅτι μέγιστον τῶν κακῶν ἐστι. 'They
    fear death *as though* they *know* well that it is the greatest of evils.

        --Plato, *Apology*

3. *Manner and Means ("in," "by")*

        τὴν ἀσπίδα ἀποβαλών, ἔφυγε τὸν θάνατον.

    By throwing away his shield, he escaped death.   (means)

            --Xenophon

        ἥκει τὰ χαλεπὰ φερόμενα.

    (lit. 'The troubles have come *being borne*.')

    The troubles have come *with a rush*.   (manner)(an idiomatic use of the
middle-passive participle of φέρω)

4. *Conditional ("if")*

        ταῦτα λέγων, οὐκ 'ἂν τὴν ἀλήθειαν ἔλεγες.

    ('Saying these things you would not be speaking the truth')

    'If you were saying these things, you would not be speaking the truth.'

    The negative in the participial clause (which represents the
if-clause or *protasis* of the condition) is μή: this will give
you a hint to translate it as a condition, since most other uses
of the participle take οὐ as negative.

        σοφοὶ μὴ ὄντες, οὐχ ἕξετε μαθητάς.

    ('Not being wise, you will not have pupils') 'If you are not wise . . .'

5. *Concession ("although")*

        πολλὰ χρήματα ἔχων, οὐκ εἰμί εὐτυχής.

    'Although I have much money, I am not happy.'

    The particles καίπερ and καί ('although', 'even though') can
also be used with the circumstantial participle of concession.

6.   *Purpose ("to," "in order to")* is usually expressed by the future participle, sometimes with ὡς.

>   ἦλθε λυσόμενος θύγατρα (= θυγατέρα)
>
> He came *to ransom* his daughter.   --*Iliad* I.13

>   ὁ ἡγησόμενος οὐδεὶς ἔσται.
>
> There will be no one *to lead* (us)/*who will lead*.   --Xenophon

7.   *Description*

>   ἦλθε πολλὰ δῶρα φέρων (or ἔχων)
>
> He came *bearing* many gifts.

The participles ἔχων, φέρων, ἄγων, λαβών are often used idiomat-
ically and may be translated as 'with'.

>   ἔρχεται τὸν υἱὸν ἔχουσα
>
> She came *bringing* her son, *or* she came *with* her son.   --Xenophon

The Genitive Absolute

The genitive absolute is a special use of the circumstantial
participle. A noun or pronoun and a participle are put into the
genitive case in an absolute construction (so called because it
does not agree with any other words in the sentence, and stands
by itself, grammatically). It is translated by a clause and can
be used to express any of the same attendant circumstances as the
circumstantial participle. In English we have such a construction, though by now it is falling into disuse: it is called the
nominative absolute (English being severely limited in the number
of its cases): for example, "*On the door being opened*, she perceived a couch." (example from Partridge). The clause in italics
is an *absolute* construction; grammatically it stands outside the
main clause. On the other hand, had we written "Upon opening the
door, she perceived a couch," the participial clause would be a
descriptive, adjectival one agreeing with "she." A common expression in English which uses a nominative absolute is "all
things being equal." In the absolute construction, then, the
participial clause which describes the circumstances stands out-

side the main sentence grammatically. The genitive absolute in
Greek (like the ablative absolute in Latin) is very common indeed, and very versatile, owing to the many forms and uses of the
Greek participle. It can express time, manner, means, cause,
condition, concession, purpose, and description, and can be used
plain or with any of the particles that can accompany the participles.

Examples:

καὶ τῶν φίλων τὴν χώραν λιπόντων, ἐμείναμεν.

Although our friends left the place, we remained.

τοῦ φίλου μὴ ἐλθόντος, ἐλίπομεν 'ἂν τὴν χώραν.

If our friend had not come, we would have left the place.

τῶν πολιτῶν δικαίων ὄντων, δικαία ἐστὶ ἡ πόλις.

Because the citizens are just, the city is just.

τοῦ πατρὸς οὐ βουλομένου, ταῦτα οὐ πράξομεν.

Since father does not wish it, we will not do these things.

λόγων γενομένων, ἀπῆλθον οἱ νεανίαι καὶ αἱ γυναῖκες.

The conversation having taken place (after the conversation), the
young men and the women departed.

Some examples from Greek authors:

1. καὶ Πολυφόντου κελεύοντος ἐκχωρεῖν, . . . Οἰδίπους
    καὶ Πολυφόντην καὶ Λάϊον ἀπέκτεινε.

                         --Apollodorus

And when Polyphontes ordered [him] to get out of the way, Oedipus
    killed Polyphontes and Laius.

2. 'Αθηναίων δὲ τὸ αὐτὸ τοῦτο παθόντων, διπλασίαν 'ἂν
    τὴν δύναμιν εἰκάζεσθαι (οἶμαι) . . .

                         --Thucydides

If the Athenians should experience this same thing, I think their
    power would be estimated as double.

3. πῶς δίκης οὔσης ὁ Ζεὺς οὐκ ἀπόλωλεν;

                         --Aristophanes

If justice exists, how is it that Zeus has not perished?

Note: A rarer construction is the accusative absolute, which is used in the same way as the genitive absolute, but is restricted to the participles of impersonal verbs: these are put into the accusative in the neuter singular.

3. *Supplementary*

The supplementary participle is more closely related to the verb: it is used to complete the meaning of the verb, and without it the idea is incomplete. The supplementary participle may go with either the subject or the object of the verb, for example:

παύω (active): παύω τὸν ἄνδρα λέγοντα

I stop the man (from) speaking.

παύομαι (middle): παύομαι λέγων/λέγουσα

I stop (myself) speaking or I cease speaking.

This construction is found with verbs meaning 'begin', 'continue', 'stop' (cf. in English "keep on keeping on," etc.). Also with those meaning 'repent', 'be weary', 'be pleased' or 'displeased', 'allow'.

ἄρξομαι λέγων 'I shall begin speaking.'

παύσω τοῦτο γιγνόμενον 'I shall stop this from happening.' (Plato)

Note: It is very interesting that some of these verbs may take both the supplementary participle and the supplementary infinitive constructions, but with different meanings.

Examples:

αἰσχύνομαι	'be ashamed'
αἰσχύνομαι λέγων	'I am ashamed speaking', i.e. 'I speak with shame'
αἰσχύνομαι λέγειν	'I am ashamed to speak' (and so, do not speak)

In the first example, the participle 'speaking' (λέγων) implies that I am actually speaking, ashamed or not; in the second, the infinitive, 'to speak' (λέγειν), implies that my shame prevents me from speaking. This subtle difference in construction can make a great deal of difference in meaning.

There are several verbs in Greek which take a supplementary participle in a way that seems odd to us at first, because it differs from English usage.

τυγχάνω 'happen' (we use the infinitive, Greek uses the participle):

> τυγχάνει δίκαιος ὤν 'He happens to be (lit. *being)* honest' or 'He really is honest'.

(Often forms of τυγχάνω are used to emphasize that something is indeed true.)

λανθάνω 'escape the notice of' (we usually translate the participle by a finite verb and express the form of λανθάνω by an adverb, 'unawares', 'without being observed'):

> οὐ λανθάνει κακὸς ὤν   Literally: 'He does not escape notice being wicked.'

> ἔλαθον ἐσελθόντες 'They got in secretly.' Thucydides (ἐσ- = εἰσ-)

φθάνω 'anticipate', 'be beforehand' (the action in which one is ahead of somebody else is expressed by the participle):

> ἔφθασαν τοὺς φίλους ἐλθόντες Literally: 'They anticipated their friends having come.' Or, 'They got there before their friends'/'They got the jump on their friends . . .'

In all these constructions, the main verbal idea is contained in the participle rather than in the finite verb.

Other Uses of the Supplementary Participle:

In *Indirect Statement:* with verbs of *knowing* (and the opposite, 'be ignorant', 'forget') and *showing,* and with verbs of sense perception ('see', 'hear', 'feel') the participle is used in indirect statement.

Examples:

> ἡ ψυχὴ ἀθάνατος φαίνεται οὖσα. --Plato

It appears that the soul is immortal.

> ὁρῶμεν πάντα ἀληθῆ ὄντα ἃ λέγετε. --Xenophon

We see that everything you say is true.

> ἤκουσε Κῦρον ἐν Κιλικίᾳ ὄντα. --Xenophon

He heard that Cyrus was in Cilicia.

With *Verbs of Perception*, you may also have the participle not in indirect statement, but modifying the object of the verb. (As in the English examples, 'I saw Mommy kissing Santa Claus' or 'I hear him coming', compare with 'I hear that he is coming'.)

The verbs ἀκούω and αἰσθάνομαι take their objects in the genitive case (except in indirect statement). Ponder the following examples:

> ἀκούω τοῦ σοφοῦ λέγοντος. 'I hear the wise man speaking.' (That is, I actually hear him.)
>
> ἀκούω τὸν σοφὸν λέγοντα. 'I hear that the wise man is speaking.'

Tenses of the Participle

The tenses of the participle (except in indirect statement) represent time only as relative to the main verb. The *present* refers to an action *at the same time* as that of the main verb ('while'); the *aorist* refers to time *previous* to that of the main verb ('after', 'having . . .'). The *future* participle is used for expressing *purpose* or *intention*, and is rarely used otherwise.

In indirect statement, however, the participle's tense represents the same tense of a finite verb, that is, the tense of the original statement (as in the infinitive construction, cf. Lesson IV).

Notes on Participles:

1. "There is but one difference between the supplementary and circumstantial participles. It lies in the fact that the circumstantial participle is an additional statement and does not form an essential part of the verbal notion of the principal verb [as does the supplementary participle]. The circumstantial participle may be removed and the sentence will not bleed." (A. T. Robertson, *A Grammar of the Greek New Testament in the Light of Historical Research*, p. 1124)

2. The problem of the *dangling* participle: in our modern education, our introduction to participles in our own language (if in fact we are introduced to them at all) is usually in connection with the problem of "the dangling participle": this is a problem which does not occur in Greek. Consider why not.

An example of a dangling participle in English is:

"I saw the Grand Canyon, *driving* through Arizona."

Actually we know what this means: that I saw it while I was driving, because the grammatically correct alternative--that the Grand Canyon was driving--is absurd (or at best the product of hallucination). On the other hand, in the sentence

"I saw that man, driving my car."

if it means that I was driving my car and saw him, it does not say so. In the first example, the probable meaning is clear and the only risk a speaker of such a sentence would run is that he would not understand the snickering, tittering, or guffawing in his audience. In the second sentence, carelessness could lead to confusion. This is true because in English *place* (position of the words) is very important. In Greek there is no confusion about what word(s) the particple 'goes with', because it will be in the same case as the word(s) it means to agree with. (For example, if it goes with the subject, it will be nominative; if with the object, accusative, and its place in the sentence is not of importance.)

3. The Greeks were φιλομέτοχοι (fond of participles). And Greek has a rich system of participles, richer than Latin or English, for example. Latin has no present passive nor perfect active participles. And English must resort to long periphrases to translate some of the participles (notably the future participle). It may be said that wherever a participle is possible, Greek has one. This wealth of participles gives a great deal of flexibility to the language, as you will see, the more you read.

Vocabulary

Verbs

αἰσθάνομαι, αἰσθήσομαι, ἠσθόμην	*perceive, sense, understand, learn, hear* (+ gen.) (aesthetic)
αἰσχύνομαι (princ. pts. Appendix II)	*be ashamed* (cf. αἰσχρός)(also in act. αἰσχύνω 'to disgrace')
βασιλεύω (reg. princ. pts.)	*be king, rule* (+ gen.)(cf. βασιλεύς)
βλέπω, βλέψομαι, ἔβλεψα	*look, see*
γιγνώσκω, γνώσομαι	*come to know, perceive* (aor. will be given later)(cf. γνώμη)
διώκω, διώξω, ἐδίωξα	*pursue, chase*
διαφέρω (see φέρω)	*carry over/across; differ, surpass*
εἶδον	*saw* (second aorist, stem ἰδ-: partic. ἰδών, infin. ἰδεῖν)(related to Latin *video*)
εὑρίσκω, εὑρήσω, εὗρον (or ηὗρον)	*find* (pf. εὕρηκα 'Eureka!'; heuristic)
κελεύω, κελεύσω, ἐκέλευσα	*urge, exhort, bid, order*
λανθάνω, λήσω, ἔλαθον	*escape notice* (+ partic.)(cf. λήθη 'Lethe')

πυνθάνομαι, πεύσομαι,   *learn*
   ἐπυθόμην
τυγχάνω, τεύξομαι, ἔ-   *happen* (+ partic.), *meet* (+ gen.)(cf. τύχη)
   τυχον
ὑπάρχω   *begin, exist, belong to* (cf. ἄρχω)
φεύγω, φεύξομαι (φευ-   *flee, take flight, avoid, escape* (cf. Latin *fugio*,
   ξοῦμαι), ἔφυγον   Engl. 'fugitive')
φθάνω, φθήσομαι, ἔφθα-   *be beforehand, outstrip* (with partic.)
   σα

Compounds of εἰμί: conjugated like εἰμί

ἄπειμι   *be away, be absent*
πάρειμι   *be present, be near, stand by* (impersonal: πάρεστι
                            + dative 'it depends on . . .')
πρόσειμι   *be added to, belong to*
σύνειμι   *be with, live with, have dealings with*

Ζεύς, Διός, ὁ   *Zeus* (dat. Διί, acc. Δία, voc. Ζεῦ)(μὰ τὸν Δία 'by
                            Zeus!')

Particles (used with participles)

ἅμα   *at once, at the same time*
ἅτε   *since, inasmuch as*
αὐτίκα   *at once, forthwith*
μεταξύ   *in the midst, while*
ὡς   *as if, as, on the ground that*

Exercises

   1. Review the verbs you have had so far, and form the participles for each (orally or in writing). For a complete verb
there will be six participles (so far; there are more yet to
come). Remember that the participle is not augmented.

   2. Form and decline the following participles

        1. Present active of ἔχω

        2. Aorist active of βάλλω

        3. Future active of φέρω

        4. Aorist active of παύω

        5. Future middle of γίγνομαι

   3. Parse:

Example: λύσαντα, aorist active participle of λύω, masc. acc. sg.
or neuter nom./acc. pl.

Note on recognizing participles:

-οντ- tells you that it is an active participle of one of the thematic tenses: future, present, or second aorist.

      1. most futures will have σ before the -οντ-

      2. the second aorist is usually accented on the
         o-sound

-αντ- tells you that you are dealing with the first aorist participle.

    -ομενος middle/middle-passive of a thematic tense.

    -αμενος middle of the first aorist.

1. γενομένου	13. λεγομένην	25. ἀκούσας	37. λανθανόντων
2. παρόν	14. ἔχουσαι	26. νομίζων	38. μέλλοντος
3. αἰσθανομένη	15. ἀποθανόντος	27. κελεύοντος	39. συνόντες
4. γιγνώσκοντες	16. εἰπών	28. κτείναντος	40. ἀγαγόντος
5. ἔχοντες	17. ἰδόντας	29. βασιλεύων	41. λύσαντας
6. ὄντας	18. πέμψασαν	30. βασιλεύοντος	42. πείσουσαν
7. ὄντων	19. λαβουσῶν	31. μαθοῦσα	43. ἄρχουσι
8. λέγοντες	20. φερόμεναι	32. ὑπάρχοντος	44. πάσχοντα
9. κτείνας	21. εἰπόντος	33. πυθομένας	45. ἐσομέναις
10. ὤν	22. εὑρόντες	34. λύσοντι	46. βαλόντες
11. γενόμενος	23. βουλόμενα	35. ἀκούσας	47. βαλλούσης
12. μανθανόντων	24. πυνθανόμενος	36. οὔσῃ	48. πραξάσας

    4. **Translate.**

1. ὁ γέρων ἦλθεν ἔχων πολλὰ δῶρα.

2. πάρεστιν ἡ γυνὴ ἄγουσα τὸν παῖδα.

3. οἱ φεύγοντες ὑπὸ τῶν διωκόντων διώκονται.

4. ὁ ἄρχων ἄρχει τῶν ἀρχομένων.

5. ὁ κόσμος ἐλέγετο τὸ 'ὸν καὶ τὰ ὄντα.

6. ὁ γὰρ ἱερεὺς ἦλθεν ὡς λυσόμενος τὴν θυγατέρα πολλοῖς χρήμασι.

7. ἀλλ' ὁ βασιλεὺς ἐθέλων τὴν γυναῖκα ἔχειν, οὐκ ἔλαβε τὰ χρήματα.

8. οἱ οὐκ ἔχοντες οὔποτε φίλοι ἔσονται τοῖς ἔχουσιν.

9. τὸν λίθον βαλὸν τὸ παιδίον ἔφυγεν.

10. εἶπε πολλὰ ὡς πείσουσα τὸν βασιλέα.

11. ὁ δαίμων τὸν ἄνδρα λέγοντα μεταξὺ ἔπαυσεν.

12. παύσομαι λέγουσα καὶ ἄρξεσθε λέγοντες.

13. τὸν πατέρα μεταξὺ θύοντα ἀπέτειναν.

14. εἶπον ὅτι ἀπέκτειναν τοῦτον ὡς ἄδικον ὄντα.

15. ξένοι ὄντες ἐρχόμεθα εἰς ταύτην τὴν χώραν.

16. ✓ τυγχάνω ᾽ὢν δίκαιος ἀνήρ. τυγχάνω οὖσα δικαία γυνή.

17. ✓ οὖσα κακὴ οὐκ ἔλαθε τοὺς θεοὺς καὶ τοὺς ἀνθρώπους.

18. ✓ τούτου παρόντος ἤρξαντο λέγοντες.

19. ✓ οὐκ αἰσχύνει ταῦτα πράττων;

20. τῶν ποιητῶν τὴν ἀλήθειαν λεγόντων, ἀθάνατος ἡ τοῦ ἀνθρώπου ψυχή.

21. ἠκούσαμεν τοὺς ποιητὰς λέγοντας.

22. ἤκουον τοῦ σοφοῦ περὶ ἀρετῆς λέγοντος.

23. ᾐσθόμεθα οὐ σοφοὶ ὄντες.

24. καίπερ οὐκ ἰδών, ᾐσθόμην ἐκεῖνον τὸν ἄνδρα παρόντα.

25. ✓ ᾐσχύνοντο οἱ δικασταὶ λαβεῖν δῶρα καὶ χρήματα.

26. οὐκ ἔξεστιν εὑρεῖν ἄνδρα δίκαιον ἐν ταύτῃ τῇ χώρᾳ.

27. χαλεπόν ἐστι γιγνώσκειν τοὺς θεοὺς εἴ εἰσιν ᾽ἢ μή.

28. ὁ γὰρ νόμος τὸν διώκοντα λέγειν κελεύει.

29. εὗρον τὴν γυναῖκα οὖσαν ἄδικον.

30. ✓ ἡ ἐλπὶς ἀποῦσα οὐ τὸν φεύγοντα λανθάνει.

31. τῆς ἐλπίδος ἀπούσης καὶ οἱ ἀγαθοὶ ἔφευγον.

32. τῆς γυναικὸς παρούσης ὁ ἀνὴρ οὐκ ἠθέλησε λέγειν.

33. ἐκείνην τὴν χώραν λιπόντες, κατὰ θάλασσαν πρὸς τὰς νήσους ἤλθομεν.

34. καίπερ τὴν χώραν λιπεῖν βουλόμενοι, ἔμενον.

35. ἄξιόν ἐστι πείθεσθαι τῷ τὴν ἀλήθειαν λέγοντι.

36. καὶ τῶν στρατιωτῶν εἰρήνην ἄγειν βουλομένων, οὐκ ἐπαύσατο ὁ πόλεμος.

37. νέοι ὄντες εὐτυχεῖς ἐστε.

38. οἱ δικασταὶ τὴν ἀλήθειαν μαθόντες ἐβουλεύσαντο καὶ ἔκριναν.

39. ἀπεθάνετε ἄν, τῶν ἀνδρῶν μὴ ἐλθόντων.

40. τῶν παίδων ὄντων εὐδαιμόνων, ὁ πατὴρ καὶ ἡ μήτηρ εἰσὶ εὐδαίμονες.

5. A. Translate into Greek:

1. ✓ He did not kill his father without being observed.

2. ✓ I happen to be speaking to the citizens about war and peace.

3. Although the poets were present, we listened to the philosophers.

4. I heard that that man was in Greece.

5. He came to find an honest man.

6. We admired this man on the ground that he was brave and just.

7. After killing the old man, he became king.

8. The one who said these things was the father of the poet.

   B.   Compose some sentences using the following expressions:

1. τυγχάνω + a participle of ἔρχομαι

2. παύω or παύομαι + a participle of βλέπω

3. αἰσθάνομαι + a participle of εἰμί

4. a genitive absolute using a participle of ἄπειμι

Readings

μνήμη, -ης, ἡ 'memory'; οὐδείς
'no one' (masc. nom. sg.); φαίη
(with ἄν) 'would say' from φημί
(3rd. sg. optative); μνημονεύω
'remember'

1. ἡ δὲ μνήμη τοῦ γενομένου· τὸ δὲ παρὸν
    ὅτε πάρεστιν, οὐδεὶς ἂν φαίη μνημονεύ-
    ειν.

    Aristotle, περὶ μνήμης

καθάπερ 'as'; εἴρηται '(it) has
been said'; πρότερον 'before';
αἴσθησις, -εως, ἡ 'feeling' (cf.
αἰσθάνομαι); ὅσα 'as many as'
(neut. pl. nom./acc.); ζῷον,
-ου, τό 'animal'

2. τοῦ δὲ νῦν ἐν τῷ νῦν οὐκ ἔστι μνήμη, κα-
    θάπερ εἴρηται καὶ πρότερον, ἀλλὰ τοῦ μὲν
    παρόντος αἴσθησις, τοῦ δὲ μέλλοντος ἐλ-
    πίς τοῦ δὲ γενομένου μνήμη. διὸ μετὰ
    χρόνου πᾶσα μνήμη. ὥσθ' ὅσα χρόνου αἰσ-
    θάνεται, ταῦτα μόνα τῶν ζῴων μνημονεύει,
    καὶ τούτῳ ᾧ αἰσθάνεται.

    Aristotle, περὶ μνήμης

σκεπτέον 'it is necessary to
consider'

3. πρῶτον μὲν οὖν σκεπτέον τί τῶν βασιλευ-
    όντων ἔργον ἐστίν.

    Isocrates

μὴ . . . ἤ 'do not be eager to
be wealthy rather than'; δοκεῖν
'to seem' (pres. inf.); δόξα,
-ης, ἡ 'reputation'; πλεῖστος,
-η, -ον 'most'; καθίστανται 'are
established'; βάρβαροι those who
are not Ἕλληνες

4. μὴ σπεύδετε πλουτεῖν μᾶλλον 'ἢ χρηστοὶ
    δοκεῖν εἶναι, γιγνώσκοντες ὅτι καὶ τῶν
    Ἑλλήνων καὶ τῶν βαρβάρων οἱ μεγίστας
    ἐπ' ἀρετῇ δόξας ἔχοντες πλείστων ἀγαθῶν
    δεσπόται καθίστανται.

    Isocrates

ὅταν 'when' (+ subjunctive);
ἀποβλέψωσιν (aor. subj. 3rd. pl.
of ἀποβλέπω) 'look at', 're-
gard'; δυναστεία, -ας, ἡ 'power'; ἰσόθεος (ἴσος + θεός)
'equal to the gods'; μοναρχία --

5. ὅταν μὲν γὰρ ἀποβλέψωσιν εἰς τὰς τιμὰς
    καὶ τοὺς πλούτους καὶ τὰς δυναστείας,
    ἰσοθέους ἅπαντας νομίζουσι τοὺς ἐν ταῖς
    μοναρχίαις ὄντας.

    Isocrates

6. πάντων χρημάτων μέτρον ἐστὶν ἄνθρωπος,
    τῶν μὲν ὄντων ὡς ἔστιν, τῶν δὲ οὐκ ὄντων
    ὡς οὐκ ἔστιν.

    Protagoras

πῶς 'how'; ὡς ἔχει (see p. 148, #44); μέντοι 'certainly', 'however'

7. πῶς λέγεις, ἔφη ὁ Διονυσόδωρος, ὦ Κτήσιππε; εἰσὶ γάρ τινες, οἳ λέγουσι τὰ πράγματα ὡς ἔχει; εἰσὶ μέντοι, ἔφη, οἱ καλοί τε κἀγαθοὶ καὶ οἱ τἀληθῆ λέγοντες.

Plato

For sight-reading in class:

[8. Προμηθεὺς δὲ ἐξ ὕδατος καὶ γῆς ἀνθρώπους πλάσας ἔδωκεν αὐτοῖς καὶ πῦρ, λάθρα Διὸς ἐν νάρθηκι κρύψας, ὡς δὲ ᾔσθετο Ζεὺς ἐπέταξεν Ἡφαίστῳ τῷ Καυκάσῳ ὄρει τὸ σῶμα αὐτοῦ προσηλῶσαι· τοῦτο δὲ Σκυθικὸν ὄρος ἐστίν. ἐν δὴ τούτῳ προσηλωθεὶς Προμηθεὺς πολλῶν ἐτῶν ἀριθμὸν ἐδέδετο· καθ' ἑκάστην δὲ ἡμέραν ἀετὸς ἐφιπτάμενος αὐτῷ τοὺς λοβοὺς ἐνέμετο τοῦ ἥπατος αὐξανομένου διὰ νυκτός. καὶ Προμηθεὺς μὲν πυρὸς κλαπέντος δίκην ἔτινε ταύτην, μέχρις Ἡρακλῆς αὐτὸν ὕστερον ἔλυσεν, ὡς ἐν τοῖς καθ' Ἡρακλέα δηλώσομεν.]

Apollodorus

γῆς gen. of γῆ; πλάσας 'having made/formed'; ἔδωκεν '(he) gave'; αὐτοῖς 'to them'; λάθρα 'in secret (from)' (+ gen.); νάρθηξ 'fennel (stalk)'; κρύπτω 'hide'; προσηλῶσαι 'to nail to' (inf.); προσηλωθείς 'nailed to' (aor. pass. partic.); αὐτοῦ 'his'; ἐπιτάττω, aor. ἐπέταξα 'enjoin', 'order'; ὄρος, -ους, τό 'mountain'; δέω 'bind', ἐδέδετο (plpf. pass.) 'he had been bound'; ἕκαστος 'each', 'every'; ἀετός, -οῦ, ὁ 'eagle'; ἐφιπτάμενος 'flying at' (+ dat.); αὐτῷ '(to) him' (dat.); λοβός, -οῦ, ὁ 'lobe'; ἧπαρ, ἥπατος, τό 'liver'; νέμω mid. 'feed', 'consume'; αὐξάνω pass. 'grow'; κλαπέντος aor. pass. pt., genitive of κλέπτω; τίνω 'pay (a penalty)'; δηλώσομεν 'we shall make clear'; μέχρις 'until'; ὕστερον 'later'; αὐτόν 'him'

ἐγέννησε 'gave birth to' (3rd sg.); ἡ δέ refers to Pasiphae; κληθέντα 'called' (aor. pass. pt., acc. masc. sg.); πρόσωπον 'face'; τινας 'some'; χρησμός 'oracle'; κατακλείω 'shut in'; φυλάττω 'guard', 'watch'; αὐτόν 'him' (acc.)

9. Minos locks up the Minotaur (Asterion), to whom his wife Pasiphae had given birth:
ἡ δὲ Ἀστέριον ἐγέννησε τὸν κληθέντα Μινώταυρον. οὗτος εἶχε ταύρου πρόσωπον, τὰ δὲ λοιπὰ ἀνδρός· Μίνως δὲ ἐν τῷ λαβυρίνθῳ κατά τινας χρησμοὺς κατακλείσας αὐτὸν ἐφύλαττεν.

Apollodorus

ἀκουσίως 'unwillingly' (adv.); ἀδελφός, -οῦ, ὁ 'brother'; καθαίρω 'cleanse', 'purify'; αὐτοῦ 'of him' (for him, here); ἔρως, -ωτος, ὁ 'love', 'desire'; ἴσχω 'conceive', 'have'; πρός + πέμπω; συνουσία, -ας, ἡ 'intercourse' (of various kinds); ἀπαρνέομαι 'deny utterly', 'reject'; φθορά, -ᾶς, ἡ 'destruction', 'seduction'

10. Bellerophon rejects Sthenoboea, Proteus' wife:
Βελλεροφόντης δὲ ὁ Γλαύκου τοῦ Σισύφου, κτείνας ἀκουσίως ἀδελφόν, πρὸς Προῖτον ἐλθὼν καθαίρεται. καὶ αὐτοῦ Σθενέβοια ἔρωτα ἴσχει, καὶ προσπέμπει λόγους περὶ συνουσίας. τοῦ δὲ ἀπαρνουμένου, λέγει πρὸς Προῖτον ὅτι Βελλεροφόντης αὐτῇ περὶ φθορᾶς προσεπέμψατο λόγους.

Apollodorus

μέμνησο 'remember!' (imper.) + gen.

11. ἄνθρωπος ὢν μέμνησο τῆς κοινῆς τύχης.

    Menander

στρατηγέω 'be general' (-εῖ 3rd sg.); ὅστις 'whoever', 'anyone who' (m. N. sg.); ἑκατόμβη 'hecatomb', 'sacrifice'; ἐκ + ἄγω; πολέμιος, -α, -ον 'hostile', οἱ πολέμιοι 'the enemy'

12. ὅστις στρατηγεῖ μὴ στρατιώτης γενόμενος, οὗτος ἑκατόμβην ἐξάγει τοῖς πολεμίοις.

    Menander

ἄνοια, -ας, ἡ 'folly', 'want of understanding'; καταγνῶναι 'lay a charge against' (+ gen. of the person charged and acc. of the charge)(aor. inf.); ξυνέχης 'constant'

[13. . . . ἄνοιαν δή μοι δοκεῖ καταγνῶναι τῶν πολλῶν ὡς οὐ μανθανόντων ὅτι πόλεμος ἀεὶ πᾶσι διὰ βίου ξυνεχής ἐστι πρὸς ἁπάσας τὰς πόλεις.]

    Plato, *Laws*

ἀπορία, -ας, ἡ 'difficulty', 'question'; τὰ πάθη 'experiences' is subject of ἔχει; πότερον . . . ἤ 'whether . . . or'; ἴδιος, -α, -ον 'peculiar'; αὐτῆς 'of herself' (with ψυχῆς); ἀναγκαῖος, -α, -ον 'necessary', 'pressing'; ῥᾴδιος, -α, -ον 'easy'

[14. Ἀπορίαν δ' ἔχει καὶ τὰ πάθη τῆς ψυχῆς, πότερόν ἐστι πάντα κοινὰ καὶ τοῦ ἔχοντος ἤ ἐστί τι καὶ τῆς ψυχῆς ἴδιον αὐτῆς· τοῦτο γὰρ λαβεῖν μὲν ἀναγκαῖον, οὗ ῥᾴδιον δέ.]

    Aristotle, περὶ ψυχῆς

μισῶν 'hating' (pres. partic. of μισέω)

15. ὡς ἐγὼ μισῶν γυναῖκας οὐδέποτε παύσομαι.

    Aristophanes

ἐνέθηκε '(she) placed in' (aor. act. 3rd sg. of ἐντίθημι); Ἀθηνᾶ, -ᾶς, ἡ 'Athena'; μέσος, -η, -ον 'mid', 'middle (of)'

16. Ἀθηνᾶ δὲ ἐν μέσῃ τῇ ἀσπίδι τῆς Γοργόνος τὴν κεφαλὴν ἐνέθηκε.

    Apollodorus

πανόπτης, -ου, ὁ 'all-seeing'; ὀφθαλμός, -οῦ, ὁ 'eye'

17. Argos, geneology and description: Ἐκβάσου δὲ Ἀγήνωρ γίνεται, τούτου δὲ Ἄργος ὁ πανόπτης λεγόμενος. εἶχε δὲ οὗτος ὀφθαλμοὺς μὲν ἐν παντὶ τῷ σώματι.

    Apollodorus

ἄπαις, ἄπαιδος (gen.), ὁ, ἡ 'childless'; ἐκλήθη 'was called/ named' (aor. pass. of καλέω, 3rd sg.)

18. Αἰγιαλέως μὲν οὖν ἄπαιδος ἀποθανόντος ἡ χώρα ἅπασα Αἰγιάλεια ἐκλήθη.

    Apollodorus

κωλύω 'hinder', 'prevent'; Κρήτη, -ης, ἡ 'Crete'

19. Ἀστερίου δὲ ἄπαιδος ἀποθανόντος Μίνως βασιλεύειν θέλων Κρήτης ἐκωλύετο.

    Apollodorus

μιᾶς gen. sg. of εἷς, μία, ἕν; κόπτω 'chop off'; κεφαλή, -ῆς, ἡ 'head'; ἀναφύω (pass.) 'grow up/back'

20. μιᾶς γὰρ κοπτομένης κεφαλῆς δύο ἀνεφύοντο.

    Apollodorus

φονεύς, -έως, ὁ 'murderer';
αὐτός . . . ἐγώ 'I myself'

21. φονεὺς οὖν αὐτὸς ἐγιγνόμην ἐγὼ μὴ εἰπὼν
ὑμῖν ἃ ἤκουσα.

    Andocides

μύλος, -ου, ὁ 'mill'; ἄλφιτον,
-ου, τό 'barley groats' (i.e.
one's daily bread)

22. ὁ φεύγων μύλον ἄλφιτα φεύγει.

    Greek Proverb

τλάς 'having endured', 'dared'
(aor. ptcpl. of τλάω)

23. ὁ πολλὰ δὴ τλὰς Ἡρακλῆς λέγει τάδε;

    Euripides, *Heracles*

For sight-reading in class:

Ὠκεανός, -οῦ, ὁ 'Oceanus';
πέτομαι 'fly'; ἤκω 'have come';
κατά + λαμβάνω 'catch'; καμάω
(mid.) 'sleep'; θνητός, -ή, -όν
'mortal'; ἐπέμφθη (aor. pass.)
'(he) was sent'; περιεσπειραμέν-
νος 'coiled around'; ἐπί + acc.
'for', 'after' (of purpose); φο-
λίς, -ίδος, ἡ 'scale'; αὐτός,
αὐτή, αὐτό (in oblique cases)
'he', 'she', 'it'; σῦς, συός, ὁ,
ἡ 'swine'; χαλκοῦς 'of bronze';
πτέρυξ, πτέρυγος, ἡ 'wing'; χρυ-
σοῦς 'golden'; ἐποίουν 'they
made' (impf. 3rd pl.); ἐπιστάς
'standing over' (aor. pt. nom.
masc. sg.); κατευθύνω 'guide',
'direct'; ἀπεστραμμένος 'turned
away' (pf. pt.); ἐκαρατόμησεν
'beheaded' (aor. act. 3rd sg.);
ἀποτμηθείσης 'having been cut
off' (gen. abs.); ἐκθρῴσκω, aor.
ἐξέθορον 'leap out of'; πτηνός,
-ή, -όν 'winged'; ἐγέννησεν
'(she) bore'; ἐνθέμενος 'having
put in' (aor. mid. pt.); κίβισις, -εως, ἡ 'pouch', 'wallet';
ὀπίσω 'back' (adv.); πάλιν
'back', 'again' (adv.); ἐχώρει
'(he) was going' (impf. 3rd.
sg.); κοίτη, -ης, ἡ 'sleep'; ἀ-
ναστᾶσαι 'having gotten up'; συ-
νιδεῖν 'to see'; ἠδύναντο
'(they) were not able'; κυνῆ,
-ῆς, ἡ 'helmet'; ἀποκρύπτω 'conceal', 'hide'

24. Perseus and the Gorgons: the story of
Perseus' decapitation of Medusa:
[Περσεὺς] πετόμενος εἰς τὸν Ὠκεανὸν ἧκε
καὶ κατέλαβε τὰς Γοργόνας κοιμωμένας.
ἦσαν δὲ αὗται Σθένω Εὐρυάλη Μέδουσα.
μόνη δὲ ἦν θνητὴ Μέδουσα· διὰ τοῦτο ἐπὶ
τὴν ταύτης κεφαλὴν Περσεὺς ἐπέμφθη. εἶχον δὲ αἱ Γοργόνες κεφαλὰς μὲν περιε-
σπειραμένας φολίσι δρακόντων, ὀδόντας δὲ
μεγάλους ὡς συῶν καὶ χεῖρας χαλκᾶς, καὶ
πτέρυγας χρυσᾶς, δι' ὧν ἐπέτοντο. τοὺς
δὲ ἰδόντας λίθους ἐποίουν. ἐπιστὰς οὖν
αὐταῖς ὁ Περσεὺς κοιμωμέναις, κατευθυ-
νούσης τὴν χεῖρα Ἀθηνᾶς, ἀπεστραμμένος
καὶ βλέπων εἰς ἀσπίδα χαλκῆν, δι' ἧς τὴν
εἰκόνα τῆς Γοργόνος ἔβλεπεν, ἐκαρατόμησεν αὐτήν. ἀποτμηθείσης δὲ τῆς κεφαλῆς,
ἐκ τῆς Γοργόνος ἐξέθορε Πήγασος πτηνὸς
ἵππος, καὶ Χρυσάωρ ὁ Γηρυόνου πατήρ·
τούτους δὲ ἐγέννησεν ἐκ Ποσειδῶνος. ὁ
μὲν οὖν Περσεὺς ἐνθέμενος εἰς τὴν κίβι-
σιν τὴν κεφαλὴν τῆς Μεδούσης ὀπίσω πάλιν
ἐχώρει, αἱ δὲ Γοργόνες ἐκ τῆς κοίτης
ἀναστᾶσαι τὸν Περσέα ἐδίωκον, καὶ συνι-
δεῖν αὐτὸν οὐκ ἠδύναντο διὰ τὴν κυνῆν.
ἀπεκρύπτετο γὰρ ὑπ' αὐτῆς.

    Apollodorus

Προμηθέως gen. of 'Prometheus';
τόπος 'place', 'region'; πλάττω
(πλάσσω) see #8; γαμεῖ '(he)
marries; ἀφανίζω 'destroy';

25. The story of Deucalion (the Greek Noah)
the son of Prometheus and husband of
Pyrrha who was the daughter of Epime-
theus and Pandora:

ὑποθέμενος 'having instructed';
τεκταίνομαι 'build'; λάρναξ, -α-
ξος, ἡ 'ark'; ἐπιτήδειος, -α,
-ον 'suitable'; τὰ ἐπιτήδεια
'provisions'; ἐνθέμενος (see
#24) 'having put in'; εἰσέβη
'went into', 'embarked' (3rd
sg.); ὑετός, -οῦ, ὁ 'rain'; χέας
'having poured' (masc. nom.
sg.); πλεῖστος 'most'; κατακλύζω
'inundate', 'flood'; διαφθαρῆναι
'to be destroyed'; ὀλίγος, -η,
-ον 'few'; χωρίς 'except' (+
gen.); σύν + φεύγω; πλησίον adv.
'near'; ὑψηλός, -ή, -όν 'high';
διέστη 'were divided' (3rd sg.);
συνεχέθη 'were demolished' (aor.
pass. of συγχέω); ἴσος, -η, -ον
'equal'; προσίσχω 'put in (to
shore)'; ἐκεῖ 'there' (adv.);
ὄμβρος, -ου, ὁ 'storm'; παῦλα,
-ης, ἡ 'rest', 'pause'; ἐκβάς
'having disembarked' (nom. masc.
sg.); φυξίος, -ον 'putting to
flight'; ἐπιτρέπω 'refer to',
'leave to'; αἱρεῖσθαι 'to
choose'; αἱρεῖται 'he chooses';
αἴρων 'picking up'; ὑπέρ 'over'
(+ gen.); ὅθεν 'whence'; λαός,
-οῦ, ὁ 'people'; μεταφορικῶς -
ως = 'ly'; ὠνομάσθην 'were
named' (from ὀνομάζω, cf. ὄνομα); λᾶας 'stone'

Προμηθέως δὲ παῖς Δευκαλίων ἐγένετο.
οὗτος βασιλεύων τῶν περὶ τὴν Φθίαν τόπων
γαμεῖ Πύρραν τὴν Ἐπιμηθέως καὶ Πανδώ-
ρας, ἣν ἔπλασαν θεοὶ πρώτην γυναῖκα.
ἐπεὶ δὲ ἀφανίσαι Ζεὺς τὸ χαλκοῦν ἠθέλησε
γένος, ὑποθεμένου Προμηθέως, Δευκαλίων
τεκτηνάμενος λάρνακα, καὶ τὰ ἐπιτήδεια
ἐνθέμενος, εἰς ταύτην μετὰ Πύρρας εἰσέ-
βη. Ζεὺς δὲ πολὺν ὑετὸν ἀπ' οὐρανοῦ χέας τὰ πλεῖστα μέρη τῆς Ἑλλάδος κατέκλυ-
σεν, ὥστε διαφθαρῆναι πάντας ἀνθρώπους,
ὀλίγων χωρὶς οἳ συνέφυγον εἰς τὰ πλησίον
ὑψηλὰ ὄρη. τότε δὲ καὶ τὰ κατὰ Θεσσαλί-
αν ὄρη διέστη, καὶ τὰ ἐκτὸς Ἰσθμοῦ καὶ
Πελοποννήσου συνεχέθη πάντα. Δευκαλίων
δὲ ἐν τῇ λάρνακι διὰ τῆς θαλάσσης φερό-
μενος ἡμέρας ἐννέα καὶ νύκτας ἴσας τῷ
Παρνασῷ προσίσχει, κἀκεῖ τῶν ὄμβρων παῦ-
λαν λαβόντων ἐκβὰς θύει Διὶ φυξίῳ. Ζεὺς
δὲ πέμψας Ἑρμῆν πρὸς αὐτὸν ἐπέτρεψεν
αἱρεῖσθαι ὅ τι βούλεται· ὁ δὲ αἱρεῖται
ἀνθρώπους αὐτῷ γενέσθαι. καὶ Διὸς εἰπόντος ὑπὲρ κεφαλῆς ἔβαλλεν αἴρων λίθους, καὶ οὓς μὲν ἔβαλλε Δευκαλίων, ἄνδρες ἐγένοντο, οὓς δὲ Πύρρα, γυναῖκες.
ὅθεν καὶ λαοὶ μεταφορικῶς ὠνομάσθησαν
ἀπο τοῦ <u>λᾶας</u> ὁ λίθος.

Apollodorus

LESSON VIII

A. *Pronouns:* Interrogative, Indefinite, Relative Indefinite, Reciprocal

The interrogative pronoun 'who?', 'what?' is τίς, τί in Greek. It always takes the acute on the first syllable (and this never changes to the grave).

The indefinite pronoun 'anyone', 'someone', 'anything', 'something' is enclitic, but otherwise is spelled the same way as the interrogative. Both are declined in the third declension with the base τιν-.

	Interrogative			Indefinite	
	M, F	N		M, F	N
Singular					
NOM	τίς	τί		τὶς	τὶ
GEN	τίνος (τοῦ)			τινός (του)	
DAT	τίνι (τῷ)			τινί (τῳ)	
ACC	τίνα	τί		τινά	τὶ
Plural					
NOM	τίνες	τίνα		τινές	τινά
GEN	τίνων			τινῶν	
DAT	τίσι			τισί	
ACC	τίνας	τίνα		τινάς	τινά

The alternate forms given in parentheses are fairly common. The student should be aware of them, and must use the context to distinguish τοῦ and τῷ from the forms of the article that look the same. The accent will help you distinguish the interrogative from the indefinite.

Both the interrogative τίς and the indefinite τις may be used as either pronouns or adjectives:

τίς ἔρχεται;	or	τίς ἀνὴρ ἔρχεται;
Who is coming?	or	What man is coming?

λέγει τις	or	λέγει ἄνθρωπός τις
Someone says.	or	Some man says.

The indefinite is sometimes equivalent to the English indefinite article ('a', 'an'):

εἶδον ἄνθρωπόν τινα. I saw *a* man. (or *a certain* man.)

The *relative indefinite* pronoun ὅστις 'whoever', 'whatever'; 'anyone who', 'anything which' consists of the relative pronoun (ὅς, ἥ, ὅ) and the indefinite pronoun (τις, τι) combined into one word (except for ὅ τι, the neuter singular, nominative and accusative), in which both elements are declined. Note that the accent of the relative is retained throughout the relative indefinite.

	M	F	N
NOM	ὅστις	ἥτις	ὅ τι
GEN	οὗτινος (ὅτου)	ἧστινος	οὗτινος (ὅτου)
DAT	ᾧτινι (ὅτῳ)	ᾗτινι	ᾧτινι (ὅτῳ)
ACC	ὅντινα	ἥντινα	ὅ τι
NOM	οὕτινες	αἵτινες	ἅτινα (ἅττα)
GEN	ὧντινων (ὅτων)	ὧντινων	ὧντινων (ὅτων)
DAT	οἷστισι (ὅτοις)	αἷστισι	οἷστισι (ὅτοις)
ACC	οὕστινας	ἅστινας	ἅτινα (ἅττα)

The shorter forms are common in poetry, but are rarely found in Attic prose.

ὅ τι (sometimes ὅ, τι is found) is written as two words in modern texts to distinguish it from ὅτι (the conjunction meaning 'that', 'because').

Examples:

οὐκ ἔστιν ὅστις βούλεται κακῶς πράττειν.

There is not *anyone who* wishes to do badly.

The indefinite relative is often used in indirect questions:

οὐ μανθάνω ὅ τι λέγεις.

I do not understand *what* you mean.

θαυμάζω ὅστις ἐστὶ ὁ βασιλεὺς ὁ τῆς χώρας τῆσδε.

I wonder *who* is king of this land.

The *reciprocal pronoun*, ἀλλήλων, '(of) each other' is used only in the oblique cases of the plural (and dual). The plural is declined as follows: (It is derived from ἄλλος doubled: ἀλλ-αλλο-.)

	M	F	N
GEN	ἀλλήλων	ἀλλήλων	ἀλλήλων
DAT	ἀλλήλοις	ἀλλήλαις	ἀλλήλοις
ACC	ἀλλήλους	ἀλλήλας	ἄλληλα

οἱ ξένοι δῶρα πρὸς ἀλλήλους ἔπεμψαν. The strangers sent gifts to *each other*.

Vocabulary

Pronouns

ἀλλήλων	*(of) each other* (reciprocal pronoun)(*parallel*)
ὅστις, ἥτις, ὅ τι	*anyone who, anything which, whoever, whatever* (indefinite relative)
τίς, τί	*who? what?* (interrogative pronoun)
τὶς, τὶ	*someone, something, anyone, anything, a, a certain* (indefinite pronoun, enclitic)
αἰτία, αἰτίας, ἡ	*cause, responsibility; guilt, blame; credit* (*aetiology*)
ἁμαρτάνω, ἁμαρτήσομαι, ἥμαρτον, ἡμάρτηκα	*miss (the mark)* + gen.; *fail, go wrong; err* (perfect, below, part B of this lesson)
ἐνθάδε	*to this/that place, hither, thither* (adv.)
κύων, κυνός, ὁ/ἡ	*dog; Cynic philosopher* (voc. κύον)
φυλάττω, φυλάξω, ἐφύλαξα, πεφύλαχα	*keep watch, guard, defend* (perfect, below, part B of this lesson)(cf. φύλαξ)
φύσις, φύσεως, ἡ	*nature, origin* (*physics*)
χθών, χθονός, ἡ	*earth* (poetic word)(*chthonic*)

Exercises

   1. Fill in (pronouns):

1. *Whom* εἶδες;

2. *To whom* ταῦτα λέγεις;

3. *Who* ἔρχεται;

4. *What* εἶπεν;

5. ἔρχεται *anyone;*

6. *Anyone who* ταῦτα λέγει, οὐκ ἀληθὲς λέγει.

7. *What* πράττετε;

8. *Who* ἔρχονται;

9. *Whom* ἀκούεις;

10. *What* βούλει;

11. *What gift* φέρεις;

12. τοὺς ἵππους ἄγουσι *some men.*

13. *Who* οὐ βούλεται ἀγαθὰ ἔχειν;

14. *What* ἤγγειλεν ὁ ἄγγελος;

15. οὐκ ἔστιν *anyone who* οὐ βούλεται ἀγαθὰ ἔχειν.

16. οὐ λέγω *anything* ἄδικον.

17. ἔστιν *anyone who* οὐ νομίζει τὴν ψυχὴν εἶναι ἀθάνατον;

18. ᾐσθόμην *something.*

19. ὁ σοφὸς βούλεται φεύγειν *anything* αἰσχρόν.

20. *What* λέγων αἰσχύνεται;

21. λέγει *anyone* τὴν ἀλήθειαν ἀεί;

22. οὗτος ὁ λόγος ἔχει ἄλογον *something.*

23. ἀνάγκη ἐστὶν εὑρεῖν ἄξιον *someone.*

24. ἔχουσι ἅπαντα *whichever* βούλονται.

25. νομίζω *some of the women* ἀπεῖναι.

26. ἔστιν *anyone who* ἀποθνῄσκειν ἐθέλει;

27. *Whom* ἀπέκτεινον;

28. ἤκουσα τοῦ σοφοῦ λέγοντος *something* περὶ ἀρετῆς.

29. *What* πράττων ἄρξομαι καὶ *what* λέγων παύσομαι;

30. *Why* νομίζεις ταυτὴν τὴν ἀρχὴν εἶναι ἀρίστην;

31. ἔτυχον *someone* ἐξ ἄστεως.

32. *Whoever* ἔχει ἀσπίδα ἀσθενῆ οὐκ ἔστι ἀσφαλής.

33. *Who* τοὺς λίθους ἔβαλλεν;

34. *Whose* ἐστι τόδε τὸ βαρὺ βιβλίον;

35. *Why* ταῦτα λέγεις;

36. *What* βασιλεὺς ἄγει βίον εὐδαίμονα;

37. ἐβουλεύσασθε *anything;*

38. *Which/what* ἐστι ἡ βραχεῖα ὁδός;

39. *Whom* ἄγεται πρὸς γάμον;

40. γέρων *a certain* ταῦτα γιγνώσκει.

41. αἱ γυναῖκες *to each other* ἔγραφον.

42. οἱ ξένοι *each other* ἐδέχοντο.

43. *Who* διώκει την δικαιοσύνην;

44. *From one another* μανθάνομεν.

45. δαίμονα *a certain* οἱ θεοὶ ἔβαλον ἐκ τοῦ οὐρανοῦ.

46. *What* ἐστι ὄνομα ἐκείνη τῇ γυναικί;

47. *To whom* χάριν φέρετε;

48. *By whom* ἀπέθανον οἱ φεύγοντες;

49. *Whom* οἱ παῖδες πείσονται;

50. οἱ πολλοὶ εἰρήνην πρὸς *each other* ἔχοντες χαίρουσιν.

Note: τί, the accusative of respect, often means 'why?'

Readings

νοῦς, νοῦ, ὁ 'mind' (dat. νῷ, acc. νοῦν); μακάριος, -α, -ον 'happy', 'blessed'; οὐσία, -ας, ἡ 'property'

1. μακάριος ὅστις οὐσίαν καὶ νοῦν ἔχει.

    Menander

ἀνελεύθερος, -ον 'not free', 'slavish'; δόξα, -ης, ἡ 'opinion'

2. ἀνελεύθερος πᾶς ὅστις εἰς δόξαν βλέπει.

    Cleanthes, the Stoic

αὑτῷ 'to himself'; οὐδείς 'no one' (masc. nom. sg.)

3. οὐκ ἔστιν οὐδεὶς ὅστις οὐχ αὑτῷ φίλον.

    Menander

μνήμη, -ης, ἡ 'memory'; μνημονεύω 'call to mind', 'remember'; πῶς 'how?'; ἀναμιμνήσκω 'remind', pass. 'remember', 'recollect'; εἴρηται 'it has been said'

4. περὶ μὲν οὖν μνήμης καὶ τοῦ μνημονεύειν, τίς ἡ φύσις αὐτῶν καὶ τίνι τῶν τῆς ψυχῆς μνημονεύει τὰ ζῷα, καὶ περὶ τοῦ ἀναμιμνήσκεσθαι, τί ἐστι καὶ πῶς γίνεται καὶ διὰ τίν' αἰτίαν εἴρηται.

    Aristotle, περὶ μνήμης

στάσις, -εως, ἡ 'faction', 'dissent'; φιλοφροσύνη, -ης, ἡ friendliness

5. τό γε μὴν ἄριστον οὔτε ὁ πόλεμος οὔτε ἡ στάσις, . . . εἰρήνη δὲ πρὸς ἀλλήλους ἅμα καὶ φιλοφροσύνη.

    Plato, νόμοι

ἤ (see voc., IV); ἐκπεσεῖν 'to fall out', 'be deposed'; ἥδοι' = ἥδοιο 'you would be glad' (+ participle); πῶς δ'οὐκ ἄν 'how would I not'

6. ΙΩ - ἦ γάρ ποτ' ἔστιν ἐκπεσεῖν ἀρχῆς Δία;
Προμηθεύς - ἥδοι' ἄν, οἶμαι, τήνδ' ἰδοῦσα συμφοράν.
ΙΩ - πῶς δ'οὐκ ἄν, ἥτις ἐκ Διὸς πάσχω κακῶς;

    Aeschylus, *Prometheus*

ἄργυρος, -ου, ὁ 'silver'; πηγή, -ῆς, ἡ 'source', 'fount'; τις 'as it were'; θησαυρός, -οῦ, ὁ (see p. 95, #28, 29)

7. ἀργύρου πηγή τις αὐτοῖς ἐστι, θησαυρὸς χθονός.

    Aeschylus, *Persae*

πῆμα, -ατος, τό 'trouble',
'pain'; ἐλαφρός, -α, -ον 'easy';
ἔξω 'outside of' (+ gen.); παραινεῖν 'exhort', 'advise'
(inf.); νουθετεῖν 'admonish'
(inf.); ἠπιστάμην 'I knew'
(impf. 1st sg.); ἀρνέομαι,
fut. ἀρνήσομαι 'deny'; ἑκών
'willingly' (adj. masc. nom.
sg.); ἀρήγω 'help', 'aid'; αὐτός
'-self' (here 'I, myself')

ἐρημία, -ας, ἡ 'solitude'; διά +
ἔρχομαι; τουτί = τοῦτο; πρὸς ἐ-
μαυτόν 'by myself'; ἀντιβολῶ σε
'I entreat you'; καινός 'new',
'fresh'; ὀψαρτυσία, ἡ 'cook-
book'; ἐπίδειξον 'show!' (imper.); ἄκουε 'listen!' (imper.);
βολβοῖο (gen. of βολβός) 'bulb';
θύννος 'tunny-fish'; τελευτάω,
fut. τελευτήσω 'finish', 'end'

ἐρωτώμενος 'asked' (pres. m./p.
ptcpl.); ὀλίγος, -η, -ον 'little', pl. 'few'; ἐκ + βάλλω;
ῥάβδος, ἡ 'rod', 'staff' (cane)

εἰπέ speak! (imper.); ἐφεστώς
'standing upon'; σῆμα, -ατος, τό
'tomb'; πίθος, -ου, ὁ 'jar' (a
large storage jar); ᾤκει (impf.
of οἰκέω) 'lived in'; καὶ μάλα
'yes', 'indeed'; ἀστήρ, ἀστέρος,
ὁ 'star'

βλάπτω 'harm'

μαίνομαι 'be mad'; σοί 'to you'
(dat. sg.)

8. Προμηθεύς--
ἐλαφρὸν ὅστις πημάτων ἔξω πόδα
ἔχει παραινεῖν νουθετεῖν τε τὸν κακῶς
πράσσοντ᾽· ἐγὼ δὲ ταῦθ᾽ ἅπαντ᾽ ἠπιστάμην
ἑκὼν ἑκὼν ἥμαρτον, οὐκ ἀρνήσομαι·
θνητοῖς ἀρήγων αὐτὸς ηὑρόμην πόνους.

Aeschylus, *Prometheus*

[9. The Best Seller
A. ἐγὼ δ᾽ ἐνθάδ᾽ ἐν τῇ ἐρημίᾳ
τουτὶ διελθεῖν βούλομαι τὸ βιβλίον
πρὸς ἐμαυτόν.
        B. ἐστὶ δ᾽, ἀντιβολῶ
    σε, τοῦτο τί;
A. Φιλοξένου καινή τις ὀψαρτυσία.
B. ἐπίδειξον αὐτὴν ἥτις ἔστ᾽.
                A. ἄκουε
    δή.
"ἄρξομαι ἐκ βολβοῖο, τελευτήσω δ᾽ ἐπὶ
    θύννον."]

Athenaeus (quoting a fragment from
    comedy)

10. ἐρωτώμενος διὰ τί ὀλίγους ἔχει μαθητάς,
ἔφη 'ὅτι ἀργυρέᾳ αὐτοὺς ἐκβάλλω ῥάβδῳ.'

Diogenes Laertius (quoting Antisthe-
    nes)

[11. α. εἰπέ, κύον, τίνος ἀνδρὸς ἐφεστὼς σῆμα
        φυλάσσεις;
β. τοῦ κυνός. α. ἀλλὰ τίς ἦν οὗτος ἀνὴρ
        ὁ κύων;
β. Διογένης. α. γένος εἰπέ. β. Σινω-
        πεύς. α. ὃς πίθον ᾤκει;
β. καὶ μάλα· νῦν δὲ θανὼν ἀστέρας οἶκον
        ἔχει.]

Greek Anthology (on Diogenes the Dog)

12. ἔστιν οὖν ὅστις βούλεται ὑπὸ τῶν συνόν-
των βλάπτεσθαι;

Plato, *Apology*

13. τίς οὕτω μαίνεται ὅστις οὐ βούλεται σοὶ
φίλος εἶναι;

Xenophon

Quotation:

Read and learn the following line from Mimnermus, the elegi-
ac poet:

τίς δὲ βίος, τί δὲ τερπνὸν ἄτερ χρυσῆς Ἀφροδίτης;

What life, what joy is there without golden Aphrodite?

B. The Perfect Active: Fourth Principal Part

The fourth principal part is the perfect active, first person singular. The perfect active stem is used only for the perfect and pluperfect *active*, there being another stem for the perfect middle-passive (the fifth principal part).

Use of the perfect: The Greek perfect is a *primary* tense:
it refers to *present* and not to past time. The Greek perfect expresses a present state resulting from a past act. For example,
τέθνηκε, 'he has died' or 'he is dead'. The perfect is used for a
completed action with the effect of the action still continuing
in the present. Often it stresses the lasting *result* of an action rather than the action itself, as in πέποιθα (perfect of
πείθω) 'I am confident' (as in the example given above, τέθνηκε 'he
is dead').

Aspect: It must be remembered that Greek tenses show aspect
(character of the action) as well as time.

The present and imperfect are used for action going on, continuous action.

The aorist for simple action.

The perfect for completed action, for action that is finished in present time, or for a present state. The pluperfect for
action finished in past time. The future perfect (which is rare)
for action to be finished in future time or for a future state.

Formation of the Perfect Active System

The Perfect Active

The perfect stem is formed by reduplication.

First Perfect:

Reduplication + stem + κ + perfect endings:

-α	-αμεν
-ας	-ατε
-ε(ν)	-ασι

Infinitive	-έναι	
Participle	-ώς, -υῖα, -ός	(base, -οτ-)

The perfect of many verbs (especially mute and liquid stems) is formed without κ (this is called the second perfect). The same endings are used. The perfect stem of these verbs is also formed by reduplication, but the stem often shows a vowel change (often to -ο-), as λείπω, perfect λέλοιπα. Sometimes the final mute appears in its rough form (π, β → φ; κ, γ → χ)(a dental or a nasal will often be dropped and a first perfect formed). Examples: πέμπω, perfect πέπομφα; πείθω, first perfect πέπεικα, second perfect πέποιθα.

Second Perfect:

Reduplication + stem + perfect endings (same as above).

How to Reduplicate

1. For verbs beginning with a single consonant or a mute and a liquid, double the first consonant with ε: λύω, perfect λέλυκα; γράφω, perfect γέγραφα; θνῆσκω, perfect τέθνηκε (note that an aspirated consonant reduplicates with its unaspirated form, θύω, perfect τέθυκα).

2. Verbs beginning with a vowel usually lengthen the vowel: ἀγγέλλω, perfect ἤγγελκα; ἄγω, perfect ἦχα (note aspirated final consonant for second perfect).

3. Verbs beginning with two or more consonants (unless a

mute and a liquid), a double consonant (ψ, ζ, ξ), or with ῥ, reduplicate with ε (a ρ is doubled):

στέλλω	perfect	ἔσταλκα	('send')
ῥίπτω	perfect	ἔρριφα	('throw')
ζητέω	perfect	ἐζήτηκα	('seek')

This is not to be confused with the augment. The reduplication is to be considered as part of the perfect stem and must be retained throughout the perfect system, in infinitive, participle and all moods.

The Perfect Active of λύω: λέλυκα 'I have released'

λε + λυ + κ + endings

Singular	Plural
λέλυκα	λελύκαμεν
λέλυκας	λελύκατε
λέλυκε(ν)	λελύκασι

Infinitive   λελυκέναι

Participle   λελυκώς, λελυκυῖα, λελυκός

(The base of the perfect participle is in -οτ-, gen. λελυκότος, declined below.)

The inflection of the second perfect is no different:

Second Perfect of πέμπω: πέπομφα 'I have sent'

πέπομφα, πέπομφας, πέπομφε
πεπόμφαμεν, πεπόμφατε, πεπόμφασι

Infinitive   πεπομφέναι
Participle   πεπομφώς, -υῖα, -ός

The Perfect Participle

The perfect participle is formed by adding the endings -ώς,
-υῖα, -ός to the perfect stem. It is declined in the third declension with base in -οτ- in the masculine and neuter. The feminine is in the first declension with base in -υια:

	M	F	N		M	F	N
S N	λελυκώς	λελυκυῖα	λελυκός	P N	λελυκότες	λελυκυῖαι	λελυκότα
G	λελυκότος	λελυκυίας	λελυκότος	G	λελυκότων	λελυκυιῶν	λελυκότων
D	λελυκότι	λελυκυίᾳ	λελυκότι	D	λελυκόσι(ν)	λελυκυίαις	λελυκοσι
A	λελυκότα	λελυκυῖαν	λελυκός	A	λελυκότας	λελυκυίας	λελυκότα

The Pluperfect Active

The pluperfect is used for a completed action in past time. The Greek pluperfect is less common than either the Latin or English pluperfects. In Greek, the aorist tense is often used where the pluperfect is found in English (or Latin). Since the pluperfect is rare, the student need not memorize it at this time, but should learn to recognize it.

The pluperfect is a secondary tense, and so is augmented. Like the imperfect, the pluperfect has only the indicative mood.

Formation:

Augment + perfect stem (including reduplication) + endings:

-η	-εμεν
-ης	-ετε
-ει(ν)	-εσαν

Example: pluperfect of λύω: ἐλελύκη 'I had released'

ἐλελύκη	ἐλελύκεμεν
ἐλελύκης	ἐλελύκετε
ἐλελύκει(ν)	ἐλελύκεσαν

The Future Perfect Active

Even rarer is the future perfect, which is used for an action to be completed in future time. For most verbs there is no special form for the future perfect, a periphrastic construction of the perfect participle and ἔσομαι (the future of εἰμί) being used instead:

λελυκώς/-υῖα ἔσομαι 'I shall have released'

λελυκὼς ἔσομαι	λελυκότες ἐσόμεθα
λελυκὼς ἔσει	λελυκότες ἔσεσθε
λελυκὼς ἔσται	λελυκότες ἔσονται

Note that the participle must agree in gender and number with the subject of the verb.

The Fourth Principal Part (Irregular)

The following verbs have irregularly formed perfects:

ἀγγέλλω	ἤγγελκα
ἄγω	ἦχα
ἀκούω	ἀκήκοα
ἀποθνῄσκω	τέθνηκα
ἀποκτείνω	ἀπέκτονα
ἄρχω	ἦρχα
βάλλω	βέβληκα
γίγνομαι	γέγονα note the perfect active (of a middle verb) (2 pf. pt. γεγώς)
γράφω	γέγραφα
ἐθέλω	ἐθέληκα
ἔρχομαι	ἐλήλυθα
εὑρίσκω	ηὕρηκα or εὕρηκα
ἔχω	ἔσχηκα regular reduplication for stem in σχ-
κομίζω	κεκόμικα
κρίνω	κέκρικα note that a nasal is often dropped before κ
λαμβάνω	εἴληφα
λανθάνω	λέληθα
λέγω	εἴρηκα cf. εἶπον used as aorist of λέγω
λείπω	λέλοιπα
μανθάνω	μεμάθηκα
μένω	μεμένηκα
νομίζω	νενόμικα
πάσχω	πέπονθα
πείθω	πέποιθα also πέπεικα (πέποιθα 'I trust (have put confidence in)'; πέπεικα 'I have persuaded')
πέμπω	πέπομφα
πράττω	πέπραχα also πέπραγα (πέπραχα 'I have done'; πέπραγα 'I have fared')
στέλλω	ἔσταλκα ('send')
τείνω	τέτακα ('stretch')
τυγχάνω	τετύχηκα
φαίνω	πέφαγκα or πέφηνα (πέφαγκα 'I have shown'; πέφηνα 'I have appeared')
φέρω	ἐνήνοχα
φεύγω	πέφευγα

Vocabulary Notes: Verb stems and vowel gradations

As has been noted in previous lessons, many verbs show vowel gradation (or a change in the stem vowel from one form to another).

1. The second aorist usually shows a shortening of the stem vowel; this is known as the *weak* grade. The present and future have the normal or *full* grade (often in ε) as does the first perfect; but the second perfect often has o.

Examples:

λείπω, λείψω present and future have ει

ἔλιπον   aorist has ι (weak or zero grade)
λέλοιπα perfect has οι (o-grade)

φεύγω aor. ἔφυγον (weak grade), pf. πέφευγα (full grade)

πείθω, first pf. πέπεικα, second pf. πέποιθα (the -o- grade)

πέμπω, pf. πέπομφα and πάσχω, pf. πέπονθα (again the -o- grade)

2. Another common grade can be seen in the liquid and nasal stems which often show -α- in the perfect.

Examples:

στέλλω pf. ἔσταλκα ('send')
τείνω pf. τέτακα ('stretch')

3. Some of the other irregularities can be explained by stem variations: many verbs add to the stem to form the present.

a. -λ added to form the present:

Present: ἀγγέλλω   Stem: ἀγγελ-
         βάλλω   βαλ-, βλη-
         στέλλω   στελ-, σταλ-

b. Many verbs add -ι- to form the present stem:

Present: φαίνω   Stem: φαν-, φην-
         τείνω   τεν-, τα-
         ἀποκτείνω   κτεν-, κτον-
         χαίρω   χαιρ-, χαρ-

c. Some verbs add -ν- or -αν- to form the present:

Present: μανθάνω   Stem: μαθ-
         λαμβάνω   λαβ-, ληβ-
         λανθάνω   λαθ-, ληθ-
         τυγχάνω   τυχ-
         φθάνω   φθα-

d. Some add -σκω (or -ισκω)

Present: ἀποθνησκω   Stem: θνη-, θαν-
         γιγνώσκω   γνω-, γνο-
         εὑρίσκω   εὑρ-

Irregular Verbs

The verb οἶδα ('know') is an irregular second perfect in form with a present meaning. (It is related to εἶδον 'I saw', and to the Latin verb *video*.) The perfect form is to be translated as a present, the pluperfect as an imperfect.

	Perfect	Pluperfect
	οἶδα	ᾔδη
	οἶσθα	ᾔδησθα
	οἶδε	ᾔδει(ν)
	ἴσμεν	ᾖσμεν
	ἴστε	ᾖστε
	ἴσασι	ᾖσαν

Infinitive εἰδέναι

Participle εἰδώς, εἰδυῖα, εἰδός

The future is εἴσομαι (a deponent future form).

The verb δέδια ('fear') is a second perfect used in a present sense (first perfect forms are also found for some persons; these are given in parentheses):

Perfect Indicative

δέδια (δέδοικα)
δέδιας (δέδοικας)
δέδιε (δέδοικε)

δέδιμεν
δέδιτε
δεδίασι (δεδοίκασι)

Infinitive δεδιέναι (δεδοικέναι)

Participle δεδιώς, δεδιυῖα, δεδιός (δεδοικώς, δεδοικυῖα, δεδοικός)

Vocabulary

δέδια/δέδοικα	*fear* (perfect with present meaning)
διδάσκω, διδάξω, ἐδί-δαξα, δεδίδαχα	*instruct, teach* (didactic)
ἔοικα	*be like, look like* (+ dative); *seem* (+ infinitive)(impersonal ἔοικε 'it seems')(perfect with present meaning)
μέμφομαι, μέμφομαι	*blame, censure* (aorist to be given later)
οἶδα, εἴσομαι	*know* (perfect with present sense)(with participle, 'know that'; with infinitive 'know how to')
πίνω, πίομαι, ἔπιον, πέπωκα	*drink*
σχολή, σχολῆς, ἡ	*leisure, rest* (school)(σχολὴν ἄγειν 'be at rest', 'enjoy leisure')

φύω, φύσω, ἔφυσα,   in pres., fut., and first aor. act. *bring forth, pro-*
   πέφυκα   *duce*; in perfect act. and in passive, *grow, be born*
                        (cf. φυτόν 'plant', φύσις 'nature')

Exercises

   1. Form the (regular) perfects of:

   1. βουλεύω   2. θύω   3. παιδεύω   4. πιστεύω   5. παύω

   2. Conjugate in perfect active with infinitive and participle:

   1. ἄγω   2. φέρω   3. ἔρχομαι   4. μανθάνω   5. κρίνω

   Conjugate in pluperfect:

       1. γράφω   2. ἀγγέλλω

   Conjugate in future perfect: πάσχω

   3. Form the perfect active participles of: (decline any
two of them)

   1. ἀκούω   2. ἀποθνήσκω   3. ἄρχω   4. βάλλω   5. ἐθέλω
   6. ἔχω   7. νομίζω   8. λαμβάνω   9. λείπω   10. πράττω

   4. Synopses: to give a synopsis, list together all the
forms for a given person (all tenses, moods, and voices). Infinitives are included because the infinitive can stand for any person, and participles because the participle can be used with any
person.

   Example: a synopsis of παύω in the third person singular.
(It is best to put down the principal parts first. Forms that
you have not had yet will be omitted for now, but filled in later.)

Principal parts: παύω, παύσω, ἔπαυσα, πέπαυκα, πέπαυμαι (ἐπαύθην: Ch. X)

ACTIVE	Pres.	Impf.	Fut.	Aor.	Perf.	Plpf.
IND	παύει	ἔπαυε	παύσει	ἔπαυσε	πέπαυκε	ἐπεπαύκει
SUB	xiii			xiii	xiii	
OPT	xiii		xiii	xiii	xiii	
INF	παύειν		παύσειν	παῦσαι	πεπαυκέναι	
PRT	παύων		παύσων	παύσας	πεπαυκώς	

MIDDLE/MIDDLE-PASSIVE

IND	παύεται	ἐπαύετο	παύσεται	ἐπαύσατο	ix	ix
SUB	xiii			xiii	xiii	
OPT	xiii		xiii	xiii	xiii	
INF	παύεσθαι		παύσεσθαι	παύσασθαι	ix	
PRT	παυόμενος		παυσόμενος	παυσάμενος	ix	

PASSIVE

IND, etc. (Only in the Future and Aorist, see Lesson X)

Write the following synopses:

1. ἔχω: third person plural
2. λύω: second person singular
3. λαμβάνω: first person singular

(Note: if a verb lacks certain forms, leave the spaces for those forms blank: e.g. λαμβάνω lacks a future active.)

5. Parse 5a. Change to the opposite number (except infinitives):

1. ἀκηκόατε	10. τέθνηκεν	19. πεπιστεύκασι	28. ἐνήνοχας
2. εἴληφε	11. λέλοιπε	20. ἐγεγράφειν	29. νενομίκατε
3. πεπωκότα	12. πεπονθὼς	21. πεπόμφατε	30. ἐμεμαθήκη
4. εἰδέναι	ἔσομαι	22. ἐμεμαθήκεσαν	31. ᾔδε
5. δεδιέναι	13. οἶδεν	23. βεβλήκασι	32. ἴσασιν
6. εἰδότες	14. γέγραφε	24. ἐλήλυθας	33. ἔοικε
7. εἰρήκασιν	15. πέποιθας	25. λέληθε	34. πεφυκότων
8. δεδίδαχεν	16. πεφευγέναι	26. τεθνηκότες	35. δεδοικέναι
9. εὔρηκεν	17. γέγραφα	27. εἰδυῖαι	36. πεπόνθαμεν
	18. πεπράχαμεν		

6. Translate:

1. τί ἀκηκόατε; ἀκηκόαμεν μὲν ὡς Σωκράτης παιδεύει ἀνθρώπους· ἴσμεν δὲ τοῦτο οὐκ ᾿ὂν ἀληθές.

2. οἶδα ὅ τι πέπονθας.

3. γέγραφεν ὁ ἀνὴρ ἐκεῖνα.

4. ἴσασιν οἱ θεοὶ πάντα.

5. οἱ σοφοὶ θάνατον οὐ δεδίασιν.

6. τί γέγραφας; γέγραφα λόγους τινάς. ἔφη γεγραφέναι τοὺς λόγους τούσδε.

7. μεμαθήκατέ τι; ναί, πολλὰ μεμαθήκαμεν.

8. σοφὸς ὁ ἄνθρωπος ᾿ὃς πολλὰ καὶ ἀγαθὰ μεμάθηκε;

9. ὁ σοφὸς ἀνὴρ τὴν ἀληθῆ γνώμην οἶδεν.

10. οἱ τότε ἔχειν αἴσθησιν τοὺς τεθνηκότας ἐνόμιζον.

11. ἀκηκόατε γὰρ τοὺς λόγους· ὥρα δ᾽ ἐστὶ βουλεύεσθαι καὶ κρίνειν.

12. οὐκ οἶδε δεδιέναι.

13. οἶδα τούτους ὄντας ἀδίκους.

14. ἐκείνη ἡ γυνὴ θεαῖς ἔοικε κάλλος καὶ σοφίαν.

15. τίς ἀνὴρ οὐ μέμφεται τύχην;

16. οὗτος ὁ ἀνὴρ ἀπὸ μητρὸς θεᾶς πέφυκεν.

17. ἡ Ἑλλὰς φύει ἄνδρας καὶ γυναῖκας ἀγαθοὺς καὶ καλοὺς καὶ ἐλευθέρους.

18. πολὺν οἶνον πεπωκὼς ἀπέθανεν.

19. πολλὰ πολλοὺς διδάσκει ὁ βίος.

20. τίνα πέπομφας; πέπομφα ἄνθρωπόν τινα ὡς τὸν παῖδα διδάξοντα.

7. Write in Greek

a. Compose sentences using the perfects of:

1. λαμβάνω

2. ἀκούω

3. βάλλω

4. λείπω

5. πέμπω

b. Translate into Greek:

1. Has the wise old man died?

2. I have found what I wanted.

3. You have heard many poets speaking.

4. In whom are you confident?

5. What do you fear? Whatever I do not know.

6. I have not done these things.

7. She said that she had not done these things.

Readings

ἐπιχειρῶ 'I try' (+ infin.); οὐδέν 'nothing' (neut. sg. nom./
acc.)(double negative confirms
the negative)

1. ἀλλὰ γὰρ οὔτε τούτων οὐδέν ἐστιν, οὐδέ
γ' εἴ τινος ἀκηκόατε ὡς ἐγὼ παιδεύειν
ἐπιχειρῶ ἀνθρώπους καὶ χρήματα πράττο-
μαι, οὐδὲ τοῦτο ἀληθές.

Plato, *Apology of Socrates*

διαθέσις, -εως, ἡ 'arrangement',
'composition'; ὑμῖν dat. pl.
'to/for you'

2. ΑΘΗΝΑΙΟΣ. θεὸς ἤ τις ἀνθρώπων ὑμῖν, ὦ
ξένοι, εἴληφε τὴν αἰτίαν τῆς τῶν νόμων
διαθέσεως;
ΚΛΕΙΝΙΑΣ. θεός, ὦ ξένε, θεός, ὥς γε τὸ
δικαιότατον εἰπεῖν.

οἷός τε ἦν (see voc IV); κατέχω
'hold back'

Plato, *Laws*

3. ὡς δὲ εἴδομεν πίνοντα καὶ πεπωκότα, οὐκέτι οἷός τε ἦν κατέχειν.

ἡγεῖτο '(he) thought' (impf. of
ἡγέομαι)(3rd sg.); σιγή, -ῆς, ἡ
'silence'

Plato, *Phaedo*

4. Σωκράτης γὰρ ἡγεῖτο πάντα θεοὺς εἰδέναι,
τά τε λεγόμενα καὶ τὰ πραττόμενα καὶ τὰ
σιγῇ βουλευόμενα.

ἤ 'than'; δοκεῖν 'to seem'; τοι
(orig. 'for you') 'you know',
'for your information'

Xenophon

5. τὸ γάρ τοι θάνατον δεδιέναι, ὦ ἄνδρες,
οὐδὲν ἄλλο ἐστὶν ἢ δοκεῖν σοφὸν εἶναι μὴ
ὄντα· δοκεῖν γὰρ εἰδέναι ἔστιν ἃ οὐκ οἶδεν. οἶδε μὲν γὰρ οὐδεὶς τὸν θάνατον
οὐδ' εἰ τυγχάνει τῷ ἀνθρώπῳ πάντων μέγιστον ὃν τῶν ἀγαθῶν, δεδίασι δ' ὡς εὖ εἰδότες ὅτι μέγιστον τῶν κακῶν ἐστί.

οὐδέν 'nothing'; μου gen. sg.
'(of/from) me'

Plato, *Apology*

6. οὗτοι μὲν οὖν, ὥσπερ ἐγὼ λέγω, ἤ τι 'ἢ
οὐδὲν ἀληθὲς εἰρήκασιν· ὑμεῖς δέ μου ἀ-
κούσεσθε πᾶσαν τὴν ἀλήθειαν.

Plato, *Apology*

δεῖ 'it is necessary'

7. δεδίδαχεν δὲ μάλιστα Ὅμηρος καὶ τοὺς
ἄλλους ψευδῆ λέγειν ὡς δεῖ.

Aristotle, *Poetics*

λαλοῦσι 'speak', 'talk' (λαλέω
3rd pl. present); μέτρα ἰαμβικά
'iambic meter' ('iambics'); γοῦν
= γε + οὖν

8. πολλοὶ γοῦν μέτρα ἰαμβικὰ λαλοῦσιν οὐκ
εἰδότες.

Demetrius

9. Davus.   εἴρηκα τόν γ' ἐμὸν λόγον.
Syriscus. εἴρηκεν;
Smicrines. οὐκ ἤκουσας; εἴρηκεν.
Syriscus. καλῶς. οὐκοῦν ἐγὼ μετὰ
ταῦτα.

Menander, *Arbitrants*

ὦζεν ἄν 'would reek', 'would
smell'; ἡ οἰκουμένη 'the inhab-
ited world'; νεκρός, -οῦ, ὁ
'corpse'

[10. οἷόν ἐστι τὸ 'οὐ τέθνηκεν Ἀλέξανδρος,
ὦ ἄνδρες Ἀθηναῖοι· ὦζεν γὰρ ἂν ἡ οἰκουμένη τοῦ νεκροῦ.']

Demetrius

μὰ τὴν Δ. 'by Demeter!'; πλήν
'except', 'but'; ἀπάγξομαι fut.
of ἀπάγχω 'strangle', mid. 'hang
oneself', pass. 'be hanged'; με
'me' (acc. sg.); Πάταικ' 'Patae-
cus' (voc.); συνήθης, -ες 'familiar', 'intimate'; πολλάκις

11. ΠΟΛΕΜΩΝ.   οὐκ οἶδ' ὅ τι
λέγω, μὰ τὴν Δήμητρα, πλὴν ἀπάγξομαι.
Γλυκέρα με καταλέλοιπε, καταλέλοιπέ με
Γλυκέρα, Πάταικ'. ἀλλ' εἴπερ οὕτω σοι
δοκεῖ
πράττειν,--συνήθης ἦσθα γὰρ καὶ πολλάκις
λελάληκας αὐτῇ--πρότερον ἐλθὼν διαλέγου·

'often'; λελάληκας pf. of λαλέω
(8); διαλέγου 'converse with'
(imperative); αὐτῇ dat. 'to
her'; πρέσβευσον 'be (my) ambassador' (imperative); ἱκετεύω
'beseech'

ἐὰν ποιῆτε 'if you do'; υἱεῖς =
υἱοί; ἐγώ 'I' (nom.); ὑφ' = ὑπό;
ὑμῶν gen. pl. '(of) you'; αὐτός
'-self' (here, 'myself')

αἰών, αἰῶνος, ὁ 'lifetime',
'age'; δολιχός, -ή, -όν 'long';
ἀμείβω 'change'; οὔνομα = ὄνομα;
μορφή, -ῆς, ἡ 'form', 'appearance'; ἠδέ 'and'

δῆτα 'then'; τέκνον, -ου, τό
'child'; μαντεῖον, -ου, τό 'oracle'; πιστός 'trusty': ποῖος 'of
what sort?', 'which?'; ἀγνοέω
'I do not know', 'I am ignorant'

κατθανεῖν 'to die' (καταθνῄσκω);
ζῆν (inf.) 'to live'; βροτός,
-οῦ, ὁ 'mortal man'

ἀπεκρίθη (aor. of ἀποκρίνομαι)
'he answered'

βεβίωκεν (pf. of βιόω 'live');
ἤδη 'already', 'by this time';
ἐνενήκοντα 'ninety'

κατηγορέω 'accuse'; δικάζετε
imperative of δικάζω 'judge';
ἑώρακα pf. of ὁράω 'see'

φιλότιμος, -ον 'ambitious';
σφοδρός, -ά, -όν 'vehement';
ξυντεταγμένως 'vigorously'; πι
θανῶς 'persuasively'; ἐμπίμπλη
μι, pf. ἐμπέπληκα 'fill full
of'; ἐμοῦ gen. sg. '(of) me';
οὖς, ὠτός, τό 'ear'; ὑμῶν gen.
pl. 'of you', 'your'; πάλαι
'long ago'; διαβάλλω 'slander'

πρέσβευσον, ἱκετεύω σε.

> Menander

12. οὐκ ἔστιν ὅστις τὴν τύχην οὐ μέμφεται.

> Menander

13. καὶ ἐὰν ταῦτα ποιῆτε δίκαια πεπονθὼς ἐγὼ
ἔσομαι ὑφ' ὑμῶν αὐτός τε καὶ οἱ υἱεῖς.

> Plato, *Apology of Socrates*

14. Αἰὼν πάντα φέρει· δολιχὸς χρόνος οἶδεν
ἀμείβειν
οὔνομα καὶ μορφὴν καὶ φύσιν ἠδὲ τύχην.

> Greek Anthology (Plato)

15. Deianeira.
ἆρ' οἶσθα δῆτ', ὦ τέκνον, ὡς ἔλειπέ μοι
μαντεῖα πιστὰ τῆσδε τῆς χώρας πέρι;
Hyllus.
τὰ ποῖα, μῆτερ; τὸν λόγον γὰρ ἀγνοῶ.

> Sophocles, *Trachiniae*

16. τίς δ' οἶδεν εἰ τὸ ζῆν μέν ἐστι κατθα
νεῖν
τὸ κατθανεῖν δὲ ζῆν νομίζεται βροτοῖς;

> Euripides (fragment)

17. ἀπεκρίθη ὁ Πιλᾶτος· ὃ γέγραφα, γέγραφα.

> John

18. ἔτη γὰρ ἤδη βεβίωκεν ἐνενήκοντα καὶ τέτ
ταρα.

> Aeschines

19. παύσομαι κατηγορῶν. ἀκηκόατε, ἑωράκατε,
πεπόνθατε, ἔχετε· δικάζετε.

> Lysias

20. ἅτε οὖν, οἶμαι, φιλότιμοι ὄντες καὶ σφο
δροὶ καὶ πολλοί, καὶ ξυντεταγμένως καὶ
πιθανῶς λέγοντες περὶ ἐμοῦ ἐμπεπλήκασιν
ὑμῶν τὰ ὦτα καὶ πάλαι καὶ νῦν σφοδρῶς
διαβάλλοντες.

> Plato, *Apology*

ἀμαθής, -ές 'ignorant'; πολλάκις
(see pp. 189-90, #11); ἕκαστος,
-η, -ον 'each', 'every'; ἡμῶν
gen. pl. 'of us'

21. πολλάκις ἀκήκοά σου λέγοντος, ὅτι ταῦτα
ἀγαθὸς ἕκαστος ἡμῶν, ἅπερ σοφός, 'ἃ δὲ
ἀμαθής, ταῦτα δὲ κακός.

Plato, *Laches* (Nicias speaking)

22. φιλοσοφίας δὲ δύο γεγόνασιν ἀρχαί, ἥ τε
ἀπὸ 'Αναξιμάνδρου καὶ ἡ ἀπὸ Πυθαγόρου.

Diogenes Laertius

ἐρωτηθείς 'asked' (aor. pass.
partic. of ἐρωτάω); θύρα, -ας, ἡ
'door'; πλούσιος (adj. cf. πλοῦτος); ὧν δέονται '(of) what they
(have) need'

23. ἐρωτηθεὶς ὑπὸ Διονυσίου διὰ τί οἱ μὲν
φιλόσοφοι ἐπὶ τὰς τῶν πλουσίων θύρας ἔρχονται, οἱ δὲ πλούσιοι ἐπὶ τὰς τῶν φιλο-
σόφων οὐκέτι, ἔφη, 'ὅτι οἱ μὲν ἴσασιν ὧν
δέονται, οἱ δ' οὐκ ἴσασιν.'

Diogenes Laertius (an anecdote about
Aristippus)

ὁ Λύσις the *Lysis*, a dialogue of
Plato; ἀναγιγνώσκω 'read'; καταψεύδομαι 'tell lies'; νεανίσκος
= νεανίας; ἀνήρ refers to Plato

[24. φασὶ δὲ καὶ Σωκράτην ἀκούσαντα τὸν Λύσιν
ἀναγινώσκοντος Πλάτωνος ''Ηράκλεις,' εἰπεῖν, 'ὡς πολλά μου καταψεύδεθ' ὁ νεανίσκος.' οὐκ ὀλίγα γὰρ ὧν οὐκ εἴρηκε Σωκράτης γέγραφεν ἀνήρ.]

Diogenes Laertius on Plato

δοκεῖ 'seems' (3rd sg. pres.);
δοκῶν 'thinking' (masc. nom.
sg.); ἀλίσκομαι 'be caught' (+
ptcpl.); ὅταν 'whenever' (with
subjunctive); τυγχάνῃ subjunctive

[25. ὅστις δὲ θνητῶν οἴεται καθ' ἡμέραν κακόν
τι πράσσων τοὺς θεοὺς λεληθέναι, δοκεῖ
πονηρὰ καὶ δοκῶν ἀλίσκεται ὅταν σχολὴν
ἄγουσα τυγχάνῃ δίκη.]

Euripides (a fragment)

ὑμεῖς 'you' (nom. pl.); κατήγορος, -ου, ὁ 'accuser'; ἐμός, -ή,
-όν 'my' (adjective)

26. ὅ τι μὲν ὑμεῖς, ὦ ἄνδρες 'Αθηναῖοι, πεπόνθατε ὑπὸ τῶν ἐμῶν κατηγόρων, οὐκ οἶδα.

Plato, *Apology of Socrates*

κρίνατε imperative (aor.)

27. 'εἴρηκα, ἀκηκόατε, ἔχετε, κρίνατε.'

Aristotle, *Rhetoric* (an appropriate
ending for a speech)

μισῶ 'I hate'; διπλοῦς 'double';
λόγοισι = λόγοις; πολέμιος, -α,
-ον 'of/like an enemy'

28. μισῶ τὸν ἄνδρα τὸν διπλοῦν πεφυκότα,
χρηστὸν λόγοισι πολέμιον δὲ τοῖς τρόποις

Greek Anthology (Palladas)

ἀληθείαισιν = ἀληθείαις; αἴσθησις 'sense perception'; ἀπηγξάμην (see #11 ἀπάγχω)

29. εἰ ταῖς ἀληθείαισιν οἱ τεθνηκότες
αἴσθησιν εἶχον, ἄνδρες ὥς φασίν τινες,
ἀπηγξάμην ἄν, ὥστ' ἰδεῖν Εὐριπίδην.

Greek Anthology (Philemon)

θεῖος, -α, -ον (adj. of θεός)
'divine'; ἄεισε aor. of ἀείδω
'sing'; ἐκγεγαώς 'born of' (pf.
ptcpl. of ἐκγίγνομαι); ἑκατοντά-
πυλος, -ον 'hundred-gated'

[30. ἐνθάδε θεῖος "Ομηρος, 'ὃς 'Ελλάδα πᾶσαν
ἄεισε,
Θήβας ἐκγεγαὼς τῆς ἑκατονταπύλου.]

Greek Anthology

φανερός, -ά, -όν 'manifest';
ἔξω 'outside'; δεῖξαι 'to show'
(aor. inf.); ἀμφισβητέω 'dispute'; οἱ ἀμφισβητοῦντες 'the
parties in a lawsuit'; διορίζω
'distinguish', 'determine'; νομοθέτης, -ου, ὁ 'law-giver'

[31. ἔτι δὲ φανερὸν ὅτι τοῦ μὲν ἀμφισβητοῦν-
τος οὐδέν ἐστιν ἔξω τοῦ δεῖξαι τὸ πρᾶγμα
ὅτι ἔστιν 'ἢ οὐκ ἔστιν 'ἢ γέγονεν 'ἢ οὐ
γέγονεν· εἰ δὲ μέγα 'ἢ μικρὸν 'ἢ δίκαιον
'ἢ ἄδικον, ὅσα μὴ ὁ νομοθέτης διώρικεν,
αὐτὸν δή που τὸν δικαστὴν δεῖ γιγνώσκειν
καὶ οὐ μανθάνειν παρὰ τῶν ἀμφισβητοῦν-
των.]

Aristotle, *Rhetoric*

ὡς ἐλαχίστων 'of as little as
possible'; κύριος 'having authority over'; προϊδεῖν (aor.
inf. of προοράω) 'foresee';
δυνατόν 'possible', 'it is possible'

[32. περὶ μὲν οὖν τῶν ἄλλων, ὥσπερ λέγομεν,
δεῖ ὡς ἐλαχίστων ποιεῖν κύριον τὸν κρι-
τήν· περὶ δὲ τοῦ γεγονέναι 'ἢ μὴ γεγονέναι 'ἢ ἔσεσθαι 'ἢ μὴ ἔσεσθαι, 'ἢ εἶναι
'ἢ μὴ εἶναι, ἀνάγκη ἐπὶ τοῖς κριταῖς
καταλείπειν· οὐ γὰρ δυνατὸν ταῦτα τὸν
νομοθέτην προϊδεῖν.]

Aristotle, *Rhetoric*

ἔνδικος, -ον 'just'

33. τίς γὰρ δεδοικὼς μηδὲν ἔνδικος βροτῶν;

Aeschylus, *Eumenides* (Athene speaking)

ζῶντα pres. ptcpl. of ζάω 'living' (masc. acc. sg.); καίνω
'kill'; ξυνῆκα (aor. of συνίημι
'understand')(1st sg.); τοὖπος =
τὸ ἔπος; αἴνιγμα --

34. Servant.
τὸν ζῶντα καίνειν τοὺς τεθνηκότας λέγω.
Clytemnestra.
οἲ 'γώ. ξυνῆκα τοὖπος ἐξ αἰνιγμάτων.

Aeschylus, *Choephoroe*

προφήτης --; ποιεῖ 'he does/
practices'; ψευδοπροφήτης --

35. πᾶς δὲ προφήτης διδάσκων τὴν ἀλήθειαν,
εἰ 'ἃ διδάσκει οὐ ποιεῖ, ψευδοπρογήτης
ἐστί.

Διδαχή

ἔνειμι 'be present in'; νόσημα,
-ατος, τό 'disease'

36. ἔνεστι γάρ πως τοῦτο τῇ τυραννίδι
νόσημα, τοῖς φίλοισι μὴ πεποιθέναι.

Aeschylus, *Prometheus*

ὁμιλῶν 'associating with', 'con-
sorting with' (masc. nom. sg.);
διδάσκω in pass. 'learn'; θούριος (= θοῦρος) 'impetuous'

37. ταῦτά τοι κακοῖς ὁμιλῶν ἀνδράσιν διδά-
σκεται
θούριος Ξέρξης . . .

Aeschylus, *Persae* (Atossa, mother of
Xerxes, speaking)

38. τίς οὐ τέθνηκε;

Aeschylus, *Persae* (Atossa, not daring
to ask directly if her son is still
alive)

39. διδάξω καὶ διδάξομαι λόγους.

Euripides, *Andromache* (Menelaus speaking)

χρησμός, -οῦ, ὁ 'oracle'; ἐργα-   40. τοιοῦσδε χρησμοῦς ἄρα χρὴ πεποιθέναι;
στέον 'it must be done'; κεἰ =   κεἰ μὴ πέποιθα, τοὔργον ἔστ' ἐργαστέον.
καὶ εἰ; τοὔργον = τὸ ἔργον

Aeschylus, *Choephoroe* (Orestes speaking)

Quotation

Read aloud and learn the following quotation from Homer's
Iliad:

ὃς ᾔδε τά τ' ἐόντα τά τ' ἐσσόμενα πρό τ' ἐόντα.

He knew the things that are, that will be, and that were
before.

LESSON IX

A. *Pronouns*: Personal and Reflexive; Possessive Adjectives

Personal Pronouns

First Person

	Singular			Plural	
NOM	ἐγώ	I		ἡμεῖς	we
GEN	ἐμοῦ, μου	of me, my		ἡμῶν	of us, our
DAT	ἐμοί, μοι	to me		ἡμῖν	to us
ACC	ἐμέ, με	me		ἡμᾶς	us

Second Person

	Singular			Plural	
NOM	σύ	you		ὑμεῖς	you
GEN	σοῦ, σου	of you, your		ὑμῶν	of you, your
DAT	σοί, σοι	to you		ὑμῖν	to you
ACC	σέ, σε	you		ὑμᾶς	you

The unaccented forms are unemphatic and enclitic; they are usually not used after prepositions. The nominative of the personal pronoun is generally omitted (since it is supplied by the verb ending) unless it is emphatic (for contrast or emphasis). For the personal pronoun of the third person, forms of αὐτός (given below) are used in the oblique cases (that is, cases other than the nominative).

The genitive of the personal pronouns goes in the predicate position (genitives of other pronouns and of nouns usually take the attributive position):

ἡ μήτηρ μου 'my mother'

but,   ἡ τοῦ παιδὸς μήτηρ 'the child's mother'

αὐτός, αὐτή, αὐτό: *Forms and Uses*

	Singular			Plural		
	M	F	N	M	F	N
NOM	αὐτός	αὐτή	αὐτό	αὐτοί	αὐταί	αὐτά
GEN	αὐτοῦ	αὐτῆς	αὐτοῦ	αὐτῶν	αὐτῶν	αὐτῶν
DAT	αὐτῷ	αὐτῇ	αὐτῷ	αὐτοῖς	αὐταῖς	αὐτοῖς
ACC	αὐτόν	αὐτήν	αὐτό	αὐτούς	αὐτάς	αὐτά

αὐτός has three uses:

1. In all cases it can be used as an intensive adjective-pronoun, '-self'. With this meaning it is found with another pronoun, as ἐγὼ αὐτός 'I myself', or with a noun, in the predicate position, αὐτὸς ὁ ἀνήρ 'the man himself'. αὐτός, αὐτή, αὐτό in the nominative may be used without another pronoun to agree with the subject (as expressed in the verb ending), as αὐτὸς ἔφη (cf. Latin *ipse dixit)* 'he himself said (it)'.

2. In all cases, when preceded by the article (i.e. in the attributive position), αὐτός means 'the same': ὁ αὐτὸς ἀνήρ 'the same man'. (Note: αὐτός often unites by crasis with the article: αὐτός, αὐτή, ταὐτό or ταὐτόν 'the same'.)

3. In the oblique cases (all except the nominative), the forms of αὐτός are the usual personal pronouns of the third person, 'him', 'her', 'it', 'them', etc. (Note that the nominative is not so used, because the nominative if used strictly as a pronoun is used as the intensive, '-self'.)

εἶδον αὐτόν I saw *him*.

Reflexive Pronouns

The reflexive pronouns are compounded from the stems of the personal pronouns (first ἐμ-, second σε-, third ἑ-) and the oblique cases of αὐτός. In the plural of the first and second persons, the two forms are declined separately (the personal pronoun and the form of αὐτός). There is no nominative of the reflexive pronoun. The reflexive pronoun refers back to the subject of its clause (or sometimes in a dependent clause it refers to the subject of the main clause).

First Person Reflexive

	Singular		Plural	
---	M	F	M	F
GEN	ἐμαυτοῦ	ἐμαυτῆς	ἡμῶν αὐτῶν	ἡμῶν αὐτῶν
DAT	ἐμαυτῷ	ἐμαυτῇ	ἡμῖν αὐτοῖς	ἡμῖν αὐταῖς
ACC	ἐμαυτόν	ἐμαυτήν	ἡμᾶς αὐτούς	ἡμᾶς αὐτάς

Second Person Reflexive

	Singular		Plural	
	M	F	M	F
GEN	σεαυτοῦ (σαυτοῦ)	σεαυτῆς (σαυτῆς)	ὑμῶν αὐτῶν	ὑμῶν αὐτῶν
DAT	σεαυτῷ (σαυτῷ)	σεαυτῇ (σαυτῇ)	ὑμῖν αὐτοῖς	ὑμῖν αὐταῖς
ACC	σεαυτόν (σαυτόν)	σεαυτήν (σαυτήν)	ὑμᾶς αὐτούς	ὑμᾶς αὐτάς

Third Person Reflexive

Singular

	M	F	N
GEN	ἑαυτοῦ (αὐτοῦ)	ἑαυτῆς (αὐτῆς)	ἑαυτοῦ (αὐτοῦ)
DAT	ἑαυτῷ (αὐτῷ)	ἑαυτῇ (αὐτῇ)	ἑαυτῷ (αὐτῷ)
ACC	ἑαυτόν (αὐτόν)	ἑαυτήν (αὐτήν)	ἑαυτό (αὐτό)

Plural

	M	F	N
GEN	ἑαυτῶν (αὐτῶν)	ἑαυτῶν (αὐτῶν)	ἑαυτῶν (αὐτῶν)
DAT	ἑαυτοῖς (αὐτοῖς)	ἑαυταῖς (αὐταῖς)	ἑαυτοῖς (αὐτοῖς)
ACC	ἑαυτούς (αὐτούς)	ἑαυτάς (αὐτάς)	ἑαυτά (αὐτά)

(Do not confuse the alternate forms of the reflexive with forms of αὐτός: note the difference in breathing.)

Οἰδίπους τὸν ἑαυτοῦ πατέρα ἀπέκτεινε.

Oedipus killed *his own* father.

The Possessive Adjectives

Adjectives meaning 'my', 'your', 'our' are derived from the personal pronouns:

ἐμός, ἐμή, ἐμόν   'my'

σός, σή, σόν   'your' (singular)

ἡμέτερος, -α, -ον   'our'

ὑμέτερος, -α, -ον   'your' (plural)

These are declined like other adjectives in -ος, -η, -ον or -ος, -α, -ον; and like any adjective they must agree with their noun in gender, number, and case. (That is, they agree with the thing possessed, not with the possessor.)

For 'his', 'her', 'its', 'their', the genitive forms of αὐτός are used: αὐτοῦ ('his', 'its'), αὐτῆς ('her'), αὐτῶν ('their').

These are not adjectives but pronouns and so agree in gender and number with the possessor; their case is the genitive (of possession).

The possessive adjectives and the genitive of the reflexive pronoun go into the attributive position:

ὁ ἐμὸς πατήρ   'my father'

ἡ ἐμὴ μήτηρ   'my mother'

ὁ ἐμαυτοῦ/ἐμαυτῆς πατήρ   'my own father'

ἡ ἐμαυτοῦ/ἐμαυτῆς μήτηρ   'my own mother'

But the possessive genitive of the personal pronoun goes into the predicate position:

ὁ πατήρ μου   'my father'

ὁ πατὴρ αὐτοῦ/αὐτῆς   'his/her father'

Vocabulary

Pronouns and Possessive Adjectives

αὐτός, αὐτή, αὐτό	1. -*self* (intensive pronoun); 2. *same* (with article; in attributive posit.); 3. *him, her, it, them* (personal pronoun)
ἐαυτοῦ, ἐαυτῆς, ἐαυτοῦ	*(of) himself, herself, itself* (reflexive)
ἐγώ, ἐμοῦ (μοῦ), κτλ.	*I, of me,* etc. (personal pronoun)
ἐμαυτοῦ, ἐμαυτῆς	*(of) myself* (reflexive)
ἐμός, ἐμή, ἐμόν	*my* (possessive adjective)
ἡμεῖς, ἡμῶν, κτλ.	*we, of us,* etc. (personal pronoun)
ἡμέτερος, ἡμετέρα, ἡμέτερον	*our* (possessive adjective)
σεαυτοῦ, σεαυτῆς	*(of) yourself* (reflexive)
σός, σή, σόν	*your* (singular: possessive adjective)
σύ, σοῦ (σου) κτλ.	*you, of you* (singular: personal pronoun)
ὑμεῖς, ὑμῶν, κτλ.	*you, of you, etc.* (plural: personal pronoun)
ὑμέτερος, ὑμετέρα, ὑμέτερον	*your* (plural: possessive adjective)
ἀγάπη, ἀγάπης, ἡ	*love, charity* (Agape)
βλάπτω, βλάψω, ἔβλαψα, βέβλαφα, βέβλαμμαι	*hinder* (from + gen.); *harm, hurt*
δεῖ	impersonal, *there is need, it is necessary* (+ acc. of person and infinitive)(ἔδει, impf.)
διαβάλλω	*throw over/across; attack, slander* (cf. βάλλω)
δόξα, δόξης, ἡ	*expectation, estimation, repute, opinion*
δύναμις, δυνάμεως, ἡ	*power, ability, influence; forces* (for war)(dynamic)
ἕκαστος, ἑκάστη, ἕκαστον	*each, every* (in predicate position, if used with article)

ἐπιστολή, ἐπιστολῆς, ἡ   (anything sent by messenger) *message, letter* (some-
                         times in plural for one letter)(epistle)
ἤδη   *already, by this time*
μέλλω, μελλήσω, ἐμέλ-   *be likely, be destined, be about to* (+ infin.) *delay*
   λησα   (usually + fut. inf.)
μετά   preposition, *with, among*
      with genitive   *in the midst of, with*
     (with dative   poetic, *between, among*)
      with accusative   *after*
μεταβάλλω   *throw into a different position, change* (cf. βάλλω)
μεταβολή, μεταβολῆς, ἡ   *change, transition*
μνῆμα, μνήματος, τό   *remembrance, memorial; memory*
μνήμη, μνήμης, ἡ   *memory* (mnemonic)
ὀνειδίζω, ---, ὠνεί-   *make a reproach, reproach* (usually with acc. of thing,
   δισα, ὠνείδικα   dat. of person)
ὄνειδος, ὀνείδους, τό   *reproach, blame*
οὔπω (οὐ . . . πω)   *not yet*
παρέχω   *furnish, supply* (cf. ἔχω)
περί   preposition, *round about*
      with genitive   *about, concerning*
     (with dative   mostly poetic, *around, about, concerning* of place or
                         cause)
      with accusative   *about, near*
πολλάκις   *often, many times*
πῶς;   *how?*
ὑπέρ   preposition, *over*
      with genitive   *over, in defense of*
      with accusative   *over, beyond*
χρή   impersonal, *it is necessary* (impf. ἔχρην, infin. χρῆ-
                         ναι/χρῆν)
χρήσιμος, χρησίμη,   *useful* (also -ος, -ον)
   χρήσιμον

Syntax: Dative of Possession

    With the **verbs** εἰμί and γίγνομαι (and similar verbs), the da-
tive may be used to denote the *possessor*. The thing possessed is
then in the nominative.

    Example: 'I have friends' may be expressed as

                 ἔχω φίλους.   or

                ἐμοί εἰσι φίλοι.

When the dative is used for the possessor, it emphasizes the interest of the possessor in the thing he possesses. Cf. this example from Thucydides:

ἄλλοις μὲν χρήματά ἐστι πολλά, ἡμῖν δὲ ξύμμαχοι ἀγαθοί.

Others have a lot of money, but *we* have good allies.

Exercises

1. Translate:

1. τίς σε βλάπτει ἀγάπης;
2. εἰ μεγάλη ἦν ἡ πόλις ἡμῶν, ἡμῖν 'ἂν πολλοὶ πόλεμοι ἐγίγνοντο.
3. τίνα πατρίδα φυγόντες ἤλθετε παρ' ἡμᾶς;
4. τί δεῖ πράττεσθαι;
5. ταύτην γε τὴν χώραν λείπειν ἡμᾶς δεῖ.
6. τί γὰρ δεῖ τάδε λέγειν;
7. ἔδει ἡμᾶς ἐκεῖνον τὸν ἄνδρα ἰδεῖν καὶ πάντα αὐτῷ εἰπεῖν.
8. δεῖ γὰρ τοὺς ἀνθρώπους ἑαυτοὺς γιγνώσκειν.
9. ὁ διώκων διέβαλε τὸν φεύγοντα.
10. τί δ' ἐμὲ διαβάλλεις;
11. ἡ πόλις ἡμῶν ἔχει τὴν δόξαν μεγάλης δυνάμεως.
12. πάντες δόξαν ἔχειν ἀγαθὴν βούλονται.
13. παῦσαί γε δεῖ ἡμᾶς τὴν τοῦ βασιλέως δύναμιν.
14. ἕκαστος ἐθέλει τὰ ἑαυτοῦ ἔχειν.
15. καθ' ἑκάστην τὴν ἡμέραν ἐπιστολὴν γράφομεν.
16. ἐπιστολὰς ἀλλήλαις ἔγραφον.
17. ἤδη αὐτὸν ἐρχόμενον αἰσθανόμεθα.
18. τοῦ μέλλοντος χρόνου οὐκ αἰσθάνεσθε.
19. ἔμελλόν γε παρεῖναι.
20. οἱ μετὰ ἀνθρώπου τινὸς οὐκ ἀεὶ φίλοι.
21. μεθ' ἡμέρας τρεῖς ὑμᾶς δεῖ λιπεῖν.
22. μετὰ ταῦτα ἔφυγεν.
23. δεῖ σε τοὺς τρόπους μεταβαλέσθαι.
24. τὰ μὲν ὀνόματα μετέβαλον, οὐ δὲ ἑαυτούς.
25. χαίρομεν μνῆμα ἀγαθῶν ἔχουσαι.
26. οὐ βούλομαι κακῶν ἔχειν μνήμην.
27. δεῖ σὲ ταῦτα ἐν μνήμῃ λαβεῖν.
28. ὁ σοφὸς ἀνὴρ λείψεται ἀθάνατον μνήμην ἑαυτοῦ.
29. οὐ πολλὰ ἔξεστιν εἰπεῖν ἀπὸ μνήμης.

30. αἰσχύνει τοῦτό μοι ὀνειδίζων;

31. χρήματα μὲν παρέσχεν ὁ βασιλεύς· σώματα δὲ παρέσχον οἱ πολῖται.

32. οὐκ ὄνειδος φέρει ἡ ἀρετή.

33. ὄνειδός ἐστι κακὰ πράττειν.

34. πολλὰ καὶ ἀγαθὰ ἔφη περὶ τοῦ πατρός σου.

35. χρή με λέγειν.

36. ὁ χρηστὸς πολίτης χρήσιμός ἐστι πόλει.

37. ἡμῶν μὴ ἐρχομένων, τί πράξεις;

38. τὴν πατρίδα ἔλιπεν οὐ βουλόμενος τὸν ἑαυτοῦ πατέρα ἀποκτεῖναι.

39. οὐ χαίρετε ἡμᾶς ἰδοῦσαι;

40. μετὰ τῶν ἐμαυτοῦ φίλων εἰς τὴν οἰκίαν σου ἔλθον.

2. Fill-in:

1. We μὲν ἔχομεν χρήματα, you δὲ οὐκ ἔχετε.

2. εἴδομεν him.

3. οὐ γιγνώσκομεν ourselves.

4. τί you πεπόνθατε;

5. I myself ἐθέλω εἶναι to you φιλία.

6. οἱ ἄρχοντες (over) us ἄρχουσιν. (what case follows ἄρχω?)

7. Them οὐκ ἐπίστευσαν.

8. (He) himself τάδε ἔφη.

9. ἐπιστολὰς to us ἔπεμψεν.

10. αὐτή ἐστιν my mother.

11. ἐνόμισα (that) he παρεῖναι.

12. ἀκηκόαμεν you λέγοντος.

13. εἶπες to me;

14. ἡ θυγάτηρ ἠθέλησε ἀποκτείνειν τὴν her own μητέρα;

15. οὐ πείθεται ὑπὸ them.

16. ὁ same πολίτης ταῦτα ἔπραξεν.

17. The poet himself ἔγραψε τάδε.

18. ἔχομεν the same opinion.

19. They themselves ἀπέκτειναν τοὺς ξένους.

20. τυγχάνω ἰδὼν these same (things).

21. The god himself ἐφαίνετο.

22. οἱ μὲν ἄλλοι us εἶδον.

23. We δὲ οὐκ εἴδομεν ourselves.

24. ἔβαλον them λίθους.

25. οἱ γέροντες you καὶ them πεπαιδεύκασιν, us δ' οὔ.

3.   Write in Greek:

1.   He killed his (someone else's) father.

2.   He killed his own father without knowing (it).

3.   This is my mother (express in two ways).

4.   I saw my (own) mother doing these things.

5.   The same man came to find me.

6.   We ourselves are hurting each other.

7.   Who knows himself?

8.   The king himself did not wish to rule over us.

9.   I myself happened to be present.

10. You are not a friend to yourself.

3b. Compose sentences using the following:

1-3   The reflexive pronoun of each person.

4-6   The three uses of αὐτός.

      Write each of the following in two ways:

7-8   We had fine houses, but you did not.

9-10 They have much money, but we have good friends.

Readings

διαφθερεῖ fut. 3rd. sg. of διαφθείρω 'destroy utterly'

1. ἥδ' ἡμέρα φύσει σε καὶ διαφθερεῖ.

   Sophocles, *Oedipus Tyrannus* (Teiresias' dire warning to Oedipus)

λιμήν, -ένος, ὁ 'harbor', 'ha-
ven'; παίζω 'play' (παίζετε is
imperative)

[2. 'ελπὶς καὶ σύ, Τύχη, μέγα χαίρετε· τὸν
      λιμέν' εὗρον·
    οὐδὲν ἐμοί χ' ὑμῖν· παίζετε τοὺς μετ'
    ἐμέ.]

   Greek Anthology (anon.)

3. οὐκ ἀκηκόατε, ὅτι οὐ σχολὴ αὐτῷ;

   Plato, *Protagoras*

4. Socrates. ἐθελήσεις οὖν καὶ σὺ ἐμοι εἰπεῖν περὶ τῆς ἀρετῆς;

Meno. ἔγωγε.

Plato, *Meno*

γνῶθι σαυτόν 'know yourself'   5. τὸ γνῶθι σαυτὸν πᾶσίν ἐστι χρήσιμον.

Menander

ἱππεύω 'ride'; Κένταυρος, -ου, ὁ   6. Κένταυρος ἑαυτὸν ἱππεύων . . . .
'Centaur'

Demetrius, *On Style*

προθύμως 'zealously'   7. τί κέρδος ἦν αὐτῷ διαβάλλειν ἐμὲ πρὸς
                                    ὑμᾶς οὕτω προθύμως;

Lysias

8. περὶ τῆς ἐμαυτοῦ ψυχῆς οὐ πολλὰς ἐλπίδας
    ἔχω.

Dionysius of Halicarnassus

9. καὶ πολλὰς μεταβολὰς μεταβαλοῦσα ἡ τρα-
    γῳδία ἐπαύσατο, ἐπεὶ ἔσχε τὴν αὑτῆς φύ-
    σιν.

Aristotle, *Poetics*

10. τοῦτ' ἤδη σόν, οἶμαι, τὸ ἔργον, ὦ ξένε,
    ἀλλ' οὐκ ἐμὸν γίγνεται.

Plato, *Politicus*

11. ἀνδρὸς καὶ γυναικὸς ἡ αὐτὴ ἀρετή.

Diogenes Laertius (referring to the
thought of Antisthenes)

ἀμπέχω 'surround', 'cover'   12. οὐ σὸν μνῆμα τόδ' ἔστ' Εὐριπίδη, ἀλλὰ σὺ
                                    τοῦδε·
                                    τῇ σῇ γὰρ δόξῃ μνῆμα τόδ' ἀμπέχεται.

Greek Anthology (anon.)

ὑπεστήσατο 'he supposed' (aor. [13. ἀρχὴν δὲ τῶν πάντων ὕδωρ ὑπεστήσατο, καὶ
mid. of ὑφίστημι); ἔμψυχος, -ον   τὸν κόσμον ἔμψυχον καὶ δαιμόνων πλήρη.
'animate'; πλήρης, -ες 'full of'   τάς τε ὥρας τοῦ ἐνιαυτοῦ φασιν αὐτὸν εὑ-
(+ gen.); ἐνιαυτός, -οῦ, ὁ =   ρεῖν καὶ εἰς τριακοσίας ἐξήκοντα πέντε
ἔτος; τριακοσίοι 'three hundred';   ἡμέρας διελεῖν.]
ἑξήκοντα 'sixty'; διελεῖν aor.
inf. of διαιρέω 'divide'   Diogenes Laertius (on Thales)

ἁπλῶς 'simply'; *νοῦς, ὁ 'mind' 14. ἐκεῖνος [ἔφη] μὲν γὰρ ἁπλῶς ταὐτὸν ψυχὴν
(G. νοῦ, D. νῷ, A. νοῦν); ἐκεῖ-   καὶ νοῦν.
νος refers to Democritus; ταὐτόν
is often found for ταὐτό (= τὸ   Aristotle, περὶ ψυχῆς
αὐτό)

     *Note: the words marked with the asterisk (*) should be studied as rec-
ognition vocabulary.

φυσικός --; *ζωή, -ῆς, ἡ 'life';
*τροφή, -ῆς, ἡ 'nurture'; αὔξη-
σις, -εως, ἡ 'growth'; φθίσις,
-εως, ἡ 'decay'

15. τῶν δὲ φυσικῶν τὰ μὲν ἔχει ζωήν, τὰ δ'
οὐκ ἔχει· ζωὴν δὲ λέγομεν τὴν δι' αὐτοῦ
τροφήν τε καὶ αὔξησιν καὶ φθίσιν.

Aristotle

*ὀφείλω 'be obliged', 'owe';
γνώρισις 'getting to know' (ac-
quaintance)

16. ἦ πολλὴν χάριν ὀφείλω σοι τῆς Θεαιτήτου
γνωρίσεως, ὦ Θεόδωρε, ἅμα καὶ τῆς τοῦ
ξένου.

Plato, *Politicus*

*πλεῖστος, -η, -ον 'most'; ἐχέτω
'let (it) have' (third person
imperative); ἠθικός 'moral',
'expressive of moral character';
διάλογος --; σχεδόν 'almost',
'as it were'; οὐδενός gen. of
οὐδέν 'nothing'

[17. πλεῖστον δὲ ἐχέτω τὸ ἠθικὸν ἡ ἐπιστολή,
ὥσπερ καὶ ὁ διάλογος· σχεδὸν γὰρ εἰκόνα
ἕκαστος τῆς ἑαυτοῦ ψυχῆς γράφει τὴν ἐπι-
στολήν. καὶ ἔστι μὲν καὶ ἐξ ἄλλου λόγου
παντὸς ἰδεῖν τὸ ἦθος τοῦ γράφοντος, ἐξ
οὐδενὸς δὲ οὕτως, ὡς ἐπιστολῆς.]

Demetrius, *On Style*

*ἡγεμών, -όνος, ὁ 'leader'; ἀ-
πευθύνω 'govern', 'restore'; ἐξ
+ οἶδα; εἰς + εἶδον

18. Creon. ἦν ἡμῖν, ὦναξ, Λάϊός ποθ' ἡγεμὼν
γῆς τῆσδε, πρὶν σὲ τήνδ' ἀπευθύνειν πόλιν.
Oedipus. ἔξοιδ' ἀκούων· οὐ γὰρ εἰσεῖδόν
γέ πω.

Sophocles, *Oedipus Tyrannus*

Σκύθης, -ου, ὁ 'Scythian'

19. ὀνειδιζόμενος ὑπὸ Ἀττικοῦ ὅτι Σκύθης
ἐστίν, ἔφη, 'ἀλλ' ἐμοῦ μὲν ὄνειδος ἡ πατρίς, σὺ δὲ τῆς πατρίδος.'

Diogenes Laertius on Anacharsis

Λυσίου gen. of 'Lysias'; φαρμα-
κοπώλης 'druggist'; ὑπολαμβάνω
'understand', 'believe'; ἐχθρός,
-ή, -όν 'hated', 'hostile'; ὅπου
'where', 'when'

[20. Λυσίου τοῦ φαρμακοπώλου πυθομένου εἰ
θεοὺς νομίζει, 'πῶς δέ,' εἶπεν, 'οὐ νομίζω, ὅπου καὶ σὲ θεοῖς ἐχθρὸν ὑπολαμβάνω;']

Diogenes Laertius on Diogenes

μύρον, -ου, τό 'perfume'
(myrrh); δύνασαι 'you can';
μυρίσαι (aor. inf.) of μυρίζω
'make to smell sweet', 'perfume'; καί adverbial

21. πέμπω σοι μύρον ἡδύ, μύρῳ παρέχων χάριν
οὐ σοί·
αὐτὴ γὰρ μυρίσαι καὶ τὸ μύρον δύνασαι.

Greek Anthology (anon.)

*ἐχθρός, -ή, -όν 'hated', 'hos-
tile'; ἐχθρός, -οῦ, ὁ 'enemy'

22. φίλος με βλάπτων οὐδὲν ἐχθροῦ διαφέρει.

Menander (with friends like you . . .)

ῥαψῳδός --; *στρατηγός, -οῦ, ὁ
'general'; πάνυ γε 'yes', 'by
all means' (γε in conversation,
'yes')

23. Socrates. 'ἀλλ' ἐκεῖνο μὴν δοκεῖ σοι,
ὅστις γε ἀγαθὸς ῥαψῳδός, καὶ στρατηγὸς
ἀγαθὸς εἶναι;
Ion. πάνυ γε.
Socrates. οὐκοῦν σὺ τῶν Ἑλλήνων ἄριστος ῥαψῳδὸς εἶ;
Ion. πολύ γε, ὦ Σώκρατες.

εὖ (adv. of ἀγαθός) 'well'; ἴσθι
'know!' (imperative); τί δή ποτ'
'why in the world?'; ῥαψῳδέω
'recite poems'; περιιών 'going
around' (pres. ptcpl.); ἀμφότερος, -α, -ον 'both'; στρατηγέω
'be general'; στέφανος, -ου, ὁ
'crown', 'wreath'; ἐστεφανωμένος
'crowned' (pf. mid. pt.); χρεία,
-ας, ἡ 'need', 'lack'; οὐδεμία
'no' (agrees with χρεία)(fem.
nom. sg. of οὐδείς)

*εὐσεβής, -ές 'pious'; θεοφιλής,
-ές 'loved by the gods'; *παντά-
πασι 'altogether'; τὸ ἐναντίον
'the opposite'; ἄρτι 'just now';
γέμω 'be full'; *ὀνομάζω (vb.
cf. ὄνομα); τί μήν 'of course'

Socrates. ἦ καὶ στρατηγός, ὦ Ἴων, τῶν
Ἑλλήνων ἄριστος εἶ;
Ion. εὖ ἴσθι, ὦ Σώκρατες· καὶ ταῦτά γε
ἐκ τῶν Ὁμήρου μαθών.
Socrates. τί δή ποτ' οὖν πρὸς τῶν θεῶν,
ὦ Ἴων, ἀμφότερα ἄριστος ὢν τῶν Ἑλλήνων, καὶ στρατηγὸς καὶ ῥαψῳδός, ῥαψῳδεῖς
μὲν περιιών τοῖς Ἕλλησι στρατηγεῖς δ'
οὔ; ἢ ῥαψῳδοῦ μὲν δοκεῖ σοι χρυσῷ στε-
φάνῳ ἐστεφανωμένου πολλὴ χρεία εἶναι
τοῖς Ἕλλησι, στρατηγοῦ δὲ οὐδεμία;

  Plato, *Ion*

[24. Socrates. δίκαιος ἀνὴρ καὶ εὐσεβὴς καὶ
ἀγαθὸς πάντως ἄρ' οὐ θεοφιλής ἐστιν;
Protarchus. τί μήν;
Socrates. τί δέ; ἄδικός τε καὶ παντάπα-
σι κακὸς ἄρ' οὐ τοὐναντίον ἐκείνῳ;
Protarchus. πῶς δ' οὔ;
Socrates. πολλῶν μὴν ἐλπίδων, ὡς ἐλέγο-
μεν ἄρτι, πᾶς ἄνθρωπος γέμει.
Protarchus. τί δ' οὔ;
Socrates. λόγοι μήν εἰσιν ἐν ἑκάστοις
ἡμῶν, ἃς ἐλπίδας ὀνομάζομεν;
Protarchus. ναί.]

  Plato, *Philebus*

*ἀμφότερος 'both of two'; πρεσ-
βεῦον participle of πρεσβεύω
'rank before', 'put first',
'honor', 'cultivate'

25. μέρη δὲ φιλοσοφίας τρία, φυσικόν, ἠθι-
κόν, διαλεκτικόν· φυσικὸν μὲν τὸ περὶ
κόσμου καὶ τῶν ἐν αὐτῷ· ἠθικὸν δὲ τὸ
περὶ βίου καὶ τῶν πρὸς ἡμᾶς· διαλεκτικὸν
δὲ τὸ ἀμφοτέρων τοὺς λόγους πρεσβεῦον.

  Diogenes Laertius

ἐκδέχομαι 'take from', 'receive
from'; ἄραντος (aor. act. pt. of
ἀείρω 'take away'); *ἀργύριον
'silver', 'money'; αἰτιασάμενον
aor. pt. of αἰτιάομαι 'accuse',
'censure'; ἐνδεής, -ές 'in need
of' (+ gen.)

26. ἐκδεξάμενος τὸ ἀργύριον παρὰ Διονυσίου,
Πλάτωνος ἄραντος βιβλίον, πρὸς τὸν αἰτιασάμενον, 'ἐγὼ μὲν γάρ,' εἰπεῖν, 'ἀργυ-
ρίων, Πλάτων δὲ βιβλίων ἐστὶν ἐνδεής.'

  Diogenes Laertius on Aristippus

Ἐμπεδοκλέους gen. of 'Empedo-
cles'; ἀνεύρετος 'not to be
found'; *εἰκότως 'reasonably'
(cf. ἔοικα); ἐπιγνωσόμενον fut.
pt. of ἐπιγιγνώσκω 'discover';
αὐτῷ refers to Xenophanes

27. Ἐμπεδοκλέους δὲ εἰπόντος αὐτῷ ὅτι ἀνεύ-
ρετός ἐστιν ὁ σοφός, 'εἰκότως,' ἔφη·
'σοφὸν γὰρ εἶναι δεῖ τὸν ἐπιγνωσόμενον
τὸν σοφόν.'

  Diogenes Laertius ("It takes one to
    know one.")

ἐφέλκω 'draw to one', 'attract';
*σίδηρος, -ου, ὁ 'iron', 'wea-
pon'

28. αὐτὸς γὰρ ἐφέλκεται ἄνδρα σίδηρος.

  Homer, *Odyssey*

εἰς τοὺς αἰῶνας (cf. *per saecula saeculorum*) 'forever and ever'

29. ὅτι σοῦ ἐστιν ἡ δόξα καὶ ἡ δύναμις διὰ Ἰησοῦ Χριστοῦ εἰς τοὺς αἰῶνας.

Διδαχή

30. ἡ μὲν οὖν ὁδὸς τῆς ζωῆς ἐστιν αὕτη.

Διδαχή

*μέντοι 'of course'; ὤπασα aor. of ὀπάζω 'give'; σφιν 'to them' (dat. pl.); φλογωπός, -όν 'flaming red'; ἐφήμερος, -ον 'of a day'; ἐφήμεροι 'creatures of a day'; ἐκ + μανθάνω; *τέχνη 'skill', 'art', 'craft'

31. Prometheus. πρὸς τοῖσδε μέντοι πῦρ ἐγώ σφιν ὤπασα.
Chorus. καὶ νῦν φλογωπὸν πῦρ ἔχουσ' ἐφήμεροι;
Prometheus. ἀφ' οὗ γε πολλὰς ἐκμαθήσονται τέχνας.

Aeschylus, *Prometheus*

32. ἔστιν ὁ φίλος ἄλλος αὐτός.

Aristotle, *Nicomachean Ethics*

ζῇ '(he) lives' (cf. Z); *φάος (φῶς), φωτός, τό 'light'; *δῶμα, -ατος, τό 'house'; λευκός, -ή, -όν 'white', 'clear'; ἦμαρ, -ατος, τό = ἡμέρα; μελάγχιμος, -ον 'black'

[33. Messenger. Ξέρξης μὲν αὐτὸς ζῇ τε καὶ βλέπει φάος.
Atossa. ἐμοῖς μὲν εἶπας δώμασιν φάος μέγα
καὶ λευκὸν ἦμαρ νυκτὸς ἐκ μελαγχίμου.]

Aeschylus, *Persae*

*πῆμα, -ατος, τό 'misery', 'calamity'

34. Κρέων δέ σοι πῆμ' οὐδέν, ἀλλ' αὐτὸς σὺ σοί.

Sophocles, *Oedipus Tyrannus* (Teiresias speaking)

*βέβαιος, -α, -ον 'steadfast', 'firm'; *σῴζω 'save'; *ἀδελφός, -οῦ, ὁ 'brother'

35. ἀγάπης γὰρ ἀληθοῦς καὶ βεβαίας ἐστίν, μὴ μόνον ἑαυτὸν θέλειν σῴζεσθαι, ἀλλὰ καὶ πάντας τοὺς ἀδελφούς.

Martyrdom of Polycarp

τέκνον, -ου, τό 'child'; *γυμνός, -ή, -όν 'naked', 'unarmed'; ἐλέησον (aor. imp. of ἐλεέω 'have mercy'); μὴ φοβοῦ 'do not be afraid'; ὑπομενῶ 'bear' (fut. 1st sg.); τόν (sc. θάνατον); στῆθι 'stay!'; πίστευσον aor. imperative; ἀποστέλλω, aor. ἀπέστειλα 'send'; 'ἂν δέῃ 'if necessary'; ἀντιδώσω fut. 1st sg. of ἀντιδίδωμι 'give in exchange', 'give in return'

[36. 'τί με φεύγεις, τέκνον, τὸν σαυτοῦ πατέρα, τὸν γυμνόν, τὸν γέροντα; ἐλέησόν με, τέκνον, μὴ φοβοῦ· ἔχεις ἔτι ζωῆς ἐλπίδας. ἐγὼ Χριστῷ λόγον δώσω ὑπὲρ σοῦ· ἂν δέῃ, τὸν σὸν θάνατον ἑκὼν ὑπομενῶ, ὡς ὁ Κύριος τὸν ὑπὲρ ἡμῶν· ὑπὲρ σοῦ τὴν ψυχὴν ἀντιδώσω τὴν ἐμήν. στῆθι, πίστευσον· Χριστός με ἀπέστειλεν.']

Eusebius (quoting Clement) (St. John speaking to the young robber who has left the fold.)

ἀσπάζομαι 'greet'; ἀντι + ἀσπάζομαι 'greet in return'

37. ἀσπάζεταί με λέγουσα· 'χαῖρε συ, ἄνθρωπε.' καὶ ἐγὼ αὐτὴν ἀντησπασάμην· 'Κυρία, χαῖρε.'

A vision of the Church in the form of

a woman, from the *Shepherd* of Hermas. The first person is the author, Hermas.

Λάϊος, -ου, ὁ 'Laius' (father of Oedipus); ἰού (a tragic noise, exclamation of distress); Λαβδακιδᾶν gen. pl. 'of the Labdacids' (descendants of Labdacus); -ᾶν gen. ending in Doric & in tragic choral sections; *ἄθλιος, -α, -ον 'unhappy'

[38. Oedipus.   Λαΐου ἴστε τιν';
Chorus.   ὦ ἰοὺ ἰού.
Oedipus.   τό τε Λαβδακιδᾶν γένος;
Chorus.   ὦ Ζεῦ.
Oedipus.   ἄθλιον Οἰδιπόδαν;
Chorus.   σὺ γὰρ ὅδ' εἶ;]

  Sophocles, *Oedipus at Colonus*

βέβηκεν perfect of βαίνω 'go' (3rd sg. 'he has gone'); φωνεῖν 'to speak'; πέλας 'near' (+ gen.)(adv.)

[39. Oedipus.   ὦ τέκνον, ἦ βέβηκεν ἡμῖν ὁ ξένος;
Antigone.   βέβηκεν, ὥστε πᾶν ἐν ἡσύχῳ, πάτερ,
ἔξεστι φωνεῖν, ὡς ἐμοῦ μόνης πέλας.]

  Sophocles, *O. C.*

*ἀλλότριος, -α, -ον 'of/belonging to another'

40. ἔστι δὲ δικαιοσύνη μὲν ἀρετὴ δι' 'ἣν τὰ αὑτῶν ἕκαστοι ἔχουσι, καὶ ὡς ὁ νόμος, ἀδικία δὲ δι' 'ἣν τὰ ἀλλότρια, οὐχ ὡς ὁ νόμος.

  Aristotle, *Rhetoric*

ὑπό (here: 'subject to')

41. τῶν γὰρ Ἑλλήνων οἱ μὲν ὑφ' ἡμῖν οἱ δ' ὑπὸ Λακεδαιμονίοις εἰσίν.

  Isocrates, *Panegyricus*

κτενεῖν (fut. inf. of (ἀπο)κτείνω)

42. τὴν παῖδα τὴν σὴν τήν τ' ἐμὴν μέλλεις κτενεῖν;

  Euripides, *Iphigenia at Aulis* (Clytemnestra addresses her husband)

*ἔνδικος, -ον 'just'; στενάζω 'groan', 'lament'; ἡδέως 'pleasantly'; ὁρᾶν (pres. inf. of ὁράω) 'to see'

[43.   . . . οὐ γὰρ ἔνδικον
σὲ μὲν στενάζειν, τἀμὰ δ' ἡδέως ἔχειν,
θνῄσκειν τε τοὺς σούς, τοὺς δ' ἐμοὺς ὁρᾶν φάος.]

  Euripides, *I. A.*

*ἔπειτα 'then'; νυνί emphatic νῦν; τὸ συμφέρον, -οντος 'advantage'; ἀντιλέγω 'contradict'

44. ἔπειτα κἀκεῖνο χρὴ σκοπεῖν· νυνὶ γὰρ περὶ μὲν τοῦ δικαίου πάντες τὴν αὐτὴν γνώμην ἔχομεν περὶ δὲ τοῦ συμφέροντος ἀντιλέγομεν.

  Isocrates, *Archidamus*

understand λέγουσι

45. οἱ αὐτοὶ περὶ τῶν αὐτῶν τοῖς αὐτοῖς τὰ αὐτά.

  Greek proverb (referring to pedants)

Quotation

Read aloud and learn:

νεκρὸν ἰατρεύειν καὶ γέροντα νουθετεῖν ταὐτόν.

To cure a corpse and to advise an old man: the same thing.
    --Greek proverb.

Who'ld advise a man whose hair is grey,
Would cure a man who's passed away.

B. The Perfect Middle-Passive: The Fifth Principal Part

The perfect and pluperfect middle-passive are formed as one would expect them to be: by adding the middle endings to the reduplicated stem. Certain complications arise because these endings are added directly to the stem (no thematic vowel is used in the perfect).

Formation:

Perfect:

Reduplicated stem + primary endings:

-μαι	-μεθα
-σαι	-σθε
-ται	-νται

Infinitive -σθαι

Participle -μένος (accented on the penult)

Pluperfect:

Augment + reduplicated stem + secondary middle endings:

-μην	-μεθα
-σο	-σθε
-το	-ντο

Perfect and Pluperfect Middle-Passive of λύω: λυ-

'I have ransomed'/'I have been released' λέ-λυ-μαι

'I had ransomed'/'I had been released' ἐ-λε-λύ-μην

Perfect		Pluperfect	
λέλυμαι	λελύμεθα	ἐλελύμην	ἐλελύμεθα
λέλυσαι	λέλυσθε	ἐλέλυσο	ἐλέλυσθε
λέλυται	λέλυνται	ἐλέλυτο	ἐλέλυντο

Infinitive λελύσθαι   Participle λελυμένος λελυμένη λελυμένον

Since these endings are added directly to the verb stem, without a thematic vowel, certain orthographic changes occur in verbs with consonant stems, as indicated in the following chart:

Before	A Labial (β, π, φ)	A Palatal (γ, κ, χ)	A Dental (δ, τ, θ, ζ)	A Nasal (ν, μ)
	changes to	becomes	changes to	
μ (μαι, μην, μεθα, μένος)	-μ	-γ	-σ	-σ
σ (σαι, σο *see below)	-ψ	-ξ	drops out	--
τ (ται, το)	-π	-κ	-σ	-ν
θ (*σθε, σθαι)	-φ	-χ	-σ	-ν

*σ between two consonants is dropped, as in the endings -σθε and -σθαι.

The endings of the third plural -νται and -ντο are not used, but rather periphrastic forms consisting of the perfect middle participle (in the nominative plural, masculine or feminine) and the third plural of the verb εἰμί (that is, εἰσί or ἦσαν).

Liquid stems follow the last two rules, but undergo no other changes.

Examples:

The Perfect and Pluperfect of Consonant Stems

Perfect

LABIAL	PALATAL	DENTAL	NASAL	LIQUID
γράφω	ἄγω	πείθω	φαίνω	ἀγγέλλω
γέγραμμαι	ἦγμαι	πέπεισμαι	πέφασμαι	ἤγγελμαι
γέγραψαι	ἦξαι	πέπεισαι	πεφασμένος εἶ	ἤγγελσαι
γέγραπται	ἦκται	πέπεισται	πέφανται	ἤγγελται
γεγράμμεθα	ἤγμεθα	πεπείσμεθα	πεφάσμεθα	ἠγγέλμεθα
γέγραφθε	ἦχθε	πέπεισθε	πέφανθε	ἤγγελθε
γεγραμμένοι εἰσι	ἠγμένοι εἰσί	πεπεισμένοι εἰσί	πεφασμένοι εἰσί	ἠγγελμένοι εἰσί
γεγράφθαι	ἦχθαι	πεπεῖσθαι	πεφάνθαι	ἠγγέλθαι
γεγραμμένος	ἠγμένος	πεπεισμένος	πεφασμένος	ἠγγελμένος

Pluperfect

ἐγεγράμμην	ἤγμην	ἐπεπείσμην	ἐπεφάσμην	ἠγγέλμην
ἐγέγραφο	ἦξο	ἐπέπεισο	πεφασμένος ἦσθα	ἤγγελσο
ἐγέγραπτο	ἦκτο	ἐπέπειστο	ἐπέφαντο	ἤγγελτο
ἐγεγράμμεθα	ἤγμεθα	ἐπεπείσμεθα	ἐπεφάσμεθα	ἠγγέλμεθα
ἐγέγραφθε	ἦχθε	ἐπέπεισθε	ἐπέφανθε	ἤγγελθε
γεγραμμένοι ἦσαν	ἠγμένοι ἦσαν	πεπεισμένοι ἦσαν	πεφασμένοι ἦσαν	ἠγγελμένοι ἦσαν

Note: If the verb stem ends in μπ (as πέμπω), drop the π before μ, otherwise π is retained, according to the rule for labial stems.

πέμπω: perfect middle stem πεπεμπ-: πέπεμμαι

πέπεμμαι   πεπέμμεθα
πέπεμψαι   πέπεμφθε
πέπεμπται   πεπεμμένοι εἰσί

Infinitive πεπέμφθαι   Participle πεπεμμένος, -η, -ον

The Future Perfect is formed by adding -σομαι to the tense stem: reduplicated stem + σ + ο/ε (thematic vowel) + primary middle endings.

Examples: λύω   λελύσομαι
               γράφω   γεγράψομαι
               λείπω   λελείψομαι
               πράττω   πεπράξομαι

The future perfect usually has a passive meaning ('I shall have been released').

Syntax: Dative of Agent

The dative which denotes the person interested (cf. the dative of possession and dative of interest) also appears as the dative of *agent* with the perfect and pluperfect passive (that is, instead of ὑπό with the genitive, we find the dative without a preposition).

ταῦτα πέπρακται αὐτῷ

This has been done by him.

ἐμοὶ καὶ τούτοις πέπρακται.

It has been done by me and these men. --Demosthenes

Some Perfect Middles (Fifth Principal Part)
    Fill in those left blank:

ἀγγέλλω   ἤγγελμαι
ἄγω   ἦγμαι
ἄρχω   ἦργμαι
βάλλω   βέβλημαι
βουλεύω
βούλομαι   βεβούλημαι
γίγνομαι   γεγένημαι

γιγνώσκω   ἔγνωσμαι
γράφω   γέγραμμαι
δέχομαι   δέδεγμαι
εὑρίσκω   ηὕρημαι
ἔχω   ἔσχημαι
θύω   τέθυμαι
κομίζω   κεκόμισμαι (ζ acts like the dentals)
κρίνω   κέκριμαι (note that some nasal stems drop the nasal
                            and form vowel stem perfect middle)
λαμβάνω   εἴλημμαι (cf. perfect active εἴληφα)
λέγω   (λέλεγμαι) εἴρημαι (cf. εἴρηκα and εἶπον)
λείπω   λέλειμμαι
λύω
νομίζω   νενόμισμαι
παιδεύω
παύω
πείθω   πέπεισμαι
πέμπω   πέπεμμαι
πιστεύω
πράττω (stem πραγ-)   πέπραγμαι
στέλλω   ἔσταλμαι
τείνω   τέταμαι
φαίνω   πέφασμαι
φέρω   ἐνήνεγμαι
χαίρω   κεχάρημαι, κέχαρμαι

Recognizing Stem Types

   If the perfect middle has a vowel before -μαι, then it is a
vowel stem, to be conjugated like λύω in the perfect middle. If
it ends in -μμαι, then it is a labial stem, to follow the pattern
of γράφω: γέγραμμαι. If it ends in -γμαι, then it is a palatal stem
and follows ἄγω: ἦγμαι. Finally, if it ends in -σμαι, it can be
either a dental or a nasal stem. Usually one can determine which
it is (and so, which pattern to follow) by going back to the original stem.

Vocabulary

θάπτω, θάψω, ἔθαψα, ---, τέθαμμαι	*honor with funeral rites* (by burial or cremation)
κωλύω	*hinder, prevent*
μαίνομαι, ---, μέμηνα, μεμάνημαι	*rage, be furious, be mad*
μιμνήσκω, μνήσω, ἔμνησα, ---, μέμνημαι	active, *remind;* middle-passive, *call to mind, remember* (perfect with present meaning)

στρέφω, στρέφω, ἔστρε-   *turn; mid-pass.* turn oneself, be engaged in
   φα, ---, ἔστραμμαι
ἀποστρέφω   *turn back/away, avert*

Exercises

   1.   Conjugate in the perfect middle:

1. παύω   2. δέχομαι   3. λαμβάνω   4. κρίνω
5. λείπω   6. νομίζω   7. φαίνω

   2.   Fill in the perfect and pluperfect middle of the synopses in Lesson VIII.

      New Synopses:

         1.   φέρω third singular
         2.   ἄγω first plural
         3.   πέμπω second plural

   3.   Parse:

1. λελεῖφθαι   13. εἰρημένα   25. ἔστραφαι   37. νενομίσθαι
2. γεγενῆσθαι   14. πεφασμένοι εἰσί   26. ἧκται   38. ἐπεπέμμην
3. πεπραγμένων   15. πεπρᾶχθαι   27. πέφανθε   39. ἐνηνέχθαι
4. βεβληκότας   16. μεμνημένος   28. νενόμισται   40. τέθυται
5. γεγενημένων   17. πεπαίδευνται   29. ἦρχθαι   41. ἐγέγραφο
6. γεγόνασι   18. τέθαπται   30. ἠγγέλμεθα   42. κέκριται
7. γεγραμμένας   19. εὔρηται   31. ἐσταλμένοι εἰσίν 43. λέλειφθε
8. γέγραπται   20. πέπεισμαι   32. ἀπεστράμμεθα   44. βεβλημένη
9. βεβλήκασιν   21. πεπραγμένων   33. ηὔρησθε   45. ἐκεκόμιστο
10. εἴληφεν   22. ἐπέπεισθε   34. πέπεισθε   46. ἐνήνεκται
11. πεπίστευται   23. τέθαμμαι   35. δεδεγμένοι ἦσαν   47. ἔσχηνται
12. πέπαυμαι   24. κεκόμισαι   36. εἴ ληπται   48. ἐδεδέγμεθα

   4.   Translate:

1. μέμνηται τῶν φίλων καὶ παρόντων καὶ ἀπόντων.

2. μεμάνηνται γὰρ αἱ τῆς πόλεως γυναῖκες τῷ θεῷ.

3. τῶν φίλων τὸ σῶμα αὐτοῦ οὐχ εὑρόντων, οὗτος ὁ ἀνὴρ οὐκ ἐτέθαπτο.

4. ὁ κόσμος οὐκ αὐτὸς στρέφει ἑαυτόν, ἀλλ' ὑπὸ θεοῦ στρέφεται.

5. τῇ τῶν ἀγαθῶν ἀρχόντων βουλῇ ὁ πόλεμος ἀπέστραπται.

6. ὁ μὲν στρατιώτης βεβλαμμένος τὸ σῶμα ἀπέθανεν.

7. ὁ δὲ ποιητὴς βεβλαμμένος τὴν ψυχὴν ἐπαύσατο γράφων.

8. τί πέπαυσαι γράφων ἐπιστολὰς τῇ μητρί;

9. γέγραπται ἡ ἐπιστολὴ καὶ ἤδη ἔσταλται.

10. οἱ νόμοι τῷ σοφῷ γεγραμμένοι ἦσαν.

Readings

ποδιαῖος, -ά, -ον 'a foot long/
high/broad'; μείζων 'greater' (+
gen. of comparison, 'than')(nom.
masc. sing.); οἰκουμένη, -ης, ἡ
'the world'

1. . . . φαίνεται μὲν ὁ ἥλιος ποδιαῖος, πεπίστευται δ' εἶναι μείζων τῆς οἰκουμέ-
νης.

Aristotle, περὶ ψυχῆς

δόγμα, -ατος, τό 'opinion'; δια-
παίζω 'jest'; τὰ διαλεκτικά
'dialectics'; ἐρωτήσας 'having
asked' (aor. ptcpl.); τύπτω
'beat', 'strike'

2. φησὶ δ' Ἡρακλείδης ἐν μὲν τοῖς δόγμασι
Πλατωνικὸν εἶναι αὐτόν, διαπαίζειν δὲ τὰ
διαλεκτικά· ὥστε Ἀλεξίνου ποτὲ ἐρωτή-
σαντος εἰ πέπαυται τὸν πατέρα τύπτων,
'ἀλλ' οὔτ' ἔτυπτον,' φάναι, 'οὔτε πέπαυμαι.'

Diogenes Laertius, referring to Mene-
demus

παράδειγμα, -ατος, τό 'example';
δρᾶσαι 'to do' (aor. inf.)

[3. παράδειγμα δ' αὐτῆς τὸ τοιοῦτον, 'οὐ γὰρ
τὸ εἰπεῖν καλῶς καλόν, ἀλλὰ τὸ εἰπόντα
δρᾶσαι τὰ εἰρημένα.']

Demetrius on style

κατὰ πολλά 'for the most part';
χρησιμώτερος, -ά, -ον 'more useful'; γνῶθι σαυτόν (see #5 in
previous reading, p. 203)

4. κατὰ πόλλ' ἄρ' ἐστὶν οὐ καλῶς εἰρημένον
τὸ γνῶθι σαυτόν· χρησιμώτερον γὰρ ἦν
τὸ γνῶθι τοὺς ἄλλους.

Menander

βουλεύου mid. imperative
(pres.); ἔπειμι (εἶμι, 'go')
'come on', ἐπιούσης pres. partic.; περιμενοῦμεν fut. of περι-
μένω 'wait around'; *ἀδύνατος,
-ον 'impossible'; *τρόπος, -ου,
ὁ 'way', 'manner'; πείθου imper.
mid.; ποίει imperative act.,
'do!'; *ἄλλως 'otherwise'; *μη-
δαμῶς/οὐδαμῶς 'in no way', 'not
at all'

5. ἀλλὰ βουλεύου, μᾶλλον δὲ οὐδὲ βουλεύεσθαι ἔτι ὥρα, ἀλλὰ βεβουλεῦσθαι. μία δὲ
βουλή. τῆς γὰρ ἐπιούσης νυκτὸς πάντα
ταῦτα δεῖ πεπρᾶχθαι. εἰ δ' ἔτι περιμενοῦμεν ἀδύνατον καὶ οὐκέτι οἷόν τε.
ἀλλὰ παντὶ τρόπῳ, ὦ Σώκρατες, πείθου μοι
καὶ μηδαμῶς ἄλλως ποίει.

Plato, *Crito* (Crito is speaking)

Σαλαμίς 'Salamis' (the subject
of the couplet); τεκνοῦ 'beget',
'bear' (3rd sg. pres.); θεσμοθέ-
της 'lawgiver'; ἱερός, -ά, -όν
'holy'

[6. ἐπὶ δὲ τῆς εἰκόνος αὐτοῦ ἐπιγέγραπται
τάδε·

ἡ Μήδων ἄδικον παύσασ' ὕβριν ἥδε
Σόλωνα
τόνδε τεκνοῖ Σαλαμὶς θεσμοθέτην
ἱερόν.]

Diogenes Laertius (on Solon's statue)

διαίρεσις, -εως, ἡ 'division';
ἄγραφος --; καλεῖται 'is
called'; πορεύω 'bring', mid.
'go'; *ἀγορά, -ᾶς, ἡ 'marketplace'; γυναικεῖος, -α, -ον 'of
a woman'; ἱμάτιον, -ου, τό
'cloak'; περιβάλλω 'throw a-
round', mid. 'put on'; οὐθείς =
οὐδείς 'nobody', 'no' (nom.
masc. sg.); πολιτεύω 'adminis-
ter the state' (pass. 'be gov-
erned')

φεῦ 'alas'; στένω 'groan'

*δοῦλος, -ου, ὁ 'slave'; οὔτις
'no one' (οὐ + τις); κέκληνται
(pf. mid. of καλέω, 'call');
φῶς, φωτός, ὁ 'man'; ὑπήκοος,
-ον 'subject'; οἱ ὑπήκοοι 'the
subjects'

μηδέν 'nothing'; *ἴσως 'equally', 'perhaps'; ἀποδέδεικται pf.
mid. ἀποδεῖξαι aor. act. inf. of
ἀποδείκνυμαι 'prove'; *θαυμαστός,
-ή, -όν 'to be wondered at',
'admirable'

ἄστεος = ἄστεως; πέρην 'on the
other side of'; καλεομένης
'called' (pres. partic.)

μικρολόγος, -ον 'stingy'; κέκτηται pf. mid. of κτάομαι 'possess' (in pf. 'to have acquired'); *οὐσία, -ας, ἡ 'substance', 'property'

*ἔνιοι, -αι, -α 'some'; Per-
sians: Magi; Babylonians or
Assyrians: Chaldaeans; Indians:
Gymnosophists; Celts and Gala-
tians: Druids; σεμνόθεοι 'Druids'; καθά 'as'

ὑπομαίνομαι 'be somewhat mad';
-ως = '-ly'; νή 'yes', 'by' (+
acc.)

7. Νόμου διαιρέσεις δύο· ὁ μὲν γὰρ αὐτοῦ
γεγραμμένος, ὁ δὲ ἄγραφος. ᾧ μὲν ἐν
ταῖς πόλεσι πολιτευόμεθα, γεγραμμένος
ἐστίν. ὁ δὲ κατὰ ἔθη γινόμενος οὗτος
ἄγραφος καλεῖται· οἷον τὸ μὴ γυμνὸν πο-
ρεύεσθαι εἰς τὴν ἀγορὰν μηδὲ γυναικεῖον
ἱμάτιον περιβάλλεσθαι. ταῦτα γὰρ οὐθεὶς
νόμος κωλύει, ἀλλ' ὅμως οὐ πράττομεν διὰ
τὸ ἀγράφῳ νόμῳ κωλύεσθαι. τοῦ ἄρα νόμου
ἐστὶν ὁ μὲν γεγραμμένος, ὁ δὲ ἄγραφος.

    Diogenes Laertius

8. φεῦ, τῶν Ἀθηνῶν ὡς στένω μεμνημένος.

    Aeschylus, *Persae*

9. οὔτινος δοῦλοι κέκληνται φωτὸς οὐδ' ὑπήκοοι.

    Aeschylus, *Persae* (the chorus, about
    the Athenians)

10. τό τε τὸν θάνατον μηδὲν εἶναι πρὸς ἡμᾶς
εἴρηται μὲν ἴσως τῷ Σώφρονι, ἀποδέδεικται δὲ Ἐπικούρῳ, καὶ ἔστιν οὐ τὸ εἰπεῖν
ἀλλὰ τὸ ἀποδεῖξαι θαυμαστόν.

    Sextus Empiricus, *Against the Profes-
    sors*

11. τέθαπται δὲ Κίμων πρὸ τοῦ ἄστεος πέρην
τῆς διὰ Κοίλης καλεομένης ὁδοῦ.

    Herodotus (written in Ionic)

12. πρὸς τὸν μικρολόγον πλούσιον, 'οὐχ οὗτος,' ἔφη, 'τὴν οὐσίαν κέκτηται, ἀλλ' ἡ
οὐσία τοῦτον.'

    Diogenes Laertius (sayings of Bion)

[13. τὸ τῆς φιλοσοφίας ἔργον ἔνιοί φασιν ἀπὸ
βαρβάρων ἄρξαι. γεγενῆσθαι γὰρ παρὰ μὲν
Πέρσαις Μάγους, παρὰ δὲ Βαβυλωνίοις ἢ
Ἀσσυρίοις Χαλδαίους, καὶ Γυμνοσοφιστὰς
παρ' Ἰνδοῖς, παρά τε Κελτοῖς καὶ Γαλά-
ταις τοὺς καλουμένους Δρυίδας καὶ Σεμνο-
θέους, καθά φησιν Ἀριστοτέλης . . . . .]

    Diogenes Laertius

14. ὑπομαίνεθ' οὗτος, νὴ τὸν Ἀπόλλω, μαίνεται,
μεμάνητ' ἀληθῶς, μαίνεται, νὴ τοὺς θέους.

τον δεσπότην λέγω, Χαρίσιον.

Menander, *The Arbitrants*

*ἑκών, -οῦσα, -όν (base -οντ-)
'willing(ly)'; ἀδικεῖν inf. of
ἀδικέω 'commit injustice', 'do
wrong (to)'; μηδένα 'no (one)'
ms. sg. acc.; διειλέγμεθα pf. of
διαλέγω (mid. 'converse with');
ἐγῷμαι = ἐγὼ οἶμαι; ἐπείσθητε
'you would have been persuaded';
διαβολή (see διαβάλλω) 'slander'; ἀπό + λύω 'release from'

15. πέπεισμαι ἐγὼ ἑκὼν εἶναι μηδένα ἀδικεῖν
    ἀνθρώπων, ἀλλὰ ὑμᾶς τοῦτο οὐ πείθω· ὀλί-
    γον γὰρ χρόνον ἀλλήλοις διειλέγμεθα·
    ἐπεὶ ὡς ἐγῷμαι, εἰ ἦν ὑμῖν νόμος, ὥσπερ
    καὶ ἄλλοις ἀνθρώποις περὶ θανάτου μὴ
    μίαν ἡμέραν μόνον κρίνειν, ἀλλὰ πολλάς,
    ἐπείσθητε ἄν· νῦν δ' οὐ ῥᾴδιον ἐν χρόνῳ
    ὀλίγῳ μεγάλας διαβολὰς ἀπολύεσθαι.

    Plato, *Apology of Socrates*

σπαργανόω 'wrap in swaddling
clothes'; καταπίνω 'swallow
down'; δέδωκε '(she) gave' (pf.
of δίδωμι); γεγεννημένος, -η,
-ον pf. mid. pt. of γεννάω 'beget', 'bear'

16. Rhea deceives Cronus: he asked for his
    son and she gave him a stone.

    Ῥέα δὲ λίθον σπαργανώσασα δέδωκε Κρόνῳ
    καταπιεῖν ὡς τὸν γεγεννημένον παῖδα.
    Apollodorus

ἀφιγμένος pf. mid. pt. of ἀφικνέομαι 'come to'; *Ἀθήναζε 'to
Athens'; Σωκράτους genitive,
'of Socrates'; καθά 'as'

17. Ἀρίστιππος τὸ μὲν γένος ἦν Κυρηναῖος,
    ἀφιγμένος δ' Ἀθήναζε, καθά φησιν Αἰσχί-
    νης, κατὰ κλέος Σωκράτους.

    Diogenes Laertius

ἔστω 'let it be'; ἴδιος, -α, -ον
'particular', 'private', 'peculiar'; πολιτεύω pass. 'be govern-
ed'; ὁμολογεῖσθαι 'to be agreed
to'; *ὅσος, -η, -ον 'as great',
'as much', pl. 'as many' (as)

18. ἔστω δὴ τὸ ἀδικεῖν τὸ βλάπτειν ἑκόντα
    παρὰ τὸν νόμον. νόμος δ' ἐστὶν ὁ μὲν
    ἴδιος ὁ δὲ κοινός. λέγω δὲ ἴδιον μὲν
    καθ' ὃν γεγραμμένον πολιτεύονται, κοι-
    νὸν δὲ ὅσα ἄγραφα παρὰ πᾶσιν ὁμολογεῖ-
    σθαι δοκεῖ.

    Aristotle, *Rhetoric*

κόρη, -ης, ἡ 'girl', 'daughter';
πεύσῃ from πυνθάνομαι; συντόμως
'concisely', 'shortly'; αἰανής,
-ες 'everlasting'; ἀρά, -ᾶς, ἡ
'curse'; ὑπαί = ὑπό; κεκλήμεθα
(see #9 above)

19. πεύσῃ τὰ πάντα συντόμως, Διὸς κόρη.
    ἡμεῖς γάρ ἐσμεν Νυκτὸς αἰανῆ τέκνα.
    Ἀραὶ δ' ἐν οἴκοις γῆς ὑπαὶ κεκλήμεθα.

    Aeschylus, *Eumenides*

*ὧδε 'thus' (adv.); ἐξερέω 'I
shall speak out'; τελέω 'accomplish'

20. ὧδε γὰρ ἐξερέω, τὸ δὲ καὶ τετελεσμένον
    ἔσται.

    Homer, *Iliad* (Athene speaks to Achil-
    les)

συναποδημέω 'go abroad/travel
with' (+ dat.); διαφερόντως 'especially', 'excellently'

21. φασὶ δὲ καὶ τὰς Μούσας αὐτῷ συναποδη-
    μεῖν, παρθένους οὔσας καὶ πεπαιδευμένας
    διαφερόντως.

    Diodorus Siculus

πάλιν 'again' (adv.); ἐκπειράσεις fut. of ἐκπειράζω 'tempt';

22. πάλιν γέγραπται· οὐκ ἐκπειράσεις Κύριον
    τὸν θεόν σου.

*κύριος, -ου, ὁ 'lord'; κύριος,   Matthew
-α, -ον 'having authority',
'dominant'

προσήκειν 'to be fitting'   [23. δοκεῖ δέ μοι καὶ περὶ τῶν πρὸς τοὺς βαρ-
                                         βάρους τῇ πόλει πεπραγμένων προσήκειν
                                         εἰπεῖν.]

                                              Isocrates, *Panegyricus*

τιμᾶν 'to honor' (pres. inf. of   24. νομίζω δὲ χρῆναί σε πάντας μὲν τιμᾶν
τιμάω)   τοὺς περὶ τῶν σοι πεπραγμένων ἀγαθόν τι
                                         λέγοντας.

                                              Isocrates, *To Philip*

τὰ πολιτικά 'affairs of state',   25. δοκεῖ δὲ καὶ ἐν τοῖς πολιτικοῖς ἄριστα
'politics' (subject is Thales);   βεβουλεῦσθαι. Κροίσου γοῦν πέμψαντος
*συμμαχία, -ας, ἡ 'alliance';   πρὸς Μιλησίους ἐπὶ συμμαχίᾳ ἐκώλυσεν·
κρατήσαντος aor. pt. of κρατέω   ὅπερ Κύρου κρατήσαντος ἔσωσε τὴν πόλιν.
'become master', 'prevail';
Κροῖσος, -ου, ὁ 'Croesus'; Κῦ-   Diogenes Laertius
ρος, -ου, ὁ 'Cyrus'; Μιλήσιος,
-α, -ον 'Milesian'

Quotation

    Read aloud and learn the following quotation:

        γέγραπται· οὐκ ἐπ' ἄρτῳ μόνῳ ζήσεται ὁ ἄνθρωπος.

    It is written: man shall not live by bread alone.
                        --Matthew

Syntax Notes, Time Constructions

    1. Genitive of time *within which:* examples:

        ταῦτα τῆς ἡμέρας ἔπραττον.

    They were doing these things during the day.

        πέντε ἡμερῶν γράψω.

    I shall write within five days.

        νυκτός

    during the night

    2. Dative of time *when:* examples:

        ταύτῃ τῇ ἡμέρᾳ γράψω.

    I shall write on this day.

τῷ αὐτῷ ἔτει ἀπέθανεν.

He died in the same year.

Often ἐν is used when there is no modifying word, as ἐν νυκτί 'at night'.

3. Accusative of *extent* of time or space: examples:

ταῦτα τὴν ἡμέραν ἔπραττον.

They were doing these things throughout the day.

πέντε ἡμέρας ἐμείναμεν.

We remained for five days.

LESSON X

A. Comparison of Adjectives

In English, adjectives are compared (1) by adding -*er* for the comparative and -*est* for the superlative (with spelling changes where necessary): nice/nicer/nicest; big/bigger/biggest; lovely/lovelier/loveliest.

Or (2) by putting *more* or *most* before the adjective (this is common for words of more than two syllables): beautiful/more beautiful/most beautiful.

(3) Some adjectives are compared irregularly, among them the very common: good/better/best; bad/worse/worst.

In Greek the most common method of comparison is:

(1) For the *comparative*, add -τερος, -τέρα, -τερον to the *masculine base* of the adjective. And for the *superlative*, add -τατος, -τάτη, -τατον. These are declined regularly, the comparative like δίκαιος, the superlative like ἄριστος.

Notes:

If the penult of an adjective in -ος is short (in the positive), -ο- is lengthened to -ω- for both comparative and superlative. The syllable is long if it contains a long vowel or diphthong or two or more consonants, or a double consonant (ζ, ξ, or ψ).

The *masculine base* of -ος adjectives is found by removing -ς from the masculine nominative.

Adjectives in -ης, -ες have their bases in -εσ- to which the regular -τερος/-τατος is added.

On the analogy of these, -εστερος/-εστατος is added to adjectives in -ων (base in -ον).

Examples:

Positive	Comparative	Superlative

-ος type, long penult

δεινός, -ή, -όν   δεινότερος, -α, -ον   δεινότατος, -η, -ον
'terrible'   'more terrible'   'most terrible'

ἐσθλός, -ή, -όν   ἐσθλότερος, -α, -ον   ἐσθλότατος, -η, -ον
'noble'   'nobler'   'noblest'

short penult

σοφός, -ή, -όν   σοφώτερος, -α, -ον   σοφώτατος, -η, -ον
'wise'   'wiser'   'wisest'

ἄξιος, -α, -ον   ἀξιώτερος, -α, -ον   ἀξιώτατος, -η, -ον
'worthy'   'worthier'   'worthiest'

-ης, -ες type (base in -εσ-)

ἀληθής, ἀληθές   ἀληθέστερος, -α, -ον   ἀληθέστατος, -η, -ον
'true'   'truer'   'truest'

-ων, -ον type (base in -ον) add -έστερος/-έστατος

εὐδαίμων, εὔδαιμον   εὐδαιμονέστερος, -α, -ον   εὐδαιμονέστατος, -η, -ον
'lucky'   'luckier'   'luckiest'

(2) Adjectives in -υς and a few in -ρος have a different comparison:

For the comparative, add -ίων, -ιον to the root (in the -ρος type, -ρ- drops out, in the -υς type, -υ- is lost: the root is found for these types by removing -ρος or -υς). For the superlative, add -ιστος, -ίστη, -ιστον.

Examples:

ἡδύς, ἡδεῖα, ἡδύ   ἡδίων, ἥδιον   ἥδιστος, ἡδίστη, ἥδιστον
'sweet'   'sweeter'   'sweetest'

αἰσχρός, αἰσχρά, αἰσχρόν αἰσχίων, αἴσχιον   αἴσχιστος, αἰσχίστη, αἴσχιστον
'base'   'baser'   'basest'

The -ίων, -ιον type of comparative is a two termination adjective (-ιων for masculine and feminine, -ιον for neuter) of the

third declension (review -ων, -ον type in Lesson VI, εὐδαίμων). It
is declined like εὐδαίμων, but has some alternate shorter forms in
addition to the regular ones: these alternate forms are often
found.

αἰσχίων, αἴσχιον 'more shameful', 'baser'

	Singular		Plural	
	M & F	N	M & F	N
N	αἰσχίων	αἴσχιον	αἰσχίονες (αἰσχίους)	αἰσχίονα (αἰσχίω)
G	αἰσχίονος	αἰσχίονος	αἰσχιόνων	αἰσχιόνων
D	αἰσχίονι	αἰσχίονι	αἰσχίοσι	αἰσχίοσι
A	αἰσχίονα (αἰσχίω)	αἴσχιον	αἰσχίονας (αἰσχίους)	αἰσχίονα (αἰσχίω)

(3) Irregular Comparison

Several of the most important adjectives are compared
irregularly. In some cases there are several comparisons for one
positive. (Most of the following are of the -ιων, -ιστος type,
though in many cases, the -ι- of the comparative has been lost.)

1. ἀγαθός, -ή, -όν

'good'	'better'	'best'
	ἀμείνων, ἄμεινον	ἄριστος, ἀρίστη, ἄριστον
	βελτίων, βέλτιον	βέλτιστος, βελτίστη, βέλτιστον
	κρείττων, κρεῖττον	κράτιστος, κρατίστη, κράτιστον

2. κακός, -ή, -όν

'bad'	'worse'	'worst'
	κακίων, κάκιον	κάκιστος, κακίστη, κάκιστον
	χείρων, χεῖρον	χείριστος, χειρίστη, χείριστον
		'least'
	ἥττων, ἧττον	ἥκιστος, ἡκίστη, ἥκιστον

3. καλός, -ή, -όν

'fine'	'finer'	'finest'
	καλλίων, κάλλιον	κάλλιστος, -η, -ον

4. μέγας, μεγάλη, μέγα

'great'	'greater'	'greatest'
	μείζων, μεῖζον	μέγιστος, -η, -ον

5. μικρός, μικρά, μικρόν

   'small'   'smaller'   'smallest'
                        ἐλάττων, ἔλαττον   ἐλάχιστος, -η, -ον
                        μείων, μεῖον

   (μικρός also has the regular comparison μικρότερος, μικρότατος)

6. ὀλίγος, -η, -ον

   'little', pl. 'few' 'fewer'   'fewest'
                        (ἐλάττων/μείων)   ὀλίγιστος, -η, -ον

7. πολύς, πολλή, πολύ

   'much'   'more'   'most'
                        πλείων, πλεῖον   πλεῖστος, -η, -ον

8. ῥᾴδιος, -α, -ον

   'easy'   'easier'   'easiest'
                        ῥᾴων, ῥᾷον   ῥᾷστος, -η, -ον

9. ταχύς, ταχεῖα, ταχύ

   'swift'   'swifter'   'swiftest'
                        θάττων, θᾶττον   τάχιστος, -η, -ον

Adverbs: Formation and Comparison

Adverbs of manner are formed from adjectives by changing the -ων of the masculine genitive plural to -ως.

For example:

δίκαιος	gen. pl.	δικαίων	adverb	δικαίως	'justly'
σοφός		σοφῶν		σοφῶς	'wisely'
ἡδύς		ἡδέων		ἡδέως	'sweetly'
ἀληθής		ἀληθῶν		ἀληθῶς	'truly'
εὐδαίμων		εὐδαιμόνων		εὐδαιμόνως	'happily
μέγας		μεγάλων		μεγάλως	'greatly
πᾶς		πάντων		πάντως	'in any case'
ἄλλος		ἄλλων		ἄλλως	'in vain'

There are many other adverbial endings, but they can be learned as they come up. The -ως type forms the largest class.

Adverbs of manner can be compared in the following way:

For the comparative, use the neuter singular accusative of the comparative of the adjective (-τερον). For the superlative, use the neuter plural accusative of the superlative of the adjective (-τατα).

Examples:

δικαίως	δικαιότερον	δικαιότατα
'justly'	'more justly'	'most justly'
σοφῶς	σοφώτερον	σοφώτατα
'wisely'	'more wisely'	'most wisely'
ἡδέως	ἥδιον	ἥδιστα
'sweetly'	'more sweetly'	'most sweetly'
ἀληθῶς	ἀληθέστερον	ἀληθέστατα
'truly'	'more truly'	'most truly'

Syntax

1. *Than* is expressed in two ways in Greek.

a. By the conjunction ἤ 'than'. In this construction the two words compared are in the same case.

ὁ υἱός ἐστι νεώτερος ᾽ἢ ὁ πατήρ.
The son is younger than his father.

νομίζω τοῦτον τὸν ἄνδρα εἶναι σοφώτερον ᾽ἢ τὸν ἀδελφόν.
I think that this man is wiser than his brother.

b. Instead of ἤ, the genitive of comparison may be used.

οὗτος ὁ υἱός ἐστι νεώτερος τοῦ ἀδελφοῦ.
This son is younger than his brother.

νομίζω τοῦτον τὸν ἄνδρα εἶναι σοφώτερον τοῦ πατρός.
I think that this man is wiser than his father.

2. The degree of difference between the two things compared is in the dative case: *how much* younger is the boy than his brother; *how much* wiser is this man than his father.

οὗτος ὁ υἱός ἐστι πέντε ἔτεσι νεώτερος τοῦ ἀδελφοῦ.

This son is *five years* younger than his brother.

νομίζω τοῦτον τὸν ἄνδρα εἶναι πολλῷ σοφώτερον τοῦ πατρός.

I think that this man is much wiser than his father.

3. *The Partitive Genitive* (or Genitive of the Whole): The whole of which a part is taken is in the genitive. It occurs after nouns, adjectives, and verbs, and is very common with superlatives and with the indefinite pronoun.

πολλοὶ τῶν ποιητῶν

many of the poets

οἱ σοφοὶ τῶν ἀνθρώπων

the wise (of) among men: men who are wise

πάντων τῶν πολιτῶν σοφώτατος

wisest of all the citizens

θεῶν τις

(some) one of the gods

The Partitive Genitive goes into the predicate position.

Notes:

1.   The superlative may be used absolutely--that is, with no comparison implied--to mean *very*:

σοφώτατος ὁ Σωκράτης.

Socrates is very wise.

as opposed to:

ὁ Σωκράτης ἦν ὁ σοφώτατος πάντων.

Socrates was the wisest of all men.

2.   ὡς with the superlative makes a "super-superlative:" *as . . . as possible:*

ὡς τάχιστα

as quickly as possible

3.   Adjectives may be compared by using μᾶλλον and μάλιστα

with the positive:

μᾶλλον σοφός   'more wise'

μάλιστα κακός   'most bad'

μᾶλλον ἑκών   'more willingly'

(ἑκών had no regular comparison, and so this is the only way to compare it.)

    4. Adverbs with ἔχω:

    ἔχω with an adverb is often used as an equivalent to an adjective with εἰμί.

καλῶς ἔχει   'it is going well'

ὡς εἶχε   'as he was'

Declension of Numerals and of οὐδείς

εἷς, μία, ἕν   'one'   'One' is naturally declined only in the singular.

M	F	N
εἷς	μία	ἕν
ἑνός	μιᾶς	ἑνός
ἑνί	μιᾷ	ἑνί
ἕνα	μίαν	ἕν

δύο 'two'   'Two' is declined in the dual only (-οῖν being a common dual ending for genitive and dative). δύο is, however, often treated as indeclinable. (Learn to recognize these forms.)

δύο
δυοῖν
δυοῖν
δύο

τρεῖς, τρία 'three'   'Three' and 'four' are both declined in the plural only. They belong to the third declension and are of the two termination type. (Learn to recognize these forms.)

τρεῖς	τρία
τριῶν	τριῶν
τρισί	τρισί
τρεῖς	τρία

τέτταρες, τέτταρα (τέσσαρες, τέσσαρα) 'four'

τέτταρες	τέτταρα
τεττάρων	τεττάρων
τέτταρσι	τέτταρσι
τέτταρας	τέτταρα

    The words for 'no one', 'none', 'nothing', οὐδεις and μηδεις, are declined like εἷς, μία, ἕν. (They are to be used depending on whether οὐ or μή is the suitable negative.)

οὐδείς	οὐδεμία	οὐδέν
οὐδενός	οὐδεμιᾶς	οὐδενός
οὐδενί	οὐδεμιᾷ	οὐδενί
οὐδένα	οὐδεμίαν	οὐδέν

Likewise μηδείς, μηδεμία, μηδέν. (Learn thoroughly.)

Vocabulary

ἀδελφός, ἀδελφοῦ, ὁ	*brother*
ἄλλως	(adv.) *otherwise, in vain, at random* (ἄλλος)(ἄλλως τε καί . . . 'both other wise and . . .', 'especially')
ἀμφότερος, ἀμφοτέρα, ἀμφότερον	*both of two*
βέβαιος, βέβαιον	*firm, steady, steadfast, sure, certain* (also -ος, -α, -ον)
βροτός, -ου, ὁ	*mortal man* (rare in prose)(ambrosial)
δεύτερος, δευτέρα, δεύτερον	*second*
ἑκάτερος, ἑκατέρα, ἑκάτερον	*each* (of two)(cf. ἕκαστος)
ἑκών, ἑκοῦσα, ἑκόν	*readily, willingly, purposely* (base ἑκοντ-)
ἄκων, ἄκουσα, ἄκον	*involuntary, unwilling(ly)* (also ἀέκων; base ἀκοντ-)
εὖ	*well* (adv. of ἀγαθός)
κράτος, κράτους, τό	*strength, might, power, rule* (autocrat, cf. κρείττων, κράτιστος)
μακρός, μακρά, μακρόν	*long, large, great*
ὀλίγος, ὀλίγη, ὀλίγον	*little* (sg.), *few* (pl.)(ὀλίγου (δεῖν) 'almost', 'all but')
ὅλος, ὅλη, ὅλον	*whole, entire*
ὅλως	*wholly, altogether, on the whole* (holograph)
πάντως	*in all ways, in any case, by all means* (adv. of πᾶς)
πότερος, ποτέρα, πότερον	*whether* (of two)(πότερον/πότερα . . . ἤ 'whether . . . or')
ῥᾴδιος, ῥᾳδία, ῥᾴδιον	*easy, ready, easy-going*
σώφρων, σῶφρον	*of sound mind, discreet, prudent, self-controlled* (σωφροσύνη)
ὕβρις, ὕβρεως, ἡ	*hubris, wanton violence, insolence, lust*
ὕστερος, ὑστέρα, ὕστερον	*latter, next, later* (hysteron-proteron: 'he put on his shoes and socks')

Exercises

1. **Compare:**

1. σώφρων	2. ἐσθλός	3. μακρός*	4. νέος	5. ἀσφαλής
6. βραχύς	7. πονηρός*	8. φοβερός*	9. ψευδής	10. γλυκύς

*Note: these are compared regularly, with -τερος, -τατος.

2. **Decline:**

1. ἡ ὕβρις
2. τὸ κράτος
3. ταχύς (all genders)
4. σώφρων
5. ἑκων
6. the comp. of μέγας
7. the comp. of καλός

3. **Form and compare the adverbs from:**

1. μέγας	2. ῥᾴδιος	3. ἀγαθός	4. εὐδαίμων
5. δίκαιος	6. ἄξιος	7. ἀληθής	8. νέος

4. **Choose the correct adjective form to agree with each of the following nouns:**

1. τοὺς πολίτας	a. ῥᾴους	b. ῥᾳδίονας	c. ῥᾴονες
2. τὴν θάλασσαν	a. καλλίονην	b. καλλίονα	c. καλλίοναν
3. τὸν ξένον	a. μείζονα	b. μείζους	c. μεῖζον
4. τὰ δῶρα	a. ἥττωνα	b. ἥττονα	c. ἥττα
5. τοῦ ποιητοῦ	a. ἀληθεστέρης	b. ἀληθεστέρου	c. ἀληθεστέρους
6. ταῖς σκηναῖς	a. ἐλαττώναις	b. ἡδιόναις	c. ἐλάττοσι
7. τῷ νεανίᾳ	a. νεοτέρᾳ	b. νεωτέρα	c. νεωτέρῳ
8. τοῦ γένους	a. βελτίους	b. βελτίονος	c. βελτίου
9. τῆς ὁδοῦ	a. μακροτέρου	b. μακρότης	c. μακροτέρας
10. τῆς ὕβρεως	a. αἰσχίονης	b. αἰσχίονος	c. αἰσχίονως
11. τοὺς βίους	a. ὀλίγοις	b. ὀλίγαις	c. ὀλιγίσταις
12. τὰ κράτη	a. κρατίστη	b. κρείττων	c. κρείττω

5. **Translate:**

1. ἄλλως λέγεις λέγων ταῦτα.

2. λίθους ἔβαλλεν ἀμφοτέραις χερσί.

3. βροτοῖς θανάτου βεβαιότερόν ἐστι οὐδέν.

4. ἄμεινόν ἐστι βεβαίους φίλους ἔχειν 'ἢ χρήματα.

5. κρεῖττον τὸ κράτος τὸ τῆς ψυχῆς 'ἢ τὸ τοῦ σώματος.

6. πάντες γὰρ βέβαιον ἀγαγεῖν εἰρήνην ἐθέλουσιν.

7. εἰρήνης οὐδέν ἐστι εὐδαιμονέστερον.

8. οὐ βέβαιος ὁ βίος βροτῶν.

9. ἑκοῦσα ταῦτα ἑκούσαις ἤγγειλα.

10. οὔποτε ἕκων οὐδένα βέβλαφα.

11. ταῦτα πράττοντες εὖ πράττετε.

12. δευτέρᾳ ἡμέρᾳ ἄκοντες παρεσόμεθα.

13. ἑκάτερος ἡμῶν βούλεται εὐδαίμων εἶναι καὶ εὖ ἔχειν.

14. εὖ οἶδα τοῦτον ὄντα δίκαιον ἄνδρα.

15. ὁ δίκαιος μέγα κράτος ἔχει.

16. κρείσσων τοῦ κράτους ἡ σωφροσύνη.

17. τὸ πᾶν κράτος ἔχει ὁ τῶν θεῶν βασιλεύς.

18. νομίζω τὸ τοῦ θεοῦ κράτος κρεῖττον εἶναι 'ἢ τῶν ἀνθρώπων.

19. πῶς ἔχεις; ἄμεινον ἔχω.

20. αὕτη ἡ ὁδὸς πάντως μακροτέρα ἦν ἐκείνης.

21. μακρὸς βίος οὐκ ἀεί ἐστι εὐδαίμων.

22. ἐν ὀλίγῳ χρόνῳ παυσόμεθα.

23. ἦσαν πολλοὶ μὲν ἄνθρωποι ἐν τῇ πόλει, ὀλίγοι δὲ ἄνδρες.

24. ὁ κόσμος λέγεται τὸ ὅλον.

25. τὸν τύραννον τὸν δίκαιον εὑρεῖν οὐ ῥᾴδιον.

26. ἡ ῥᾴστη ὁδὸς ἄγει εἰς τὸν θάνατον.

27. ἡ ὁδὸς ἡ ῥᾳδία οὐκ ἔστιν ἀρίστη.

28. ἐκεῖνος ὁ ἄνθρωπος σοφώτατός ἐστι 'ὃς οἶδεν οὐδὲν εἰδώς.

29. ὕβρις τόδ' ἐστί, θεόν εἶναι βούλεσθαι.

30. ἄκοντος θεοῦ, οὐδὲν γίγνεται.

6. Write in Greek:

1. There is no one who is more wicked than this man.
2. Socrates is the wisest of all men, but he knows nothing.
3. It is necessary to hurt our enemies, who are more wicked than we.
4. He wrote not wisely but well.
5. Some men are good, but others are better.
6. It is easier to avoid death than wickedness.
7. In no respect (in nothing) is he wiser than you.
8. I am a little younger than my brother.
9. Not every man is taller than his wife. ('tall' μέγας)
10. I myself wish to become better in all things.

Readings

ἡγοῦμαι 'I think' (+ inf.)

1. ἐγὼ δὲ μεγίστην ἡγοῦμαι συμμαχίαν εἶναι καὶ βεβαιοτάτην τὸ τὰ δίκαια πράττειν.

   Isocrates, *Archidamus*

ἀναρχία, -ας, ἡ --

2. ἀναρχίας δὲ μεῖζον οὐκ ἔστιν κακόν.

   Sophocles, *Antigone*

κοὐδέν = καὶ οὐδέν; πέλει 'is'

3. πολλὰ τὰ δεινὰ κοὐδὲν ἀνθρώπου δεινότερον πέλει . . . .

   Sophocles, *Antigone*

στέργω 'love', 'be pleased with'

4. πάρειμι δ' ἄκων οὐχ ἑκοῦσιν οἶδ' ὅτι· στέργει γὰρ οὐδεὶς ἄγγελον κακῶν ἔργων.

   Sophocles, *Antigone*

5. (οἶον) εἰ ὁ μέγιστος ἀνὴρ γυναικὸς τῆς μεγίστης μείζων καὶ ὅλως οἱ ἄνδρες τῶν γυναικῶν μείζους· καὶ εἰ οἱ ἄνδρες ὅλως τῶν γυναικῶν μείζους, καὶ ἀνὴρ ὁ μέγιστος τῆς μεγίστης γυναικὸς μείζων.

   Aristotle, *Rhetoric*

πειθαρχεῖν 'obey', 'be obedient to' (+ dat.)

6. 'πειθαρχεῖν δεῖ θεῷ μᾶλλον 'ἢ ἀνθρώποις.'

   Eusebius

καταργεῖται 'is abolished'; ἐπουράνιος, -ον 'in heaven'; ἐπίγειος, -ον 'on earth'

7. οὐδέν ἐστιν ἄμεινον εἰρήνης, ἐν ᾗ πᾶς πόλεμος καταργεῖται ἐπουρανίων καὶ ἐπιγείων.

   St. Ignatius

γνήσιος, -α, -ον 'genuine', 'true'

8. οὐδεὶς γνησιώτερον ἔμαθεν ἀπ' ἐμοῦ λόγον· ἀλλὰ οἶδα, ὅτι ἄξιοί ἐστε ὑμεῖς.

   Barnabas

σάφα 'clearly' (adv.); νοστέω fut. νοστήσω 'return home'; υἶες = υἱοί; ἦε = ἤ

9. οὐδέ τί πω σάφα ἴδμεν ὅπως ἔσται τάδε ἔργα,
   'ἢ εὖ ἦε κακῶς νοστήσομεν υἶες 'Αχαιῶν.

   Homer, *Iliad*

10. αἴσχιστος δὲ ἀνὴρ ὑπὸ ῏Ιλιον ἦλθε.

    Homer, *Iliad* (on Thersites)

μή . . . κρύψῃς 'do not conceal'; μήτοι 'in no way'

11. Prometheus. τὸ μὴ μαθεῖν σοι κρεῖσσον 'ἢ μαθεῖν τάδε.
    Ιο. μήτοι με κρύψῃς τοῦθ' ὅπερ μέλλω παθεῖν.

    Aeschylus, *Prometheus*

τοιγάρ 'so then', 'therefore';
δράσαντες 'having done'

12. τοιγάρ κακῶς δράσαντες οὐκ ἐλάσσονα
πάσχουσι . . . .

Aeschylus, *Persae*

θεμιτός, -ή, -όν 'lawful'

13. οὐ γὰρ οἶμαι θεμιτὸν εἶναι ἀμείνονι ἀνδρὶ ὑπὸ χείρονος βλάπτεσθαι.

Plato, *Apology of Socrates*

*διδάσκαλος, -ου, ὁ 'teacher'

14. πολλοὶ μαθηταὶ κρείσσονες διδασκάλων.

Greek Anthology, Lucillius

διαφέρω + gen. of comparison
(= 'differ from')

15. οὐδὲν ἔφη τὸν θάνατον διαφέρειν τοῦ ζῆν.
'σὺ οὖν,' ἔφη τις, 'διὰ τί οὐκ ἀποθνή-
σκεις;' 'ὅτι,' ἔφη, 'οὐδὲν διαφέρει.'

Diogenes Laertius (about Thales, but
the same story is also told of
others)

μακαρίζω 'call/esteem happy'
(+ acc. and gen.); ἔγωγε = ἐγω
+ γε

16. Μακαρίζω ἄρ' ὑμᾶς ἔγωγε τοῦ κτήματος πολὺ μᾶλλον 'ἢ μέγαν βασιλέα τῆς ἀρχῆς.

Plato, *Euthydemus* (Socrates ironical-
ly congratulates the two brothers
Euthydemus and Dionysodorus that
they possess the knowledge and are
able to teach *virtue,* ἀρετή.)

17. πρῶτον μὲν ὅτι οὐδὲν γίνεται ἐκ τοῦ μὴ
ὄντος.

Diogenes Laertius (the first point of
Epicurus' physical doctrine)

*φρόνησις 'thought', 'wisdom';
φρόνιμος, -η, -ον 'wise', 'sen-
sible'; τίμιος, -α, -ον 'held
in honor', 'esteemed'; διό
'therefore'; *λοιπός, -ή, -όν
'rest of', 'remaining'; ἄνευ
(+ gen.) 'without'; συμφύω 'make
to grow together'; ἀχώριστος,
-ον 'inseparable'

[18. τούτων δὲ πάντων ἀρχὴ καὶ τὸ μέγιστον
ἀγαθὸν φρόνησις· διὸ καὶ φιλοσοφίας τιμιώτερον ὑπάρχει φρόνησις, ἐξ ἧς αἱ λοι-
παὶ πᾶσαι πεφύκασιν ἀρεταί, διδάσκουσα
ὡς οὐκ ἔστιν ἡδέως ζῆν ἄνευ τοῦ φρονίμως
καὶ καλῶς καὶ δικαίως, οὐδὲ φρονίμως καὶ
καλῶς καὶ δικαίως ἄνευ τοῦ ἡδέως· συμπε-
φύκασι γὰρ αἱ ἀρεταὶ τῷ ζῆν ἡδέως, καὶ
τὸ ζῆν ἡδέως τούτων ἐστὶν ἀχώριστον.]

Diogenes Laertius (on Epicurus)

*ζῷον, τό 'living thing', 'ani-
mal'

19. τὸ γὰρ ζῷον τοῦ μὴ ζῴου κρεῖττον· οὐδὲν
δὲ τοῦ κόσμου κρεῖττον· ζῷον ἄρ' ὁ κόσμος.

Diogenes Laertius (on Zeno)

τῦφος, -ου, ὁ 'smoke', 'con-
ceit'; *ἀπρεπής, -ές 'unseemly',
'unbecoming'

[20. πάντων ἔλεγεν ἀπρεπέστερον εἶναι τὸν τῦ-
φον, καὶ μάλιστα ἐπὶ τῶν νέων.]

Diogenes Laertius (Zeno)

*μάχομαι 'fight'

21. κρεῖττόν ἐστι μετ' ὀλίγων ἀγαθῶν πρὸς
ἅπαντας τοὺς κακοὺς 'ἢ μετὰ πολλῶν κακῶν
πρὸς ὀλίγους ἀγαθοὺς μάχεσθαι.

    Diogenes Laertius (a saying of Antis-
      thenes)

'Ισοκράτους gen. of 'Isocrates'

22. ἔστιν [Πλάτων] οὖν 'Ισοκράτους νεώτερος
ἔτεσιν ἕξ.

    Diogenes Laertius

ἐπισφαλής, -ές 'precarious';
προπέτεια, -ας, ἡ 'rashness';
φθαρτός, -ή, -όν 'transitory'

23. ἔλεγε δὲ καὶ τάδε· καλὸν ἡσυχία· ἐπισφα-
λὲς προπέτεια· κέρδος αἰσχρόν· δημοκρατία κρεῖττον τυραννίδος· αἱ μὲν ἡδοναὶ
φθαρταί, αἱ δὲ τιμαὶ ἀθάνατοι.

    Diogenes Laertius (sayings of Perian-
      der)

24. κρεῖττον ἔλεγεν ἕνα φίλον ἔχειν πολλοῦ
ἄξιον 'ἢ πολλοὺς μηδενὸς ἀξίους.

    Diogenes Laertius (Anacharsis)

ἀνδρεῖος, -α, -ον 'manly',
'brave'; ἀπάτη, -ης, ἡ 'deceit',
'strategem'; συνιέντων pres.
act. pt. gen. pl. of συνίημι
'perceive', 'understand'; ἐπισταμένων pres. mid. pt. gen. pl.
of ἐπίσταμαι 'know'; δέος, -ους,
τό 'fear'; σιωπώντων pres. act.
pt. gen. pl. of σιωπάω 'keep silence'

25. 'ἄνδρες 'Αθηναῖοι, τῶν μὲν σοφώτερος,
τῶν δὲ ἀνδρειότερός εἰμι· σοφώτερος μὲν
τῶν τὴν ἀπάτην τοῦ Πεισιστράτου μὴ συνιέντων, ἀνδρειότερος δὲ τῶν ἐπισταμένων
μέν, διὰ δέος δὲ σιωπώντων.'

    Diogenes Laertius, quoting Solon

ἀπόφθεγμα 'terse saying'; *πρέσβυς, -εως, ὁ 'old man' (also
used as an adjective); ἀγένητος,
-ον 'unborn'; ποίημα 'creation',
'poem'; *τόπος, -ου, ὁ 'place';
χωρέω 'makes room for'(-εῖ 3rd
sg. pres.); *τρέχω 'run'; *ἰσχυρός, -ά, -όν 'strong'; κρατέω
'be master of'; ἀνά + εὑρίσκω;
*ἀνά 'up' prep. mostly with acc.
'up', 'throughout'

26. φέρεται δὲ καὶ ἀποφθέγματα αὐτοῦ τάδε·

    πρεσβύτατον τῶν ὄντων θεός, ἀγενητὸν
      γάρ.
    κάλλιστον κόσμος· ποίημα γὰρ θεοῦ.
    μέγιστον τόπος· ἅπαντα γὰρ χωρεῖ.
    τάχιστον νοῦς· διὰ παντὸς γὰρ τρέχει.
    ἰσχυρότατον ἀνάγκη· κρατεῖ γὰρ πάντων.
    σοφώτατον χρόνος· ἀνευρίσκει γὰρ πάν-
      τα.
    Diogenes Laertius, quoting Thales

27. Protarchus. οὐδέν γε, ἀλλ' ἅπερ ἀκούω,
λέγω.

    Plato, *Philebus* (Protarchus is denying
    responsibility for what he has been
    saying.)

*θνητός, -ή, -όν 'mortal'

28. βέβαιον οὐδέν ἐστιν ἐν θνητῷ βίῳ.

    Menander

29. γνώμη γερόντων ἀσφαλεστέρα νέων.

Menander

30. ἐν ταῖς ἀνάγκαις χρημάτων κρείττων φίλος.

Menander

φιλότεκνος 'loving one's children'; ὄνθ' = ὄντα

31. ἔστιν δὲ μήτηρ φιλότεκνος μᾶλλον πατρός·
ἡ μὲν γὰρ αὐτῆς οἶδεν ὄνθ', ὁ δ' οἴεται.

Menander

32. κάλλιστόν ἐστι κτῆμα παιδεία βροτοῖς.

Menander

33. Prometheus to Io. σχολὴ δὲ πλείων 'ἢ
θέλω πάρεστί μοι.

Aeschylus, *Prometheus*

*τίκτω, τέξομαι 'bring forth',
'bear', 'beget'; φέρτερος 'better', 'mightier'

34. 'ἢ τέξεταί γε παῖδα φέρτερον πατρός.

Aeschylus, *Prometheus*

35. οἱ πλεῖστοι κακοί.

Diogenes Laertius, quoting Bias

ἐς = εἰς; αὔδα imperative of
αὐδάω 'speak', 'tell'; *πένθος,
-ους, τό 'grief'; τῶνδε and ψυχῆς depend on πέρι (= περί):
the accent shifts when the preposition follows the noun

φρόνησις, -εως, ἡ 'thought',
'wisdom'

οὐθέν = a later form of οὐδέν

36. Oedipus tells Creon to announce his message before all the people:

ἐς πάντας αὔδα· τῶνδε γὰρ πλέον φέρω τὸ
πένθος 'ἢ καὶ τῆς ἐμῆς ψυχῆς πέρι.

Sophocles, *Oedipus Tyrannus*

37. ἀγαθὸν μέγιστον ἡ φρόνησίς ἐστ' ἀεί.

Menander

38. αἰσθάνεται δ' οὐθὲν 'ὃ μὴ ἔχει ψυχήν.

Aristotle, περὶ ψυχῆς

39. καιρὸς γάρ ἐστι τῶν νόμων κρεῖττον πολύ.

Menander

40. ὕβρις κακὸν μέγιστον ἀνθρώποις ἔφυ.

Menander

εὔφυων 'cheerful', 'well-dis-
posed'

πενία, -ας, ἡ 'poverty'

41. υἱῷ μέγιστον ἀγαθόν ἐστι' εὔφυων πατήρ.

Menander

42. οὐκ ἔστι πενίας οὐδὲ 'ἓν μεῖζον κακόν.

Menander

43. οὐκ ἔστιν οὐδὲν κτῆμα κάλλιον φίλου.

Menander

44. οὐκ ἔσθ' ὑγιείας κρεῖττον οὐδὲν ἐν βίῳ.

Menander

45. ἰσχυρότερον δέ γ' οὐδέν ἐστι τοῦ λόγου.

Menander

γαμεῖν 'to marry' (pres. inf.)

46. γυναῖκα θάπτειν κρεῖσσον ἐστιν 'ἢ γαμεῖν.

Menander

47. γυνὴ γὰρ οὐδὲν οἶδε πλὴν 'ὃ βούλεται.

Menander

ποιεῖ 'makes' (3rd sg. pres.)

48. ἅπαντας αὐτῶν κρείσσονας ἀνάγκη ποιεῖ.

Menander

κακῶς ἀκούων = κακῶς λεγόμενος (i.e. hearing oneself called κακός); ὀργίζομαι 'be angry'; *πονηρία, -ας, ἡ 'wickedness'; *τεκμήριον, -ου, τό 'evidence'

49. κακῶς ἀκούων ὅστις οὐκ ὀργίζεται πονηρίας πλείστης τεκμήριον φέρει.

Menander

50. οὐδὲν γλυκύτερόν ἐστιν 'ἢ πάντ' εἰδέναι.

Menander, *Arbitrants*

ἦ subjunctive of εἰμί third person sg.; θεῖ 'runs' (3rd sg. pres.); ἑάλων 'I have been caught'; βραδύς, -εῖα, -ύ 'slow'; *κατήγορος, -ου, ὁ 'accuser'; *κακία, -ας, ἡ 'wickedness'; ἄπειμι 'I will go away'; ὄφλων (with δίκην) 'convicted' (participle, aorist); ὠφληκότες 'convicted' (perfect participle); μοχθηρία, -ας, τό 'wickedness'; τίμημα, -ατος, τό 'penalty'; ἐμμένω 'abide by'; μετρίως 'fairly', 'moderately'

51. ἀλλὰ μὴ οὐ τοῦτ' ἦ χαλεπόν, ὦ ἄνδρες, θάνατον ἐκφυγεῖν, ἀλλὰ πολὺ χαλεπώτερον πονηρίαν· θᾶττον γὰρ θανάτου θεῖ. καὶ νῦν ἐγὼ μὲν ἅτε βραδὺς ὢν καὶ πρεσβύτης ὑπὸ τοῦ βραδυτέρου ἑάλων, οἱ δ' ἐμοὶ κατήγοροι ἅτε δεινοὶ καὶ ὀξεῖς ὄντες ὑπὸ τοῦ θάττονος, τῆς κακίας. καὶ νῦν ἐγὼ μὲν ἄπειμι ὑφ' ὑμῶν θανάτου δίκην ὄφλων, οὗτοι δ' ὑπὸ τῆς ἀληθείας ὠφληκότες μοχθηρίαν καὶ ἀδικίαν. καὶ ἐγώ τε τῷ τιμήματι ἐμμένω καὶ οὗτοι. ταῦτα μέν που ἴσως οὕτως καὶ ἔδει σχεῖν, καὶ οἶμαι αὐτὰ μετρίως ἔχειν.

Plato, *Apology of Socrates*

ξηρός, -ά, -όν 'dry'; ὑδρωπικός 'dropsical'

[52. οὐδὲν γάρ, φασί, ξηρότερον ὑδρωπικοῦ.]

Longinus

οἰκονομέω 'manage' (-εῖ 3rd sg. pres.); τραγικός --

53. καὶ ὁ Εὐριπίδης εἰ καὶ τὰ ἄλλα μὴ εὖ οἰκονομεῖ ἀλλὰ τραγικώτατός γε τῶν ποιητῶν φαίνεται.

Aristotle, *Poetics*

ὑποκριτής, -οῦ, ὁ 'actor'; πλῆθος, -ους, τό 'multitude', 'number'; ἐλαττόω (aor. ἠλάττωσα) 'diminish'; λόγος (here) dialogue;

[54. καὶ τό τε τῶν ὑποκριτῶν πλῆθος ἐξ ἑνὸς εἰς δύο πρῶτος Αἰσχύλος ἤγαγε καὶ τὰ τοῦ χοροῦ ἠλάττωσε καὶ τὸν λόγον πρωταγωνιστὴν παρεσκεύασεν· τρεῖς δὲ καὶ σκηνογρα-

πρωταγωνιστής, -οῦ, ὁ 'main part'; παρασκευάζω 'furnish'; σκηνογραφία, -ας, ἡ 'scene painting'

χειμών, -ῶνος, ὁ 'winter', 'storm'; εὐδία, -ας, ἡ 'calm weather'

*ὄλβιος, -α, -ον 'happy'

*ἀείδω 'sing'

ὅρος, -ου, ὁ 'boundary', 'limit'

φίαν Σοφοκλῆς.]

Aristotle, *Poetics*

55. χειμὼν μεταβάλλει ῥᾳδίως εἰς εὐδίαν.

Menander

56. ὄλβιος δ' οὐδεὶς βροτῶν πάντα χρόνον.

Bacchylides

57. βροτοῖς ἥδιστον ἀείδειν.

Musaeus

58. εἷς ὅρος, μία βροτοῖσιν εὐτυχίας ὁδός.

Bacchylides

59. ὕβρις τάδ' ἐστί, κρείσσω δαιμόνων εἶναι θέλειν.

Euripides, *Hippolytus*

Quotation

Read and learn the following saying:

εἷς ἀνήρ, οὐδεὶς ἀνήρ.

One man, no man.

Greek Proverb

B. The Aorist Passive: Sixth Principal Part: The Passive System (Aorist and Future Passive)

1. The regular (or first) aorist passive is formed by:

augment + stem + θη/θε + endings (a type of secondary endings)

θη is used for the indicative and infinitive. θε is used for the participle, the subjunctive, and the optative.

The endings are:

	Singular	Plural
	-ν	-μεν
	-ς	-τε
	-	-σαν

Infinitive -ναι   Participle -είς, -εῖσα, -έν (base in εντ)

Example: λύω in the aorist passive ἐλύθην 'I was released'

ἐ + λύ + θη + ν

    ἐλύθην   ἐλύθημεν
    ἐλύθης   ἐλύθητε
    ἐλύθη   ἐλύθησαν

Infinitive λυθῆναι

Participle λυθείς, λυθεῖσα, λυθέ ς (λυθεντ-)

Before -θ- consonant changes take place (as in the perfect middle):

    π, β → φ   κ, γ → χ   τ, δ, θ, ζ → σ

Examples:

πέμπω	stem, πεμπ-	aorist passive,	ἐπέμφθην
ἄγω	ἀγ-		ἤχθην
πείθω	πειθ-		ἐπείσθην
νομίζω	νομιζ-		ἐνομίσθην

2. A second aorist passive is formed without -θ- (cf. the second perfect active without -κ-):

    augment + stem (often vowel gradation) + η/ε
        + endings

Both first and second aorist passive systems are conjugated in the same way.

Some examples:

στέλλω	aorist passive	ἐστάλην
φαίνω		ἐφάνην
γράφω		ἐγράφην

The Aorist Passive Participle is declined in the same way as the active participles with bases in -ντ- except that the base is in -εντ- rather than -οντ- or -αντ-. The masculine nominative singular and the dative plural masculine and neuter are in -είς and -εισι, formed by the lengthening of the vowel when -ντ- is dropped before -σ-. The feminine is declined in the first declension (like θάλαττα).

λυθείς, base (M & N) λυθεντ-; (F) λυθεισ- ('having been freed')

Singular

N.	λυθείς	λυθεῖσα	λυθέν
G.	λυθέντος	λυθείσης	λυθέντος
D.	λυθέντι	λυθείσῃ	λυθέντι
A.	λυθέντα	λυθεῖσαν	λυθέν

Plural

N.	λυθέντες	λυθεῖσαι	λυθέντα
G.	λυθέντων	λυθεισῶν	λυθέντων
D.	λυθεῖσι	λυθείσαις	λυθεῖσι
A.	λυθέντας	λυθείσας	λυθέντα

The Future Passive

Formation:

aorist passive stem (-η- form) + σ + ο/ε + primary middle endings

The long form of the stem (in -θη or -η) is used throughout the future passive. Note that active endings are used in the aorist passive and that middle endings are used in the future passive.

Example: λύω in the future passive λυθήσομαι ('I shall be released')

λυ + θή + σ + ο + μαι

λυθήσομαι	λυθησόμεθα
λυθήσει/-ῃ	λυθήσεσθε
λυθήσεται	λυθήσονται

Infinitive   λυθήσεσθαι

Participle   λυθησόμενος

Vocabulary

διαφθείρω, διαφθερῶ, διέφθειρα, διέφθαρκα, διέφθαρμαι, διεφθάρην	*destroy utterly, corrupt*
ἐρρήθην	used as aorist passive of εἶπον 'I said'
ἐχθρός, ἐχθρά, ἐχθρόν	*hated, hateful*
ὁ ἐχθρός	*enemy*
οἴομαι (οἶμαι), ᾠόμην, οἰήσομαι, ᾠήθην	*think, believe* (+ infinitive)

σώζω, σώσω, ἔσωσα, σέ-   *save*; passive, *be saved, escape*
  σωκα, σέσωμαι, ἐσώ-
  θην

Aorist Passive, Sixth Principal Part

ἀγγέλλω   (stem ἀγγελ-) ἠγγέλθην
ἄγω   ἤχθην
ἀκούω   ἠκούσθην
ἄρχω   ἤρχθην
βάλλω   ἐβλήθην (stems βαλ- and βλη-)
βουλεύω   ἐβουλεύθην
βούλομαι   ἐβουλήθην (βούλομαι is a passive deponent)
γιγνώσκω   ἐγνώσθην
γράφω   ἐγράφην
εὑρίσκω   ηὑρέθην
ἔχω   ἐσχέθην
θύω   ἐτύθην (Note: θυ- becomes τυ- before -θην)
κομίζω   ἐκομίσθην
κρίνω   ἐκρίθην
λαμβάνω   ἐλήφθην
λέγω   ἐλέχθην, ἐρρήθην
λείπω   ἐλείφθην
λύω   ἐλύθην
νομίζω   ἐνομίσθην
παιδεύω   ἐπαιδεύθην
παύω   ἐπαύθην
πείθω   ἐπείσθην
πέμπω   ἐπέμφθην
πιστεύω   ἐπιστεύθην
πράττω   (stem πραγ-) ἐπράχθην
φαίνω   ἐφάνην, ἐφάνθην
φέρω   ἠνέχθην
χαίρω   ἐχάρην

Exercises

1. Form the future passive of the verbs given above.

2. a. Conjugate in the Aorist Passive:

1. γράφω   2. νομίζω   3. παιδεύω   4. πράττω   5. λαμβάνω

b. Decline the Aorist Passive Participle of:

1. βάλλω   2. βούλομαι   3. πέμπω

c. Conjugate in the Future Passive:

1. ἀκούω   2. παύω

3. Fill in the Aorist Passive and Future Passive in the
synopses given in Lessons VIII and IX.

> New Synopses:
>
> > 7. γράφω second singular
> > 8. παύω first singular
> > 9. βούλομαι third singular

4. Parse:

1. πεμφθεῖσιν	10. ἤρχθην	19. γνωσθείς	28. παιδευθείσης
2. σωθήσεσθαι	11. λειφθέντος	20. ἐκομίσθης	29. ἐτάθησαν (τείνω)
3. ἐσώθησαν	12. ἤχθησαν	21. ἐχάρην	30. ἀκουσθέντα
4. πεμφθέντες	13. ἐβλήθη	22. ἐνεχθεῖσι	31. παυθεῖσαι
5. σωθῆναι	14. ἐλέχθητε	23. γραφθήσεσθαι	32. ἐπράχθημεν
6. ἠγγέλθημεν	15. βουλευθήσει	24. τυθήσομαι	33. πεμφθήσονται
7. γραφησόμενος	16. ἐλήφθη	25. ἐσχέθησαν	34. πιστευθησόμεθα
8. ἐλύθης	17. βουληθέντι	26. νομισθῆναι	35. ἠνέχθησαν
9. ἀκουσθῆναι	18. ἐκρίθησαν	27. ἐφάνην	36. ἐγράφη

5. Translate:

1. εἰς τήνδε τὴν χώραν ἐπέμφθημεν.

2. οὗτοι οἱ ἵπποι ἅμα λυθέντες ἔφυγον.

3. αὗται αἱ ἐπιστολαὶ ἐγράφησαν ὑφ' ἡμῶν.

4. τῶν ὑπὸ τῶν τότε λεχθέντων τὰ μὲν ἀληθῆ ἐστι, τὰ δὲ ψευδῆ.

5. ἐν δημοκρατίᾳ οὐκ ἤρχθησαν ὑπὸ τῶν ὀλίγων.

6. εἰς λίθους ἐγράφησαν οἱ νόμοι οἱ τῶν Ἑλλήνων.

7. ἐβουλήθημεν τοῦ σοφοῦ ἀκούειν.

8. ᾠήθησαν οἱ ποιηταὶ τὴν τοῦ ἀνθρώπου ψυχὴν εἶναι ἀθάνατον.

9. ὑφ' ἡμῶν ἐσώθητε.

10. ὁ φεύγων ὑπὸ τῶν δικαστῶν κριθήσεται.

11. ταῖς θεαῖς τὰ δῶρα ἐνεχθήσεται τῇδε τῇ ἡμέρᾳ.

12. ἄκων ἐν τῇ νήσῳ ὁ γέρων ἐλείφθη ὑπο τῶν ἐχθρῶν.

13. ἐπείσθητε τοῖς λόγοις τοῖς τῶν πολλὰ καὶ ψευδῆ λεγόντων;

14. καλὰ τὰ ὑφ' ὑμῶν πραχθέντα.

15. τῇ θεᾷ ἡ καλλίστη θυγάτηρ ἡ τοῦ στρατηγοῦ ἐτύθη.

16. τὰ παιδία ἐπαιδεύθη ὑπὸ τῶν πατέρων καὶ τῶν μητέρων.

17. ἐπέμφθην ὡς οὖσιν ὑμῖν ταῦτα.

18. ἄμεινόν ἐστι τὸ σωθῆναι 'ἢ τὸ ἀποθνήσκειν.

19. τούτων πραχθέντων ἑκόντες σοι πιστεύσομεν.

20. τοῦ ἀδίκου ληφθέντος ἔξεστιν ἡμῖν εἰρήνην ἄγειν.

21. σωθήσεσθαι γὰρ οἱ κακοὶ ᾠήθησαν φεύγοντες.

22. οἱ διώκοντες ᾠήθησαν ὑπ' αὐτοῦ τοὺς νέους διαφθαρῆναι.

23. οἱ σωθέντες χάριν ταῖς σωζούσαις οὐκ ἴσασιν. (χάριν εἰδέναι τινί 'feel grateful to someone')

6. Composition: Translate into Greek:

1. By whom were you sent?

2. We wished to be led to the king.

3. What was written on the stones?

4. By whom are the citizens ruled in this city?

5. They thought that they had been saved.

6. He happened to have been found in the same place.

7. They were not persuaded by the gifts, but by the words and deeds of the just.

8. Why were you left alone in this place?

9. He was brought here by wicked men who wished to kill him, but he was saved by his friends.

10. I was sent to find a just man.

Readings

ἡγεῖ 'you think' (2 sg. of ἡγέομαι); δῆτα 'indeed', 'then'

1. Neoptolemus. οὐκ αἰσχρὸν ἡγεῖ δῆτα τὸ ψευδῆ λέγειν;
   Odysseus. οὐκ εἰ τὸ σωθῆναί γε τὸ ψεῦδος φέρει.

   Sophocles, *Philoctetes*

*πρόσωπον, -ου, τό 'face', 'person'

2. 'εἶδον γὰρ θεὸν πρόσωπον πρὸς πρόσωπον, καὶ ἐσώθη μου ἡ ψυχή.'

   Eusebius

*πῶς 'how'; *ἀγών, -ῶνος, ὁ 'contest'

3. μένω ἀκοῦσαι πῶς ἀγὼν κριθήσεται.

   Aeschylus, *Eumenides*

ἀπολείπω 'leave to'; συναπολείπω 'leave along with'; ἐπιστήμη 'understanding'; χρησόμενος fut. pt. of χράομαι 'use' + dat.

4. οἱ ἄνθρωποι χρήματα μὲν ἀπολείπουσι τοῖς παισίν, ἐπιστήμην δὲ οὐ συναπολείπουσιν, τὴν χρησομένην τοῖς ἀπολειφθεῖσιν.

   Demetrius

ἐρωτηθείς aor. pass. pt. of ἐρωτάω 'ask'

5. ἐρωτηθεὶς τίς ἐστι φίλος, 'ἄλλος,' ἔφη, 'ἐγώ.'

   Diogenes Laertius (Zeno)

ποῖος, -α, -ον 'of what kind?'; 'what sort of?'; 'what?'

6. ἐρωτηθεὶς ὑπό τινος, 'ποῖός τίς σοι Διογένης δοκεῖ;' 'Σωκράτης,' εἶπε, 'μαινόμενος.'

Diogenes Laertius (Diogenes)

ἀλλότριος, -α, -ον 'of/belonging to another'

7. ἐρωτηθεὶς ποῖον οἶνον ἡδέως πίνει, ἔφη 'τὸν ἀλλότριον.'

Diogenes Laertius (Diogenes)

ἀπαίδευτος, -ον 'uneducated'; οἱ ζῶντες 'the living' (ptcpl. of ζάω); τεθνεώτων pf. pt. act. of θνήσκω/ἀποθνήσκω; *ὅσος, -η, -ον 'as great as', 'as much as', 'how great'

8. ἐρωτηθεὶς τίνι διαφέρουσιν οἱ πεπαιδευμένοι τῶν ἀπαιδεύτων, 'ὅσῳ,' εἶπεν, 'οἱ ζῶντες τῶν τεθνεώτων.'

Diogenes Laertius (Aristotle)

ἐνοικοῦσα pres. act. pt. fem. of ἐνοικέω 'inhabit'

9. ἐρωτηθεὶς τί ἐστι φίλος, ἔφη 'μία ψυχὴ δύο σώμασιν ἐνοικοῦσα.'

Diogenes Laertius (Aristotle)

θέατρον, -ου, τό 'theatre'; καθεδεῖται fut. of καθέζομαι 'sit'; *γοῦν 'at least then' (γε + οὖν)

10. ἐρωτηθεὶς ὑπό τινος τί αὐτοῦ ὁ υἱὸς ἀμείνων ἔσται παιδευθείς, 'καὶ εἰ μηδὲν ἄλλο,' εἶπεν, 'ἐν γοῦν τῷ θεάτρῳ οὐ καθεδεῖται λίθος ἐπὶ λίθῳ.'

Diogenes Laertius (Aristippus)

καταλαμβάνω 'catch'; λαλῶν 'talking'; μελετᾶν (inf. of μελετάω 'practise')

[11. καταληφθεὶς δέ ποτε καὶ αὐτῷ λαλῶν καὶ ἐρωτηθεὶς τὴν αἰτίαν ἔφη μελετᾶν χρηστὸς εἶναι.]

Diogenes Laertius (Pyrrho)

γένεσις, -εως, ἡ --; ἰλύς, ἰλύος, ἡ 'mud'; *θερμός, -ή, -όν 'hot'; ψυχρός, -ά, -όν 'cold'; γεννηθῆναι from γεννάω 'beget', 'bear'

12. ἔλεγε δὲ δύο αἰτίας εἶναι γενέσεως θερμὸν καὶ ψυχρόν. καὶ τὰ ζῷα ἀπὸ τῆς ἰλύος γεννηθῆναι· καὶ τὸ δίκαιον εἶναι καὶ τὸ αἰσχρὸν οὐ φύσει, ἀλλὰ νόμῳ.

Diogenes Laertius (Archelaus)

ἐκλήθη aor. pass. of καλέω 'call'; παρό 'wherefore'; λήγω 'cease' (aor. ἔληξα); μετάγω 'convey from one place to another'; εἰς + ἄγω

[13. οὗτος πρῶτος ἐκ τῆς Ἰωνίας τὴν φυσικὴν φιλοσοφίαν μετήγαγεν Ἀθήναζε, καὶ ἐκλήθη φυσικός, παρὸ καὶ ἔληξεν ἐν αὐτῷ ἡ φυσικὴ φιλοσοφία, Σωκράτους τὴν ἠθικὴν εἰσαγαγόντος.]

Diogenes Laertius (Archelaus)

*δικάζω 'judge'

14. ἐρωτηθεὶς τί γλυκὺ ἀνθρώποις, 'ἐλπίς,' ἔφη. ἥδιον ἔλεγε δικάζειν μεταξὺ ἐχθρῶν 'ἢ φίλων· τῶν μὲν γὰρ φίλων πάντως ἐχθρὸν ἔσεσθαι τὸν ἕτερον, τῶν δὲ ἐχθρῶν τὸν ἕτερον φίλον.

Diogenes Laertius (Bias)

πατρικός, -ή, -όν 'of one's father', 'hereditary'; *ἑταῖρος, -ου, ὁ 'companion'; ἐτελεύτησε 'he died'; ἑταίρω and φίλω dual nom.

[15. δίκαιος δ' εἶ· καὶ γὰρ πατρικὸς ἡμῖν φίλος τυγχάνεις ὤν· ἀεὶ γὰρ ἐγὼ καὶ ὁ σὸς πατὴρ ἑταίρω τε καὶ φίλω ἦμεν, καὶ πρότερον ἐκεῖνος ἐτελεύτησε, πρίν τι ἐμοὶ διενεχθῆναι.]

Plato, *Laches* (the speaker is Lysimachus)

*πλήρης, ˉες 'full of' + gen.

16. Θαλῆς ᾠήθη πάντα πλήρη θεῶν εἶναι.

Aristotle, περὶ ψυχῆς

ἀχάριστος, -ον 'thankless', 'ungrateful'

17. ἀεὶ δ' ὁ σωθεὶς ἐστιν ἀχάριστος φύσει.

Menander

ἀλλαχοῦ 'elsewhere', 'somewhere else'; ἔχω + infin. 'be able'; ἀδηλότης, -ητος, ἡ 'uncertainty'; σύγγραμα, -ατος, τό 'writing', 'book'; ἐκ + βάλλω; κατακαίω aor. κατέκαυσα 'burn'; κεκτημένων pf. pt. of κτάομαι 'possess' (pf. 'to have acquired'); ἀναλέγω 'gather up'

18. The Book Burning

καὶ ἀλλαχοῦ δὲ τοῦτον ἤρξατο τὸν τρόπον· 'περὶ μὲν θεῶν οὐκ ἔχω εἰδέναι οὔθ' ὡς εἰσίν, οὔθ' ὡς οὐκ εἰσίν· πολλὰ γὰρ τὰ κωλύοντα εἰδέναι, ἥ τ' ἀδηλότης καὶ βραχὺς ὢν ὁ βίος τοῦ ἀνθρώπου.' διὰ ταύτην δὲ τὴν ἀρχὴν τοῦ συγγράμματος ἐξεβλήθη πρὸς Ἀθηναίων· καὶ τὰ βιβλί' αὐτοῦ κατέκαυσαν ἐν τῇ ἀγορᾷ ὑπὸ κήρυκι ἀναλεξάμενοι παρ' ἑκάστου τῶν κεκτημένων.

Diogenes Laertius (Protagoras)

ὀκταμηνιαῖος 'eight months old'; ὑπερμεγέθης, -ες 'enormous'; εὐνή, -ῆς, ἡ 'bed'; βρέφος, -ους, τό 'babe', 'infant'; ἐπιβοάω (ἐπιβοωμένης pres. pt. mid.) 'call for help'; διαναστάς aor. pt. of διανίστημι 'awaken'; ἄγχω 'strangle'

[19. Heracles and the Snakes

τοῦ δὲ παιδὸς ὄντος ὀκταμηνιαίου δύο δράκοντας ὑπερμεγέθεις Ἥρα ἐπὶ τὴν εὐνὴν ἔπεμψε, διαφθαρῆναι τὸ βρέφος θέλουσα. ἐπιβοωμένης δὲ Ἀλκμήνης Ἀμφιτρύωνα, Ἡρακλῆς διαναστὰς ἄγχων ἑκατέραις ταῖς χερσὶν αὐτοὺς διέφθειρε.]

Apollodorus

δεῖμα, -ατος, τό 'fear'; εἰς + ἰδεῖν; θαυμαστός, -ή, -όν 'to be admired'; 'ἂν γένοιτ' 'would be' (optative, 3rd sg.); ὑπεύθυνος, -ον 'accountable'; κοιρανεῖ 'be lord' + gen. (pres. 3rd sg. act. of κοιρανέω)

[20. Atossa. . . . ταῦτ' ἔμοιγε δείματ' εἰσιδεῖν
ὑμῖν δ' ἀκούειν. εὖ γὰρ ἴστε παῖς ἐμὸς πράξας μὲν εὖ θαυμαστὸς 'ἂν γένοιτ' ἀνήρ, κακῶς δὲ πράξας οὐχ ὑπεύθυνος πόλει, σωθεὶς δὲ ὁμοίως τῆσδε κοιρανεῖ χθονός.]

Aeschylus, *Persae*

βασίλισσα = βασίλεια 'queen'; νομοθετέω 'make laws'; δύναται 'is able' (3rd sg. pres.); ἀδελφή, -ῆς, ἡ (cf. ἀδελφός); *καρπός, -οῦ, ὁ 'fruit'; *τρέφω, θρέψω, ἔθρεψα, τέτροφα, τέθραμμαι, ἐτρέφθην/ἐτράφην 'nourish', 'rear'

21. ἐγὼ Ἶσίς εἰμι ἡ βασίλισσα πάσης χώρας, ἡ παιδευθεῖσα ὑπὸ Ἑρμοῦ, καὶ ὅσα ἐγὼ ἐνομοθέτησα, οὐδεὶς αὐτὰ δύναται λῦσαι. ἐγώ εἰμι ἡ τοῦ νεωτάτου Κρόνου θεοῦ θυγάτηρ πρεσβυτάτη· ἐγώ εἰμι γυνὴ καὶ ἀδελφὴ Ὀσίριδος βασιλέως· ἐγώ εἰμι ἡ πρώτη καρπὸν ἀνθρώποις εὑροῦσα· ἐγώ εἰμι μήτηρ Ὥρου τοῦ βασιλέως . . . χαῖρε

χαῖρε Αἴγυπτε ἡ θρέψασά με.'
Diodorus Siculus (inscription on the
stele of Isis)

Quotation

Read and learn:

μάντις δ᾽ ἄριστος ὅστις εἰκάζει καλῶς.
The best soothsayer is the one who guesses well.
Greek Proverb

LESSON XI

A. *Contract Verbs*

In Attic Greek, ω-type verbs with stems ending in α, ε, or ο contract the stem vowel with the thematic vowel in the present system (present and imperfect tenses).

The rules for each type of contract verb should be memorized, since they apply to all the contracted forms of that type (with a few exceptions).

Accent of contract verbs:

1. If the accent does not fall on one of the original syllables of the contraction, it remains unchanged.

$$ἐνίκα\text{-}ον → ἐνίκων$$

2. If the accent falls on the first of the original syllables of the contraction, the contracted syllable receives the circumflex.

$$νικά\text{-}ουσι → νικῶσι$$

3. If the accent falls on the second, the contraction receives the acute.

$$νικα\text{-}όμενος → νικώμενος$$

The uncontracted forms of these verbs were not used in Attic Greek, but are found in other dialects.

I. α-contracts

Rules for contraction:

1. ι is written subscript
2. α + o-sound becomes ω
3. α + e-sound becomes α

1. An iota of the ending is written subscript:

$$νικάω: \text{ stem } νικα\text{-} \quad νικά\text{-}εις → νικᾷς$$

2. α contracts with any *o* sound (i.e. ο, ω, ου, οι, ῳ) to become ω:

νικά-ομαι → νικῶμαι

νικά-ω → νικῶ

3. α contracts with any *e* sound (i.e. ε, η, ει, ῃ) to become α:

ἐνίκα-ε → ἐνίκα

νικά-ει → νικᾷ

νικά-ῃ → νικᾷ

The one exception (in fact, only an apparent exception) is that the present active infinitive does not have ι-subscript: νικάειν becomes νικᾶν (NOT νικᾷν). The explanation of this is that the -ειν infinitive ending is itself a contraction for ε-εν, so that the ι was not originally part of the ending.

Conjugation of νικάω ('conquer') in the present system indicative, infinitive and participle (stem, νικα-):

PRESENT

Active		Middle-Passive	
	Singular		
(νικά-ω)	νικῶ	(νικά-ομαι)	νικῶμαι
(νικά-εις)	νικᾷς	(νικά-ει/-ῃ)	νικᾷ
(νικά-ει)	νικᾷ	(νικά-εται)	νικᾶται
	Plural		
(νικά-ομεν)	νικῶμεν	(νικα-ώμεθα)	νικώμεθα
(νικά-ετε)	νικᾶτε	(νικά-εσθε)	νικᾶσθε
(νικά-ουσι)	νικῶσι	(νικά-ονται)	νικῶνται
	Infinitive		
-ε-εν			
(νικά-ειν)	νικᾶν	(νικά-εσθαι)	νικᾶσθαι
	Participle		
ων			
(νικά-ουσα)	νικῶν, νικῶσα,	(νικα-όμενος)	νικώμενος
ον	νικῶν		

IMPERFECT

	Singular		
(ἐνίκα-ον)	ἐνίκων	(ἐνικα-όμην)	ἐνικώμην
(ἐνίκα-ες)	ἐνίκας	(ἐνικά-ου)	ἐνικῶ

(ἐνίκα-ε)	ἐνίκα	(ἐνίκά-ετο)	ἐνικᾶτο

Plural

(ἐνίκά-ομεν)	ἐνικῶμεν	(ἐνίκα-όμεθα)	ἐνικώμεθα
(ἐνίκά-ετε)	ἐνικᾶτε	(ἐνίκά-εσθε)	ἐνικᾶσθε
(ἐνίκα-ον)	ἐνίκων	(ἐνίκά-οντο)	ἐνικῶντο

Exception:

ζάω ('live') contracts to -η- instead of -α-:

Present		Imperfect	
ζῶ	ζῶμεν	ἔζων	ἐζῶμεν
ζῇς	ζῆτε	ἔζης	ἐζῆτε
ζῇ	ζῶσι	ἔζη	ἔζων

Infinitive ζῆν
Participle ζῶν

A few other verbs in -αω have -η rather than -α in the contracted forms. Among them are διψάω 'be thirsty', πεινάω 'be hungry', χράω 'give oracles', χράομαι 'use'.

χράομαι ('use') is thus conjugated:

Present		Imperfect	
χρῶμαι	χρώμεθα	ἐχρώμην	ἐχρώμεθα
χρῇ	χρῆσθε	ἐχρῶ	ἐχρῆσθε
χρῆται	χρῶνται	ἐχρῆτο	ἐχρῶντο

Infinitive χρῆσθαι
Participle χρώμενος

II.   ε-contracts

Rules for contraction:

1. ε + ε becomes ει
2. ε + ο becomes
3. ε before any long vowel or diphthong is absorbed

Present system of φιλέω ('love') (stem φιλε-):

PRESENT

Active		Middle-Passive	

Singular

(φιλέ-ω)	φιλῶ	(φιλέ-ομαι)	φιλοῦμαι
(φιλέ-εις)	φιλεῖς	(φιλέ-ει/-ῃ)	φιλεῖ/-ῇ
(φιλέ-ει)	φιλεῖ	(φιλέ-εται)	φιλεῖται

Plural

(φιλέ-ομεν)	φιλοῦμεν	(φιλε-όμεθα)	φιλούμεθα
(φιλέ-ετε)	φιλεῖτε	(φιλέ-εσθε)	φιλεῖσθε
(φιλέ-ουσι)	φιλοῦσι	(φιλέ-ονται)	φιλοῦνται

Infinitive

| (φιλέ-ειν) | φιλεῖν | (φιλέ-εσθαι) | φιλεῖσθαι |

Participle

	ων		
(φιλέ-ουσα)	φιλῶν, φιλοῦσα	(φιλε-όμενος)	φιλούμενος
	ον	φιλοῦν		

IMPERFECT

Singular

(ἐφίλε-ον)	ἐφίλουν	(ἐφιλε-όμην)	ἐφιλούμην
(ἐφίλε-ες)	ἐφίλεις	(ἐφιλέ-ου)	ἐφιλοῦ
(ἐφίλε-ε)	ἐφίλει	(ἐφιλέ-ετο)	ἐφιλεῖτο

Plural

(ἐφιλέ-ομεν)	ἐφιλοῦμεν	(ἐφιλε-όμεθα)	ἐφιλούμεθα
(ἐφιλέ-ετε)	ἐφιλεῖτε	(ἐφιλέ-εσθε)	ἐφιλεῖσθε
(ἐφίλε-ον)	ἐφίλουν	(ἐφιλέ-οντο)	ἐφιλοῦντο

There are a few verbs of two syllables which have uncontracted forms: πλέω 'sail', δέω 'need', 'want' contract only before -ε or -ει.

Present of πλέω:

πλέω	πλέομεν
πλεῖς	πλεῖτε
πλεῖ	πλέουσι

Infinitive πλεῖν
Participle πλέων, πλέουσα, πλέον

Other verbs of this type are:

θέω	'run'
πνέω	'breathe'
ῥέω	'flow'
χέω	'pour'

III. o-contracts

Rules for contraction:

1. o + η or ω becomes ω
2. o + ε or o or ου becomes ου
3. o + any ι-diphthong becomes οι

Again the one exception is that the present infinitive does not have οι: δηλό-ειν contracts to δηλοῦν (NOT δηλοῖν).

PRESENT

	Active		Middle-Passive

Singular

(δηλό-ω)	δηλῶ	(δηλό-ομαι)	δηλοῦμαι
(δηλό-εις)	δηλοῖς	(δηλό-ει/-ῃ)	δηλοῖ
(δηλό-ει)	δηλοῖ	(δηλό-εται)	δηλοῦται

Plural

(δηλό-ομεν)	δηλοῦμεν	(δηλο-όμεθα)	δηλούμεθα
(δηλό-ετε)	δηλοῦτε	(δηλό-εσθε)	δηλοῦσθε
(δηλό-ουσι)	δηλοῦσι	(δηλό-ονται)	δηλοῦνται

Infinitive

ε-εν
| (δηλό-ειν) | δηλοῦν | (δηλό-εσθαι) | δηλοῦσθαι |

Participle

ων
| (δηλό-ουσα) | δηλῶν, δηλοῦσα, | (δηλο-όμενος) | δηλούμενος |
ον | | δηλοῦν | | |

IMPERFECT

Singular

(ἐδήλο-ον)	ἐδήλουν	(ἐδηλο-όμην)	ἐδηλούμην
(ἐδήλο-ες)	ἐδήλους	(ἐδηλό-ου)	ἐδηλοῦ
(ἐδήλο-ε)	ἐδήλου	(ἐδηλό-ετο)	ἐδηλοῦτο

Plural

(ἐδηλό-ομεν)	ἐδηλοῦμεν	(ἐδηλο-όμεθα)	ἐδηλούμεθα
(ἐδηλό-ετε)	ἐδηλοῦτε	(ἐδηλό-εσθε)	ἐδηλοῦσθε
(ἐδήλο-ον)	ἐδήλουν	(ἐδηλό-οντο)	ἐδηλοῦντο

The Present Active Participles of Contract Verbs

The participles of contract verbs follow the rules for contraction.

1.   -αω

α-contracts have -ω- throughout the declension of the participle, resulting from α contracting with the o-sound (-ω-, -ο-, -ου-) of the participial ending.

Singular			Plural		
νικῶν	νικῶσα	νικῶν	νικῶντες	νικῶσαι	νικῶντα
νικῶντος	νικώσης	νικῶντος	νικώντων	νικωσῶν	νικώντων
νικῶντι	νικώσῃ	νικῶντι	νικῶσι	νικώσαις	νικῶσι
νικῶντα	νικῶσαν	νικῶν	νικῶντας	νικώσας	νικῶντα

2.   -εω

ε-contracts have -ου- where other verbs have -ο-; otherwise their participles are declined in the same way as those of
other -ω verbs.   (ε + ο → ου)(ε is absorbed before a long vowel
or diphthong, ω, ου)

	Singular				Plural	
φιλῶν	φιλοῦσα	φιλοῦν	φιλοῦντες	φιλοῦσαι	φιλοῦντα
φιλοῦντος	φιλούσης	φιλοῦντος	φιλούντων	φιλουσῶν	φιλούντων
φιλοῦντι	φιλούσῃ	φιλοῦντι	φιλοῦσι	φιλούσαις	φιλοῦσι
φιλοῦντα	φιλοῦσαν	φιλοῦν	φιλοῦντας	φιλούσας	φιλοῦντα

3.   -οω

Present participles of ο-contracts are declined like
those of ε-contracts.   (ο + ο → ου)

	Singular				Plural	
δηλῶν	δηλοῦσα	δηλοῦν	δηλοῦντες	δηλοῦσαι	δηλοῦντα
δηλοῦντος	δηλούσης	δηλοῦντος	δηλούντων	δηλουσῶν	δηλούντων
δηλοῦντι	δηλούσῃ	δηλοῦντι	δηλοῦσι	δηλούσαις	δηλοῦσι
δηλοῦντα	δηλοῦσαν	δηλοῦν	δηλοῦντας	δηλούσας	δηλοῦντα

Principal Parts of Contract Verbs

The principal parts of most contract verbs are regular.

1.   α- and ε-contracts regularly lengthen α or ε to η in the
principal parts:

| νικάω | νικήσω | ἐνίκησα | νενίκηκα | νενίκημαι | ἐνικήθην |
| φιλέω | φιλήσω | ἐφίλησα | πεφίληκα | πεφίλημαι | ἐφιλήθην |

2.   ο-contracts regularly lengthen the ο to ω.

| δηλόω | δηλώσω | ἐδήλωσα | δεδήλωκα | δεδήλωμαι | ἐδηλώθην |

Not all contract verbs have regular principal parts; the irregular ones are given in the vocabulary and are to be learned in
the usual way.

Note that the contract verbs have contracted forms in the
present system only.   Their other tenses are conjugated regularly.   There are some exceptions, as καλέω and γαμέω which have con-

tracted futures (treated below).

The Contract Futures

1. Liquid and Nasal Stems (i.e. stems ending in λ, μ, ν, ρ) originally formed their futures by adding -εσ- + thematic vowel + endings. Between two vowels, -σ- drops out, resulting in an ε-contract future (conjugated like the present of φιλέω).

> Example: μένω: stem, μεν-
>
>> future: [μενέσω → μενέω] → μενῶ
>>
>> κρίνω: stem, κριν- future, κρινῶ

Often the verb stem appears in a simpler form in the future than in the present.

Examples:

> ἀγγέλλω: stem ἀγγελ-   future, ἀγγελῶ
> φαίνω: stem φαν-   future, φανῶ
> τείνω: stem τεν-   future, τενῶ

(The liquid aorists, also formed without -σ-, on the other hand often appear in an extended form because of the phenomenon of compensatory lengthening, e.g. μένω, aorist ἔμεινα; ἀγγέλλω, aorist ἤγγειλα.)

2. Verbs with presents in -ίζω usually form their futures similarly to liquid and nasal futures.

> Example: νομίζω: future, [νομίσω → νομιέω] → νομιῶ

3. The "Attic Future:" In Attic Greek, contraction is more prevalent than in other dialects. Certain types of verbs which show the sigmatic future in other dialects have contract futures in Attic. Among these are some ε-stem verbs, such as καλέω and γαμέω, which in Attic have futures which are identical to their presents. Like the liquid and nasal futures, these "Attic futures" are ε-contract futures, and will present no difficulty. There are, however, certain -α- stems (not always immediately apparent as such) which have -α- contract futures.

Example: ἐλαύνω stem, ἐλα- (aorist ἤλασα) which has the future:

$$[\dot{\epsilon}\lambda\acute{\alpha}\sigma\omega \to \dot{\epsilon}\lambda\acute{\alpha}\omega] \to \dot{\epsilon}\lambda\tilde{\omega}$$

The few verbs of this sort will be identified in the following way:

ἐλαύνω, ἐλῶ (-άω), ἤλασα, etc.

Verbs in -αννυμι form futures in -αω; those in -εννυμι, in -εω. Some verbs in -αζω also have -αω futures (βιβάζω: fut. [βιβάω] → βιβῶ). (βιβάζω 'make to go')

Examples of Liquid Future and "Attic Future"

the future of κρίνω		the future of ἐλαύνω	
Active	Middle	Active	Middle
κρινῶ	κρινοῦμαι	ἐλῶ	ἐλῶμαι
κρινεῖς	κρινεῖ (-ῇ)	ἐλᾷς	ἐλᾷ
κρινεῖ	κρινεῖται	ἐλᾷ	ἐλᾶται
κρινοῦμεν	κρινούμεθα	ἐλῶμεν	ἐλώμεθα
κρινεῖτε	κρινεῖσθε	ἐλᾶτε	ἐλᾶσθε
κρινοῦσι	κρινοῦνται	ἐλῶσι	ἐλῶνται
κρινεῖν	κρινεῖσθαι	ἐλᾶν	ἐλᾶσθαι
κρινῶν	κρινούμενος	ἐλῶν	ἐλώμενος

Vocabulary

I. Learn well:

ἀγαπάω	*love, greet with affection* (ἀγάπη)
ἀδικέω	*be* ἄδικος, *do wrong* (often used with the participle which states the particular charge of wrongdoing)
αἱρέω, αἱρήσω, εἷλον, ἥρηκα, ἥρημαι, ἡρέθην	*take,* mid. *choose* (2nd aor. stem ἑλ-)
ἀξιόω	*think worthy, expect, claim* (ἄξιος)
ἀποκρίνομαι, ἀποκρινοῦμαι, ἀποκέκριμαι, ἀπεκρίθην	*answer*
ἀφικνέομαι, ἀφίξομαι, ἀφικόμην, ἀφῖγμαι	*arrive at, come to, reach*
δέω	*lack, want, stand in need of* (+ genitive)
δέομαι	*beg, ask*
δεῖ	*there is need, one ought* (impersonal)
δηλόω	*make visible, show, reveal* (δῆλος)

διανοέομαι, διανοήσο-   *intend, have in mind, think* (νοῦς)
  μαι, διενοήθην
διάνοια, (διανοία)   *thought, intellect, mind, intention, belief*
  -ας, ἡ
δοκέω, δόξω, ἔδοξα,   *expect, think* (+ acc. and inf.)(δοκῶ μοι 'I seem to
  ---, δέδογμαι   myself', 'I am determined')(impersonal δοκεῖ 'it
                            seems', 'seems best'; often in formulas, 'it is de-
                            cided by (+ dat.)')
δράω, δράσω, ἔδρασα,   *do, accomplish*
  δέδρακα, δέδραμαι,
  ἐδράσθην
ἐλαύνω, ἐλῶ (-άω), ἤ-   *drive, march*
  λασα, ἐλήλακα, ἐλή-
  λαμαι, ἠλάθην
ἐάω (impf. εἴων)   *suffer, permit* (+ acc. and inf.); *let alone* (other
                            principal parts in principal part list)
ἐπιθυμέω   *set one's heart* (θυμός) *upon (a thing), long for, de-*
                            sire (+ gen.)
ἐράω (impf. ἤρων)   *love, be in love with* (+ gen.)(only pres. and imperf.
                            in active; aor. pass. ἠράσθην)
ἐρωτάω   *ask* (+ 2 acc.), *question*
ζητέω   *seek, inquire, search into/after, demand*
ζάω, ζήσω/ζήσομαι   *live, pass one's life* (ἔζησα, ἔζηκα late forms)
ἡγέομαι   *go before, lead; believe*
καλέω, καλῶ, ἐκάλεσα,   *call, summon; invoke* (act. or mid.); *pass. to be*
  κέκληκα, κέκλημαι,   *called*
  ἐκλήθην
κατηγορέω   *speak against, accuse*
μισέω   *hate*
νικάω   *conquer, prevail, win*
νοέω   *think, intend*
ὁράω (impf. ἑώρων),   *see, look* (2nd aor. stem ἰδ-)
  ὄψομαι, εἶδον, ἑόρα-
  κα (ἑώρακα), ὦμμαι
  (ἑώραμαι), ὤφθην
ποιέω   *make, produce, cause* (ποιητής)
σκοπέω   *contemplate, inspect, examine, look to*
τιμάω   *honor, esteem, value* (τιμή)
φιλέω   *love, kiss* (show outward signs of love)
φοβέομαι, φοβήσομαι,   *fear, be frightened* (for object clause with μή, see
  πεφόβημαι, ἐφοβήθην   Lesson XIII); *be afraid to* (+ inf.)(φόβος)
φρονέω   *be minded, be wise*
χράομαι   *use* (+ dat.), *make use of, take part in*
χράω   *proclaim* (of oracles); mid. *consult an oracle*

II. Learn the following as recognition vocabulary:

βοάω, βοήσομαι, ἐβόησα   *cry aloud, shout, howl*
γαμέω, γαμῶ, ἔγημα,   *marry* (act. of the man; mid. of the woman or the par-
  γεγάμηκα, γεγάμημαι   ents)
γεννάω   *beget,* mid. *create* (causal of γίγνομαι)

διψάω   be thirsty, (+ gen.) thirst after (dipsomaniac)
δουλόω   enslave (δοῦλος)
εὐτυχέω   be prosperous (εὐτυχής)
θέω, θεύσομαι   run (other forms from τρέχω)
νοσέω   be sick (νόσος, ἡ)
οἰκέω   inhabit, colonize; live, dwell (οἶκος)
πεινάω   be hungry
πλέω, πλεύσομαι, ἔ-   sail, go by sea
  πλευσα, πέπλευκα,
  πέπλευσμαι, ἐπλεύ-
  σθην
πνέω, πνεύσομαι, ἔ-   blow, breathe (πνεῦμα)
  πνευσα, πέπνευκα,
  (πέπνευμαι), ἐπνεύ-
  σθην
ῥέω (ῥυήσομαι, ἐρρύην,   flow, run
  ἐρρύηκα)
σιγάω   keep silence
σιωπάω   keep silence; keep secret
συμμαχέω   be an ally (to)(+ dat.)
τεκνόω   furnish with children; (of the man, active) beget; (of
                                 the woman, middle) bear
τελευτάω   bring to pass, come to an end (die); pass. happen
τελέω   accomplish, fulfil; pay, initiate (τέλος)
τολμάω   undertake; (+ inf.) dare, bring oneself (to do)
ὑπισχνέομαι   promise (+ fut. inf.); profess (+ pres. inf.)

Vocabulary Note:

    The contract verbs are mostly denominative, that is, derived from nouns.

        1. The -αω verbs are often derived from -α (or -η) base nouns:

            διψάω from δίψα, δίψης, ἡ 'thirst'
            σιγάω   σιγή, σιγῆς, ἡ 'silence'
            νικάω   νίκη, -ης, ἡ 'victory'
            τιμάω   τιμή, -ῆς, ἡ 'honor'

        2. The -εω verbs are sometimes derived from -o bases:

            φιλέω from φίλος   'friend', 'friendly', 'dear'
            οἰκέω   οἶκος   'house'
            γαμέω   γάμος   'marriage'
            μισέω   μῖσος, -ους, τό 'hate', 'hatred'
            τελέω   τέλος, -ους, τό 'end'

        3. The -οω verbs are derived from nouns or adjectives in -o.

            δηλόω from δῆλος 'clear'
            δουλόω   δοῦλος 'slave'
            ἀξιόω   ἄξιος 'worthy'

Exercises

1. Conjugate in full:

   1. ὁράω   2. δοκέω   3. οἰκέω   4. ἀγαπάω

2. Conjugate in the present system only:

1. ἀξιόω   2. ἐράω   3. πλέω   4. τελέω   5. τιμάω

3. Decline the present active participles of:

   1. ποιέω   2. τιμάω   3. δουλόω   4. δέω

   Decline the future active participle of βάλλω.

4. Synopses:

      10. ἐλαύνω   first plural

      11. νομίζω   second plural

      12. βάλλω   third plural

5. Parse:

1. ζῶμεν	6. βοῶμεν	11. ἑώρα	16. τιμᾶν
2. ἠδίκεις	7. ἐλῶ	12. ὑπισχνεῖται	17. ἠξιοῦντο
3. ἐφοβεῖσθε	8. ἐποίουν	13. ἀξιοῦν	18. ᾠκεῖτο
4. καλεῖς	9. σιγᾷς	14. ἐτελεύτα	19. νοσοῦμεν
5. ἀφικνοῦνται	10. ἐγάμει	15. νοεῖν	20. φοβεῖσθαι

6. Translate:

1. οἱ πατέρες τὰ παιδία ἀγαπῶσι.
2. οἱ μὲν τὰ χρήματα, οἱ δὲ τὴν ἀρετὴν ἀγαπῶσι.
3. πάντες τὸ ἀγαθὸν καὶ καλὸν ἀγαπῶμεν καὶ ζητοῦμεν.
4. οὐ γὰρ τοῖς παροῦσιν ἀγαπᾷ. (ἀγαπάω + dative 'be contented with')
5. ταῦτα ποιῶν ἀδικεῖς.
6. ὁ δικαστὴς ὁ ἄδικος πολλὰ ἠδίκει.
7. οἱ νομίζοντες τοὺς θεοὺς ἀδικοῦσιν.
8. ἀδικήσας οὐδὲν ἄξιον θανάτου ἐλύθη ὑπὸ τῶν πολιτῶν.
9. πολλὰ καὶ καλὰ πράξαντες οὐχ ἑαυτοὺς κακοῦ τινος ἠξίουν.
10. ἀξιῶ σε ἀληθῆ λέγειν.
11. τὸ ἐκείνου τοῦ ἀνδρὸς κλέος εἰς οὐρανὸν ἀφικνεῖται.
12. ἐβόων ὅτι ἀφικόμεθα.
13. ἐβοῶμεν ἀλλήλοις μὴ φεύγειν.
14. τί βοᾷς; τί οὐ σιγᾷς;
15. τὴν τοῦ βασιλέως θυγατέρα ἔγημεν.

16. οἱ Ἕλληνες οὔποτε δουλωθύσονται ὑπὸ τῶν βαρβάρων.

17. ὁ πλοῦτος τὰς τῶν ἀνθρώπων ψυχὰς δουλοῖ.

18. αἱ γυναῖκες ὑπὸ τῶν ἀνδρῶν ἐδουλοῦντο.

19. πολλοῦ δεῖ τὰ ἀληθῆ λέγειν.   (πολλοῦ δεῖ 'lacks much', 'is far from')

20. ὁ γεννήσας σέ ἐστι ὁ σὸς πατήρ.

21. πολλοῦ δέουσι ἄνθρωποι δίκαιοι εἶναι.

22. αὐτὸν δηλώσω καλὸν καὶ ἀγαθὸν ὄντα.

23. τῷ πατρὶ ἐσθλὸς ᾽ὢν ἐβουλήθη δηλοῦν.

24. οἱ δίκαιοι δικαιοσύνην διψῶσιν.

25. ζῶν καὶ ὁρῶν τὸν ἥλιον, οὐ παύσομαι τὴν ἀλήθειαν ζητῶν.

26. ταῦτα πράξομεν ὡς ἡμῖν δοκεῖ εἶναι ἄριστα.

27. ἐν ὕπνῳ τάδε ἰδεῖν ἐδόκουν.

28. οὐκ ἐμὲ ἐᾷ ἐλθεῖν.

29. πάντες οἱ ἄνθρωποι τῆς δικαιοσύνης ἐπιθυμοῦσιν.

30. ὁ δὲ ἀνὴρ ὁ δίκαιος τοῦ ἀδίκου πλούτου οὐκ ἐπιθυμεῖ.

31. ὁ νεώτερος ἀδελφὸς τυραννίδος ἤρα.

32. ὁ ἐρῶν καὶ ὁ ἐρώμενος οὔκ εἰσιν οἱ αὐτοί.

33. ἠρωτῶμεν αὐτὸν τὸ ὄνομα.

34. τί ἐρωτᾷς με τo ὄνομά μου;

35. ἡ μεν ἐρωμένη ὑπο τοῦ ἐρῶντος ἐρᾶται, ὁ δε ἐρῶν οὐκ ἐρᾶται ὑπο τῆς ἐρωμένης.

36. ἐρωτῶμεν· τίς εἶ καὶ τί ζητεῖς;

37. οἱ εὐτυχοῦντες πολλοὺς φίλους ἔχουσιν.

38. μὴ ζητῶν οὐχ εὑρήσεις.

39. εὐτυχοῦντες τοὺς θεοὺς οὐ καλούμεθα.

40. ἐκεῖνοι τοὺς ξένους ἐπὶ δεῖπνον ἐκάλουν.

41. ἡ μήτηρ αὐτοῦ καλοῦμαι.

42. ὑπὸ τῶν θεῶν ὁ θάνατος ἐμισεῖτο.

43. τὸν μισοῦντά σε δεῖ ἀγαπᾶν.

44. ὁ μὲν νικήσας ὑπὸ πάντων τιμᾶται, ὁ δὲ νικηθεὶς μισεῖται.

45. αὕτη πάσας γυναῖκας κάλλει καὶ σωφροσύνῃ ἐνίκα.

46. τῆς κακῆς βουλῆς νικησάσης τὸν πόλεμον οὐκ ἔπαυσεν.

47. ταῖς συμφοραῖς νικῶμαι.

48. νοεῖς γὰρ ἔρχεσθαι;

49. νοσεῖ ἡ πόλις ᾗ οὐκ ἔστι ἄρχων.

50. οἰκοῦμεν τὰς πλείστας τῶν νήσων.

51. τί ὁρᾷς; θαῦμά τι ὁρῶ.

52. ὁρᾶτε ὅ τι λέγω;

53. οἱ ἄδικοι χρημάτων πεινῶσιν.

54. ἐν τῇ θαλάττῃ πλέομεν.

55. εἰς την νῆσον πλεῖτε;

56. τόνδε τὸν ἄνδρα ποιεῖν βασιλέα βούλει;

57. τὰ ἑαυτοῦ σκοπεῖν δεῖ.

58. ταῦτα ποιεῖν τολμᾷς;

59. δεῖ τοὺς ἐχθροὺς φιλεῖν, οὐ μόνον τοὺς φίλους.

60. ἐφίλει τοὺς αὐτὸν μισοῦντας.

61. ὑπισχνούμεθα σιωπήσειν.

62. μεγάλα ποιεῖν ἐτόλμησεν.

63. οὐδὲν καὶ οὐδένα ἐφοβοῦντο.

64. οὐ λέγεις ἃ φρονεῖς.

65. οὐ φοβούμεθα τοὺς εὖ φρονοῦντας.

7. Write in Greek:

1. We love those who love us.

2. He is guilty of corrupting the young men.   (He does injustice by corrupting the young men.)

3. I think you worthy to receive these gifts.

4. The good help (are allies to) each other.

5. In silence (keeping silent) they dared to do many fine deeds.

6. Do you promise to finish these works?

7. We ourselves were seeking the same man, but we did not find him.

8. We do not see the soul, but we think it exists (is).

9. Good men honor each others' opinions.

10. If you were doing these things, you would be doing well.

Readings

Ἡράκλειος, -α, -ον 'of Heracles'

1. ἐμοῦ γὰρ ζῶντος οὐ κτενεῖς ποτε τοὺς Ἡρακλείους παῖδας.

Euripides, *Heracles*

*ποίημα, -ατος, τό 'poem', 'cre-
ation'

2. ὥσπερ . . . οἱ ποιηταὶ τὰ αὑτῶν ποιήματα
καὶ οἱ πατέρες τοὺς παῖδας ἀγαπῶσι.

    Plato, *Republic*

ὑποπτεύω 'suspect'

3. οὐκ ἀξιῶ ὑποπτεύεσθαι.

    Thucydides

4. ἄλλο τι ἀξιοῖς 'ἢ ἀποθανεῖν;

    Lysias

*ἐλεύθερος, -α, -ον 'free'

5. ἐλεύθερος πᾶς ἑνὶ δεδούλωται, νόμῳ.

    Menander

6. χαλεπὸν τὸ ποιεῖν, τὸ δὲ κελεῦσαι ῥᾴδιον.

    Philemon (a comic poet)

7. βέλτιόν ἐστι σῶμά γ' 'ἢ ψυχὴν νοσεῖν.

    Menander

8. ὁ μὴ γαμῶν ἄνθρωπος οὐκ ἔχει κακά.

    Menander

9. φιλεῖ δ' ἑαυτοῦ πλεῖον οὐδεὶς οὐδένα.

    Menander

10. 'ὃν γὰρ θεοὶ φιλοῦσιν ἀποθνήσκει νέος.

    Menander

λίαν 'too much' (adv.)

11. λίαν φιλῶν σεαυτὸν οὐχ ἕξεις φίλον.

    Menander

12. οὐδεὶς 'ὃ νοεῖς μὲν οἶδεν, 'ὃ δὲ ποιεῖς
βλέπει.

    Menander

*πένης, -ητος, ὁ 'poor man'; δω-
ρέω 'give', 'make gifts'

13. μισῶ πένητα πλουσίῳ δωρούμενον.

    Menander

*ὀφθαλμός, -οῦ, ὁ 'eye'

14. ἔστιν Δίκης ὀφθαλμός, 'ὃς τὰ πάνθ' ὁρᾷ.

    Menander

ὥρη = ὥρα

15. ὥρη ἐρᾶν, ὥρη δὲ γαμεῖν, ὥρη δὲ πεπαῦ-
σθαι.

    Greek Anthology (Dionysius)

16. σοφία γάρ ἐστι καὶ μαθεῖν 'ἃ μὴ νοεῖς.

    Menander

17. ἡδύ 'γε δικαίους ἄνδρας εὐτυχεῖς ὁρᾶν.

    Menander

18. τούτους ἀγαπᾷ καὶ περὶ αὑτὸν ἔχει.

    Demosthenes

ἀνθρώπινος, -η, -ον 'of/from/be-   19. ἄνθρωπον ὄντα δεῖ φρονεῖν τἀνθρώπινα.
longing to man', 'human'
                                        Menander

ἐνίοτε 'at times', 'sometimes'   20. ἔρχεται τἀληθὲς ἐς φῶς ἐνίοτ' οὐ ζητού-
                                        μενον.

                                        Menander

                                    21. ὁ μηδὲν ἀδικῶν οὐδενὸς δεῖται νόμου.

                                        Menander

ἐξεργάζομαι 'work out', 'accom-   22. ἄπαντα σιγῶν ὁ θεὸς ἐξεργάζεται.
plish'
                                        Menander

ἀτυχέω 'be unlucky'   23. ἄνθρωπος ἀτυχῶν σῴζεθ' ὑπὸ τῆς ἐλπίδος.

                                        Menander

*ὀργή, -ῆς, ἡ 'anger'; ἰσχύω 'be   24. ὀργὴ φιλούντων ὀλίγον ἰσχύει χρόνον.
strong'
                                        Menander

σωφρονέω 'be of sound mind', 'be   [25. οὐκ ἔστι μείζων ἡδονὴ ταύτης πατρὶ 'ἢ
discreet'   σωφρονοῦντα καὶ φρονοῦντ' ἰδεῖν τινα
                                        τῶν ἐξ ἑαυτοῦ.]

                                        Menander

μάγειρος, -ου, ὁ 'cook'; ἀθῷος,   26.   οὐδὲ εἷς
-ον 'unpunished'; διαφεύγω 'get   μάγειρον ἀδικήσας ἀθῷος διέφυγεν·
away', 'escape'; πως (encl.)   ἱεροπρεπὴς πώς ἐστιν ἡμῶν ἡ τέχνη.
'somehow'; ἱεροπρεπής, -ές 'sa-
cred', 'holy'; *τέχνη, -ης, ἡ   Menander
'craft', 'profession', 'art',
'skill'; 'treatise'

                                    27. καὶ μὴν ὁρᾶν μοι δύο μὲν ἡλίους δοκῶ.

                                        Euripides, *Bacchae*

παμμεγέθης, -ες 'of enormous   28. Getas. κακόν τι, Δᾶέ, μοι δοκεῖς πεποη-
size'; πεποηκέναι = πεποιηκέναι   κέναι παμμέγεθες . . .

                                        Menander

προσδοκάω 'expect'   [29. ὃ βούλεται γὰρ μόνον ὁρῶν καὶ προσδοκῶν
                                        ἀλόγιστος ἔσται τῆς ἀληθείας κριτής.]

                                        Menander

ἀναχορεύω 'celebrate in dance';   30. Pentheus. ἦλθες δὲ πρῶτα δεῦρ' ἄγων τὸν
ὄργια, τά 'rites', 'mysteries';   δαίμονα;
διάφορος, -ον 'different'   Dionysus. πᾶς ἀναχορεύει βαρβάρων τάδ'
                                                ὄργια.
                                        Pentheus. φρονοῦσι γὰρ κάκιον Ἑλλήνων
                                                πολύ.

Dionysus. τάδ' εὖ γε μᾶλλον· οἱ νόμοι
δε διάφοροι.

Euripides, *Bacchae*

χορεύω 'dance'; βάκχιος 'Bac-
chic'; ὁ Βάκχιος 'Bacchus'

31. Cadmus. μόνοι δὲ πόλεως Βακχίῳ χορεύσο-
μεν;
Teiresias. μόνοι γὰρ εὖ φρονοῦμεν, οἱ
δ' ἄλλοι κακῶς.

Euripides, *Bacchae*

*σπουδή, -ῆς, ἡ 'haste', 'eager-
ness', 'seriousness'; ἀξιομνη-
μόνευτος, -ον 'worthy of men-
tion'; παιδία, -ᾱς, ἡ 'child's
play', 'fun', 'sport'

[32. ἀλλ' ἐμοὶ δοκεῖ τῶν καλῶν κἀγαθῶν ἀνδρῶν
ἔργα οὐ μόνον τὰ μετὰ σπουδῆς πραττόμενα
ἀξιομνημόνευτα εἶναι ἀλλὰ καὶ τὰ ἐν ταῖς
παιδιαῖς.]

Xenophon, *Symposium*

χρέων, τό (used in nom. and
acc.) 'necessity'; often = χρή
'it is necessary'

[33. ἢ τὴν τύχην μὲν δαίμον' ἡγεῖσθαι χρέων,
τὰ δαιμόνων δὲ τῆς τύχης ἐλάσσονα.]

Euripides, *Cyclops*

ἀπειθέω 'be disobedient'

34. τὸ δὲ ἀδικεῖν καὶ ἀπειθεῖν τῷ βελτίονι,
καὶ θεῷ καὶ ἀνθρώπῳ, ὅτι κακὸν καὶ αἰσχρόν ἐστιν οἶδα.

Plato, *Apology*

σκόπει 'consider!' (imper.); ἱ-
κανῶς 'sufficiently'; *φρόνιμος,
-ον 'wise', 'prudent'; ἄφρων,
-ον (gen. ἄφρονος) 'mindless',
'witless'

35. Socrates. σκόπει δή· οὐχ ἱκανῶς δοκεῖ
σοι λέγεσθαι, ὅτι οὐ πάσας χρὴ τὰς δόξας
τῶν ἀνθρώπων τιμᾶν, ἀλλὰ τὰς μέν, τὰς δ'
οὔ; τί φής; ταῦτα οὐχὶ καλῶς λέγεται;
Crito. καλῶς.
Socrates. οὐκοῦν τὰς μὲν χρηστὰς τιμᾶν,
τὰς δὲ πονηρὰς μή;
Crito. ναί.
Socrates. χρησταὶ δὲ οὐχ αἱ τῶν φρονί-
μων, πονηραὶ δὲ αἱ τῶν ἀφρόνων;
Crito. πῶς δ' οὔ;

Plato, *Crito*

εὔελπις (n. εὔελπι, gen. -ιδος)
'of good hope'; ἀμελέω 'be care-
less', 'neglect'; ἀπὸ τοῦ αὐτομάτου 'by chance'; *δῆλος, -η,
-ον 'visible', 'clear'; ἀπηλλά-
χθαι pf. mid. inf. of ἀπαλλάττω
'set free', mid. 'be released
from'; ἀποτρέπω 'turn away
from'; *σημεῖον, -ου, τό 'sign';
καταψηφίζομαι 'vote against',
'vote for conviction'; χαλεπαίνω
'be angry'; *καί τοι 'and yet';
τοσόσδε, -ήδε, -όνδε 'so great',
n. 'so much'; υἱεῖς = υἱούς;

36. ἀλλὰ καὶ ὑμᾶς χρή, ὦ ἄνδρες δικασταί,
εὐέλπιδας εἶναι πρὸς τὸν θάνατον, καὶ
ἕν τι τοῦτο διανοεῖσθαι ἀληθές, ὅτι οὐκ
ἔστιν ἀνδρὶ ἀγαθῷ κακὸν οὐδὲν οὔτε ζῶντι
οὔτε τελευτήσαντι, οὐδὲ ἀμελεῖται ὑπὸ
θεῶν τὰ τούτου πράγματα· οὐδὲ τὰ ἐμὰ νῦν
ἀπὸ τοῦ αὐτομάτου γέγονεν, ἀλλά μοι δῆ-
λόν ἐστι τοῦτο, ὅτι ἤδη τεθνάναι καὶ ἀ-
πηλλάχθαι πραγμάτων βέλτιον ἦν μοι. διὰ
τοῦτο καὶ ἐμὲ οὐδαμοῦ ἀπέτρεψεν τὸ σημεῖον, καὶ ἔγωγε τοῖς καταψηφισαμένοις
μου καὶ τοῖς κατηγόροις οὐ πάνυ χαλεπαίνω. καί τοι οὐ ταύτῃ τῇ διανοίᾳ κατεψη-
φίζοντό μου καὶ κατηγόρουν ἀλλ' οἰόμενοι

ἡβάω 'reach manhood'; τιμωρέω 'punish', τιμωρήσασθε aor. mid. imperative; λυπέω 'grieve', 'give pain'; ἐπιμελέομαι 'pay attention to'; ὀνειδίζετε imperative; ἀπιέναι (inf.) 'to go away'; βιόω 'live'; ὁπότερος, -α, -ον 'which of two'; ἄδηλος, -ον 'unknown'; πλὴν ἤ 'except'; ἐὰν ταῦτα ποιῆτε 'if you do these things'

βλάπτειν· τοῦτο αὐτοῖς ἄξιον μέμφεσθαι. τοσόνδε μέντοι αὐτῶν δέομαι· τοὺς υἱεῖς μου, ἐπειδὰν ἡβήσωσι, τιμωρήσασθε, ὦ ἄνδρες, ταὐτὰ ταῦτα λυποῦντες, ἅπερ ἐγὼ ὑμᾶς ἐλύπουν, ἐὰν ὑμῖν δοκῶσιν ἢ χρημάτων ἢ ἄλλου του πρότερον ἐπιμελεῖσθαι ἢ ἀρετῆς, καὶ ἐὰν δοκῶσί τι εἶναι μηδὲν ὄντες, ὀνειδίζετε αὐτοῖς, ὥσπερ ἐγὼ ὑμῖν, ὅτι οὐκ ἐπιμελοῦνται ὧν δεῖ, καὶ οἴονταί τι εἶναι ὄντες οὐδενὸς ἄξιοι. καὶ ἐὰν ταῦτα ποιῆτε δίκαια πεπονθὼς ἐγὼ ἔσομαι ὑφ' ὑμῶν αὐτός τε καὶ οἱ υἱεῖς.

ἀλλὰ γὰρ ἤδη ὥρα ἀπιέναι, ἐμοὶ μὲν ἀποθανουμένῳ, ὑμῖν δὲ βιωσομένοις· ὁπότεροι δὲ ἡμῶν ἔρχονται ἐπὶ ἄμεινον πρᾶγμα, ἄδηλον παντὶ πλὴν ἢ τῷ θεῷ.

Plato, *Apology of Socrates*

*ἄναξ, -κτος, ὁ 'lord', 'king'; ἐξαμαρτάνω 'err greatly'

[37. Neoptolemus to Odysseus. . . . βούλομαι δ', ἄναξ, καλῶς δρῶν ἐξαμαρτεῖν μᾶλλον ἢ νικᾶν κακῶς.]

Sophocles, *Philoctetes*

ἐραστής, -οῦ, ὁ 'lover'

38. οὐδεὶς ἐραστὴς ὅς τις οὐκ ἀεὶ φιλεῖ.

Euripides, *Trojan Women*

ὑγιαίνω 'be healthy'

39. ἀνδρὶ δ' ὑγιαίνειν ἄριστόν ἐστιν, ὥς γ' ἡμῖν δοκεῖ.

Aristotle, *Rhetoric* (quoting Simonides or Epicharmus)

*φονεύς, -έως, ὁ 'murderer'

40. φονεὺς γὰρ εἶναι μητρὸς ἠξιώσατο.

Aeschylus, *Eumenides*

41. καὶ οὐ δεῖ ἡμᾶς φοβεῖσθαι τοὺς ἀνθρώπους μᾶλλον, ἀλλὰ τὸν θεόν.

II Clement

ἔα imperative of ἐάω; κέρδιστος 'most profitable'

[42. ἔα με τῇδε τῇ νόσῳ νοσεῖν, ἐπεὶ κέρδιστον εὖ φρονοῦντα μὴ φρονεῖν δοκεῖν.]

Aeschylus, *Prometheus*

οὖλος Ionic for ὅλος

43. οὖλος ὁρᾷ, οὖλος δὲ νοεῖ, οὖλος δὲ τ' ἀκούει. (sc. ὁ θεός)

Xenophanes

ἐπαινέω 'approve'

44. οὐ χαλεπὸν Ἀθηναίους ἐν Ἀθηναίοις ἐπαινεῖν.

Aristotle, *Rhetoric*

*ὀργή, -ῆς, ἡ 'anger', 'tempera-
ment'

45. Oceanus.
   οὔκουν, Προμηθεῦ, τοῦτο γιγνώσκεις, ὅτι
   ὀργῆς νοσούσης εἰσὶν ἰατροὶ λόγοι;

   Aeschylus, *Prometheus*

ἐξειργασμένη pf. mid. pt. of ἐξεργάζομαι 'work out', 'accomplish'; ποῦ 'where'

46. ἥδ' ἔστ' ἐκείνη τοὔργον ἡ 'ξειργασμένη·
   τήνδ' εἵλομεν θάπτουσαν. ἀλλὰ ποῦ
                           Κρέων;

   Sophocles, *Antigone*

47. Eteocles.
   αὐτὴ σὺ δουλοῖς κἀμὲ καὶ πᾶσαν πόλιν.

   Aeschylus, *Seven against Thebes*

εἴσω 'inside' (adv. + gen.)

48. Eteocles.
   σὸν δ' αὖ τὸ σιγᾶν καὶ μένειν εἴσω
   δόμων.

   Aeschylus, *Seven*

a play on the two meanings of
φιλέω 'love' and 'kiss'; φίλει
imper. 2nd sg. pres. act. (note
accent: from φιλε-ε)

[49. εἴ με φιλεῖς, μισεῖς με· καὶ εἰ μισεῖς,
       σὺ φιλεῖς με·
   εἰ δέ με μὴ μισεῖς, φίλτατε, μή με φίλει.]

   Greek Anthology

Ἔρως, -ωτος, ὁ --; αἷμα, -ατος,
τό 'blood'; μειδιάω 'smile'

[50. τίς θεὸν εἶπεν Ἔρωτα; θεοῦ κακὸν οὐδὲν
       ὁρῶμεν
   ἔργον· ὁ δ' ἀνθρώπων αἵματι μειδιάει.]

   Greek Anthology

τέρπομαι 'enjoy'; κερδαίνω 'make
a profit'

51. ἐρωτηθεὶς τί ποιῶν ἄνθρωπος τέρπεται,
   ἔφη 'κερδαίνων.'

   Diogenes Laertius (Bias)

[52. The opening of Athenaeus.
    Ἀθήναιος μὲν ὁ τῆς βίβλιου πατήρ·
   ποιεῖται δὲ τὸν λόγον πρὸς Τιμοκράτην·
   Δειπνοσοφιστης δὲ ταύτῃ τὸ ὄνομα.]

ἀσεβής, -ές 'ungodly'; εὐσέβεια,
-ας, ἡ 'piety'

53. ἐρωτηθεὶς ὑπὸ ἀσεβοῦς ἀνθρώπου τί ποτέ
   ἐστιν εὐσέβεια, ἐσίγα.

   Diogenes Laertius (Bias)

δυνάμενος 'being able' (pres.
ptcpl. of δύναμαι)

54. ἀνὴρ δίκαιός ἐστιν οὐχ ὁ μὴ ἀδικῶν,
   ἀλλ' ὅστις ἀδικεῖν δυνάμενος μὴ βούλεται.

   Menander

ἐπαινέω 'approve', 'praise'

55. πρὸς τὸν εἰπόντα, 'πολλοί σε ἐπαινοῦσι,'
   'τί γάρ,' ἔφη, 'κακὸν πεποίηκα;'

   Diogenes Laertius (Antisthenes)

μυθέομαι 'say', 'tell'; γελοῖος,
-α, -ον 'laughable', 'absurd'
(also γέλοιος); ἀληθέα = ἀληθῆ

56. Ἑκαταῖος Μιλήσιος ὧδε μυθεῖται· τάδε
     γράφω, ὥς μοι δοκεῖ ἀληθέα εἶναι· οἱ γὰρ
     Ἑλλήνων λόγοι πολλοί τε καὶ γελοῖοι, ὡς
     ἐμοὶ φαίνονται, εἰσίν.

          Hecataeus

[57. ἐπὶ σαυτὸν καλεῖς, ἐπὶ τοὺς νόμους κα-
      λεῖς, ἐπὶ τὴν δημοκρατίαν καλεῖς.]

          Aeschines

58. πάντα δὲ τὰ τῶν νικωμένων ἀγαθὰ τῶν νι-
     κώντων γίγνεσθαι.

          Plato, *Laws*

δεῖμα, -ατος, τό 'fear'; ἀρά,
-ᾶς, ἡ 'curse'; *τοιόσδε, τοιά-
δε, τοιόνδε 'of such kind'

[59. Oedipus.
      ἤκουσα κἀγώ· τὸν δ᾽ ἰδόντ᾽ οὐδεὶς ὁρᾷ.
      Chorus.
      ἀλλ᾽ εἴ τι μὲν δὴ δείματός γ᾽ ἔχει μέ-
          ρος,
      τὰς σὰς ἀκούων οὐ μενεῖ τοιάσδ᾽ ἀράς.]

          Sophocles, *Oedipus Tyrannus*

B. Contract Nouns and Adjectives

Nouns and adjectives with bases in -οο and -εο are contracted according to the rules for -ο- and -ε- contractions. The most
important noun of this kind is νοῦς 'mind', declined as follows:

Singular		Plural	
ὁ νοῦς (νό-ος)		οἱ νοῖ (νό-οι)	
τοῦ νοῦ (νό-ου)		τῶν νῶν (νό-ων)	
τῷ νῷ (νό-ῳ)		τοῖς νοῖς (νό-οις)	
τὸν νοῦν (νό-ον)		τοὺς νοῦς (νό-ους)	
(νοῦ) (νό-ε)			

A very common contracted noun of the first declension is γῆ,
γῆς, ἡ 'earth': (a contraction of γέα)

              ἡ γῆ
             τῆς γῆς
              τῇ γῇ
             τὴν γῆν

(The plural is rare.)

Readings

*γαῖα, -ας (Ionic γαίης) 'earth'

1. ἐκ γαίης γαρ πάντα καὶ εἰς γῆν πάντα τελευτᾷ.

    Xenophanes

ὄχλος, -ου, ὁ 'crowd', 'mob'

2. ἰσχυρὸν ὄχλος ἐστίν, οὐκ ἔχει δὲ νοῦν.

    Menander

*πάλιν adv. 'again'; συγκεκαυμένον pf. mid. pt. of συγκαίω 'burn up with' (but also of the effect of intense cold); *χειμών, -ῶνος, ὁ 'winter'; χρεία, -ας, ἡ 'need'; ἱμάτιον, -ου, τό 'cloak'; καινός, -ή, -όν 'new'; καινοῦ or καὶ νοῦ

3. A pun. πάλιν δὲ ἰδὼν τὸν Κράτητα χειμῶνος συγκεκαυμένον, 'ὦ Κράτης,' εἶπε, 'δοκεῖς μοι χρείαν ἔχειν ἱματίου καινοῦ.'

    Diogenes Laertius (Stilpo)

ὁμοῦ 'together'; διακοσμέω 'separate', 'arrange'; *εἶτα 'then'

4. 'πάντα χρήματα ἦν ὁμοῦ· εἶτα νοῦς ἐλθὼν αὐτὰ διεκόσμησε.'

    Diogenes Laertius (Anaxagoras)

5. νοῦς ἐστὶ βασιλεὺς ἡμῖν οὐρανοῦ τε καὶ γῆς.

    Plato, *Philebus*

εὐδαιμονία, -ας, ἡ the state of being εὐδαίμων

6. Happiness is . . .
εὐδαιμονία τοῦτ' ἐστὶν υἱὸς νοῦν ἔχων.

    Menander

χαλινός, -οῦ, ὁ 'bridle', 'bit'

7. ψυχῆς μέγας χαλινὸς ἀνθρώποις ὁ νοῦς.

    Menander

8. γράμματα μαθεῖν δεῖ καὶ μαθόντα νοῦν ἔχειν.

    Menander

ξίφος, -ους, τό 'sword'; τιτρώσκω 'wound', 'hurt'

9. ξίφος τιτρώσκει σῶμα, τὸν δὲ νοῦν λόγος.

    Menander

10. ὁ νοῦς γὰρ ἡμῶν ἐστιν ἐν ἑκάστῳ θεός.

    Menander

[11.   θεός ἐστι τοῖς χρηστοῖς ἀεὶ
ὁ νοῦς γάρ, ὡς ἔοικεν, ὦ σοφώτατοι.]

    Menander

*νεκρός, -οῦ, ὁ 'corpse'; κόπρος, ἡ 'dung', 'dirt'

[12. εἰμὶ νεκρός· νεκρὸς δὲ κόπρος, γῆ δ' ἡ κόπρος ἐστίν·
εἰ δ' ἡ γῆ θεός ἐστ', οὐ νεκρός, ἀλλὰ θεός.]

    Epicharmus

πολυμαθία, -ας, ἡ (Ion. πολυμαθίη) 'much learning'; αὖτις 'a-
gain', 'moreover'; ἐπίστασθαι
'to know'; (Hesiod, Pythagoras,
Xenophanes, Hecataeus)

*ἀσπάζομαι 'greet'; πῶ = ποιῶ;
ὅταν εἰσίδω 'whenever I see';
χωρίον, -ου, τό 'place', 'country'; τρέφω 'feed', 'nourish'

κείνοις = ἐκείνοις; πέλει 'is'

13. πολυμαθίη νόον οὐ διδάσκει· Ἡσίοδον γὰρ
    ἂν ἐδίδαξε καὶ Πυθαγόρην, αὖτίς τε Ξε-
    νοφάνεά τε καὶ Ἑκαταῖον. ʽεἶναι γὰρ
    ʽἓν τὸ σοφόν, ἐπίστασθαι γνώμην . . .ʼ

    Diogenes Laertius (Heraclitus)

[14. χαῖρ', ὦ φίλη γῆ, διὰ χρόνου πολλοῦ σ'
        ἰδὼν
    ἀσπάζομαι· τουτὶ γὰρ οὐ πᾶσαν ποῶ
    τὴν γῆν, ὅταν δὲ τοὐμὸν ἐσίδω χωρίον·
    τὸ γὰρ τρέφον με τοῦτ' ἐγὼ κρίνω θεόν.]

    Menander

15. Darius.
    αὐτὴ γὰρ ἡ γῆ ξύμμαχος κείνοις πέλει.
    Chorus.
    πῶς τοῦτ' ἔλεξας, τίνι τρόπῳ δὲ συμμα-
        χεῖ.

    Aeschylus, *Persae*

Quotation

Read and learn the following saying:

μία χελιδὼν ἔαρ οὐ ποιεῖ.

One swallow does not make a spring.

Greek Proverb

LESSON XII

The -μι Verbs

A second type of Greek verb is the -μι or athematic conjugation. A characteristic of the -ω conjugation (or thematic conjugation) is the thematic vowel (ο/ε) before the personal endings (in certain tenses); the -μι verbs, on the other hand, have no thematic vowel in the present, imperfect, and second aorist: that is, they add their endings directly to the stem in these tenses. Other tense systems of these verbs are usually of the same type as those of -ω verbs (whether thematic or not: for example, the future is a thematic tense, the first aorist, perfect, and aorist passive are not).

The -μι conjugation is so called because the first person singular, present active indicative ending is -μι (rather than -ω). The -μι verbs are divided into three categories.

1. *Irregular* (also called *Root* class), such as εἰμί, φημί.

2. *Reduplicating* class, so called because in the original form, the first consonant was reduplicated with ι in the present system. (These verbs are also called the -ωμι/-ημι type, because their first forms end in either -ωμι or -ημι.) Although there are a few irregularities in each of the verbs of this type, they do follow a pattern, which will be described below.

3. The -νυμι type, in which the syllable -νυ- is inserted before the endings (in the present stem only). The -νυμι class is the most regular type of the -μι verbs. Except for the present system, they follow the -ω conjugation.

-μι Verb Endings:

Singular

Primary		Secondary	
Active	Middle	Active	Middle
-μι	-μαι	-ν	-μην
-ς	-σαι	-ς	-σο
-σι	-ται	--	-το

Plural

Primary			Secondary	
Active	Middle		Active	Middle
-μεν	-μεθα		-μεν	-μεθα
-τε	-σθε		-τε	-σθε
-ασι	-νται		-σαν	-ντο
-ναι	-σθαι	Infinitive	-ναι	-σθαι

(Note that the middle endings are the same as those for other verbs.)

Reduplicating Class

The four most common verbs of the reduplicating class are: ἵστημι, δίδωμι, τίθημι, and ἵημι. They are conjugated as follows in their athematic tenses (insofar as they differ from -ω verbs.)

I. ἵστημι (Principal parts: ἵστημι, στήσω, ἔστησα (first aorist), ἔστην (second aorist), ἔστηκα, ἔσταμαι, ἐστάθην) 'make stand', 'stand'

ACTIVE

Present	Imperfect	2nd Aorist	1st Aorist	Perfect active
ἵστημι	ἵστην	ἔστην	ἔστησα	ἔστηκα
ἵστης	ἵστης	ἔστης	ἔστησας	ἔστηκας
ἵστησι	ἵστη	ἔστη	ἔστησε	ἔστηκε
ἵσταμεν	ἵσταμεν	ἔστημεν	ἐστήσαμεν	ἔσταμεν
ἵστατε	ἵστατε	ἔστητε	ἐστήσατε	ἔστατε
ἱστᾶσι	ἵστασαν	ἔστησαν	ἔστησαν	ἑστᾶσι

Infinitive

ἱστάναι		στῆναι	στῆσαι	ἑστάναι

Participle

ἱστάς		στάς	στήσας	ἑστῶς, ἑστῶσα, ἑστός

MIDDLE

ἵσταμαι	ἱστάμην	no	ἐστησάμην
ἵστασαι	ἵστασο		ἐστήσω
ἵσταται	ἵστατο	second	ἐστήσατο
ἱστάμεθα	ἱστάμεθα	aorist	ἐστησάμεθα
ἵστασθε	ἵστασθε	middle	ἐστήσασθε
ἵστανται	ἵσταντο		ἐστήσαντο

Infinitive

ἵστασθαι			στήσασθαι

Participle

ἱστάμενος			στησάμενος

Notes:

One very important thing to remember about ἵστημι and the other verbs of its class is that the stem is variable, showing a long and a short form. The stem of ἵστημι is στη-/στα-. For the present stem, it is reduplicated, originally to σίστημι; but initial σ often changes to the rough breathing, resulting in ἵστημι, present stem, ἱστη/ἱστα.

The present, imperfect, and second aorist must be studied until their peculiarities are familiar. Note that in the present system active, the long (-η) form of the stem is used in the singular, the short (-α) in the plural.

The middle voice of ἵστημι and the other verbs of its type is very simple: the middle endings are added to the short form of the stem.

There are some special peculiarities of ἵστημι:

1. It has two aorist forms. A few verbs have both first and second aorists, and when they do usually the two aorists have different meanings. So it is with ἵστημι. The first aorist is transitive, 'I made stand', 'I set up'; the second aorist is intransitive, 'I stood'. There is no second aorist middle. The transitive forms of ἵστημι ('make to *stand, set, place*') and of its compounds, are the present, imperfect, future, and first aorist active. The intransitive forms ('stand', 'be set') are the second aorist, the perfect and pluperfect (ἕστηκα, εἱστήκη) and the passive forms of the present, imperfect and future.

2. There is a special form of the perfect (given above) and of the *pluperfect*:

εἱστήκη	ἕσταμεν
εἱστήκας	ἕστατε
εἱστήκει	ἕστασαν

3. ἵστημι is one of few verbs that has a future perfect active, ἑστήξω.

II. δίδωμι (Principal parts: δίδωμι, δώσω, ἕδωκα, δέδωκα, δέδομαι, ἐδόθην) 'give'

	Present	Imperfect	Second Aorist
	δίδωμι	ἐδίδουν	ἕδωκα
	δίδως	ἐδίδους	ἕδωκας
	δίδωσι	ἐδίδου	ἕδωκε
	δίδομεν	ἐδίδομεν	ἕδομεν
	δίδοτε	ἐδίδοτε	ἕδοτε
	διδόασι	ἐδίδοσαν	ἕδοσαν
Infinitive	διδόναι		δοῦναι
Participle	διδούς		δούς
	δίδομαι	ἐδιδόμην	ἐδόμην
	δίδοσαι	ἐδίδοσο	ἕδου
	δίδοται	ἐδίδοτο	ἕδοτο

	διδόμεθα	ἐδιδόμεθα	ἐδόμεθα
	δίδοσθε	ἐδίδοσθε	ἔδοσθε
	δίδονται	ἐδίδοντο	ἔδοντο
Infinitive	δίδοσθαι		δόσθαι
Participle	διδόμενος		δόμενος

Notes:

δίδωμι has the stem δω/δο, which is reduplicated to δίδω-μι for the present system (with the present stem διδω-/διδο-). Again, the long form is used in the singular (with the variation ου in the imperfect) and the short form in the plural and throughout the middle voice.

III. τίθημι (Principal parts: τίθημι, θήσω, ἔθηκα, τέθηκα, τέθειμαι, ἐτέθην) 'set', 'place'

	Present	Imperfect	Second Aorist
	τίθημι	ἐτίθην	ἔθηκα
	τίθης	ἐτίθεις	ἔθηκας
	τίθησι	ἐτίθει	ἔθηκε
	τίθεμεν	ἐτίθεμεν	ἔθεμεν
	τίθετε	ἐτίθετε	ἔθετε
	τιθέασι	ἐτίθεσαν	ἔθεσαν
Infinitive	τιθέναι		θεῖναι
Participle	τιθείς		θείς
	τίθεμαι	ἐτιθέμην	ἐθέμην
	τίθεσαι	ἐτίθεσο	ἔθου
	τίθεται	ἐτίθετο	ἔθετο
	τιθέμεθα	ἐτιθέμεθα	ἐθέμεθα
	τίθεσθε	ἐτίθεσθε	ἔθεσθε
	τίθενται	ἐτίθεντο	ἔθεντο
Infinitive	τίθεσθαι		θέσθαι
Participle	τιθέμενος		θέμενος

Notes:

τίθημι has the stem θη/θε, reduplicated for the present system to θίθη-μι. But the initial aspirated consonant changes to its unaspirated form for ease in pronunciation before another aspiration, hence τίθημι (present stem, τιθη/τιθε). Note the use of the diphthong -ει for -η (as ου for ω in forms of δίδωμι) in forms of the imperfect and in the aorist infinitive.

IV. ἵημι (Principal parts: ἵημι, -ήσω, -ἧκα, -εἷκα, -εἷμαι, -εἵθην)(The dash -ἧκα, etc. indicates that the form is found only in compounds, as ἀφῆκα.) 'throw', 'send'

Present	Imperfect	Aorist	Present	Imperfect	Aorist
ἵημι	ἵην	-ἧκα	ἵεμαι	ἱέμην	-εἵμην
ἵης	ἵεις	-ἧκας	ἵεσαι	ἵεσο	-εἷσο
ἵησι	ἵει	-ἧκε	ἵεται	ἵετο	-εἷτο
ἵεμεν	ἵεμεν	-εἷμεν	ἱέμεθα	ἱέμεθα	-εἵμεθα
ἵετε	ἵετε	-εἷτε	ἵεσθε	ἵεσθε	-εἷσθε
ἱᾶσι	ἵεσαν	-εἷσαν	ἵενται	ἵεντο	-εἷντο
ἱέναι		-εἷναι	ἵεσθαι		-ἕσθαι
ἱείς		-εἵς, -εἷσα, -ἕν	ἱέμενος		-ἕμενος

Notes:

ἵημι has the stem ἡ/ἑ which is reduplicated to ἱη-μι (present stem, ἱη/ἱε). Again the diphthong (-ει) is found in the imperfect and in the aorist infinitive.

The Reduplicating Class of -μι Verbs: Review

Although the verbs of the reduplicating class must be studied carefully so that their individual peculiarities may be learned, the following summary of their mutual similarities may be useful:

1. All of them end in -ημι or -ωμι in the first form.

2. All have a long and a short form of the stem (the long form being used in the present and imperfect singular and the aorist infinitive; the short form in the present and imperfect plural, in the present infinitive, and throughout the middle). The long form is usually the stem vowel in its long form, but sometimes a diphthong is substituted (ου for ω and ει for η).

3. A syllable (originally a reduplication) is added to each to form the present stem. This extra syllable occurs throughout the present system and only there.

4. δίδωμι, ἵημι, and τίθημι have irregular second aorists, with -κα, -κας, -κε and the long form of the stem in the singular; -μεν, -τε, -σαν with the short form in the plural.

Verbs in -νυμι

The third type of -μι verbs is that in which the syllable -νυ is added before the endings to form the present stem. In all other tense systems they are conjugated like -ω verbs. These are the most regular of the -μι verbs. δείκνυμι (stem δεικ-; principal parts δείξω, ἔδειξα, δέδειχα, δέδειγμαι, ἐδείχθην), 'show'.

Present System of δείκνυμι (present stem, δεικνυ-)

Present	Imperfect	Present	Imperfect
δείκνυμι	ἐδείκνυν	δείκνυμαι	ἐδεικνύμην
δείκνυς	ἐδείκνυς	δείκνυσαι	ἐδείκνυσο
δείκνυσι	ἐδείκνυ	δείκνυται	ἐδείκνυτο
δείκνυμεν	ἐδείκνυμεν	δεικνύμεθα	ἐδεικνύμεθα
δείκνυτε	ἐδείκνυτε	δείκνυσθε	ἐδείκνυσθε
δεικνύασι	ἐδείκνυσαν	δείκνυνται	ἐδείκνυντο

Inf. δεικνύναι   δείκνυσθαι

Part. δεικνύς, δεικνῦσα, δεικνύν   δεικνύμενος, -η, -ον

The Participles of -μι Verbs (Active)

The participles (active) of -μι verbs are declined in the same way as those of other verbs, but are formed with the characteristic vowel of the verb.

ἵστημι	present participle,	ἱστάς	(base: ἱσταντ-)
	second aorist,	στάς	(base: σταντ-)
	(first aorist)	στήσας	(base: στησαντ-)
δίδωμι	present,	διδούς	(base: διδοντ-)
	aorist,	δούς	(base: δοντ-)
τίθημι	present,	τιθείς	(base: τιθεντ-)
	aorist,	θείς	(base: θεντ-)
ἵημι	present,	ἵεις	(base: ἱεντ-)
	aorist,	-εἵς	(base: -ἑντ-)
δείκνυμι	present,	δεικνύς	(base: δεικνυντ-)

These participles are not difficult if it is remembered that the characteristic active participial ending (-ντ-) is added to the stem of the verb (short form, except when compensatory lengthening takes place).

Do not try to form the aorist participles of δίδωμι, τίθημι, ἵημι from the principal parts, but rather from the stem.

The Participles Declined

	Present			Second Aorist	

1. ἵστημι

ἱστάς	ἱστᾶσα	ἱστάν	στάς	στᾶσα	στάν
ἱστάντος	ἱστάσης	ἱστάντος	στάντος	στάσης	στάντος
ἱστάντι	ἱστάση	ἱστάντι	στάντι	στάση	στάντι
ἱστάντα	ἱστᾶσαν	ἱστάν	στάντα	στᾶσαν	στάν
ἱστάντες	ἱστᾶσαι	ἱστάντα	στάντες	στᾶσαι	στάντα
ἱστάντων	ἱστασῶν	ἱστάντων	στάντων	στασῶν	στάντων
ἱστᾶσι	ἱστάσαις	ἱστᾶσι	στᾶσι	στάσαις	στᾶσι
ἱστάντας	ἱστάσας	ἱστάντα	στάντα	στάσας	στάντα

2. δίδωμι

διδούς	διδοῦσα	διδόν	δούς	δοῦσα	δόν
διδόντος	διδούσης	διδόντος	δόντος	δούσης	δόντος
διδόντι	διδούση	διδόντι	δόντι	δούση	δόντι
διδόντα	διδοῦσαν	διδόν	δόντα	δοῦσαν	δόν
διδόντες	διδοῦσαι	διδόντα	δόντες	δοῦσαι	δόντα
διδόντων	διδουσῶν	διδόντων	δόντων	δουσῶν	δόντων
διδοῦσι	διδούσαις	διδοῦσι	δοῦσι	δούσαις	δοῦσι
διδόντας	διδούσας	διδόντα	δόντας	δούσας	δόντα

3. τίθημι

τιθείς	τιθεῖσα	τιθέν	θείς	θεῖσα	θέν
τιθέντος	τιθείσης	τιθέντος	θέντος	θείσης	θέντος
τιθέντι	τιθείση	τιθέντι	θέντι	θείση	θέντι
τιθέντα	τιθεῖσαν	τιθέν	θέντα	θεῖσαν	θέν
τιθέντες	τιθεῖσαι	τιθέντα	θέντες	θεῖσαι	θέντα
τιθέντων	τιθεισῶν	τιθέντων	θέντων	θεισῶν	θέντων
τιθεῖσι	τιθείσαις	τιθεῖσι	θεῖσι	θείσαις	θεῖσι
τιθέντας	τιθείσας	τιθέντα	θένιας	θείσας	θέντα

4. ἵημι

ἱείς	ἱεῖσα	ἱέν	-είς	-εῖσα	-έν
ἱέντος	ἱείσης	ἱέντος	-έντος	-είσης	-έντος
ἱέντι	ἱείση	ἱέντι	-έντι	-είση	-έντι
ἱέντα	ἱεῖσαν	ἱέν	-έντα	-εῖσαν	-έν
ἱέντες	ἱεῖσαι	ἱέντα	-έντες	-εῖσαι	-έντα
ἱέντων	ἱεισῶν	ἱέντων	-έντων	-εισῶν	-έντων
ἱεῖσι	ἱείσαις	ἱεῖσι	-εῖσι	-είσαις	-εῖσι
ἱέντας	ἱείσας	ἱέντα	-έντας	-είσας	-έντα

Note that for each verb, the present and aorist participles
are declined exactly alike, the only difference being that the
present participle has one more syllable than the aorist.

5. Present Participle of δείκνυμι

δεικνύς	δεικνῦσα	δεικνύν
δεικνύντος	δεικνύσης	δεικνύντος
δεικνύντι	δεικνύσῃ	δεικνύντι
δεικνύντα	δεικνῦσαν	δεικνύν
δεικνύντες	δεικνῦσαι	δεικνύντα
δεικνύντων	δεικνυσῶν	δεικνύντων
δεικνῦσι	δεικνύσαις	δεικνῦσι
δεικνύντας	δεικνύσας	δεικνύντα

Deponent Verbs of the -μι type

There are a number of deponent verbs of the athematic type, but these usually present no difficulty, since the middle voice is regular. For example, δύναμαι ('be able'), ἐπίσταμαι (impf. ἠπιστάμην 'understand') keep -α- before their endings throughout the present system. Similarly, κάθημαι 'sit' and κεῖμαι 'lie' retain their stem vowels η or ει.

Irregular Second Aorist

A few verbs of the -ω conjugation have athematic second aorists. For example:

γιγνώσκω	aorist	ἔγνων
βαίνω	aorist	ἔβην
ἁλίσκομαι	aorist	ἑάλων or ἥλων
φθάνω	aorist	ἔφθην
πέτομαι ('fly')	aorist	ἔπτην

These are inflected like second aorists of -μι verbs, by adding the personal endings directly to the stem.

Aorist Active of βαίνω			of γιγνώσκω	
ἔβην	ἔβημεν	βῆναι	ἔγνων	ἔγνωμεν
ἔβης	ἔβητε		ἔγνως	ἔγνωτε
ἔβη	ἔβησαν		ἔγνω	ἔγνωσαν
Infinitive	βῆναι			γνῶναι
Participle	βάς, βᾶσα, βάν			γνούς, γνοῦσα, γνόν
	(stem βαντ-)			(stem γνοντ-)

Vocabulary

ἁλίσκομαι, ἁλώσομαι, ἑάλων, ἑάλωκα, impf. ἡλισκόμην	*be caught* (passive in meaning, for active use forms of αἱρέω)
ἀνοίγνυμι or ἀνοίγω, ἀνοίξω, ἀνέῳξα, ἀνέῳχα, ἀνέῳγμαι, ἀνεῴχθην	*open*; pass. *be open, stand open* (the simple verb οἴγνυμι/οἴγω is much less common in prose)
βαίνω, βήσομαι, ἔβην, βέβηκα	*walk, step, go*
συμβαίνω	*meet, come to pass, happen, result*
δείκνυμι, δείξω, ἔδειξα, δέδειχα, δέδειγμαι, ἐδείχθην	*show, explain*
ἐπιδείκνυμι	*exhibit, display*
δύναμαι, δυνήσομαι, δεδύνημαι, ἐδυνήθην	*be able, be strong enough* (to do)(+ infin.)
δίδωμι, δώσω, ἔδωκα, δέδωκα, δέδομαι, ἐδόθην	*give, grant*
ἀποδίδωμι	*give up/back, concede*; mid. *sell* (+ gen.)(of price)
προδίδωμι	*betray, give up*
ἐπίσταμαι, ἐπιστήσομαι, ἠπιστήθην, impf. ἠπιστάμην	*understand*
ἐπιστήμη, ἐπιστήμης, ἡ	*understanding, knowledge*
ἵημι, -ἥσω, -ἧκα, -εἷκα, -εἷμαι, -εἵθην	*send, release, throw*
ἀφίημι	*send forth; release from* (+ partitive gen.)
ἵστημι, στήσω, ἔστησα, ἔστην, ἕστηκα, (ἕσταμαι) ἐστάθην	transitive, causal: (act. pres., impr., fut.; aor. 1 act. & mid.) *make to stand, set, establish, appoint* intransitive: (aor. 2, perfect, and passive) *stand, halt*
ἀφίστημι	causal: *put away, cause to revolt* intransitive: *stand away, revolt from*
καθίστημι	causal: *set down, establish, restore* intransitive: *set oneself down, settle*
κάθημαι	(present system only), impf. ἐκαθήμην or καθήμην *sit, lie idle, reside*
κεῖμαι, κείσομαι	(no other principal parts) *lie, lie down to rest, be situated*
ὄλλυμι (or ὀλλύω), ὀλῶ, ὤλεσα, ὠλόμην, ὀλώλεκα, ὄλωλα	transitive: (active, 1 aor. & 1 perf.) *kill, destroy* intransitive: (middle, 2 aor. & 2 perf.) *be destroyed, perish*
ἀπόλλυμι	trans. *destroy utterly, kill* intrans. *perish, die; fall into ruin* (The simple verb, ὄλλυμι, is found only in poetry and late prose.)
πίμπλημι, πλήσω, ἔπλησα, πέπληκα, πέπλησμαι, ἐπλήσθην	*fill* (+ gen. *fill full of*; + dat. *fill with*)

Exercises

1. Write the following synopses:

    1. ἀνατίθημι   first singular

    2. ἐπιδείκνυμι   second singular

    3. προδίδωμι   third singular

    4. δύναμαι   first plural

    5. καθίστημι   second plural

    7. ἀφίημι   third plural

2. Parse the following:

1. διδόναι	26. ἀναθήσεις	51. τιθεῖσα	76. θέσθαι
2. ἁλώσεται	27. ἀποστάντος	52. ἀφέντες	77. ἠπίσταντο
3. ἀνεῳγμένος	28. ἐδείκνυν	53. ἱέντα	78. ἴασι
4. ἀποδούς	29. ἐδύνατο	54. καθιστάναι	79. στῆσαι
5. ἀφίης	30. ἡλισκόμεθα	55. ἱείς	80. ἱστάναι
6. ἀπέστην	31. ἀφῆκα	56. ἱέντος	81. στῆναι
7. βάντος	32. ἐδίδουν	57. ἐπιστάμενα	82. καταστῆναι
8. ἐπιδείκνυντος	33. ἀνατιθέναι	58. δόσθαι	83. καταστῆσαι
9. ἀνέθηκε	34. βέβηκα	59. στάσης	84. καθεστάναι
10. ἀνοίγνυται	35. δεικνύμενος	60. ἱστᾶσαν	85. ἔκειντο
11. ἀπεδίδους	36. ἔδωκας	61. ἵστασαν	86. προυδίδους
12. ἀποστήσαντες	37. δύναται	62. κατέστην	87. προδοθέν
13. ἀφέστηκα	38. ἀφεῖναι	63. κεῖται	88. θεῖναι
14. ἐδείκνυσαν	39. ἀπεῖναι	64. κειμένοις	89. ἐκάθησο
15. ἐδίδοσαν	40. ἔβη	65. δόντες	90. ἦσθα
16. ἑάλωκε	41. δοῦναι	66. τιθέντων	91. δόντα
17. ἀνατεθῆναι	42. ἱστάντα	67. θέν	92. διδόντα
18. ἀνέῳξε	43. στάντι	68. δυνήσεται	93. δώσοντα
19. ἀφιᾶσι	44. θέντος	69. ἑστῶς	94. ἔφασαν
20. εἶναι	45. ἐδυνήθη	70. κείμεθα	95. δοθέντα
21. εἶναι	46. ἐδόμην	71. ἐπέδειξαν	96. θήσεις
22. δείκνυσι	47. ἐπεδείκνυ	72. ἱστᾶσι	97. ἐτέθην
23. ἑάλωσαν	48. ἵης	73. στησόμεθα	98. ἔβησαν
24. ἀπεδίδοτο	49. καθήμενος	74. προύδωκε	99. γνοῦσαι
25. ἀφίεσαν	50. θείσης	75. πίμπλησι	100. γνῶναι

3. Translate (Some special meanings of the verbs are given in parentheses.)

1. οἱ ἐχθροὶ θανάτῳ ἑάλωσαν.

2. τοῦτο πράττων ἑάλως.

3. ἀδικοῦντες οὐχ ἁλωσόμεθα.

4. ὁ ποιητὴς τῷ σοφῷ τὸ ἑαυτοῦ βιβλίον ἀνέθηκε.

5. τῇ θεᾷ ταῦτα τὰ δῶρα ἀναθήσομεν.

6. τοῖς θεοῖς οἱ πολῖται ἀνέθησαν τάδε.

7. οὐ γὰρ σοὶ ἀνατιθέασι τὴν αἰτίαν ἐκείνης τῆς συμφορᾶς.

8. οὐχ ὁρᾷ τὰς Ἅιδου πύλας ἀνεῳγμένας. ('the gates of Hades')

9. αὐτὸν ἀνοιγνύναι τὰς πύλας τὰς τῆς οἰκίας νομίζω.

10. τί οὐκ ἀνοίγνυς τὴν θύραν; (θύρα, -ας, ἡ 'door')

11. τοῖς φίλοις χάριτας ἀπεδίδοσαν.

12. οὐκ αἰσχύνει τὴν ἐπιστήμην ἀποδιδόμενος;

13. τὸν τοῦ φίλου βίον ἀπέδοτο.

14. οἱ κακοὶ τῶν κινδύνων ἀφίσταντο.

15. ὁ ἄρχων τῆς ἀρχῆς ἀφέστη. ('resigned/was deposed from')

16. οἱ σοφοὶ τοὺς πολίτας ἀπὸ τοῦ τυράννου ἀπέστησαν.

17. χαλεπόν ἐστι ἔργων καὶ κινδύνων καὶ πόνων ἀποστῆναι.

18. ὁ γὰρ βασιλεὺς τὸν ἱερέα ἀφῆκεν οὐ βουλόμενος τὴν θυγατέρα αὐτοῦ λύειν.

19. ὁ δὲ γέρων ἀφίει δάκρυα. (δάκρυ, -υος, τό 'tear')

20. ὁ ἀνὴρ βουλόμενος γαμεῖν τὴν τοῦ βασιλέως θυγατέρα ἔδοξε τὴν γυναῖκα ἀφεῖναι. ('divorce')

21. τοῖς σοῖς λόγοις κινδύνου ἀφιέμεθα.

22. ταῦτα ὁ χρόνος δείξει.

23. ἐδείκνυσαν φίλοι ὄντες.

24. πολλὰ ὁ θεὸς ἡμῖν δείκνυσιν.

25. τὴν ὁδὸν ὑμῖν δείξομεν.

26. εἰς τὴν ἀγορὰν βαίνεις;

27. βαίνομέν γε ὡς ὀψόμενοι τὰ θαύματα.

28. ἔβησαν φεύγοντες.

29. τί μοι δίδως;

30. οὗτος ὁ ἀνὴρ ἑαυτὸν ταῖς τοῦ σώματος ἡδοναῖς ἐδίδου.

31. οἱ θεοὶ τοῖς δικαίοις τὴν νίκην διδόασιν;

32. δῶρα γὰρ πολλὰ καὶ καλὰ τοῖς δαίμοσι δώσομεν.

33. τὰ διδόμενα οὐ βουλόμεθα λαβεῖν.

34. δίκην ἔδωκε ὁ ἄδικος. (δ. δίκην 'pay the penalty')

35. ὁ πατὴρ καὶ ἡ μήτηρ τὴν θυγατέρα τούτῳ τῷ ἀνδρὶ γυναῖκα ἔδοσαν. (δ. γυναῖκα 'give in marriage' as wife)

36. οἱ φεύγοντες τοῖς διώκουσιν ἑαυτοὺς ἔδοσαν.

37. ταῦτά γε ἡμῖν ἐδόθη ὑπὸ τῶν γερόντων.

38. δύνασαι ταῦτα πράττειν; δύναμαι μέν, ἐθέλω δ' οὔ.

39. Ζεὺς ἅπαντα δύναται.

40. τί μοι δοῦναι δύνασθε;

41. ἐδύνατο δε τὸν βασιλέα ὁρᾶν;

42. ταῦτα γὰρ ποιῶν πολλὰ χρήματα λαμβάνειν δυνήσομαι.

43. ὁ τύραννος τὴν αὐτοῦ δύναμιν ἐπεδείκνυτο.

44. ἐπέδειξά σε ἄδικον ὄντα.

45. τοῖς ξένοις πᾶσαν τὴν πόλιν ἐπιδείξουσιν.

46. ὁ ἄδικος δικαστὴς οὐκ ἐδυνήθη τὴν δικαιοσύνην ἐπιδείκνυσθαι.

47. ἡ μάντις τὸ μέλλον ἐπίσταται.

48. πολλὰ δὲ ἠπίσταντο οἱ σοφοί.

49. οὗτοι οὔκ εἰσιν οἱ λόγοι ἀνδρὸς ἐπισταμένου.

50. πάντες γὰρ τὰ γράμματα ἐπιστάμεθα.

51. τίς γὰρ ἡμῖν τοῦτον τὸν ἄγγελον ἧκε;

52. πολλοὺς δὲ λίθους ἐφ' ἡμῖν ἵεσαν.

53. οἱ ἵπποι ἔστησαν ἐν τῷ πεδίῳ.

54. τοὺς ἵππους ἵσταμεν.

55. οἱ πολῖται αὐτὸν ἔστησαν βασιλέα.

56. ἱστάμην παρὰ τῷ ἀδελφῷ.

57. οὐδὲν γὰρ λέγοντες κάθησθε.

58. ὑμεῖς οἱ καθήμενοί με κρινεῖτε.

59. ἐπὶ τῶν ἵππων ἐκάθηντο.

60. οἱ πολῖται δημοκρατίαν καθιστάναι ἐβούλοντο.

61. χαλεπόν ἐστι καλοὺς νόμους καθιστάναι.

62. κατέστη ἡ θάλαττα.

63. τὰ ἄνθη ἐπὶ τὴν ὁδὸν κεῖται. (ἄνθος, -ους, τό 'flower')

64. ἡμᾶς χρὴ πείθεσθαι τοῖς ὑπὸ τῶν θεῶν κειμένοις νόμοις. (κεῖμαι 'be set up', 'laid down')

65. ἡ νῆσος ἐν μέσῃ τῇ θαλάττῃ κεῖται.

66. ἐν ταύταις ταῖς οἰκίαις κεῖται πολλὰ κτήματα.

67. ἄθαπτοι οἱ ἐν ἐκείνῳ τῷ πολέμῳ ἀποθανόντες κεῖνται. (ἄθαπτοι 'unburied')

68. φόβῳ πιμπλήμενοι ἐφύγομεν καὶ τὴν Ἑλλάδα προύδομεν.

69. ἐπίμπλη τὰς κύλικας οἴνου.

70. ὑπὸ τῶν φίλων προδοθέντες ἥλωσαν.

71. οὔ σέ ποτε προδώσομεν.

72. τί ταῦτα πράττων προδίδως τὴν πόλιν καὶ τὴν μητέρα καὶ τὰ παιδία;

73. ἡ θεὰ τὸν ἄνδρα ἀθάνατον ἔθηκεν.

74. ἐν μὲν δημοκρατίᾳ οἱ πολῖται τοὺς νόμους τίθενται.

75. ἐν δὲ τυραννίδι τοὺς νόμους τίθησιν ὁ τύραννος.

76. ὁ σοφὸς τοὺς ἀνθρώπους ἀγαθοὺς καὶ καλοὺς βούλεται θεῖναι.

77. βούλομαί σε φίλον ἐμὸν θέσθαι.

78. ἡ μήτηρ τῇ παιδὶ ὄνομα τίθεται.

79. τιμὴν τοῖς σοφοῖς ἔθεσαν.

80. εἰ τὰ χρήματά μοι ἔδωκεν, εἶχον 'ἂν αὐτά.

4. Translate into Greek:

1. The citizens made (for themselves) good laws.

2. Are you able to know the future?

3. The gods reveal all things to men during the night. (see p. 216)

4. We were caught telling many lies.

5. You have given me the greatest of gifts.

6. It is good to understand all things.

7. We are not always able to live well.

8. The poet attributed all things to the gods.

9. The soldiers stand beside their leader.

10. After they had been victorious (having won) the soldiers set up their shields to the gods.

4b. Compose sentences using:

    1. ἵστημι   (as causal)

    2. ἵστημι   (as intransitive)

    3. ἵημι

4. βαίνω

5. προδίδωμι

Readings

1. πάντα τύχη καὶ μοῖρα, Περίκλεεις, ἀνδρὶ
   δίδωσιν.

   Archilochus

νῆ Δία 'by Zeus'; τελέως 'per-
fectly' (adv.); ἑστιάω 'entertain', 'feast'; *δεῖπνον, -ου,
τό 'dinner'; ἄμεμπτος, -ον
'blameless'; παρατίθημι 'place
before', 'provide'; θέαμα, -ατος,
τό 'sight', 'spectacle'; ἀκρόαμα,
-ατος, τό 'anything heard'

2. εἶπεν ὁ Σωκράτης· Νὴ Δί᾽, ὦ Καλλία, τελέως ἡμᾶς ἑστιᾷς. οὐ γὰρ μόνον δεῖπνον
   ἄμεμπτον παρέθηκας, ἀλλὰ καὶ θεάματα καὶ
   ἀκροάματα ἥδιστα παρέχεις.

   Xenophon, *Symposium*

πρός 'to the advantage of' (+
gen.); Φοῖβε (voc. of Phoebus =
Apollo)

3. πρὸς τῶν ἐχόντων, Φοῖβε, τὸν νόμον τί-
   θης.

   Euripides, *Alcestis*

Ἅλυς, -υος, ὁ 'the Halys' (a
river in Asia Minor); δια + βαίνω; καταλύω 'destroy'

4. Κροῖσος Ἅλυν διαβὰς μεγάλην ἀρχὴν κατα-
   λύσει.

   Herodotus (the oracle to Croesus)

πημονή, -ῆς, ἡ = πῆμα

5. ὅμως δ᾽ ἀνάγκη πημονὰς βροτοῖς φέρειν
   θεῶν διδόντων.

   Aeschylus, *Persae* (Atossa)

6. ἀρχὴ ἄνδρα δείκνυσιν.

   Diogenes Laertius (saying of Pittacus)

Αἰσχίνης, -ου, ὁ 'Aeschines'

7. Αἰσχίνου δὲ εἰπόντος, ʼπένης εἰμὶ καὶ
   ἄλλο μὲν οὐδὲν ἔχω, δίδωμι δέ σοι ἐμαυτόν,ʼ ʼἆρ᾽ οὖν,ʼ εἶπεν, ʼοὐκ αἰσθάνῃ τὰ
   μέγιστά μοι διδούς;ʼ

   Diogenes Laertius (Socrates)

αὖ adv. 'back', 'again', 'moreover'

[8. πρὸς δὲ αὖ τούτοις μνήμην τινὰ δοκεῖ τίς
   μοι δεδωκέναι θεῶν ἡμῖν.]

   Plato, *Philebus*

*θέλω = ἐθέλω

9. θέλομεν καλῶς ζῆν πάντες ἀλλ᾽ οὐ δυνάμε-
   θα.

   Menander

10. ζῶμεν γὰρ οὐχ ὡς θέλομεν, ἀλλ᾽ ὡς δυνά-
    μεθα.

    Menander

πλουτέω 'be wealthy'

11. βουλόμεθα πλουτεῖν πάντες, ἀλλ᾽ οὐ δυνά-
μεθα.

Menander

12. ὡς μέγα τὸ μικρόν ἐστιν ἐν καιρῷ δοθέν.

Menander

ἀνέθηκαν = ἀνέθεσαν; ὅσσα = ὅσα;
ἀνθρώποισιν = ἀνθρώποις; ὀνείδεα
= ὀνείδη; φόγος, -ου, ὁ 'blame',
'censure'; μοιχεύω 'commit adul-
tery'; ἀπατεύω 'cheat', 'deceive'

[13. πάντα θεοῖς ἀνέθηκαν Ὅμηρός θ᾽ Ἡσίοδός
τε,
ὅσσα παρ᾽ ἀνθρώποισιν ὀνείδεα καὶ φόγος
ἐστίν,
κλέπτειν μοιχεύειν τε καὶ ἀλλήλους ἀπα-
τεύειν.]

Xenophanes

γυμνός, -ή, -όν 'naked'; ἐπι +
βαίνω; ἄπειμι 'go away', 'depart'; μάτην 'in vain'; μοχθῶ
'be weary with toil'

[14. Γῆς ἐπέβην γυμνός, γυμνός θ᾽ ὑπὸ γαῖαν
ἄπειμι·
καὶ τί μάτην μοχθῶ, γυμνὸν ὁρῶν τὸ τέλος.]

Greek Anthology (Palladas)

συνίστημι (intr.) 'stand with'
(ξύν = σύν); κασίγνητος, -ου, ὁ
'brother'; κάσις, -ιος, ὁ 'brother'; φέρ᾽ = φέρε 'come'; ὡς
τάχος 'with all speed'; κνημίς,
-ῖδος, ἡ 'greave' (leg-armor);
αἰχμή, -ῆς, ἡ 'spear'; πέτρος,
-ου, ὁ 'rock', 'stone'; πρόβλη-
μα, -ατος, τό 'a defence against'

15. τούτοις πεποιθὼς εἶμι καὶ ξυστήσομαι
αὐτός· τίς ἄλλος μᾶλλον ἐνδικώτερος;
ἄρχοντί τ᾽ ἄρχων καὶ κασιγνήτῳ κάσις,
ἐχθρὸς σὺν ἐχθρῷ στήσομαι. φέρ᾽ ὡς
τάχος
κνημῖδας αἰχμῆς καὶ πέτρων προβλήματα.

Aeschylus, *Seven against Thebes*
(Eteocles, after naming his other
generals announces that he will
fight his brother.)

ἱμερτός, -ή, -όν 'lovely'; ᾠδή,
-ῆς, ἡ 'song'; ἀντί 'before',
'instead of' (+ gen.)

[16. αὐτὸς κῆρυξ ἦλθον ἀφ᾽ ἱμερτῆς Σαλαμῖνος,
κόσμον ἐπέων ᾠδὴν ἀντ᾽ ἀγορῆς θέμενος.]

Solon

*οὔτοι 'indeed not'; ὑποδείκνυμι
'show', 'display'; ἐφευρίσκω
'find by chance', 'discover'

[17. οὔτοι ἀπ᾽ ἀρχῆς πάντα θεοὶ θνητοῖς ὑπέ-
δειξαν,
ἀλλὰ χρόνῳ ζητοῦντες ἐφευρίσκουσιν ἄμεινον.]

Xenophanes

ἔκθαμβος, -ον 'amazed'; ὡσεί 'as
if'; τρόμος, -ου, ὁ 'trembling';
*θρίξ, τριχός, ἡ 'hair'; *ὀρθός,
-ή, -όν 'straight', 'upright';
φρίκη, -ής, ἡ 'shuddering'; πρός
+ ἔρχομαι; μνησθείς aor. pass.
pt. of μιμνήσκω (+ gen.); θάρσος,
-ους, τό 'courage'; γόνυ, -ατος,
τό 'knee'; τιθέναι τὰ γόνατα 'to
kneel down'; ἐξομολογέομαι 'con-

18. ἰδὼν ταῦτα κείμενα καὶ μηδένα ὄντα ἐν τῷ
τόπῳ ἔκθαμβος ἐγενόμην, καὶ ὡσεὶ τρόμος
με ἔλαβεν καὶ αἱ τρίχες μου ὀρθαί· καὶ
ὡσεὶ φρίκη μοι προσῆλθεν μόνου μου ὄντος.
ἐν ἐμαυτῷ οὖν γενόμενος καὶ μνησθεὶς τῆς
δόξης τοῦ θεοῦ καὶ λαβὼν θάρσος, θεὶς τὰ
γόνατα ἐξωμολογούμην τῷ κυρίῳ πάλιν τὰς
ἁμαρτίας μου ὡς καὶ πρότερον.

Hermas, *The Shepherd*

fess fully'; *ἁμαρτία, -ας, ἡ
'error', 'sin'

19. πολλὰ πιών καὶ πολλὰ φαγών, καὶ πολλὰ
          κάκ᾽ εἰπὼν
   ἀνθρώπους, κεῦμαι Τιμοκρέων Ῥόδιος.

    Simonides

*εἶεν 'well', 'okay'; κατοικτίζω
'have compassion', 'pity'; mid.
'lament'; μάτην 'in vain'; στυγέω 'hate'; ἔχθιστος superl. of
ἐχθρός; γέρας, -αος, τό 'gift of
honor', 'prerogative'

20. εἶεν, τί μέλλεις καὶ κατοικτίζῃ μάτην;
   τί τὸν θεοῖς ἔχθιστον οὐ στυγεῖς θεόν,
   ὅστις τὸ σὸν θνητοῖσι προὔδωκεν γέρας;

    Aeschylus, *Prometheus*

παραδίδωμι 'give', 'transmit',
'hand over'; δεσμός, -οῦ, ὁ
'bond', 'fetter'; καταλαμβάνω
'seize', 'catch'; παρίστημι
'place beside'; ἀετός, -οῦ, ὁ
'eagle'; *ἐσθίω, ἔδομαι, ἔφαγον
'eat'; ἧπαρ, ἥπατος, τό 'liver';
τιμωρία, -ας, ἡ 'punishment'
(gen. with τυγχάνω); εὐεργεσία,
-ας, ἡ 'well-doing', 'service';
κατατοξεύω 'shoot down'; *λήγω
'allay', 'cease from'; εὐεργέτης,
-ου, ὁ 'benefactor', 'do-gooder'

21. Ζεὺς δέ, Προμηθέως παραδόντος τὸ πῦρ
τοῖς ἀνθρώποις, δεσμοῖς κατελάβετο καὶ
παρέστησεν ἀετὸν τὸν ἐσθίοντα τὸ ἧπαρ
αὐτοῦ. Ἡρακλῆς δ᾽ ὁρῶν τῆς τιμωρίας
αὐτὸν τυγχάνοντα διὰ τὴν τῶν ἀνθρώπων
εὐεργεσίαν, τὸν μὲν ἀετὸν κατετόξευσε,
τὸν δὲ Δία πείσας λῆξαι τῆς ὀργῆς ἔσωσε
τὸν κοινὸν εὐεργέτην.

    Diodorus Siculus

*πρέσβυς, -εως, ὁ 'old man';
ὠφελέω 'help', 'aid', 'benefit'

[22. ὑμεῖς δέ, πρέσβεις, χαίρετ᾽ ἐν κακοῖς
       ὅμως
   ψυχῇ διδόντες ἡδονὴν καθ᾽ ἡμέραν,
   ὡς τοῖς θανοῦσι πλοῦτος οὐδὲν ὠφελεῖ.]

    Aeschylus, *Persae*

ἡμῶν gen. with κατηγορέω; παρα-
λαμβάνω 'receive', 'succeed to';
αἴτιος, -α, -ον 'guilty'; ἀνδρα-
ποδισμός, ὁ 'enslaving'; Σκιω-
ναῖος 'Scionean'; Μήλιος 'Me-
lian'; ὄλεθρος, -ου, ὁ 'destruction'; προφέρω 'bring forward',
'throw in one's teeth'; *πολεμέω
'fight' (against + dat.); διῳκοῦμεν from διοικέω 'conduct', 'manage'; σφόδρα 'very' (adv.); *κολάζω 'check', 'punish'; περιπίπτω
'fall around', 'fall into'

[23. μετὰ δὲ ταῦτ᾽ ἤδη τινὲς ἡμῶν κατηγοροῦ-
σιν, ὡς ἐπειδὴ τὴν ἀρχὴν τῆς θαλάττης
παρελάβομεν, πολλῶν κακῶν αἴτιοι τοῖς
Ἕλλησι κατέστημεν, καὶ τόν τε Μηλίων
ἀνδραποδισμὸν καὶ τὸν Σκιωναίων ὄλεθρον
ἐν τούτοις τοῖς λόγοις ἡμῖν προφέρουσιν.
ἐγὼ δ᾽ ἡγοῦμαι πρῶτον μὲν οὐδὲν εἶναι
τοῦτο σημεῖον ὡς κακῶς ἤρχομεν, εἴ τινες
τῶν πολεμησάντων ἡμῖν σφόδρα φαίνονται
κολασθέντες, ἀλλὰ πολὺ τόδε μεῖζον τεκμήριον ὡς καλῶς διῳκοῦμεν τὰ τῶν συμμα-
χῶν, ὅτι τῶν πόλεων τῶν ὑφ᾽ ἡμῖν οὐσῶν
οὐδεμία ταύταις ταῖς συμφοραῖς περιέπε-
σεν.]

    Isocrates, *Panegyricus*

Θῆβαι, Θηβῶν, αἱ 'Thebes'; ἄ-
παις, ἄπαιδος, ὁ/ἡ 'childless';
*ἱκανός, -ή, -όν 'sufficient';
ἐπερωτάω 'consult', 'question';
*τέκνον, -ου, τό 'child'; χρησ-
μός, -οῦ, ὁ 'oracle'; *συμφέρω
'be useful', 'be profitable';
τεκνόω 'bear', 'beget'; πατρο-
κτόνος, -ον 'murdering one's
father'; πληρόω 'fill'; ἀτύχημα,
-ατος, τό 'misfortune'; ἐπιλανθάνομαι 'forget'; ἐκτίθημι 'put
out', 'expose'; *βρέφος, -ους,
τό 'infant'; σφυρόν, -οῦ, τό
'ankle'; διαπερονάω 'pierce
through'; οἰκέτης, -ου, ὁ 'servant'; δωρέω 'give'; ἀνδρόω
pass. 'become a man'; *ἐπιχειρέω
'try', 'attempt'; γονεύς, -εως,
ὁ 'father', pl. 'parents'; ὑπο-
βολή, -ῆς, ἡ 'substitution'; Φω-
κίς, -ίδος, ἡ 'Phocis'; ἀπαντάω
'meet'; ὑπερηφάνως 'arrogantly'
(adv.); ἐκχωρέω 'depart', 'get
out of the way'; προστάττω 'order'; ὀργίζω 'provoke', 'anger';
ἀγνοέω 'be ignorant', 'not know'

24. Λάϊος ὁ Θηβῶν βασιλεὺς γήμας Ἰοκάστην
τὴν Κρέοντος, καὶ χρόνον ἱκανὸν ἄπαις
ὤν, ἐπηρώτησε τὸν θεὸν περὶ τέκνων γενέσεως. τῆς δὲ Πυθίας δούσης χρησμὸν αὐτῷ
μὴ συμφέρειν γενέσθαι τέκνα (τὸν γὰρ ἐξ
αὐτοῦ τεκνωθέντα παῖδα πατροκτόνον ἔσεσθαι καὶ πᾶσαν τὴν οἰκίαν πληρώσειν μεγά-
λων ἀτυχημάτων), ἐπιλαθόμενος τοῦ χρησ-
μοῦ καὶ γεννήσας υἱόν, ἐξέθηκε τὸ βρέφος
διαπερονήσας αὐτοῦ τὰ σφυρὰ σιδήρῳ· δι᾽
ἣν αἰτίαν Οἰδίπους ὕστερον ὠνομάσθη.
οἱ δ᾽ οἰκέται λαβόντες τὸ παιδίον ἐκθεῖ-
ναι μὲν οὐκ ἠθέλησαν, ἐδωρήσαντο δὲ τῇ
Πολύβου γυναικί, οὐ δυναμένῃ γεννῆσαι
παῖδας. μετὰ δὲ ταῦτα ἀνδρωθέντος τοῦ
παιδός, ὁ μὲν Λάϊος ἔκρινεν ἐπερωτῆσαι
τὸν θεὸν περὶ τοῦ βρέφους τοῦ ἐκτεθέν-
τος, ὁ δὲ Οἰδίπους μαθὼν παρά τινος τὴν
καθ᾽ ἑαυτὸν ὑποβολήν, ἐπεχείρησεν ἐπερωτῆσαι τὴν Πυθίαν περὶ τῶν κατ᾽ ἀλήθειαν
γονέων. κατὰ δὲ τὴν Φωκίδα τούτων ἀλλήλοις ἀπαντησάντων, ὁ μὲν Λάϊος ὑπερηφάνως ἐκχωρεῖν τῆς ὁδοῦ προσέταττεν, ὁ δ᾽
Οἰδίπους ὀργισθεὶς ἀπέκτεινε τὸν Λάϊον,
ἀγνοῶν ὅτι πατὴρ ἦν αὐτοῦ.

Diodorus Siculus

[25. Πραξαγόρας τάδε δῶρα θεοῖς ἀνέθηκε, Λυ-
καίου
υἱός· ἐποίησεν δ᾽ ἔργον Ἀναξαγόρας.]

Anacreon

26. 'ἦλθον γάρ,' φησίν, 'εἰς Ἀθήνας καὶ οὔτις μὲ ἔγνωκεν.'

Diogenes Laertius (Democritus)

ἄτεχνος, -ον 'without skill';
*τυφλός, -ή, -όν 'blind'; ὁδηγέω
'lead', 'show the way'; τεχνίτης, -ου, ὁ 'artist', 'crafts-
man'; μάθησις, -εως, ἡ 'learning'

[27. οὔτε δὲ ὁ ἄτεχνος τὸν ἄτεχνον δύναται
διδάσκειν, ὡς οὐδὲ ὁ τυφλὸς τὸν τυφλὸν
ὁδηγεῖν, οὔτε ὁ τεχνίτης τὸν ὁμοίως τεχ-
νίτην· οὐδέτερος γὰρ αὐτῶν ἐδεῖτο μαθή-
σεως . . .]

Sextus Empiricus (Against the Professors)

ἐφίστημι 'set upon', 'stand over'   28. πρὸς Ἀλέξανδρον ἐπιστάντα καὶ εἰπόντα,
'οὐ φοβῇ με;' 'τί γάρ,' εἶπεν, 'εἰ ἀγαθὸν
ἢ κακόν;' τοῦ δὲ εἰπόντος, 'ἀγαθόν,'
'τίς οὖν,' εἶπε, 'τὸ ἀγαθὸν φοβεῖται;'

Diogenes Laertius (Diogenes)

ἐλεημοσύνη, -ης, ἡ 'pity';
'alms'; ἐλεέω 'have pity on'
(aor. ἠλέησα)

29. ὀνειδιζόμενός ποτε ὅτι πονηρῷ ἀνθρώπῳ
ἐλεημοσύνην ἔδωκεν, 'οὐ τὸν τρόπον,' εἶπεν, 'ἀλλὰ τὸν ἄνθρωπον ἠλέησα.'

Diogenes Laertius (Aristotle)

ὅταν 'whenever' (+ subj. δύνωνται); *φαῦλος, -η, -ον 'mean',
'bad', 'cheap'; *σπουδαῖος, -α,
-ον 'serious', 'good'; διακρίνω
'separate', 'distinguish'

30. τότ' ἔφη τὰς πόλεις ἀπόλλυσθαι, ὅταν μὴ
δύνωνται τοὺς φαύλους ἀπὸ τῶν σπουδαίων
διακρίνειν.

Diogenes Laertius (Antisthenes)

συνίστημι 'set together', 'introduce (as a student)'; πεντα-
κόσιοι 'five hundred'; *δραχμή,
-ῆς, ἡ 'drachma'; *τοσοῦτος,
τοσαύτη, τοσοῦτο 'so great', 'so
much'; ἀνδράποδον, -ου, τό
'slave'; ὠνέομαι 'buy'; πρίω
aor. imper. 'buy!'

31. συνιστάντος τινὸς αὐτῷ υἱὸν ᾔτησε πεντα-
κοσίας δραχμάς· τοῦ δ' εἰπόντος, 'τοσού-
του δύναμαι ἀνδράποδον ὠνήσασθαι,' 'πρί-
ω,' ἔφη, 'καὶ ἕξεις δύο.'

Diogenes Laertius (Aristippus)

*οὐδαμοῦ 'nowhere'

[32.   'ἦ θεοὶ μὲν οὐδαμοῦ
τὰ θνητὰ δ' ἔσται μεγάλα, μὴ δόντος
δίκην.]

Euripides, *Heracles* (Iris speaking)

ἀποκρύπτω 'hide from', 'conceal'; ἐρῶ 'I will tell'; ὅταν
'whenever'; ἐλεεινός, -ή, -όν
'pitiable'; δάκρυ, -υος, τό
'tear'; *ἐμπίμπλημι 'fill full
of' (+ gen.); *καρδία, -ας, ἡ
'heart'; πηδάω 'leap', 'throb'

33. οὐ γάρ σε ἀποκρυψάμενος ἐρῶ. ἐγὼ γὰρ
ὅταν ἐλεεινόν τι λέγω, δακρύων ἐμπίμ-
πλαταί μου οἱ ὀφθαλμοί· ὅταν τε φοβερὸν
ἢ δεινόν, ὀρθαὶ αἱ τρίχες ἵστανται ὑπὸ
φόβου καὶ ἡ καρδία πηδᾷ.

Plato, *Ion*

ὁστισοῦν, ὁτιοῦν 'anybody/any-
thing whatsoever'

34. ἀλλ' ἔστι μέν, ὦ Νικία, χαλεπὸν λέγειν
περὶ ὁτουοῦν μαθήματος, ὡς οὐ χρὴ μανθά-
νειν· πάντα γὰρ ἐπίστασθαι ἀγαθὸν δοκεῖ
εἶναι.

Plato, *Laches*

35. βούλονται μέν, δύνανται δ' οὔ.

Thucydides

ἔνδον 'within', 'at home'; μάλα
'very', 'exceedingly'; προσκεφά-
λαιον, -ου, τό 'cushion', 'pil-
low'; δίφρος, -ου, ὁ 'seat',
'couch'; αὐλή, -ῆς, ἡ 'court',
'hall'; αὐτόθι 'there'; κύκλος,
-ου, ὁ 'ring', 'circle'; στεφα-
νόω '(to) crown'

[36. ἦν δ' ἔνδον καὶ ὁ πατὴρ ὁ τοῦ Πολεμάρχου
Κέφαλος. καὶ μάλα πρεσβύτης μοι ἔδοξεν
εἶναι· διὰ χρόνου γὰρ καὶ ἑωράκη αὐτόν.
καθῆστο δὲ ἐστεφανωμένος ἐπί τινος προσ-
κεφαλαίου τε καὶ δίφρου· τεθυκὼς γὰρ
ἐτύγχανεν ἐν τῇ αὐλῇ. ἐκαθεζόμεθα οὖν
παρ' αὐτόν· ἔκειντο γὰρ δίφροι τινὲς
αὐτόθι κύκλῳ.]

Plato, *Republic*

Quotation

Read and learn the following Greek Proverb:

τῶν ὤτων ἔχω τὸν λύκον, οὔτ᾽ ἔχειν, οὔτ᾽ ἀφεῖναι δυνάμαι.

I have the wolf by the ears: I can neither hold him nor let him go.

LESSON XIII

The Subjunctive and Optative Moods

The subjunctive and optative are two moods expressing degrees of unreality (as opposed to the indicative mood, which, generally speaking, expresses a statement of fact). *Mood*, you may remember, indicates the manner (or mode) in which the speaker/writer conceives of the assertion made by the verb. The use of the subjunctive or optative implies that this assertion is not strictly factual: an intention, a wish, an order, a 'maybe', or a 'might have been' may be implied. Various uses of the two moods will be explained below.

A. *The Subjunctive*

The subjunctive is found in the present, aorist, and perfect tenses. It has no future, but the basic idea of the subjunctive is future. The tenses of the subjunctive have no time value, but express the *aspect*. The present is used for an action going on (continuous), the aorist for a single action, the perfect for a completed action (or a present state). The most commonly used tenses of the subjunctive are the present and the aorist. The subjunctive, having no time value, is never augmented.

Formation:

The subjunctive is formed by lengthening the thematic vowel. The indicative has o/ε, the subjunctive ω/η:

Active Indicative:	-ω	-εις -ει	-ομεν	-ετε	-ουσι
Active Subjunctive:	-ω	-ῃς -ῃ	-ωμεν	-ητε	-ωσι
Middle Indicative:	-ομαι	-ει	-εται	-ομεθα	-εσθε -ονται
Middle Subjunctive:	-ωμαι	-ῃ	-ηται	-ωμεθα	-ησθε -ωνται

Primary endings are always used for the subjunctive. It refers to the future and is associated with primary tenses. Even the aorist subjunctive uses the primary endings. Also the athe-

matic verbs use these endings with the long thematic vowel (by
analogy with the other verbs). Contract verbs follow their rules
for contraction. The perfect subjunctive usually consists of the
perfect participle and the subjunctive of εἰμί.

Subjunctive Forms of εἰμί:

$$\begin{array}{ll} ὦ & ὦμεν \\ ᾖς & ἦτε \\ ᾖ & ὦσι \end{array}$$

Each tense of the subjunctive, optative, etc. is formed from
the corresponding tense stem (from the appropriate principal
part).

Subjunctive Forms of λύω:

ACTIVE

Present	Aorist	Perfect
λύω	λύσω	λελυκὼς ὦ
λύῃς	λύσῃς	λελυκὼς ᾖς
λύῃ	λύσῃ	λελυκὼς ᾖ
λύωμεν	λύσωμεν	λελυκότες ὦμεν
λύητε	λύσητε	λελυκότες ἦτε
λύωσι	λύσωσι	λελυκότες ὦσι

MIDDLE

λύωμαι	λύσωμαι	λελυμένος ὦ
λύῃ	λύσῃ	λελυμένος ᾖς
λύηται	λύσηται	λελυμένος ᾖ
λυώμεθα	λυσώμεθα	λελυμένοι ὦμεν
λύησθε	λύσησθε	λελυμένοι ἦτε
λύωνται	λύσωνται	λελυμένοι ὦσι

PASSIVE

λυθῶ
λυθῇς
λυθῇ

λυθῶμεν
λυθῆτε
λυθῶσι

Note that the participle must agree with the verb in number and gender,
so that if the subject is feminine or neuter λελυκυῖα ὦ, ᾖς, ᾖ or λελυκὸς ᾖ
must be used. For the perfect active subjunctive there is another form: λε-
λύκω, λελύκῃς, λελύκῃ, λελύκωμεν, λελύκητε, λελύκωσι, which is also found, but
is less common than the periphrastic form given above.

The aorist passive is inflected as a contract verb. The short form of the aorist passive stem, in θε- (or ε-) is used for the subjunctive (and for the optative); the ε- is absorbed before the long vowel of the endings.

Second Aorist Subjunctive of λείπω (ἔλιπον, aorist stem, λιπ-)

	ACTIVE	MIDDLE
	λίπω	λίπωμαι
	λίπῃς	λίπῃ
	λίπῃ	λίπηται
	λίπωμεν	λιπώμεθα
	λίπητε	λίπησθε
	λίπωσι	λίπωνται

Present Subjunctive of Contract Verbs

Review of Contraction used for the Subjunctive

1. -εω: ε is absorbed before a long vowel.

2. -αω: α + o-sound becomes ω. α + e-sound becomes α.

3. -οω: o + η or ω contracts to ω. o + any ι-diphthong yields οι.

	-εω	-αω	-οω
ACTIVE			
	φιλῶ	νικῶ	δηλῶ
	φιλῇς	νικᾷς	δηλοῖς
	φιλῇ	νικᾷ	δηλοῖ
	φιλῶμεν	νικῶμεν	δηλῶμεν
	φιλῆτε	νικᾶτε	δηλῶτε
	φιλῶσι	νικῶσι	δηλῶσι
MIDDLE-PASSIVE			
	φιλῶμαι	νικῶμαι	δηλῶμαι
	φιλῇ	νικᾷ	δηλοῖ
	φιλῆται	νικᾶται	δηλῶται
	φιλώμεθα	νικώμεθα	δηλώμεθα
	φιλῆσθε	νικᾶσθε	δηλῶσθε
	φιλῶνται	νικῶνται	δηλῶνται

Subjunctive of -μι Verbs

ἵστημι		τίθημι		ἵημι		δίδωμι	
ACTIVE							
Present	Aorist	Present	Aorist	Present	Aorist	Present	Aorist
ἱστῶ	στῶ	τιθῶ	θῶ	ἱῶ	-ὧ	διδῶ	δῶ
ἱστῇς	στῇς	τιθῇς	θῇς	ἱῇς	-ἧς	διδῷς	δῷς
ἱστῇ	στῇ	τιθῇ	θῇ	ἱῇ	-ἧ	διδῷ	δῷ

Present	Aorist	Present	Aorist	Present	Aorist	Present	Aorist
ἱστῶμεν	στῶμεν	τιθῶμεν	θῶμεν	ἱῶμεν	-ῶμεν	διδῶμεν	δῶμεν
ἱστῆτε	στῆτε	τιθῆτε	θῆτε	ἱῆτε	-ῆτε	διδῶτε	δῶτε
ἱστῶσι	στῶσι	τιθῶσι	θῶσι	ἱῶσι	-ῶσι	διδῶσι	δῶσι

MIDDLE

ἱστῶμαι		τιθῶμαι	θῶμαι	ἱῶμαι	-ῶμαι	διδῶμαι	δῶμαι
ἱστῇ		τιθῇ	θῇ	ἱῇ	-ῇ	διδῷ	δῷ
ἱστῆται		τιθῆται	θῆται	ἱῆται	-ῆται	διδῶται	δῶται
ἱστώμεθα		τιθώμεθα	θώμεθα	ἱώμεθα	-ώμεθα	διδώμεθα	δώμεθα
ἱστῆσθε		τιθῆσθε	θῆσθε	ἱῆσθε	-ῆσθε	διδῶσθε	δῶσθε
ἱστῶνται		τιθῶνται	θῶνται	ἱῶνται	-ῶνται	διδῶνται	δῶνται

(There is no second aorist middle of ἵστημι.)

Subjunctive of δείκνυμι, Present:

ACTIVE	MIDDLE
δεικνύω	δεικνύωμαι
δεικνύῃς	δεικνύῃ
δεικνύῃ	δεικνύηται
δεικνύωμεν	δεικνυώμεθα
δεικνύητε	δεικνύησθε
δεικνύωσι	δεικνύωνται

Review of the Subjunctive Forms:

Nearly all the subjunctive forms have the same set of endings, the primary endings with the long form of the thematic vowel. Even the -μι verbs are
for the most part inflected in the same way as the others and are accented
like the ε-contracts (the stem vowel contracting with the long thematic vowel). The exceptions are (1) α-contracts whose subjunctive and indicative are
identical; (2) the o-contracts which have -ω- except where there is an ι-subscript in the ending (in which case they have -οι-), and (3) the -μι verb, δίδωμι, which has -ω throughout the present and aorist subjunctive (-ω super-
cedes any other vowel).

Characteristics of the Subjunctive:

1. Long thematic vowel.

2. Primary endings.

Some Uses of the Subjunctive

The subjunctive in general refers to the future. Among its
uses are exhortations, commands, expressions of purpose, and conditions: in most of these uses, the idea of futurity can still

be seen: a command refers to the future, a purpose is future
relative to another action. In conditions, the subjunctive refers either directly to the future, or to an indefinite time (it
is never strictly present).

Independent Uses of the Subjunctive

The three most common uses of the subjunctive in the main
clause are:

1. *Hortatory:* The first person (usually plural) of
the subjunctive is used in exhortations. The negative is μή.

ἴδωμεν   Let us (Let's) see!

μὴ ταῦτα ποιῶμεν   Let us not do these things!

2. *Prohibitions:* A negative command is expressed by
the aorist subjunctive in the second person with μή (or by the
present imperative with μή: see Lesson XIV).

μὴ ποιήσῃς τοῦτο   Do not do that!

3. *Deliberative:* The first person of the subjunctive
is used in questions in which a person asks himself what he is to
do.

τί εἴπω;   What am I to say?

ταῦτα ποιῶμεν;   Are we to do these things?

The Subjunctive in Conditions

1. Future (more vivid) Conditions: when a hypothetical future case is stated distinctly and vividly, the subjunctive is
used with ἐάν (also spelled ἄν or ἤν) in the protasis (*if*-clause)
and the future indicative (or its equivalent) in the apodosis
(*conclusion*-clause). The negative in the protasis is μή, in the
apodosis οὐ.

Protasis (IF)(μή)   Apodosis (THEN)(οὐ)

ἐάν + Subjunctive   Future Indicative

ἐὰν εἴπῃ τι, αὐτοῦ ἀκουσόμεθα.

If he says anything, we will hear him.

ἐὰν μὴ ἔλθῃ, ταῦτα οὐ ποιήσομεν.

If he does not come, we shall not do these things.

2.   Present General Conditions: refer to a customary or repeated action or to a general truth.   The time is indefinite.
The subjunctive with ἐάν is used in the protasis, the present indicative in the apodosis.

ἐὰν ἔλθῃ τις, ταῦτα ποιοῦμεν

If (ever) anyone comes, we (always) do these things.

ἐὰν εἴπῃς τι, οὐκ ἀκούομεν.

If (ever) you say anything, we do not listen.

Other uses of the subjunctive will be treated in a later
section.

Exercises

1.   Form and conjugate the following subjunctives:

1.   Present active and middle of δοκέω

2.   Aorist active, middle, and passive of τίθημι

3.   All the subjunctive forms of παιδεύω

2.   Fill in the subjunctive forms of the synopses given in
previous lessons (IX, X, XI, XII).

3.   Parse the following forms:

1. εἴπω   2. δοκῶμεν   3. ἔλθωσι   4. τιμῶνται   5. ἀξιῶσθε

6. θῶ   7. παυθῆτε   8. ἕλωμαι   9. γράψωμεν 10. τεθνηκότες ὦσι

11. διδῷς   12. λίπωσι   13. ἔρχῃ   14. δεικνύῃς 15. βάλωμαι

16. βουλεύσῃς 17. γένηται   18. ἀποθνῄσκῃ 19. ἀγάγωσι   20. κληθῇς

4.   Read the following sentences:

1.   τί ποιῶμεν;

2.   ἀλλήλους ἀγαπῶμεν.

3.   μὴ τούτῳ πιστεύσητε

4.   μηδὲν ποιήσῃς.

5. ἐάν μοι ταῦτα διδῷς, φιλήσω σε.

6. ἐὰν τὴν πατρίδα προδῶτε, οὐδεὶς ὑμᾶς τιμήσει.

7. τί βουλευώμεθα;

8. τούτου τοῦ σοφοῦ ἀκούωμεν.

9. μὴ θάψῃς τοῦτον τὸν νεκρόν. (νεκρός 'corpse')

10. ἐὰν ἀποθάνῃ ὁ ἀδελφός, βουλόμεθα αὐτὸν θάψαι.

11. τὸν τοῦ ἀδελφοῦ νεκρὸν θαψώμεθα.

12. μὴ τὸν μὲν τοῦ βασιλέως νόμον φοβώμεθα.

13. τῷ δὲ τῶν θεῶν νόμῳ πειθώμεθα.

14. ἐὰν τὴν ἀλήθειαν μὴ λέγητε, οὐδεὶς ὑμῖν πιστεύει.

15. τοῦτον εἶναι κακὸν καὶ αἰσχρὸν μὴ νομίσῃς.

16. ἐὰν ἀδικῶσιν, δίκην δώσουσιν.

17. μηδὲν ψευδὲς εἴπῃς. μηδὲν αἰσχρὸν εἴπωμεν.

18. ἐὰν ἐκείνην τὴν χώραν λίπῃς, οὐ μενοῦμεν.

19. ἐὰν χρήματα σχῶμεν, εἰς τὰς νήσους κατὰ θάλασσαν ἐλευσόμεθα.

20. ἐὰν αὐτὸν ἴδω, ἀποφεύγω.

21. ἐὰν ζητῇς τι, εὑρήσεις.

Readings

What type of condition?

1. βίον καλὸν ζῇς, 'ἂν γυναῖκα μὴ ἔχῃς.

     Menander

Parse ἔχωμεν & ἔξομεν. What type of condition?

2. ἐὰν δ' ἔχωμεν χρήμαθ', ἔξομεν φίλους.

     Menander

Parse γαμεῖς. παραινέω 'recommend', 'advise'

3. . . . οὐ γαμεῖς, 'ἂν νοῦν ἔχῃς,
   τοῦτον καταλιπὼν τὸν βίον· γεγάμηκα γὰρ
   αὐτός· διὰ τοῦτο σοι παραινῶ μὴ γαμεῖν.

     Menander

4. καλὸν τὸ διδάσκειν, ἐὰν ὁ λέγων ποιῇ.

     Ignatius

genitives depend on ἀξίως; πρᾶγμα 'subject'; *δόξα, -ης, ἡ 'opinion', 'reputation', 'glory'; *διατρίβω 'rub away', 'spend time'; ἡμῖν dat. of agent; παρακελεύομαι 'exhort', 'recommend'; *συγγνώμη 'forgiveness', 'pardon'; καταγελάω 'laugh at'; καταφρονέω 'despise'

[5. "Accustomed as I am . . ."
ἐγὼ δ' 'ἢν μὴ καὶ τοῦ πράγματος ἀξίως
εἴπω καὶ τῆς δόξης τῆς ἐμαυτοῦ καὶ τοῦ
χρόνου, μὴ μόνον τοῦ περὶ τὸν λόγον ἡμῖν
διατριφθέντος ἀλλὰ καὶ σύμπαντος οὗ βεβί-
ωκα, παρακελεύομαι μηδεμίαν συγγνώμην
ἔχειν ἀλλὰ καταγελᾶν καὶ καταφρονεῖν.]

     Isocrates, *Panegyricus*

ἴωμεν subj. of εἶμι 'go'

6. ἀλλ' ἴωμεν ἀγαθῇ τύχῃ . . .

Plato, *Laws*

φιλομαθής, -ές 'fond of learning'; πολυμαθής, -ές 'very learned'

7. ἐὰν ᾖς φιλομαθής, ἔσει πολυμαθής.

Isocrates

οἷον 'for example'; εἴα (impf. of ἐάω); ἱέρεια, -ας, ἡ (fem. of ἱερεύς); δημηγορέω 'be a public orator'

8. οἷον ἱέρεια οὐκ εἴα τὸν υἱὸν δημηγορεῖν· ἐὰν μὲν γάρ, ἔφη, τὰ δίκαια λέγῃς, οἱ ἄνθρωποί σε μισήσουσιν, ἐὰν δὲ τὰ ἄδικα, οἱ θεοί. δεῖ μὲν οὖν δημηγορεῖν· ἐὰν μὲν γὰρ τὰ δίκαια λέγῃς, οἱ θεοί σε φιλήσουσιν, ἐὰν δὲ τὰ ἄδικα, οἱ ἄνθρωποι.

Aristotle, *Rhetoric*

*ἀναγκαῖος, -α, -ον 'necessary'; *σκοπέω 'look at/after/into'

9. τὸ γαμεῖν, ἐάν τις τὴν ἀλήθειαν σκοπῇ, κακὸν μέν ἐστιν, ἀλλ' ἀναγκαῖον κακόν.

Menander

πλύνω 'beat'

10. ἐὰν κακῶς μου τὴν γυναῖχ' οὕτω λέγῃς, τὸν πατέρα καὶ σὲ τούς τε σοὺς ἐγὼ πλυνῶ.

Menander

ἴωμεν 'let's go', subjunct. of εἶμι 'go'

11. νῦν ἴωμεν καὶ ἀκούσωμεν τοῦ ἀνδρός.

Plato, *Protagoras*

12. εἴπωμεν ἢ σιγῶμεν;

Euripides, *Ion*

ὡς 'how'; *μάθησις, -εως, ἡ 'learning'

13. ὡς οὐδὲν ἡ μάθησις, ἂν μὴ νοῦς παρῇ.

Menander

φράζω 'speak'; ἐγκώμιον, -ου, τό 'song' or 'speech of praise', 'encomium'

14. ὑπὲρ σεαυτοῦ μὴ φράσῃς ἐγκώμιον.

Menander

μῶρος, -α, -ον 'dull', 'stupid'; *γέλοιος, -α, -ον 'humorous'

15. γελᾷ δ' ὁ μῶρος, κἄν τι μὴ γέλοιον ᾖ.

Menander

ψέγω 'blame'; μιμέομαι 'imitate'

16. ἃ ψέγομεν ἡμεῖς, ταῦτα μὴ μιμώμεθα.

Menander

*ἔγγυς (adv.) 'near'

17. ἢν ἐγγὺς ἔλθῃ θάνατος, οὐδεὶς βούλεται θνήσκειν.

Euripides, *Alcestis*

ἦ introduces the question; σφ' = σφε 'him'; ἀπόρρητος, -ον 'forbidden'

18. Ismene.
ἦ γὰρ νοεῖς θάπτειν σφ', ἀπόρρητον πόλει;
Antigone.
τὸν γοῦν ἐμὸν καὶ τὸν σόν, ἢν σὺ μὴ θέλῃς,
ἀδελφόν· οὐ γὰρ δὴ προδοῦσ' ἁλώσομαι.

Sophocles, *Antigone*

19. ἀρετὴ δὲ κἂν θάνῃ τις οὐκ ἀπόλλυται.

Euripides (fragment)

ἀναιρέω 'take away', 'destroy';   [20. ἐρωτηθεὶς ποτε τί πλέον ἔχουσιν οἱ φιλό-
*βιόω 'live'   σοφοι, ἔφη, 'ἐὰν πάντες οἱ νόμοι ἀναιρε-
                                   θῶσιν, ὁμοίως βιωσόμεθα.']

Diogenes Laertius (Aristippus)

χὠ = καὶ ὁ; *κτάομαι 'acquire'   [21. μὴ Πλοῦτον εἴπῃς· οὐχὶ θαυμάζω θεὸν
                                 ὃν χὠ κάκιστος ῥᾳδίως ἐκτήσατο.]

Euripides (fragment)

ῥόδον, -ου, τό 'rose'; ἀκμάζω   [22. τὸ ῥόδον ἀκμάζει βαιὸν χρόνον· ἢν δὲ
'bloom'; βαιός, -ά, -όν 'little',   παρέλθῃ
'short'; παρέρχομαι 'pass away';   ζητῶν εὑρήσεις οὐ ῥόδον, ἀλλὰ βάτον.]
βάτος, -ου, ἡ 'bramble'

Greek Anthology (anon.)

παρίσθμια, τά 'tonsils', 'an in-   [23. Poet-fever
flammation of the tonsils'; ἐξ-   Ποιητὴς ἐλθὼν εἰς Ἴσθμια πρὸς τὸν ἀγῶνα,
ορμάω 'set out'; παραπύθια (an   εὑρὼν ποιητάς, εἶπε παρίσθμι' ἔχειν.
illness which keeps one from   μέλλει δ' ἐξορμᾶν εἰς Πύθια· κἂν πάλιν
taking part in the Pythian games)   εὕρῃ,
                              εἰπεῖν οὐ δύναται, 'καὶ παραπύθι'
                              ἔχω.']

Anthology (Cerealius) (an elaborate
pun)

Relative Conditions

Conditions may also be expressed as relative conditions, using a relative pronoun ("who," etc.) or a relative adverb ("when," etc.). The subjunctive relative conditions follow their simple counterparts.

Present General:

Protasis	Apodosis
relative word + ἄν + subjunctive	present indicative

ὅταν τις ἔλθῃ, ταῦτα ποιοῦμεν. (ὅταν = ὅτε + ἄν)

Whenever anyone comes, we do these things.

Future (More Vivid)

Protasis	Apodosis
relative word + ἄν + subjunctive	future indicative

ὅταν ἔλθῃ ταῦτα ποιήσομεν.

When he comes, we will do these things.

Readings

*κάλλος, -ους, τό 'beauty'

1. ὡς ἡδὺ κάλλος, ὅταν ἔχῃ νοῦν σώφρονα.

   Menander

*γῆρας, -αος (-ως), τό 'old age'; ἐπάν 'whenever'; *εὔχομαι 'pray (for)'; *ὀφείλω 'owe'

[2. γῆρας ἐπὰν μὲν ἀπῇ, πᾶς εὔχεται· ἢν δέ ποτ' ἔλθῃ
    μέμφεται· ἔστι δ' ἀεὶ κρεῖσσον ὀφειλόμενον.]

   Anthology (Menecrates)

περιγίγνομαι 'survive', 'result'

3. ἐρωτηθεὶς τί περιγίνεται κέρδος τοῖς ψευδομένοις, 'ὅταν' ἔφη, 'λέγωμεν ἀληθῆ, μὴ πιστεύεσθαι.'

   Diogenes Laertius (Aristotle)

φρικώδης, -ες 'awful', 'horrible'; οὐθέν = οὐδέν; ἐπειδήπερ 'since really'; τόθ' = τότε (before rough breathing)

4. τὸ φρικωδέστατον οὖν τῶν κακῶν ὁ θάνατος οὐθὲν πρὸς ἡμᾶς, ἐπειδήπερ ὅταν μὲν ἡμεῖς ὦμεν, ὁ θάνατος οὐ πάρεστιν· ὅταν δ' ὁ θάνατος παρῇ τόθ' ἡμεῖς οὐκ ἐσμέν.

   Diogenes Laertius (Epicurus)

*σπεύδω 'hasten', 'strive after'; χὠ = καὶ ὁ; συνάπτομαι 'join with'

5. ἀλλ' ὅταν σπεύδῃ τις αὐτός, χὠ θεὸς συνάπτεται.

   Aeschylus *Persae* (refers to one hastening to his ruin)

ὑπερβολή, -ῆς, ἡ 'excess'; ἀγαθότης, -τητος, ἡ 'goodness'; βλασφημέω 'blaspheme'; καταγελάω 'laugh at' (+ gen.)

6. ὅταν γὰρ ἀκούσωσιν παρ' ἡμῶν, ὅτι λέγει ὁ θεός· οὐ χάρις ὑμῖν, εἰ ἀγαπᾶτε τοὺς ἀγαπῶντας ὑμᾶς, ἀλλὰ χάρις ὑμῖν, εἰ ἀγαπᾶτε τοὺς ἐχθροὺς καὶ τοὺς μισοῦντας ὑμᾶς· ταῦτα ὅταν ἀκούσωσιν, θαυμάζουσιν τὴν ὑπερβολὴν τῆς ἀγαθότητος· ὅταν δὲ ἴδωσιν, ὅτι οὐ μόνον τοὺς μισοῦντας οὐκ ἀγαπῶμεν ἀλλ' ὅτι οὐδὲ τους ἀγαπῶντας, καταγελῶσιν ἡμῶν, καὶ βλασφημεῖται τὸ ὄνομα.

   Clement of Rome

[7. καὶ ὃ μή ἐστιν ὑπερβολή, τοῦτο ἀγαθόν, 'ὃ δ' ἂν ᾖ μεῖζον 'ἢ δεῖ, κακόν.]

   Aristotle, *Rhetoric*

πλοῦς, ὁ 'a sailing voyage' (a contraction of πλόος)

8. ἀεὶ καλὸς πλοῦς ἔσθ' ὅταν φεύγῃς κακά.

   Sophocles, *Philoctetes*

9. μισῶ πονηρόν, χρηστὸν ὅταν εἴπῃ λόγον.

          Menander

χαρίεις, χαρίεσσα, χαρίεν or   [10. ὡς χάριέν ἐστ' ἄνθρωπος ʽὃς ʼὰν ἄνθρωπος
χάριεν 'pleasing', 'agreeable'   ᾖ.]

          Menander

ἵνα (as rel. adv.) 'where'   11. πατρὶς γάρ ἐστι πᾶσ' ἵν' ʼὰν πράττῃ τις
                     εὖ.

          Proverb

Quotation

    Read and learn the following:

        φάγωμεν καὶ πίωμεν· αὔριον γὰρ ἀποθνήσκομεν.

    Let us eat and drink; for tomorrow we die.   (Doctrine of Epicurus as quoted by Paul, I Corinthians)

B.   *The Optative*

    The optative is found in the present, future, aorist, and perfect tenses. It is a somewhat vaguer mood than the subjunctive: some of its uses will be discussed below. The tenses of the optative usually refer to aspect rather than time (there is, however, one exception to this generalization: namely in indirect statement, see below). The future optative is not common and is used only in indirect statement, to represent the future indicative. The optative is *not* augmented.

    There are two forms of the optative (i.e. two sets of endings).

        1. The ι-type: used for -ω verbs, -νυμι verbs, and all middles (and generally in the plural of the active).

        2. The -ιη-type: for the present of contract verbs (and liquid futures), for the present and aorist of -μι verbs (except -νυμι verbs) and for the aorist passive.

    Thus one characteristic of the optative is the presence of ι.

Another is that the optative has secondary endings and is often associated with past tenses.

Formation of the Optative

    I. *ι-type*

Present, Future, and Second Aorist

Tense stem + thematic vowel -ο- + ι (characteristic vowel of optative) + endings:

	ACTIVE	MIDDLE/MIDDLE-PASSIVE
	(οι)-μι	(οι)-μην
	(οι)-ς	(οι)-ο (← οισο)
	(οι)-	(οι)-το
	(οι)-μεν	(οι)-μεθα
	(οι)-τε	(οι)-σθε
	(οι)-εν	(οι)-ντο

    Examples: present and future of λύω; second aorist of λείπω:

Present	Future	Second Aorist
λύοιμι	λύσοιμι	λίποιμι
λύοις	λύσοις	λίποις
λύοι	λύσοι	λίποι
λύοιμεν	λύσοιμεν	λίποιμεν
λύοιτε	λύσοιτε	λίποιτε
λύοιεν	λύσοιεν	λίποιεν

MIDDLE

λυοίμην	λυσοίμην	λιποίμην
λύοιο	λύσοιο	λίποιο
λύοιτο	λύσοιτο	λίποιτο
λυοίμεθα	λυσοίμεθα	λιποίμεθα
λύοισθε	λύσοισθε	λίποισθε
λύοιντο	λύσοιντο	λίποιντο

First Aorist Optative

First Aorist Stem (with characteristic α of first aorist) + ι + endings.

ACTIVE		MIDDLE	
λύσαιμι	λύσαιμεν	λυσαίμην	λυσαίμεθα
λύσαις (λύσειας)	λύσαιτε	λύσαιο	λύσαισθε
λύσαι (λύσειε)	λύσαιεν (λύσειαν)	λυσαίτο	λύσαιντο

The forms given in parentheses are the more common ones in most prose and it is recommended that the student learn to recognize them.

Note that the -οι and -αι of the optative third person singular (as in λύοι, λύσοι, λίποι, and λύσαι) are considered *long* for the purposes of accent.

The present optative of δείκνυμι is formed by adding the endings in -οι to the stem δεικνυ-: δεικνύοιμι, δεικνύοις, etc.

II. *The ιη-type*

Stem + ιη + endings:

$$-ιη-ν$$
$$-ιη-ς$$
$$-ιη-$$

$$-ιη-μεν \text{ or } -ι-μεν$$
$$-ιη-τε \text{ or } -ι-τε$$
$$-ιη-σαν \text{ or } -ι-εν$$

The ιη endings are used in the singular, but are seldom found in the plural. The ι type is used throughout the middle.

1. The present optative of εἰμί

$$εἴην$$
$$εἴης$$
$$εἴη$$

$$εἶμεν \text{ or } εἴημεν$$
$$εἶτε \text{ or } εἴητε$$
$$εἶεν \text{ or } εἴησαν$$

The perfect optative is formed by using the perfect participle (active or middle) with the optative of εἰμί: λελυκὼς εἴην (active), λελυμένος εἴην (middle-passive).

2. Present optative of contract verbs (and of liquid futures)

The thematic vowel ο joined with ιη (or ι) contracts with the stem vowel:

$$α + οι \rightarrow ῳ$$
$$ε + οι \rightarrow οι$$
$$ο + οι \rightarrow οι$$

} These two types have the same *form* in the optative, though it results from different contractions.

Examples:

-αω	-εω	-οω
νικῴην	φιλοίην	δηλοίην
νικῴης	φιλοίης	δηλοίης
νικῴη	φιλοίη	δηλοίη

νικῷμεν (νικῴημεν)	φιλοῖμεν (φιλοίημεν)	δηλοῖμεν (δηλοίημεν)
νικῷτε (νικῴητε)	φιλοῖτε (φιλοίητε)	δηλοῖτε (δηλοίητε)
νικῷεν (νικῴησαν)	φιλοῖεν (φιλοίησαν)	δηλοῖεν (δηλοίησαν)

νικῴμην	φιλοίμην	δηλοίμην
νικῷο	φιλοῖο	δηλοῖο
νικῷτο	φιλοῖτο	δηλοῖτο

νικῴμεθα	φιλοίμεθα	δηλοίμεθα
νικῷσθε	φιλοῖσθε	δηλοῖσθε
νικῷντο	φιλοῖντο	δηλοῖντο

The liquid futures follow φιλέω in the optative.

Monosyllabic stem verbs like πλέω, δέω, which contract only before ε or ει, show the ι-type optative: πλέοιμι, πλέοις, πλέοι, etc.

3.   The Present and Aorist Optative of -μι verbs

-μι verbs use the short form of the stem before ι of the optative. The vowel before the ι depends on the stem vowel of the verb.

ἵστημι   Present   Aorist

                      ἱσταίην   σταίην
                      ἱσταίης   σταίης
                      ἱσταίη   σταίη

          ἱσταῖμεν (ἱσταίημεν)   σταῖμεν (σταίημεν)
          ἱσταῖτε (ἱσταίητε)   σταῖτε (σταίητε)
          ἱσταῖεν (ἱσταίησαν)   σταῖεν (σταίησαν)

          ἱσταίμην
          ἱσταῖο
          ἱσταῖτο

          ἱσταίμεθα
          ἱσταῖσθε
          ἱσταῖντο

Other -μι verbs   Present   Aorist

          δίδωμι   Active   διδοίην   δοίην
                     Middle   διδοίμην   δοίμην

		Present	Aorist
τίθημι	Active	τιθείην	θείην
	Middle	τιθείμην	θείμην
ἵημι	Active	ἱείην	-εἵην
	Middle	ἱείμην	-εἵμην

(For full conjugation of these and other verbs, see appendix.)

    4. *The Aorist Passive Optative*

stem + θε + ιη + endings

$$\lambda υθείην$$
$$\lambda υθείης$$
$$\lambda υθείη$$

λυθεῖμεν (λυθείημεν)
λυθεῖτε   (λυθείητε)
λυθεῖεν   (λυθείησαν)

    The Future Passive Optative

Stem + θη + σο + the regular ι-type ending in the middle

λυθησοίμην	λυθησοίμεθα
λυθήσοιο	λυθήσοισθε
λυθήσοιτο	λυθήσοιντο

Some Uses of the Optative

    I. The Optative in Independent Clauses

1. *The Potential Optative*

    The optative with ἄν expresses a future possibility: this use corresponds to the English potential forms using such auxiliaries as *may, can, might, could, would.*

    ἔλθοι ἄν   'He may/might/could/would come.'

The negative used with the potential optative is οὐ.

2. *Optative of Wish* ('Optative Optative': the name *optative* is derived from the Latin *opto* 'wish')

    A future wish is expressed by the optative; εἴθε or εἰ γάρ 'O that', 'O if', may be used with this construction. The negative is μή.

ἔλθοι   εἴθε ἔλθοι   'may he come!'

μὴ ἔλθοι   εἴθε μὴ ἔλθοι   'may he not come!'

Note:

Wishes which refer to the past are expressed by the secondary tenses of the indicative (imperfect or aorist) with εἴθε or εἰ γάρ (which cannot be omitted). The negative is μή.

εἴθε ἤρχετο   'would that he were coming!'

εἴθε ἦλθεν   'would that he had come!'

II. The Optative in Conditions (and relative conditional clauses)

1. *Past General Conditions* refer to a customary or repeated action or to a general truth *in past time*. They have εἰ with the optative in the protasis and (usually) the imperfect indicative in the apodosis.

Protasis   Apodosis

εἰ + optative   imperfect indicative

εἰ ἔλθοι τις, ταῦτα ἐποιοῦμεν.

If (ever) anyone came, we (always) did/used to do/would do these things.

A relative word may be substituted for εἰ:

ὅτε ἔλθοι τις, ταῦτα ἐποιοῦμεν.

Whenever anyone came, we did these things.

2. *Future* (less vivid) *Conditions*:

When the future condition is stated less distinctly, the optative is used in both clauses. Compare this with the English 'should-would' condition: "If I should go (*or* if I went), I would do these things."

Protasis (μή)   Apodosis (οὐ)

εἰ + optative   optative + ἄν (cf. potential opt.)

εἰ ἔλθοιμι, ταῦτα ᾽ἂν ποιήσαιμι.

If I should come, I would do these things.

This can also be expressed as a relative condition:

ὅτε ἔλθοιμι, ταῦτα 'ἂν ποιήσαιμι.

Whenever I should come, I would do these things.

Exercises

1. Give all the optative forms of παύω
    present active and middle
    future active, middle, and passive
    aorist active, middle, and passive
    perfect active and middle

   Of τιμάω and ποιέω, the present optative only

   Of ἀποδίδωμι, ἀφίστημι, ἀνατίθημι present and aorist optative

2. Fill in the optative forms in the synopses given in previous lessons.

3. Parse:

1. γένοιτο   2. βάλοιμι   3. τιθείην   4. λάβοιεν   5. πέμψοις
6. ζῴην   7. ἀποκτείναιμεν 8. γένοιο   9. βουλεύσαιντο 10. λειφθεῖεν
11. τιμήσειαν   12. ἀκουσοίμην 13. εἶησαν   14. βάλλοισθε   15. ἀγαπῷμεν
16. βουληθείη   17. λαμβάνοιτε 18. δοῖεν   19. δοκοίης   20. τεθήσοιο

4. Translate:

1. πάντες τοῦτον 'ἂν τιμήσειαν.

2. εἰ γὰρ νικῷμεν.

3. μὴ γένοιτο.

4. εἴποι ἄν τις τάδε.

5. καλῶς ἔχοιτε.

6. οὐκ 'ἂν εἴη ἄλογον εἰ τούτῳ τῷ ἀνδρὶ πιστεύοιτε;

7. τίς 'ἂν ὑμῖν πείθοιτο;

8. εἴ τις ψευδῆ εἴποι, οὐκ ἐπιστεύετο.

9. ὑμῖν βίον μακρὸν καὶ εὐτυχῆ θεοὶ δοῖεν.

10. αἰσχρὸν γὰρ 'ἂν εἴη εἰ ταῦτα ποιήσαιμεν.

11. εἰρήνην ἄγοιτε ἀεί.

12. ἡδέως 'ἂν μάθοιμι καὶ ἡδέως διδάσκοιμι.

13. ἡδέως ἄν σε ἴδοιμι.

14. τί 'ἂν ἔχειν βούλοιο;

15. εἴ τι ποιεῖν δύναιντο, ἐποίουν.

16. τί ᾽ἂν εἴη ἡ ἀρετή;

17. εἰ αὐτὸν ἴδοιμεν, ἀπηρχόμεθα.

18. εἰ γὰρ καλὸς κἀγαθὸς γένοιο.

19. οὐ ταῦτα ποιοίην ἄν.

20. εἰ γάρ μοι χρήματα πολλὰ εἴη.

Readings

παῖ **voc.** of παῖς

1. ὦ παῖ, γένοιο πατρὸς εὐτυχέστερος.

   Sophocles, *Aias*

2. εἴθε φίλος ἡμῖν γένοιο.

   Xenophon

ἄτοπος, -ον 'strange'; φαίη opt.
of φημί (3rd sg., pres.)

3. ἄτοπον γὰρ ᾽ἂν εἴη εἰ τις φαίη φιλεῖν
   τὸν Δία.

   Magna Moralia

4. ἀρετὴ ᾽ἂν εἴη κάλλος ψυχῆς.

   Plato, *Republic*

5. δοῦλοι γὰρ ᾽ἂν καὶ δεσπόται οὐκ ἄν ποτε
   γένοιντο φίλοι . . .

   Plato, *Laws*

σχῆμα, -ατος, τό 'form', pl.
'steps (of a dance)'; χρήσει
fut. of χράομαι (with dative);
ὀρχέομαι 'dance'; *γελάω 'laugh'

[6. Socrates has been admiring some young
dancers and addresses their trainer, a
Syracusan:
   καὶ ἐγὼ μὲν, ἔφη, πάνυ ᾽ἂν ἡδέως, ὦ Συ-
   ρακόσιε, μάθοιμι τὰ σχήματα παρὰ σοῦ.
   καὶ ὅς, τί οὖν χρήσει αὐτοῖς; ἔφη.
   ὀρχήσομαι νὴ Δία.
   ἐνταῦθα δὴ ἐγέλασαν ἅπαντες.]

   Xenophon, *Symposium*

φαίης pres. opt. 2nd sg. of φημί

[7. ἢ πῶς ᾽ἂν φαίης σὺ περὶ τούτων;]

   Plato, *Philebus*

τάχα ἄν 'probably', 'perhaps';
*ἕπομαι 'follow'

[8. εἴ μοι σαφέστερον ἔτι περὶ αὐτῶν εἴποις,
   τάχ᾽ ᾽ἂν ἑποίμην.]

   Plato, *Philebus*

ξύλον, -ου, τό 'wood'; ἔμψυχος, -ον 'animate'; *κινέω 'set in motion'

9. Animal, Vegetable, or Mineral?
εἰ μή ἐστι ζῷον ὁ ἄνθρωπος, λίθος 'ἀν εἴη 'ἢ ξύλον. οὐκ ἔστι δὲ λίθος 'ἢ ξύλον· ἔμψυχον γάρ ἐστι καὶ ἐξ αὐτοῦ κινεῖται· ζῷον ἄρα ἐστίν.

   Diogenes Laertius (Plato)

*ποῦ 'where'; *οὐδαμοῦ 'nowhere'; Λακεδαίμων, -ονος, ἡ 'Lacedaemon', 'Sparta'

10. ἐρωτηθεὶς ποῦ τῆς Ἑλλάδος ἴδοι ἀγαθοὺς ἄνδρας, 'ἄνδρας μέν,' εἶπεν, 'οὐδαμοῦ, παῖδας δ' ἐν Λακεδαίμονι.'

   Diogenes Laertius (Diogenes)

οὐθέν = οὐδέν

11. καὶ μὴν καὶ τὸ πᾶν ἀεὶ τοιοῦτον ἦν οἷον νῦν ἐστι, καὶ ἀεὶ τοιοῦτον ἔσται. οὐθέν γάρ ἐστιν εἰς 'ὃ μεταβαλεῖ. παρὰ γὰρ τὸ πᾶν οὐθέν ἐστιν, 'ὃ 'ἂν εἰσελθὸν εἰς αὐτὸ τὴν μεταβολὴν ποιήσαιτο.

   Diogenes Laertius (Epicurus)

φονεύω 'murder'; καθόλου 'in general'; βίαιος, -ᾱ, -ον 'violent'; ῥύομαι 'rescue', 'protect'; περιπίπτω 'meet with' + dat.; ὀφείλω 'owe', 'be obliged'

12. A Law of the Egyptians
ἔπειτα εἴ τις ἐν ὁδῷ κατὰ τὴν χώραν ἰδὼν φονευόμενον ἄνθρωπον 'ἢ τὸ καθόλου βίαιόν τι πάσχοντα μὴ ῥύσαιτο δυνατὸς ὤν, θανάτῳ περιπεσεῖν ὤφειλεν . . .

   Diodorus Siculus

εὐτυχία, -ας, ἡ 'success', 'good luck'; ἦν δ' ἐγώ 'said I'; γνοίη aor. opt. of γιγνώσκω

[13. ἡ σοφία δήπου, ἦν δ' ἐγώ, εὐτυχία ἐστί· τοῦτο δὲ κἂν παῖς γνοίη.]

   Plato, *Euthydemus*

διδακτός, -όν 'taught', 'teachable'

14. εἰ δέ γ' ἐστὶν ἐπιστήμη τις ἡ ἀρετή, δῆλον ὅτι διδακτὸν 'ἂν εἴη.

   Plato, *Meno*

15. τούτῳ μὲν οὕτως εὐτυχεῖν δοῖεν θεοί.

   Aeschylus, *Seven*

ἐκ + φεύγω

16. θεῶν διδόντων οὐκ 'ἂν ἐκφύγοις κακά.

   Aeschylus, *Seven*

μόρσιμος, -ον 'doomed', 'destined'

[17. τί δ' 'ἂν φοβοίμην ᾧ θανεῖν οὐ μόρσιμον;]

   Aeschylus, *Prometheus*

νόσημα, -ατος, τό = νόσος; *στυγέω 'hate'; φορητός, -όν 'bearable'; ἐκ + διδάσκω; γηράσκω 'grow old'

18. Prometheus and Hermes
Prometheus. νοσοῖμ' ἄν, εἰ νόσημα τοὺς ἐχθροὺς στυγεῖν.
Hermes. εἴης φορητὸς οὐκ ἄν, εἰ πράσσοις καλῶς.

P. ὤμοι.

H. ὤμοι; τόδε Ζεὺς τοὖπος οὐκ ἐπίσταται.

P. ἀλλ' ἐκδιδάσκει πανθ' ὁ γηράσκων
χρόνος.

   Aeschylus, *Prometheus*

ἐκπέρσαι aor. inf. of ἐκπέρθω   19. ὑμῖν θεοὶ δοῖεν ἐκπέρσαι Πριάμοιο πόλιν.
'destroy utterly'; Πριάμοιο gen.
of 'Priam'   Homer, *Iliad*

ἀλογία, -ας, ἡ 'lack of reason',   20. οὐ πολλὴ 'ἂν ἀλογία εἴη, εἰ φοβοῖτο τὸν
'folly'   θάνατον ὁ τοιοῦτος;

                                     Plato, *Phaedo*

ἱκνέομαι 'come', aor. ἱκόμην   [21. ἀλλ' εὐτυχὴς ἵκοιτο τῇ θ' αὐτοῦ πόλει
                                     ἐμοί τε· τίς γὰρ ἐσθλὸς οὐχ αὑτῷ φίλος;]

                                     Sophocles, *Oedipus at Colonus*

*κρατέω 'be strong'; ἔρημος, -η,   [22. Creon and Haemon
-ον 'lonely', 'desert'   C. ἄλλῳ γὰρ 'ἢ 'μοι χρή με τῆσδ' ἄρχειν
                                          χθονός;
                                     H. πόλις γὰρ οὐκ ἔσθ' ἥτις ἀνδρός ἐσθ'
                                          ἑνός.
                                     C. οὐ τοῦ κρατοῦντος ἡ πόλις νομίζεται;
                                     H. καλῶς ἐρήμης γ' 'ἂν σὺ γῆς ἄρχοις
                                          μόνος.]

                                     Sophocles, *Antigone*

*συμβουλεύω 'advise', mid. 'take   [23. Anytus' warning to Socrates.
counsel with'; εὐλαβέομαι 'be   Ὦ Σώκρατες, ῥᾳδίως μοι δοκεῖς κακῶς
cautious'   λέγειν ἀνθρώπους. ἐγὼ μὲν οὖν ἄν σοι
                                     συμβουλεύσαιμι, εἰ ἐθέλεις ἐμοὶ πείθεσ-
                                     θαι, εὐλαβεῖσθαι· ὡς ἴσως μὲν καὶ ἐν
                                     ἄλλῃ πόλει ῥᾷόν ἐστι κακῶς ποιεῖν ἀνθρώ-
                                     πους 'ἢ εὖ, ἐν τῇδε δὲ καὶ πάνυ· οἶμαι
                                     δὲ σὲ καὶ αὐτὸν εἰδέναι.]

                                     Plato, *Meno*

ἕλκος, -ους, τό 'wound', 'ulcer'   24.   . . . τί γὰρ
                                   γένοιτ' 'ἂν ἕλκος μεῖζον 'ἢ φίλος κακός;

                                     Sophocles, *Antigone*

γνοίης aor. opt. of γιγνώσκω   25. ἀλλ' ἐν χρόνῳ γνώσει τάδ' ἀσφαλῶς ἐπεὶ
                                   χρόνος δίκαιον ἄνδρα δείκνυσιν μόνος·
                                   κακὸν δὲ κἂν ἐν ἡμέρᾳ γνοίης μιᾷ.

                                     Sophocles, *Oedipus Tyrannus* (Creon
                                     speaking)

-οιο = -ου (epic gen. form)

βοῦς, βοός, ὁ/ἡ 'bull', 'cow', 'ox'; φθογγή, -ῆς, ἡ 'voice'; αὐδάω 'talk', 'speak'; λήθομαι (= λανθάνομαι) 'forget'; κοὔ = καὶ οὐ

*ἐλαύνω 'drive', 'march'

*ἄθλιος, -α, -ον 'unhappy', 'wretched', 'sorry'

ἐπιορκέω 'swear falsely'; *τιμω-ρία, -ας, ἡ 'retribution', 'pun-ishment'; *αἰσχύνη, -ης, ἡ 'shame', 'disgrace'

βοηθέω 'assist'

ἴστε imperative 2 pl. of οἶδα; θεμιτός 'lawful'; ἐξελαύνω 'drive out', 'exile'; ἀτιμόω 'dishonor', 'deprive of civic rights'; ἀποκτείνυμι (ἀποκτιν-νυμι) = ἀποκτείνω

[26. μηδ' ἔτι Τηλεμάχοιο πατὴρ κεκλημένος εἴην.]

    Homer, *Iliad*

27. τὰ δ' ἄλλα σιγῶ· βοῦς ἐπὶ γλώσσῃ μέγας
βέβηκεν· οἶκος δ' αὐτός, εἰ φθογγὴν λά-
βοι,
σαφέστατ' ἂν λέξειεν· ὡς ἑκὼν ἐγὼ
μαθοῦσιν αὐδῶ κοὐ μαθοῦσι λήθομαι.

    Aeschylus, *Agamemnon* (the watchman
    speaks)

28. ὑμεῖς μὲν οὐχ ὁρᾶτε, ἐγὼ δ' ὁρῶ
ἐλαύνομαι δὲ κοὐκέτ' ἂν μείναιμ' ἐγώ.

    Aeschylus, *Choephoroe* (Orestes, upon
    first seeing the Furies)

[29. οὐκ ἂν γένοιτ' ἐρῶντος ἀθλιώτερον
οὐδὲν γέροντος πλὴν ἕτερος γέρων ἐρῶν.]

    Menander

[30. οὐδεὶς ἂν ἐπιορκεῖν βούλοιτο, φοβούμε-
νος τήν τε παρὰ τῶν θεῶν τιμωρίαν καὶ
τὴν παρὰ τοῖς ἀνθρώποις αἰσχύνην.]

    "Aristotle," *Rhetoric to Alexander*

31. εἰ τοὺς ἀδικηθέντας, πάτερ, φευξούμεθα,
τίσιν ἂν βοηθήσαιμεν ἄλλοις ῥᾳδίως;

    Menander

32. εὖ γὰρ ἴστε, ἐὰν ἐμὲ ἀποκτείνητε τοιοῦτον ὄντα οἷον ἐγὼ λέγω, οὐκ ἐμὲ μείζω
βλάψετε ἢ ὑμᾶς αὐτούς· ἐμὲ μὲν γὰρ οὐδὲν ἂν βλάψειεν οὔτε Μέλητος οὔτε Ἄνυ-
τος· οὐδὲ γὰρ ἂν δύναιτο· οὐ γὰρ οἶμαι
θεμιτὸν εἶναι ἀμείνονι ἀνδρὶ ὑπὸ χείρονος βλάπτεσθαι. ἀποκτείνειε μεντἂν ἴσως
ἢ ἐξελάσειεν ἢ ἀτιμώσειεν· ἀλλὰ ταῦτα
οὗτος μὲν ἴσως οἴεται καὶ ἄλλος τίς που
μεγάλα κακά ἐγὼ δ' οὐκ οἴομαι, ἀλλὰ πολὺ
μᾶλλον ποιεῖν ἃ οὗτος νυνὶ ποιεῖ, ἄνδρα
ἀδίκως ἐπιχειρεῖν ἀποκτεινύναι.

    Plato, *Apology*

Quotation

Read and learn this prayer from Plato's *Phaedrus:*

ὦ φίλε Πάν τε καὶ ἄλλοι ὅσοι τῇδε θεοί, δοίητέ μοι καλῷ γενέσθαι τἄνδο-
θεν· ἔξωθεν δὲ ὅσα ἔχω, τοῖς ἐντὸς εἶναί μοι φίλια. πλούσιον δὲ νομίζοιμι τὸν
σοφόν· τὸ δὲ χρυσοῦ πλῆθος εἴη μοι ὅσον μήτε φέρειν μήτε ἄγειν δύναιτο ἄλλος
ἢ ὁ σώφρων.

        ἔνδοθεν '(from) within'; ἔξωθεν '(from) without'

C.   Uses of the Subjunctive and Optative in Subordinate Clauses

Sequence of Moods

        In certain types of subordinate clauses, either the subjunc-
tive or the optative may be used. Which mood is to be used depends upon the tense of the verb in the main clause. The subjunctive, you will remember, has primary endings: it is associated with primary tenses of the indicative; the optative has secondary endings and is used, as a rule, with secondary tenses of
the indicative.

Primary Tenses	Secondary Tenses
present	imperfect
future	aorist
perfect	pluperfect
(future perfect)	
subjunctive (all tenses)	optative (all tenses)

        Some examples:

1.   *Purpose Clauses* express the purpose of the action of the main
verb. These take the subjunctive if the tense of the main verb
is primary, the optative if it is secondary. ἵνα or ὅπως ('in
order that'/'that') is used in this construction. The negative
is μή.

        ἐρχόμεθα ἵνα ταῦτα ποιῶμεν/ποιήσωμεν.
    We are coming so that we may do these things.

        ἤλθομεν ἵνα ταῦτα ποιοῖμεν/ποιήσαιμεν.
    We went so that we might do these things.

(Compare this to the English sequence in:
I go that I *may* . . .
I went that I *might* . . .)

2. *Object Clauses* with μή after verbs of *fearing*:

After verbs of <u>fearing</u>, <u>μή</u> introduces a construction in
which the <u>subjunctive</u> is used if the main verb is of <u>primary</u>
tense, the <u>optative</u> if it is of a <u>secondary</u> tense.   μή in this
type of clause means 'that', 'lest'.   The negative is μὴ οὐ.

φοβούμεθα μὴ αὐτὸν ἴδωμεν.

We fear lest/that we may see him.

φοβούμεθα μὴ οὐκ αὐτὸν ἴδωμεν.

We fear that we may not see him.

ἐφοβούμεθα μὴ οὐκ αὐτὸν ἴδοιμεν.

We feared lest/that we might not see him.

The Optative in Indirect Statement after ὅτι *or* ὡς

After secondary tenses (of the verb of saying), a tense of
the optative may be substituted for the same tense of the indicative after ὅτι or ὡς in indirect statement.

Examples:

εἶπεν ὅτι ταῦτα ποιεῖ. or
εἶπεν ὅτι ταῦτα ποιοίη.

He said that he was doing these things. ('ταῦτα ποιῶ')

εἶπεν ὅτι ταῦτα ποιήσει. or
εἶπεν ὅτι ταῦτα ποιήσοι.

He said that he would do these things. ('ταῦτα ποιήσω')

εἶπεν ὅτι ταῦτα ἐποίησεν. or
εἶπεν ὅτι ταῦτα ποιήσαι/ποιήσειεν.

He said that he had done these things. ('ταῦτα ἐποίησα')

εἶπεν ὅτι ταῦτα πεποίηκεν. or
εἶπεν ὅτι ταῦτα πεποιηκὼς εἴη.

He said that he had done these things. (ʹταῦτα πεποίηκαʹ)

Exercises

1. Write in Greek:

1. Oh, may that wicked man not come!
2. Let us go that we may see the philosopher (wise man).
3. I would like to see her (I would gladly . . .).
4. If you should leave this place, you would not see them.
5. If you leave this place, you will not see them.
6. It would be difficult to know all things well.
7. We went to the philosopher's house that we might learn many fine things.
8. A wise and just man would not say the things which you are saying.
9. If (ever) a man speaks the truth, he is (always) believed by good men.
10. We wrote letters to our absent friends that we might tell them that these things had taken place.
11. He said that he would write. (two forms)
12. We feared that something bad might happen.

Readings

*ἐπιμελέομαι 'take care of', 'pay attention to'; ἀναγκάζω 'force', 'compel'; ἀπὸ στόματος i.e. 'by heart'

1. καὶ ʹὃς εἶπεν· ʹὁ πατὴρ ἐπιμελούμενος ὅπως ἀνὴρ ἀγαθὸς γενοίμην, ἠνάγκασέ με πάντα τὰ ʹΟμήρου ἔπη μαθεῖν· καὶ νῦν δυναίμην ʹἂν Ἰλιάδα ὅλην καὶ ʹΟδύσσειαν ἀπὸ στόματος εἰπεῖν.ʹ

    Xenophon, *Symposium*

ἐπʹ αὐτοφώρῳ 'in the very act', 'red-handed'

2. Lycon has just told the party that the thing he takes most pride in is his son.
    καὶ ὁ Καλλίας ἰδών, ῏Αρʹ οἶσθα, ἔφη, ὦ Λύκων, ὅτι πλουσιώτατος εἶ ἀνθρώπων; Μὰ Δίʹ, ἔφη, τοῦτο μέντοι ἐγὼ οὐκ οἶδα. ʹΑλλὰ λανθάνει σε ὅτι οὐκ ʹἂν δέξοιο τὰ βασιλέως χρήματα ἀντὶ τοῦ υἱοῦ; ʹΕπʹ αὐτοφώρῳ εἴλημμαι, ἔφη, πλουσιώτατος ὡς ἔοικεν, ἀνθρώπων ὤν.

    Xenophon, *Symposium*

ἦ δ' ὅς 'said he'

κόσμιος, -ον 'well-ordered'; εὔ-κολος, -ον 'good-natured'; ἐπί-πονος, -ον 'painful'; γῆρας, τό 'old age'; νεότης, νεότητος, ἡ 'youth'; *συμβαίνω 'happen', 'meet', 'result'

προοράω 'foresee'

τηνικάδε 'so early' (adv.); ἥκω 'have come', 'be present'; πρῴην 'the day before yesterday'; ἄρτι 'just now'; ἦ δ' ὅς see #3; ἦν δ' ἐγώ 'said I'

φλυαρέω 'talk nonsense'; μειρά-κιον, -ου, τό 'lad'; *οὖς, ὠτός, τό 'ear'

*πόσις (no genitive), ὁ 'hus-band', 'spouse'

δίδασχ' imperative; ἱκάνω 'I have come'; δέμας, τό 'body' (only in nom. & acc.); *σπουδαῖ-ος, -α, -ον 'serious', 'good'; ὄψις, -εως, ἡ 'sight', 'appear-ance'; μορφή, -ῆς, ἡ 'form'; που (encl.) 'anywhere', 'somewhere'

[3. Ἦ καὶ δύναισθ' ἄν, ἦ δ' ὅς, πεῖσαι μὴ ἀκούοντας;]

Plato, *Republic*

[4. ἂν μὲν γὰρ κόσμιοι καὶ εὔκολοι ὦσι, καὶ τὸ γῆρας μετρίως ἐστὶν ἐπίπονον· εἰ δὲ μή, καὶ γῆρας, ὦ Σώκρατες, καὶ νεότης χαλεπὴ τῷ τοιούτῳ ξυμβαίνει.]

Plato, *Republic*

5. οὐδὲ τῶν πραγμάτων προορᾶτε οὐδὲν πρὶν ἂν ἢ γεγενημένον ἢ γιγνόμενόν τι πύ-θησθε.

Demosthenes

[6. Hippocrates has just arrived at Socra-tes' house, waking him before dawn with the exciting news:
Socrates. μή τι νεώτερον ἀγγέλλεις;
   Οὐδέν γ', ἦ δ' ὅς, εἰ μὴ ἀγαθά γε.
   Εὖ ἂν λέγοις, ἦν δ' ἐγώ· ἔστι δὲ τί, καὶ τοῦ ἕνεκα τηνικάδε ἀφίκου;
   Πρωταγόρας, ἔφη, ἥκει, στὰς παρ' ἐμοι.
   Πρῴην, ἔφην ἐγώ· σὺ δὲ ἄρτι πέπυσαι;]

Plato, *Protagoras*

7. ἀνὴρ πονηρὸς δυστυχεῖ κἂν εὐτυχῇ.

Menander

8. πρὸς τὸ φλυαροῦν μειράκιον, 'διὰ τοῦτο,' εἶπε, 'δύο ὦτα ἔχομεν, στόμα δὲ ἕν, ἵνα πλείονα μὲν ἀκούωμεν, ἥττονα δὲ λέγω-μεν.'

Diogenes Laertius (Zeno)

9. ταῦτ' οὖν φοβοῦμαι μὴ πόσις μὲν Ἡρακλῆς ἐμὸς καλῆται, τῆς νεωτέρας δ' ἀνήρ.

Sophocles, *Trachiniae* (Deianeira speaking)

[10. Theseus and Oedipus
Th. τοῦτ' αὐτὸ νῦν δίδασχ' ὅπως 'ἂν ἐκ-μάθω.
Oed. δώσων ἱκάνω τοὐμὸν ἄθλιον δέμας σοὶ δῶρον, οὐ σπουδαῖον εἰς ὄψιν· τὰ δὲ κέρδη παρ' αὐτοῦ κρείσσον' ἢ μορφὴ καλή.
Th. ποῖον δὲ κέρδος ἀξιοῖς ἥκειν φέρων;
Oed. χρόνῳ μάθοις ἄν, οὐχὶ τῷ παρόντι

που.]

Sophocles, *Oedipus at Colonus*

*κρύπτω 'hide'; στόλος, -ου, ὁ
'expedition'; στενάζω 'groan'
(imperative)

11. Philoctetes and Neoptolemus
    Ph. τί ποτε λέγεις, ὦ τέκνον; ὡς οὐ μαν-
         θάνω.
    Ν. οὐδέν σε κρύψω· δεῖ γὰρ ἐς Τροίαν σε
         πλεῖν
    πρὸς τοὺς Ἀχαιοὺς καὶ τὸν Ἀτρειδῶν
         στόλον.
    Ph. οἴμοι, τί εἶπας;
                            Ν. μὴ στέναζε, πρὶν
         μάθῃς.
    Ph. ποῖον μάθημα; τί με νοεῖς δρᾶσαί
         ποτε;

Sophocles, *Philoctetes*

Θετταλία, -ας, ἡ 'Thessaly';
ἀπολαύω 'enjoy', 'profit'; αὐτοῦ
(adv.) 'here', 'there'; ἀποδημάω
'go abroad'; ἐπιτήδειος, -ου, ὁ
(as noun) 'close friend'; ἐκθρέ-
ψῃς: ἐκ + τρέφω; εἰς Ἅιδου 'to
(the house of) Hades'

12. λόγοι δὲ ἐκεῖνοι οἱ περὶ δικαιοσύνης τε
    καὶ τῆς ἄλλης ἀρετῆς ποῦ ἡμῖν ἔσονται;
    ἀλλὰ δὴ τῶν παίδων ἕνεκα βούλει ζῆν, ἵνα
    αὐτοὺς ἐκθρέψῃς καὶ παιδεύσῃς. τί δέ
    εἰς Θετταλίαν αὐτοὺς ἀγαγὼν θρέψεις τε
    καὶ παιδεύσεις, ξένους ποιήσας, ἵνα καὶ
    τοῦτο ἀπολαύσωσιν; ἢ τοῦτο μὲν οὔ, αὐ-
    τοῦ δὲ τρεφόμενοι σοῦ ζῶντος βέλτιον
    θρέψονται καὶ παιδεύσονται, μὴ ξυνόντος
    σοῦ αὐτοῖς; οἱ γὰρ ἐπιτήδειοι οἱ σοὶ
    ἐπιμελήσονται αὐτῶν. πότερον ἐὰν εἰς
    Θετταλίαν ἀποδημήσῃς, ἐπιμελήσονται, ἐὰν
    δὲ εἰς Ἅιδου ἀποδημήσῃς, οὐχὶ ἐπιμελή-
    σονται;

Plato, *Crito*

χάριν οἶδα 'be grateful'; ἀκούετε imperative (2nd pl.)

[13. Socrates. . . . καὶ χάριν γε εἴσομαι,
     ἐὰν ἀκούητε.
     Friend. καὶ μὴν καὶ ἡμεῖς σοί, ἐὰν
     λέγῃς.
     Socrates. διπλῆ 'ἂν εἴη ἡ χάρις. ἀλλ'
     οὖν ἀκούετε.]

Plato, *Protagoras*

πρότερος, -α, -ον 'before',
'earlier'

14. "Ask a foolish question . . ."
    πρὸς τὸν πυθόμενον τί πρότερον γεγό-
    νοι, νὺξ 'ἢ ἡμέρα, 'ἡ νύξ,' ἔφη, 'μιᾷ
    ἡμέρᾳ πρότερον.'

Diogenes Laertius (Thales)

15. ἔλεγέ τε τοὺς μὲν ἄλλους ἀνθρώπους ζῆν
    ἵν' ἐσθίοιεν· αὐτὸς δὲ ἐσθίειν ἵνα ζῴη.

Diogenes Laertius (Socrates)

*ἄφρων, -ον (gen. -ονος) 'fool-
ish', 'witless'; κοῦφος, -η, -ον
'light'; νόος = νοῦς

16. ἄφρονος ἀνδρὸς ὁμῶς καὶ σώφρονος οἶνος
       ὅταν δὴ
    πίνῃ ὑπὲρ μέτρον, κοῦφον ἔθηκε νόον.

    Theognis

τοι 'you know', 'for your information'; κόρος, -ου, ὁ 'satie-
ty', 'surfeit; ὄλβος, -ου, ὁ
'happiness', 'wealth'; *ἕπομαι
'follow'; ἄρτιος, -α, -ον 'complete', 'perfect', 'just right'

17. τίκτει τοι κόρος ὕβριν, ὅταν κακῷ ὄλβος
       ἕπηται
    ἀνθρώπῳ, καὶ ὅτῳ μὴ νόος ἄρτιος ᾖ.

    Theognis

λήθω = λανθάνω

18. ἠρώτησέ τις αὐτὸν εἰ λήθοι θεοὺς ἄνθρω-
    πος ἀδικῶν· 'ἀλλ' οὐδὲ διανοούμενος,'
    ἔφη.

    Diogenes Laertius (Thales)

γαμβρός, -οῦ, ὁ 'brother-in-
law', "in-law"; φωνέω 'speak';
ῥύομαι 'rescue'

[19. . . . παῖδα γὰρ Μενοικέως
    Κρέοντ', ἐμαυτοῦ γαμβρόν, ἐς τὰ Πυθικὰ
    ἔπεμψα Φοίβου δώμαθ' ὡς πύθοθ' ὅ τι
    δρῶν ἢ τί φωνῶν τήνδε ῥυσαίμην πόλιν.]

    Sophocles, *Oedipus Tyrannus* (Oedipus
    speaking)

μεμπτός, -ή, -όν 'to be blamed'

[20. Agamemnon and Clytemnestra
    Cl. Θέτις δ' ἔθρεψεν ἢ πατὴρ Ἀχιλλέα;
    Ag. Χείρων ἵν' ἤθη μὴ μάθοι κακῶν βροτῶν.
    Cl. φεῦ
         σοφός γ' ὁ θρέψας χὠ διδοὺς σοφώτε-
           ρος.
    Ag. τοιόσδε παιδὸς σῆς ἀνὴρ ἔσται πόσις.
    Cl. οὐ μεμπτός. οἰκεῖ δ' ἄστυ ποῖον
         Ἑλλάδος;]

    Euripides, *Iphigenia at Aulis*

LESSON XIV

A. *The Imperative Mood*

One last mood of the Greek verb remains to be studied: the imperative. Its meaning is simple enough: it gives an order (makes a command) or issues a prohibition. It is found in three tenses: present, aorist and perfect. All commands refer to the future time, and so, once more, the tenses of the imperative refer to aspect rather than time. The imperative is not augmented.

Present Imperative: 'Do it: keep on doing, be doing!'

Aorist: 'Do it (once)!'

Perfect: 'Get it done!' It expresses a command that should be *decisive* or *permanent*. (The perfect Imperative is very rare.)

The imperative is found in the second and third persons: (you) 'do it!'; 'let him/her/them do it!'; 'let it be done!' There is no first person imperative, the hortatory subjunctive ('let's do it!') being used instead.

The negative used with the imperative is μή. But μή with the aorist subjunctive is used instead of the aorist imperative. That is to say: for a prohibition, use:

μή + the present imperative *or*

μή + the aorist subjunctive

Forms of the imperative:

Endings:

	Active	Middle

Singular

2nd	- (-θι)	-σο
3rd	-τω	-σθω

Plural

2nd	-τε	-σθε
3rd	-ντων	-σθων

Imperatives of -ω verbs (endings with thematic vowel)

Present	(Active)		(Middle)	
λῦε	(-ε)	2nd	λύου	(-ου)(←ε-σο)
λυέτω	(-ετω)	3rd	λυέσθω	(-εσθω)
λύετε	(-ετε)	2nd	λύεσθε	(-εσθε)
λυόντων	(-οντων)	3rd	λυέσθων	(-εσθων)

First Aorist Imperative   Aorist Passive

Active	Middle		
λῦσον	λῦσαι	2nd	λύθητι
λυσάτω	λυσάσθω	3rd	λυθήτω
λύσατε	λύσασθε	2nd	λύθητε
λυσάντων	λυσάσθων	3rd	λυθέντων

Second Aorist Imperative

λίπε	λιποῦ	2nd
λιπέτω	λιπέσθω	3rd
λίπετε	λίπεσθε	2nd
λιπόντων	λιπέσθων	3rd

(For Perfect Imperative, see Appendix.)

The Imperatives of Contract Verbs follow the rules for contraction. The endings with thematic vowel as given with the present of λύω are the ones to be used for the present of contract
verbs. Form the imperatives of the contract verbs νικάω, φιλέω,
δηλόω, and check your results against the forms given in the appendix.

The Present Imperative of εἰμί

2nd	ἴσθι
3rd	ἔστω
2nd	ἔστε
3rd	ἔστων *or* ὄντων

(For the imperatives of the other -μι verbs, see appendix.)

Note on the endings of the imperative:

The only forms of the imperative which will present any difficulty are the second person singular forms. The others are easily recognizable from their distinctive endings which are added with the thematic vowel in thematic tenses, or directly to the stem in non-thematic forms. The second plural of the present is identical to the second plural indicative, but in most instances the context will tell which is intended.

The second singular:

Active and Passive: The original ending of the second person singular active imperative is -θι: this is retained in the -μι verbs and in the aorist passive (but changes to -τι after θη-). The thematic tenses of -ω verbs (present and second aorist) have only the thematic vowel -ε as ending. The first aorist has -ον in the active.

Middle: The middle second person singular imperative ending is -σο. In the thematic tenses, σ drops out: εσο → εο → ου. The -μι verbs usually retain the σ. The first aorist has -αι.

Note: An imperative (or hortatory subjunctive) may be strengthened by having ἄγε, φέρε, ἴθι (the present active second singular imperatives of ἄγω, φέρω, εἶμι 'go') precede it. They can be translated as "come!" or "come on!"

The Vocative Case

The vocative case is used when addressing a person directly.

The first declension -η or -α types, all neuters, and all plurals (of any declension) have vocatives like the nominative.

ὦ ἄνδρες Ἀθηναῖοι	gentlemen of Athens!
ὦ Μοῦσα	Oh Muse!
ὦ δόξα, δόξα	Ah reputation, reputation!

The first declension masculines in -ης or -ας have vocative singular in -α. Those in -της have short -ᾰ: most others have long -ᾱ.)

ὦ πολῖτα (-ᾰ)

ὦ νεανία (-ᾱ)

The second declension nouns in -ος have vocative in -ε.

ὦ ἄνθρωπε   sir!

The third declension vocative singular presents some variety.

It is sometimes the same as the nominative and sometimes the same as the base.

Most nouns ending in a mute (except those in -ιδ-), in a nasal or liquid (if accented on the ultima) have vocative like the nominative.

ὦ φύλαξ

ὦ ποιμήν

Most others have vocative like the base:

ὦ δαῖμον	(δαίμων)	
ὦ ἐλπί	(ἐλπίς)	(base ἐλπιδ-)
ὦ παῖ	(παῖς)	(base παιδ-)
ὦ πόλι	(πόλις)	(base πολι-)
ὦ Σώκρατες	(Σωκράτης)	
ὦ πάτερ	(πατήρ)	
ὦ ἄνερ	(ἀνήρ)	

Exercises

1. Fill in the imperative forms of the synopses given in previous lessons.

2. Form all the imperatives of

    1. παύω
    2. ὁράω
    3. ποιέω

Readings

1. ἢ λέγε τι σιγῆς κρεῖττον ἢ σιγὴν ἔχε.

    Menander

σμικρός = μικρός; subject of ἔφη is Euthydemus; ἐγώ = Socrates

2. φέρε δή μοι ἀπόκριναι, ἔφη· ἔστιν ὅ τι ἐπίστασαι; πάνυ γε ἦν δ᾽ ἐγώ, καὶ πολλά, σμικρά γε.

    Plato, *Euthydemus*

ἔστω often used in definitions; *ἕνεκα prep. with gen., 'for the sake of', 'on account of'

[3. ἔστω δὴ τὸ φιλεῖν τὸ βούλεσθαί τινι ἃ οἴεται ἀγαθά, ἐκείνου ἕνεκα ἀλλὰ μὴ αὑτοῦ.]

ὅρκος, -ου, ὁ 'oath'; πιστός,
-ή, -όν 'true', 'trusty'; ψεύδομαι 'lie', 'speak falsely'; ὁμι-
λέω 'associate with'; *αἰδέομαι
'respect', 'be ashamed'; γονεύς,
-εως, ὁ 'father', pl. 'parents';
καλοκἀγαθία = the character and
conduct of one who is καλὸς καὶ
ἀγαθός (καλοκἀγαθός by crasis)

Aristotle, *Rhetoric*

4. καλοκἀγαθίαν ὅρκου πιστοτέρον ἔχε. μὴ
   ψεύδου . . . ἄρχε πρῶτον μαθὼν ἄρχεσθαι.
   συμβούλευε μὴ τὰ ἥδιστα ἀλλὰ τὰ ἄριστα.
   νοῦν ἡγεμόνα ποιοῦ. μὴ κακοῖς ὁμίλει.
   θεοὺς τίμα, γονέας αἰδοῦ.

Diogenes Laertius (Solon)

ὑπολαμβάνω 'suppose', 'inter-
pose'; *διαβολή, ἡ 'slander';
πόθεν 'whence', 'from where';
αὐτοσχεδιάζω 'judge unadvised-
ly'; ταυτί = ταῦτα; *πειράομαι
'try'; παίζω 'play', 'jest',
'joke'; ἐρῶ 'I shall tell'

5. ὑπολάβοι 'ἂν οὖν τις ὑμῶν ἴσως· ἀλλ', ὦ
   Σώκρατες, τὸ σὸν τί ἐστι πρᾶγμα; πόθεν
   αἱ διαβολαί σοι αὗται γεγόνασιν; . . .
   λέγε οὖν ἡμῖν τί ἐστιν, ἵνα μὴ ἡμεῖς
   περὶ σοῦ αὐτοσχεδιάζωμεν. ταυτί μοι
   δοκεῖ δίκαια λέγειν ὁ λέγων, κἀγὼ ὑμῖν
   πειράσομαι ἀποδεῖξαι, τί ποτ' ἔστιν τοῦτο ὃ ἐμοὶ πεποίηκε τό τε ὄνομα καὶ τὴν
   διαβολήν. ἀκούετε δή. καὶ ἴσως μὲν δόξω τισὶν ὑμῶν παίζειν, εὖ μέντοι ἴστε,
   πᾶσαν ὑμῖν τὴν ἀλήθειαν ἐρῶ. ἐγὼ γὰρ,
   ὦ ἄνδρες Ἀθηναῖοι, δι' οὐδὲν ἀλλ' ἢ
   διὰ σοφίαν τινὰ τοῦτο τὸ ὄνομα ἔσχηκα.

Plato, *Apology*

σχολάζω 'have leisure'; ἀντιλέγω
'speak against', 'dispute'; *μέλει '(it) is a care to' (+ dat.);
διαλύω 'release', 'reconcile';
ἀπολούμενος 'villain', 'scoun-
drel' (fut. mid. pt. of ἀπόλλυμι);
περιπατέω 'walk around'; διφθέρα
'leather clothes' (as peasants
wore'; ἐπικρατέω 'rule over'; ἁ-
πανταχοῦ 'everywhere'; παρατυγχά-
νω 'be present at', 'happen
along'; πρόνοια, -ας, ἡ 'fore-
thought'; ἐμμένω 'stand by'; *καταφρονέω 'despise'; δικάζω 'judge',
'decide' ('for' + dat.)

[6. Syriscus, Smicrines, Daos
Syr.   πρὸς τῶν θεῶν,
    βέλτιστε, μικρὸν 'ἂν σχολάσαις ἡμῖν
        χρόνον;
Sm.   ὑμῖν; περὶ τίνος;
Syr. ἀντιλέγομεν πρᾶγμά τι.
Sm.   τί οὖν ἐμοὶ μέλει;
Syr.   κριτὴν τούτου τινὰ
    ζητοῦμεν ἴσον· εἰ δή σε μηδὲν κωλύει,
    διάλυσον ἡμᾶς.
Sm.   ὦ κάκιστ' ἀπολούμενοι
    δίκας λέγοντες περιπατεῖτε, διφθέρας
    ἔχοντες;
Syr.   ἀλλ' ὅμως--τὸ πρᾶγμ' ἐστὶν
    βραχὺ
    καὶ ῥᾴδιον μαθεῖν, πάτερ,--δὸς τὴν
        χάριν.
    μὴ καταφρονήσῃς πρὸς θεῶν. ἐν παντὶ
        δεῖ
    καιρῷ τὸ δίκαιον ἐπικρατεῖν ἀπανταχοῦ,
    καὶ τὸν παρατυγχάνοντα τούτου τοῦ μέ-
        ρους
    ἔχειν πρόνοιαν· κοινόν ἐστι τῷ βίῳ
    πάντων.

. . . .   Sm.   ἐμμενεῖτ' οὖν, εἰπέ μοι,
οἷς 'ἂν δικάσω.
                        πάντως.
              ἀκούσομαι· τί γὰρ
τὸ κωλῦον; σὺ πρότερος, ὁ σιωπῶν λέγε.]

Menander

*αὖθις (adv.) 'again'; πρόβατον, -ου, τό 'sheep'; τράγος, -ου, ὁ 'goat'; εἱμαρμένος, -η, -ον 'decreed by fate'; βιόω aor. ἐβίωσα or ἐβίων (irreg. 2 aor.) 'live'; *εὐθύς, -εῖα, -ύ 'straight', 'direct'; εὐθύς, εὐθύ (as adverb) 'at once'

7. εἴ τις προσελθών μοι θεῶν λέγοι, 'Κρά-
τ́ων,
ἐπὰν ἀποθάνῃς, αὖθις ἐξ ἀρχῆς ἔσει·
ἔσει δ' ὅ τι 'ἂν βούλῃ, κύων, πρόβατον,
τράγος,
ἄνθρωπος, ἵππος· δὶς βιῶναι γάρ σε δεῖ·
εἱμαρμένον τοῦτ' ἐστίν, ὅ τι βούλει δ'
ἑλοῦ·'
'ἅπαντα μᾶλλον,' εὐθὺς εἰπεῖν 'ἂν δοκῶ,
'ποίει με πλὴν ἄνθρωπον· ἀδίκως εὐτυχεῖ
κακῶς τε πράττει τοῦτο τὸ ζῷον μόνον.

Menander

ἄρκτος, ὁ/ἡ 'bear'; ἴχνος, -ους, τό 'track'

8. ἄρκτου παρούσης ἴχνη μὴ ζήτει.

Bacchylides

συνηβάω 'be young with'; συστε-φανηφορέω 'wear a crown with'; σωφρονέω 'be sober'

[9. σύν μοι πῖνε, συνήβα, συστεφανηφόρει
σύν μοι μαινομένῳ μαίνεο, σὺν σώφρονι
σωφρόνει.]

Attic Scolion

10. μῆτερ, πάρειμι· τὴν χάριν δὲ σοὶ δίδους
ἦλθον. τί χρὴ δρᾶν; ἀρχέτω δέ τις λόγου.

Euripides, *Phoenissae*

δουλεύω 'be a slave'; ἐπιθυμία, -ας, ἡ 'desire', 'lust'

[11. ἄρχε σαυτοῦ μηδὲν ἧττον 'ἢ τῶν ἄλλων,
καὶ τοῦθ' ἡγοῦ βασιλικώτατον, 'ἂν μηδε-
μίᾳ δουλεύῃς τῶν ἡδονῶν ἀλλὰ κρατῇς τῶν
ἐπιθυμιῶν μᾶλλον 'ἢ τῶν πολιτῶν.]

Isocrates, *Nicocles*

προσδοκάω 'expect', 'think'

12. πιστεύω γὰρ δίκαια εἶναι 'ἃ λέγω καὶ μη-
δεὶς ὑμῶν προσδοκησάτω ἄλλως.

Plato, *Apology*

κριθή, -ῆς, ἡ 'barley'

13. A charm to cure styes: take nine barley-corns, prick the stye with each, saying:

φεῦγε, φεῦγε· / κριθή σε διώκει.

ὕει 'it is raining'; ὗσον aor.
imper. 'rain!'; ἄρουρα, -ας, ἡ
'cornland'; Πεδιῶν refers to the
plain of Attica

14. ὗσον, ὗσον, ὦ φίλε Ζεῦ,
    κατὰ τῆς ἀρούρας τῆς Ἀθηνῶν
    καὶ κατὰ τῆς Πεδιῶν.

    A Folk-Song

'ταῖρε = ἑταῖρε; σκορπίος, ἡ
'scorpion'; φυλάσσεο = φυλάττου

15. ὑπὸ παντὶ λίθῳ σκορπίον, ὦ 'ταῖρε φυλάσ-
    σεο.

    Praxilla

[16. 'ἐπὶ τοῦτ' ἐλήλυθα, ἐπὶ τὸν ἄρχοντα ὑμῶν
    ἀγάγετέ με.']

    Eusebius (John the evangelist to the
    young robber)

ἐντολή, -ῆς, ἡ 'commandment';
διάβολος, -ου, ὁ 'the devil'

17. φοβήθητι, φησί, τὸν κύριον καὶ φύλασσε
    τὰς ἐντολὰς αὐτοῦ.
    τὸν δὲ διάβολον μὴ φοβηθῇς.
    φοβήθητι δὲ τὰ ἔργα τοῦ διαβόλου, ὅτι
    πονηρά ἐστι.

    The Shepherd of Hermas

18. πρῶτον πάντων πίστευσον, ὅτι εἷς ἐστιν
    ὁ θεός.

    The Shepherd of Hermas

19. ἀλλ' εἰπὲ πᾶν τἀληθές.

    Sophocles, *Trachiniae*

προσδέχομαι 'receive'

[20. ὦ φίλτατ' ἀνδρῶν, πρῶθ' ἃ πρῶτα βούλο-
                                    μαι
    δίδαξον, εἰ ζῶνθ' Ἡρακλῆ προσδέξομαι.]

    Sophocles, *Trachiniae*

21. ἔστω δὴ τὸ ἀδικεῖν τὸ βλάπτειν ἑκόντα
    παρὰ τὸν νόμον.

    Aristotle, *Rhetoric*

*φρήν, φρενός, ἡ 'heart',
'mind'; φόβος, -ου, ὁ 'fear'

22. μέμνησο, μὴ φόβος σε νικάτω φρένας.

    Aeschylus, *Eumenides*

μίμνω = μένω; ἐϋκνήμιδες Ἀχαιοί
'well-greaved Achaeans'; εἰς ὅ
'until'; *αὐτοῦ 'here'; κεν = ἄν

[23. 'ἀλλ' ἄγε, μίμνετε πάντες, ἐϋκνήμιδες
                          Ἀχαιοί
    αὐτοῦ, εἰς ὅ κεν ἄστυ μέγα Πριάμοιο ἕλω-
                          μεν.']

    Homer, *Iliad* (Odysseus)

βαδίζω 'go', 'walk'

24. καὶ βάδιζε μετ᾽ εἰρήνης.

Eusebius

*μνημονεύω 'remember'; προσευχή, -ῆς, ἡ 'prayer'

25. μνημονεύετε μου ἐν ταῖς προσευχαῖς ὑμῶν.

Ignatius

26. ὑμεῖς δὲ ἀγαπᾶτε τοὺς μισοῦντας ὑμᾶς, καὶ οὐχ ἕξετε ἐχθρόν.

Didache

ὁ πλησίον 'one's neighbor'

27. ἡ μὲν οὖν ὁδὸς τῆς ζωῆς ἐστιν αὕτη· πρῶ-τον ἀγαπήσεις τὸν θεὸν τὸν ποιήσαντά σε, δεύτερον τὸν πλησίον σου, ὡς σεαυτόν· πάντα δὲ ὅσα ἐὰν θελήσῃς μὴ γίνεσθαί σοι, καὶ σὺ ἄλλῳ μὴ ποίει.

Didache (Teaching of the Twelve Apos-tles)

ἴτε imper. of εἶμι 'go', 'come'; ἐλευθερόω 'set free'; πατρῷος 'of/from the father'; ἕδος, -ους, τό 'seat', 'abode'; θήκη, -ης, ἡ 'grave'; πρόγονος, -ου, ὁ 'ancestor'

28. ὦ παῖδες Ἑλλήνων ἴτε ἐλευθεροῦτε πατρίδ᾽, ἐλευθεροῦτε δὲ παῖδας, γυναῖκας, θεῶν τε πατρῴων ἕδη θήκας τε προγόνων, νῦν ὑπὲρ πάντων ἀγών.

Aeschylus, *Persae*

παίγνιον, -ου, τό 'plaything', 'game'; μετατίθημι 'change', 'retract', 'change from'; σπου-δή, -ῆς, ἡ 'haste', 'serious-ness'; ὀδύνη, -ης, ἡ 'pain', 'grief'

[29. σκηνὴ πᾶς ὁ βίος καὶ παίγνιον· ἢ μάθε παίζειν, τὴν σπουδὴν μεταθείς, ἢ φέρε τὰς ὀδύ-νας.]

Palladas (Anthology)

σκοπέω 'look for'

30. σκόπει δέ με ἐξ ἐμαυτοῦ.

Diogenes Laertius (Bion)

ξεῖν᾽ = ξένε; τῇδε 'here', 'in this place'; κείνων = ἐκείνων; ῥῆμα, -ατος, τό 'word'

31. In memory of the Spartans who died at Thermopylae

ὦ ξεῖν᾽, ἄγγειλον Λακεδαιμονίοις ὅτι τῇδε κείμεθα, τοῖς κείνων ῥήμασι πειθόμενοι.

Simonides

32. χάριτας δικαίας καὶ δίδου καὶ λάμβανε.

Menander

μηδέποτε 'never'

33. κέρδος πονηρὸν μηδέποτε βούλου λαβεῖν.

Menander

*ἐπιλανθάνομαι 'forget'

34. χάριν λαβὼν μέμνησο καὶ δοὺς ἐπιλάθου.
    Menander

ποτέ 'at some time', 'some day'

35. μέμνησο νέος 'ὢν ὡς γέρων ἔσῃ ποτέ.
    Menander

πανήγυρις, -εως, ἡ 'festival'

36. πανήγυριν νόμιζε τόνδε τὸν βίον.
    Menander

θησαυρός, -οῦ, ὁ 'treasure'

37. φίλους ἔχων νόμιζε θησαυροὺς ἔχειν.
    Menander

προίξ, -ῖκος, ἡ 'gift', 'dowry'

38. γάμει δὲ μὴ τὴν προῖκα, τὴν γυναῖκα δέ.
    Menander

ὅρκος, -ου, ὁ 'oath'; *φαῦλος, -η, -ον 'cheap', 'petty', 'bad'

39. ἀνδρῶν δὲ φαύλων ὅρκον εἰς ὕδωρ γράφε.
    Menander

40. αἰσχρὸν δὲ μηδὲν πρᾶττε μηδὲ μάνθανε.
    Menander

σωτήρ, -ῆρος, ὁ 'savior', 'deliverer'

41. Ζεῦ σῶτερ, εἴπερ ἐστὶ δυνατόν, σῷζέ με.
    Menander

*πύλη, -ης, ἡ 'gate'; κλείω 'close'; ἐξ + ἔρχομαι; θεάομαι '(to) view'

42. εἰς Μύνδον ἐλθὼν καὶ θεασάμενος μεγάλας τὰς πύλας, μικρὰν δὲ τὴν πόλιν, 'ἄνδρες Μύνδιοι,' ἔφη, 'κλείσατε τὰς πύλας, μὴ ἡ πόλις ὑμῶν ἐξέλθῃ.'
    Diogenes Laertius (Diogenes)

πηλίκος, -η, -ον 'how great'; νικάω 'surpass'

43. "Look upon my works, ye mighty, and despair."
'βασιλεὺς βασιλέων 'Οσυμανδύας εἰμί. εἰ δέ τις εἰδέναι βούλεται πηλίκος εἰμὶ καὶ ποῦ κεῖμαι, νικάτω τι τῶν ἐμῶν ἔργων.'
    Diodorus Siculus

Saying

δός που στῶ καὶ τὴν γῆν κινήσω.

Give (me) a place to stand and I will move the earth.
    --Archimedes

B. Verbals in -τέος, -τέον

Verbal adjectives ending in -τέος, -τέον are derived from verb stems (mostly from the aorist passive stem, omitting the -θη; but some from the present stem).

ποιητέος   (ἐποιήθην)

ἀκουστέος   (ἠκούσθην)

They express necessity and are used with the dative of agent. The neuter is used as an impersonal.

ἐμοὶ ἀκουστέον It is necessary for me to hear . . .

ποιητέον   It must be done . . .

Readings

τὸ γνῶθι σαυτόν see p. 203, #5

1. τὸ γνῶθι σαυτόν ἐστιν, 'ἂν τὰ πράγματα εἰδῇς τὰ σαυτοῦ καὶ τί σοι ποιητέον.

    Menander

κἄγωγ' = καὶ ἔγωγε

2. Herdsman.
οἴμοι, πρὸς αὐτῷ γ' εἰμὶ δεινῷ λέγειν.
Oedipus.
κἄγωγ' ἀκούειν· ἀλλ' ὅμως ἀκουστέον.

    Sophocles, *Oedipus Tyrannus*

ἀδυνατέω 'lack the ability (to do . . .)'

[3. . . . ἀλλ' εἰ δρᾶν τοῦθ' ἡμεῖς ἀδυνατοῦμεν, σοὶ δραστέον· ὑπέσχου.]

    Plato, *Philebus*

μόριον, -ου, τό 'part'; *συμβαίνει 'meets', 'has to do with'; ἐπὶ τὸ πολύ 'for the most part'; μνημονικός, -όν 'of good memory'; ἀναμνηστικός, -όν 'able to recall to mind readily'; εὐμαθής, -ές 'quick to learn'; μνημονεύω 'remember'; ἀναμιμνήσκω 'recollect'

[4. περὶ μνήμης καὶ τοῦ μνημονεύειν λεκτέον τί ἐστι, καὶ διὰ τίν' αἰτίαν γίγνεται, καὶ τίνι τῶν τῆς ψυχῆς μορίων συμβαίνει τοῦτο τὸ πάθος καὶ τὸ ἀναμιμνήσκεσθαι· οὐ γὰρ οἱ αὐτοί εἰσι μνημονικοὶ καὶ ἀναμνηστικοί, ἀλλ' ὡς ἐπὶ τὸ πολὺ μνημονικώτεροι μὲν οἱ βραδεῖς, ἀναμνηστικώτεροι δὲ οἱ ταχεῖς καὶ εὐμαθεῖς.]

    Aristotle, περὶ μνήμης

*δικαστήριον, -ου, τό 'court'; *πανταχοῦ 'everywhere'; βιάζομαι 'do violence to'; *ὅσιος, -α, -ον 'sanctioned by the law of nature'; ᾗ 'in what (course)'

5. ἀλλα καὶ ἐν πολέμῳ καὶ ἐν δικαστηρίῳ καὶ πανταχοῦ ποιητέον, 'ἃ 'ἂν κελεύῃ ἡ πόλις καὶ ἡ πατρίς, 'ἢ πείθειν αὐτὴν ᾗ τὸ δίκαιον πέφυκε, βιάζεσθαι δὲ οὐχ ὅσιον μητέρα οὔτε πατέρα, πολὺ δὲ τούτων ἔτι ἧτ-

τον τὴν πατρίδα;

Plato, *Crito*

6. ἤδη σοι τέλος ἐχέτω ὁ λόγος.

Plato, *Phaedrus*

Saying:

μὴ εἰς τὴν αὔριον ἀναβάλλου· ἡ γὰρ αὔριον οὐδέ ποτε
λαμβάνει τέλος.

Do not put off until tomorrow; for tomorrow never
admits fulfillment.

--St. John Chrysostom

Translate the following, and rejoice:

τὸ δὲ τέλος μέγιστον ἀπάντων.

--Aristotle, *Poetics*

APPENDICES

APPENDIX I: CASE DECLENSION

Adjectives, Article, Nouns, Participles, Pronouns

A. *Indices*

B. *The Cases*

For fuller descriptions and more examples, the student is directed to Herbert Weir Smyth, *Greek Grammar* (revised by Gordon M. Messing) and to William Watson Goodwin, *Greek Grammar* (revised by Charles Burton Gulick); and for diversion to Basil L. Gildersleeve, "A Sexual System of the Cases," *American Journal of Philology* 36, p. 108ff.

The examples are taken from Plato's *Euthyphro* and Euripides' *Alcestis* (unless otherwise noted).

The Nominative Case

1. The most common nominative endings are:

> First declension: -η, -α, -(τ)ης, -ας, -αι
> Second declension: -ος, -ον; -οι, -α
> Third declension: -ς (-ξ, -ψ), -ων, -ος, -(μ)α; -ες,
>   -α (-η), (-εις)

2. Uses

a. The *subject* of a finite verb is nominative (p. 35). A finite verb is one in which the ending defines the person, as in the indicative, subjunctive, optative, and imperative (which have personal endings), as opposed to the infinitive.

Examples:

(1) ἀπωλόμεσθα πάντες, οὐ κείνη μόνη. --*Alcestis* 825

We are all lost, not she only.

Notes: -μεσθα = -μεθα
        κεῖνος, -η, -ο = ἐκεῖνος, -η, -ο

(2) ἢ σκεπτέον τί λέγει ὁ λέγων; --*Euthyphro* 3c

Or is it necessary to examine what the sayer (speaker) is saying (i.e., means)?

Note: σκεπτέον verbal, see p. 322

(3) Ὦ φίλε Εὐθύφρων, ἀλλὰ τὸ μὲν καταγελασθῆναι ἴσως οὐδὲν πρᾶγμα. --*Euthyphro* 3c

My dear Euthyphro, perhaps being laughed down is no matter.

Notes: τὸ καταγελασθῆναι is an articular infinitive (pp. 71-75)
        The verb of the sentence, ἐστί, is omitted.

(4) ἔσται τάδ᾽ ἔσται. --*Alcestis* 327

These things will be, (they) will be.

Note: the neuter plural is like *spaghetti*, it is
thought of collectively and takes a singular
verb. (36)

b. *Predicate nominative*: a nominative is used in the predicate
after verbs meaning 'be', 'become', 'appear', 'be named', and the like, in
agreement with the subject. A few such verbs are εἰμι 'I am', γίγνομαι 'I become', αἱρέομαι 'I am chosen', καλέομαι 'I am called', λέγομαι 'I am said/
called', δοκέω 'I seem'.

Examples:

(1) μαθητὴς δὴ γέγονα σός . . .   --*Euthyphro* 5a

I have, then, become your pupil.

(2) Οὐκοῦν τὸ θύειν δωρεῖσθαί ἐστι τοῖς θεοῖς, τὸ δ᾽
εὔχεσθαι αἰτεῖν τοὺς θεούς; --*Euthyphro* 14c

To sacrifice, then is to give to the gods, to pray
is to ask of the gods (is that not so)?

Notes: τὸ θύειν and τὸ εὔχεσθαι are the subjects
of the two clauses: the article identifies them
as such: the predicate nominative usually does
not have the article.

(3) αὐτοὶ γὰρ οἱ ἄνθρωποι τυγχάνουσι νομίζοντες τὸν
Δία τῶν θεῶν ἄριστον καὶ δικαιότατον. --*Euthyphro* 5e

For men themselves happen to believe (that) Zeus
(is) the best and most just of the gods.

Note: The supplementary participle is used in the
nominative case if it refers to the same person
as the subject of the main verb (cf. pp. 160-62).

(4) οὐχ ὁμολογήσω ἄκλητος ἥκειν. --Plato, *Symposium*
174d

I shall not admit that I have come uninvited.

Note: The subject of an infinitive in indirect
statement is usually omitted if it is the same
as the subject of the main verb, but any adjective agreeing with it is nominative (109-10).

The Genitive Case

1. The most common genitive endings are:

First declension: -ης, -ας, -ου; -ῶν
Second declension: -ου; -ων
Third declension: -ος (-ους, -ως); -ων

2. Uses: Most of the uses of the genitive come under two headings:
the defining (or adjectival) genitive, which denotes the dependence of one
noun upon another; and the ablatival genitive which denotes separation.

a. Possessive (p. 37): The genitive (in the attributive
position) is used for possession or other close relationship.

Examples:

(1) γυνὴ μὲν οὖν ὄλωλεν Ἀδμήτου, ξένε. --*Alcestis* 821

Rather, the wife of Admetus is dead, stranger.

(2) use in the predicate:

τοῦ ἡμετέρου προγόνου, ὦ Εὐθύφρων, ἔοικεν εἶναι
Δαιδάλου τὰ ὑπὸ σοῦ λεγόμενα. --*Euthyphro* 11c

The things said by you, Euthyphro, seem to be of
our ancestor, Daedalus (i.e. seem to belong to
Daedalus).

b. The Partitive Genitive (p. 224) (in the predicate position) denotes the whole from which a part is taken, and is used
with nouns, adjectives, verbs.

Examples:

(1) οἶσθα γὰρ εἴπερ τις ἄλλος ἀνθρώπων. --*Euthyphro*
15d

For you know, if indeed anyone else of men (does).

(2) This genitive is common with verbs of touching,
remembering, forgetting.

ἔθιγες ψυχᾶς, ἔθιγες δὲ φρενῶν. --*Alcestis* 109

You have touched my soul, you have touched my
senses.

Notes: ψυχᾶς = ψυχῆς; ἔθιγες 2 per. sg. of
ἔθιγον, aor. of θιγγάνω 'touch'.

c. The Genitive of Comparison (pp. 223-24): With comparative adjectives and adverbs, and with verbs implying comparison or
distinction, the genitive is used.

Examples:

(1) Μανθάνω· ὅτι σοι δοκῶ τῶν δικαστῶν δυσμαθέστερος
εἶναι. *Euthyphro* 9b

I understand, that I seem to you to be more thick-
witted than the jurors.

(2) ψυχῆς γὰρ οὐδέν ἐστι τιμιώτερον. --*Alcestis* 301

For nothing is more precious than life.

d. The Genitive of Agent (p. 89): the agent, i.e., the one
by whom something is done, is expressed by the genitive with ὑπό
'by'.

Examples:

    (1) . . . φιλεῖται <u>ὑπὸ θεῶν πάντων</u> . . .   *--Euthyphro*
        10d

        It is loved <u>by all the gods</u> . . .

    (2) καὶ πόλεμον ἄρα ἡγῇ σὺ εἶναι τῷ ὄντι ἐν τοῖς θεοῖς
        πρὸς ἀλλήλους καὶ ἔχθρας γε δεινὰς καὶ μάχας καὶ
        ἄλλα τοιαῦτα πολλά, οἷα λέγεταί τε <u>ὑπὸ τῶν ποιη-</u>
        <u>τῶν</u>.   *--Euthyphro* 6b

        And do you think that in reality there is war
        among the gods against each other, and terrible
        enmities and battles and the many other things
        of this sort that are told <u>by the poets</u>.

    e. The Genitive of Cause: Verbs of emotion take a genitive of the cause.

Examples:

    (1) <u>οὗ</u> δὴ χολωθεὶς τέκτονας Δίου πυρὸς
        κτείνω Κύκλωπας.   *--Alcestis* 5

        In anger <u>for which/whom</u> I kill(ed) the Cyclopes,
        workers of Zeus' fire.

        This genitive is also frequently used in excla-
mations:

    (2) Ἰώ μοι <u>τύχας</u>.   *--Alcestis* 398

        Ah me, for my (ill) <u>fortune</u>!

        Note: τύχας = τύχης

    f. Genitive of Source (p. 77): With verbs of hearing the genitive is used for the person or thing whose sound is heard. (The sound heard is accusative.)

Examples:

    (1) ἀλλ' ἄκουέ <u>μου</u>.   *--Alcestis* 781

        But hear <u>me</u>.

    (2) ὦ παῖδες, αὐτοὶ δὴ τάδ' εἰσηκούσατε
        <u>πατρὸς λέγοντος</u> μὴ γαμεῖν ἄλλην τινὰ
        γυναῖκ' ἐφ' ὑμῖν μηδ' ἀτιμάσειν ἐμέ.
                             --Alcestis 371-73

        Children, you yourselves have heard your <u>father</u>
        <u>asserting</u> these things, that he will not marry
        another woman (to be) over you, and that he will
        not dishonor me.

        Note: The attributive participle is common in
this expression, in agreement with the person actually
heard from.

      g. Genitive with verbs of ruling (p. 48): Verbs of ruling take a genitive which depends on the nominal idea of the verb (e.g. βασιλεύω 'be king of').

Example:

       πολλῶν μεν ἄρχεις. *Alcestis* 687

       You rule <u>over many</u>.

      h. Verbs of reaching and obtaining take a genitive of the end attained.

Example:

       τύγχανω with genitive

       ὁσίου γὰρ ἀνδρὸς ὅσιος 'ὢν ἐτύγχανον
       παιδὸς Φέρητος, 'ὃν θανεῖν ἐρρυσάμην.
                   --*Alcestis* 10-11

       Being holy, I met (kept meeting) <u>with a holy man</u>,
       <u>the son</u> of Pheres, whom I saved from death.

      i. Genitive of Separation (pp. 37, 89): The genitive in Greek has taken over the ablatival case (separation). A genitive is used with verbs, adjectives, adverbs, prepositions implying separation from.

Examples:

     (1) <u>ἐσθλῆς</u> γάρ, οὐδεῖς ἀντερεῖ, καὶ <u>σώφρονος</u>
        <u>γυναικὸς</u> ἡμάρτηκας. --*Alcestis* 615-16

        For you have lost <u>a noble</u>--no one will deny it--
          and <u>chaste wife</u>.

     (2) οὐκ ἠθέλησα ζῆν ἀποσπασθεῖσά σου
        σὺν παισὶν ὀρφανοῖσιν. --*Alcestis* 287-88

        I did not wish to live deprived <u>of you</u> with the
          children as orphans.

     (3) καὶ νοσφιεῖς με <u>τοῦδε δευτέρου νεκροῦ</u>;
                  --*Alcestis* 43

        And will you rob me <u>of this second corpse</u>?

     (4) ἀλλὰ <u>σμικροῦ τινος</u> ἔτι ἐνδεής εἰμι. --*Euthyphro*
        12e

        But I am still in need <u>of a little</u> something.

     (5) Θρῄκης ἐκ <u>τόπων δυσχειμέρων</u> . . . --*Alcestis* 67

        <u>from the wintry regions</u> of Thrace . . .

      j. Genitive of time within which (p. 216): The genitive is used for the period of time within which anything takes place.

Example:

       ταῦτα <u>τῆς ἡμέρας</u> ἐγένετο. Xenophon, *Anabasis*
       7, 4, 14

These things took place <u>during</u> <u>the</u> <u>day</u>.

k. Genitive Absolute (pp. 158-60): A participial clause in the genitive gives the attendant circumstances of the main action.

Examples:

(1) τόδε δέ <u>σου</u> ἐνενόησα ἅμα <u>λέγοντος</u>. --*Euthyphro* 9c

<u>While</u> <u>you</u> <u>were</u> <u>speaking</u>, I was thinking about this
. . .

(2) <u>νέων</u> <u>φθινόντων</u> μεῖζον ἄρνυμαι γέρας. --*Alcestis* 55

<u>When</u> <u>the</u> <u>young</u> <u>die</u> I amass greater honor.

l. Other uses of the genitive: objective, subjective, material.

(1) The subjective genitive denotes the subject of a feeling or action expressed in the noun:

<u>τῶν</u> <u>βαρβάρων</u> φόβος . . . Xenophon, *Anabasis* 1,
2, 17

the fear <u>of</u> <u>the</u> <u>barbarians</u> (i.e. the fear which
they feel) . . .

(2) The objective genitive denotes the object of the feeling or action expressed by the noun:

τοῦ <u>ὕδατος</u> ἐπιθυμία . . . Thucydides 2, 52

Desire <u>for</u> <u>water</u> . . .

(3) The genitive is used for material or contents:

ἕρκος <u>ὀδόντων</u> . . . Homer, *Iliad* 4, 850

The barrier <u>of</u> <u>teeth</u> (i.e. consisting of teeth)
. . .

The Dative Case

The dative case is used for the indirect object, for the person interested; it also has taken over the locative (place where), instrumental (means), and sociative (accompaniment).

1. The most common dative endings are:

First declension: -ῃ, -ᾳ; -αις (-αισι)
Second declension: -ῳ; -οις (-οισι)
Third declension: -ι; -σι

2. Uses

a. Indirect Object

Examples:

(1) θάψεις δ' αὐτὸς ὢν αὐτῆς φονεύς,
δίκας τε δώσεις <u>σοῖσι</u> <u>κηδεσταῖς</u> ἔτι.
                              --*Alcestis* 731

You will bury her, yourself being her murderer,
and you will yet pay the penalty (lit. give justice) <u>to your in-laws</u>. (σοῖσι = σοῖς)

Many intransitive and impersonal verbs take a
dative:

(2) οὐκ ἤρκεσέ <u>σοι</u> μόρον Ἀδμήτου
διακωλῦσαι; --*Alcestis* 32

Isn't it enough <u>for</u> <u>you</u> to have prevented the
death of Admetus?

Note: ἀρκέω, aor. ἤρκεσα 'be enough', 'suffice'

(3) <u>τῇ σῇ</u> πέποιθα <u>χειρὶ δεξιᾷ μόνῃ</u>. --*Alcestis* 1115

I have confidence (trust) <u>in your right hand only</u>.

Note: The intransitive forms of πείθω take a
dative.

(4) βλέψον δ' ἐς αὐτήν, εἴ τι <u>σῇ</u> δοκεῖ πρέπειν
<u>γυναικί</u>. --*Alcestis* 1121-22

Look upon her (to see) if she resembles <u>your wife</u>
at all.

Other verbs which take the dative are those meaning: benefit, serve, obey, assist, please, satisfy, advise, and their op-
posites, and those expressing friendliness, hostility, blame, anger, reproach, likeness.

(5) καὶ <u>τοῖσδέ</u> γ' <u>οἴκοις</u> ἐκδίκως προσωφελεῖν.
                                        --*Alcestis* 41

And to help <u>this house</u> unjustly . . .

Compound verbs in σύν and some compounds in πρός, παρά, ἐν,
ἐπί take the dative.

(6) Ἥκω <u>κακοῖσι σοῖσι</u> συγκάμνων, τέκνον . . .
                                        --*Alcestis* 614

I have come sympathizing <u>with your troubles</u>, my
boy.

Note: -οισι = -οις

With verbs expressing *accompaniment* and agreement and dis-
agreement, the dative is used (sociative).

(7) ἕπομαι 'follow', with the dative:

        οὐχ ἕπομαι, ὦ Σώκρατες, <u>τοῖς λεγομένοις</u>.
                                --*Euthyphro* 12a

I do not follow the <u>argument</u> (lit. <u>the things</u>
<u>being said</u>), Socrates.

(8) διαφέρομαι 'disagree', with the dative:

        ἐγὼ οὖν <u>τούτῳ</u> διαφέρομαι <u>τῷ ποιητῇ</u>. --*Euthyphro* 12b

I, accordingly, disagree <u>with</u> <u>this</u> <u>poet</u>.

    b.   Dative with Adjectives expressing likeness, friendliness, hostility, and meanings similar to those of verbs given above (a).

Examples:

    (1) σὺ δ᾽ εἶ παλαιὸς <u>δεσπόταις</u> <u>ἐμοῖς</u> φίλος.
                                --*Alcestis* 212

    You are a friend of long standing <u>to</u> <u>my</u> <u>masters</u>.

    (2) Θάνατος -- οὐ δῆτ᾽· ἐπίστασαι δὲ τοὺς ἐμοὺς τρόπους.
        Ἀπόλλων -- ἐχθρούς γε <u>θνητοῖς</u> καὶ θεοῖς στυγουμένους.
                            --*Alcestis* 61-62

    Death: No, indeed: you know my ways.
    Apollo: Yes, hateful <u>to</u> <u>men</u> and abhorred by the
       gods.

    (3)   μηδὲ γὰρ θανών ποτε
    σοῦ χωρὶς εἴην τῆς μονῆς πιστῆς <u>ἐμοί</u>.
                        --*Alcestis* 367-68

    For not even if you die would I ever be separated
       from you, the only one faithful <u>to</u> <u>me</u>.

    c.   Dative of Advantage or Disadvantage: The person or thing for whose advantage or disadvantage anything is or is done is in the dative: it is usually translated by the English preposition "for."

Examples:

    (1) <u>Τιρυνθίῳ</u> πράσσω τιν᾽ Εὐρυσθεῖ πόνον.
                    --*Alcestis* 481

    I am performing a labor <u>for</u> <u>Eurystheus</u> <u>of</u> <u>Tiryns</u>.

    (2) πάσαις δ᾽ ἔθηκεν εὐκλεέστατον βίον
    <u>γυναιξίν</u>, ἔργον τλᾶσα γενναῖον τόδε.
                    --*Alcestis* 623-24

    But she has made life most illustrious <u>for</u> <u>all</u>
       <u>women</u>, having endured this noble deed.

    (3) σαυτῷ γὰρ εἴτε δυστυχὴς εἴτ᾽ εὐτυχὴς
    ἔφυς·᾽ἃ δ᾽ ἡμῶν χρῆν σε τυγχάνειν, ἔχεις.
                    --*Alcestis* 685-86

    For you were born <u>for</u> <u>yourself</u>, whether happy or
       unhappy; what it was necessary for you to get
       from us, you have.

    The *ethical* dative is a special type of dative of advantage in which the personal pronoun has the force of 'for my sake', 'for your sake', etc.

    (4) οὐ γὰρ ἐθέλουσι <u>σοὶ</u> μένειν, ὡς καὶ αὐτῷ σοι δοκεῖ.
                  --*Euthyphro* 11c

> For they do not wish to stand still <u>for you</u>, as it
> seems to you yourself.

d. Dative of Possession: With εἰμί and γίγνομαι, the dative
may denote the possessor, the thing possessed being nominative.
(pp. 199-200)

Examples:

(1) μόνος γὰρ <u>αὐτοῖς</u> ἦσθα, κοὔτις ἐλπὶς ἦν
σοῦ κατθανόντος ἄλλα φιτεύσειν τέκνα.
                                    --*Alcestis* 293-94

> For you were alone <u>to them</u> (i.e. you were <u>their</u>
> only child) and there was no hope--once you were
> dead--to produce other children.

(2) οὐ γάρ που καὶ <u>σού</u> γε δίκη τις οὖσα τυγχάνει
πρὸς τὸν βασιλέα ὥσπερ <u>ἐμοί</u>. --*Euthyphro* 2a

> For there does not happen to be <u>for you</u> a suit be-
> fore the 'king' as there is <u>to me</u> (i.e. <u>you</u> do
> not have a suit as <u>I</u> do).

(3)   βραχὺς δὲ <u>σοι</u>
πάντως ὁ λοιπὸς ἦν βιώσιμος <u>χρόνος</u>.
                                    --*Alcestis* 649-50

> But the time left to live in any case was short
> <u>for you</u> (i.e. <u>you</u> did not have much time left).

e. The Dative Agent is used with perfect and pluperfect
passive (but seldom with other tenses of the passive). (p. 210)
(see genitive of agent, d, above)

Example:

πολλαὶ θεραπεῖαι <u>τοῖς ἰατροῖς</u> ηὕρηνται . . .
                                    --Isocrates 8, 39

> Many cures have been found <u>by the doctors</u>.

f. Instrumental Dative: Cause, manner, and means are expressed by the dative. (pp. 37, 48)

Examples: Cause

(1) φίλου γὰρ ἀνδρὸς <u>συμφοραῖς</u> βαρύνομαι.
                                    --*Alcestis* 42

> Yes, I am weighted down <u>by the misfortunes</u> of a
> man (who is) my friend.

    Means

(2) <u>βαρείᾳ συμφορᾷ</u> πεπλήγμεθα. --*Alcestis* 405

> We are smitten <u>by a grievous misfortune</u>.

(3) οὐδ' ἁλίσκεται <u>τέχνῃ</u> . . . --*Alcestis* 786

> And it is not grasped <u>by art/skill</u> . . .

g. The dative of *respect* is a form of the dative of manner. (p. 70)

Example:

λόγῳ γὰρ ἦσαν οὐκ ἔργῳ φίλοι.   --*Alcestis* 339

For they were friends <u>in</u> <u>word</u>, not <u>in</u> <u>deed</u>.

h. A dative of manner is used with comparatives to denote the *degree of difference*. (pp. 223-24)

Example:

κινδυνεύω ἄρα, ὦ ἑταῖρε, ἐκείνου τοῦ ἀνδρὸς
δεινότερος γεγονέναι τὴν τέχνην, <u>τοσούτῳ</u> <u>ὅσῳ</u>
ὁ μὲν τὰ αὑτοῦ μόνα ἐποίει οὐ μένοντα, ἐγὼ δὲ
πρὸς τοῖς ἐμαυτοῦ, ὡς ἔοικε, καὶ τὰ ἀλλότρια.
                              --*Euthyphro* 11d

I am likely, then, my friend, to be more clev-
er than that man, <u>insofar</u> <u>as</u> he made only his
own (creations) not (to) stay put, but I, in addition to my own, as it seems, also (make) other
people's . . .

i. Locative Dative: The dative is used to represent the lost locative case for place where or time when.

Place where is usually expressed by the dative with a preposition in prose; the preposition is frequently omitted in poetry. (p. 37)

Examples:

(1) Ἄδμητον <u>ἐν</u> <u>δόμοισιν</u> κιγχάνω; --*Alcestis* 477

Do I find Admetus <u>in</u> <u>the</u> <u>house</u>?

Time when is expressed without or with a preposition.

(2)   συμμέτρως δ᾽ ἀφίκετο
φρουρῶν τόδ᾽ ἦμαρ <u>ᾧ</u> θανεῖν αὐτὴν χρεών.
                              --*Alcestis* 26-27

But he has come in good time, watching this day <u>on</u>
    <u>which</u> she must die.

(3) θάπτειν τιν᾽ <u>ἐν</u> <u>τῇδ᾽</u> <u>ἡμέρᾳ</u> μέλλω νεκρόν.
                              --*Alcestis* 477

I am going to bury a corpse <u>on</u> <u>this</u> <u>day</u>.

The Accusative Case

1. The most common accusative endings are:

First declension: -ην, -αν; -ας
Second declension: -ον; -ους
Third declension: -ν, -α, -ος, -(μ)α; -ας, (-εις), -α

2. Uses: The accusative is used for the direct object, for the end of motion (terminal), as subject of an infinitive, and in a number of adverbial expressions.

  a. The direct object of a transitive verb is accusative.

Examples:

(1) οὗτοι δὴ ᾿Αθηναῖοί γε, ὦ Εὐθύφρων, δίκην αὐτὴν
  καλοῦσιν ἀλλὰ γραφήν. --*Euthyphro* 2a

The Athenians do not, to be sure, call it a suit, Euthyphro, but an indictment.

(2) ὀνομάζουσι μέντοι αὐτόν, ὡς ἐγῷμαι, Μέλητον.
       --*Euthyphro* 2b

They call him, I think, Meletus.

(3) ἦ μὴν πολύν γε τὸν κάτω λογίζομαι
  χρόνον, τὸ δὲ ζῆν μικρόν, ἀλλ᾿ ὅμως γλυκύ.
       --*Alcestis* 692-93

Surely indeed, I reckon the time below (to be) long, but the (time for) living short, but still sweet.

(4) ἐγὼ δὲ σ᾿ οἴκων δεσπότην ἐγεινάμην
  κἄθρεψ᾿, ὀφείλω δ᾿ οὐχ ὑπερθνῄσκειν σέθεν.
       --*Alcestis* 681-82

I begot you and reared you (as) master of the house; I do not owe (it to you) to die for you.

(5)   ἀλλὰ ταῦτα μὲν
  φέρειν ἀνάγκη καίπερ ὄντα δύσφορα.
       --*Alcestis* 616-17

But it is necessary to bear these things though they are hard to bear.

(6) καὶ τῶν θεῶν ἄρα, ὦ γενναῖε Εὐθύφρων, ἄλλοι ἄλλα
  δίκαια ἡγοῦνται κατὰ τὸν σὸν λόγον, καὶ καλὰ καὶ
  αἰσχρὰ καὶ ἀγαθὰ καὶ κακά . . .
       --*Euthyphro* 7e

And of the gods then, my dear Euthyphro, different ones think different things just (according to your statement) and fair and ugly and good and evil.

Note the use of ἄλλος . . . ἄλλος.

(7) μακροῦ βίου γὰρ ᾐσθόμην ἐρῶντά σε.
       --*Alcestis* 715

I perceive that you are in love with a long life.

See p. 162.

Two accusative objects may be used with one verb.

(8) τί φῄς; <u>γραφὴν</u> <u>σέ</u> τις, ὡς ἔοικε, γέγραπται . . . *Euthyphro* 2b

What are you saying? Someone, as it seems, has
drawn up <u>an indictment against</u> <u>you</u>.

(9) τί δῆτά <u>σ᾿</u> ἠδίκησα;   σ᾿ = σε   *Alcestis* 689

<u>What</u> wrong have I done <u>you</u>?

b. Cognate accusative (internal object): the cognate accusative repeats the meaning already contained in the verb, and may
be used with transitive or intransitive verbs.

Examples:

(1) καὶ δὴ καὶ <u>τὸν</u> <u>ἄλλον</u> <u>βίον</u> ὅτι ἄμεινον βιωσοίμην.
                      --*Euthyphro* 16a

and in particular, that I will live <u>the rest of my</u>
<u>life</u> better . . .

(2)   ὅστις ἀρίστης
ἀπλακὼν ἀλόχου τῆσδ᾿ <u>ἀβίωτον</u>
τὸν ἔπειτα <u>χρόνον</u> βιοτεύσει. --*Alcestis* 241-43

For he, having lost this most excellent wife, will
live <u>the</u> <u>time</u> thereafter <u>unlivable</u> (<u>-ly</u>).

c. The accusative is used as subject of an infinitive.

Examples:

(1) φησὶ γάρ <u>με</u> <u>ποιητὴν</u> εἶναι θεῶν --*Euthyphro* 3b

For he says that <u>I</u> am a <u>maker</u> (<u>poet</u>) of gods . . .

(2) καὶ <u>μ᾿</u> οὐ νομίζω <u>παῖδα</u> <u>σὸν</u> πεφυκέναι. μ᾿ = με
                      --*Alcestis* 641

And I do not think that <u>I</u> am <u>your</u> <u>son</u>.

Note: Usually the subject of an infinitive in
indirect statement is omitted if it is the same as the
subject of the leading verb and adjectives or nouns in
agreement with it are nominative. But if it is included for special emphasis, it is in the accusative case,
as are all words agreeing with it.

(3) δεῖ γὰρ θανεῖν <u>με</u> . . . --*Alcestis* 320

For it is necessary <u>for</u> <u>me</u> to die.

d. The terminal accusative (place to which) is usually used
with a preposition (e.g. εἰς, πρός, παρά), but in poetry is sometimes found without a preposition.

Examples:

(1) εἰς Ἅιδου <u>δόμους</u> . . . --*Alcestis* 25

<u>into</u> <u>the</u> <u>house</u> of Hades . . .

(2) τοῖος Φέρητος εἶσι πρὸς <u>δόμους</u> ἀνήρ . . .
                      --*Alcestis* 65

Such a man will come <u>to the house</u> of Pheres . . .

(3) ἐλθὼν δὲ <u>γαῖαν τηνδ</u>᾽ ἐβουφόρβουν ξένῳ . . .
                              --*Alcestis* 8

Having come <u>to this land</u>, I herded cattle for a
stranger.

    e.   The accusative of respect is an adverbial accusative
which tells in what respect something is true. (pp. 69-70)

Example:

        <u>οὐδὲν</u> μὲν οὖν παύονται ταῦτα ἀμφισβητοῦντες καὶ
        ἄλλοθι καὶ ἐν τοῖς δικαστηρίοις . . .
                              --*Euthyphro* 8c

<u>In no way</u> do they cease disputing these things,
both elsewhere and in the courts (i.e. especially in the courts).

    f.   The accusative is used for the extent of space or time.
(p. 217)

Example:

                            ἡδὺ γὰρ φίλους
        κἀν νυκτὶ λεύσσειν, <u>ὅντιν</u>᾽ ἂν παρῇ <u>χρόνον</u>.
                              --*Alcestis* 355-56

For it is sweet to see friends even at night,
<u>for whatever time</u> he is there.

    g.   The accusative absolute (p. 160) is used instead of the
genitive absolute, when the participle represents an impersonal
verb.

Example:

        θνῄσκω <u>παρόν</u> μοι μὴ θανεῖν ὑπὲρ σέθεν . . .
                              --*Alcestis* 284

I am dying, <u>it being possible</u> for me not to die
on your behalf.

The Vocative Case

1.   The most common vocative endings are:

    First declension: -η, -α; -αι
    Second declension: -ε, -ον; -οι, -α
    Third declension: like nominative, or like stem

2.   Use: The vocative is used for direct address, either with or without ὦ (oh!).

Examples:

    (1) χαῖρ᾽, ὦ Διὸς <u>παῖ</u> Περσέως ἀφ᾽ αἵματος.
                              --*Alcestis* 509

Hail, <u>son</u> of Zeus, from the blood of Perseus.

(2) Ἄδμητε, καὶ σὺ χαῖρε, Θεσσαλῶν ἄναξ.
                              --*Alcestis* 510

Admetus, hail you too, king of the Thessalians.

C. *The Prepositions*

A. The Prepositions: their basic meanings, the cases used with them, their meanings when used to form compounds.

    A = with the accusative case
    D = with the dative case   (D) = with the dative only in poetry
    G = with the genitive case

ἀμφί   G A   *on both sides*
in compounds: about, on both sides, in two ways

ἀνά   A (D)   *up*
in compounds: up, back, again

ἀντί   G   *in the face of, opposite to*
in compounds: against, in opposition, in return, instead

ἀπό   G   *off*
in compounds: from, off, in return, back; also used as a negative and
       as an intensive

διά   G A   *through*
in compounds: through, thoroughly, apart; also used as an intensive
       (completely), and to indicate endurance, and rivalry

εἰς (ἐς)   A   *into, to*
in compounds: into, in, to

ἐν   D   *in*
in compounds: in, at, on, among

ἐξ, ἐκ   G   *from within*
in compounds: out, from, away, off, thoroughly

ἐπί   G D A   *upon*
in compounds: upon, after, toward, to, over, against, besides

κατά   G A   *down*
in compounds: down, against, completely; intensity

μετά   G (D) A   *amid, among*
in compounds: with (sharing), after; change

παρά   G D A   *alongside*
in compounds: beside, along by, wrongly

περί   G D A   *around, about (on all sides)*
in compounds: around, about, over

πρό   G   *before*
in compounds: before, for, in preference

πρός   G D A   *in front of, at, by*
in compounds: to, toward, against, besides

σύν (ξύν)   D   *with*
    in compounds: with, together, altogether

ὑπέρ   G A   *over*
    in compounds: over, above, beyond, in defence of

ὑπό   G D A   *under*
    in compounds: under, gradually

    B. The Prepositions arranged according to the cases used with them.
(The basic meaning of each is in upper case.)

       1. With *genitive* only:

ἀντί   OPPOSITE to: 'in the face of', 'opposite to', 'for', 'instead of',
    'in return for'

ἀπό   OFF: 'from', 'off from', 'away from'

ἐξ, ἐκ   OUT: 'from', 'out of', 'from within'

πρό   BEFORE: 'before' (of time or place), 'in front of', 'in defence
    of', 'in preference to'

       2. With *dative* only:

ἐν   IN: 'in' (of place), 'at', 'near', 'on', 'by', 'among'; 'in',
    'on', 'during' (of time)

σύν (ξύν)   WITH: 'with' (instrumental dative), 'along with', 'with the help
    of', 'together with'

       3. With *accusative* only:

ἀνά   UP: 'up to', 'up'; 'up along', 'over', 'through' (ἀνά is used in
    poetry with the dative, for 'upon')

εἰς   INTO, TO: 'into', 'to'; 'against', 'up to', 'until'

       4. With *genitive* and *accusative*:

ἀμφί   ON BOTH SIDES
    1. with genitive: 'about', 'concerning' (of cause)
    2. with accusative: 'about' (of place), 'towards' (of time), 'with'
    (of attendance on a person)

διά   THROUGH
    1. with genitive: 'through and out of', 'through' (of place and time),
    'by' (of means or agency)
    2. with accusative: 'through', 'over' (of space covered), 'because of',
    'on account of'

κατά   DOWN
    1. with genitive: 'down from', 'down toward', 'under', 'against'
    2. with accusative: 'down', 'throughout', 'during'; 'for the purpose
    of', 'according to'; 'about' (approximately)

μετά   AMID, AMONG
    1. with genitive: 'among', 'together with', 'amid', 'in accordance

with'
2. with accusative: 'into the midst of', 'after' (purpose), 'next to'
(3. in epic poetry, with dative: 'amid', locative)

ὑπέρ   OVER
1. with genitive: 'from over', 'in defence of'; 'concerning'
2. with accusative: 'over', 'beyond', 'exceeding'

        5. With *genitive, dative,* and *accusative:*

ἐπί   UPON (on the surface of)
1. with genitive: 'upon' (of place), 'in the time of'
2. with dative: 'on', 'by' (proximity), 'in addition to'; 'on condition of', 'because of'
3. with accusative: 'to' (of the goal); 'against', 'for' (extension of
time, purpose)

παρά   ALONGSIDE
1. with genitive: 'from' (separation or source)
2. with dative: 'with', 'by the side of'
3. with accusative: 'to' (of persons); 'along', 'by', 'past'; 'throughout' (of time); 'in consequence of', 'depending on', 'in comparison to';
'beyond', 'contrary to'

περί   AROUND, ABOUT
1. with genitive: 'about', 'concerning'
2. with dative: 'about' (of place or cause)
3. with accusative: 'around', 'about' (of position); 'approximately'
(of time), 'engaged in', 'connected with'

πρός   in FRONT of, AT, BY
1. with genitive: 'facing' (of place), 'from' (on the part of), 'from
the point of view of'
2. with dative: 'at', 'near' (of *place*, rather than of persons); 'in
addition to', 'in the presence of'
3. with accusative: 'to', 'towards' ('to' face to face); 'against',
'with', 'for' (purpose), 'with reference to', 'in consequence of'

ὑπό   UNDER
1. with genitive: 'out from under'; 'by' (agent)
2. with dative: 'under', 'beneath', 'subjected to'
3. with accusative: 'under', 'to (a place) under'; 'toward' (of time)

D. *Participles*

    1. Uses: see pages 149-50, 153-163, 164-171.

    2. Identification:

    -ντ- is the sign for all active participles in the masculine and neuter,
except for the perfect active; -ντ- is also the sign for the aorist passive
participle.

    -οντ- (fem. in -ουσ-) for the thematic tenses: present, future, second
aorist (150-51), and for the present and aorist of δίδωμι (271).

-ουντ- (fem. -ουσ-) for the ε-contracts and o-contracts and for liquid future (p. 248)

-ωντ- (fem. -ωσ-) for the α-contracts (p. 247)

-αντ- (fem. -ασ-) for the first aorist (p. 151), and for the present and second aorist of ἵστημι (p. 271)

-εντ- (fem. -εισ-) for the aorist passive (pp. 235-36), and for the present and second aorist of τίθημι and ἵημι (p. 271)

-υντ- (fem. -υσ-) for present of -νυμι verbs (p. 272)

-οτ- (fem. -υι-) is the sign for the perfect active participle (p. 181).

-μενος, -η, -ον is the sign for middle (or middle-passive) participles, and for the future passive (pp. 152-53).

-όμενος for thematic tenses: present, future, second aorist middle; future passive; and present and aorist of δίδωμι (p. 268)

-ούμενος for ε-contract and o-contract verbs and for the liquid future (pp. 245-47)

-ώμενος for α-contracts (p. 244)

-άμενος for the first aorist (p. 152) and for the present of ἵστημι (p. 266)

-έμενος for present and aorist of τίθημι and ἵημι (pp. 268, 269)

-ύμενος for present of -νυμι verbs (p. 270)

-μένος (note accent) for perfect middle-passive (p. 208)

A few examples:

1. Attributive participle: (used with the article)

> πῶς οὖν ἔκρυπτες τὸν παρόντα δαίμονα,
> φίλου μολόντος ἀνδρός, ὡς αὐτὸς λέγεις;
>   --*Alcestis* 561-62

> How then did you hide the <u>present</u> fortune
> from a man who came (here) as your friend,
> as you yourself say?

2. Circumstantial participle (participle used to relate such things as time, cause, concession, condition, purpose)

> . . . καὶ ὡς <u>διαβαλῶν</u> δὴ ἔρχεται εἰς τὸ δι-
> καστέριον. --*Euthyphro* 3b

> And he goes into the court <u>for</u> <u>the</u> <u>purpose</u>
> <u>of</u> <u>slandering</u> . . .

3. Supplementary participle: (completes the action)

> ἀλλ᾽ ἦ καὶ σοφὸς λέληθας <u>ὤν</u>; --*Alcestis* 58

> But have you escaped my notice <u>being</u> clever?

APPENDIX II: VERBS

A. Principal Parts (The most important verbs are marked with an asterisk (*).)

A

*ἀγγέλλω, ἀγγελῶ, ἤγγειλα, ἤγγελκα, ἤγγελμαι, ἠγγέλθην   'announce'
*ἄγω, ἄξω, ἤγαγον (ἀγαγ-), ἦχα, ἦγμαι, ἤχθην (ἀχθ-) 'lead'
 ᾄδω (ἀείδω), ᾄσομαι, ᾖσα, ᾖσμαι, ᾔσθην 'sing'
 αἰδέομαι, αἰδέσομαι, ᾔδεσμαι, ᾐδέσθην 'respect', 'feel shame'
*αἱρέω, αἱρήσω, εἷλον (ἑλ-), ᾕρηκα, ᾕρημαι, ᾑρέθην 'take', mid. 'choose'
 αἴρω, ἀρῶ, ἦρα, ἦρκα, ἦρμαι, ἤρθην 'raise'
*αἰσθάνομαι, αἰσθήσομαι, ᾐσθόμην, ᾔσθημαι 'perceive'
 αἰσχύνω, αἰσχυνῶ, ᾔσχυνα, ᾐσχύνθην 'disgrace', mid. 'feel ashamed'
*ἀκούω, ἀκούσομαι, ἤκουσα, ἀκήκοα (plpf. ἠκηκόη/ἀκηκόη), ἠκούσθην   'hear'
 ἁλίσκομαι, ἁλώσομαι, ἑάλων/ἥλων (p. 273), ἑάλωκα/ἥλωκα   'be captured'
*ἁμαρτάνω, ἁμαρτήσομαι, ἥμαρτον, ἡμάρτηκα, ἡμάρτημαι, ἡμαρτήθην 'err'
*ἀνοίγνυμι/ἀνοίγω, impf. ἀνέῳγον, ἀνοίξω, ἀνέῳξα, ἀνέῳχα/ἀνέῳγα, ἀνέῳγμαι,
       ἀνεῴχθην (fut. pf. ἀνεῴξομαι) 'open'
*ἀποθνήσκω, ἀποθανοῦμαι, ἀπέθανον, τέθνηκα (fut. pf. τεθνήξω)   'die'
*ἀποκρίνομαι (cf. κρίνω), ἀποκρινοῦμαι, ἀποκέκριμαι, ἀπεκρίθην   'answer'
*ἀποκτείνω, ἀποκτενῶ, ἀπέκτεινα, ἀπέκτονα 'kill'
*ἀπόλλυμι, -ολῶ, -ώλεσα, -ωλόμην (2 aor. mid.), -ολώλεκα/-όλωλα   'destroy',
       mid. 'perish'
 ἅπτω, ἅψω, ἧψα, ἧμμαι, ἥφθην 'fasten', mid. 'touch'
*ἀφικνέομαι, ἀφίξομαι, ἀφικόμην, ἀφῖγμαι   'arrive'
*ἄρχω, ἄρξω, ἦρξα, ἦρχα, ἦργμαι, ἤρχθην 'begin', 'rule', mid. 'begin'

B

*βαίνω, -βήσομαι, -έβην, βέβηκα (p. 272) 'go'
*βάλλω, βαλῶ, ἔβαλον, βέβληκα, βέβλημαι, ἐβλήθην 'throw', 'hit'
 βιβάζω, -βιβάσω/-ομαι, ἐβίβασα; fut. also βιβῶ (-άω) 'make go'
 βλάπτω, βλάψω, ἔβλαψα, βέβλαφα, βέβλαμμαι, ἐβλάφθην/ἐβλάβην   'harm'
 βλέπω, βλέψομαι, ἔβλεψα 'see'
 βοάω, βοήσομαι, ἐβόησα 'shout'
*βούλομαι, βουλήσομαι, βεβούλημαι, ἐβουλήθην   'will', 'wish'

Γ

*γαμέω, γαμῶ, ἔγημα, γεγάμηκα, γεγάμημαι 'marry' (act. of the man, mid. of
       the woman)
 γελάω, γελάσομαι, ἐγέλασα, ἐγελάσθην 'laugh'
 γηράσκω (or γηράω), γηράσομαι, ἐγήρασα, γεγήρακα 'grow old'
*γίγνομαι, γενήσομαι, ἐγενόμην, γέγονα ('am'), γεγένημαι, (ἐγενήθην late)
       perf. ptcpl. γεγώς 'become', 'be'
*γιγνώσκω, γνώσομαι, ἔγνων (p. 272), ἔγνωκα, ἔγνωσμαι, ἐγνώσθην   'know'
*γράφω, γράφω, ἔγραψα, γέγραφα, γέγραμμαι, ἐγράφην 'write'

Δ

 δέδια/δέδοικα (δείδω)(p. 185) 'fear'
*δείκνυμι (p. 270)(or δεικνύω), δείξω, ἔδειξα, δέδειχα, δέδειγμαι, ἐδείχθην
    'show'

*δέχομαι, δέξομαι, ἐδεξάμην, δέδεγμαι, (-εδέχθην)   'receive', 'await'
 δέω, δήσω, ἔδησα, δέδεκα, δέδεμαι, ἐδέθην   'bind'
*δέω, δεήσω, ἐδέησα, δεδέηκα, δεδέημαι, ἐδεήθην   'need', 'lack'; mid. 'ask'
       impers. δεῖ (impf. ἔδει), δεήσει, ἐδέησε   'it is necessary'
*διανοέομαι (cf. νοέω), διανοήσομαι, διενοήθην   'think', 'perceive'
*διαφθείρω (φθείρω), διαφθερῶ, διέφθειρα, διέφθαρκα/διέφθορα, διέφθαρμαι, διε-
       φθάρην   'corrupt', 'destroy'; 2 perf. 'am ruined'
 διδάσκω, διδάξω, ἐδίδαξα, δεδίδαχα, δεδίδαγμαι, ἐδιδάχθην   'teach'
*δίδωμι (pp. 267-68), δώσω, ἔδωκα (pl. ἔδομεν), δέδωκα, δέδομαι, ἐδόθην
       'give'
 διώκω, διώξομαι (or διώξω), ἐδίωξα, δεδίωχα, ἐδιώχθην   'pursue', 'prosecute'
*δοκέω, δόξω, ἔδοξα, δέδογμαι, (-εδόχθην)   'seem', 'think'
 δράω, δράσω, ἔδρασα, δέδρακα, δέδραμαι, ἐδράσθην   'do'
*δύναμαι (p. 272), δυνήσομαι, δεδύνημαι, ἐδυνήθην   'be able'

E

*ἐάω (impf. εἴων), ἐάσω, εἴασα, εἴακα, εἴαμαι, εἰάθην   'permit', 'let alone'
*ἐθέλω, ἐθελήσω, ἠθέλησα, ἠθέληκα, (pres. also θέλω)   'wish', 'be willing'
 εἶδον (see under ὁράω)
*εἰμί, ἔσομαι   'be'
*εἶμι   'go'
*εἶπον (see under λέγω)
 ἐλαύνω, ἐλῶ (-άω)(pp. 249-50), ἤλασα, -ελήλακα, ἐλήλαμαι, ἠλάθην 'drive',
       'march'
*ἔοικα (p. 185)   'seem'
*ἐπίσταμαι (p. 272)(impf. ἠπιστάμην), ἐπιστήσομαι, ἠπιστήθην   'understand'
 ἕπομαι (impf. εἱπόμην), ἕψομαι, ἑσπόμην (σπ-)   'follow'
 ἐράω (impf. ἤρων), aor. ἠράσθην   'love'
 ἐρρήθην (see under λέγω)
*ἔρχομαι, ἐλεύσομαι (εἶμι used in prose), ἦλθον (ἐλθ-), ἐλήλυθα   'come', 'go'
 ἐσθίω (impf. ἤσθιον), fut. ἔδομαι, ἔφαγον, ἐδήδοκα, -εδήδεσμαι, (ἠδέσθην poet-
       ic)   'eat'
*εὑρίσκω (aug. εὑ/ηὑ), εὑρήσω, ηὗρον/εὗρον, ηὕρηκα/εὕρηκα, εὕρημαι, εὑρέθην
       'find'
 εὔχομαι, εὔξομαι, ηὐξάμην, ηὖγμαι   'pray', 'boast'
*ἔχω, (impf. εἶχον), ἕξω/σχήσω, ἔσχον (σχ-), ἔσχηκα, -έσχημαι, (ἐσχέθην late)
       'have'

Z

 ζάω (p. 245, contr. to -η), ζήσω/ζήσομαι, (ἔζησα, ἔζηκα late)   'live'

H

 ἥδομαι, ἡσθήσομαι, ἥσθην   'am pleased'
 ἥκω (impf. ἧκον), fut. ἥξω   'have come', 'am here'

Θ

 θάπτω, θάψω, ἔθαψα, τέθαμμαι, ἐτάφην   'bury'
 θαυμάζω, θαυμάσομαι, ἐθαύμασα, τεθαύμακα, ἐθαυμάσθην   'wonder', 'admire'
 θέω, θεύσομαι (other tenses from τρέχω)   'run'
 θνήσκω (see under ἀποθνήσκω)

θύω, θύσω, ἔθυσα, τέθυκα, τέθυμαι, ἐτύθην   'sacrifice'

I

*ἵημι (pp. 268-69), -ἥσω, -ἧκα, -εἷκα, -εἷμαι, -εἵθην   'send'
 ἱκνέομαι (see under ἀφικνέομαι)
*ἵστημι (p. 266), στήσω, ἔστησα/ἔστην, ἔστηκα (plpf. εἱστήκη), (ἔσταμαι rare),
     fut. pf. ἑστήξω, ἐστάθην   'stand', 'make stand'

K

 καθέζομαι (or καθίζομαι) impf. ἐκαθεζόμην, fut. καθεδοῦμαι, fut. of καθίζο-
     μαι: καθιζήσομαι, aor. ἐκαθισάμην   'sit'
 κάθημαι (ἧμαι) impf. ἐκαθήμην (p. 272)   'sit'
 καίω, καύσω, ἔκαυσα, -κέκαυκα, κέκαυμαι, ἐκαύθην   'burn'
*καλέω, καλῶ (pp. 249-50), ἐκάλεσα, κέκληκα, κέκλημαι, ἐκλήθην   'call'
*κεῖμαι, κείσομαι (p. 272)   'lie'
 κελεύω, κελεύσω, ἐκέλευσα, κεκέλευκα, κεκέλευσμαι, ἐκελεύσθην   'command'
 κλείω, κλείσω/κλήσω, ἔκλεισα/ἔκλησα, -κέκληκα, κέκλειμαι/κέκλημαι, ἐκλείσθην/
     ἐκλήσθην   'shut'
 κλέπτω, κλέψω/κλέψομαι, ἔκλεψα, κέκλοφα, κέκλεμμαι, ἐκλάπην   'steal'
 κομίζω, κομιῶ, ἐκόμισα, κεκόμικα, κεκόμισμαι, ἐκομίσθην   'care for', 'carry'
*κρίνω, κρινῶ, ἔκρινα, κέκρικα, κέκριμαι, ἐκρίθην   'judge'
 κρύπτω, κρύψω, ἔκρυψα, κέκρυμμαι, ἐκρύφθην   'hide'
*κτάομαι, κτήσομαι, ἐκτησάμην, κέκτημαι   'acquire', pf. 'possess'
 κτείνω (see ἀποκτείνω)

Λ

*λαμβάνω, λήψομαι, ἔλαβον, εἴληφα, εἴλημμαι, ἐλήφθην   'take'
 λανθάνω, λήσω, ἔλαθον, λέληθα 'escape notice', 'lie hid'
     ἐπι-λανθάνομαι, ἐπιλήσομαι, ἐπελαθόμην, ἐπιλέλησμαι   'forget'
*λέγω, λέξω, ἔλεξα/εἶπον (εἰπ-), εἴρηκα, λέλεγμαι/εἴρημαι, ἐλέχθην/ἐρρήθην
     'say'
*λείπω, λείψω, ἔλιπον, λέλοιπα, λέλειμμαι, ἐλείφθην   'leave'

M

 μαίνομαι, ἔμηνα, μέμηνα, ἐμάνην (aor. pass.)   'be mad'
*μανθάνω, μαθήσομαι, ἔμαθον, μεμάθηκα   'learn'
*μέλλω, μελλήσω, ἐμέλλησα   'intend', 'be about to'
*μένω, μενῶ, ἔμεινα, μεμένηκα   'remain'
 μιμνήσκω (μιμνήσκω), -μνήσω, -έμνησα, μέμνημαι, ἐμνήσθην   'remind', mid. 're-
     member'

N

*νομίζω, νομιῶ, ἐνόμισα, νενόμικα, νενόμισμαι, ἐνομίσθην   'believe', 'think'

O

 οἴγνυμι (see under ἀνοίγνυμι)
*οἶδα (pp. 184-85), plpf. ᾔδη, fut. εἴσομαι   'know'
*οἴομαι (1st pers. usually οἶμαι, ᾤμην), οἰήσομαι, ᾠήθην   'think'
 ὄλλυμι (see ἀπόλλυμι)

*ὁράω, impf. ἑώρων, ὄψομαι, εἶδον (ἰδ-), ἑόρακα/ἑώρακα (plpf. ἑωράκη), ἑώραμαι/
    ὦμμαι, ὤφθην (ὀφθ-) 'see'
ὀφείλω, ἐφειλήσω, ὠφείλησα, 2 aor. ὤφελον (= would that!), ὠφείληκα 'owe'
    (aor. pass. ptcpl. ὀφειληθείς)

Π

*πάσχω, πείσομαι, ἔπαθον, πέπονθα 'suffer', 'experience'
*πείθω, πείσω, ἔπεισα, πέπεικα/πέποιθα (trust), πέπεισμαι, ἐπείσθην 'per-
    suade', mid. 'obey'
πειράομαι, πειράσομαι, ἐπειρασάμην, πεπείραμαι, ἐπειράθην 'try'
*πέμπω, πέμψω, ἔπεμψα, πέπομφα, πέπεμμαι, ἐπέμφθην 'send'
πίμπλημι, -πλήσω, -έπλησα, -πέπληκα, -πέπλησμαι, -επλήσθην 'fill'
πίνω, πίομαι, ἔπιον, πέπωκα, -πέπομαι, -επόθην 'drink'
*πίπτω, πεσοῦμαι, ἔπεσον, πέπτωκα 'fall'
πλέω (p. 246), πλεύσομαι/πλευσοῦμαι, ἔπλευσα, πέπλευκα, πέπλευσμαι 'sail'
πνέω, πνευσοῦμαι/-πνεύσομαι, ἔπνευσα, -πέπνευκα 'breathe', 'blow'
*πράττω (stem πραγ-), πράξω, ἔπραξα, πέπραχα/πέπραγα, πέπραγμαι, ἐπράχθην 'do'
*πυνθάνομαι, πεύσομαι, ἐπυθόμην, πέπυσμαι 'learn', 'inquire'

Ρ

ῥήγνυμι, -ρήξω, ἔρρηξα, -ἔρρωγα, ἐρράγην 'break'
ῥίπτω, ῥίψω, ἔρριψα, ἔρριφα, ἔρριμμαι, ἐρρίφθην 'throw'
ῥύομαι, ῥύσομαι, ἐρρυσάμην 'rescue', 'defend'

Σ

σιγάω, σιγήσομαι, ἐσίγησα, σεσίγηκα, σεσίγημαι, ἐσιγήθην 'be silent'
*σκοπέω (pres. & impf.) other tenses from σκέπτομαι, σκέψομαι, ἐσκεψάμην,
    ἔσκεμμαι, fut. pf. ἐσκέψομαι, verbal σκεπτέος 'view'
*στέλλω, στελῶ, ἔστειλα, -ἔσταλκα, ἔσταλμαι, ἐστάλην 'send'
*στρέφω, -στρέψω, ἔστρεφα, ἔστραμμαι, ἐστρέφθην/ἐστράφην 'turn'
σῴζω/σώζω, σώσω, ἔσωσα, σέσωκα, σέσωμαι/σέσωσμαι, ἐσώθην 'save'

Τ

τάττω, τάξω, ἔταξα, τέταχα, τέταγμαι, ἐτάχθην 'arrange'
τείνω, τενῶ, -έτεινα, -τέτακα, τέταγμαι, -ετάθην 'stretch'
*τίθημι (p. 268), θήσω, ἔθηκα (pl. ἔθεμεν), τέθηκα, τέθειμαι, ἐτέθην 'put'
*τίκτω, τέξομαι, ἔτεκον, τέτοκα 'beget', 'bring forth'
τιτρώσκω, τρώσω, ἔτρωσα, τέτρωμαι, ἐτρώθην 'wound'
*τρέπω, τρέψω, ἔτρεψα, 2 aor. mid. ἐτραπόμην, τέτροφα, τέτραμμαι, ἐτρέφθην/
    ἐτράπην 'turn', mid. 'flee'
τρέφω, θρέψω, ἔθρεψα, τέτροφα, τέθραμμαι, ἐθρέφθην/ἐτράφην 'support',
    'nourish'
τρέχω, δραμοῦμαι, ἔδραμον, -δεδράμηκα, -δεδράμημαι 'run'
*τρίβω, τρίψω, ἔτριψα, τέτριφα, τέτριμμαι, ἐτρίφθην/ἐτρίβην 'rub'
*τυγχάνω, τεύξομαι, ἔτυχον, τετύχηκα 'hit', 'happen', 'obtain'

Υ

ὑπισχνέομαι, ὑποσχήσομαι, ὑπεσχόμην, ὑπέσχημαι 'promise'

Φ

*φαίνω, φανῶ, ἔφηνα, πέφαγκα/πέφηνα, πέφασμαι, ἐφάνθην/ἐφάνην   'show'
*φέρω, οἴσω, ἤνεγκα/ἤνεγκον, ἐνήνοχα, ἐνήνεγμαι, ἠνέχθην   'bear', 'carry'
*φεύγω, φεύξομαι/φευγοῦμαι, ἔφυγον, πέφευγα   'flee'
*φημί, φήσω, ἔφησα   'say'
 φθάνω, φθήσομαι, ἔφθασα, ἔφθην (act. p. 278)   'anticipate'
 φθείρω (see διαφθείρω)
*φοβέομαι, φοβήσομαι, πεφόβημαι, ἐφοβήθην   'fear'
 φράζω, φράσω, ἔφρασα, πέφρακα, πέφρασμαι, ἐφράσθην   'tell', mid. 'devise'
*φυλάττω, φυλάξω, ἐφύλαξα, πεφύλαχα, πεφύλαγμαι, ἐφυλάχθην   'guard'
*φύω, φύσω, ἔφυσα/ἔφυν, πέφυκα   'produce'; 2 aor. 'grew', 'was', pf. 'am by
     nature'

Χ

 χαίρω, χαιρήσω, κεχάρηκα, ἐχάρην   'rejoice'
 χέω, χέω (fut.), ἔχεα, κέχυκα, κέχυμαι, ἐχύθην   'pour'
*χράομαι (p. 245), χρήσομαι, ἐχρησάμην, κέχρημαι, ἐχρήσθην   'use'
 χράω, χρήσω, ἔχρησα, κέχρηκα   'utter an oracle', mid. 'consult an oracle'
 χρή (subj. χρῇ, opt. χρείη, inf. χρῆναι) impf. χρῆν (= χρὴ ἦν) or ἐχρῆν   'it
     is necessary'

Ψ

 ψεύδω, ψεύσω, ἔψευσα, ἔψευσμαι, ἐψεύσθην   'deceive', mid. 'lie'

Ω

 ὠνέομαι (impf. ἐωνούμην), ὠνήσομαι, ἐώνημαι, ἐωνήθην   'buy'

λύω, λύσω, ἔλυσα, λέλυκα, λέλυμαι, ἐλύθην

Active Voice

IND	Present	Imperfect	Future	Aorist	Perfect	Pluperfect
S 1	λύω	ἔλυον	λύσω	ἔλυσα	λέλυκα	ἐλελύκη
S 2	λύεις	ἔλυες	λύσεις	ἔλυσας	λέλυκας	ἐλελύκης
S 3	λύει	ἔλυε(ν)	λύσει	ἔλυσε(ν)	λέλυκε(ν)	ἐλελύκει
D 2	(λύετον)	(ἐλύετον)	(λύσετον)	(ἐλύσατον)	(λελύκατον)	(ἐλελύκετον)
D 3	(λύετον)	(ἐλυέτην)	(λύσετον)	(ἐλυσάτην)	(λελύκατον)	(ἐλελυκέτην)
P 1	λύομεν	ἐλύομεν	λύσομεν	ἐλύσαμεν	λελύκαμεν	ἐλελύκεμεν
P 2	λύετε	ἐλύετε	λύσετε	ἐλύσατε	λελύκατε	ἐλελύκετε
P 3	λύουσι(ν)	ἔλυον	λύσουσι(ν)	ἔλυσαν	λελύκασι	ἐλελύκεσαν

SUBJ

	Present			Aorist	Perfect	
S 1	λύω			λύσω	λελυκὼς ὦ / λελύκω	
S 2	λύῃς			λύσῃς	λελυκὼς ᾖς / λελύκῃς	
S 3	λύῃ			λύσῃ	λελυκὼς ᾖ / λελύκῃ	
D 2	(λύητον)			(λύσητον)	(λελυκότε ἦτον / λελύκητον)	
D 3	(λύητον)			(λύσητον)	(λελυκότε ἦτον / λελύκητον)	
P 1	λύωμεν			λύσωμεν	λελυκότες ὦμεν / λελύκωμεν	
P 2	λύητε			λύσητε	λελυκότες ἦτε / λελύκητε	
P 3	λύωσι(ν)			λύσωσι	λελυκότες ὦσι / λελύκωσι	

OPT

	Present		Future	Aorist	Perfect	
S 1	λύοιμι		λύσοιμι	λύσαιμι	λελυκὼς εἴην / λελύκοιμι / -οίην	
S 2	λύοις		λύσοις	λύσαις / λύσειας	λελυκὼς εἴης / λελύκοις / -οίης	
S 3	λύοι		λύσοι	λύσαι / λύσειε	λελυκὼς εἴη / λελύκοι / -οίη	
D 2	(λύοιτον)		(λύσοιτον)	(λύσαιτον)	(λελυκότε εἴητον, εἶτον / λελύκοιτον)	
D 3	(λυοίτην)		(λυσοίτην)	(λυσαίτην)	(λελυκότε εἰήτην, εἴτην / λελυκοίτην)	
P 1	λύοιμεν		λύσοιμεν	λύσαιμεν	λελυκότες εἴημεν, εἶμεν / λελύκοιμεν	
P 2	λύοιτε		λύσοιτε	λύσαιτε	λελυκότες εἴητε, εἶτε / λελύκοιτε	
P 3	λύοιεν		λύσοιεν	λύσαιεν / λύσειαν	λελυκότες εἴησαν, εἶεν / λελύκοιεν	

IMP

	Present			Aorist	Perfect	
S 2	λῦε			λῦσον	λελυκὼς ἴσθι / λέλυκε	
S 3	λυέτω			λυσάτω	λελυκὼς ἔστω / λελύκέτω	
D 2	(λύετον)			(λύσατον)	(λελυκότε ἔστον / λελύκετον)	
D 3	(λυέτων)			(λυσάτων)	(λελυκότε ἔστων / λελυκέτων)	
P 2	λύετε			λύσατε	λελυκότες ἔστε / λελύκετε	
P 3	λυόντων			λυσάντων	λελυκότες ὄντων	

INF   λύειν   λύσειν   λῦσαι   λελυκέναι

PT   λύων (-οντ-)   λύσων   λύσας   λελυκώς (-οτ-)
      λύουσα   (-οντ-)   (-αντ-)   λελυκυῖα
      λῦον   λύσουσα   λύσασα   λελυκός
                               λῦσον   λῦσαν

Middle Voice of λύω (and Middle-Passive)

IND	Present (M-P)	Imperfect (M-P)	Future (M)	Aorist (M)	Perfect (M-P)	Pluperfect (M-P)
S 1	λύομαι	ἐλυόμην	λύσομαι	ἐλυσάμην	λέλυμαι	ἐλελύμην
S 2	λύει, λύῃ	ἐλύου	λύσει, -ῃ	ἐλύσω	λέλυσαι	ἐλέλυσο
S 3	λύεται	ἐλύετο	λύσεται	ἐλύσατο	λέλυται	ἐλέλυτο
D 2	(λύεσθον)	(ἐλύεσθον)	(λύσεσθον)	(ἐλύσασθον)	(λέλυσθον)	(ἐλέλυσθον)
D 3	(λύεσθον)	(ἐλυέσθην)	(λύσεσθον)	(ἐλυσάσθην)	(λέλυσθον)	(ἐλελύσθην)
P 1	λυόμεθα	ἐλυόμεθα	λυσόμεθα	ἐλυσάμεθα	λελύμεθα	ἐλελύμεθα
P 2	λύεσθε	ἐλύεσθε	λύσεσθε	ἐλύσασθε	λέλυσθε	ἐλέλυσθε
P 3	λύονται	ἐλύοντο	λύσονται	ἐλύσαντο	λέλυνται	ἐλέλυντο

SUBJ

	Present		Aorist	Perfect
S 1	λύωμαι		λύσωμαι	λελυμένος ὦ
S 2	λύῃ		λύσῃ	λελυμένος ᾖς
S 3	λύηται		λύσηται	λελυμένος ᾖ
D 2	(λύησθον)		(λύσησθον)	(λελυμένω ἦτον)
D 3	(λύησθον)		(λύσησθον)	(λελυμένω ἦτον)
P 1	λυώμεθα		λυσώμεθα	λελυμένοι ὦμεν
P 2	λύησθε		λύσησθε	λελυμένοι ἦτε
P 3	λύωνται		λύσωνται	λελυμένοι ὦσι

OPT

	Present	Future	Aorist	Perfect
S 1	λυοίμην	λυσοίμην	λυσαίμην	λελυμένος εἴην
S 2	λύοιο	λύσοιο	λύσαιο	λελυμένος εἴης
S 3	λύοιτο	λύσοιτο	λύσαιτο	λελυμένος εἴη
D 2	(λύοισθον)	(λύσοισθον)	(λύσαισθον)	(λελυμένω εἴητον / εἶτον)
D 3	(λυοίσθην)	(λυσοίσθην)	(λυσαίσθην)	(λελυμένω εἰήτην / εἴτην)
P 1	λυοίμεθα	λυσοίμεθα	λυσαίμεθα	λελυμένοι εἴημεν / εἶμεν
P 2	λύοισθε	λύσοισθε	λύσαισθε	λελυμένοι εἴητε / εἶτε
P 3	λύοιντο	λύσοιντο	λύσαιντο	λελυμένοι εἴησαν / εἶεν

IMP

	Present		Aorist	Perfect
S 2	λύου		λῦσαι	λέλυσο
S 3	λυέσθω		λυσάσθω	λελύσθω
D 2	(λύεσθον)		(λύσασθον)	(λέλυσθον)
D 3	(λυέσθων)		(λυσάσθων)	(λελύσθων)
P 2	λύεσθε		λύσασθε	λέλυσθε
P 3	λυέσθων		λυσάσθων	λελύσθων

INF   λύεσθαι   λύσεσθαι   λύσασθαι   λελύσθαι

PT	λυόμενος	λυσόμενος	λυσάμενος	λελυμένος
	λυομένη	λυσομένη	λυσαμένη	λελυμένη
	λυόμενον	λυσόμενον	λυσάμενον	λελυμένον

		Passive Voice of λύω		Second Aorist of λείπω	
IND	Future Perfect	Aorist	Future	Active	Middle
S 1	λελύσομαι	ἐλύθην	λυθήσομαι	ἔλιπον	ἐλιπόμην
S 2	λελύσει, λελύσῃ	ἐλύθης	λυθήσει, λυθήσῃ	ἔλιπες	ἐλίπου
S 3	λελύσεται	ἐλύθη	λυθήσεται	ἔλιπε	ἐλίπετο
D 2	(λελύσεσθον)	(ἐλύθητον)	(λυθήσεσθον)	(ἐλίπετον)	(ἐλίπεσθον)
D 3	(λελύσεσθον)	(ἐλυθήτην)	(λυθήσεσθον)	(ἐλιπέτην)	(ἐλιπέσθην)
P 1	λελυσόμεθα	ἐλύθημεν	λυθησόμεθα	ἐλίπομεν	ἐλιπόμεθα
P 2	λελύσεσθε	ἐλύθητε	λυθήσεσθε	ἐλίπετε	ἐλίπεσθε
P 3	λελύσονται	ἐλύθησαν	λυθήσονται	ἔλιπον	ἐλίποντο

SUBJ

S 1		λυθῶ		λίπω	λίπωμαι
S 2		λυθῇς		λίπῃς	λίπῃ
S 3		λυθῇ		λίπῃ	λίπηται
D 2		(λυθῆτον)		(λίπητον)	(λίπησθον)
D 3		(λυθῆτον)		(λίπητον)	(λίπησθον)
P 1		λυθῶμεν		λίπωμεν	λιπώμεθα
P 2		λυθῆτε		λίπητε	λίπησθε
P 3		λυθῶσι		λίπωσι	λίπωνται

OPT

S 1	λελυσοίμην	λυθείην	λυθησοίμην	λίποιμι	λιποίμην
S 2	λελύσοιο	λυθείης	λυθήσοιο	λίποις	λίποιο
S 3	λελύσοιτο	λυθείη	λυθήσοιτο	λίποι	λίποιτο
D 2	(λελύσοισθον)	(λυθεῖτον / λυθείητον)	(λυθήσοισθον)	(λίποιτον)	(λίποισθον)
D 3	(λελυσοίσθην)	(λυθείτην / λυθειήτην)	(λυθησοίσθην)	(λιποίτην)	(λιποίσθην)
P 1	λελυσοίμεθα	λυθεῖμεν / λυθείημεν	λυθησοίμεθα	λίποιμεν	λιποίμεθα
P 2	λελύσοισθε	λυθεῖτε / λυθείητε	λυθήσοισθε	λίποιτε	λίποισθε
P 3	λελύσοιντο	λυθεῖεν / λυθείησαν	λυθήσοιντο	λίποιεν	λίποιντο

IMP

S 2		λύθητι		λίπε	λιποῦ
S 3		λυθήτω		λιπέτω	λιπέσθω
D 2		(λύθητον)		(λίπετον)	(λίπεσθον)
D 3		(λυθήτων)		(λιπέτων)	(λιπέσθων)
P 2		λύθητε		λίπετε	λίπεσθε
P 3		λυθέντων		λιπόντων	λιπέσθων

INF   λελύσεσθαι   λυθῆναι   λυθήσεσθαι   λιπεῖν   λιπέσθαι

PT   λελυσόμενος   λυθείς   λυθησόμενος   λιπών   λιπόμενος
       λελυσομένη   λυθεῖσα   λυθησομένη   λιποῦσα   λιπομένη
       λελυσόμενον   λυθέν   λυθησόμενον   λιπόν   λιπόμενον

Contract Verbs: Present System

-άω   Active   Middle-Passive

IND Pres.

		Active	Middle-Passive
	1	νικῶ (-άω)	νικῶμαι (-άομαι)
S	2	νικᾷς (-άεις)	νικᾷ (-άει, -άῃ)
	3	νικᾷ (-άει)	νικᾶται (-άεται)
D	2	(νικᾶτον (-άετον))	(νικᾶσθον (-άεσθον))
	3	(νικᾶτον (-άετον))	(νικᾶσθον (-άεσθον))
	1	νικῶμεν (-άομεν)	νικώμεθα (-αόμεθα)
P	2	νικᾶτε (-άετε)	νικᾶσθε (-άεσθε)
	3	νικῶσι (-άουσι)	νικῶνται (-άονται)

Imperf.

		Active	Middle-Passive
	1	ἐνίκων (-ͅαον)	ἐνικώμην (-αόμην)
S	2	ἐνίκας (-ͅαες)	ἐνικῶ (-άου)
	3	ἐνίκα (-ͅαε)	ἐνικᾶτο (-άετο)
D	2	(ἐνικᾶτον (-άετον))	(ἐνικᾶσθον (-άεσθον))
	3	(ἐνικάτην (-αέτην))	(ἐνικάσθην (-αέσθην))
	1	ἐνικῶμεν (-άομεν)	ἐνικώμεσθα (-αόμεσθα)
P	2	ἐνικᾶτε (-άετε)	ἐνικᾶσθε (-άεσθε)
	3	ἐνίκων (-ͅαον)	ἐνικῶντο (-άοντο)

SUBJ Pres.

		Active	Middle-Passive
	1	νικῶ (-άω)	νικῶμαι (-άωμαι)
S	2	νικᾷς (-άῃς)	νικᾷ (-άῃ)
	3	νικᾷ (-άῃ)	νικᾶται (-άηται)
D	2	(νικᾶτον (-άητον))	(νικᾶσθον (-άησθον))
	3	(νικᾶτον (-άητον))	(νικᾶσθον (-άησθον))
	1	νικῶμεν (-άωμεν)	νικώμεθα (-αώμεθα)
P	2	νικᾶτε (-άητε)	νικᾶσθε (-άησθε)
	3	νικῶσι (-άωσι)	νικῶνται (-άωνται)

OPT Pres.

		Active	Middle-Passive
	1	νικῴην (-αοίην)	νικῴμην (-αοίμην)
S	2	νικῴης (-αοίης)	νικῷο (-άοιο)
	3	νικῴη (-αοίη)	νικῷτο (-άοιτο)
D	2	(νικῷητον (-αοίητον) / νικῷτον (-άοιτον))	(νικῷσθον (-άοισθον))
	3	(νικῴήτην (-αοιήτην) / νικῴτην (-αοίτην))	(νικῷσθην (-αοίσθην))

		Active	Middle-Passive
	1	νικῷημεν (-αοίημεν) / νικῷμεν (-άοιμεν)	νικῴμεθα (-αοίμεθα)
P	2	νικῷητε (-αοίητε) / νικῷτε (-άοιτε)	νικῷσθε (-άοισθε)
	3	νικῷησαν (-αοίησαν) / νικῷεν (-άοιεν)	νικῷντο (-άοιντο)

IMP

		Active	Middle-Passive
S	2	νίκα (-άε)	νικῶ (-άου)
	3	νικάτω (-αέτω)	νικάσθω (-αέσθω)
D	2	(νικᾶτον (-άετον))	(νικᾶσθον (-άεσθον))
	3	(νικάτων (-αέτων))	(νικάσθων (-αέσθων))
P	2	νικᾶτε (-άετε)	νικᾶσθε (-άεσθε)
	3	νικώντων (-αόντων)	νικάσθων (-αέσθων)

INF   νικᾶν (-άειν)   νικᾶσθαι (-άεσθαι)

PT   νικῶν (-άων)   νικώμενος, -η, -ον
           νικῶσα (-άουσα)   (-αόμενος)
           νικῶν (-άον)

-εω		Active	Middle-Passive

IND Pres.

		Active	Middle-Passive
S	1	φιλῶ (-έω)	φιλοῦμαι (-έομαι)
	2	φιλεῖς (-έεις)	φιλεῖ / -ῇ (-έει, -έῃ)
	3	φιλεῖ (-έει)	φιλεῖται (-έεται)
D	2	(φιλεῖτον (-έετον))	(φιλεῖσθον (-έεσθον))
	3	(φιλεῖτον (-έετον))	(φιλεῖσθον (-έεσθον))
P	1	φιλοῦμεν (-έομεν)	φιλούμεθα (-εόμεθα)
	2	φιλεῖτε (-έετε)	φιλεῖσθε (-έεσθε)
	3	φιλοῦσι (-έουσι)	φιλοῦνται (-έονται)

Imperf.

		Active	Middle-Passive
S	1	ἐφίλουν (-εον)	ἐφιλούμην (-εόμην)
	2	ἐφίλεις (-εες)	ἐφιλοῦ (-έου)
	3	ἐφίλει (-εε)	ἐφιλεῖτο (-έετο)
D	2	(ἐφιλεῖτον (-έετον))	(ἐφιλεῖσθον (-έεσθον))
	3	(ἐφιλείτην (-εέτην))	(ἐφιλείσθην (-εέσθην))
P	1	ἐφιλοῦμεν (-έομεν)	φιλούμεθα (-εόμεθα)
	2	ἐφιλεῖτε (-έετε)	ἐφιλεῖσθε (-έεσθε)
	3	ἐφίλουν (-εον)	ἐφιλοῦντο (-έοντο)

SUBJ

		Active	Middle-Passive
S	1	φιλῶ (-έω)	φιλῶμαι (-έωμαι)
	2	φιλῇς (-έῃς)	φιλῇ (-έῃ)
	3	φιλῇ (-έῃ)	φιλῆται (-έηται)
D	2	(φιλῆτον (-έητον))	(φιλῆσθον (-έησθον))
	3	(φιλῆτον (-έητον))	(φιλῆσθον (-έησθον))

		Active	Middle-Passive
	1	φιλῶμεν (-έωμεν)	φιλώμεθα (-εώμεθα)
P	2	φιλῆτε (-έητε)	φιλῆσθε (-έησθε)
	3	φιλῶσι (-έωσι)	φιλῶνται (-έωνται)

OPT

		Active	Middle-Passive
	1	φιλοίην (-εοίην)	φιλοίμην (-εοίμην)
S	2	φιλοίης (-εοίης)	φιλοῖο (-έοιο)
	3	φιλοίη (-εοίη)	φιλοῖτο (-έοιτο)
	2	(φιλοίητον (-εοιήτον) / φιλοῖτον (-έοιτον))	(φιλοῖσθον (-έοισθον))
D	3	(φιλοιήτην (-εοιήτην) / φιλοίτην (-εοίτην))	(φιλοίσθην (-εοίσθην))
	1	φιλοίημεν (-εοίημεν) / φιλοῖμεν (-έοιμεν)	φιλοίμεθα (-εοίμεθα)
P	2	φιλοίητε (-εοίητε) / φιλοῖτε (-έοιτε)	φιλοῖσθε (-έοισθε)
	3	φιλοίησαν (-εοίησαν) / φιλοῖεν (-έοιεν)	φιλοῖντο (-έοιντο)

IMP

		Active	Middle-Passive
S	2	φίλει (-εε)	φιλοῦ (-έου)
	3	φιλείτω (-εέτω)	φιλείσθω (-εέσθω)
D	2	(φιλεῖτον (-έετον))	(φιλεῖσθον (-έεσθον))
	3	(φιλείτων (-εέτων))	(φιλείσθων (-εέσθων))
P	2	φιλεῖτε (-έετε)	φιλεῖσθε (-έεσθε)
	3	φιλούντων (-εόντων)	φιλείσθων (-εέσθων)

| INF | | φιλεῖν (-έειν) | φιλεῖσθαι (-έεσθαι) |

| PT | | φιλῶν (-έων) φιλοῦσα (-έουσα) φιλοῦν (-έον) | φιλούμενος, -η, -ον (-εόμενος) |

| -όω | | Active | Middle-Passive |

IND Pres.

		Active	Middle-Passive
	1	δηλῶ (-όω)	δηλοῦμαι (-όομαι)
S	2	δηλοῖς (-όεις)	δηλοῖ (-όει, -όῃ)
	3	δηλοῖ (-όει)	δηλοῦται (-όεται)
D	2	(δηλοῦτον (-όετον))	(δηλοῦσθον (-όεσθον))
	3	(δηλοῦτον (-όετον))	(δηλοῦσθον (-όεσθον))
	1	δηλοῦμεν (-όομεν)	δηλούμεθα (-οόμεθα)
P	2	δηλοῦτε (-όετε)	δηλοῦσθε (-όεσθε)
	3	δηλοῦσι (-όουσι)	δηλοῦνται (-όονται)

Imperf.

		Active	Middle-Passive
	1	ἐδήλουν (-οον)	ἐδηλούμην (-οόμην)
S	2	ἐδήλους (-οες)	ἐδηλοῦ (-όου)
	3	ἐδήλου (-οε)	ἐδηλοῦτο (-όετο)

D	2	(ἐδηλοῦτον (-όετον))	(ἐδηλοῦσθον (-όεσθον))
	3	(ἐδηλούτην (-οέτην))	(ἐδηλούσθην (-οέσθην))
	1	ἐδηλοῦμεν (-όομεν)	ἐδηλούμεθα (-οόμεθα)
P	2	ἐδηλοῦτε (-όετε)	ἐδηλοῦσθε (-όεσθε)
	3	ἐδήλουν (-́οον)	ἐδηλοῦντο (-όοντο)

SUBJ

S	1	δηλῶ (-όω)	δηλῶμαι (-όωμαι)
	2	δηλοῖς (-όῃς)	δηλοῖ (-όῃ)
	3	δηλοῖ (-όῃ)	δηλῶται (-όηται)
D	2	(δηλῶτον (-όητον))	(δηλῶσθον (-όησθον))
	3	(δηλῶτον (-όητον))	(δηλῶσθον (-όησθον))
P	1	δηλῶμεν (-όωμεν)	δηλώμεθα (-οώμεθα)
	2	δηλῶτε (-όητε)	δηλῶσθε (-όησθε)
	3	δηλῶσι (-όωσι)	δηλῶνται (-όωνται)

OPT

S	1	δηλοίην (-οοίην)	δηλοίμην (-οοίμην)
	2	δηλοίης (-οοίης)	δηλοῖο (-όοιο)
	3	δηλοίη (-οοίη)	δηλοῖτο (-όοιτο)
D	2	(δηλοίητον (-οοίητον) / δηλοῖτον (-όοιτον))	(δηλοῖσθον (-όοισθον))
	3	(δηλοιήτην (-οοιήτην) / δηλοίτην (-οοίτην))	(δηλοίσθην (-οοίσθην))
P	1	δηλοίημεν (-οοίημεν) / δηλοῖμεν (-όοιμεν)	δηλοίμεθα (-οοίμεθα)
	2	δηλοίητε (-οοίητε) / δηλοῖτε (-όοιτε)	δηλοῖσθε (-όοισθε)
	3	δηλοίησαν (-οοίησαν) / δηλοῖεν (-όοιεν)	δηλοῖντο (-όοιντο)

IMP

S	2	δήλου (-́οε)	δηλοῦ (-όου)
	3	δηλούτω (-οέτω)	δηλούσθω (-οέσθω)
D	2	(δηλοῦτον (-όετον))	(δηλοῦσθον (-όεσθον))
	3	(δηλούτων (-οέτων))	(δηλούσθων (-οέσθων))
P	2	δηλοῦτε (-όετε)	δηλοῦσθε (-όεσθε)
	3	δηλούντων (-οόντων)	δηλούσθων (-οέσθων)

INF	δηλοῦν (-όειν)	δηλοῦσθαι (-όεσθαι)
PT	δηλῶν (-όων) δηλοῦσα (-όουσα) δηλοῦν (-όον)	δηλούμενος, -́η, -ον (-οόμενος)

Liquid Future (future of κρίνω)

		Active	Middle
IND			
	1	κρινῶ	κρινοῦμαι
S	2	κρινεῖς	κρινεῖ / -ῇ
	3	κρινεῖ	κρινεῖται
D	2	(κρινεῖτον)	(κρινεῖσθον)
	3	(κρινεῖτον)	(κρινεῖσθον)
	1	κρινοῦμεν	κρινούμεθα
P	2	κρινεῖτε	κρινεῖσθε
	3	κρινοῦσι	κρινοῦνται
OPT			
	1	κρινοίην / κρινοῖμι	κρινοίμην
S	2	κρινοίης / κρινοῖς	κρινοῖο
	3	κρινοίη / κρινοῖ	κρινοῖτο
D	2	(κρινοῖτον)	(κρινοῖσθον)
	3	(κρινοίτην)	(κρινοίσθην)
	1	κρινοῖμεν	κρινοίμεθα
P	2	κρινοῖτε	κρινοῖσθε
	3	κρινοῖεν	κρινοῖντο
INF		κρινεῖν	κρινεῖσθαι
PT		κρινῶν κρινοῦσα κρινοῦν	κρινούμενος, -η, -ον

-MI Verbs

1. ἵστημι

		Present System Active	Middle-Passive	2nd Aorist Active	Perfect System Active
IND					
	1	ἵστημι	ἵσταμαι	ἔστην	ἕστηκα
S	2	ἵστης	ἵστασαι	ἔστης	ἕστηκας
	3	ἵστησι	ἵσταται	ἔστη	ἕστηκε
D	2	(ἵστατον)	(ἵστασθον)	(ἔστητον)	(ἕστατον)
	3	(ἵστατον)	(ἵστασθον)	(ἐστήτην)	(ἕστατον)
	1	ἵσταμεν	ἱστάμεθα	ἔστημεν	ἕσταμεν
P	2	ἵστατε	ἵστασθε	ἔστητε	ἕστατε
	3	ἱστᾶσι	ἵστανται	ἔστησαν	ἑστᾶσι

		Imperfect			Pluperfect
	1	ἵστην	ἱστάμην		εἱστήκη
S	2	ἵστης	ἵστασο		εἱστήκης
	3	ἵστη	ἵστατο		εἱστήκει
D	2	(ἵστατον)	(ἵστασθον)		(ἕστατον)
	3	(ἱστάτην)	(ἱστάσθην)		(ἑστάτην)
	1	ἵσταμεν	ἱστάμεθα		ἕσταμεν
P	2	ἵστατε	ἵστασθε		ἕστατε
	3	ἵστασαν	ἵσταντο		ἕστασαν

SUBJ		Present			Perfect
	1	ἱστῶ	ἱστῶμαι	στῶ	ἑστῶ
S	2	ἱστῇς	ἱστῇ	στῇς	ἑστῇς
	3	ἱστῇ	ἱστῆται	στῇ	ἑστῇ
D	2	(ἱστῆτον)	(ἱστῆσθον)	(στῆτον)	(ἑστῆτον)
	3	(ἱστῆτον)	(ἱστῆσθον)	(στῆτον)	(ἑστῆτον)
	1	ἱστῶμεν	ἱστώμεθα	στῶμεν	ἑστῶμεν
P	2	ἱστῆτε	ἱστῆσθε	στῆτε	ἑστῆτε
	3	ἱστῶσι	ἱστῶνται	στῶσι	ἑστῶσι

OPT					
	1	ἱσταίην	ἱσταίμην	σταίην	ἑσταίην
S	2	ἱσταίης	ἱσταῖο	σταίης	ἑσταίης
	3	ἱσταίη	ἱσταῖτο	σταίη	ἑσταίη
D	2	(ἱσταίητον / ἱσταῖτον)	(ἱσταῖσθον)	(σταίητον / σταῖτον)	(ἑσταίητον / ἑσταῖτον)
	3	(ἱσταιήτην / ἱσταίτην)	(ἱσταίσθην)	(σταιήτην / σταίτην)	(ἑσταιήτην / ἑσταίτην)
	1	ἱσταίημεν / ἱσταῖμεν	ἱσταίμεθα	σταίημεν / σταῖμεν	ἑσταίημεν / ἑσταῖμεν
P	2	ἱσταίητε / ἱσταῖτε	ἱσταῖσθε	σταίητε / σταῖτε	ἑσταίητε / ἑσταῖτε
	3	ἱσταίησαν / ἱσταῖεν	ἱσταῖντο	σταίησαν / σταῖεν	ἑσταίησαν / ἑσταῖεν

IMP					
S	2	ἵστη	ἵστασο	στῆθι	ἕσταθι
	3	ἱστάτω	ἱστάσθω	στήτω	ἑστάτω
D	2	(ἵστατον)	(ἵστασθον)	(στῆτον)	(ἕστατον)
	3	(ἱστάτων)	(ἱστάσθων)	(στήτων)	(ἑστάτων)
P	2	ἵστατε	ἵστασθε	στῆτε	ἕστατε
	3	ἱστάντων	ἱστάσθων	στάντων	ἑστάντων
INF		ἱστάναι	ἵστασθαι	στῆναι	ἑστάναι
PT		ἱστάς, ἱστᾶσα, ἱστάν	ἱστάμενος, -η, -ον	στάς, στᾶσα, στάν	ἑστώς, ἑστῶσα, ἑστός

2. τίθημι

		Present System		2nd Aorist	
		Active	Middle-Passive	Active	Middle
IND					
	1	τίθημι	τίθεμαι	ἔθηκα	ἐθέμην
S	2	τίθης	τίθεσαι	ἔθηκας	ἔθου
	3	τίθησι	τίθεται	ἔθηκε	ἔθετο
D	2	(τίθετον)	(τίθεσθον)	(ἔθετον)	(ἔθεσθον)
	3	(τίθετον)	(τίθεσθον)	(ἐθέτην)	(ἐθέσθην)
	1	τίθεμεν	τιθέμεθα	ἔθεμεν	ἐθέμεθα
P	2	τίθετε	τίθεσθε	ἔθετε	ἔθεσθε
	3	τιθέασι	τίθενται	ἔθεσαν	ἔθεντο

		Imperfect	
	1	ἐτίθην	ἐτιθέμην
S	2	ἐτίθεις	ἐτίθεσο
	3	ἐτίθει	ἐτίθετο
D	2	(ἐτίθετον)	(ἐτίθεσθον)
	3	(ἐτιθέτην)	(ἐτιθέσθην)
	1	ἐτίθεμεν	ἐτιθέμεθα
P	2	ἐτίθετε	ἐτίθεσθε
	3	ἐτίθεσαν	ἐτίθεντο

SUBJ		Present			
	1	τιθῶ	τιθῶμαι	θῶ	θῶμαι
S	2	τιθῇς	τιθῇ	θῇς	θῇ
	3	τιθῇ	τιθῆται	θῇ	θῆται
D	2	(τιθῆτον)	(τιθῆσθον)	(θῆτον)	(θῆσθον)
	3	(τιθῆτον)	(τιθῆσθον)	(θῆτον)	(θῆσθον)
	1	τιθῶμεν	τιθώμεθα	θῶμεν	θώμεθα
P	2	τιθῆτε	τιθῆσθε	θῆτε	θῆσθε
	3	τιθῶσι	τιθῶνται	θῶσι	θῶνται

OPT				
	τιθείην	τιθείμην	θείην	θείμην
	τιθείης	τιθεῖο	θείης	θεῖο
	τιθείη	τιθεῖτο	θείη	θεῖτο
	(τιθείητον / τιθεῖτον)	(τιθεῖσθον)	(θείητον / θεῖτον)	(θεῖσθον)
	(τιθειήτην / τιθείτην)	(τιθείσθην)	(θειήτην / θείτην)	(θείσθην)
	τιθείημεν / τιθεῖμεν	τιθείμεθα	θείημεν / θεῖμεν	θείμεθα
	τιθείητε / τιθεῖτε	τιθεῖσθε	θείητε / θεῖτε	θεῖσθε
	τιθείησαν / τιθεῖεν	τιθεῖντο	θείησαν / θεῖεν	θεῖντο

IMP

S	2	τίθει	τίθεσο	θές	θοῦ
	3	τιθέτω	τιθέσθω	θέτω	θέσθω

D	2	(τίθετον)	(τίθεσθον)	(θέτον)	(θέσθον)
	3	(τιθέτων)	(τιθέσθων)	(θέτων)	(θέσθων)

P	2	τίθετε	τίθεσθε	θέτε	θέσθε
	3	τιθέντων	τιθέσθων	θέντων	θέσθων

INF   τιθέναι   τίθεσθαι   θεῖναι   θέσθαι

PT   τιθείς   τιθέμενος,   θείς   θέμενος,
          τιθεῖσα   -η, -ον   θεῖσα   -η, -ον
          τιθέν   θέν

3. δίδωμι

	Present System		2nd Aorist	
	Active	Middle-Passive	Active	Middle

IND

	1	δίδωμι	δίδομαι	ἔδωκα	ἐδόμην
S	2	δίδως	δίδοσαι	ἔδωκας	ἔδου
	3	δίδωσι	δίδοται	ἔδωκε	ἔδοτο

D	2	(δίδοτον)	(δίδοσθον)	(ἔδοτον)	(ἔδοσθον)
	3	(δίδοτον)	(δίδοσθον)	(ἐδότην)	(ἐδόσθην)

	1	δίδομεν	διδόμεθα	ἔδομεν	ἐδόμεθα
P	2	δίδοτε	δίδοσθε	ἔδοτε	ἔδοσθε
	3	διδόασι	δίδονται	ἔδοσαν	ἔδοντο

Imperfect

	1	ἐδίδουν	ἐδιδόμην
S	2	ἐδίδους	ἐδίδοσο
	3	ἐδίδου	ἐδίδοτο

D	2	(ἐδίδοτον)	(ἐδίδοσθον)
	3	(ἐδιδότην)	(ἐδιδόσθην)

	1	ἐδίδομεν	ἐδιδόμεθα
P	2	ἐδίδοτε	ἐδίδοσθε
	3	ἐδίδοσαν	ἐδίδοντο

SUBJ   Present

	1	διδῶ	διδῶμαι	δῶ	δῶμαι
S	2	διδῷς	διδῷ	δῷς	δῷ
	3	διδῷ	διδῶται	δῷ	δῶται

D	2	(διδῶτον)	(διδῶσθον)	(δῶτον)	(δῶσθον)
	3	(διδῶτον)	(διδῶσθον)	(δῶτον)	(δῶσθον)

	1	διδῶμεν	διδώμεθα	δῶμεν	δώμεθα
P	2	διδῶτε	διδῶσθε	δῶτε	δῶσθε
	3	διδῶσι	διδῶνται	δῶσι	δῶνται

OPT

S	1	διδοίην	διδοίμην	δοίην	δοίμην
	2	διδοίης	διδοῖο	δοίης	δοῖο
	3	διδοίη	διδοῖτο	δοίη	δοῖτο
D	2	(διδοίητον / διδοῖτον)	(διδοῖσθον)	(δοίητον / δοῖτον)	(δοῖσθον)
	3	(διδοιήτην / διδοίτην)	(διδοίσθην)	(δοιήτην / δοίτην)	(δοίσθην)
P	1	διδοίημεν / διδοῖμεν	διδοίμεθα	δοίημεν / δοῖμεν	δοίμεθα
	2	διδοίητε / διδοῖτε	διδοῖσθε	δοίητε / δοῖτε	δοῖσθε
	3	διδοίησαν / διδοῖεν	διδοῖντο	δοίησαν / δοῖεν	δοῖντο

IMP

S	2	δίδου	δίδοσο	δός	δοῦ
	3	διδότω	διδόσθω	δότω	δόσθω
D	2	(δίδοτον)	(δίδοσθον)	(δότον)	(δόσθον)
	3	(διδότων)	(διδόσθων)	(δότων)	(δόσθων)
P	2	δίδοτε	δίδοσθε	δότε	δόσθε
	3	διδόντων	διδόσθων	δόντων	δόσθων

INF	διδόναι	δίδοσθαι	δοῦναι	δόσθαι
PT	διδούς διδοῦσα διδόν	διδόμενος, -η, -ον	δούς δοῦσα δόν	δόμενος, -η, -ον

4. -νυμι verbs

Present System of δείκνυμι

		Active	Middle-Passive	Active	Middle-Passive
IND		Present		Imperfect	
S	1	δείκνυμι	δείκνυμαι	ἐδείκνυν	ἐδεικνύμην
	2	δείκνυς	δείκνυσαι	ἐδείκνυς	ἐδείκνυσο
	3	δείκνυσι	δείκνυται	ἐδείκνυ	ἐδείκνυτο
D	2	(δείκνυτον)	(δείκνυσθον)	(ἐδείκνυτον)	(ἐδείκνυσθον)
	3	(δείκνυτον)	(δείκνυσθον)	(ἐδεικνύτην)	(ἐδεικνύσθην)
P	1	δείκνυμεν	δεικνύμεθα	ἐδείκνυμεν	ἐδεικνύμεθα
	2	δείκνυτε	δείκνυσθε	ἐδείκνυτε	ἐδείκνυσθε
	3	δεικνύασι	δείκνυνται	ἐδείκνυσαν	ἐδείκνυντο
SUBJ		Present		OPT	
S	1	δεικνύω	δεικνύωμαι	δεικνύοιμι	δεικνυοίμην
	2	δεικνύῃς	δεικνύῃ	δεικνύοις	δεικνύοιο
	3	δεικνύῃ	δεικνύηται	δεικνύοι	δεικνύοιτο
D	2	(δεικνύητον)	(δεικνύησθον)	(δεικνύοιτον)	(δεικνύοισθον)
	3	(δεικνύητον)	(δεικνύησθον)	(δεικνυοίτην)	(δεικνυοίσθην)

	1	δεικνύωμεν	δεικνυώμεθα	δεικνύοιμεν	δεικνυοίμεθα
P	2	δεικνύητε	δεικνύησθε	δεικνύοιτε	δεικνύοισθε
	3	δεικνύωσι	δεικνύωνται	δεικνύοιεν	δεικνύοιντο

IMP   INF

S	2	δείκνυ	δείκνυσο	δεικνύναι	δείκνυσθαι
	3	δεικνύτω	δεικνύσθω		

PT

D	2	(δείκνυτον)	(δείκνυσθον)	δεικνύς	δεικνύμενος,
	3	(δεικνύτων)	(δεικνύσθων)	δεικνῦσα	-η, -ον
P	2	δείκνυτε	δείκνυσθε	δεικνύν	
	3	δεικνύντων	δεικνύσθων		

IRREGULAR VERBS

εἰμί 'be'

		Present				Imperfect	Future	
		IND	SUBJ	OPT	IMP	IND	IND	OPT
	1	εἰμι	ὦ	εἴην		ἦ / ἦν	ἔσομαι	ἐσοίμην
S	2	εἶ	ἦς	εἴης	ἴσθι	ἦσθα	ἔσῃ / -ει	ἔσοιο
	3	ἐστί	ᾖ	εἴη	ἔστω	ἦν	ἔσται	ἔσοιτο
D	2	(ἐστόν)	(ἦτον)	(εἴητον / εἶτον)	(ἔστον)	(ἦστον)	(ἔσεσθον)	(ἔσοισθον)
	3	(ἐστόν)	(ἦτον)	(εἰήτην / εἴτην)	(ἔστων)	(ἤστην)	(ἔσεσθον)	(ἐσοίσθην)
P	1	ἐσμέν	ὦμεν	εἴημεν / εἶμεν		ἦμεν	ἐσόμεθα	ἐσοίμεθα
	2	ἐστέ	ἦτε	εἴητε / εἶτε	ἔστε	ἦτε / (ἦστε)	ἔσεσθε	ἔσοισθε
	3	εἰσί	ὦσι	εἴησαν / εἶεν	ἔστων / ὄντων	ἦσαν	ἔσονται	ἔσοιντο

INF   εἶναι   ἔσεσθαι

PT   ὤν, οὖσα, ὄν   ἐσόμενος, -η, -ον

εἶμι 'go'

		Present				Imperfect
		IND	SUBJ	OPT	IMP	IND
	1	εἶμι	ἴω	ἴοιμι/ἰοίην		ἦα / ἤειν
S	2	εἶ	ἴῃς	ἴοις	ἴθι	ἤεισθα / ἤεις
	3	εἶσι	ἴῃ	ἴοι	ἴτω	ἤειν / ἤει
D	2	(ἴτον)	(ἴητον)	(ἴοιτον)	(ἴτον)	(ᾖτον)
	3	(ἴτον)	(ἴητον)	(ἰοίτην)	(ἴτων)	(ᾔτην)
P	1	ἴμεν	ἴωμεν	ἴοιμεν		ᾖμεν
	2	ἴτε	ἴητε	ἴοιτε	ἴτε	ᾖτε
	3	ἴασι	ἴωσι	ἴοιεν	ἰόντων	ᾖσαν / ᾔεσαν

INF   ἰέναι

PT   ἰών, ἰοῦσα, ἰόν

φημί 'say'

		IND	SUBJ	OPT	IMP	IND
		Present			**Imperfect**	
	1	φημί	φῶ	φαίην		ἔφην
S	2	φής	φῆς	φαίης	φαθί/φάθι	ἔφησθα / ἔφης
	3	φησί	φῇ	φαίη	φάτω	ἔφη
D	2	(φατόν)	(φῆτον)	---	(φάτον)	(ἔφατον)
	3	(φατόν)	(φῆτον)	---	(φάτων)	(ἐφάτην)
	1	φαμέν	φῶμεν	φαῖμεν / φαίημεν		ἔφαμεν
P	2	φατέ	φῆτε	φαίητε	φάτε	ἔφατε
	3	φασί	φῶσι	φαῖεν / φαίησαν	φάντων	ἔφασαν

INF	φάναι	Future	φήσω
PT	φάς, φᾶσα, φάν (poetic)	Aorist	ἔφησα
	Attic prose uses φάσκων		

English-Greek Vocabulary

(for translation exercises)

A

about   περί

absent: use participle of ἄπειμι

    be absent   ἄπειμι

admire   θαυμάζω

aforesaid (the)   ταῦτα

after   (use aorist participle, see p. 155f.)

all   πᾶς, πᾶσα, πᾶν (pp. 136-37)

alone   μόνος, μόνη, μόνον

although   (see concessive participle with καί, καίπερ, pp. 157-59)

and   καί

anyone   τις (p. 173)

anyone who   ὅστις (p. 174)

anything   τι (p. 173)

anything which   ὅ τι (p. 174)

archon   ἄρχων, ἄρχοντος, ὁ (p. 120)

attribute   ἀνατίθημι (p. 268) principal parts follow τίθημι*

avoid   φεύγω*

B

bad   κακός, κακή, κακόν

be   εἰμί*, ἔσομαι (p. 57), γίγνομαι*

be able   δύναμαι* (p. 272), οἷός τε εἰμί (p. 113)

be caught   ἁλίσκομαι* (p. 272)

be confident   πέποιθα (perfect of πείθω*, p. 179) + dat.

be guilty   ἀδικέω (pp. 245-46)

be present   πάρειμι (cf. εἰμί)

be victorious   νικάω (pp. 244-45)

be willing   ἐθέλω*

beautiful   καλός, καλή, καλόν

become   γίγνομαι*

better   ἀμείνων, βελτίων, κρείττων (pp. 220-21)

before   πρίν (pp. 141-42)

begin   ἄρχω*, + gen. + participle (p. 160)

believe   νομίζω*, πιστεύω

best   ἄριστος, ἀρίστη, ἄριστον

    the best of men   οἱ ἄριστοι

bird   ὄρνις, ὄρνιθος, ὁ/ἡ (p. 120)

both . . . and   καί . . . καί

brave   ἀγαθός, -ή, -όν; ἐσθλός, -ή, -όν

bring   φέρω*, ἄγω*

brother   ἀδελφός, -οῦ, ὁ

business   ἔργον, -ου, τό

    it is the business of   ἔργον ἐστί + gen.

but   ἀλλά; δέ (postpositive)

by, dat. of means (p. 48); agent: ὑπό + gen. (p. 89)

    *to be found in the principle parts list

C

carry   φέρω*
catch   αἱρέω*
      be caught   ἁλίσκομαι*
cease (i.e. stop oneself)   παύομαι
certain (a certain one)   τις, τι (p. 173)
child   παιδίον, -ου, τό; παῖς, παιδός, ὁ/ἡ (pp. 120, 125)
citizen   πολίτης, -ου, ὁ (p. 83)
city   πόλις, πόλεως, ἡ (p. 122)
come   ἔρχομαι*
come into being   γίγνομαι*
common, in common   κοινός, -ή, -όν
concerning   περί (+ gen.)
confident, be   πέποιθα + dat. (see p. 179)
consent   ἐθέλω*
corrupt   διαφθείρω*
court   δικαστήριον, δίκη
      to take someone to court   ἄγειν πρὸς τὴν δίκην

D

dare   τολμάω
death   θάνατος, θανάτου, ὁ
deed   ἔργον, ἔργου, τό
deny   οὔ φημι
destroy   λύω, ἀπόλλυμι*
die   ἀποθνῄσκω*
difficult   χαλεπός, -ή, -όν
divinity   δαίμων, δαίμονος, ὁ (p. 120)
do   πράττω*, ποιέω (pp. 245-46)

E

each other   ἀλλήλων (p. 175)
educate   παιδεύω
      have (someone) educated   παιδεύομαι
either . . . or   ἤ . . . ἤ
enemy   ἐχθρός, -ά, -όν
evil   κακός, -ή, -όν; πονηρός, -ά, -όν
      the evils   τὰ κακά

F

father   πατήρ, πατρός, ὁ (pp. 122-23)
fear   δέδια, δέδοικα (p. 185), φοβέομαι* (pp. 245-46, 251)
find   εὑρίσκω*
fine   καλός, -ή, -όν
flee   φεύγω*
following, the   τάδε
for (as conjunction)   γάρ (postpositive)
      as preposition, use dative case
forever   ἀεί, εἰς ἀεί

former times, in expression   οἱ τότε 'men of former times'
free   λύω
friend   φίλος, -ου, ὁ
friendship   φιλία, φιλίας, ἡ
future   τὰ μέλλοντα, ὁ μέλλων χρόνος

G

gain   κέρδος, κέρδους, τό
gift   δῶρον, δώρου, τό
give   δίδωμι (pp. 267-68)
gladly   ἡδέως
go   ἔρχομαι*, εἶμι
god   θεός, -οῦ, ὁ; δαίμων, δαίμονος, ὁ
goddess   θεά, -ᾶς, ἡ; θεός, -οῦ, ἡ
good   ἀγαθός, -ή, -όν; καλός, -ή, -όν; ἐσθλός, -ή, -όν; χρηστός, -ή, -όν
    good things   τὰ ἀγαθά
    good men   οἱ ἀγαθοί
greatest   μέγιστος, μεγίστη, μέγιστον
Greece   Ἑλλάς, Ἑλλάδος, ἡ (p. 120)
ground, as in expression "on the ground that"   ὡς + ptcpl. (p. 157)
guest   ξένος, -ου, ὁ
guilty, be   ἀδικέω (pp. 245-46)

H

happen   γίγνομαι*, συμβαίνω (pp. 272, 273), τυγχάνω (p. 161)
have   ἔχω*
have (someone) educated   παιδεύομαι (mid. of παιδεύω)
hear   ἀκούω* + gen. (of person heard from), + acc. (of thing heard)
heaven(s)   οὐρανός, -οῦ, ὁ
help (be ally to)   συμμαχέω + dat. (pp. 245-46)
her   oblique cases of αὐτός, -ή, -ό in fem. (pp. 195-96)
    as reflexive   ἑαυτῆς, -ῇ, -ήν (p. 197)
    as possessive, use article (p. 39), αὐτῆς (pp. 195-96), ἑαυτῆς 'her own'
here   ἐνθάδε, ἐνταῦθα
herald   κῆρυξ, κήρυκος, ὁ (p. 120)
him   oblique cases of αὐτός in masculine (pp. 195-96)
    himself, as emphatic   αὐτός (pp. 195-96)
         as reflexive   ἑαυτοῦ (p. 197)
his   article (p. 39), αὐτοῦ (pp. 195-96), ἑαυτοῦ 'his own'
hit   βάλλω*, hit with + dat. of means
honest (= just)   δίκαιος, δικαία, δίκαιον
honor (n.)   τιμή, -ῆς, ἡ   (vb.) τιμάω (pp. 244-45)
host   ξένος, -ου, ὁ
house   οἰκία, -ας, ἡ (p. 83)
hurt   βλάπτω*

I

I   ἐγώ (p. 195); unless emphatic, expressed by first person verb ending in
    the singular
if   εἰ, ἐάν (conditions, pp. 142-43, 289-90, 293-94, 300-01)

immortal   ἀθάνατος, -ον (p. 62)
in, loc. prep.   ἐν + dat., as dat. or acc. of respect (p. 70)
in common (common)   κοινός, -ή, -όν
into   εἰς + acc.
is   ἐστί = he/she/it is/there is (p. 57)
island   νῆσος, νήσου, ἡ
it is necessary   ἀνάγκη (ἐστί), δεῖ, χρή

J

judge (n)   δικαστής, -οῦ, ὁ   (vb) κρίνω
justice   δίκη, δικαιοσύνη

K

keep silence   σιγάω, σιωπάω
kill   ἀποκτείνω*
     be killed   ἀποθνῄσκω*
king   βασιλεύς, βασιλέως, ὁ   (p. 122)
know   γιγνώσκω*, οἶδα* (pp. 184-85), ἐπίσταμαι* (pp. 272-73)

L

law   νόμος, -ου, ὁ
lead   ἄγω*
learn   μανθάνω*
leave   λείπω*
letter (epistle)   ἐπιστολή, -ῆς, ἡ; (of alphabet) letters   τὰ γράμματα
lie (falsehood)   ψευδές, τό; (vb) κεῖμαι
life   βίος, -ου, ὁ
listen to   ἀκούω* (+ gen. of source)
     in sense of 'heed', 'obey'   πείθομαι + dat.
little   μικρός, -ά, -όν; ὀλίγος, -η, -ον
live   ζάω* (pp. 244-45)
     live in peace εἰρήνην ἄγειν
love   ἀγαπάω, φιλέω, ἐράω (pp. 244-46)

M

make   τίθημι* (p. 268), make for oneself   τίθεμαι (mid.), ποιέω (pp. 245-46),
     πράττω*
man   ἄνθρωπος, ἀνήρ (pp. 122-23, 126)
many   πολλοί, πολλαί, πολλά (pl. of πολύς, p. 138)
master   δεσπότης, -ου, ὁ (p. 83)
me, oblique cases of ἐγώ (p. 195)
men of former times   οἱ τότε
money   χρήματα, -ων, τά (pl. of χρῆμα, (p. 120)
mother   μήτηρ, μητρός, ἡ (pp. 122-23)
much   πολύς, πολλή, πολύ (p. 138)
my   ἐμός, -ή, -όν (p. 197), μου, ἐμοῦ (p. 195), ἐμαυτῆς, -οῦ (p. 196)
myself, as emphatic   αὐτός, αὐτή (pp. 195-96), ἐμαυτῆς, -οῦ refl. (p. 196)

N

native land   πατρίς, -ίδος, ἡ (p. 120)

necessary, it is   ἀνάγκη (ἐστί), χρή, δεῖ
never   οὔποτε, οὐ . . . ποτε
night   νύξ, νυκτός, ἡ
        during the night   νυκτός
no one   οὐδείς, οὐδεμία (p. 226)
not   οὐ (οὐκ, οὐχ); μή
nothing   οὐδέν, μηδέν (p. 226)

O

obey   πείθομαι (mid. of πείθω*) + dat.
observe, as in the expression, 'not without being observed' (see p. 161)
       λανθάνω*
of, use genitive case
old man   γέρων, γέροντος, ὁ (p. 120)
on   ἐν + dat., ἐπί + gen. or dat.
        on, with expression of time, use dat. (pp. 216-17)
on account of   διά + acc.
on the ground that   ὡς + ptcpl. (pp. 156-57)
one another   ἀλλήλων (p. 175)
opinion   γνώμη, γνώμης, ἡ
or   ἤ
ourselves   ἡμῶν αὐτῶν (pp. 196-97)
over, in "rule over"   ἄρχω + gen.

P

peace   εἰρήνη, -ης, ἡ
        live in peace   εἰρήνην ἄγειν
persuade   πείθω*
philosopher   σοφός, -οῦ, ὁ
place   χώρα, -ας, ἡ; τόπος, -ου, ὁ
plan   βουλεύω
        plan for oneself   βουλεύομαι
poet   ποιητής, -οῦ, ὁ (p. 83)
possessions   τά + gen. (e.g. the possessions of wise men = τὰ τῶν σοφῶν)
present, participle of πάρειμι
        be present   πάρειμι (cf. εἰμί*)
profit   κέρδος, κέρδους, τό
        it is profitable   κέρδος ἐστί (p. 129)

R

receive   λαμβάνω*
release   λύω
remain   μένω*
reveal   ἐπιδείκνυμι (pp. 269-70)
road   ὁδός, ὁδοῦ, ἡ
rule   ἄρχω
        rule over   ἄρχω + gen.

S

sacrifice   θύω; sacrifice to   θύω + dat.

same   αὐτός, αὐτή, αὐτό (in attributive position, p. 196)
save   σῴζω*
say   λέγω*, φημί* (p. 107), εἶπον* (said)
sea   θάλαττα (θάλασσα), θαλάττης, ἡ (p. 83)
        by sea   κατὰ θάλατταν
see   ὁράω*
seek   ζητέω (pp. 245-46)
send   πέμπω*, στέλλω*
servant   θεράπων, θεράποντος, ὁ (p. 120)
set up   τίθημι*, ἀνατίθημι (p. 268)
shield   ἀσπίς, ἀσπίδος, ἡ (p. 120)
silence   σίγη, -ης, ἡ
        keep silence   σιγάω, σιωπάω
small   μικρός, -ά, -όν (p. 83)
so   οὕτω/οὕτως
soldier   στρατιώτης, -ου, ὁ (p. 83)
some   τις, τι (p. 173)
some . . . others   οἱ/αἱ/τὰ μέν . . . οἱ/αἱ/τὰ δέ
someone   τις (p. 173)
something   τι (p. 173)
soul   ψυχή, -ῆς, ἡ
speak   λέγω*
stand   ἵστημι* (pp. 267, 273)
stone   λίθος, λίθου, ὁ
stop   παύω
        stop oneself (cease)   παύομαι
sun   ἥλιος, ἡλίου, ὁ

                                    T

take   λαμβάνω*, αἱρέω*
take away   ἀπάγω (ἄγω*)
take counsel   βουλεύω; --for oneself   βουλεύομαι
take place   γίγνομαι*
tall   μέγας, μεγάλη, μέγα (p. 138)
teach   παιδεύω, διδάσκω*
tell   λέγω*
than   gen. of comparison; ἤ (p. 223)
that   ἐκεῖνος, ἐκείνη, ἐκεῖνο; οὗτος, αὕτη, τοῦτο (pp. 84-85)
that (in order that)   ὡς + fut. participle (p. 158); ἵνα + subj. or opt. (pp. 306-07)
that (introducing indirect statement) pp. 108-10, 161-62, 307-08
the   ὁ, ἡ, τό (p. 39)
the one . . . the other   ὁ/ἡ/τὸ μέν . . . ὁ/ἡ/τὸ δέ (pp. 44, 65)
their   article (p. 39), αὐτῶν (not reflexive, pp. 195-96), ἑαυτῶν (reflexive, pp. 196-97)
them   oblique cases of αὐτός, αὐτή, αὐτό in plural (pp. 195-96)
there is   ἐστί, there are   εἰσί, there was   ἦν, there were   ἦσαν
thing   express by neuter of adj.; χρῆμα, χρήματος, τό
think   νομίζω*
think worthy   ἀξιόω (p. 247)
this   οὗτος, αὕτη, τοῦτο; ὅδε, ἥδε, τόδε (p. 84)
        this man   οὗτος

time   χρόνος, ὥρα
     it is time   ὥρα [ἐστί] + infin.
to   dat. case without preposition; εἰς + acc.; παρά + acc.; πρός + acc.
trust   πιστεύω + dat.; πείθομαι (mid. of πείθω*) + dat.
truth   ἀλήθεια, -ας, ἡ; ἀληθῆ, τά (p. 135)
two   δύο (p. 225)
tyranny   τυραννίς, -ίδος, ἡ (p. 120)

                    U

unjust   ἄδικος, -ον
     unjust men   οἱ ἄδικοι
understand   ἐπίσταμαι* (p. 272), μανθάνω*
until   πρίν (p. 142)
us   oblique cases of ἡμεῖς (p. 195)
used to, use imperfect tense (p. 57)

                    V

victorious, be   νικάω (pp. 244-45)
virtue   ἀρετή, -ῆς, ἡ

                    W

wait   μένω*
want   βούλομαι*
war   πόλεμος, -ου, ὁ
we   ἡμεῖς (p. 195); implied in -μεν, -μεθα endings
wealth   πλοῦτος, -ου, ὁ
well   εὖ, καλῶς
what (relative)   ὅς, ἥ, ὅ (pp. 65-66)
what (?)(interrogative)   τίς, τί (p. 173)
whatever   ὅστις, ἥτις, ὅ τι (p. 174)
which (relative)   ὅς, ἥ, ὅ (pp. 65-66)
whichever   ὅστις, ἥτις, ὅ τι (p. 174)
who (relative)   ὅς, ἥ, ὅ (pp. 65-66)
who (?)(interrogative   τίς (p. 173)
whoever   ὅστις, ἥτις (p. 174)
whole   ὅλος, -η, -ον; πᾶς, πᾶσα, πᾶν (p. 137)
why   τί, διὰ τί
wicked   κακός, -ή, -όν; πονηρός, -ά, -όν
     wicked things   τὰ κακά
wickedness   πονηρία, -ας, ἡ; κακία, -ας, ἡ; τὸ κακόν
wife   γυνή, γυναικός, ἡ (p. 124)
willing   ἑκών, ἑκοῦσα, ἑκόν
     be willing   ἐθέλω*
win   νικάω (pp. 244-45)
wise   σοφός, -ή, -όν
     wise man   ὁ σοφός
wisely   σοφῶς
wish   βούλομαι*, ἐθέλω*
with   dat. of means; σύν + dat.; μετά + gen.
woman   γυνή, γυναικός, ἡ (p. 124)

word   λόγος, λόγου, ὁ
world   κόσμος, -ου, ὁ
worthy   ἄξιος, ἀξία, ἄξιον
       think/deem worthy   ἀξιόω (pp. 246-47)
write   γράφω*

Y

you   singular σύ, plural ὑμεῖς (p. 195)
young   νέος, -α, -ον
       young man   νεανίας, -ου, ὁ (p. 83)
yourself   as emphatic αὐτός, -ή, -ό (pp. 195-96)
       as reflexive σεαυτοῦ, σεαυτῆς; ὑμῶν αὐτῶν (pp. 196-97)

Greek-English Vocabulary

* principal parts in list, pp. 345-49
v entry appears in lesson vocabulary

A

v	ἀγαθός, -ή, -όν	good, well-born, brave, capable, serviceable
	τὰ ἀγαθά	goods, wealth (for comparative and superlative see p. 221)
	ἀγαθότης, -τητος, -ἡ	goodness
	ἄγαν	very much, too much (Ion., Dor.)
v	ἀγάπη, -ης, ἡ	love (of God for man and man for God), brotherly love, alms, charity
v	ἀγαπάω	love, greet with affection, desire
	ἀγένητος, -ον	unborn, uncreated
v *	ἀγγέλλω	announce, bear a message
	ἀγνοέω	not to perceive, be ignorant
v	ἀγορά, -ᾶς, ἡ	assembly, marketplace, agora
	ἄγραφος, -ον	unwritten
	ἄγχω	press tight, strangle, hang
v *	ἄγω	lead, drive, bring, carry
v	ἀγῶν, ἀγῶνος, ὁ	gathering, assembly, place for contests, contest, struggle, lawsuit
v	ἀδελφή, -ῆς, ἡ	sister
v	ἀδελφός, -οῦ, ὁ	brother
	ἄδηλος, -ον	unknown, ignoble, unseen
	ἀδηλότης, -ητος, ἡ	uncertainty
v	ἀδικέω	to be ἄδικος, do wrong (with ptcpl. of particular charge of wrong-doing)
v	ἄδικος, -ον	unjust
v	ἀδίκως	unjustly
	ἀδυνατέω	be unable, lack ability
v	ἀδύνατος, -ον	unable, impossible
	τὸ ἀδύνατον	impossibility
v	ἀεί	always, ever
*	ᾄδω (ἀείδω)	sing, sing of, chant
	ἀετός, -οῦ, ὁ	eagle
	ἀήρ, ἀέρος, ὁ (ἡ)	mist, haze, lower air; air; pl. climates
v	ἀθάνατος, -ον	immortal, deathless, everlasting
	οἱ ἀθάνατοι	the immortals
	Ἀθήναζε	to/towards Athens
	Ἀθῆναι, Ἀθηνῶν, αἱ	the city of Athens
v	Ἀθηναῖος, -α, -ον	Athenian
v	ἄθλιος, -α, -ον	struggling, unhappy, wretched, sorry
	ἄθῳος, -ον	unpunished
	αἰανής, -ές	everlasting, wearisome
v *	αἰδέομαι	be ashamed, respect
	Ἅιδης, -ου, ὁ (ᾅδης)	Hades
	αἷμα, αἵματος, τό	blood
	αἴνιγμα, -ατος, τό	dark saying, riddle
v *	αἱρέω	take, mid. choose
*	αἴρω (ἀείρω)	lift, raise up

v *	αἰσθάνομαι	perceive, apprehend by the senses; understand, learn
	αἴσθησις, -εως, ἡ	sense-perception, sensation
v	αἰσχρός, -ά, -όν	shameful, base, causing shame; ugly
	αἰσχύνη	shame, disgrace
v	αἰσχύνομαι	to be dishonored, be ashamed
*	αἰσχύνω	make ugly, disfigure
v	αἰτία, αἰτίας, ἡ	responsibility, guilt, blame, cause, motive, credit
	αἰτιάομαι	accuse, censure
	αἰτιατικός, -ή, -όν	causal
	ἡ αἰτιατική (πτῶσις)	the accusative case
	αἴτιος, -α, -ον	blamable, guilty, causing
	αἰχμή, -ῆς, ἡ	the point of a spear, spear
	αἰών αἰῶνος, ὁ	lifetime, age, generation, epoch (eon)
	ἄκαιρος, -ον	ill-timed, unseasonable; importunate
	ἀκρόαμα, -ατος, τό	anything heard; a play, musical piece
v	ἄκων, ἄκουσα, ἄκον (ἀκοντ-)	involuntary, unwilling(ly)
	ἀλγέω, -ήσω	feel pain, suffer
v	ἀλήθεια, ἀληθείας, ἡ	truth, reality, sincerity
	ἀκήρυκτος, -ον	unannounced, unproclaimed
	ἀκμάζω	be in full bloom
	ἀκουσίως	involuntarily
v *	ἀκούω	hear, listen (with acc. of thing heard, gen. of person heard from)
v	ἀληθής, -ές	true
v *	ἀλίσκομαι	be caught (used as passive of αἱρέω)
v	ἀλλά (ἀλλ')	but
	ἀλλαχοῦ	elsewhere, somewhere else
v	ἀλλήλων	each other, one another
v	ἄλλος, -η, -ον	other, another
	ἀλλότριος, -α, -ον	of/belonging to another
v	ἄλλως	otherwise, at random, in vain
	ἀλογία, -ας, ἡ	want of reason, folly, contempt
v	ἄλογος, -ον	irrational, unreasoning, without speech
	ἄλφιτον, -ου, τό	barley groats, one's daily bread
v	ἅμα	at once, at the same time
	ἀμαθής, -ές	ignorant, stupid
	ἅμαξα, -ας, ἡ	wagon
v *	ἁμαρτάνω	miss (the mark), fail, go wrong, err
v	ἁμαρτία, -ας, ἡ	failure, error, sin
	ἀμείβω	change, exchange
	ἀμελέω	neglect, be careless
	ἄμεμπτος, -ον	blameless
	ἀμπέχω	surround, cover, enclose, embrace; mid. put around oneself
v	ἀμφί	on both sides, G about, concerning, A about, near
	ἀμφισβητέω	stand apart, disagree, dispute
	οἱ ἀμφισβητοῦντες	the parties in a lawsuit
v	ἀμφότερος, -α, -ον	both of two
v	ἀνά	up; D on, upon; A up, throughout

	ἀναγιγνώσκω	know well, perceive, read
	ἀναγκάζω	force, compel, constrain
v	ἀναγκαῖος, -α, -ον	constraining, necessary
v	ἀνάγκη, -ης, ἡ	necessity, force, constraint, tie of blood
	ἀναιρέω	take up/away, destroy; mid. gain, win
	ἀναλέγω	pick up, gather; read aloud
	ἀναμιμνῄσκω	remind; pass. remember, recall
	ἀναμνηστικός, -όν	able to call to mind readily
v	ἄναξ, ἄνακτος, ὁ	lord, master
	ἀναρχία, -ας, ἡ	anarchy
	ἀνατίθημι (*τίθημι)	lay upon, refer, attribute, entrust, dedicate, set up, put back
	ἀναφαίρετος, -ον	not to be taken away
	ἀναφύω	produce again; pass. grow up
	ἀναχορεύω	begin a choral dance, celebrate in the chorus
	ἀνδραποδισμός, -οῦ, ὁ	enslaving, selling into slavery
	ἀνδράπεδον, -ου, τό	slave
v	ἀνδρεία, -ας, ἡ	manliness, manly spirit; pl. brave deeds
	ἀνδρεῖος, -α, -ον	belonging to a man, manly
	ἀνδρόω	rear up to manhood; pass. become a man
	ἀνελεύθερος	not free, slavish
	ἄνευ	without (G)
	ἀνεύρετος, -ον	undiscovered
	ἀνευρίσκω	find out, discover
v	ἀνήρ, ἀνδρός, ὁ	man, husband
	ἄνθος, -ους, τό	flower, bloom
	ἀνθρώπινος, -η, -ον	of, from, belonging to man, human
v	ἄνθρωπος, -ου, ὁ	man; pl. mankind
	ἀνίστημι (*ἵστημι)	make to stand up, set up; stand up
	ἄνοια, -ας, ἡ	lack of understanding, folly
v *	ἀνοίγνυμι (ἀνοίγω)	open; pass. be open, stand open
	ἀντασπάζομαι	welcome, greet in return
v	ἀντί	in the face of, opposite to (G)
	ἀντιβολέω	meet, entreat; partake of (with G)
	ἀντιλέγω	speak against, contradict, dispute
	ἀντωνυμία, -ας, ἡ	pronoun
	ἀξιομνημόνευτος, -ον	worthy of mention
v	ἄξιος, -α, -ον	worthy, deserving, counterbalancing
v	ἀξιόω	think/deem worthy, think fit, expect, consent, dare, make a claim
	ἀπάγχω	strangle, throttle; mid. hang oneself; pass. be hanged
	ἀπαίδευτος, -ον	uneducated, ignorant
	ἄπαις, ἄπαιδος, ὁ/ἡ	childless
	ἀπαλλάσσω	set free, release; mid. be set free from
	ἀπαντάω	meet, encounter
	ἀπανταχοῦ	everywhere
	ἀπαρνέομαι	deny utterly, reject, refuse
v	ἅπας, ἅπᾶσα, ἅπαν	quite all, everyone; the whole
	ἀπατεύω	cheat, deceive
	ἀπάτη, -ης, ἡ	cheating, trickery, fraud, stratagem
	ἀπειθέω	be disobedient

v	ἄπειμι (*εἰμί)	be away, be far from, be absent
	ἄπειμι (*εἶμι)	go away, depart
	ἀπευθύνω	make straight, restore, direct, correct
	ἁπλῶς	singly, in one way, simply, generally
	ἀπό	from, off from, away from (G)
	ἀποβλέπω	look away from, gaze steadily, regard
	ἀποδημέω	go abroad
	ἀποδίδωμι	give up, give back, return, pay, assign, concede, allow; mid. sell
	ἀποδείκνυμι	point out, show forth, bring forward, prove
v *	ἀποθνῄσκω	die, be killed
v *	ἀποκρίνομαι	answer
	ἀποκρύπτω	hide from, keep hidden, conceal
v *	ἀποκτείνω	kill, slay, put to death
	ἀπολαύω	enjoy, profit by
	ἀπολείπω (*λείπω)	be wanting, leave behind, lose, forsake
v *	ἀπόλλυμι	act. destroy utterly, kill, slay; mid. perish, die, fall into ruin
	ἀπολύω	loose from, mid. release for oneself, redeem, defend oneself
	ἀπονέμω, ἀπονεμῶ	portion out, assign
	ἀπορία, -ας, ἡ	difficulty (of passing), perplexity, embarrassment, question for discussion
	ἄπορος, -ον	without passage, impassable, unmanagable, impossible
	ἀπόρρητος, -ον	forbidden, not to be spoken
	ἀποστέλλω (*στέλλω)	send away, banish; pass. go away, depart
	ἀποστρέφω (*στρέφω)	turn back/away, avert
	ἀποτελέω	bring to an end, complete, produce, accomplish
	ἀποτέμνω	cut off
	ἀποτρέπω (*τρέπω)	turn away from, dissuade from
	ἀποφθέγμα	a thing uttered, terse saying
	ἀπρεπής, -ές	unseemly, unbecoming
*	ἅπτω	hasten, kindle
	ἄρα	particle denoting interest or surprise, then
	ἆρα	an interrogative particle which leaves the question open
	ἀρά, -ᾶς, ἡ	prayer, curse
	ἀργύριον, -ου, τό	silver, coin
	ἄργυρος, -ου, ὁ	white metal, silver
v	ἀρετή, -ῆς, ἡ	goodness, excellence, moral virtue
	ἀρήγω	aid, succor
	ἄρθρον, -ου, τό	joint, connecting word, the article (gram.)
v	ἄριστος, -η, -ον	best, noblest, bravest
	ἄρκτος, -ου, ὁ/ἡ	bear
	ἀρνέομαι, -ήσομαι	deny, disown
	ἄρουρα, -ας, ἡ	tilled land, corn land
	ἀρσενικός, -ή, -όν	male, of masculine gender
	ἄρτι	just exactly, just now
	ἄρτιος, -α, -ον	complete, exactly fitted; active, ready
v	ἄρχω	begin, rule (with Gen)
v	ἄρχων, -οντος, ὁ	archon, ruler

	ἀσεβής, -ές	ungodly, unholy, profane
v	ἀσθενής, -ές	weak, feeble, poor
	ἀσπάζομαι	welcome, greet
v	ἀσπίς, ἀσπίδος, ἡ	shield
	ἀστήρ, ἀστέρος, ὁ	star, flame, fire
v	ἄστυ, ἀστέως, τό	city, town
v	ἀσφαλής, -ές	safe, steadfast, sure
v	ἄτε	just as, as if, inasmuch as (with ptcpl.)
	ἄτερ	without
	ἄτεχνος, -ον	without art, unskilled
	ἀτιμόω	dishonor, punish with ἀτιμία (i.e., deprive of civil rights)
	ἄτομος, -ον	uncut, that cannot be cut
	ἄτοπος, -ον	out of place, strange, unnatural, bad
	ἀττικίζω	Atticize, speak in the Attic dialect
	ἀτυχέω	be unlucky
	ἀτύχημα, -ατος, τό	misfortune, mishap
	αὖ	back, again, moreover, besides
	αὐδάω	talk, speak, say
	αὐλή, -ῆς, ἡ	open court, hall, dwelling
	αὐξάνω (αὔξω)	increase; pass. grow
	αὔξησις, -εως, ἡ	growth, increase; the augment (gram.)
	αὔριον	tomorrow
v	αὐτίκα	forthwith, at once, immediately
	αὖτις/αὖθις	back, anew, again, moreover
	αὐτοσχεδιάζω	act/speak off-hand, judge unadvisedly
	αὐτόθι	on the very spot, there
	αὐτόματος (-η) -ον	acting of one's own will, self-moving, without cause, accidental
	αὐτοῦ	there, here
	αὐτόφωρος, -ον	caught in the act of theft
	ἀφανίζω	make unseen, do away with, destroy
v	ἀφίημι (*ἵημι)	send forth, discharge, release from
v *	ἀφικνέομαι	arrive at, come to, reach
v	ἀφίστημι (*ἵστημι)	put away, remove, cause to revolt, pay; stand away, revolt from
v	ἄφρων, -ον (gen. -ονος)	senseless, witless, foolish, crazed
	ἄφωνος, -ον	voiceless, dumb
	τὰ ἄφωνα	consonants, esp. mutes
	Ἀχαιός, -ά, -όν	Achaean
	ἀχάριστος, -ον	unpleasing, without grace, thankless
	ἀχώριστος, -οω	not parted, undivided, inseparable

B

	βαδίζω	go on foot, walk, go
v *	βαίνω	walk, step, go
	βαιός, -ά, -όν	little, slight, short
	Βάκχιος, -α, -ον	Bacchic, inspired
	ὁ Βάκχιος (θεός)	the Bacchic god, Bacchus
v *	βάλλω	throw, hit
v	βάρβαρος, -ον	barbarous, non-Greek, foreign
	οἱ βάρβαροι	all non-Greek-speaking peoples

v	βαρύς, βαρεῖα, βαρύ	heavy, tiresome, oppressive
v	βασιλεύς, βασιλέως, ὁ	king
v	βασιλεύω	to be king, rule, reign (with Gen.)
	βασίλισσα, -ας, ἡ (= βασίλεια)	queen
	βάτος	bramble
v	βέβαιος (-α) -ον	firm, steady, steadfast, durable, sure
	βιάζω/βιάζομαι	force, do violence to
	βίαιος (-α) -ον	forcible, violent, acting with violence
v	βιβλίον, -ου, τό	paper, book
v	βίος, βίου, ὁ	life, livelihood, mode of life
	βίοτος, -ου, ὁ	life, means of living
v	βιόω	live, pass one's life
v *	βλάπτω	disable, hinder, harm, hurt, damage
	βλασφημέω	blaspheme, speak profanely
v *	βλέπω	see, have the power of sight, look
v *	βοάω	cry aloud, shout, roar, howl
v *	βοηθέω	assist, come to the rescue
	βολβός, ὁ	a bulbous plant
v	βουλεύω	plan, take counsel, deliberate
v	βουλή, -ῆς, ἡ	counsel, will, determination, Senate
	βουλιμιάω	be hungry as an ox
v *	βούλομαι	wish, be willing, be wont
	βοῦς, βοός, ὁ/ἡ	bull, cow, ox; pl. cattle
v	βραδύς, -εῖα, -ύ	slow, heavy, late
v	βραχύς, -εῖα, -ύ	short, brief
	βρέφος, -ους, τό	new-born babe
	βροντάω	thunder, impers. it thunders
v	βροτός, -οῦ, ὁ	mortal man
	βυθός, -οῦ, ὁ	the depth, bottom, abyss

Γ

	γαῖα, -ας (-ης), ἡ	land, country, earth (poetic for γῆ)
	γαμβρός, -οῦ, ὁ	-in-law, any connection by marriage
v *	γαμέω	marry (act. of the man, mid. of woman)
v	γάμος, -ου, ὁ	wedding, marriage, wedlock
v	γάρ	for (postpositive particle)
v	γέ	at least, yes (postpositive particle)
v *	γελάω	laugh, laugh at, sneer at
	γέλοιος, -α, -ον	laughable, absurd, humorous
	γέλοια	jokes
	γέλως, γέλωτος, ὁ	laughter
	γέμω	be full, be laden (only pres. and impf.)
	γένεσις, -εως, ἡ	origin, source, birth, descent
	γενικός, -ή, -όν	of/belonging to the γένος, typical
	ἡ γενική (πτῶσις)	genitive case
v	γεννάω	beget; mid. create
v	γένος, γένους, τό	race, birth, offspring, stock, clan
	γέρας, γέραος, τό	gift of honor, prize, prerogative
v	γέρων, γέροντος, ὁ	old man
	γεωργός, -οῦ, ὁ	farmer

		γῆ, γῆς, ἡ	earth (land and sea), land, country
	*	γηράσκω	grow old
		γῆρας, γήραος, τό	old age
		γηράω	grow old
v	*	γίγνομαι	become, be born, be, come into being
v	*	γιγνώσκω	know (know by observation), come to know, perceive
		γλαῦξ, γλαυκός, ἡ	the little owl, *Athene noctua*
v		γλυκύς, -εῖα, -ύ	sweet, pleasant
v		γλῶσσα, -ης, ἡ (γλῶττα)	tongue, language
		γνήσιος, -α, -ον	legitimate, genuine, true
v		γνώμη, -ης, ἡ	thought, opinion, means of knowing, organ by which one perceives; intelligence
		αἱ γνῶμαι	practical maxims
		γνωρίζω	make known, gain knowledge of
		γνώρισις, -εως, ἡ	a making known, a getting to know
		γονεύς, -έως, ὁ	father, pl. parents
		γόνυ, γόνατος, τό	knee
		γοῦν (γε οὖν)	at least then, at any rate
		γράμμα, -ατος, τό	that which is drawn, letter
		γραμματική, -ῆς, ἡ	grammar
		γραμματικός, -ή, -όν	knowing one's letters
		γραμματικός, -οῦ, ὁ	grammarian, teacher of reading and writing
		γραφική, -ῆς, ἡ	the art of writing
		γραφικός, -ή, -όν	of painting/drawing/writing
v	*	γράφω	scratch, draw, write
v		γυμνός, -ή, -όν	naked, unarmed
		γυναικεῖος, (-α), -ον	of/belonging to women, feminine
v		γυνή, γυναικός, ἡ	woman, wife

Δ

v		δαίμων, δαίμονος, ὁ	divinity
		δάκρυ, δάκρυος, τό (δάκρυον)	tear, drop
		δασύς, -εῖα, -ύ	hairy, shaggy, hoarse, aspirated
		δέ	but, and (postpositive conjunction)
v	*	δέδια, δέδοικα	fear
v		δεῖ	there is need (impers. from *δέω)
v	*	δείκνυμι	show, bring to light, explain
		δεῖμα, -ατος, τό	fear, terror, object of fear
v		δεινός, -ή, -όν	fearful, dreadful, terrible, awful
		δειπνέω	make/take a meal, entertain
v		δεῖπνον, -ου, τό	meal, dinner, supper
		δέκα	ten
		δέμας	the body
		δεξιός, -ά, -όν	on the right hand/side, ready, skillful, fortunate; northerly
		δέος, δέους, τό	fear, alarm, awe, reverence
		δεσμός, -οῦ, ὁ	bond(s), fetter(s)
v		δέσποινα, δεσποίνης, ἡ	mistress, lady of the house, queen
v		δεσπότης, -ου, ὁ	master, lord, master of the house

		δεύτερος, -α, -ον	second
v	*	δέχομαι	receive, take, accept, welcome, await
v	*	δέω	lack, want, stand in need of (with Gen)
		δέομαι	beg, ask
		δεῖ	there is need, one ought
	*	δέω	bind, tie, fetter
v		δή	of course, indeed, quite (postpositive)
		δηλαδή	clearly, manifestly (adv.)
v		δῆλος, -η, -ον	visible, clear, manifest, evident
v		δηλόω	make visible, show, reveal
		δημηγορέω	be a public orator, harangue the people
v		δημοκρατία, -ας, ἡ	democracy, popular government
		δῆμος, -ου, ὁ	district, common people, the popular assembly
		δήπου	probably, doubtless, I presume, certainly not, is it not so
		δῆτα	aye, indeed, truly, then
v		διά	through: through, over, in the midst of (G) because of, for the sake of (A)
		διαβαίνω (*βαίνω)	stand firm, step across/over, cross over
v		διαβάλλω (*βάλλω)	throw/carry over/across, set against, bring into discredit, attack, slander
v		διαβολή, -ῆς, ἡ	false accusation, misrepresentation, slander, calumny
		διάβολος, -ου, ὁ	the devil, the slanderer
		διαθέσις, -εως, ἡ	arrangement, composition, delivery, condition
		διαίρεσις, -εως, ἡ	a dividing, division
		διαιρέω (*αἱρέω)	take apart, divide, distinguish, determine
		διακρίνω (*κρίνω)	separate, divide, distinguish
		διαλέγω	pick out
		διαλέγομαι	talk, hold conversation with
		διαλεκτικός, -ή, -όν	skilled in discourse
		ἡ διαλεκτική	the art of debating
		διάλογος, -ου, ὁ	dialogue, conversation
		διαλύω	loose, part; reconcile
		διακοσμέω	divide, arrange
		διακριβόω	portray exactly, examine with precision
		διανίστημι (*ἵστημι)	awaken, arouse; stand up, rise
v	*	διανοέομαι	to be minded, intend, have in mind, think
v		διάνοια, -ας, ἡ (διανοία)	thought, intellect, mind, intention, belief
		διαπαίζω	jest
		διαπερονάω	pierce through
v		διατρίβω (*τρίβω)	rub between, rub away, waste, spend time
		διαφερόντως	differently from, especially, extremely
v		διαφέρω (*φέρω)	carry over/across; differ, surpass
		οὐδὲν διαφέρει	it makes no difference
		διαφεύγω (*φεύγω)	flee through, get away, escape
v	*	διαφθείρω	destroy utterly, corrupt, pass. be destroyed
		διαφορά, -ᾶς, ἡ	difference
		διάφορος, -ον	different; superior
		διδακτός, -ή, -όν	taught, teachable
v		διδάσκαλος, -ου, ὁ	teacher, master

v *	διδάσκω	instruct, teach
v *	δίδωμι	give, grant
	διέρχομαι (*ἔρχομαι)	go through, pass through
	διΐστημι (*ἵστημι)	set apart, separate; stand apart, be divided
v	δικάζω	judge, decide, determine
v	δίκαιος, -α, -ον	just
v	δικαιοσύνη, -ης, ἡ	righteousness, justice
v	δικαίως	justly
v	δικαστήριον, -ου, τό	court (of law)
v	δικαστής, -οῦ, ὁ	judge, juryman, juror
v	δίκη, δίκης, ἡ	justice, order, right; lawsuit, trial
	διό	wherefore, therefore
	διορίζω	draw a boundary through, distinguish, define, separate
	διπλοῦς, -ῆ, -οῦν	twofold, double
	δίς (ῐ)	twice, doubly
	διφθέρα, -ας, ἡ	leather, leather garment worn by peasants
	δίφθογγος, -ον	with two sounds
	ἡ δίφθογγος	diphthong
	δίφρος, -ου, ὁ	chariot-board, seat, couch, stool
	δίχρονος, -ον	of two quantities
	διψάω	thirst, be thirsty, thirst after (gen)
v *	διώκω	pursue, chase
	δόγμα, -ατος, τό	opinion, resolution, decree
v *	δοκέω	expect, think, suppose, imagine
	δοκῶ μοι	I seem to myself, I am determined
	δοκεῖ	it seems, it seems best to (dat)
	δολιχός, -ή, -όν	long
	δόμος, -ου, ὁ	house, temple, room (often in pl. for one house)
	δόξα, -ης, ἡ	expectation, opinion, estimation; glory
	δοτικός, -ή, -όν	inclined to give
	ἡ δοτική (πτῶσις)	the dative case
	δουλεύω	be a slave
	δοῦλος, -ου, ὁ	slave
v	δουλόω	enslave
v	δράκων, δράκοντος, ὁ	snake, serpent
	δραχμή, -ῆς, ἡ	drachma
v *	δράω	do, accomplish
	δυϊκός, -ή, -όν	dual
v *	δύναμαι	be able, be strong enough (to do)(infin)
	δύναται	it is possible
v	δύναμις, -εως, ἡ	power, might, ability, influence, authority
	δυναστεία, -ας, ἡ	power, lordship; pl. mighty deeds
	δυναστεύω	hold power/lordship, be lord over (gen)
	δυνατός, -ή, -όν	strong, mighty, possible
v	δύο	two
v	δυσδαίμων, δύσδαιμον	ill-fated
v	δυστυχής, -ές	unfortunate, unlucky
v	δώδεκα	twelve
v	δῶμα, -ατος, τό	house, chief room, hall
v	δῶρον, -ου, τό	gift
	δωρέω	give, present

E

v *	ἐάω	suffer, permit (acc & inf), let alone
v	ἐγγύς	near, nearly, like
	ἐγκώμιον, -ου, τό	hymn of praise, encomium
v	ἐγώ	I (first person pronoun)
	ἕδος, -ους, τό	seat, abode (esp. of a god)
v *	ἐθέλω	wish, be willing, consent
v	ἔθνος, -ους, τό	nation, tribe
v	ἔθος, -ους, τό	custom
v	εἰ	if, whether
v	εἴκοσι	twenty
v	εἶδον	saw (as second aorist of *ὁράω, see)
	εἴδωλον, -ου, τό	phantom, image reflected
	εἶεν	particle used in dialogue and oratory in passing to the next point: well, very good, so far so good
	εἰκότως	fairly, reasonably, suitably
v	εἰκών, -όνος, ἡ	likeness, image
v	εἴπερ	even if, if indeed
v	εἶπον	said (2 aor., defective vb.)
v	εἰρήνη	peace
v	εἰς	into, to (acc)
	εἷς, μία, ἕν	one
	εἰσάγω (*ἄγω)	lead in/into, bring in, bring before
	εἰσβαίνω (*βαίνω)	go on board, embark, enter
	εἰσοράω (*ὁράω)	look into, behold, discern, look upon
	εἴσω	into, within (acc); inside
v	εἶτα	then, after, and so then, indeed?
v	ἕκαστος, -η, -ον	each, every (pred. pos.)
v	ἑκάτερος, -α, -ον	each (of two)
	ἑκατόμβη, -ης, ἡ	an offering of a hundred oxen, sacrifice
	ἑκατοντάπυλος, -ον	hundred-gated
	ἐκβαίνω (*βαίνω)	step out, disembark
	ἐκβάλλω (*βάλλω)	throw/cast out, produce, put forth
	ἐκγίγνομαι (*γίγνομαι)	be born of (gen), be born to (dat), come into being
	ἐκδέχομαι (*δέχομαι)	take, receive from, wait for, expect, take/understand in a certain sense
	ἐκδιδάσκω (*διδάσκω)	teach thoroughly
	ἐκεῖ	there, in that place; then
v	ἐκεῖνος, ἐκείνη, ἐκεῖνο	that
	ἔκθαμβρος, -ον	amazed, astounded
	ἐκθρώσκω, aor. ἐξέθορον	leap out of
	ἐκμανθάνω (*μανθάνω)	learn thoroughly
	ἑκούσιος, -α, -ον	voluntary
	ἐκπειράζω	tempt
	ἐκπέρθω	destroy utterly
	ἐκπίπτω (*πίπτω)	fall out, be driven out
	ἐκπορίζω	invent, contrive, provide, furnish, procure; mid. provide for oneself
	ἐκτίθημι (*τίθημι)	set out, expose, exhibit
	ἐκτός	without, outside (adv.); beyond, outside of (gen)

	ἐκφεύγω (*φεύγω)	flee away, escape
	ἐκχωρέω	go out/away, depart, give way
v	ἑκών, ἑκοῦσα, ἑκόν (ἑκοντ-)	readily, willingly, purposely
	ἐλαττόω	make less/smaller/worse; lessen, damage
	ἐλαφρός, -ά, -όν	light, easy
	ἐλεέω, aor. ἠλέησα	have pity on, show mercy to; feel pity
	ἐλεεινός, -ή, -όν	pitiable, pitied
	ἐλεημοσύνη, -ης, ἡ	pity, mercy, alms
v	ἐλεύθερος, -α, -ον	free
	ἐλευθερόω	set free, deliver
	ἕλκος, -ους, τό	wound, sore, ulcer
	ἕλκω	drag, draw
	Ἑλλάς, Ἑλλάδος, ἡ	Hellas, Greece
v	Ἕλλην, Ἕλληνος, ὁ	(a) Greek (man)
	ἑλληνίζω	speak Greek
	Ἑλληνικός, -ή, -όν	Greek, Hellenic
	τὰ Ἑλληνικά	the history of Greek affairs, Greek Lit.
v	Ἑλληνίς, Ἑλληνίδος, ἡ	(a) Greek (woman)
v	ἐλπίς, ἐλπίδος, ἡ	hope, expectation
	ἐμμένω (*μένω)	abide by, stand by
	ἐμπειρία, -ας, ἡ	experience, practice
v	ἐμπίμπλημι (*πίμπλημι)	fill quite full, fill full of (gen)
	ἔμψυχος, ἔμψυχον	having life in one, animate; vivid
v	ἐν	in, among (dat)
v	ἐναντίος	opposite, facing (as prep. with gen)
	ἐναντίος, -α, -ον	opposite, face to face
	ἐνδεής, -ές	wanting, lacking, in need of
v	ἕνδεκα	eleven
	ἔνδικος, -ον	according to right, legitimate
	ἔνδοθεν	from within, within (gen)
	ἔνδον	within, at home (gen)
	ἔνειμι (*εἰμί)	be among, be present in a place, be possible
v	ἕνεκα	for the sake of, on account of (gen)
	ἐνενήκοντα	ninety
v	ἐνθάδε	thither, hither
	ἐνιαυτός, -οῦ, ὁ	anniversary, year
	ἐνικός, -ή, -όν	single
	ἀριθμὸς ἐνικός	the singular number
v	ἔνιοι, -αι, -α	some
	ἐνίοτε	at times, sometimes
v	ἐννέα	nine
	ἐνοικέω	dwell in, inhabit
	ἐντίθημι (*τίθημι)	put in/into/on
	ἐντολή, -ῆς, ἡ	command, commandment
v	ἐξ (ἐκ)	from, out of (gen)
v	ἕξ	six
	ἐξαγγέλλω (*ἀγγέλλω)	tell out, proclaim
	ἐξάγω (*ἄγω)	lead out/away, bring out/forth
	ἐξαμαρτάνω (*ἁμαρτάνω)	mistake utterly, err greatly; pass. be mismanaged
	ἐξελαύνω (*ἐλαύνω)	drive out, chase out
	ἐξεργάζομαι	work out, accomplish, finish

	ἐξερέω	I shall speak out, proclaim (future, without pres.)
	ἐξέρχομαι (*ἔρχομαι)	go/come out, go forth
	ἐξήκοντα	sixty
	ἐξοῖδα (*οἶδα)	know thoroughly, know well
	ἐξομολογέομαι	confess in full, admit, make full acknowledgement for
	ἐξορμάω	set out, start from, send forth, stir up
	ἔξω	out, out of, outside
	ἔξωθεν	from without, without
v *	ἔοικα	be like, look like (dat.); seem
	ἐπαινέω	approve, sanction, agree to
	ἐπάν (ἐπήν)	whenever
v	ἐπεί	after that, since, seeing that
v	ἐπειδή	when
	ἐπειδήπερ	since really
	ἔπειμι (*εἶμι)	go/come to, attack, come upon
v	ἔπειτα	thereupon, thereafter, then
	ἐπερωτάω	consult, question, inquire of
	ἐπί	on, upon (G, D, A)
	ἐπιβαίνω (*βαίνω)	set foot on (G); arrive at, come to
	ἐπιβοάω (*βοάω)	call upon, cry out to, call for help
	ἐπιγιγνώσκω (*γιγνώσκω)	observe, witness; find out, discover, learn to know; find out too late
	ἐπιδείκνυμι (*δείκνυμι)	exhibit as a specimen; exhibit, display
	ἐπίγειος, -ον	on/of the earth
v	ἐπιθυμέω	set one's heart (θυμός) upon a thing, long for, desire (gen.)
	ἐπιθυμητής, -οῦ, ὁ	one who longs for, lover, follower
	ἐπιθυμία, -ας, ἡ	desire, longing, lust
	ἐπικρατέω	rule over, govern, prevail, conquer
	ἐπίκτητος, -ον	gained in addition, acquired
v	ἐπιλανθάνω (*λανθάνω)	escape notice; mid. forget; pass. be forgotten
v	ἐπιμελέομαι	take care of, pay attention to
	ἐπιορκέω	swear falsely
	ἐπίπονος	painful, toilsome, laborious
	ἐπίρρημα, -ατος, τό	that which is said afterwards; adverb
v *	ἐπίσταμαι	know how (to do), understand
	ἐπιστάμενος, -η, -ον	knowing, understanding, skilful
	ἐπιστέλλω (*στέλλω)	send to, enjoin, command
	ἐπιστήμη, -ης, ἡ	understanding, skill, knowledge
	ἐπιστολή, -ῆς, ἡ	anything sent by a messenger, message, order; letter
	ἐπισφαλής, -ές	prone to fall, unsteady, precarious
	ἐπιτάττω	put upon one as a duty, enjoin, order, place next to/beside
	ἐπιτήδειος, -α, -ον	suitable, useful
	τὰ ἐπιτήδεια	supplies, provisions
	ὁ ἐπιτήδειος	close friend
	ἐπιτρέπω (τρέπω)	turn to, transfer, refer to, leave to
	ἐπιχειρέω	put one's hand to, try, attempt
v *	ἕπομαι	follow

	ἐπουράνιος, -α, -ον	in heaven, heavenly
	ἐπριάμην	buy (used as aor. of ὠνέομαι)
v	ἑπτά	seven
v	ἔπος, -ους, τό	word
	ἐραστής, -οῦ, ὁ	lover, partisan
v *	ἐράω	love, be in love with
	ἐργαστέον	it must be done, one must do it
v	ἔργον, -ου, τό	deed, work
	ἐρημία, -ας, ἡ	solitude, desert, wilderness, desolation
	ἔρημος (-η) -ον	lonely, lone, desert
	ἐρρήθην	said (used as aor. pass. of εἶπον)
v *	ἔρχομαι	come, go
	ἐρῶ (ἐρέω)	I will say/tell/speak (fut., no pres.)
	ἔρως, ἔρωτος, ὁ	love, desire
v	ἐρωτάω	ask (with two acc.), question
v *	ἐσθίω	eat
v	ἐσθλός, -ή, -όν	noble, good, brave
	ἔσοπτρον, -ου, τό	looking glass, mirror
	ἑστιάω	entertain, feast
v	ἑταῖρος, -ου, ὁ	companion, comrade
	ἐτεός, -ά, -όν	true, genuine
	ἐτεή, ἡ / ἐτεῇ	reality, in reality
v	ἕτερος, -α, -ον	one or the other of two (usu. with article)
v	ἔτι	yet, still, besides, already
v	ἔτος, -ους, τό	year
v	εὖ	well (adv. of ἀγαθός)
v	εὐγενής, -ές	well-born, noble-minded, generous
	εὐδαιμονία, -ας, ἡ	prosperity, good fortune, happiness
v	εὐδαίμων, εὔδαιμον	lucky, happy, wealthy
	εὐδία, -ας, ἡ	fair weather
	εὔελπις, -ιδος, ὁ/ἡ	of good hope, hopeful, cheerful (n. εὔελπι)
	εὐεξία, -ας, ἡ	good habit of body, good health/condition
	εὐεργεσία, -ας, ἡ	service, good deed
	εὐεργέτης, -ου, ὁ	well-doer, benefactor, do-gooder
v	εὐκλεής, -ές	glorious, of good fame, famous
	εὐκνήμις, -ῖδος	well-greaved
	εὔκολος, -ον	good-natured, of good digestion
	εὐκταῖος, -α, -ον	of/for prayer, votive; prayed for, desired
	εὐλαβέομαι	be cautious, be discreet, beware of
	εὐμαθής, -ές	quick at learning, easy to learn, well-known
	εὐνή, -ῆς, ἡ	bed, lair; the marriage-bed, wedlock
	εὔνοια, -ας, ἡ	goodwill, favor
	εὐπιθής, -ές	ready to obey, obedient, compliant
	Εὐριπίδης, Εὐριπίδου, ὁ	Euripides
v *	εὑρίσκω	find
v	εὐρύς, εὐρεῖα, εὐρύ	wide, spacious, far-reaching
v	εὐσέβεια, -ας, ἡ	reverence toward the gods, piety
v	εὐσεβής, -ές	pious, religious
v	εὐτυχέω	to be prosperous
v	εὐτυχής, -ές	lucky, fortunate, successful
	εὐτυχία, -ας, ἡ	success, good luck, prosperity
v	εὔχομαι	pray (for), vow

	εὔφρων, -ον	cheerful, merry, well-disposed, gracious
	ἐφέλκω (*ἕλκω)	drag after one, lead, bring on, attract
	ἐφευρίσκω (*εὑρίσκω)	find by chance, discover
	ἐφήμερος, -ον	living but a day, short-lived
	ἐφίπταμαι (*ἐπιπέτομαι)	fly to/towards, fly over
	ἐφίστημι (*ἵστημι)	set/place upon; stand upon/over
v	ἐχθρός, -ά, -όν	hated, hateful; as noun, enemy
v *	ἔχω	have, possess, keep
v	ἕως	until; while, so long as

Z

v *	ζάω	live, pass one's life
v	Ζεύς, Διός, Διί, Δία	Zeus
	μὰ Δία	by Zeus
v	ζητέω	seek, ask for, search after/into, require
v	ζωή, -ῆς, ἡ	living, one's substance, property; life, existence
v	ζῷον, -ου, τό	living being, animal

H

v	ἤ	or
	ἤ . . . ἤ	either . . . or
	ἦ	in truth (affirmative); is it that (interrog.)
	ἡβάω	be young, be in the prime of life
v	ἡγεμών, -όνος, ὁ	guide, leader, chief
v	ἡγέομαι	go before, lead the way, command; believe
	ἠδέ	and
v	ἤδη	already, by this time
*	ἥδομαι	enjoy oneself, be glad (with participle)
v	ἡδονή, -ῆς, ἡ	enjoyment, pleasure
v	ἡδύς, ἡδεῖα, ἡδύ	sweet, pleasant
	ἠθικός, -ή, -όν	moral, showing moral character
	ἦθος, -ους, τό	an accustomed place (pl. haunts, abodes); custom, usage (pl. manners); character
v *	ἥκω	have come, be present
v	ἥλιος, ἡλίου, ὁ	sun, sunlight; pl. sunbeams
	ἦμαρ, -ατος, τό	day (cf. ἡμέρα)
v	ἡμέρα, -ας, ἡ	day, time
v	ἥμισυς, ἡμίσεια, ἥμισυ	half
v	ἡνίκα	at the time when
	ἧπαρ, ἥπατος, τό	liver
	Ἡράκλειος (-α) -ον	of Heracles
v	ἡσυχία, -ας, ἡ	rest, quiet, silence, stillness

θ

v	θάλαττα, θαλάττης, ἡ	sea (-σσ-)
v	θάνατος, -ου, ὁ	death
v *	θάπτω	honor with funeral rites, bury, cremate
	θάρσος, -ους, τό	courage, confidence
	θαῦμα, -ατος, τό	marvel

v *	θαυμάζω	wonder at, marvel
	θαυμαστός, -ή, -όν	to be wondered at, admirable
v	θεά, θεᾶς, ἡ	goddess
	θέαμα, -ατος, τό	sight, spectacle
	θέατρον, -ου, τό	a place for seeing, theatre
	θεῖος, -α, -ον	of/from the gods, divine
	θελκτήριον, -ου, τό	charm, spell
	θέλω (*ἐθέλω)	wish, be willing, consent
	θεμιτός, -ή, -όν	lawful
v	θεός, θεοῦ, ὁ/ἡ	god, goddess (voc. θεός)
	θεοφιλής, -ές	dear to the gods; loving the gods
v	θεραπεύω	be an attendant, do service, pay court to
v	θεράπων, θεράποντος, ὁ	henchman, squire, companion in arms, attendant, servant
	θερμός, -ή, -όν	hot; neuter as noun, heat
	θεσμοθέτης, -ου, ὁ	a lawgiver
	Θετταλία (-σσ-), -ας, ἡ	Thessaly
v *	θέω	run
	θήκη, -ης, ἡ	box, chest, grave, vault
	θηλυκός, -ή, -όν	like the female, feminine
v	θῆλυς, θήλεια, θῆλυ	female, feminine, of/belonging to a woman, soft, gentle, effeminate
	θησαυρός, -οῦ, ὁ	treasure, treasury, strong-room, safe
	θνητός, -ή, -όν	mortal
	θούριος, -α, -ον	rushing, impetuous, furious
v	θρίξ, τριχός, ἡ	hair
v	θυγατήρ, θυγατρός, ἡ	daughter
	θύννος, -ου, ὁ	tunny-fish, tuna
	θύρα, -ας, ἡ	door; pl. double/folding doors
v *	θύω	sacrifice

I

	ἰαμβικός, -ή, -όν	iambic
	ἰατρεύω	treat medically, cure, practice medicine
v	ἰατρός, -οῦ, ὁ	physician
v	ἴδιος, ἰδία, ἴδιον	one's own, private, peculiar
	ἰδιότης, ἰδιότητος, ἡ	peculiar nature/property, special character
	ἰδίως	peculiarly; as a proper noun
	ἱέρεια, -ας, ἡ	priestess
v	ἱερεύς, ἱερέως, ὁ	priest
	ἱεροπρεπής, -ές	sacred, holy
	ἱερός, -ά, -όν	supernatural, consecrated, holy
	τὰ ἱερά	offerings, rites
v *	ἵημι	release, let go; utter, throw, hurl, send, mid. hasten, desire to
v	ἱκανός, -ή, -όν	befitting, becoming, sufficient, able, enough
	ἱκάνω	come, reach, attain to
	ἱκανῶς	sufficiently
	ἱκετεύω	approach as a suppliant, supplicate, beseech
*	ἱκνέομαι	come
	ἰλύς, ἰλύος, ἡ	mud, slime, dirt

ἱμάτιον, -ου, τό   an outer garment, cloak, mantle
ἱμερτός, -ή, -όν   longed for, lovely
ἵνα   where; that, in order that
v   ἱππεύς, ἱππέως, ὁ   horseman, rider, knight
ἱππεύω   be a horseman, ride
v   ἵππος, -ου, ὁ   horse
ἰσόθεος, -ον   equal to the gods, godlike
v   ἴσος, -η, -ον   equal
v * ἵστημι   intr.: stand, halt, stand firm
v   ἰσχυρός, -ά, -όν   strong, mighty, powerful
ἰσχύς, -ύος, ἡ   strength, might, power
ἰσχύω   be strong
ἴσχω   keep back, restrain, hold fast, conceive
ἴσως   equally; probably, perhaps
ἴχνος, -ους, τό   track, trace, clue

K

καθά   just as
καθαίρω   cleanse, purify
καθάπερ   as, exactly as, like as if
v * καθέζομαι   sit down, take up a position
v * κάθημαι   be seated, sit, lie idle; reside
v   καθίστημι (*ἵστημι)   trans.: set down, establish, restore; intrans.:
                           set oneself down, settle, stand before
καθόλου   on the whole, in general
v   καί   and; even, also, just
καί . . . καί   not only . . . but also; both . . . and
καινός, -ή, -όν   new, fresh, novel
καίνω   kill, slay
καίπερ   even, although
v   καιρός, -οῦ, ὁ   due measure, proportion, exact time, critical
                           time, opportunity
καίτοι   and indeed, and yet, although
κακία, -ας, ἡ   badness, cowardice; pl. defects
κακοδαίμων, -ον   ill-starred
v   κακός, -ή, -όν   bad, evil, base, cowardly, ugly, worthless
v * καλέω   call, summon, invoke; pass. to be called
Καλλίμαχος, -ου, ὁ   Callimachus (Hellenistic poet and librarian)
v   κάλλος, -ους, τό   beauty; pl. beautiful things
v   καλός, -ή, -όν   good, fine, fair, beautiful
καρατομέω   behead
v   καρδία, -ας, ἡ   heart
v   καρπός, -οῦ, ὁ   fruit, profit, returns
καρτερός, -ά, -όν   strong, staunch
κασίγνητος, -ου, ὁ   brother; any blood relative
κάσις, κάσιος, ὁ/ἡ   brother, sister
κατά   down: G, down from, down upon, against; A, down
                           along, over, through, during, according to,
                           against, opposite
καταγελάω (*γελάω)   laugh at, mock
καταγιγνώσκω (*γιγνώ-   remark/observe against; condemn, lay as a charge
σκω)   against (G of pers., A of crime)

καταθνῄσκω (*ἀποθνῄσκω)   die away, be dying
κατακαίω (*καίω)   burn, burn down, consume
κατακλείω (*κλείω)   shut in, enclose
κατακλύζω   deluge, innundate, overwhelm
καταλαμβάνω (*λαμβάνω)   seize, lay hold of, catch, overtake
καταλείπω (*λείπω)   leave behind
καταλύω (λύω)   dissolve, destroy
καταπίνω (*πίνω)   gulp, swallow down/up
καταργέω   make barren/useless; pass. be abolished, be set
                            free
κατασκευάζω   equip, furnish, construct, build
κατασκευή, -ῆς, ἡ   preparation, construction, furniture, state,
                            condition, constitution
κατατοξεύω   shoot down (with bow and arrow)
καταφρονέω   disdain, scorn, despise
καταψεύδομαι   tell lies against, speak falsely of
καταψηφίζομαι   vote against/in condemnation of; pass. be con-
                            demned
κατευθύνω   make/keep straight, guide, direct
κατέχω, (*ἔχω)   hold back, withhold

v κατηγορέω   speak against, allege in accusation
   κατήγορος, -ου, ὁ   accuser
   κατοικτίζω   have compassion for

v * κεῖμαι   lie, be laid down, be set up; lie sick; lie
                            buried, be situated

v κελεύω   urge, drive on; exhort, bid
   κεν/κε   Epic and Ionic for ἄν
   κενός, -ή, -όν   empty, void (G); the void
   κερδαίνω   gain, make gain/profit from
   κέρδιστος, -η, -ον   most cunning/crafty; most profitable

v κέρδος, -ους, τό   gain, profit
   κεφαλή, -ῆς, ἡ   head

v κῆρυξ, κήρυκος, ὁ   herald, public messenger, envoy, crier
   κίβισις, -εως, ἡ   pouch, wallet
   κινδυνεύω   run the risk, be likely to
   κινέω   move, set in motion

 * κλείω   shut, close
 * κλέπτω   steal

v κλέος, τό   rumor, report, fame (only nom. & acc., sg. & pl.)
   κλητικός, -ή, -όν   of/for invitation
     ἡ κλητική (πτῶσις)   the vocative case
   κλύζω   wash, dash over, wash away, purge

v κλώψ, κλωπός, ὁ   thief
   κνημίς, κνημῖδος, ἡ   greave
   κοιμάω   lull, put to sleep; m-p. go to sleep

v κοινός, -ή, -όν   common, public; shared in common
   κοιρανέω   be lord/master; rule, command
   κοίτη, -ης, ἡ   bed
   κολάζω   check, chastise, punish

 * κομίζω   carry, convey; take care of, provide for, con-
                            duct, bring back; mid. get back

   κόπρος, -ου, ὁ   dung dirt

	κόπτω	smite, cut off, chop off
	κόρος, -ου, ὁ	satiety, surfeit; insolence
	κόσμιος, -α, -ον	well-ordered, moderate, regular, modest
v	κόσμος, -ου, ὁ	order, good order, discipline; ornament, honor, credit; world-order, universe
	κοῦφος, -η, -ον	light, nimble
	κρατέω	be strong, rule, prevail against
v	κράτος, -ους, τό	strength, might, power, rule
	κριθή, -ῆς, ἡ	barley
v *	κρίνω	judge, separate, distinguish, decide, choose; give judgement
	κρίσις, -εως, ἡ	separating, decision, judgment, trial
	Κρόνος, -ου, ὁ	Cronus (Kronos), father of Zeus
	κρυπτός, -ή, -όν	hidden, secret
*	κρύπτω	hide, cover
*	κτάομαι	procure for oneself, get, acquire; incur
v	κτῆμα, κτήματος, τό	anything gotten, possession
	κτῆσις, κτήσεως, ἡ	acquisition, possession, ownership
	κυβερνάω	steer, govern
	κύκλος, -ου, ὁ	ring, circle
	κύκνος, -ου, ὁ	swan
v	κύλιξ, κύλικος, ἡ	cup, wine-cup
	κυνῆ, -ῆς, ἡ	dog's skin, helmet
	κύριος, -α, -ον	having power/authority over (G), lawful
	ὁ κύριος	lord, master, guardian
v	κύων, κυνός, ὁ/ἡ	dog, Cynic (voc. κύον)
v	κωλύω	hinder, prevent (with infin., hinder from)

Λ

	λάθρα	secretly, by stealth; unknown to (G)
	λᾶας, ὁ (λᾶος, λᾶι, λᾶαν)	stone
	Λακεδαιμόνιος, -α, -ον	Lacedaemonian, Spartan
	Λακεδαίμων, -ονος, ἡ	Lacedaemon, Sparta
	λαλέω	talk, chat, prattle; speak
v *	λαμβάνω	take, seize, receive
	λάμπω	give light, shine
v *	λανθάνω	escape notice (with ptcpl., p. 161)
	λαός, -οῦ, ὁ	men, people
	λάρναξ, -ακος, ἡ	box, ark
v *	λέγω	say, mean
v *	λείπω	leave, quit, leave behind, spare
	λευκός, -ή, -όν	speech, word, diction, style
v	λέων, λέοντος, ὁ	lion
	λήγω	allay, abate
	λήθομαι	forget
	λίαν	too much
v	λίθος, -ου, ὁ	stone
	λιμήν, -ένος, ὁ	harbor, haven, retreat
	λιμός, -οῦ, ὁ	hunger, famine
	λιπαρός, -ά, -όν	oily, shiny, fatty; sleak, rich, easy

	λοβός, -οῦ, ὁ	lobe (of ear or liver)
v	λόγος, -ου, ὁ	reason, word, speech, account, principle
	λοιπός, -ή, -όν	remaining over
	καὶ τὰ λοιπά (κτλ.)	etc.
	λυπέω	give pain, to pain, grieve, annoy
	λύπη, -ης, ἡ	pain, grief
	λύχνος, -ου, ὁ	light, lamp
v	λύω	free, loosen, untie, release, destroy, break

M

	μάγειρος, -ου, ὁ	cook
v	μάθημα, μαθήματος, τό	that which is learned: lesson, knowledge
	μάθησις, μαθήσεως, ἡ	act of learning, acquiring information
v	μαθητής, μαθητοῦ, ὁ	learner, pupil, disciple
v *	μαίνομαι	rage, be furious, be mad
	μακαρίζω	call/esteem happy, bless
	μακάριος, -α, -ον	happy, blessed
	μακρολόγος, -ον	speaking at length
v	μακρός, -ά, -όν	long, large, great
	μάλα	very, exceedingly, yes certainly
v	μάλιστα	especially; yes of course
v *	μανθάνω	learn, understand; learn, esp. by study, but also by practice or experience
	μανία, -ας, ἡ	madness
v	μάντις, μάντεως, ὁ/ἡ	seer, prophet
v	μάτην	in vain
v	μάχομαι, μαχοῦμαι	fight, fight with (D)
	Μέγαρα, -ων, τά	Megara
v	μέγας, μεγάλη, μέγα	big, great
	μέθοδος, -ου, ἡ	pursuit, investigation, method, system
	μεθύσκω	make drunk, intoxicate; pass. get drunk (aor. pass. ἐμεθύσθην)
	μειδιάω	smile
	μειράκιον, -ου, τό	lad, stripling
	μείρομαι	receive one's portion/share/lot
	εἱμαρμένος	pf. pt. allotted, decreed by fate
	μελάγχιμος, -ον	black, dark
v	μέλει	impersonal: it is a care to (D)
	μελετάω	care for (G), practise, exercise oneself
	μέλλω	be destined, be likely; delay
	μεμπτός, -ή, -όν	to be blamed, contemptible
	μέμφομαι	blame, censure
v	μέν . . . δέ	on the one hand . . . on the other hand; postpos. conj. used for contrast
v	μέντοι	yet, nevertheless, of course
v *	μένω	remain, wait (for); stand fast (in battle)(no mid. or pass.)
v	μέρος, -ους, τό	share, portion, heritage, lot, destiny
	μεσημβρία, -ας, ἡ	midday
	μέσος, -η, -ον	middle, in the middle
	μετά	G: in the midst of, among, between, with; A: in pursuit of, after (of place or time)

v	μεταβάλλω (*βάλλω)	throw into a different position, change
v	μεταβολή, -ῆς, ἡ	change, transition
	μετάγω (*ἄγω)	convey from one place to another, change one's course
	μεταξύ	in the midst; between, meanwhile
	μετατίθημι (*τίθημι)	place among; change; change one's mind
	μεταφορικῶς	metaphorically
	μετέχω (*ἔχω)	partake of (G), share
	μετοχή, -ῆς, ἡ	sharing, participation; participle
	μετρίως	moderately, modestly, on fair terms
v	μέτρον, -ου, τό	measure; due measure, limit, proportion
	μέχρι	to, up to, as far as
v	μή	not
v	μηδαμῶς	in no way, not at all
v	μηδείς, μηδεμία, μηδέν	not one, not even one, nobody, nothing
	μηδέποτε	never
	Μήλιος, -ου, ὁ	Melian, inhabitant of Melos
	μήν	verily, truly, indeed, then
v	μητήρ, μητρός, ἡ	mother
	μήτοι	in no wise, nay
v *	μιμνήσκω	act. remind; m-p call to mind, remember
	μικρολόγος, -ον	mean, stingy
v	μικρός, -ά, -όν	small, little, petty, trivial; young
	μιμέομαι	imitate, mimic, copy
	μίμνω (= μένω)	remain, stay, wait
v	μισέω	hate
	μνῆμα, μνήματος, τό	remembrance, memory; memorial, mound
	μνήμη, -ης, ἡ	remembrance, memory
	μνημονεύω	call to mind, remember, think
	μνημονικός, -όν	of memory, of good memory
v	μοῖρα, -ας, ἡ	part, portion, division, political party, fate, lot, share, destiny
	μοιχεύω	commit adultery
	μοναρχία, -ίας, ἡ	monarchy, government by a single ruler
	μόνιμος (-η) -ον	staying in one's place, stationary, lasting, stable, steady, steadfast
v	μόνος, -η, -ον	alone, solitary, only, single
	μόριον, -ου, τό	piece, portion, constituent part, member
	μόρσιμος, -ον	appointed by fate, doomed, destined
	μορφή, -ῆς, ἡ	form, shape, figure; beauty, appearance
	Μοῦσα, Μούσης, ἡ	Muse; music, song
	μοχθέω	be weary with toil, suffer greatly
	μοχθηρία, -ας, ἡ	wretchedness; badness, wickedness
	μυθέομαι	say, speak, tell, name
	μύλος, -ου, ὁ	mill
	μυρίζω	rub with ointment, anoint; m. anoint oneself
	μύρον, -ου, τό	sweet oil, unguent, perfume
	μωρός, -ά, -όν / μῶρος	dull, heavy, stupid, foolish

N

	ναί	yes
	νάρθηξ, -ηκος, ὁ	giant fennel

ναῦς, νεώς, ἡ | ship (νηί, ναῦν, pl. νῆες/ναῦς, νεῶν, ναυσί, ναῦς/νῆας)

v ναύτης, ναύτου, ὁ | sailor
v νεανίας, νεανίου, ὁ | youth, young man
   νεανίσκος, -ου, ὁ | youth, young man (dimin.)
   νεκρός, -ου, ὁ | corpse
   νέμω | deal out, distribute; graze
v νέος, -α, -ον | new, young; strange, unexpected
   νεότης, -ητος, ἡ | youth, youthful spirit, rashness
   νή (νὴ τοὺς θεούς) | particle of strong affirmation (yes, by the gods)
v νῆσος, νήσου, ἡ | island
v νικάω | conquer, prevail, win
   νιν (= μιν) | him, her
v νοέω | perceive, observe, think, intend
v * νομίζω | think, believe
   νομοθετέω | lawgiver
v νόμος, -ου, ὁ | usage, custom, law
   κατὰ νόμον | according to law
   παρὰ νόμον | contrary to law
v νόος, νόου (νοῦς, νοῦ), ὁ | mind
v νοσέω | be sick, suffer
   νόσημα, -ατος, τό | disease
v νόσος, -ου, ἡ | disease, sickness
   νοστέω | return, come back home
   νουθετέω | put in mind, admonish, warn, advise
v νοῦς, νοῦ, ὁ (= νόος) | mind
v νῦν (νυν) | now, as it is
v νύξ, νυκτός, ἡ | night

Ξ

   ξενίζω | receive/entertain as a guest
v ξένος, -ου, ὁ | guest-friend, stranger, foreigner
   ξηρός, -ά, -όν | dry, parched
   ξίφος, -ους, τό | sword
   ξύλον, -ου, τό | wood
   ξύν = σύν | with
   ξύμπας = σύμπας | all together, all at once; whole

Ο

v ὁ, ἡ, τό | the (definite article)
v ὅδε, ἥδε, τόδε | this, that
   ὁδηγέω | show the way, lead the way, guide
v ὁδός, ὁδοῦ, ἡ | road, street, way; manner
v ὁδούς, ὁδόντος, ὁ | tooth
   ὀδύνη, -ης, ἡ | pain, grief
   ὄζω | smell
   οἴγνυμι (οἴγω)(*ἀνοιγ-νυμι) | open
v * οἶδα | know (by reflection)
   οἰκέτης, -ου, ὁ | house-slave, servant; pl. one's family

v	οἰκέω	inhabit, colonize; live, dwell
v	οἰκία, -ας, ἡ	building, house, dwelling; household
	οἰκονομέω	be a householder, manage, order, arrange
	οἰκτρός, -ά, -όν	pitiable
	οἶνος, -ου, ὁ	wine
v *	οἶμαι/οἴομαι	think, believe (+ inf)
v	οἶος, οἴα, οἶον	such, what a
	οἶός τε εἰμί	be able
	οἶον	such as
	ὀκταμνιαῖος, -α, -ον	eight months old
	ὀκτώ	eight
	ὄλβιος, -ον	happy, blessed, prosperous, wealthy
	ὄλβος, -ου, ὁ	happiness, wealth
	ὄλεθρος, -ου, ὁ	ruin, destruction; bane, pest
v	ὀλίγος, -η, -ον	little; pl. few
	ὀλίγου δεῖν	almost, all but
	ὄλλυμι (*ἀπόλλυμι)	destroy, make an end of, kill; perish
v	ὅλος, ὅλη, ὅλον	whole, entire, complete
	κατὰ ὅλον	on the whole
	ὅλως	wholly, altogether, on the whole
	ὄμβρος, -ου, ὁ	storm of rain, thunderstorm, heavy rain
	ὁμιλέω	be in company with, consort with, speak to
v	ὄμμα, -ατος, τό	eye
	ὄμνυμι, ὀμοῦμαι, ὤμοσα	swear
v	ὁμοίως	in like manner
	ὁμολογέω	speak together, agree, allow, admit
	ὁμοῦ	together, along with; near, almost
v	ὅμως	still, nevertheless, all the same
	ὀνειδίζω	cast in one's teeth; reproach
v	ὄνειδος, -ους, τό	reproach, censure, blame
v	ὄνομα, -ατος, τό	name, fame
v	ὀνομάζω	speak by name, call by name, name
v	ὀξύς, -εῖα, -ύ	sharp, keen
	ὀπάζω, aor. ὤπασα	make to follow, send with one, give
	ὀπίσω	(adv.) backwards, back, hereafter
v	ὅποτε	when
	ὁπότερος, -α, -ον	which of two, one of two
v *	ὁράω	see, look
v	ὀργή, -ῆς, ἡ	natural impulse, temperament, anger
	ὄργια, -ίων, τά	secret rites, orgies, mysteries
	ὀργίζω	provoke, make angry; mid. be angry
	ὀρθός, -ή, -όν	straight, upright
	ἡ ὀρθή (πτῶσις)	nominative case
	ὅρκος, -ου, ὁ	oath; the object by which one swears
v	ὄρνις, ὄρνιθος, ὁ/ἡ	bird; omen
	Ὀρόντας, Ὀρόντα, ὁ	Orontas
v	ὄρος, -ους, τό	mountain, hill
	ὅρος, -ου, ὁ	boundary, limit, frontier; rule, standard
	ὀρχέομαι	dance
v	ὅς, ἥ, ὅ	who, which
v	ὅσιος, -α, -ον	sanctioned by the law of nature; pious, devout, scrupulous

	ὁσιότης, -ητος, ἡ	piety
	ὁσίως	piously
v	ὅσος, -η, -ον	as great as, how great, as long as, how long, as much as, as many as, how much/many
	ὁστισοῦν, ὁτιοῦν	anybody whatsoever, anything
v	ὅτε	when, at the time when (ὅστις, see p. 174)
v	ὅτι	that, because
	ὅττι	Epic form for ὅτι or ὅ,τι (ὅ τι)
v	οὐ (οὐκ, οὐχ, οὐκί, οὐχί)	not
	οὐδαμοῦ	nowhere
v	οὐδαμῶς	in no way, by no means
v	οὐδέ, μηδέ	but not, not even
	οὐδείς, οὐδεμία, οὐδέν	no one, nothing, none, no (adj.)
	οὐδέτερος, -α, -ον	not either, neither of two; neuter
	οὐθείς, οὐθέν	later form of οὐδείς, οὐδέν
v	οὐκέτι	no more, no longer, not now
	οὔκουν	not therefore/then?, and so not?
	οὐκοῦν	therefore, then
v	οὖν	therefore, then, in fact, at all events (post-positive)
v	οὔποτε (οὔ . . . ποτε)	not ever, never
v	οὔπω (οὔ . . . πω)	not yet
v	οὐρανός, -οῦ, ὁ	heaven, sky
	οὖς, ὠτός, τό	ear
	οὐσία, -ας, ἡ	that which is one's own, property; reality
v	οὔτε (οὔτε . . . οὔτε)	and not (mostly repeated: neither . . . nor)
	οὔτις (Οὔτις)	no one, nobody (Noman)
v	οὔτοι	indeed not
v	οὗτος, αὕτη, τοῦτο	this
v	οὕτως (οὕτω)	in this way, manner, so, thus
v	ὀφείλω	owe, have to pay, be obliged
v	ὀφθαλμός, -οῦ, ὁ	eye
	ὀφλισκάνω (aor. pt. ὄφλων)	owe, incur a debt, lose (a case); be found guilty of a capital crime
	ὄχλος, -ου, ὁ	throng, multitude, mob, crowd
	ὀφαρτυσία, -ας, ἡ	cook-book
	ὄψις, -εως, ἡ	sight, appearance; eyesight

Π

	πᾶ Doric for πῆ	how, where? whither?
v	πάθος, πάθους, τό	that which happens to a person or thing, experience, emotion, state, condition
	παίγνιον, -ου, τό	plaything, toy, game
v	παιδεία, -ας, ἡ	rearing of a child, education; youth
v	παιδεύω	educate, bring up/rear a child, teach, train
	παιδιά, -ᾶς, ἡ	child's play, sport, pastime, game
v	παιδίον, -ου, τό	little child, young slave (m. or f.)
	παίζω	play, jest, sport
v	παῖς, παιδός, ὁ/ἡ	child, slave (gen. pl. παίδων, voc. sg. παῖ)
	πάλαι	long ago, once upon a time
v	παλαιός, -ά, -όν	ancient, old

		πάλιν	back, backwards; again, in turn
		παμμεγέθης, -ες	of enormous size
		πανήγυρις, -εως, ἡ	festival
		πανόπτης, -ου, ὁ	all-seeing
		παντάπασι	all in all, altogether, wholly
v		πανταχοῦ	everywhere
v		πάντως	in all ways, in any case, by all means
v		πάνυ	altogether, by all means
v		παρά	G: from the side of, from beside, from; D: by the side of, beside; A: to the side of, along, past, beyond
		παράδειγμα, -ατος, τό	pattern, model, plan, exemplar, example
		παραδίδωμι (*δίδωμι)	give/hand over, deliver; betray, hand down
		παραινέω	exhort, recommend, advise
		παρακελεύομαι	exhort, cheer, encourage by shouting
		παραλαμβάνω (*λαμβάνω)	receive from another, succeed to, entertain
		παραμυθία, -ας, ἡ	encouragement, reassurance, consolation
		παραπύθια, -ων, τά	an allergy to the Pythian games (comic word)
		παρασκευάζω	get ready, prepare, provide; mid. prepare for oneself
		παρατίθημι (*τίθημι)	place beside/before, provide, set before
		παρατυγχάνω (*τυγχάνω)	happen to be by, be present at
v		πάρειμι (*εἰμί)	be present, be near, stand by
		πάρεστι μοί	it depends on me
		παρέρχομαι (*ἔρχομαι)	pass away, pass
v		παρέχω (*ἔχω)	furnish, supply
		παρθένος, -ου, ἡ	maiden, girl
		παρίσθμια, -ων, τά	tonsils, inflammation of the tonsils
		παρίστημι (*ἵστημι)	place beside, by; stand beside
		παρό	wherefore
		παρουσία, -ας, ἡ	presence, arrival, occasion
v		πᾶς, πᾶσα, πᾶν	sg. every, pl. all; + art. all, the whole
v	*	πάσχω	suffer, be affected
v		πατήρ, πατρός, ὁ	father
		πατρικός, -ή, -όν	hereditary, belonging to one's father
		ἡ πατρική (οὐσία)	patrimony
v		πατρίς, πατρίδος, ἡ	fatherland, country
		πατροκτόνος, -ον	murdering one's father, parricidal
		πατρῷος (-α) -ον	of/from a father, hereditary
		παῦλα, -ης, ἡ	rest, pause
		παύω	stop, bring to an end, check; mid. cease
		πεδίον, -ου, τό	plain
		πειθαρχέω	obey one in authority, be obedient
v	*	πείθω	persuade; m-p obey, trust in
		Πειθώ	Peitho, persuasion
		πεινάω	be hungry
v		πεῖρα, πείρας, ἡ	test, trial, attempt
	*	πειράομαι	try, attempt
		πέλας	near, hard by (+G)
		οἱ πέλας	one's neighbors
		Πελοποννήσιοι, οἱ	Peloponnesians
		Πελοπόννησος, ἡ	Peloponnese (Πέλοπος νῆσος)

	πέλω	go, come, rise; be, become
v *	πέμπω	send, conduct, escort
v	πένης, -ητος, ὁ	one who works for a living, laborer, poor man
	πενία, -ας, ἡ	poverty, need
	πένθος, -ους, τό	grief, sorrow, mourning, misfortune
	πεντακόσιοι, -αι, -α	five hundred
v	πέντε	five
	πέρην (πέραν)	on the other side of, across
v	περί	G. about, concerning; D. about (poetic); A. a-bout, around, near
	περιβάλλω (*βάλλω)	throw around, embrace; mid. put on
	περιγίγνομαι (*γίγνο-μαι)	be superior, survive, result from
	περίειμι (*εἶμι)	go around, go about
	περιέχω (*ἔχω)	encompass, surround, embrace, excel
	περιμένω (*μένω)	wait for, await, expect, wait, abide
	περίμετρον, -ου, τό	circumference
	περιπατέω	walk around, walk, live
	περιπίπτω (*πίπτω)	fall around, fall foul of, fall into
	περισπώμενος (τόνος)	the circumflex (from περισπάω draw around)
	πέτομαι	fly
	πέτρα, -ας, ἡ	rock, cliffs
	πέτρος, -ου, ὁ	piece of rock, stone
	πηγή, -ῆς, ἡ	running water, source, fount
	πηδάω	spring, leap, throb
	πηλίκος, -η, -ον	how great, how much, how old
v	πῆμα, -ατος, τό	misery, calamity, bane
	πημονή, ῆς, ἡ	suffering
	πηνίκα	(adv.) at what point in time? at what hour?
	πιθανός, -ή, -όν	persuasive, plausible
	πίθος, -ου, ὁ	pithos, large wine jar
	πικρός, -ά, -όν	pointed, sharp, pungent, bitter
v *	πίμπλημι	fill
v *	πίνω	drink
v *	πίπτω	fall
v	πιστεύω	trust, put one's faith in, rely on (+D)
	πιστός, -ή, -όν	to be trusted, faithful, trusty, genuine, trust-worthy, sure, credible
	πλάσσω (-ττ-)	form, mould
v *	πλέω	sail, go by sea
v	πλῆθος, -ους, τό	multitude, mass, populace, mob, size
	πληθυντικός, -ή, -όν	plural
v	πλήν	except (+G)
v	πλήρης, =ες	full (of), infected
	πληρόω	fill, make full
	πλησίον	near (ὁ πλησίον (ὤν) one's neighbor)
	πλοῦς (πλόος) ὁ	a sailing voyage
	πλούσιος, -α, -ον	wealthy, opulent
	πλουτέω	be rich/wealthy
v	πλοῦτος, πλούτου, ὁ	wealth, riches
	Πλοῦτος	Plutus, god of wealth
	πλύνω	wash, beat

	πνεῦμα, πνεύματος, τό	blast, wind, breath, breathing, spirit
*	πνέω	blow, breathe, smell of a thing
	ποδιαῖος, -α, -ον	a foot long/high/broad
	πόθεν	whence, from what place?
v	ποιέω	make, produce, cause
	περὶ πολλοῦ/πλείονος ποιοῦμαι	consider of great/greater importance
	ποίημα, -ατος, τό	anything made/done; poem, act, deed
	ποιητής, -οῦ, ὁ	poet, author
v	ποῖος, -α, -ον	of what kind/sort? what? which?
	πολεμέω	be at war, wage war with, fight, attack
	πολέμιος, -α, -ον	of/belonging to war; of/like an enemy, hostile
	οἱ πολέμιοι	the enemy
v	πόλεμος, -ου, ὁ	war
v	πόλις, πόλεως, ἡ	city-state
	πολιτεύω	be a citizen, administer the state; pass. be governed
v	πολίτης, πολίτου, ὁ (ῑ)	citizen
	πολιτικός, -ή, -όν	of/for/relating to citizens, civic, political
v	πολλάκις	often, many times
	πολλοστός, -ή, -όν	far on in the ordinal series; long (of time)
	πολυμαθής, -ές	knowing much
	πολυμαθία, ἡ	much learning
v	πολύς, πολλή, πολύ	many, much
	ἐπὶ τὸ πολύ	for the most part
v	πονηρός, -ά, -όν	oppressed by toils; wicked, worthless
v	πόνος, πόνου, ὁ	toil, labor, hard work; trouble, pain
v	πορεύω	bring, carry; mid. go, walk, march
v	πορίζω	bring about, provide; mid. furnish oneself with, procure
	πόρος, -ου, ὁ	means of passing; way/means of achieving
v	πόσις, ὁ	husband, spouse (no gen. in Attic, dat. πόσει, voc. πόσι)
v	πούς, ποδός, ὁ	foot (acc. πόδα, dat. pl. ποσί)
	ποτέ	at some/any time
v	πότερον (π. . . . ἤ)	whether (whether . . . or)
	πότερος, -α, -ον	whether of two
v	πρᾶγμα, πράγματος, τό	deed, act, occurrence, thing, concrete reality; pl. affairs, circumstances
	πραγματεύομαι	busy oneself, be engaged in business, undertake, elaborate
v *	πράττω	do, make, achieve
	πρεσβεύω	be elder, rank before, represent, urge
v	πρέσβυς, -εως, ὁ	old man, elder
	πρεσβύτης, -ου, ὁ	old man
v	πρίν	until, before
	πρό	gen.: before, in behalf of, in preference to
	πρόβατον, τό	sheep
	πρόβλημα, -ατος, τό	anything that juts out, barrier, defence
	πρόγονος, ὁ	ancestor
v	προδίδωμι	betray, give up, give beforehand
	προεῖδον (προοράω)	foresee, portend

	πρόθεσις, -εως, ἡ	placing in public, placing first; preposit.
	προθύμως	zealously, readily, actively
	προίξ, προικός, ἡ	gift, dowry
	πρόνοια, -ας, ἡ	foresight
	προοράω	foresee
	προπέτεια, -ας, ἡ	rashness, reckless haste
v	πρός	gen.: from; dat.: at, near, by; acc.: to, towards
	προσδέχομαι (*δέχομαι)	accept, receive, expect
	προσδοκάω	expect, think
	πρόσειμι (*εἰμί)	be added to, belong to, be present as well
	προσεπιμετρέω	assign over and above
	προσέρχομαι (*ἔρχομαι)	come/go to, approach
	προσευχή, -ῆς, ἡ	prayer
	προσηγορία, -ας, ἡ	friendly greeting, familiarity; common noun
	προσήκω	to have come to, be at hand; impersonal: it concerns, befits, has reference to
	προσηλόω	nail, rivet, fix to
	προσίσχω (= προσέχω)	hold against
	προσκεφάλαιον, τό	cushion, pillow
	προσπέμπω	send to
	προστάττω (*τάττω)	place on post, assign, order
	προστίθημι (*τίθημι)	put to, hand over, add, impose, give besides
v	πρόσωπον, -ου, τό	face, mask, character, person
	πρότερος, -α, -ον	before, in front, former, earlier
	πρότερον (πρ. . . . πρίν)	adv. before, earlier than
	προφέρω	bring before/forward, propose, publish; throw in one's teeth
	προφήτης, -ου, ὁ	interpreter, prophet
	πρῴην	lately, just now, not long ago, the day before yesterday
	πρωταγωνιστής, -οῦ, ὁ	one who plays the first part, chief actor
v	πρῶτος, -η, -ον	foremost, first
	πτέρυξ, πτέρυγος, ἡ	wing
	πτηνός, -ή, -ον	flying, winged
	πτῶσις, -εως, ἡ	falling, fall; mode, modification, case, etc.
	πτωτικός, -ή, -όν	capable of inflection
	πύλη, -ης, ἡ	gate
v *	πυνθάνομαι	learn (by hearsay or inquiry)
v	πῦρ, πυρός, τό	fire (not used in pl.; τὰ πυρά = watchfires, dat. πυροῖς)
v	πῶς	how

P

	ῥάβδος, -ου, ἡ	rod, wand, staff
v	ῥάδιος, -α, -ον	easy, ready; easy-going
	ῥαθυμία, -ας, ἡ	easiness of temper, relaxation, indifference
	ῥαψῳδέω	recite poems
	ῥαψῳδός, -οῦ, ὁ	reciter of Epic poems, professional reciter
	ῥέω	flow, run, stream, gush

v *	ῥήγνυμι	break, shatter, rend
	ῥῆμα, -ατος, τό	word, saying; phrase; verb
v	ῥήτωρ, ῥήτορος, ὁ	public speaker
	ῥίζα, -ης, ἡ	root
	ῥόδον, -ου, τό	the rose
*	ῥύομαι	rescue, deliver, protect
	ῥώμη, -ης, ἡ	bodily strength, might

Σ

	σᾶμα	Doric for σῆμα
	σάτυρος, -ου, ὁ	satyr
	σάφα	clearly, plainly, truly
	σαφής, -ές	clear, plain, distinct
	σεμνόθεοι, οἱ	Druids
	σημεῖον, -ου, τό	mark, sign, token, omen, signal
	σῆμα, -ατος, τό	sign, mark; omen; mound, cairn, tomb
	σημαίνω	show, indicate, signify
v *	σιγάω	keep silence, keep secret
	σιγή, -ῆς, ἡ	silence
v	σίδηρος, -ου, ὁ	iron; tool, sword, knife
	σιωπάω	keep silence, keep secret
	σκεπτέον	one must reflect, consider
v	σκηνή, -ῆς, ἡ	tent, stage
	σκηνογραφία, -ας, ἡ	scene-painting
	σκιά, -ᾶς, ἡ	shadow, reflection, image, phantom
	Σκιωναῖος, -α, -ον	Scionean, of Scione (city in Macedonia)
v *	σκοπέω	behold, contemplate, examine, look to
	σκορπίος, -ου, ἡ	scorpion
	Σκύθης, -ου, ὁ	Scythian; (at Athens) police
	σμικρός = μικρός	small
	σοφία, -ας, ἡ	cleverness, skill, practical wisdom, learning
	σοφός, -ή, -όν	skilled, clever, learned, wise, prudent
	σπαργανόω	swathe in swaddling clothes
v	σπεύδω	hasten, seek eagerly, strive after
v	σπουδαῖος, -α, -ον	serious, grave, earnest, good
v	σπουδή, -ῆς, ἡ	haste, speed, eagerness, seriousness
	στάσις, -εως, ἡ	placing, setting, position; party, faction
	στενάζω	groan, moan, bemoan, bewail
	στένω	sigh, groan, moan
	στέργω	love, be fond of, like, be content/pleased
	στερέω	deprive, rob; pass. be deprived of
	στέφανος, -ου, ὁ	crown, wreath
	στεφανόω	to crown, wreathe
	στοά, -ᾶς, ἡ	stoa, roofed colonnade; the Stoic school
	στόλος, -ου, ὁ	equipment for war; expedition, journey, army
v	στόμα, -ατος, τό	mouth
	στρατηγέω	be general
v	στρατηγός, -οῦ, ὁ	general, commander of an army
v	στρατιώτης, -ου, ὁ	soldier
	στρατόπεδον, -ου, τό	camp, encampment; army
v *	στρέφω	turn; m-p turn oneself, be engaged in

	στυγέω	hate
v	σύ, σοῦ, σοί, σέ	you (sg.)
	συγγνώμη, -ης, ἡ	fellow-feeling, pardon, forgiveness, excuse
	σύγγραμα, -ατος, τό	a written paper, book, prose work
	συγγραφεύς, -έως, ὁ	historian, prose-writer
	συγγράφω (*γράφω)	write/note down; compose a work in writing
	συγκαίω (*καίω)	set on fire with, burn up, inflame
	συγκεκαυμένον	pf. mid.-pass. ptcpl. of συγκαίω
	σύγκαιμαι (*κεῖμαι)	lie together, be composed of
	συγχέω (*χέω)	pour together, confound, obliterate
v	συμβαίνω (*βαίνω)	meet, come to an agreement; happen, result
	συμβόλαιον, -ου, τό	mark, sign, contract, covenant
	συμβουλεύω	advise; mid. take counsel with
	συμμαχέω	be an ally/in alliance with, help, succour + D
	συμμαχία, -ας, ἡ	alliance
	συμφέρω (*φέρω)	bring together, collect, be useful
	συμφέρων	ptcpl., useful, expedient, fitting, profitable
	συμφεύγω (*φεύγω)	flee along with, take refuge
v	συμφορά, -ᾶς, ἡ	mishap, misfortune; event, circumstance
	συμφύω (*φύω)	make to grow together; pf. & pass. grow together, grow into one
	σύμφωνος, -ον	agreeing in sound; n. pl. the consonants
v	σύν (ξύν)	with, in company with
	συναποδημέω	go abroad, travel with
	συναπολείπω (*λείπω)	leave behind along with
	συνάπτω	tie, join together, unite; mid. take part with
	σύνδεσμος, -ου, ὁ	that which binds; conjunction
v	σύνειμι (*εἰμί)	be with, live with, have dealings with
	συνεχής, -ές (ξυν-)	holding together, continuous, successive
	συνηβάω	be young together
	συνήθεια, -ας, ἡ	acquaintance, intimacy, habit, custom
	συνήθης, -ες	dwelling/living together, intimate, accustomed
	συνίημι (*ἵημι)	bring/set/come together; perceive, understand
	συνίστημι (*ἵστημι)	place together, introduce, recommend; stand together
	συνοράω (*ὁράω)	be able to see, see, comprehend
	συνουσία, -ας, ἡ	being with, intercourse
	συντάσσω (-ττ-)	put in array, arrange
	συντεταμένως	in set terms; earnestly, eagerly, vigorously
	συντόμως	concisely, shortly
	σῦς (= ὗς), συός, ὁ/ἡ	swine
	συστεφανηφορέω	wear a crown with
	σφαῖρα, -ας, ἡ	ball, globe, sphere
	σφαλερός, -ά, -όν	slippery, perilous, uncertain, precarious
	σφε	him, her, them (acc. sg. or pl.)
	σφόδρα	very, very much, exceedingly
	σφοδρός, -ά, -όν	vehement, violent, excessive
	σφυρόν, -οῦ, τό	ankle
	σχεδόν	near, hard by, almost
	σχῆμα, -ατος, τό	form, shape, appearance, figure (in dance: steps), pretence, fashion
	σχολάζω	be at leisure

v	σχολή, -ῆς, ἡ	leisure, rest, ease
v *	σῴζω (σῴζω)	save; pass. be saved, escape
v	σῶμα, -ατος, τό	body
	σωτήρ, -ῆρος, ὁ	savior, deliverer
	σωτηρία, -ας, ἡ	deliverance, preservation, safe return
	σωφρονέω	be of sound mind, practise self-control, be discreet, be temperate
v	σωφροσύνη, -ης, ἡ	soundness of mind, prudence, discretion, moderation, self-control
	σώφρων, σῶφρον	of sound mind, discreet, temeprate, prudent, self-controlled

T

v	ταμίας, -ου, ὁ	steward, dispenser, treasurer
	ταῦρος, -ου, ὁ	bull
	τάφος, -ου, ὁ	funeral rites; grave, tomb
	τάχα	quickly, soon
	τάχα ἄν	probably, perhaps
	τάχος, -εος, τό	speed, quickness
	ὡς τάχος	with all speed
v	ταχύς, -εῖα, -ύ	swift, fleet
v	τε	and (enclitic)
v	τεῖχος, τείχους, τό	wall, esp. city-wall
	τεκμήριον, -ου, τό	sure sign, proof, evidence, demonstration
v	τέκνον, -ου, τό	child
	τεκνόω	furnish with children, beget; mid. bear
	τεκταίνομαι	frame, devise, plan
	τέκτων, -ονος, ὁ (ἡ)	carpenter; craftsman, workman, master in any art
v	τελευτάω	bring to pass, accomplish, fulfil, finish, die, pass. be fulfilled, happen, come to end
v	τελέω	fulfil, accomplish; pay, initiate
	τελέως	completely, perfectly
v	τέλος, τέλους, τό	coming to pass, fulfilment, result, end
	τερπνός, -ή, -όν (τερπνόν, -οῦ, τό)	delightful, pleasant; as noun: enjoyment (n)
	τέρπω	delight; m-p. be cheered, enjoy oneself
v	τέτταρες, τέτταρα (σσ)	four
v	τέχνη, -ης, ἡ	art, skill, craft; treatise
	τεχνίτης, -ου, ὁ	artist, craftsman
	τηνικάδε	at this time, so early
	τί δή ποτε;	why ever? why in the world? what do you mean?
v *	τίθημι	set, place, put, set up, establish, make, institute, order, dispose
v *	τίκτω	bring forth, bear, beget
v	τιμάω	honor, esteem, rever, value; estimate
	τιμή, -ῆς, ἡ	honor, esteem, dignity; office, worth, value
	τίμημα, -ατος, τό	worth, price, value, penalty
	τίμιος (-α) -ον	valued, esteemed, held in honor, precious
	τιμωρέω	help, avenge; mid. punish
	τιμωρία, -ας, ἡ	help, aid, vengeance, retribution, torture
	τίνω	pay a price/penalty/debt

v	τίς, τί	who? what? (pronoun or adj.)
	τις, τι	anyone/someone, anything/something, any, some
	τιτρώσκω	wound, hurt
	τλάω (aor. ἔτλην)	endure, dare
	τοι	let me tell you; look here
	τοιγάρ	so then, wherefore, therefore
	τοίνυν	well then, well, now then, again
	τοιόσδε, τοιάδε, τοιόν-δε	of such a kind/quality
v	τοιοῦτος, τοιαύτη, τοι-οῦτο	such, such as this
v	τολμάω	undertake, dare, endure, bring oneself to do
	τόνος, -ου, ὁ	that which can be stretched, pitch, accent
	τόπος, -ου, ὁ	place, region
	τοσόσδε, -ήδε, -όνδε	so great, so large
	τοσόνδε (adv.)	so very, so much, to such a degree
v	τοσοῦτος, τοσαύτη, το-οῦτο	so great, so large, so much
v	τότε	at that time, then, next
	οἱ τότε	men of that time
	τραγικός, -ή, -όν	tragic, stately
	τράγος, -ου, ὁ	goat
v	τρεῖς, τρία	three
v *	τρέφω	nourish, feed, cherish, foster; mid. rear for oneself; pass. grow (up)
v *	τρέχω	run
	τριακοσίοι, -αι, -α	three hundred
	τρίπους, -ποδος, ὁ/ἡ	three-footed; as noun: tripod (m.)
	τρόμος, -ου, ὁ	trembling, quaking
v	τρόπος, -ου, ὁ	turn, direction, way, manner
v	τροφή, -ῆς, ἡ	nourishment, food, nurture, rearing
	τροφός, -οῦ, ὁ/ἡ	feeder, rearer, nurse
v *	τυγχάνω	happen, meet (G), attain, obtain
	τύπτω	beat, strike
v	τυραννίς, -ίδος, ἡ	monarchy, sovereignty, tyranny
v	τύραννος, -ου, ὁ	absolute ruler, monarch, tyrant
	τυφλός, -ή, -όν	blind
	τῦφος, -ου, ὁ	smoke, mist, cloud, conceit, vanity
v	τύχη, -ης, ἡ	fortune, fate, chance, success, ill fortune

Υ

v	ὕβρις, ὕβρεως, ἡ	hubris, wanton violence, insolence, lust, rape
	ὑγιαίνω	be healthy
v	ὑγίεια, -ας, ἡ	health
v	ὑγιής, -ές	healthy
	ὑδρωπικός, -ή, -όν	dropsical
v	ὕδωρ, ὕδατος, τό	water
	ὕει (ὕω)	it is raining
	ὑετός, -οῦ, ὁ	rain
v	υἱός, -οῦ, ὁ	son (also in third declension as ι-stem)
	ὕλη, -ης, ἡ	forest, woodland; material, stuff

	ὑπαί = ὑπό	(poetic)
v	ὑπάρχω	begin, exist, belong to, accrue
v	ὑπέρ	gen.: over, in defence of; acc.: over, beyond
	ὑπερβάλλω (*βάλλω)	throw over/beyond a mark, overshoot, outdo, surpass, exceed; cross
	ὑπερβολή, -ῆς, ἡ	a throwing beyond, excess, excessive praise
	ὑπερηφάνως	magnificently, arrogantly
	ὑπερμεγέθης, -ες	excessively large, enormous
	ὑπεύθυνος, -ον	liable to give account, accountable, responsible
	ὑπήκοος, -ον	giving ear, obedient, subject
	οἱ ὑπήκοοι	subjects
v *	ὑπισχνέομαι	promise; profess
v	ὕπνος, -ου, ὁ	sleep
v	ὑπό	gen.: under, by, through; dat.: beneath, under, below; acc.: under, to (a place) under, toward
	ὑποβολή, -ῆς, ἡ	throwing under, substitution by stealth, suggesting; foundation
	ὑποδείκνυμι (*δείκνυμι)	show secretly, mark out; make a display
	ὑποκριτής, -οῦ, ὁ	one who answers, actor, player, hypocrite
	ὑπολαμβάνω (*λαμβάνω)	take up by getting under, take up, seize, interpret, understand, accept, believe
	ὑπομαίνομαι	be somewhat mad
	ὑπομένω (*μένω)	stay behind, remain alive, abide, submit, await, bear, dare
	ὑποπτεύω	be suspicious, suspect; pass. be suspected
	ὑποτίθημι (*τίθημι)	place under, suggest, propose; m. instruct
v	ὕστερος, -α, -ον	latter, behind, next, later
	ὑφίστημι (*ἵστημι)	place/set under; stand under, sink, promise, submit, undertake
	ὑψηλός, -ή, -όν	high, lofty

Φ

v *	φαίνω	bring to light; pass. appear, seem
	φανερός (-ά) -όν	visible, shining, illustrious, conspicuous
	φαρμακοπώλης, -ου, ὁ	druggist, apothecary
	φαῦλος, -η, -ον	cheap, easy, mean, bad
	φαύλως πράττειν	be in a sorry plight
	φείδομαι	spare, pay heed to
v *	φέρω	bring, carry, bear
	φεῦ	alas, woe
v *	φεύγω	flee, take flight, avoid, escape
v *	φθάνω	be beforehand, outstrip (+ ptcpl.)
	φθαρτός, -ή, -όν	corruptible, destructible, mortal, transitory
	φθίσις, -εως, ἡ	wasting away, perishing, decay, atrophy
	φθογγή, -ῆς, ἡ	voice, cry
	φθορά, -ᾶς, ἡ	destruction, ruin, seduction
v	φιλέω	love, welcome, kiss
v	φιλία, -ας, ἡ	friendship, affection
v	φίλιος, -α, -ον	friendly
	φιλομαθής, -ες	fond of learning, eager for learning

v	φίλος, -ου, ὁ	friend, loved one (including family); dear
	φιλότεκνος, -ον	loving one's children/offspring
	φιλότιμος, -ον	loving honor, ambitious
	φιλοφροσύνη, -ης, ἡ	friendliness, kindliness, welcome
	φλογωπός, -όν	fiery-looking, flaming red
	φλυαρέω	talk nonsense, trifle
	φοβέομαι	be seized with fear, be frightened
	φοβερός, -ά, -όν	fearful, afraid, timid
	φολίς, -ίδος, ἡ	scale
v	φονεύς, -έως, ὁ	slayer, murderer
	φονεύω	murder, kill, slay
	φορητός (-ή) -όν	borne, carried, bearable
	φράζω	tell, declare, advise, bid, order
v	φρήν, φρενός, ἡ	midriff, heart, mind
	φρίκη, -ης, ἡ	a shuddering
	φρικώδης, -ες	awful, horrible
v	φρονέω	be minded, have understanding, be wise
	φρόνησις, -εως, ἡ	purpose, intention, thought, sense, judgment, pride, wisdom, prudence
	φρόνιμος, -ον	understanding, discreet, sensible, wise
v	φύλαξ, φύλακος, ὁ	watcher, guard, sentinel
v	φυλάττω (-σσ-)	keep watch, guard, defend
	φυξίος, -ον	of banishment, putting to flight
	φυσικός, -ή, -όν	natural, physical
v	φύσις, σύσεως, ἡ	nature, origin
	φυτεύω	plant, beget, engender, produce, cause
v *	φύω	bring forth, produce; pass. & pf. act.: grow, be born
	Φωκίς, -ίδος, ἡ	Phocis
	φωνέω	produce a sound/tone; speak, tell of
	φωνή, -ῆς, ἡ	voice, sound
	φωνήεις, -εσσα, -εν	endowed with speech, vocal
	τὰ φωνήεντα	the vowels
	φώς, φωτός, ὁ	man
v	φῶς (= φάος), φωτός, τό	light, daylight

X

v *	χαίρω	rejoice
	χαλεπαίνω	be hard, be angry
v	χαλεπός, -ή, -όν	difficult, hard to bear, painful
	χαλινός, -οῦ, ὁ	bridle, bit
	χαλκοῦς, -ῆ, -οῦν	of copper/bronze
	χαρακτήρ, -ῆρος, ὁ	distinctive mark, type, character
	χαρίεις, -εσσα, -εν	graceful, pleasant, lovely
v	χάρις, χάριτος, ἡ	grace, favor
	χειμών, -ῶνος, ὁ	winter, storm, tempest
v	χείρ, χειρός, ἡ	hand
	χειροτονία, -ας, ἡ	extension of the hand, voting by show of hands
*	χέω	pour
	χθές	yesterday
v	χθών, χθονός, ἡ	earth, land, country

	χορεύω	dance, set dancing
v	χράομαι	use (+ D)
	χράω	proclaim (an oracle); mid. consult an oracle
	χρεία, -ας, ἡ	need, want (of +G)
v	χρή	it is necessary
v	χρῆμα, -ατος, τό	thing, matter, affair; pl. money
v	χρήσιμος, -η, -ον	useful, serviceable
	χρησμός, -οῦ, ὁ	oracular response, oracle
v	χρηστός, -ή, -όν	useful, good, honest; pl. n. benefits
v	χρόνος, -ου, ὁ	time; tense
v	χρυσίον, -ου, τό	gold
	Χρύσιππος, -ου, ὁ	Chrysippus
	χρυσός, -οῦ, ὁ	gold
	χρυσοῦς, -ῆ, -οῦν	of gold, golden
v	χώρα, χώρας, ἡ	space, place; land, country
	χωρέω	make room for another, go, come, advance
	χωρίον, -ου, τό	place, spot, country
	χωρίς	separately, apart, without

ψ

	ψέγω	blame, find fault with
v	ψευδής, -ές	false, lying, untrue
	ψευδοπροφήτης, -ου, ὁ	false prophet
	ψηφηγορία, -ας, ἡ	vote by ballot
	ψιλός, -ή, -όν	bare, bald, smooth
	ψόγος, -ου, ὁ	blame, censure
v	ψυχή, -ῆς, ἡ	life, soul
	ψυχρός, -ά, -όν	cold

Ω

	ὧδε	in this way, so, thus; hither, here
	ᾠδή, -ῆς, ἡ (ἀοιδή)	song
*	ὠνέομαι	buy, purchase
v	ὥρα, ὥρας, ἡ	season, time of day, hour (any fixed period)
v	ὡς	as; as if; prep. + acc.: to; how
	ὡσεί	as if, as though, just as
	ὥσπερ	just as, even as
v	ὥστε	so that, so as to, and so
	ὠφελέω	help, aid, benefit, be of service to